THE LAW OF TREATIES BEYOND THE VIENNA CONVENTION

The Law of Treaties Beyond the Vienna Convention

Edited by
ENZO CANNIZZARO

Contributors:
Mahnoush H. Arsanjani, Enzo Cannizzaro, Annalisa Ciampi, Benedetto Conforti, Olivier Corten, Pierre-Marie Dupuy, Serena Forlati, Alessandra Gianelli, Gleider I. Hernández, Jan Klabbers, Pierre Klein, Marcelo G. Kohen, Pieter Jan Kuijper, Donald McRae, Daniel Müller, Georg Nolte, Paolo Palchetti, Alain Pellet, Paolo Picone, Fausto Pocar, W. Michael Reisman, Francesco Salerno, Luigi Sbolci, Bruno Simma, Christian Tomuschat, Joe Verhoeven, Mark E. Villiger, Michael Wood, Karl Zemanek.

OXFORD
UNIVERSITY PRESS

OXFORD
UNIVERSITY PRESS

Great Clarendon Street, Oxford, OX2 6DP,
United Kingdom

Oxford University Press is a department of the University of Oxford. It furthers the University's objective of excellence in research, scholarship, and education by publishing worldwide. Oxford is a registered trade mark of Oxford University Press in the UK and in certain other countries

First published 2011

Published in the United States of America by Oxford University Press
198 Madison Avenue, New York, NY 10016, United States of America

British Library Cataloguing in Publication Data
Data available

Library of Congress Cataloging in Publication Data
Data available

ISBN 978–0–19–958891–6

Professor Giorgio Gaja

Preface

Law Beyond the Law

There are a number of reasons for reappraising the state of the law of treaties now that more than 40 years have passed since the Vienna Convention.

First, there is a broad need to assess the impact of the Vienna Convention on the pre-existing customary law of treaties, and vice versa.

The Vienna Convention is undoubtedly one of the most successful works of codification ever undertaken in international law. It includes rules which, at the time of the conclusion of the Convention, had already acquired the status of customary law; but it also contains innovative rules that move beyond pre-existing custom and establish new legal regimes.

Examples of the latter category are well known: the legal regime of reservations; the regime of treaty conflict; the rules on treaty interpretation; the entire regime of invalidity and termination, including the procedure for their determination; and the unprecedented concept of *jus cogens*.

More generally, the impact of the Vienna Convention on the Law of Treaties went well beyond the normal impact of a treaty of codification. The Convention has become the new source of authority for determining the state of the law, a sort of 'rule of recognition' for determining, almost univocally, the general character of the law of treaties. By virtue of some quite mysterious effect, the new law introduced by the Vienna Convention (with a few notable exceptions) crossed the line separating conventional law from customary law and became, in the case law of international courts and tribunals, part of a heritage of general law.

Equally momentous has been the impact of the subsequent practice on the Vienna Convention. Not long after the entry into force of the Convention, the International Law Commission decided to study specific areas of the law of treaties, a project that reflects the rapid obsolescence, or at least the insufficiency, of some of the solutions adopted by the Vienna Convention. Furthermore, the codification of other fields of international law, such as, for example, the law of state responsibility, has helped to highlight the scope and content of certain rules of the Convention. The flourishing of studies concerning the mutual impact between these two branches illustrates the need for a global approach to the law of treaties, one that makes constant reference to the rules which determine the consequences of their breach.

A further reason for a focus on the relationship between custom and the Vienna Convention emerges if one considers the changing legal paradigms of the law of treaties.

In the classical view, legal relations established by treaties were mainly framed in a bilateralistic conceptual scheme. The Vienna Convention has slightly altered this fundamental paradigm, and has sought to establish a balanced compromise between the need to maintain the traditional bilateralistic approach and a new emerging approach which increasingly takes into account collective and universal values that are mainstreamed within the international legal order by treaties.

There are plenty of fields, in the Vienna Convention and in subsequent practice, in which the classical bilateralist is confronted with the new communitarian approach: the effects of a treaty for third parties is one of these fields where recent practice shows an increasing tendency to use treaties in order to create objective law. Another one is the law of reservations, with its inherent tension between, on the one hand, the tendency to split the content of multilateral treaties into a bundle of bilateral legal relations and, on the other, the need to assert the existence of a core content of obligations uniformly incumbent upon all the parties to the treaty. In the field of treaty interpretation, the tension is between methods based on objective and uniform construction and methods giving much weight to the position of the parties to the dispute. The difficulty of drawing the line separating bilateralism from communitarianism is the origin of the uncertainties in determining the rules of treaty conflict.

The tension between bilateralism and communitarianism pervades the full range of the rules on invalidity and termination of treaties, where classical bilateralism must increasingly accommodate the interests of the international community. The paradigmatic example of this pendulum is the relationship between treaties and *jus cogens*. Although this issue seldom arises in practice, it is crucial for the law of treaties. *Jus cogens* is a conceptual crossroads from which a number of different roads depart: one leading back to classical bilateralism; one which increasingly admits the priority of collective over individual interests; and a variety of intermediate solutions, including the solution endorsed by the Vienna Conference, whose systematic coherence appears controversial.

Finally, the diverse roles of the Vienna Convention provide an excellent opportunity to assess the philosophically controversial function of codification in contemporary international law. The interplay between the Vienna Convention and previous and subsequent practice constitutes a living example, perhaps the most vivid one available to contemporary scholars, of the incessant recurrence of factual law and formal law in the never-ending search for coincidence between legal reality and social reality.

* * *

Yet the reasons given above cannot explain sufficiently why, toward the middle of 2009, a research project was launched, to which leading international law scholars enthusiastically agreed to lend their talents, for the purpose of examining such a fascinating but intractable topic. The explanation lies in the fact that this book was conceived from the very beginning as a tribute to Professor Giorgio Gaja.

This is easily understood, as the scientific community regards Prof. Gaja as one of the greatest contemporary international lawyers. Such eminent stature has been earned by the sense of systematic coherence and authoritativeness that emanates from his writings, by his creativity in pointing out new directions for legal research, and by his capacity for finding remote logical connections among apparently unrelated aspects of legal experience. It was by virtue of these qualities, universally recognized, that Prof. Gaja was also called on to exert an influential role in the International Law Commission, and, with remarkable frequency, in the International Court of Justice as ad hoc judge in a number of proceedings.

Although Prof. Gaja's writings cover almost every field of international and European law,[1] it is to the law of treaties, by itself and in its relations with other international law fields, that he has devoted constant attention throughout his entire professional life. A common trait of these writings is the observation of how law develops through the interplay of its different sources, in order to reflect more and more the reality of the international relations. The search for the 'law beyond the law' is thus, in the scientific and personal itinerary of Giorgio Gaja, more than an invaluable methodological direction; it is his way to attain the essence of cognition. Writing a book on 'The Law of Treaties Beyond the Vienna Convention' seemed, to the circle of contributors, the best possible way to honour him.

* * *

A last word must be said by the current editor, speaking now on his own behalf.

Sitting today in my office, at the University of Rome, and writing the preface to this book, I am reminiscing about the many years during which my professional and human interlocution with Giorgio Gaja unfolded. I can appreciate, now more than ever, how deeply he has changed my way of looking at the law and beyond it.

E.C.
Rome, June 2010

[1] A list of his contributions to public international law may be found at <http://untreaty.un.org/cod/avl/faculty/Gaja.html>.

Acknowledgements

In finalizing this book I wish to acknowledge the invaluable yet obscure work of the many without whom this book would probably never have come to light.

I owe much to Paolo Palchetti, who considerably contributed to the architecture of the book and whose constant advice has been indispensable throughout its process of realization. Beatrice Bonafé coordinated the work of a group of young scholars who repeatedly checked the manuscript and carried out significant editorial work: Eugenia Bartoloni, Benedetta Ubertazzi, Federica Vincenzetti, Maura Marchegiani, Alessandro Bufalini, Giulia D'Agnone, and Luca Pantaleo. Mel Marquis has provided superb linguistic assistance in regard to various parts of the book.

I am also indebted to Oxford University Press, which graciously agreed to publish this book. In particular, credit is due to John Louth and Merel Alstein, who, from the beginning, have given their support to the research project.

Royalties and other financial advantages gained from this book will be donated to Oxfam International, a non-profit organization whose activities include fighting poverty and injustice, evils which, hélas, international law has been unable, thus far, to extinguish.

Contents

V. *JUS COGENS* BEYOND THE VIENNA CONVENTION

List of Abbreviations

AFDI	Annuaire français de droit International
AJIL	American Journal of International Law
Annu. de l'Inst. de Droit Internat.	Annuaire de l'Institut de Droit International
Anu. de Derecho Internac.	Anuario de Derecho Internacional
ArchivVR	Archiv des Völkerrecht
ARIEL	Austrian Review of International and European Law
ASIL Proc.	Proceedings of the Annual Meetings of the American Society of International Law
Australian YIL	Australian Yearbook of International Law
BYIL	British Yearbook of International Law
Calif. L Rev.	California Law Review
Columb. J of Transnat'l L	Columbia Journal of Transnational Law
Columb. L R	Columbia Law Review
Comun. e Studi	Comunicazione e studi
DGVR Berichte	Berichte der Deutschen Gesellschaft für Völkerrecht
EJIL	European Journal of International Law
Finnish YIL	Finnish Yearbook of International Law
Georgetown L J	Georgetown Law Journal
GYIL	German Yearbook of International Law
Harv. Int'l L J	Harvard International Law Journal
Harv. L Rev.	Harvard Law Review
HRLJ	Human Rights Law Journal
ICLQ	International and Comparative Law Quarterly
ILM	International Legal Materials
ILQ	International Law Quarterly
ILR	International Law Reports
Ital. Yb. of Int'l L	Italian Yearbook of International Law
JDI	Journal du droit international
Leiden J Int'l L	Leiden Journal of International Law
Max Planck UNYB	Max Planck Yearbook of United Nations Law
Mich. J Int'l L	Michigan Journal of International Law
NILR	Netherlands International Law Review
Nordic JIL	Nordic Journal of International Law
NYUJ of Int'l L & Pol.	New York University Journal of International Law and Politics
Pol. Yb. Int'l L	Polish Yearbook of International Law
RBDI	Revue belge de droit international
Recueil des Cours	Recueil des Cours de l'Académie de Droit International
Rev. Egypt. de Droit Internat.	Revue Egyptienne de Droit International

Rev. Esp. de Derecho Internac.	Revista española de derecho internacional
RGDIP	Revue générale de droit international public
RIAA	Reports of International Arbitral Awards
Riv. di Diritto Internaz.	Rivista di Diritto Internazionale
Stanford J Int'l L	Stanford Journal of International Law
SZIER	Schweizerische Zeitschrift für Internationales und Europäisches Recht
United Nations Conference on the Law of Treaties, *Official Records*, vol. I	United Nations Conference on the Law of Treaties, First Session, Vienna 26 March–24 May 1968, Official Records, Summary Records of the Plenary Meetings and of the Meetings of the Committee of the Whole (New York: United Nations, 1969)
United Nations Conference on the Law of Treaties, *Official Records*, vol. II	United Nations Conference on the Law of Treaties, Second Session, Vienna 9 April–22 May 1969, Official Records, Summary Records of the Plenary Meetings and of the Meetings of the Committee of the Whole (New York: United Nations, 1970)
United Nations Conference on the Law of Treaties, *Official Records*, vol. III	United Nations Conference on the Law of Treaties, First and Second Sessions, Vienna, 26 March–24 May 1968 and 9 April–22 May 1969, Official Records, Documents of the Conference (New York: United Nations, 1971)
UNTS	United Nations Treaty Series
Va. J Int'l L	Virginia Journal of International Law
Yale L J	Yale Law Journal
YILC	Yearbook of the International Law Commission
ZaöRV	Zeitschrift für ausländisches öffentliches Recht und Völkerrecht

List of Contributors

Mahnoush H. Arsanjani, Former Director of the Codification Division of the United Nations Office of Legal Affairs; Member of the *Institut de Droit International.*

Enzo Cannizzaro, Professor of International and European Union Law at the University of Rome 'La Sapienza'.

Annalisa Ciampi, Associate Professor of European Union Law at the University of Verona.

Benedetto Conforti, Emeritus Professor of International Law at the University of Naples 'Federico II'; former Judge at the European Court of Human Rights; Member of the *Institut de Droit International.*

Olivier Corten, Professor of International Law at the Université libre de Bruxelles, Center of International Law.

Pierre-Marie Dupuy, Professor of International Law at the Graduate Institute of International and Development Studies, Geneva and at the University of Panthéon-Assas, Paris 2.

Serena Forlati, Associate Professor of International Law at the University of Ferrara.

Alessandra Gianelli, Professor of International Law at the University of Teramo.

Gleider I. Hernández, Associate Legal Officer/Law Clerk at the International Court of Justice; PhD candidate, Wadham College, Oxford.

Jan Klabbers, Professor of International Organizations Law at the University of Helsinki.

Pierre Klein, Professor of International Law at the Université libre de Bruxelles, Center of International Law.

Marcelo G. Kohen, Professor of International Law at the Graduate Institute of International and Development Studies, Geneva; Member of the *Institut de Droit International.*

Pieter Jan Kuijper, Professor of the Law of International Organizations at the University of Amsterdam; former Director for External Relations and Trade Law in the Legal Service of the European Commission.

Donald McRae, Hyman Soloway Professor at the University of Ottawa; Member of the International Law Commission.

Daniel Müller, Researcher at the *Centre de droit international de Nanterre (CEDIN)*, University of Paris X-Nanterre.

Georg Nolte, Professor of Law at the Humboldt University of Berlin; Member of the International Law Commission.

Paolo Palchetti, Associate Professor of International Law at the University of Macerata.

Alain Pellet, Professor of International Law at the University of Paris X-Nanterre; Member and former President of the International Law Commission; Member of the *Institut de Droit International*.

Paolo Picone, Professor of International Law at the University of Rome 'La Sapienza'; Member of the *Institut de Droit International*.

Fausto Pocar, Professor of International Law at the University of Milan; Judge and former President of the International Criminal Tribunal for the Former Yugoslavia; Member of the *Institut de Droit International*.

W. Michael Reisman, Myres S. McDougal Professor of International Law, Yale Law School; Member of the *Institut de Droit International*.

Francesco Salerno, Professor of International Law at the University of Ferrara.

Luigi Sbolci, Professor of International Law at the University of Florence.

Bruno Simma, Judge at the International Court of Justice; William W. Cook Global Law Professor at the University of Michigan Law School (on leave); Professor (ret.) at the Ludwig-Maximilians-Universität, Munich; Member of the *Institut de Droit International*.

Christian Tomuschat, Emeritus Professor at the Humboldt University of Berlin; former Member and President of the International Law Commission; Member of the *Institut de Droit International*.

Joe Verhoeven, Professor of International Law at the University of Paris II Panthéon-Assas; Member and Secretary General of the *Institut de Droit International*.

Mark E. Villiger, Professor of Law at the University of Zurich; Judge at the European Court of Human Rights.

Michael Wood, Senior Fellow of the Lauterpacht Centre for International Law, University of Cambridge; Member of the International Law Commission.

Karl Zemanek, Emeritus Professor of Law at the University of Vienna; Member of the *Institut de Droit International*.

Table of Cases

PERMANENT COURT OF INTERNATIONAL JUSTICE

INTERNATIONAL COURT OF JUSTICE

Contentious cases

Advisory Opinions

WTO DISPUTE SETTLEMENT SYSTEM

WTO Appellate Body Reports

WTO Panel Reports

ARBITRAL TRIBUNALS

Permanent Court of Arbitration

Iran-US Claims Tribunal

Eritrea–Ethiopia Claims Commission

ICSID

Other arbitral Tribunals

COURT OF JUSTICE OF THE EUROPEAN UNION

General Court

Court of Justice

EUROPEAN COMMISSION OF HUMAN RIGHTS

EUROPEAN COURT OF HUMAN RIGHTS

INTER-AMERICAN COURT OF HUMAN RIGHTS

INTERNATIONAL CRIMINAL TRIBUNAL FOR THE FORMER YUGOSLAVIA

NATIONAL COURTS

PART I

CONCLUSION OF TREATIES

1

Are Agreements between States and Non-State Entities Rooted in the International Legal Order?

*Olivier Corten and Pierre Klein**

According to Article 3 of the 1969 Vienna Convention on the Law of Treaties between States:

The fact that the present Convention does not apply to international agreements concluded between States and other subjects of international law or between such other subjects of international law, or to international agreements not in written form, shall not affect:

(a) the legal force of such agreements;
(b) the application to them of any of the rules set forth in the present Convention to which they would be subject under international law independently of the Convention;
(c) the application of the Convention to the relations of States as between themselves under international agreements to which other subjects of international law are also parties.[1]

A provision to the same effect is to be found in the 1986 Vienna Convention on the Law of Treaties between International Organizations or between International Organizations and States.[2]

Ever more numerous situations seem to come within the ambit of this provision.[3] Over the years, a growing number of agreements have thus been concluded with entities which are neither states nor international organizations.[4] Examples of such entities range from the Holy See to components of federal states, and

* The authors wish to express their sincere gratitude to Ms Martyna Falkowska for her very able research assistance.

[1] 1969 Vienna Convention on the Law of Treaties, 1155 *UNTS*, 331.

[2] 1986 Vienna Convention on the Law of Treaties, A/CONF.129/15.

[3] This study will not deal with agreements concluded with indigenous peoples; see, eg, M.A. Martinez, 'Study on Treaties, Agreements and Other Constructive Arrangements between States and Indigenous Populations', UNHCHR (Sub-commission) 'Final report by Miguel Alfonso Martínez, Special Rapporteur' (1999) E/CN.4/Sub.2/1999/20, available at <http://www.unhchr.ch/huridocda/huridoca.nsf/0/696c51cf6f20b8bc802567c4003793ec?opendocument>; see also <http://cwis.org/fwdp/treaties.html>.

[4] See generally on the definition of entities parties to treaties J. Klabbers, *The Concept of Treaty in International Law* (The Hague: Kluwer Law International, 1996) 47–8.

have also included non-state parties to armed conflicts—insurrectional movements, and later on national liberation movements.[5] As far as this latter category of non-state entity is concerned, however, the vast majority of territories under colonial domination or foreign occupation having gained independence, there is nowadays hardly any group involved in armed confrontation with the authorities of a state—be it to attempt to overthrow these authorities, to create a new state, or simply to claim a better treatment for (part of) the population—which can successfully claim such status—and the aura of legitimacy conferred upon it by international law.[6] But while their status under international law may be quite different from that of national liberation movements, such armed opposition groups and movements have, over the past 20 years or so, become parties to an impressive number of agreements with states, aiming mostly at bringing internal conflicts to an end. These agreements—and more specifically the issue of their legal status—have recently begun to draw the attention of authors and, in at least one case, of tribunals.[7] Even though any answer to this latter question is dependent upon the very content of each particular agreement and on the circumstances of its drawing up, it is often queried whether these new types of agreements do reflect the emergence—in legal terms—of non-state entities in international relations. It could indeed be argued that, by entering into agreements akin to treaties with such entities, states would tend to recognize that such groups have a limited form of international legal personality. Such 'international agreements' would therefore be endowed with 'legal force' (Article 3(a) of the Vienna Conventions), and could be subject to 'any of the rules [...] to which they would be subject under international law independently of the Convention' (Article 3(b)). The purpose of this contribution will be to assess to what extent this could indeed be said to be the case. This chapter is based on a selection of agreements aiming at bringing an end to a violent conflict within a state. This sample includes several dozens of such agreements, covering all regions of the world.[8] We have attempted to establish whether, beyond the specificities of each agreement, these reflected

[5] On the various categories of entities that have concluded agreements deemed to come within the ambit of Article 3 of the Vienna Convention on the Law of Treaties over the years, see, eg, the Commentary to that provision by Y. Le Bouthillier and J.-F. Bonin, in O. Corten and P. Klein (eds), *Les Conventions de Vienne sur le droit des traités—Commentaire article par article* (Brussels: Bruylant, 2006) 106–9, para. 16. See also O. Lissitzyn, 'Territorial Entities other than States in the Law of Treaties' 125 *Recueil des Cours* (1968-III) 1–90.

[6] See generally T. Christakis, *Le droit à l'autodétermination en dehors des situations de décolonisation* (Paris: La documentation française, 1999).

[7] See in particular C. Bell, *On the Law of Peace. Peace Agreements and the Lex Pacificatoria* (Oxford: Oxford University Press, 2008) and the bibiliography, 345–70; C. Bell, 'Peace Agreements: Their Nature and Legal Status' 100 *AJIL* (2006) 373–412; V.P. Fortna, *Peace Time: Cease-Fire Agreements and the Durability of Peace* (Princeton: Princeton University Press, 2004). Sierra Leone (Special Criminal Court), *Prosecutor v. Morris Kallon, Brima Bazzy Kamara*, case n. SCSL-2004-15-AR72(E), SCSL-2004-16-AR72(E), 13 march 2004.

[8] Use has been made of the Uppsala Conflict Data Program database, available at <http://www.pcr.uu.se/gpdatabase/search.php> (consulted in March and April 2010). Unless specified otherwise, all texts quoted below are to be found in this database.

the parties' will to endow them with any kind of 'legal force' under international law, and more generally to ground them in the international legal sphere.

We have focused to that end on the two constituents that are generally to be found in peace agreements:

- First, such agreements aim at a suspension of combats and hostilities; the parties reciprocally commit not to use force against each other.[9] Traditionally, however, the use of force within a state is deemed to be a matter pertaining to the latter's sovereignty. The prohibition on the use of force expressed in the United Nations Charter applies in 'international relations' only—ie between states.[10] Do peace agreements, when they provide for ceasefire arrangements, confirm the thesis according to which the scope of this rule now extends to conflict situations *within* states?[11] Are non-state entities which are parties to such agreements given as a consequence a form—or 'measure'—of international legal personality akin to states, to the extent that those entities would benefit from this rule which is traditionally aimed at protecting state sovereignty vis-à-vis third states?
- The second typical constituent of peace agreements is clauses aimed at the political settlement of the conflict. Here again, such settlement *a priori* pertains to the exclusive jurisdiction of states, which have the sovereign right to determine their political, economic, social, and cultural regime.[12] It may therefore be wondered, here too, whether peace agreements evidence a drastic reduction of the area of domestic jurisdiction of states, rebel groups being entitled to rely on rights and obligations under international law to require compliance with rules providing for a particular form of power sharing.

These two issues will be addressed in turn (Sections 1 and 2), based on an analysis of the aforementioned selection of agreements aiming at bringing an end to violent conflicts within a state, in order to assess the parties' will to ground them in the international legal order. Lastly, a move will be made away from the position—and perceptions—of the parties themselves to consider how such agreements are envisaged by third parties—mainly the United Nations and third states—when it comes to their implementation. Section 3 will therefore attempt to determine whether such third parties consider that the implementation and breaches of such agreements are to be dealt with as a matter of international law—or not. Our general assumption,

[9] See H. Levie, 'The Nature and Scope of the Armistice Agreement' 50 *AJIL* (1956) 880–906; R.R. Baxter, 'Armistices and other Forms of Suspension of Hostilities', 149 *Recueil des Cours* (1976-I) 351–99; S.D. Bailey, 'Cease-Fires, Truces, and Armistices in the practice of the UN Security Council' 71 *AJIL* (1977) 461–72.

[10] O. Corten, *The Law Against War* (Oxford: Hart Publishing 2010) 126–98.

[11] See, eg, A. Cassese, 'Article 51', in J.P. Cot and A. Pellet (eds), *La Charte des Nations Unies* (Paris: Economica, 3rd edn, 2005) 1333.

[12] See, eg, UNGA resolution 2625 (XXV) and ICJ, *Military and Paramilitary Activities in and against Nicaragua (Nicaragua v USA)*, Merits, Judgment of 27 June 1986, *ICJ Reports* (1986) at 133, para. 263.

based on the sample we have been working on, is that the 'move to international law' that those agreements evidence is only limited. Due to the numerous ambiguities which characterize these texts and to the treatment they have been given by both parties and non-parties, they do not appear to be clearly rooted in the international legal order. It is therefore far from obvious that they come under the category of agreements envisaged in Article 3 of the Vienna Conventions on the Law of Treaties and that they could be considered as such to be subject to rules of international law pertaining to treaties, even independently of the Conventions.

1. The Text of the Agreements: Ceasefires as an Application of the International Prohibition on the Use of Force?

According to Article 1 of the Agreement between Sierra Leone and RUF concluded in 2000, the parties agree '[t]o declare and observe a cease-fire and to halt hostilities with effect from Friday 10th November 2000 starting at 23:59 hours'.[13] Similar commitments are expressed in a number of agreements concluded between states and armed opposition groups. These often proclaim or take note of a ceasefire that is to come into effect at a certain time, or express in less specific terms a renunciation of violence or of the use of armed force by one or both parties.[14] Do such clauses reflect a will to apply, within states, the rule prohibiting the use of force 'in international relations' set out in Article 2(4) of the United Nations Charter? In the affirmative, peace agreements should clearly be viewed as rooted in the international legal order.

The very broad terms used in those provisions do not appear to allow for such a conclusion. One would even be inclined to reach the opposite conclusion if

[13] Available at <http://www.pcr.uu.se/gpdatabase/search.php>; see also Agreement on a Permanent Ceasefire Juba, Sudan, (23 February 2008).

[14] See, eg, 'Clause 1: The immediate ceasing of hostilities and the abstention of all military acts or other forms of violence, and the ceasing of all media campaigns liable to harm the efforts aiming at asserting the spirit of brotherhood and concord' (Peace Agreement between the Government of the Central African Republic and the political and military movements designated below: 'Front Démocratique du Peuple Centrafricain' (FDPC) (The Democratic Front for the Central African People); 'Union des Forces Démocratiques pour le Rassemblement' (UFDR) (the Union of Democratic Forces for Unity), 2 Feb 2007; 'The Parties to this Agreement hereby declare that they renounce, deplore and do solemnly give up violence and the use of armed force and undertake to settle their differences through consultation and peaceful negociation [...]' (*Salomon Islands—The Townville Peace Agreement*, 15 October 2000, Part Eight.); 'condition for lasting peace and a cessation of violence in Burundi'(Article II, Arusha Peace and Reconciliation Agreement for Burundi, 28 August 2000, available at <http://ocha-gwapps1.unog.ch/rw/rwb.nsf/db900SID/MHII-6ABBHY?OpenDocument>). See also Accord de paix Sénégal et 'mouvement des forces démocratiques de la Casamance', 30 December 2004, Article 1(2)); Rwanda, Peace Agreement between the Government of the Republic of Rwanda and the Rwandese Patriotic Front, Arusha, 4 August 1993, annexed to A/48/824, S/26915, 23 December 1993 ('The war between the Government of the Republic of Rwanda and the Rwandese Patriotic Front is hereby brought to an end'); Pretoria Agreement on the Peace Process in Côte d'Ivoire, 6 April 2005; letter dated 25 April 2005 from the Permanent Representative of South Africa to the United Nations addressed to the President of the Security Council, 25 April 2005, S/2005/270, Article 3.

account is taken of the definition of acts which are deemed to amount to a breach of the ceasefire, as they are sometimes listed in those instruments. The following excerpts of the peace accord signed in 2006 between the government of Nepal and the Communist Party of Nepal, and of the Bicesse Agreement of May 1991 between the government of Angola and UNITA, respectively, are particularly telling in that regard:

'Ceasefire' refers to the act of prohibiting all forms of attack, kidnapping, disappearance, obstruction, carried out between Nepal Government and CPN (Maoist) by aiming at each other, mobilization of armed forces, strengthening, aggressive and violent activities, and activities spreading destruction, incitement and instigation through whatever means;[15]

The cease-fire will, beginning on the date and time agreed upon for its entry into force, entail the cessation of: (a) All armed air, land or sea attacks, as well as all actions of sabotage; (b) All offensive movement of troops or armed groups; (c) Attempts to occupy new ground positions and the movement of military forces and resources from one area to another without prior agreement between the parties; (d) All military manoeuvres aimed at installing weapons with the capability to endanger the safety of settlements and the economic, administrative and military infrastructures; (e) Patrol activities outside the areas to be demarcated around the areas of assembly for the troops of the Government of the People's Republic of Angola and UNITA; (f) All acts of violence against the civilian population; (g) The planting of new mines and actions aimed at impeding activities to deactivate mines; (h) Unjustified restrictions or impediments on the free circulation of persons and goods; (i) Any other actions that may impede the normal evolution of the cease-fire process; (j) Receipt of lethal material, regardless of its origin.[16]

The types of conduct targeted in these provisions go far beyond the 'use of force' within the meaning of Article 2(4) of the Charter, in the context of which this concept is generally understood as an attack—or the threat of such attack—with military means, and does not encompass any coercive—or even merely hostile—action.[17] In this regard, it should be noted that some agreements provide not only

[15] Comprehensive Peace Accord signed between the Nepal Government and the Communist Party of Nepal, 22 November 2006, Article 2.

[16] The Bicesse Agreement, Angola, Peace Accords for Angola, May 1991. See also The Uganda Peace Talks Agreement for the Restoration of Peace to the Sovereign State of the Republic of Uganda, 17 November 1985, Article 1; Agreement on a Permanent Ceasefire Juba, Sudan (23 February 2008), Article 5; Agreement on a Ceasefire between the Government of the Democratic Socialist Republic of Sri Lanka and the Liberation Tigers of Tamil Eelam (23 February 2002), Article 1; Sierra Leone and RUF, Abuja, 10 November 2000, Article 9; Arusha Peace and Reconciliation Agreement for Burundi, 28 August 2000, available at <http://ocha-gwapps1.unog.ch/rw/rwb.nsf/db900SID/MHII-6ABBHY?OpenDocument>, Protocol III—Peace and Security for all, Article 25; Ceasefire Agreement between the Transitional Government of Burundi and the Conseil national pour la défense de la démocratie—Forces pour la défense de la démocratie, Arusha, 2 December 2002, (Doc. S/2002/1329, 4 December 2002, Article II); Comprehensive Ceasefire Agreement between the Government of the Republic of Burundi and the Palipehutu–FNL, Dar es Salaam, 7 September 2006, Article II (and annex); Agreement between the governement of the Republic of Angola and UNITA, Doc. S/2002/483, Luanda, 26 April 2002, Article 3.

[17] O. Corten, *supra* note 10, 50–92.

for a ceasefire, but also for the 'cessation of hostilities'. The scope of this latter notion is sometimes defined in very broad terms, including for instance

Political hostilities: (i) Verbal aggression and denigration; (ii) Political imprisonment; (iii) Forced regroupment camps; (iv) Violation of political rights and freedoms, or '[...] (c) [...] murders, the taking of hostages, unlawful arrest and detention, and acts of pillage against the civilian population and servicemen in the Republic and other countries; (d) [...] blockades of populated areas, national economic and military installations and of all means of communication; (e) [...] the use of all forms of communication and mass media to undermine the process of national reconciliation; (f) [the use of] religion and the religious feelings of believers, as well as any ideology, for hostile purposes.[18]

In the same sense, the October 1995 agreement for peace between the government of the Philippines and rebel groups provides that

... [c]essation of hostilities shall cover not only armed activities and conflicts but such other acts considered as hostile, including, but not limited to, surveillance, special operations, unlawful arrests and seizures, and any exercise of police authority which is violative of civil and political rights or recruitment, agitation, propaganda, and any illegal act or activity which may destabilize the State or which is in contravention of the letter and spirit of this Agreement.[19]

One may still quote, to the same effect, the Burundi Ceasefire Agreement of 2002, according to which '[u]pon signing the Ceasefire Agreement, the parties shall cease all acts of violence and shall desist from public campaigns against the other parties. In other words, the media and public forums, among others, shall not be used to incite hostility.'[20] Such provisions are obviously very remote from the wording and meaning of Article 2(4), which is indeed never referred to in any of these agreements.[21]

In the same perspective, it should be noted that no mention is ever made of the right of self-defence, be it under general international law or under Article 51 of the UN Charter. To the contrary, a number of the agreements under analysis provide

[18] Agreement on a Temporary Cease-fire and the Cessation of Other Hostile Acts on the Tajik–Afghan Border and within the Country for the Duration of the Talks, Article 2 (in Report of the Secretary-General on the Situation in Tajikistan, Doc. S/1994/1102, 27 September 1994, pp. 4–5; Annex I).

[19] General Agreement for Peace between the Government of the Republic of the Philippines and the Rebolusyonaryong Alyansang Makabansa–Soldiers of the Filipino People–Young Officers'Union, done in Quezon City this 13 day of October 1995, Article 1, section 1.

[20] Annex 1 to the Burundi Ceasefire Agreement (Ceasefire Agreement between the Transitional Government of Burundi and the Conseil national pour la défense de la démocratie–Forces pour la défense de la démocratie), Arusha, 2 December 2002, S/2002/1329, 4 December 2002, Article 1(2).

[21] Practice shows that whenever parties to an agreement intend to refer to the prohibition on the use of force within the meaning of the UN Charter, they do so in unambiguous terms; see, for instance, Article 1 of the 1949 Washington Treaty creating NATO or the Preamble of ECOWAS Protocol on non-aggression of 22 April 1978, available at <http://bibliotecavirtual.clacso.org.ar/ar/libros/iss/pdfs/ecowas/14ProtNonAggre.pdf>. See also Article 301 of the 1982 Convention on the Law of the Sea.

for a specific procedure to be followed in the event of a breach of the ceasefire that has been proclaimed. To give but one example of such mechanism, the 1994 agreement concluded between Liberia and rebel groups provides in that respect that

> ... [a]ll violations of the cease-fire shall be reported to UNOMIL, which shall, on immediate receipt of the information on violation, commence an investigation and make findings thereof. In the event the violation can be cured by the party, UNOMIL shall pursue such a course. However, should such a course not be possible, UNOMIL shall submit its findings to the Cease-fire Violations Committee. The Violations Committee shall invite the violating party(ies) for the purpose of having such party(ies) take corrective measures to cure violations within such time-frame as may be stipulated by the Committee. Should the violating party not take the required corrective measures, and the use of peace enforcement powers are [sic] recommended against the violator, the Liberia National Transitional Government, in collaboration with ECOMOG, shall thereupon take the necessary action.[22]

Such a mechanism *a contrario* excludes the right to unilaterally use force in self-defence, as an exception to the general prohibition on the use of force in public international law. All in all, the very wording and the overall conception of these agreements tend to show that the parties to these instruments never had the intent to have their relations in that respect ruled by *jus contra bellum* within the meaning of public international law.

Mention nevertheless has to be made of some agreements whose wording is far more ambiguous in that respect. Three of these, concerning secessionist conflicts in Eastern Europe, may more particularly be singled out. In the first of these agreements, Georgia and South Ossetia undertake 'to settle all the issues in dispute exclusively by peaceful means, without resort to force or threat of resort to force'[23] and to 'denounce application of force or threat of force'.[24] In the second, the Republic of Moldova and Transdniestria 'reaffirm their commitment not to resort to the use of force or the threat of force in their mutual relations. Any differences shall be resolved exclusively by peaceful means.'[25] Finally,

[22] S/1994/1174, 16 October 1994, Article 8. See also Memorandum of Understanding between the Government of the Republic of Indonesia and the Free Aceh Movement, Signed in triplicate in Helsinki, Finland on the 15 of August in the year 2005, Article VI(1); The Uganda Peace Talks Agreement for the Restoration of Peace to the Sovereign State of the Republic of Uganda, 17 November 1985, Article 17; Arusha Peace and Reconciliation Agreement for Burundi, 28 August 2000, available at <http://ocha-gwapps1.unog.ch/rw/rwb.nsf/db900SID/MHII-6ABBHY?OpenDocument>, Protocol III. Peace and Security for all, Article 27; Ceasefire Agreement between the Transitional Government of Burundi and the Conseil national pour la défense de la démocratie-Forces pour la défense de la démocratie, Arusha, 2 December, 2002, S/2002/1329, 4 December 2002, Article III; The Bicesse Agreement, Angola, Peace Accords for Angola, May 1991, Article 4.

[23] Agreement on Further Development of the Process of Peaceful Settlement of the Georgian-Ossetian Conflict and the Joint Controlling Commission, 31 October 1994, Article 5, available at <http://www.rrc.ge/law/Agrea_1994_10_31_e.htm?lawid=440&lng_3=en>.

[24] Memorandum on Measures to Provide Security and Strengthen Mutual Trust between Sides in the Georgian–South Ossetian Conflict, 16 May 1996, Article 1, available at <http://www.rrc.ge/law/memr_1996_05_16_e.htm?lawid=472&lng_3=en>.

[25] Memorandum on the Bases for Normalization of Relations between the Republic of Moldova and Transdniestria, Article 1.

Russia and Chechnya have undertaken in an instrument expressly identified as a 'treaty' 'to reject forever the use of force or threat of force in resolving all matters of dispute'.[26] Such formulas appear much closer to the wording of Article 2(4) of the Charter. While the latter is not explicitly mentioned in these agreements, it could be argued that the parties intended to refer to it, at least indirectly. Such argument could be supported by the fact that the states and secessionist entities concerned simultaneously reiterate their 'commitment to the UN Charter, fundamental principles and decisions of the OSCE, and universally recognized norms of international law'[27] or undertake to 'develop their relations on generally recognized principles and norms of international law'[28]—this being subject to the conclusion of further agreements aiming at regulating these new relations.[29] Should one conclude therefrom that these agreements evidence the parties' will to have their mutual relations governed by the rules of *jus contra bellum* under international law? Such a conclusion is indeed possible on the basis of a literal analysis of the instruments concerned. It would, however, appear excessive if the interpretation and application these agreements have been given in practice is taken into account. This indeed shows that the relations between these states and the secessionist entities that they were fighting have generally not been approached under the angle of the prohibition on the use of force in international relations.[30]

At this stage, it will only be pointed out that the vast majority of agreements under analysis does not reflect any intention to make applicable within states the prohibition on the use of force as this concept is understood in public international law. To that extent, it is far from obvious that these instruments evidence the will of the parties to have their relations governed by international law. It could nevertheless be argued that by agreeing not to resort to violent action under a peace agreement, the parties intend to create some type of international obligation which would not amount to the prohibition set out in Article 2(4) of the UN Charter and whose validity and scope would be limited to the agreement in question. The breach of such obligation would therefore not give rise to the right to use force in self-defence under Article 51 of the Charter, but to—potential—specific consequences provided for by the agreement (eg activation of third party monitoring mechanism, etc).

Ultimately, much will depend on the terms of each particular agreement. The question of whether the parties have intended to create international obligations and provide for the application of rules of international law in their mutual

[26] Peace Treaty and Principles of Interrelation between Russian Federation and Chechen Republic Ichkeria, 12 May 1997, Article 1.

[27] Memorandum on Necessary Measures to be undertaken in order to Ensure Security and Strengthening of Mutual Trust Between the Parties to the Georgian–Ossetian Conflict, available at <http://www.rrc.ge/law/memr_1996_05_16_e.htm?lawid=472&lng_3=en>, Preamble.

[28] Peace Treaty and Principles of Interrelation between Russian Federation and Chechen Republic Ichkeria, 12 May 1997, Article 2.

[29] Ibid., Article 3.

[30] See *infra*, Part 3.

relations will have to be answered on the basis of the content of each instrument. As was the case in some of these agreements, the parties may even have specifically identified the law applicable to the instrument at stake. Such situations shall be considered in the following section, since provisions of that kind are often related to the principles agreed on by the parties in order to achieve the political settlement of the conflict.

2. The Text of the Agreements: Principles of Governance as International Legal Obligations?

According to the Agreement on comprehensive solutions concluded by the government of the Republic of Uganda and the Lord's Resistance Army/Movement in 2007:

2.1 The Parties shall adhere to the following objectives and directive principles enshrined in the Constitution as the guiding principles in the implementation of this Agreement:

a) The State shall be based on democratic principles, which empower and encourage the active participation of all citizens at all levels in their own governance.

b) The composition of Government shall be broadly representative of the national character, gender and social diversity of the country.

c) Every effort shall be made to integrate all the peoples of Uganda in governance while at the same time recognizing the existence of their ethnic, religious, ideological, political and cultural diversities.

d) The Government shall take necessary measures to bring about balanced development of different areas of Uganda and between the rural and urban areas.

e) The Government shall take special measures in favor of development of the least developed areas.

f) The Government shall take affirmative action in favor of groups marginalized on the basis of gender, age, disability or any other reason created by history, tradition or custom, for the purpose of redressing imbalances, which may exist against them.

g) All persons are equal before and under the law in all spheres of political, social and cultural life, and in every other respect and shall enjoy equal protection of the law.

h) The Parties affirm that there shall be no arbitrary detentions.[31]

[31] Juba, Sudan, 2 May 2007.

Similar provisions may be found in numerous other agreements, which often provide for reforms of the constitutional,[32] executive,[33] legislative,[34] and judiciary[35] systems, or of police and security forces.[36] Such provisions often aim at securing the (re-)integration of rebel forces within the state apparatus, so as to make possible the restoration of peace and order in the long term—an objective that will not be reached through the mere proclamation of a ceasefire, which generally provides for a temporary respite in the conflict only, if more radical reforms are not undertaken.[37] In that perspective, some agreements expressly put the emphasis on '[t]he founding of a State governed by the rule of law, based on national unity, democracy, pluralism and respect for human rights'.[38] Globally, references to the concepts of democracy, governance, or rule of law seem to extend far beyond the traditional international obligations limiting the national competence of states in determining their system of government.[39] It may, however, be asked whether by referring to such concepts the parties actually intend to undertake obligations under international law.

One point calls for clarification from the outset in that respect. When agreements express undertakings to comply with human rights enshrined in

[32] See, eg, the Arusha Peace and Reconciliation Agreement for Burundi, 28 August 2000, available at<http://ocha-gwapps1.unog.ch/rw/rwb.nsf/db900SID/MHII-6ABBHY?OpenDocument>, Protocol II. Democracy and Good Governance, Article 1; The Bicesse Agreement, Angola, Peace Accords for Angola, May 1991, Article IV(1); Agreement between the Interim Government of National Unity of Liberia (IGNU) of the first part and the National Patriotic Front of Liberia (NPFL) of the second part and the United Liberation Movement of Liberia for Democracy (ULIMO) of the third part, S/26272, 9 August 1993, Article 14(8).

[33] See, eg, the Peace Agreement between the Government of Uganda and the Ugandan People's Democratic Movement, 3 June 1988, A (1).

[34] See, eg, the Agreement on Provisional Arrangements in Afghanistan pending the re-establishment of permanent Government institutions, Bonn, 5 December 2001, S/2001/1154, 5 December 2001, II.

[35] See, eg, the Agreement between the Interim Government of National Unity of Liberia (IGNU) of the first part and the National Patriotic Front of Liberia (NPFL) of the second part and the United Liberation Movement of Liberia for Democracy (ULIMO) of the third part, S/26272, 9 August 1993, Article 14(8).

[36] See, eg, Peace Agreement between the Government of Liberia, the Liberians United for Reconciliation and Democracy, the Movement for Democracy in Liberia and the political parties, Accra, 18 August 2003, S/2003/850, 29 August 2003, Article VII.

[37] See, eg, Linas–Marcoussis Agreement, 23 January 2003, S/2003/99.

[38] Ceasefire Agreement between the Transitional Government of Burundi and the Conseil national pour la défense de la démocratie–Forces pour la défense de la démocratie, Arusha, 2 December 2002, S/2002/1329, 4 December 2002, Article VI(1)(1); see also the Peace Agreement between the Government of the Republic of Rwanda and the Rwandese Patriotic Front, Arusha, 4 August 1993, annexed to A/48/824-S/26915, 23 December 1993, Preamble; Agreement between the governement of the Republic of Angola and UNITA, S/2002/483, Luanda, 26 April 2002, Article 2(1); Peace Agreement between the Government of the Central African Republic and the political and military movements designated below: 'Front Démocratique du Peuple Centrafricain' (FDPC) (The Democratic Front for the Central African People); 'Union des Forces Démocratiques pour le Rassemblement' (UFDR) (the Union of Democratic Forces for Unity), 2 Feb 2007, Preamble.

[39] See, eg, T. Carothers (ed.), *Promoting the Rule of Law Abroad. In Search of Knowledge* (Washington: Carnegie Endowment for International Peace, 2006).

international conventions, it is beyond doubt that they refer to obligations pertaining to the international legal sphere.[40] The Pretoria Agreement concluded in 2002 in the framework of the inter-Congolese dialogue thus provides that '[t]he Parties shall reaffirm their support for the Universal Declaration of Human Rights, the International Pact on Civil and Political Rights of 1966, the International Pact on Economic and Socio-Cultural Rights of 1966, the African Charter on Human Rights and the Rights of Peoples of 1981, and duly ratified international conventions'.[41]

As such, clauses of that kind do not, however, reflect the parties' will to have the ceasefire and/or power-sharing agreement they have concluded governed by international law. It is indeed quite common for domestic law instruments (constitutions, acts, decrees, etc.) to refer to or to incorporate public international law norms. This obviously does not entail that the instrument in question itself pertains to the international legal sphere. Such practice is merely reflective of the state's commitment to comply with specific international obligations binding upon it by enacting measures for the implementation of those obligations in the domestic legal order. The same conclusion could *a priori* be drawn in respect of agreements aiming at putting an end to internal conflicts whenever they refer to compliance with international human rights.

References to overarching principles such as governance or the rule of law appear more original in that regard. It may seem more difficult to argue here that such references are nothing more than a way to incorporate traditional human rights. It is, however, far from obvious that, by including references to such principles in the agreements they conclude to bring an end to internal conflicts, the parties intend to have these agreements governed by international law. There are two reasons for this. First, the wording used in a significant number of agreements appears to be too general and unspecific to be characterized as juridical. In other words, doubts can be expressed as to the actual will of the parties to commit themselves in legal—rather than political, in particular—terms. Besides the abovementioned reference to 'objectives and directive principles' in the Uganda/

[40] See generally C. Bell, *Peace Agreements and Human Rights* (Oxford: Oxford University Press, 2000).

[41] Inter-Congolese Dialogue, Pretoria Agreement, 16 December 2002, Article III(3). See also Niger, Accord entre le gouvernement et l'organisation de la résistance armée, Ouagadougou, 15 April 1995, Preamble; Comprehensive Peace Accord signed between Nepal Government and the Communist Party of Nepal, 22 November 2006, Articles 7 and 10(3); Agreement on Provisional Arrangements in Afghanistan pending the re-establishment of permanent Government institutions, Bonn, 5 December 2001, S/2001/1154, 5 December 2001, I; Arusha Peace and Reconciliation Agreement for Burundi, 28 August 2000, available at <http://ocha-gwapps1.unog.ch/rw/rwb.nsf/db900SID/MHII-6ABBHY?OpenDocument>, Protocol II. Democracy and Good Governance, Article 3; Peace Agreement between the Government of Liberia, the Liberians United for Reconciliation and Democracy, the Movement for Democracy in Liberia and the political parties, Accra, 18 August 2003, S/2003/850, 29 August 2003, Article XII; Memorandum of Understanding between the Government of the Republic of Indonesia and the Free Aceh Movement, Signed in triplicate in Helsinki, 15 August 2005, Article 2.

LRA Agreement of 2007, mention could be made, for instance of Article 3 of the Arusha Peace and Reconciliation Agreement for Burundi, according to which

> The Parties commit themselves to refrain from any act or behaviour contrary to the provisions of the Agreement, and to spare no effort to ensure that the said provisions are respected and implemented in their letter and spirit in order to ensure the attainment of genuine unity, reconciliation, lasting peace, security for all, solid democracy and on equitable sharing of resources in Burundi.[42]

Such language appears closer to 'soft law', ambiguous as this notion may be. The ambiguity as to the rooting of such agreements in the legal sphere is perfectly evidenced by the following description of one of these instruments by the parties themselves: '[T]he Lusaka Protocol, signed 20 November 1994 by the Government and by the UNITA with the mediation of the UN and in the presence of Observer Countries to the Angolan Peace Process, was undertaken *as the political-juridical instrument* for the resolution of the Angolan conflict, in order to achieve peace and national reconciliation [...]'[43]

Such ambiguity actually appears to reflect the rather elusive character of the concept of rule of law when envisaged from the perspective of international law. Strong doubts have indeed been expressed as to the rooting of this concept in the international legal order as it stands presently, at least when its use aims at encompassing rights and obligations reaching beyond well-established civil and political rights, such as the right to the safety of persons, the right to take part in free and fair elections, etc.[44]

Secondly, even if these agreements were interpreted as pertaining exclusively to the legal sphere, it should still be established that the legal sphere in question is that of public international, rather than national, law. What is striking in that regard is the fact that the provisions on applicable law, whenever such provisions are included in the instruments under examination, very often refer to national constitutions[45] or laws[46] and not to international legal instruments. Article 3 of the Peace Agreement concluded between the government of the Republic of

[42] Arusha Peace and Reconciliation Agreement for Burundi, 28 August 2000, available at <http://ocha-gwapps1.unog.ch/rw/rwb.nsf/db900SID/MHII-6ABBHY?OpenDocument>.

[43] Agreement between the governement of the Republic of Angola and UNITA, S/2002/483, Luanda, 26 April 2002, Preamble (see also Article 2(2)); emphasis added.

[44] See in particular the proceedings of the 2008 annual conference of the French Society for International Law (SFDI, *L'Etat de droit en droit international* (Paris: Pedone, 2009)).

[45] 'Both Parties uphold the supremacy of the Constitution, the Rule of the Law and the preservation of democratic processes and institutions' (General Agreement for Peace between the Government of the Republic of the Philippines and the Rebolusyonaryong Alyansang Makabansa–Soldiers of the Filipino People–Young Officers' Union, done in Quezon City this 13 day of October 1995); 'The obligation derived from the above, should be undertaken with full respect to the constitution of the Republic of Angola and for Human Rights' (Agreement signed by the Government of the Republic of Angola and UNITA Renovada on 18 Feb 1999, Luanda, S/1999/268, 11 March 1999). See also Ouagadougou Peace Agreement, 4 March 2007, S/2007/144, Preamble.

[46] S/26272, 9 August 1993, Article 14(5); Protocol on the fundamental Principles for establishing peace and national accord in Tajikistan, 17 August 1995, Preamble.

Rwanda and the Rwandese Patriotic Front in August 1993 provides a perfect illustration of this:

The two parties also agree that the Constitution of 10th June, 1991, and the Arusha Peace Agreement, shall constitute indissolubly the Fundamental Law that shall govern the Country during the Transition period, taking into account the following provisions:

1. The following Articles of the Constitution shall be replaced by the provisions of the Peace Agreement relating to the same matters. The Articles in question are: 34, 35, 38, 39, 40, 41, 42, 43, 44, 45, 46, 47, 48, 49, 50, 51, 52, 54, 55, 56, 57, 58, 59, 60, 63, 65, 66, 67, 68, 70, 71, 73, 74, 75 paragraph 2, 77 paragraphs 3 and 4, 81, 82, 83, 84, 85, 86, 87, 88 paragraph 1, 90, 96, 99, 101.
2. In case of conflict between the other provisions of the Constitution and those of the Peace Agreement, the provisions of the Peace Agreement shall prevail.
3. The Constitutional Court shall verify the conformity of Laws and Orders in Council with the Fundamental Law thus defined. Pending the enactment of the law on the Supreme Court, the existing Constitutional Court shall remain composed of both the Court of Cassation and the Council of State. The Presiding Judge of the Constitutional Court shall assume the presidency.[47]

The peace agreement is thus conceived as a component of the state's 'Fundamental Law', and while it provides for its own primacy over the constitution in the formal sense of the term, its status is akin to that of a national constitution in the material sense. It therefore appears to sit at the top of the hierarchy of norms in the national legal order.[48] In that perspective, the various provisions entailing the reform of legislative, executive, and judiciary powers have to be interpreted as being part of the domestic legal order, even if some of the sources of obligations referred to or if monitoring mechanisms—possibly—established are of an international character.[49] Provisions relating to ceasefires *stricto sensu* which have been analysed in the first section of this study should indeed be interpreted under the same perspective.[50]

[47] Rwanda, Peace Agreement between the Government of the Republic of Rwanda and the Rwandese Patriotic Front, Arusha, 4 August 1993 (annexed to A/48/824-S/26915, 23 December 1993); see also Peace Agreement between the Government of Liberia, the Liberians United for Reconciliation and Democracy, the Movement for Democracy in Liberia and the political parties, Accra, 18 August 2003, S/2003/850, 29 August 2003, Article XXXV.

[48] See also Inter-Congolese Dialogue, Pretoria Agreement, 16 December 2002, Article VII(a), Sun City, 1 April 2003, Article I(3); Memorandum of Understanding between the Government of the Republic of Indonesia and the Free Aceh Movement, Signed in triplicate in Helsinki, Finland on the 15 of August in the year 2005, Preamble.

[49] See also Niger, Accord entre le gouvernement et l'organisation de la résistance armée, Ouagadougou, 15 April 1995, clause 27 (publication of the agreement in the *Official Journal of the Republic of Niger*).

[50] See, eg, the following clause: '*In upholding the supremacy of the Constitution* and the rule of the law, the Second Party commits itself to peaceful democratic processes in the attainment of its political goals, renounces violence and resort to arms against the First Party and shall not propose or conspire to undertake activities inimical and injurious to the security and stability of the State' (General Agreement for Peace between the Government of the Republic of the Philippines and the Rebolusyonaryong Alyansang Makabansa–Soldiers of the Filipino People–Young Officers'

Keeping in mind that any general conclusion could be nuanced in accordance with the specificities of each agreement, it therefore appears at this stage that the instruments under examination are not devoid of ambiguities. On the one hand, their form is often very similar to that of an international treaty, and they frequently provide for international mechanisms of guarantee by including third states and/or international organizations as 'witnesses'[51] or as members of monitoring bodies.[52] References are sometimes made to obligations flowing from international conventions, and wording similar to that of international law rules is sometimes used. On the other hand, peace agreements concluded between states and armed opposition groups include numerous provisions which, by reason both of the rules they set out and of the applicable law they refer to, tend to evidence the grounding of these agreements in the national legal order. If their content is the only element being taken into account, the international status of such instruments thus appears far from obvious. An attempt shall therefore be made at dispelling this ambiguity by examining how they are perceived by states and international organizations.

3. The Implementation of Peace Agreements: Are They Perceived as International Legal Instruments?

It appears particularly difficult to assess the way in which the various agreements analysed in this study have been implemented. This would indeed suppose a thorough review of the context in which each of these instruments has been adopted and implemented—and thus a detailed analysis of each of the conflicts at stake, from Angola to Senegal, from Nepal to Georgia, from the Philippines to the Solomon Islands. This would obviously by far exceed the bounds of this contribution. We have therefore limited ourselves to situations which have been dealt with

Union, done in Quezon City this 13th day of October 1995, Article I, section 2; emphasis added). See also Protocol on the fundamental Principles for establishing peace and national accord in Tajikistan, 17 August 1995. Comp. Peace Agreement Between the Government of the Central African Republic and the political and military movement designated below: 'Union des Forces Démocratiques pour le Rassemblement' (UFDR) (the Union of Democratic Forces for Unity), 13 April 2007, Preamble; Peace agreement between the Government of the Republic of Chad and the Movement for Democracy and Justice in Chad, S/2002/45, 11 January 2002, Preamble; Accord de paix global entre le gouvernement de la République centrafricaine et les mouvements politico-militaires designed below: 'Armée Populaire pour la Restauration de la Démocratie' (APRD), Front démocratique du Peuple Centrafricain (FDPC), Union des Forces Démocratiques pour le Rassemblement (UFDR), 21 June 2008, Preamble.

[51] See, eg, the Bicesse Agreement, Angola, Peace Accords for Angola, May 1991.

[52] See, eg, the Afghan Peace Accord, 7 March 1993, S/25435, 19 March 1993, Article 9; the Arusha Peace and Reconciliation Agreement for Burundi, 28 August 2000, available at <http://ocha-gwapps1.unog.ch/rw/rwb.nsf/db900SID/MHII-6ABBHY?OpenDocument>, Protocol III. Peace and Security for all, Article 27; Peace Agreement between the Government of Liberia, the Liberians United for Reconciliation and Democracy, the Movement for Democracy in Liberia and the political parties, Accra, 18 August 2003, S/2003/850, 29 August 2003, Article XXIII.

by the UN Security Council. Debates within the Security Council indeed give States the opportunity to express their views on various aspects of the internal conflicts at stake, including—and this will obviously be the most relevant point here—on the legal status of the obligations set out in peace agreements. It will therefore be enquired whether this practice—to take up the issue again from the angle of Article 3 of the Vienna Conventions on the law of treaties—evidence any recognition of such agreements as being governed by rules pertaining to general international law.

The way in which the Security Council dealt with such agreements may be said to reflect certain patterns. In some cases, the Council calls upon the parties to an internal conflict to agree on a ceasefire. In the case of Yemen, for instance, the Council adopted two resolutions in June 1994 '[c]all[ing] for an immediate cease-fire', '[r]emind[ing] all concerned that their political differences cannot be resolved through the use of force and urg[ing] them to return immediately to negotiations which will permit a peaceful resolution of their differences and a restoration of peace and stability'.[53] In the same perspective, the Council sometimes expresses its satisfaction at the actual conclusion of such an agreement, as it did for instance when it 'welcome[d] the signing of the ceasefire agreement between the Transitional Government of Burundi and the Conseil national pour la défense de la démocratie-Front de défense de la démocratie (CNDD-FDD) on 2 December 2002 in Arusha'.[54] It may also express 'its intention to support the immediate and full implementation of [a] Ceasefire Agreement'.[55] Such statements are, however, of little value when it comes to pronouncing on the legal force and value of such agreements. The only observation that may be made at this stage is that the Security Council deems the conclusion of peace agreements appropriate, even though the context is that of an internal conflict.

Another hypothesis is that of the 'endorsement' of a peace agreement by the Council. It did so, amongst others, in a resolution of 4 February 2003, where it '*[e]ndorse[d]* the agreement signed by the Ivorian political forces in Linas-Marcoussis on 24 January 2003 (S/2003/99) ("the Linas-Marcoussis Agreement") and adopted by the Conference of Heads of State and *call[ed] on* all Ivorian political forces to implement it fully and without delay'.[56]

This endorsement will be subsequently extended to further peace agreements concluded by the parties to the Ivorian conflict after the Linas-Marcoussis agreement and reaffirmed in several resolutions dealing with the situation in Côte d'Ivoire.[57] The Security Council thus on several occasions '*[c]all[ed]* on the

[53] UNSC resolution 924 (1994), para. 3; see also UNSC resolution 941.

[54] UNSC Presidential Statement 40 S/PRST/2002/40 (2002); UNSC Presidential Statement 30 S/PRST/2003/30 (2003).

[55] UNSC Presidential Statement 40 S/PRST/2002/40 (2002) .

[56] UNSC resolution 1464 (2003), para. 1.

[57] UNSC resolution 1514 (2003), Preamble; UNSC resolution 1527 (2004), Preamble; UNSC resolution 1528 (2004), Preamble; UNSC resolution 1572 (2004), Preamble; UNSC resolution 1594 (2005), Preamble; UNSC resolution 1600 (2005), Preamble; UNSC resolution 1603 (2005),

signatories of the Linas-Marcoussis Agreement to carry out expeditiously their responsibilities under the Linas-Marcoussis Agreement'[58] or '*demand[ed]* that the parties fulfil their obligations under the Linas-Marcoussis Agreement'.[59] In other cases, the Council adopted coercive measures aimed at ensuring compliance with peace agreements, as in Liberia[60] or Sierra Leone.[61] It could be thought that in such cases, the provisions of these agreements are considered to produce legal effects in the international sphere, even if terms such as 'calls on' or 'responsibilities under' are arguably not the most explicit in that regard. However, the source of this binding character appears to be Article 25 of the Charter according to which resolutions of the Security Council are binding on members of the Organization. Of course, this provision is directed at member states only, and not at non-state entities, but these are generally deemed to be bound by Security Council resolutions inasmuch as they are among their addressees.[62] It could thus be argued that by endorsing peace agreements concluded between a state and non-state entities and by calling for their respect, the Security Council confers upon the provisions of such instruments some legal effects in the international order. But it is clear that such legal effect will then be a consequence of the resolutions, rather than of the agreement in itself.

In other cases, however, the Council uses a terminology which may be said to evidence the binding character of such agreements, whether or not it has previously endorsed them. Regarding the situation in Tajikistan, for example, the Council '[e]mphasize[d] the absolute necessity for the parties to comply fully with all the obligations they have assumed and urge[d] them, in particular, to observe strictly the Agreement of 17 September 1994 and to agree to its substantial extension'.[63]

In other situations again, the Council expressed its 'support' for the peace process[64] and in this context 'recall[ed] strongly the obligations [of the parties]' to comply with a ceasefire agreement, or to act 'in accordance with their obligations'.[65] It also 'request[ed] the parties to continue to respect their commitments'[66]

Preamble; UNSC resolution 1609 (2005), Preamble; UNSC resolution 1633 (2005), Preamble; UNSC resolution 1643 (2005), Preamble; UNSC resolution 1763 (2007), Preamble; UNSC resolution 1765 (2007), Preamble; UNSC resolution 1795 (2008), Preamble; UNSC resolution 1826 (2008), Preamble; UNSC 1865 (2009), Preamble; UNSC resolution 1880 (2009), Preamble; UNSC resolution 1911 (2010), Preamble.

58 UNSC resolution 1527 (2004), para. 4.

59 UNSC resolution 1528 (2004), para. 10.

60 UNSC resolution 788 (1992).

61 UNSC resolution 1171 (1998).

62 See P.H. Kooijmans, 'The Security Council and Non-State Entities as Parties to Conflicts' in *International Law. Theory and Practice. Essays in Honour of Erik Suy* (The Hague: Martinus Nijhoff, 1998) 333–46; T. Kalala, *Les résolutions de l'ONU et les destinataires non étatiques* (Brussels: Larcier, 2009) 137 *et seq*.

63 UNSC resolution 999 (16 June 1995), para. 10.

64 UNSC Presidential Statement 40 S/PRST/2002/40 (2002); UNSC Presidential Statement 30 S/PRST/2003/30 (2003); UNSC resolution 1545 (2004), Preamble; UNSC resolution 1577 (2004), Preamble; UNSC resolution 1602 (2005), Preamble; UNSC resolution 1606 (2005).

65 UNSC resolution 1643 (2005), para. 2.

66 UNSC Presidential Statement 40 S/PRST/2002/40 (2002); UNSC resolution 1545 (2004), Preamble.

or 'urge[d] [the parties] to begin resolutely implementing all the commitments they have made under these agreements'.[67] On various occasions, the Council also decided 'to investigate violations of the ceasefire',[68] deplored 'the repeated violations of the ceasefire agreement',[69] or condemned 'flagrant violations of the ceasefire agreement'.[70] Could it be concluded from these various statements that the peace agreements at stake are equated with treaties, or are at least given 'legal force' within the meaning of Article 3 of the Vienna Conventions on the Law of Treaties? The wording of the relevant resolutions clearly does not dispel all ambiguities in that regard. The Security Council does not expressly refer to international obligations, nor does it characterize those agreements as treaties or as legally binding instruments. It does not hint at any sort of responsibility that may flow for the parties from a breach of the agreements, as it frequently does when it mentions human rights or international humanitarian law violations.[71]

How, then, is the emphasis placed by the Council on the necessity to conclude and abide with such agreements to be interpreted? Recalling the limits upon the Security Council's competences appears to be a useful first step in answering this question. In theory, the Council is not endowed with the competence to pronounce on issues pertaining to the national jurisdiction of states—a category under which agreements aiming at bringing internal conflicts to an end *a priori* appear to come. It is precisely for this reason that the government of Yemen, having learned that a meeting of the Council had been called to address the situation in that country, opposed the convening of such a meeting and claimed that it would constitute an 'interference in the internal affairs of the Republic of Yemen, contrary to Article 2, paragraph 7 of the Charter of the United Nations'.[72] The Council did not follow suit and adopted two resolutions dealing with this—clearly internal—conflict,[73] even though the representative of China insisted that this stance should not constitute a precedent.[74] The Council founded its competence to deal with that situation on its responsibilities for the maintenance of international peace and security, as is apparent from the French representative's statement according to which '[i]n adopting this new resolution, the Security Council has affirmed that it is determined to contribute to the peaceful settlement of a dispute that is unleashing a humanitarian disaster and shaking

[67] UNSC resolution 1572 (2004), para. 4.

[68] UNSC resolution 1609 (2005), para. 3; UNSC resolution 1739 (2007), para. 3.

[69] UNSC resolution 1572 (2004), Preamble; see also UNSC resolution 1584 (2005), Preamble.

[70] See, eg, UNSC resolution 1572 (2004), para. 1; UNSC resolution 1545 (2004), Preamble; UNSC resolution 1602 (2005), Preamble.

[71] See, eg, UNSC 1865 (2009), Preamble; UNSC resolution 1602 (2005), Preamble; UNSC resolution 1791 (2007), para. 7.

[72] Letter dated 31 May 1994 from the Permanent Representative of Yemen to the United Nations addressed to the President of the Security Council, Doc. S/1994/644, 31 May 1994; see also message dated 27 May 1994 from Yemeni political parties and organizations addressed to the President of the Security Council, S/1994/641.

[73] UNSC resolution 924 (1994); UNSC resolution 931 (1994).

[74] S/PV.3386, at 3.

the foundations of regional security. That is why our Council stresses the immediate cessation of military operations.'[75]

This precedent sheds light on the logic behind the Security Council's treatment of agreements aiming at bringing an end to internal conflicts. The broad interpretation of the concept of international peace and security that the Council developed over the years enables it to consider that the breach of such agreements constitutes a threat to the peace within the meaning of Article 39 of the Charter.[76] By encouraging the conclusion of such instruments, calling upon the parties to comply with their terms, monitoring their implementation, and reacting to their violation, the Council ensures that the situations in question do not evolve into regional conflicts.[77] In this perspective, the Council does not pronounce on the legal value and status of the agreements concluded by parties to internal conflicts, nor does it pass judgment on their violations, as would a judicial organ. It more simply holds that compliance with a peace agreement and the global political settlement of the situation which gave birth to the conflict are measures that may contribute to the restoration of peace and security.[78] To that extent, no general conclusion may be drawn as to the legal value of such commitments in the international legal order whenever the Council requires that the parties abide by the terms of the settlement they have accepted (by organizing elections, or not challenging their result, for instance). Likewise, it is obvious that when it condemns not only the use of force, but more generally all acts of violence,[79] the Security Council does not refer to any rule of international law, such as that expressed in Article 2(4) of the Charter—a provision which is indeed never mentioned when the Council deals with such agreements.[80]

One may nevertheless wonder whether states themselves—and not only the Security Council as a political organ, the competences of which explain to a large extent its treatment of peace agreements—consider such instruments to express commitments pertaining to the international legal sphere.

The conflict that took place in Georgia in 2008 is an interesting case in point in that regard. In the section of its report dedicated to relations between Georgia and South Ossetia, the independent international fact-finding mission on the conflict in Georgia asserts that by concluding several ceasefire agreements, the

[75] S/PV.3394, 29 June 1994, at 2. See also Report of the Secretary-General on the situation in Yemen, S/1994/764, 7 June 1994, at 4, para. 20.

[76] See, for an earlier application, O. Corten, 'La résolution 940 du Conseil de sécurité autorisant une intervention militaire en Haïti: la consécration d'un principe de légitimité démocratique ?', 6 *EJIL* (1995) 116–33.

[77] See also, regarding the situation in Côte d'Ivoire, S/PV.5078, 15 November 2004.

[78] T. Kalala, *supra* note 62, 125 *et seq.*

[79] See, eg, UNSC resolution 1719 (2006), Preamble.

[80] See, eg, regarding the situation in Côte d'Ivoire, UNSC resolution 1584 (2005), UNSC resolution 1643 (2005); regarding the situation in Angola; UNSC resolution 1127 (1997), UNSC resolution 1173 (1998), UNSC resolution 1237 (1999), UNSC resolution 1295 (2000); regarding the situation in the DRC, UNSC resolution 1279 (1999), UNSC resolution 1304 (2000), UNSC resolution 1332 (2000), UNSC resolution 1355 (2001).

parties have acknowledged the applicability of the prohibition on the use of force within the meaning of the UN Charter. According to the Mission,

> . . . the legal obligation of Georgia to refrain from the use of force in its relations with South Ossetia is enshrined in the 1994 Agreement 'On the further development of the process of the peaceful regulation of the Georgian-Ossetian conflict and on the Joint Control Commission'. This Agreement states: 'The Parties to the conflict reiterate pledged commitments to settle all the issues in dispute exclusively by peaceful means, without resort to force or threat of resort to force'.[81]

Thus, while observing in passing that '[t]he legal nature of the document is not that of a treaty in its own right', the Mission interprets this agreement as evidencing the will of the parties (among which Georgia and South Ossetia) to create international legal obligations, and even to make applicable between them the *jus contra bellum* regime under general international law. Such an understanding of the agreement may certainly be upheld, if one relies on its wording, as it has been quoted in the first section of this study.[82] It nevertheless appears to be contradicted to a large extent by the interpretation sustained by states.

When Russia attempted to give legal grounds to the military actions it had undertaken in August 2008 it did not claim that Georgia had initially breached Article 2(4) of the Charter vis-à-vis South Ossetia and that Russian troops were exercising collective self-defence on behalf of the latter under Article 51 of the Charter. Russian authorities indeed relied on this latter provision, but only to justify individual self-defence, as a consequence of the armed attack carried out by Georgia against Russian troops—and thus in 'international relations', as requested by Article 2(4).[83] Nor did Georgia rely on the latter provision. While they complained of attacks by Ossetian troops, the Georgian authorities never argued before the Security Council that they had exercised self-defence in virtue of Article 51 of the Charter as a consequence of an 'armed attack' by South Ossetia.[84] Other states have not argued otherwise. To the best of our knowledge, none has claimed that the prohibition on the use of force within the meaning of

[81] Independent International Fact-Finding Mission on the Conflict in Georgia, Report, September 2009, vol. I, 41, available at <http://www.ceiig.ch/>, at 240. See O. Corten, 'Le rapport de la Mission d'enquête internationale indépendante sur le conflit en Géorgie: quel apport au *jus contra bellum* ?', 114 *RGDIP* (2010) 35–61.

[82] See above.

[83] Letter dated 11 August 2008 from the Permanent Representative of the Russian Federation to the United Nations addressed to the President of the Security Council, S/2008/545. In its observations transmitted to the Mission, Russia confirmed that it relied on individual, and not collective, self-defence; it did not claim that Georgia had breached Article 2(4) towards South Ossetia (Report, vol. III, 436–7).

[84] See identical letters dated 7 August 2008 from the Permanent Representative of Georgia to the United Nations addressed to the Secretary-General and the President of the Security Council, A/62/923; letter dated 8 August 2008 from the Permanent Representative of Georgia to the United Nations addressed to the President of the Security Council, S/2008/536; letter dated 9 August 2008 from the Permanent Representative of Georgia to the United Nations addressed to the President of the Security Council, S/2008/537. See also Georgia's position regarding the peace agreements, as it has been presented to the Mission (Report, vol. III, 223–7, 234, 265–7—Georgia

the Charter applied in an internal conflict.[85] Even South Ossetia and Abkhazia, in their observations on issues of fact and law to the Mission, have not explicitly argued that Articles 2(4) and 51 of the Charter applied in their relations with Georgia and have logically preferred to base their claim on breaches of the ceasefire agreements or of relevant resolutions of the Security Council.[86] While the more general issue of the legal nature of such agreements is thus left open, it is clear that they are not perceived as making the classical international law rule of the prohibition on the use of force applicable in internal conflicts.

In addition, it should be noted that such transposition of this rule in the context of internal conflicts would not be uniform, and would vary in accordance with the terms of each particular agreement. This would obviously raise serious problems in consideration of the peremptory character of the rule—and of the ensuing impossibility to derogate from it by way of a convention. This is most probably one reason why, beyond the specific case of the Georgian conflict, the same position may be observed more generally.[87] In cases as different as the internal conflicts in the Democratic Republic of the Congo, in Sudan, or in Tajikistan, no state or international organization appears to have claimed that Article 2(4) was applicable to relations between the parties to these conflicts, in spite of the fact that they had undertaken not to use force—a commitment that had sometimes been taken note of by the Security Council.[88] Mention could also be made in that respect of the conflict between Russia and Chechnya. Here again, both parties had concluded an agreement prohibiting the use of force in their mutual relations.[89] When, in spite of this agreement, Russia undertook military operations against Chechnya, no state or international organization claimed that Russia had carried out an armed attack enabling Chechnya to use force in self-defence, in accordance with the UN Charter. In each of these precedents, as long as the relations between the parties to an internal conflict were the only ones at stake, a peace agreement—the international legal value of which remains uncertain—or resolutions adopted by the Security Council, if any, remained the only applicable instruments.[90]

makes it clear that it was acting in self-defence as a consequence of Russia's armed attack, making no mention of South Ossetia in that respect).

85 See the positions taken by states during debates at the Security Council (especially S/PV.5951, 8 August 2008, and <http://en.wikipedia.org/wiki/International_reaction_to_the_2008_South_Ossetia_war>).

86 For South Ossetia, see Report, vol. III, 518–22; for Abkhazia, see ibid., at 547–57.

87 See O. Corten and A. Lagerwall, 'La violation d'un cessez-le-feu constitue-t-elle nécessairement une violation de l'article 2 § 4 de la Charte des Nations Unies?', 61 *Revue hellénique de droit international* (2008) 92 *et seq.*

88 For the DRC, see, for instance, resolution 1304 (2002); for Sudan, see, for instance, resolutions 1590 (2005) and 1591 (2005); for Tajikistan, see resolution 1089 (1996).

89 See in particular the agreement of 17 May 1997, quoted above.

90 See also the situation in Yemen in 1994, in the context described above; when the governmental authorities denounced a violation of the ceasefire by the insurrectional elements, they did not refer to Article 2(4) or Article 51 of the UN Charter; letter dated 27 June 1994 from the

The situation is not different when it comes to reactions to breaches of provisions of peace agreements relating to human rights or, more globally, to issues of governance. When the Security Council and third states have been faced with such situations, they have called upon parties to these agreements to comply with the latter and/or with international human rights norms.[91] Reference, however, appears to have been made to such norms merely on the basis of the fact that they were applicable in the state concerned under general international law, irrespective of any peace agreement. States have not hinted in any way at the fact that a breach of the relevant provisions of the peace agreements amounted *ipso facto* to a breach of any international legal obligation. Here again, nothing seems to point to a conception of peace agreements as being grounded in the international legal order.

4. Conclusion

Can peace agreements concluded between a state and a non-state entity produce legal effects in the international sphere, as mentioned in Article 3 of the Vienna Conventions on the Law of Treaties? Could it be considered that, following the conclusion of such agreements, some areas that were traditionally conceived as pertaining to the national jurisdiction of states (such as the use of violence within national borders, or the choice of a political system) are as of now governed by international law? On the basis of the agreements that have been reviewed in this study, a clearly affirmative answer would appear excessive—especially in relation to this latter question. As far as the international legal effects of such instruments are concerned, it should be recalled that much will depend on the specificities of each agreement and on the way it has been implemented. It could well be that the parties have intended to generate such international legal effects in their mutual relations, even though the agreements under examination have evidenced very little elements in that sense. Most of these agreements proved to be rather ambiguous, a significant portion of their components evidencing that they are rooted in the domestic legal order. In a small number of cases, elements tended rather to point to some degree of internationalization of the legal relations thus established

Permanent Representative of Yemen to the United Nations addressed to the Secretary-General, S/1994/761. For another example, regarding the situation in Côte d'Ivoire, see Annex to the letter dated 9 November 2004 from the Permanent Representative of Nigeria to the United Nations addressed to the President of the Security Council, Communiqué of the nineteenth session of the Peace and Security Council of the AU, S/2004/896, 11 November 2004; annex to the letter dated 6 October 2005 from the Permanent Representative of Nigeria to the United Nations addressed to the President of the Security Council, Communiqué of the 40th meeting of the Peace and Security Council of the AU, S/2005/639.

91 See, eg, for Burundi, S/PV.4341, 29 June 2001, at 2; S/PV.4673, 18 December 2002, at 3; S/PV.5686, 30 May 2007, at 2.

between the parties. Such ambiguity may probably find some explanation in the political tensions between official authorities, which clearly have more interest in providing for the application of domestic law—upon which they exercise an optimal degree of control—on the one hand, and insurrectional movements which will be inclined to argue for a degree of internationalization of the situation, in particular in secessionist conflicts, on the other hand. This ambiguity finds confirmation in the very pragmatic treatment of peace agreements by the Security Council and states when they call for compliance with these instruments. In the vast majority of cases, such demands are made in the name of the maintenance of international peace and security, without much attention being paid to the characterization in legal terms of the parties' undertakings under these agreements. It therefore appears difficult to reach clear-cut conclusions as to the legal effects of such peace agreements in the international sphere—and, as a consequence, as to their possible characterization as 'treaties' under international law. This is all the more so given that this study is based on a limited sample of peace agreements—which nevertheless appears to be large enough to evidence the general trends that have been highlighted above. But these should definitely be viewed mainly as working hypotheses which could be nuanced—or even refuted—on the basis of a more far-reaching investigation of this question.

2

Article 18 of the 1969 Vienna Convention: A Vague and Ineffective Obligation or a Useful Means for Strengthening Legal Cooperation?

Paolo Palchetti

1. Introduction

Under Article 18 of the 1969 Vienna Convention on the Law of Treaties, a state which has signed or ratified a treaty has the obligation to refrain from acts which would defeat the object and purpose of that Treaty prior to its entry into force. In its Commentary to Article 15 of the Draft Articles on the Law of Treaties, which ultimately became Article 18 of the 1969 Convention, the International Law Commission seemed to regard this provision as corresponding to a rule of general international law. It observed '[t]hat an obligation of good faith to refrain from acts calculated to frustrate the objects of the treaty attaches to a State which has signed a treaty subject to ratification appears to be generally accepted'.[1] Regardless of whether a rule of general international law corresponding to Article 18 existed at the time when the International Law Commission was undertaking the codification of the rules on the law of treaties, the prevailing view among legal scholars is to consider that such a rule has 'crystallized' into customary law as a consequence of its unanimous adoption by states at the Vienna Conference and its incorporation in Article 18 of the Vienna Convention.[2] Indeed, state

[1] *YILC* (1966), vol. II, at 202.

[2] See especially P.V. McDade, 'The Interim Obligation Between Signature and Ratification of a Treaty', 32 *NILR* (1985) 5 *et seq.*, at 25; R. Kolb, *La bonne foi en droit international public* (Genève: PUF, 2000) 186; L. Boisson de Chazournes, A.-M. La Rosa, and M.M. Mbengue, 'Article 18', in O. Corten and P. Klein (eds), *Les Conventions de Vienne sur le droit des traités* (Bruxelles: Bruylant, 2006) vol. I, 594 *et seq.*; M. Villiger, *Commentary on the 1969 Vienna Convention on the Law of Treaties* (The Hague: Martinus Nijhoff, 2009) 247. For the view that 'this provision in all probability constitutes at least a measure of progressive development', see I. Sinclair, *The Vienna Convention on the Law of Treaties* (Manchester: Manchester University Press, 2nd edn, 1984) 43. According to A. Aust, *Modern Treaty Law and Practice* (Cambridge: Cambridge University Press, 2000) 94, there is uncertainty as to whether the provision reflects customary law. G. Gaja, 'Trattati internazionali',

practice subsequent to the 1969 Vienna Convention, while certainly not widespread, tends to support the view that Article 18 corresponds to a rule of general international law. A recent example is provided by a letter sent on 6 May 2002 by the United States to the United Nations Secretary-General. The letter stated that 'the United States does not intend to become a party' to the Statute of the International Criminal Court and that, '[a]ccordingly, the United States has no legal obligations arising from its signature on December 31, 2000'.[3] Since the United States is not a party to the Vienna Convention, this indirect reference to Article 18 may be regarded as an implicit recognition that this provision reflects customary international law.

While the rule enshrined in Article 18 appears to have been well received by states, this certainly does not mean that the existence of an obligation not to defeat the object and purpose of a treaty prior to its entry into force may be regarded as unproblematic. Indeed, Article 18 raises considerable difficulties. In the first place, there is the question concerning the determination of the exact content of the obligation laid down in this provision. Different views have been taken regarding the test for determining when a signatory state may be regarded as defeating the object and purpose of the treaty. The uncertainty surrounding the content of this obligation has led several commentators to criticize Article 18 as being too vague.[4] A further question relates to the effectiveness of the rule contained in the Article. State practice with regard to this rule mainly consists of statements by states in which, directly or indirectly, they recognize the existence of an interim obligation upon signatory states pending the treaty's entry into force. Concrete cases in which a state has denounced the breach of such obligation by another state are extremely rare.[5] It has been held that this lack of substantial practice is simply a consequence of the fact that the situation referred to in Article 18 occurs only exceptionally.[6] However, a different explanation can be given: it may be submitted that, while in principle states seem to be ready to admit the existence of this obligation, in fact they are less keen to take the steps necessary to ensure its fulfilment.

Vagueness and ineffectiveness are often indicated as the two major shortcomings affecting the obligation laid down in Article 18. Is this criticism justified? The present contribution seeks to provide an answer to this question, but at the same time, and more comprehensively, it endeavours to reassess the impact Article 18 has had on state practice over the 40 years since the adoption of the Vienna Convention.

Digesto delle Discipline Pubblicistiche (Torino: UTET, 1998) vol. XV, at 349, finds it difficult to assert the existence of a customary rule corresponding to Article 18.

[3] Letter from J.R. Bolton to K. Annan, 6 May 2002, available at <http://www.freerepublic.com/focus/news/678762/posts>.

[4] See G. Gaja, *supra* note 2, at 349; A. Aust, *supra* note 2, at 94; P. Daillier and A. Pellet, *Droit international public* (Paris: LGDJ, 7th edn, 2002) 136.

[5] For a recent overview of the relevant practice see L. Boisson de Chazournes, A.-M. La Rosa, and M.M. Mbengue, *supra* note 2, 605 *et seq.*

[6] R. Kolb, *supra* note 2, at 194.

2. An Overly Vague Obligation?

There is little doubt that Article 18 does not impose on states, in the period between the signature and the entry into force of a treaty, a general obligation to refrain from acting in a manner inconsistent with that treaty. As the International Law Commission recently observed, '[i]t is unanimously accepted that article 18, paragraph (a), of the Convention does not oblige a signatory state to *respect* the treaty, but merely to refrain from rendering the treaty inoperative prior to its expression of consent to be bound'.[7] Similarly, while the rule laid down in Article 18 is closely linked to the obligation to act in good faith, it seems clear that the provision does not impose a general obligation to refrain from frustrating the legitimate expectations of states which have become, or which have the intention to become, parties to the treaty. In particular, the situation envisaged in Article 18 must not be confused with other situations in which a signatory state may be held to be bound by certain treaty provisions, or by the entire treaty, by virtue of other general legal concepts, such as estoppel, which themselves flow from the principle of good faith.[8]

The problems with Article 18 arise when one has to determine what this provision actually requires from states. The definition of the content of this obligation presents a twofold difficulty. First, the 'object and purpose of the treaty' must be identified. Secondly, there is the issue of when a state's conduct may be regarded as having the effect of 'defeating' the object and purpose of the treaty. Attempting to provide a clear answer to these difficult questions would require an extensive analysis beyond the scope of the present contribution. I will therefore confine myself to a few observations whose aim is to indicate a possible direction for approaching the problems involved in defining the content of the obligation laid down in Article 18.

As is well known, the notion of a treaty's object and purpose appears in several provisions of the Vienna Convention. Most notably, under Article 19, subparagraph c), the admissibility of a reservation is made conditional on its compatibility

[7] See *GAOR, Sixty-second Session, Supplement No. 10* (A/62/10) at 67 (italics in the original).

[8] In the *North Sea Continental Shelf* case, the question was raised as to whether the 1958 Geneva Convention on the Continental Shelf was binding for all the parties in the case. The Federal Republic of Germany had signed but not ratified the Convention. Denmark and the Netherlands argued that the Convention had become binding on Germany because, by its conduct and public statements, Germany had unilaterally assumed the obligations of the Convention. After examining the arguments of the parties, the International Court of Justice concluded: 'Having regard to these considerations of principle, it appears to the Court that only the existence of a situation of estoppel could suffice to lend substance to this contention—that is to say if the Federal Republic were now precluded from denying the applicability of the conventional régime, by reason of past conduct, declarations, etc., which not only clearly and consistently evidenced acceptance of that régime, but also had caused Denmark and the Netherlands, in reliance on such conduct, detrimentally to change position or suffer prejudice.' ICJ, *North Sea Continental Shelf (Federal Republic of Germany/Denmark; Federal Republic of Germany/Netherlands)*, Judgment of 20 February 1969, *ICJ Reports* (1969) 3 *et seq.*, at 26.

with the treaty's object and purpose. The reference to object and purpose in the context of the rules governing treaty reservations, and more broadly in the context of the law of treaties, has often been criticized because of the difficulties involved in defining this notion.[9] In this respect, the critical remarks addressed towards the manner in which Article 18 was formulated may be regarded, to a certain extant, as a reflection of a broader criticism addressed towards the use of the notion of object and purpose more generally in the Vienna Convention. However, as the International Law Commission's work on the reservations to treaties seems to indicate, the difficulties arising in connection with the identification of a treaty's object and purpose should not be overstated. Moreover, as the Commission observed with regard to the criterion laid down in Article 19, subparagraph c), the reference to a treaty's object and purpose, notwithstanding its inevitable margin of subjectivity, 'has considerable merit'.[10] One of the most valuable effects of the use of this notion is that, by focusing on the specificity of each treaty, it introduces an element of flexibility into rules—such as those codified by the Vienna Convention—which in principle are conceived as applicable to a great variety of treaties.[11] With regard to Article 18, this implies that an approach which purports to identify a rigid criterion to be applied in respect to any treaty would be inappropriate to the problem of determining the scope of the obligation placed upon signatory states. Whether an act of a state may be regarded as defeating the object and purpose of a treaty must be assessed taking into account the specificity of each treaty or category of treaties.

As to the method for determining a treaty's object and purpose, some guidance on this point may now be found in the draft guidelines elaborated by the International Law Commission in the context of its work on reservations to treaties. A reference to the draft guidelines on reservations would be justified also in view of the fact that, according to the Commission 'there is little doubt that the expression "object and purpose of the treaty" has the same meaning in all of these provisions' (ie the provisions of the Vienna Convention containing a reference to this expression).[12] Reference may be made, in particular, to draft

[9] For a recent examination of the difficulties raised by the reference to object and purpose of a treaty, see the work of the International Law Commission on the topic of reservations to treaties, *GAOR, Sixty-second Session, Supplement No. 10* (A/62/10) at 66 *et seq*. For the view that the reference to object and purpose 'raises more problem than it solves and is liable of becoming a bone of contention', see I. Buffard and K. Zemanek, 'The "Object and Purpose" of a Treaty: An Enigma?', 3 *ARIEL* (1998) 311 *et seq*., at 343.

[10] *GAOR, Sixty-second Session, Supplement No. 10* (A/62/10) at 70.

[11] On this point see especially P. Reuter, 'Solidarité et divisibilité des engagements conventionnels', in Y. Dinstein (ed.), *International Law at a Time of Perplexity* (Dordrecht: Martinus Nijhoff, 1988) 623 *et seq*., at 627; J. Klabbers, 'Treaties, Object and Purpose', in R. Wolfrum (ed.), *Max Planck Encyclopedia of Public International Law* (Oxford: Oxford University Press, 2010) 4.

[12] *GAOR, Sixty-second Session, Supplement No. 10* (A/62/10) at 68. The view that the notion of object and purpose has the same meaning regardless of the specific legal issue concerned is not unanimously shared. For a different view see J. Klabbers, 'Some Problems Regarding the Object and Purpose of Treaties', 8 *Finnish YIL* (1997) 138 *et seq*., at 148 *et seq*.

Guideline 3.1.6, which provides as follows: 'The object and purpose of the treaty is to be determined in good faith, taking account of the terms of the treaty in their context. Recourse may also be had in particular to the title of the treaty, the preparatory work of the treaty and the circumstances of its conclusion and, where appropriate, the subsequent practice agreed upon by the parties.'[13] The treaty's provisions which must be taken into account for the purposes of determining the scope of the obligation arising under Article 18 include those dealing with the conditions for a treaty's entry into force. Thus, with regard to the Comprehensive Nuclear-Test-Ban Treaty, it has been persuasively argued that, when determining the object and purpose of this Treaty for the purposes of defining a signatory state's obligation under Article 18, account must be had to the fact that Article XIV of the Treaty makes entry into force conditional upon ratification by each of the 44 states possessing nuclear power reactors, which are listed in Annex 2.[14] Since this provision is clearly indicative of the fact that one of the states' major concerns when adopting the text of the Treaty was to ensure that participation in the treaty regime would not put one of these 44 states in an unfavourable position in respect to the other states, it could not be maintained that, by signing a treaty, a state could assume the obligation not to carry out a nuclear weapons test explosion. To attach this effect to the signature would run counter to what appears to be an essential element in the overall balance of rights and obligations created by the Treaty.

The scope of the obligation laid down in Article 18 is further defined by reference to the impact of the state's conduct on the accomplishment of the treaty's object and purpose. The prohibition only refers to 'acts which would defeat the object and purpose of a treaty'. By using the term 'defeat', Article 18 appears to set a very high threshold, thereby reducing the scope of the obligation imposed on states prior to a treaty's entry into force.

The expression 'defeat the object and purpose of a treaty' is not used elsewhere in the Vienna Convention. It is not clear what elements are to be taken into account for the determination of whether this threshold has been met. However, during the drafting of the provision several examples were given. Ago, for instance, referred to the case of 'a treaty relating to the return by a State of works of art formerly taken from the territory of another State'. In his view, if the state which was to return the works of art destroyed them or allowed them to be destroyed, 'that was obviously a breach of the obligation of good faith'.[15] Lachs mentioned the case of a disarmament treaty which obliges the parties to reduce their armies by one-third. He observed that, 'if there was no specific provision on the subject, signatory States were under an obligation to maintain the

[13] *GAOR, Sixty-second Session, Supplement No. 10* (A/62/10) at 77. It must be noted that reference to subsequent practice is not pertinent in regard to Article 18.

[14] G. Gaja, 'Quali effetti ha la firma del Trattato per il divieto totale degli esperimenti nucleari?' 79 *Riv. di Diritto Internaz.* (1996) 973 *et seq.*

[15] *YILC* (1966), vol. I, 92.

status quo, so as not to invalidate the basic presumption of the agreement'.[16] If one considers these cases, which are generally regarded as typical examples of acts which may 'defeat the object and purpose of a treaty',[17] it may be suggested that a certain parallelism exists between the situations falling within the scope of the prohibition contained in Article 18 and the situations in which a state party to a treaty, by its unilateral conduct, creates such conditions that enable the other parties to suspend or terminate the treaty. In particular, while the example given by Ago finds a clear parallel in the case contemplated in Article 61 of the Vienna Convention, which concerns the termination of a treaty for supervening impossibility of performance, the case referred to by Lachs evokes the situation of a fundamental change of circumstances contemplated in Article 62. Taking this parallelism into account, it may be argued that the criteria for the termination of treaties laid down in Articles 61 and 62 may also provide useful indications for assessing whether certain conduct amounts to an act defeating the object and purpose of the treaty within the meaning of Article 18. Thus, it appears that a state would certainly violate the obligation set forth in Article 18 if it causes the permanent disappearance or destruction of an object indispensable for the execution of the treaty.[18] Equally, when a signatory state, by its unilateral conduct, produces a change of the circumstances existing at the time of the signature, such conduct may be regarded as amounting to a violation of Article 18 if the treaty obligations are based on the *status quo* at the time of the signature and the effect of the change is to radically transform the extent of the obligations to be performed by the parties when the treaty enters into force.[19]

It may be asked whether one can push this parallelism even further and conclude that, under certain circumstances, a violation of Article 18 would occur when a state engages in conduct which would amount to a 'material breach' within the meaning of Article 60 of the Vienna Convention if the treaty were already in force. Analogies between these two provisions are suggested by the fact that, under Article 60, a 'material breach' is defined, *inter alia*, as 'the violation of a provision essential to the accomplishment of the object or purpose of the treaty'—a formula which clearly resembles that which appears in Article 18. The idea of linking the notion of 'acts defeating the object and purpose of a treaty' with that of 'material breach' may prove to be particularly useful with regard to certain categories of multilateral treaties, such as human rights treaties. With respect to such treaties, criteria such as that based on impossibility of performance or on a radical change of the status quo are clearly inadequate.[20] In one

[16] Ibid., 97. [17] See M. Villiger, *supra* note 2, at 249.

[18] See J. Klabbers, 'How to Defeat a Treaty's Object and Purpose Pending Entry into Force: Toward Manifest Intent', 34 *Vanderbilt Journal of International Law* (2001) 283 *et seq*., at 293 note 40.

[19] See R. Kolb, *supra* note 2, 184, who referred to the possibility of applying by analogy the principle *rebus sic stantibus*.

[20] See C.A. Bradley, 'Unratified Treaties, Domestic Politics, and the U.S. Constitution', 48 *Harv. Int'l LJ* (2007) 307 *et seq*., at 308. According to J. Klabbers, 'How to Defeat', *supra* note 18,

isolated case where the question of the application of Article 18 in the context of human rights treaties was incidentally raised, the European Court of Human Rights seemed to endorse the view that a state which has signed but not yet ratified a treaty is bound to respect certain core obligations imposed by that treaty on states parties. In its judgment of 12 March 2003 in the *Öcalan v Turkey* case, the Court excluded that the imposition of the death penalty by a Turkish court amounted to a violation of Article 2 of the European Convention on Human Rights. In reaching this conclusion, it noted, *inter alia*, that

> ... [i]t must also be borne in mind in this context that Turkey has now signed Protocol No. 6 [...] and that the non-implementation of the capital sentence is in keeping with Turkey's obligations as a signatory State to this Protocol, in accordance with Article 18 of the Vienna Convention of 23 May 1969 on the Law of Treaties, to 'refrain from acts which would defeat the object and purpose' of the Protocol.[21]

Thus, in the Court's view, the mere signature of a Treaty, such as Protocol No. 6 to the European Convention, whose main object and purpose is to promote the abolition of the death penalty, has the effect of imposing on the signing state the obligation to refrain from acts of capital punishment.

3. An Ineffective Obligation?

Article 18 imposes an obligation of conduct. If a state breaches this obligation, it will incur international responsibility. While neither Article 18 nor the International Law Commission's Commentary identifies the states to which the obligation is owed, it seems reasonable to hold that the states entitled to invoke the responsibility are only those which are already parties to the treaty or those which, having signed the treaty, have agreed to be bound by the same obligation.

As it has already been observed, there is an almost complete lack of practice relating to claims of responsibility for breaches of the obligation laid down in Article 18. The absence of relevant practice may be regarded as indicative of the fact that states do not have a particular interest in taking action to secure the *mise en œuvre* of responsibility in case of a breach of this obligation. If one considers what a state may hope to gain from such an action, this is hardly surprising. To better assess this point, however, a distinction must be drawn between two different situations.

331, 'where [...] international agreements are concluded to further the community interest, Article 18 as drafted and conceived can only disappoint'. With respect to such treaties, Klabbers held the view that a 'manifest intent test' should be applied, according to which, 'where behavior pending entry into force of an agreement is generally held to be morally obnoxious in light of what the agreement itself represents, then it violates the interim obligation'. Ibid., at 331.

[21] *Öcalan v Turkey*, Judgment of 12 March 2003, para. 185.

A first case relates to the situation where the wrongdoing state later becomes a party to the treaty. In such a scenario, the other parties to the treaty may well have an interest in ensuring that the wrongdoing state is held accountable for its conduct prior to the treaty's entry into force.[22] In particular, the other parties would be entitled to claim from the responsible state the performance of the obligation of reparation, which may include, when materially possible, the re-establishment of the situation which existed before the wrongful act. Not surprisingly, the few cases which are generally regarded as the most notable precedents in relation to the obligation now laid down in Article 18 mainly concern claims addressed to a state which ultimately became party to the treaty. Thus, for instance, in the *Megalidis v Turkey* case, the Turkish-Greek Mixed Arbitral Tribunal found that the seizure of a Greek national's property by Turkish authorities, which took place after signature but before the entry into force for Turkey of the Treaty of Lausanne, was invalid. The Arbitral Tribunal held the view that 'il est de principe que déjà avec la signature d'un Traité et avant sa mise en vigueur, il existe pour les parties contractantes une obligation de ne rien faire qui puisse nuire au Traité en diminuant la portée de ses clauses'.[23]

The scenario changes considerably if the wrongdoing state, after having signed the treaty, has refrained from ratifying it. Certainly, even in this case, the other parties or signatories would be entitled to claim from that state the cessation of the wrongful conduct and the performance of the obligation of reparation. However, since the wrongdoing state is free to decide to put an end to its obligation simply by making its intention clear not to become a party to the treaty, there would be little to gain from taking such an action. Thus, particularly in the case of bilateral treaties, if the signatory state, by taking acts which defeat the treaty's object and purpose, renders the treaty inoperative—for instance, because it causes the destruction of an object indispensable for the execution of treaty—the most probable consequence will simply be that the other signatory state will decide not to ratify the treaty. With regard to multilateral 'normative' treaties—such as, for instance, human rights treaties—a further consideration comes into play. In this context, the advantages that may be gained from invoking the responsibility of the wrongdoing state must be balanced against the risk of deterring that state from ratifying the treaty. Since in respect of such treaties the attainment of broad

[22] It has been rightly observed that responsibility cannot be invoked by a state if, by becoming party to the treaty, it appears to have acquiesced in the 'defeating' act. See M. Villiger, *supra* note 2, 248. See also A.D. McNair, *The Law of Treaties* (Oxford: Clarendon Press, 1962) 203.

[23] *Recueil des decisions des tribunaux arbitraux mixtes*, vol. VIII, 386. In its Commentary to draft Article 15, the International Law Commission referred to the judgment of the Permanent Court of International Justice in the *Certain German Interests in Polish Upper Silesia* case. *YILC* (1966), vol. II, 202. It is worth noting that also in that case the state which invoked responsibility ultimately had become party to the treaty.

ratification is generally regarded as an important goal, such a risk may render the invocation of Article 18 even less appealing.[24]

4. The Use of Article 18 in Cases before Domestic Judges

While Article 18 has been rarely invoked at the inter-state level, it is somewhat surprising to observe that this provision has been applied in several cases before domestic judges. This practice is significant in that it seems to suggest a possible role for domestic judges in contributing to the effectiveness of the obligation to refrain from acts defeating a treaty's object and purpose pending its entry into force.[25]

In cases before domestic courts, Article 18 may be invoked for a variety of purposes. In the first place, the obligation not to defeat a treaty's object and purpose can be relied upon by domestic judges in order to review the conduct of the Executive or to assess the validity of domestic rules. Practice provides several examples to this effect. In 2003, the Supreme Court of Benin was called upon to assess whether a draft bilateral agreement between Benin and the United States, which concerned the surrender of United States nationals to the International Criminal Court—a so-called 'Article 98 agreement'—was compatible with the obligations of Benin under the Rome Statute. While Article 18 was not directly relevant in this case, Benin being a party to the Rome Statute, the Supreme Court of Benin also alluded to that provision, implicitly suggesting that, by concluding this agreement with the United States, Benin's conduct would have defeated the object and purpose of the Rome Statute.[26] In a judgment of 2004 rendered by a Chilean court, Article 18 was relied on in order to justify the decision to set aside an amnesty law which prevented the criminal prosecution

[24] According to E.T. Swaine, 'Unsigning', 55 *Stanford Law Review* (2002–03) 2061 *et seq.*, at 2083, 'states interested in pressing mere signatories into compliance must weigh the possibility that their actions will *widen* the gap between ratification and nonratification by driving signatories to unsign'. See also C.A. Bradley, *supra* note 20, 330; P.V. McDade, *supra* note 2, 46.

[25] The view that domestic courts may play an important role in the enforcement of the obligation laid down in Article 18 was expressed by J.S. Charme, 'The Interim Obligation of Article 18 of the Vienna Convention on the Law of Treaties: Making Sense of an Enigma', 25 *George Washington Journal of International Law & Economics* (1991) 71 *et seq.*, at 111 *et seq.*

[26] Benin, Supreme Court, *Legal Opinion on the Compatibility of the Bilateral Agreement Between the Governments of the United States and Benin with Article 98 of the Rome Statute of the International Criminal Court*, 25 July 2003, *Oxford Reports on International Law in Domestic Courts*, ILDC 844 (BJ2003). It is interesting to note that the same view was expressed by the Parliamentary Assembly of the Council of Europe in its resolution 1336 (2002) of 25 June 2003, where it stated: 'The Assembly considers such agreements [Article 98 agreements] to be violations of the Rome Statute of the ICC (in particular Articles 27 and 86, Article 98(2) allowing only narrowly defined exceptions in the framework of status of force agreements) and of the Vienna Convention on the Law of Treaties (Article 18), according to which States must refrain from any action which would not be consistent with the object and purpose of a treaty.'

of state agents suspected of involvement in the disappearance of a Chilean national. While Chile had signed but not ratified the 1994 Inter-American Convention on the Forced Disappearance of Persons, the court found that to apply the amnesty law in the case at hand would have amounted to an act that defeated the object and purposes of the Convention.[27] A final example that can be mentioned here is a 2005 decision of the Constitutional Court of Latvia. The case concerned the constitutional review of a law that had imposed the substantial use of the Latvian language in education. Claimants argued that this measure was contrary to Article 18, since it defeated the object and purpose of the 1995 Framework Convention for the Protection of National Minorities, which Latvia had signed but not ratified. While admitting in principle the possibility of reviewing the validity of a domestic law in the light of its compatibility with the obligation laid down in Article 18, the Constitutional Court rejected the complaints, finding that the law in question did not defeat the object and purpose of the Framework Convention.[28]

In certain cases, Article 18 has also been invoked by individuals in order to protect their interests against measures taken by the state in the period between the signature and the entry into force of a treaty. A situation of this kind is likely to arise when the proposed treaty accords some benefits to individuals, and the state, by taking actions which defeat the treaty's object and purpose before its entry into force, causes the legitimate expectations of these individuals to be frustrated. A notable example in this respect is provided by the *Opel Austria v Council* case, decided by the European Court of First Instance in 1997. In this case, the applicant claimed that, by adopting a Council regulation imposing certain tariffs a few weeks before the entry into force of the Agreement on the European Economic Area between Austria and the European Communities, the European Communities had defeated the object and purpose of that Agreement; it also argued that Article 18 is 'capable of conferring on individuals rights which they may invoke before the Court'.[29] The Court of First Instance annulled the Regulation, finding that, 'by adopting the contested regulation in the period preceding the entry into force of the EEA Agreement after the Communities had deposited their instruments of approval, the Council infringed the applicant's

[27] Chile, Court of Appeals of Santiago, *Miguel Angel Sandoval Case*, 5 January 2004. For a summary and commentary of the decision see X. Fuentes, *Oxford Reports on International Law in Domestic Courts*, ILDC 394 (CL 2004).

[28] Latvia, Constitutional Court, *Re Latvia Education Law*, 13 May 2005, *Oxford Reports on International Law in Domestic Courts*, ILDC 190 (LV 2005). It must be observed that the Latvian Constitutional Court took a very strict view regarding the content of the obligation imposed by Article 18.

[29] European Court of First Instance, Case T-115/94, *Opel Austria v Council* [1997] ECR II-43, 67. On this judgment see P.J. Kuijper, 'Customary International Law, Decisions of International Organisations and Other Techniques for Ensuring Respect for International Legal Rules in European Community Law', in J. Wouters, A. Nollkaemper, and E. de Wet (eds), *The Europeanisation of International Law* (The Hague: Asser Press, 2008) 87 *et seq.*, at 94 *et seq.*; J. Klabbers, 'How to Defeat', *supra* note 18, 321 *et seq.*

legitimate expectations'.[30] It must be observed, however, that in reaching this conclusion the Court relied not so much on the international obligation to refrain from defeating a treaty's object and purpose as it relied on the principle of the protection of legitimate expectations. In the Court's view, this principle was a sort of equivalent within the European legal order of the international principle set forth in Article 18.[31]

It is worth noting that reference to signed but unratified treaties is not limited to the two abovementioned situations. Domestic courts have accorded relevance to signed treaties for wider purposes. Thus, for instance, in a judgment of 2007, the Italian Court of Cassation held the view that domestic rules on the medical treatment of patients had to be interpreted in accordance with the 1997 Oviedo Convention on Human Rights and Biomedicine—a treaty signed but not yet ratified by Italy.[32] In its judgment of 2005 in *Roper v Simmons*—a case dealing with the question of whether it was permissible under the United States Constitution to execute juvenile offenders—the Supreme Court also took note of the provisions of the United Nations Convention on the Rights of the Child—again, a treaty signed but not ratified by the United States.[33] It has been suggested that it is because of Article 18 that domestic courts are inclined to accord legal relevance to signed but unratified treaties.[34] This view goes too far. While it cannot be excluded that, under certain circumstances, the recognition of legal effects to signed but unratified treaties can serve to ensure the performance of the obligation laid down in Article 18, it seems that, in most cases, relevance is accorded to signed treaties regardless of whether this may appear justified by that obligation. Taking this into account, it would be excessive to regard Article 18 as the only reason why domestic judges may decide to attach legal effects to unratified treaties.

5. Conclusions

It has been said that Article 18 'is more exhortatory than normative'.[35] This view seems to capture an important feature of Article 18. This is not to say that, as the first Special Rapporteur on the topic of the Law of the Treaties, James Brierly,

[30] [1997] ECR II-43, 81. [31] Ibid., 71.

[32] Italy, Court of Cassation, Case No. 21748, 16 October 2007, 57 *Giustizia civile* (2007) 2366 *et seq*. For an analysis of this and of other decisions of Italian courts giving relevance to the Oviedo Convention see V. Tonini, 'La rilevanza della Convenzione di Oviedo sulla biomedicina secondo la giurisprudenza italiana', 92 *Riv. di Diritto Internaz.* (2009) 116 *et seq*.

[33] 543 U.S. 576 (2005). For other judgments of United States courts giving relevance to signed but unratified treaties, see J.S. Charme, *supra* note 25, 112, note 188.

[34] J.S. Charme, *supra* note 25, 113.

[35] S. Rosenne, 'Vienna Convention on the Law of Treaties', in R. Bernhardt (ed.), *Encyclopedia of Public International Law* (Amsterdam: North Holland Publishing Company, 1984) vol. VII, 525 *et seq*., 532.

suggested, the obligation not to defeat a treaty's object and purpose must be regarded as a moral rather than a legal obligation.[36] There is no doubt that the obligation laid down in Article 18 constitutes a legal, enforceable duty. However, it is true that Article 18 seems to suffer from certain shortcomings, which inevitably weaken its normative force. On the one hand, the notion of acts defeating a treaty's object and purpose, with its inevitable margin of subjectivity, makes it difficult to identify the exact content of the obligation; this uncertainty, in turn, may discourage the invocation of the rule for the purposes of ensuring its enforcement. On the other hand, the risk of incurring responsibility for non-compliance does not seem to provide a real incentive to ensure its respect. In most cases, since the wrongdoing state can freely decide to put an end to its obligation by indicating clearly that it does not intend to become a party to the treaty, the other signatories or parties will have little interest in enforcing this obligation through the invocation of responsibility.

Still, despite all its shortcomings, Article 18 is by no means a rule devoid of any practical relevance. In this regard, an interesting development is the increasing recourse to this provision in cases before domestic courts. By reviewing the conduct of the political organs of the state or by protecting the legitimate expectation of injured individuals, domestic courts can certainly contribute to the effectiveness of the obligation not to defeat a treaty's object and purpose pending its entry into force. In so doing, such courts can ultimately help to compel their respective states to conduct themselves in good faith in the delicate process of treaty formation.

[36] J.L. Brierly, 'Second Report on the Law of Treaties', *YILC* (1951), vol. II, 73.

3

Reservations to Treaties: An Objection to a Reservation is Definitely not an Acceptance

Alain Pellet and Daniel Müller

Professor Gaja, a leading member of the International Law Commission (ILC) since 1999, has taken a prominent part in the elaboration of the Guide to Practice on reservations to treaties,[1] a topic on which he has written extensively.[2] His views, expressed both in the plenary sessions of the Commission and in the Drafting Committee, have greatly influenced the drafting of the guidelines which compose the Guide, which should be finalized in 2011.

'[T]he question of reservations has always been a thorny and controversial issue, and even the provisions of the Vienna Convention have not eliminated all these difficulties.'[3] But, amongst the very many difficult questions it raises, probably the most vexing issue is that of the respective effects of an acceptance of a reservation, on the one hand, and of an objection to a reservation on the other.

The 1969 and 1986 Vienna Conventions on the Law of Treaties[4] are so ambiguous and, in some respects, so sibylline, that it is sometimes alleged that

[1] As the Special Rapporteur on reservations to treaties stated in 1995, the ILC 'should try to adopt a guide to practice in respect of reservations. In accordance with the Commission's statute and its usual practice, this guide would take the form of draft articles whose provisions, together with commentaries, would be guidelines for the practice of states and international organizations in respect of reservations; these provisions would, if necessary, be accompanied by model clauses' (*YILC* (1995), vol. II(1), at 108, para. 487 (*b*)).

[2] 'Reservations to Treaties and the Newly Independent States', 1 *Ital. Yb. of Int'l L* (1975) 52–68; 'Unruly Treaty Reservations', in *Le droit international à l'heure de sa codification: Études en honneur de Roberto Ago* (Milano: Giuffrè, 1987) 307–30; 'Le riserve tardive ai trattati: un fenomeno a molti inviso (ma non sempre visto bene)', 86 *Riv. di Diritto Internaz.* (2003) 463–6; 'Il regime della Convenzione di Vienna concernente le riserve inammissibili', in *Studi in onore di Vincenzo Starace* (Napoli: Editoriale Scientifica, 2008) 349–61.

[3] P. Reuter, 'Tenth Report on the Question of Treaties Concluded between States and International Organizations or Between Two or More International Organizations', *YILC* (1981), vol. II(1), at 56, para. 53.

[4] Except where otherwise specified, in the remainder of this paper the expression 'Vienna Convention' will encompass both the Vienna Convention of 23 May 1969 on the Law of

an acceptance of a reservation and an objection to it have the same effect[5]—at least when the objecting state does not 'definitely express' the intention that its objection preclude the entry into force of the treaty between itself and the reserving state.[6] Indeed, apart from this situation (commonly known as 'objection with maximum effect'), envisaged in Article 20(4)(b), the Vienna Convention is extremely discreet with respect to the 'normal'[7] consequence of an objection, which is only addressed in Article 21(3). According to this rather obscure[8] provision: 'When a State objecting to a reservation has not opposed the entry into force of the treaty between itself and the reserving State, the provisions to which the reservation relates do not apply as between the two States to the extent of the reservation.'

However, absent a definition in the Vienna Convention of the words 'acceptance' and 'objection', according to Article 31(1) they must be interpreted in accordance with their ordinary meaning; and this clearly implies that they have opposite meanings and invite the conclusion that they generate different effects. The drafting of Articles 20 ('Acceptance and objection to reservations') and 21 ('Legal effects of reservations and of objections to reservations') calls for distinguishing the effects an acceptance or an objection may have on the entry into force of the treaty, on the one hand (1)—and on the relations between the parties if and when the treaty enters into force between them, regardless of whether the reservation is permissible—on the other hand (2). The first aspect is not exempt from difficulties, but the second one is immensely complex.

1. Acceptance, Objection, and the Entry into Force of the Treaty

Under the traditional unanimity régime, the impact of acceptances and objections on the entry into force of the treaty was clear-cut: failing unanimous acceptance of the reservation by the other parties, the treaty could not enter into force for the reserving state; in other words, any objection prevented a unanimous acceptance and therefore precluded the latter from becoming a party.[9] It was

Treaties and the Vienna Convention of 21 March 1986 on the Law of Treaties between States and International Organisations or between Organisations, and we will use the word 'state(s)' as including international organisations.

5 J. Klabbers, 'Accepting the Unacceptable? A New Nordic Approach to Reservations to Multilateral Treaties', 69 *Nordic JIL* (2000) 179–93, at 179.

6 Article 20(4)(*b*) of the Vienna Convention.

7 Or 'minimum' effect—in contrast to the exceptional situation of an objection with maximum effect.

8 The US representative at the 1968–69 Vienna Conference noted that one can be 'rather puzzled' about the meaning of that provision (United Nations Conference on the Law of Treaties, *Official Records*, vol. II, at 181, para. 9).

9 This is also the reason why the first Special Rapporteur of the ILC on the subject of the law of treaties did not consider specifically the issue of 'objections'. See D. Müller, 'Article 21 (1969)', in O. Corten and P. Klein (eds), *Les Conventions de Vienne sur le droit des traités, Commentaire*

therefore crystal clear that an objection constituted the very opposite of an acceptance. Moreover, the acceptance of the reservation was deemed to result from the absence of an objection.[10] It is thus apparent that the opposition and complementarity between acceptance and objection is not a new element introduced by the 'flexible' approach launched at the universal level by the ICJ in 1951,[11] before being advocated by Sir Humphrey Waldock, endorsed by the ILC after much procrastination, and finally enshrined in the 1969 Vienna Convention.[12]

In the framework of the elaboration of the Guide to practice on reservations to treaties, the ILC Special Rapporteur took up the same idea. In view of the fact that 'it follows from article 20, paragraph 5, of the 1969 Vienna Convention on the Law of Treaties that in most cases, acceptance of a reservation results from the absence of an objection',[13] he proposed to define the term 'acceptance' as follows in draft Guideline 2.8: 'The acceptance of a reservation arises from the absence of objections to the reservation formulated by a State or international organization on the part of [a][14] contracting State or contracting international organization.'[15]

The opposition between acceptances and objections is particularly clear with respect to the entry into force of the treaty vis-à-vis the reserving state (Section 1.1). However, it is also relevant for the entry into force of the treaty with regard to all its contracting parties (Section 1.2).

1.1. Acceptance of the reservation and constitution of the reserving state as a party

One cannot consider Article 21 of the Vienna Conventions without taking into account that an acceptance of a reservation—whether it be given in advance,[16] unanimously,[17] or by the competent organ of an international organization[18]—makes the author of this reservation a contracting state.

article par article (Bruxelles: Bruylant, 2006) at 887, paras 5–6 (to be published in English, Oxford University Press, 2011).

[10] On this point, see D. Müller, ibid., at 814–15, paras 31–32.

[11] ICJ, *Reservations to the Convention on the Prevention and Punishment of the Crime of Genocide*, Advisory Opinion of 28 May 1951, *ICJ Reports* (1951) 15.

[12] For a summary of this sinuous history, see A. Pellet, 'Article 19 (1969)', in O. Corten and P. Klein (eds), *supra* note 9, at 652–73, paras 16–67.

[13] A. Pellet, 'Eighth Report on Reservations to Treaties' (2003), A/CN.4/535/Add.1, para. 69.

[14] The English translation of the Special Rapporteur's Report (originally in French) erroneously translated the word '*un*' as 'the'.

[15] A. Pellet, 'Twelfth Report on Reservations to Treaties' (2007), A/CN.4/584, para. 195. The ILC has included the idea a broader definition which includes express and tacit reservations in a single guideline (provisionally numbered 2.8.0—see *GAOR, Sixty-fourth Session, Supplement No. 10* (A/64/10) at 212).

[16] In the treaty itself—Vienna Convention, Article 20(1).

[17] In case it appears that 'the application of the treaty in its entirety between all the parties is an essential condition of the consent of each one to be bound by the treaty'—Article 20(2).

[18] Article 20(3).

Guideline 4.2.1 states the obvious: 'As soon as a reservation is established in accordance with guidelines 4.1 to 4.1.3 [relating to the "establishment" of a reservation], its author becomes a contracting State or contracting organization to the treaty.'[19]

On the contrary, an objection does not have this effect, or at least, the objection cannot produce it alone. Traditionally, in keeping with the unanimity principle, the immediate and radical effect of an objection was that the reserving state could not claim to be a state party to the treaty;[20] this is what is nowadays commonly called the 'maximum' effect of an objection.[21] That outcome was unavoidable under the system of unanimity, in which even a single objection neutralized the otherwise unanimous consent of the other contracting states, which could therefore produce no effect; no derogation was possible. Sir Humphrey Waldock's reference to the 'revolution' introduced by the 'flexible' system did not lead him to propose a complete rejection of the unanimity principle whereby 'the objections shall preclude the entry into force of the treaty as between the objecting and the reserving States'—this was a reflection of the traditional rule—'but shall not preclude its entry into force as between the reserving State and any other State which does not object to the reservation'[22]—and this was the introduction of an element of flexibility.

However, in 1951, the ICJ considered that '... each State objecting to [a reservation] will or will not ... consider the reserving State to be a party to the Convention'.[23] In order to align the draft with the solution proposed in the Advisory Opinion, and in response to the criticisms and misgivings expressed by many members of the ILC,[24] the radical (but traditional) solution proposed by Sir Humphrey in respect of the relations between the reserving and the objecting states was abandoned in favour of a simple presumption of 'maximum effect', leaving 'minimum effect' available as an option. Thus, draft Article 20(2)(b), as adopted by the ILC on first reading, provided:

An objection to a reservation by a State which considers it to be incompatible with the object and purpose of the treaty precludes the entry into force of the treaty as between the

[19] *GAOR, Sixty-fifth Session, Supplement No. 10* (A/65/10) at 63.

[20] P.-H. Imbert, *Les réserves aux traités multilatéraux* (Paris: Pedone, 1979) at 155 and 260. See also D. Müller, *supra* note 10, at 911, para. 48.

[21] A. Pellet, 'Eighth Report on Reservations to Treaties' (2003), A/CN.4/535/Add.1, para. 95.

[22] Draft Article 19, para. 4(*c*), presented by Sir Humphrey in 1962 in his first Report on the law of treaties (A/CN.4/144, *YILC* (1962), vol. II, at 62). This solution is, moreover, frequently offered as the only one that makes sense. See, for example, P. Reuter, *Introduction au droit des traités* (Paris: PUF, 2nd edn, 1985) at 75, para. 132.

[23] ICJ, *Reservations to the Convention on the Prevention and Punishment of the Crime of Genocide*, Advisory Opinion of 28 May 1951, *ICJ Reports* (1951) at 26.

[24] See, for example, Tunkin (*YILC* (1962), vol. I, at 156, para. 26 and 654th meeting, 30 May 1962, at 161, para. 11), Rosenne (ibid., at 156–7, para. 30), Jiménez de Aréchaga (ibid., at 158, para. 48), de Luna (ibid., at 160, para. 66), Yasseen (ibid., at 161, para. 6). The Special Rapporteur was also in favour of introducing the presumption (ibid., at 162, paras 17 and 20).

objecting and the reserving State, unless a contrary intention shall have been expressed by the objecting State.[25]

This formulation of the presumption had the advantage of underlining what was then the main function of an objection: even if its author could no longer prevent the reserving state from becoming a contracting state to the treaty, it would nevertheless exclude any treaty relationship between itself and the reserving state.[26] However:

1. the permissibility of the objection was limited to cases when the objecting state considered that the reservation was incompatible with the object and purpose of the treaty;
2. the presumption was not conclusive, since it entered into play only in the absence of a contrary view expressed by the objecting state; and
3. the provision as drafted left open the question of whether a 'minimum effect' objection produces the same effect as an acceptance, making the reserving state a contracting party. However, subparagraph (c) of paragraph 4 of the ILC draft Article suggested otherwise, and the Commentary of the ILC confirmed that only the expression of at least one acceptance 'determines the moment at which a reserving State may be considered as a State which has ratified, accepted or otherwise become bound by the treaty'.[27]

The controversial reversal of the presumption in favour of 'minimum' instead of 'maximum' effect objections seemed motivated by the desire 'to broaden treaty relations among States and to prevent the formation of an undesirable vacuum in the legal ties between States',[28] just as if a 'minimum effect' objection would *ipso facto* create treaty relations between the reserving and the objecting state. The Explanatory Memorandum on the Question of Reservations to Multilateral Treaties submitted by the USSR to the second session of the Vienna Conference very openly criticized the ILC proposal which, according to the Memorandum, was 'based on the erroneous idea that a reservation made to an international treaty by one of the parties to that treaty requires "acceptance" by the other parties to the treaty'.[29] However, the amendment as it was finally adopted does not even come close to the idea that a 'minimum effect' objection is tantamount to an acceptance. Quite to the contrary, Article 20(4) (b),

[25] *YILC* (1962), vol. II, at 175 and at 181, para. 23.

[26] The Commentary of draft Article 17 prepared by the ILC explained in this regard: 'Although an objection to a reservation normally indicates a refusal to enter into treaty relations on the basis of the reservation, objections are sometimes made to reservations for reasons of principle or policy without the intention of precluding the entry into force of the treaty between the objecting and reserving States' (*YILC* (1966), vol. II, at 207, para. 17).

[27] *YILC* (1966), vol. II, at 207, para. 17.

[28] See the summary of the Czechoslovak and Romanian observations in Sir Humphrey Waldock's Fourth Report on the Law of Treaties, *YILC* (1965), vol. II, at 48.

[29] United Nations Conference on the Law of Treaties, *Official Records*, vol. III, at 265.

as finally amended in conformity with the Soviet proposal, makes it clear that, rather than creating a treaty relationship between the objecting state and the reserving state, 'an objection by another contracting State to a reservation *does not preclude* the entry into force of the treaty as between the objecting and reserving States ...'.

1.2. Objection to the reservation and entry into force of the treaty

In the now 'normal' case, an objection (with 'minimum effect') still has no immediate effect on the entry into force of the treaty in relations between the two states, and, *a fortiori*, it cannot make the author of the reservation a contracting state, as is the case for an acceptance of the reservation.[30] This is probably one of the most fundamental differences between acceptances and objections. As Article 20(4)(c) of the Convention unmistakably makes clear, the (permissible)[31] reservation needs to be accepted by at least one other contracting state in order for the author of the reservation to be part of the circle of contracting states. Failing such a critical acceptance—in whatever way it might have been expressed—an objection with a 'minimum effect' produces no specific consequence and certainly does not establish a treaty relationship between the reserving state and the objecting state. Concretely, a treaty which is subject to the general régime of consent as established in Article 20(4) of the Vienna Convention enters into force for the reserving state only if the reservation has been accepted by at least one other contracting party. It is only if the reservation is thus established that treaty relations may exist between the reserving state and the author of a simple objection.[32] As long as there has been no acceptance of the reservation there can be no treaty relationship whatsoever for its author; its consent to be bound by the treaty will not produce any effect.

It is nevertheless true, as Professor Gaja explained as early as 1987,[33] that the practice followed in particular by the United Nations Secretary-General in his capacity of depositary of international treaties does not seem to be consistent with the rule contained in Article 20(4)(c). As explained in the *Summary of Practice of the Secretary-General as Depositary of Multilateral Treaties*, the Secretary-General

[30] See *supra* pp. 39–40.

[31] As for the effects of acceptances and objections in the case of impermissible reservations, see *infra* pp. 54–9.

[32] This treaty relationship is nevertheless subject to the provision of Article 21(3) of the Vienna Convention: 'the provisions to which the reservation relates do not apply between the reserving State and the objecting State to the extent of the reservation'. See also *infra* pp. 46–54.

[33] 'Unruly Treaty Reservations', *supra* note 2, at 323–4. See also P.-H. Imbert, 'À l'occasion de l'entrée en vigueur de la Convention de Vienne sur le droit des traités, réflexions sur la pratique suivie par le Secrétaire général des Nations Unies dans l'exercice de ses fonctions de dépositaire', 26 *AFDI* (1980) 524–41; R. Riquelme Cortado, *Las reservas a los tratados, Lagunas y ambigüedades del Régimen de Viena* (Murcia: Universidad de Murcia, 2004) at 245–50; or D. Müller, *supra* note 10, at 821–2, para. 48.

agrees that any instrument expressing consent to be bound by a treaty which is accompanied by a reservation may be deposited; however, he refuses to adopt a position on the issue of the permissibility or the effects of the reservation, and therefore he 'indicates the date on which, in accordance with the treaty provisions, the instrument would normally produce its effect, leaving it to each party to draw the legal consequences of the reservations that it deems fit'.[34] The Secretary-General does not wait for the expression of at least one acceptance (as is provided for under Article 20(4)(c)), but treats an instrument of ratification or accession containing a reservation in the same way as any other notification of ratification or accession:

Since he is not to pass judgement, the Secretary-General is not therefore in a position to ascertain the effects, if any, of the instrument containing reservations thereto, *inter alia*, whether the treaty enters into force as between the reserving State and any other State, *a fortiori* between a reserving State and an objecting State if there have been objections. As a consequence, if the final clauses of the treaty in question stipulate that the treaty shall enter into force after the deposit of a certain number of instruments of ratification, approval, acceptance or accession, the Secretary-General as depositary will, subject to the considerations in the following paragraph, include in the number of instruments required for entry into force all those that have been accepted for deposit, whether or not they are accompanied by reservations and whether or not those reservations have met with objections.[35]

Just to give a recent example, Pakistan has thus acceded to the International Convention for the Suppression of the Financing of Terrorism through a notification dated 17 June 2009. This instrument was accompanied by reservations to Articles 11, 14, and 24 of the Convention. Despite these reservations, the Secretary-General noted in his depositary notification of 19 June 2009 that:

The Convention will enter into force for Pakistan on 17 July 2009 in accordance with its article 26 (2) which reads as follows: 'For each State ratifying, accepting, approving or acceding to the Convention after the deposit of the twenty-second instrument of ratification, acceptance, approval or accession, the Convention shall enter into force on the thirtieth day after deposit by such State of its instrument of ratification, acceptance, approval or accession.'[36]

Pakistan's instrument is therefore considered by the depositary as taking immediate effect, notwithstanding the twelve-month delay envisaged in Article 20(5) of the Vienna Convention. For the depositary, Pakistan is one of the contracting states, and is indeed a party to the International Convention for the Suppression

[34] United Nations, *Summary of Practice of the Secretary-General as Depositary of Multilateral Treaties* (New York: United Nations, 1999) (ST/LEG/7/Rev.1) para. 187.

[35] Ibid., para. 184.

[36] *Status of Multilateral Treaties Deposited with the Secretary-General*, Chapter XVIII, 11 (available at <http://treaties.un.org>). This practice is constant. See, eg, the examples given in R. Riquelme Cortado, *supra* note 33, at 546–7.

of the Financing of Terrorism, independently of whether its reservations have been accepted by at least one other contracting party.

This position has been justified by the Secretary-General by the fact that:

> ... [f]inally, for a State's instrument not to be counted, it might conceivably be required that all other contracting States, without exception, would have not only objected to the participation of the reserving State, but that those objecting States would all have definitely expressed their intention that their objection would preclude the entry into force of the treaty as between them and the objecting State.[37]

The Secretary-General thus contests neither the validity nor the correctness of the rule expressed in Article 20(4)(c); he simply ignores the delay for reversing the presumption of acceptance expressed in Article 20(5). Indeed, he does not express the view, as the USSR did,[38] that no acceptance is necessary but that, in any event, it is hardly conceivable that there would not always be at least one state which makes no objection and which therefore will be considered to have accepted the reservation (under Article 20(5)). Waiting for the necessary period for the presumption to trigger its effects would, in the opinion of the Secretary-General, unduly 'delay the announcement of the entry into force of the treaty as well as its registration under Article 102 of the Charter of the United Nations'.[39]

The mere existence of this practice[40] gave rise to a harsh discussion during the re-consideration of the question by the ILC in 2010. Some members of the Commission considered that the rule enunciated in Article 20(4)(c) has no value any more, and that it has been modified by this 'subsequent' practice. However, when considering and evaluating this practice, it should be kept in mind that the depositary of an international treaty does not, as such, have the authority to determine the date of entry into force of the treaty. In relation to the Secretary-General's practice, at the relevant time, with regard to the Genocide Convention (which concerned the very same issue), the ICJ pointed out that 'the existence of an administrative practice does not in itself constitute a decisive factor in ascertaining what views the contracting States to the Genocide Convention may have had concerning the rights and duties resulting therefrom'. Moreover, the ILC did not overlook the issue during the elaboration of the Draft Articles on the Law of Treaties. In its Commentary of draft Article 72(1)(f), it noted:

> Paragraph 1(f) notes the duty of the depositary to inform the States entitled to become parties to the treaty when the number of signatures or of instruments of ratification, etc. required for the entry into force of the treaty have been received or deposited. The question whether the required number has been reached may sometimes pose a problem, as when questionable reservations have been made. In this connexion, as in others, although

[37] *Summary of Practice of the Secretary-General*, *supra* note 34, para. 186.

[38] See *supra* pp. 41–2.

[39] *Summary of Practice of the Secretary-General*, *supra* note 34, para. 186.

[40] Also followed by other depositaries (see 'Depositary Practice in Relation to Reservations', Report of the Secretary-General, A/5687, *YILC* (1965), vol. II, at 74).

the depositary has the function of making a preliminary examination of the matter, it is not invested with competence to make a final determination of the entry into force of the treaty binding upon the other States concerned. However normal it may be for States to accept the depositary's appreciation of the date of the entry into force of a treaty, it seems clear that this appreciation may be challenged by another State and that then it would be the duty of the depositary to consult all the other interested States as provided in paragraph 2 of the present article.[41]

In 2010, the ILC finally took into account the existence of the discrepancy between the rule provided for in the Vienna Convention and the dominant depositary practice. While reconfirming the rule enunciated in Article 20(4)(c) of the Convention,[42] the Commission also stated that: '[t]he author of the reservation may however be included at an earlier date [ie before the reservation has been accepted and established] in the number of contracting States and contracting organizations required for the treaty to enter into force, if no contracting State or contracting organization is opposed in a particular case'.[43]

Even if the drafting seems to suggest otherwise, this guideline cannot dispense with the reservation to be accepted, which reduces the difference between acceptances and objections practically to the vanishing point.[44] It only allows the states parties to presume that the reservation has been accepted at an earlier date (eg the date of the act of ratification or accession of the treaty) as the date at which the reservation would normally have been established under the Vienna Convention (the date of an express acceptance, or twelve months after the formulation of the reservation).

In its celebrated Advisory Opinion of 1951, the ICJ very logically considered that:

- 'it is the compatibility of a reservation with the object and purpose of the Convention that must furnish the criterion for the attitude of a State in making the reservation on accession as well as for the appraisal by a State in objecting to the reservation';[45]

[41] *YILC* (1966), vol. II, at 270, para. 6 of the Commentary.

[42] Paragraph 1 of Guideline 4.2.2 (Effect of the establishment of a reservation on the entry into force of a treaty) reads: '1. When a treaty has not yet entered into force, the author of a reservation shall be included in the number of contracting States and contracting organizations required for the treaty to enter into force once the reservation is established' (*GAOR, Sixty-fifth Session, Supplement No. 10* (A/65/10) at 63).

[43] Guideline 4.2.2 (Effect of the establishment of a reservation on the entry into force of a treaty), para. 2, ibid.

[44] This is all the more so since the Secretary-General (wrongly) seems to equate an objection with minimum effect with an acceptance ('Finally, for a State's instrument not to be counted, it might conceivably be required that all other contracting States, without exception, would have not only objected to the participation of the reserving State, *but that those objecting States would all have definitely expressed their intention that their objection would preclude the entry into force of the treaty as between them and the objecting State*'—see *supra* p. 44).

[45] ICJ, *Reservations to the Convention on the Prevention and Punishment of the Crime of Genocide*, Advisory Opinion of 28 May 1951, *ICJ Reports* (1951) at 24.

- 'As no State can be bound by a reservation to which it has not consented, it necessarily follows that each State objecting to it will or will not, on the basis of its individual appraisal within the limits of the criterion of the object and purpose stated above, consider the reserving State to be a party to the Convention';[46] but
- only in that case, the ICJ had linked the automatic preclusion of the entry into force of the treaty between the two states; it admitted that 'it may be that a State, whilst not claiming that a reservation is incompatible with the object and purpose of the Convention, will nevertheless object to it, but that an understanding between that State and the reserving State will have the effect that the Convention will enter into force between them, except for the clauses affected by the reservation'.[47]

By delinking the 'maximum effect' of an objection from the criterion of the compatibility with the object and purpose of the treaty, the Vienna Convention has put this impeccable reasoning in jeopardy: the presumption laid down in Article 20(4)(b) results in the (widely used) possibility that a state may in fact agree to be bound with another state by a treaty that it considered to be devoid of object and purpose by means of the reservation. Absurd as it might be, this situation threatens but does not eliminate the distinction between an acceptance and an objection in the relations between the states in question.

2. Acceptance, Objection, and the Relations between the Reserving and the Objecting States

Acceptances and objections do not only have different legal effects regarding the entry into force of the treaty. If and when the treaty has entered into force, they also have different legal effects with regard to the content of the treaty relations between the reserving and the objecting states. However, the Vienna Convention provides only an *obscure clarté* as to the effect of an acceptance of or an objection to a permissible reservation (Section 2.1); it is mute as to the effects (if any) of an acceptance of, or an objection to, an impermissible reservation (Section 2.2).

2.1. Acceptance of, and objection to, a permissible reservation

Article 21(1) makes clear that the acceptance of a permissible reservation has a fundamental role to play in the relations between the reserving and the objecting states since it 'establishes' the reservation, to use the word in the *chapeau* of Article

[46] Ibid., at 26. [47] Ibid.

21(1) of the Vienna Convention[48] whereas, by contrast, an objection prevents a reservation from producing effects. However, Article 20 and—in spite of its title ('Legal effects of reservations and of objections to reservations')—Article 21 leave many questions unanswered with regard to the consequences of an objection to a permissible reservation. Indeed, this is one of the core issues.

However, deficient as they may be, these provisions confirm the dialectical relation existing between the two possible reactions to reservations: an acceptance is the opposite of an objection, and vice versa. Article 20(5), according to which a state is presumed to have accepted a reservation if it has not objected to it, clearly illustrates this basic idea. As the representative of the French Republic put it during the Vienna Conference: '[A]cceptance and objection [are] the obverse and reverse sides of the same idea. A State which [accepts] a reservation thereby [surrenders] the right to object to it; a State which [raises] an objection thereby [expresses] its refusal to accept a reservation.'[49]

In contrast to an acceptance, which conditions the establishment of a reservation and cannot but modify the treaty as and to the extent provided for by the reservation, an objection to a reservation can have various consequences on the treaty relationship between the reserving state and the objecting state. The choice of these different legal effects, which are, at least partially, envisaged by the Vienna Convention, is left to a certain extent to the objecting state alone.[50]

As provided for in Article 20(4)(b) of the Vienna Convention, an objecting state can choose, at its own discretion and without any condition, whether to establish a treaty relationship between itself and the reserving state. This choice is not open to the accepting state: its acceptance *ipso facto* makes the author of the reservation a contracting state.

In addition, as Professor Gaja has noted,[51] objecting states have a certain degree of freedom[52] to determine the extent of the treaty relations they want to have with

[48] According to the definition given in Guideline 4.1 of the Guide to Practice (Establishment of a reservation with regard to another state or organization): 'A reservation formulated by a State or an international organization is established with regard to a contracting State or contracting organization if it is permissible and was formulated in accordance with the required form and procedures, and if that contracting State or contracting organization has accepted it.'

[49] United Nations Conference on the Law of Treaties, *Official Records*, vol. I, at 116, para. 14.

[50] At least when the reservation is permissible; the situation is appreciably different with regard to an objection made to an impermissible reservation. See *infra* Section 2.2.

[51] 'Unruly Treaty Reservations', *supra* note 2, at 325–6.

[52] There are limits to that freedom. In particular, it is not open to the objecting state to impose on the reserving state an obligation to respect the treaty without the benefit of its reservation. These objections purport to produce what has been called a 'super-maximum effect' (see B. Simma, 'Reservations to Human Rights Treaties—Some Recent Developments', in *Liber amicorum Professor Ignaz Seidl-Hohenveldern in Honour of his 80th Birthday* (The Hague: Kluwer, 1998, at 667–8; or A. Pellet, 'Eighth Report on Reservations to Treaties' (2003), A/CN.4/535/Add.1, para. 96). It is quite clear that such an effect of an objection (including objections with intermediate effect) is not only not envisaged by the Vienna Conventions, but is also clearly incompatible with the principle of mutual consent. Accordingly, a super-maximum effect is excluded in the case of a valid reservation: the author of an objection cannot force the author of the reservation to be bound by more than what it is prepared to consent to. Guideline 4.3.7 of the Guide to Practice

the reserving state in that they can choose a (narrow) road between the maximum and the minimum effects of their objection. Such objections, intended to have an 'intermediary effect', were made in relation to the 1969 Vienna Convention itself, and they consisted in accepting the entry into force of the Convention with the exclusion not only of the provisions to which the reservation related[53] but also to other provisions linked to those excluded by the reservation.[54] This 'new generation'[55] of objections purports to produce effects exceeding those provided for under Article 21(3) without, however, reaching the clear-cut effect of a 'maximum effect' reservation, ie the non-entry into force of the treaty between the two states.

The ILC has decided to take note of this—limited—practice of objections with 'intermediary effect' in its Guide to practice.[56] Nevertheless, they are not entirely unproblematic. First, the question arises whether the objecting state can modulate the legal relationship to be established with the reserving state at its full discretion. The limited practice described above seems to suggest that only treaty provisions which have a specific link with the provisions affected by the reservation can be excluded. The United Kingdom, in its objection of 5 June 1987 in respect of the Soviet reservation to Article 66 of the Vienna Convention, stated that:

> Article 66 provides in certain circumstances for the compulsory settlement of disputes by the International Court of Justice [...] or by a conciliation procedure [...]. These provisions are inextricably linked with the provisions of Part V to which they relate. Their

(Right of the author of a valid reservation not to be compelled to comply with the treaty without the benefit of its reservation) adopted in 2010 unmistakably recognizes that: '[t]he author of a reservation which is permissible and which has been formulated in accordance with the required form and procedures cannot be compelled to comply with the provisions of the treaty without the benefit of its reservation'. (*GAOR, Sixty-fifth Session, Supplement No.10* (A/65/10) at 66).

[53] Usually Article 66 of the Vienna Convention (see the reservations formulated by Algeria (*Multilateral treaties deposited with the Secretary-General*, available at <http://treaties.un.org/>, Chapter XXIII, 1), Belarus (ibid.), China (ibid.), Cuba (ibid.), Guatemala (ibid.), the Russian Federation (ibid.), the Syrian Arab Republic (ibid.), Tunisia (ibid.), Ukraine (ibid.), and Viet Nam (ibid.). Bulgaria, the Czech Republic, Hungary, and Mongolia had formulated similar reservations but withdrew them in the early 1990s (ibid.). The German Democratic Republic had also formulated a reservation excluding the application of Article 66 (ibid.).

[54] The other articles of the Vienna Convention relating to *jus cogens* (Articles 53 and 64)—see the objections of Canada, Egypt, Japan, the Netherlands, New Zealand, Sweden, the United Kingdom, and the United States (ibid).

[55] *'Nueva generación'* (our translation), Riquelme Cortado, *supra* note 33, at 293. R. Baratta expressed the idea that 'the practice has generated new legal models of objections, dictated probably by the necessity of responding to needs which had not emerged and had not been considered at the time of the "codification"' (our translation—*'la prassi abbia generato nuovi modelli giuridici di obiezioni, dettati verosimilmente della necessità di rispondere a bisogni non emersi e comunque non considerati al momento della "codificazione"'*) (*Gli effetti delle riserve ai trattati* (Milano: Giuffré, 1999) at 387).

[56] See Commentary to Guideline 2.6.1 (Definition of objections to reservations), in *GAOR, Sixtieth Session, Supplement No. 10* (A/60/10) at 199, para. 23). See also 'Eighth Report on Reservations to Treaties' (2003), A/CN.4/535/Add.1, para 95.

inclusion was the basis on which those parts of Part V which represent progressive development of international law were accepted by the Vienna Conference.[57]

But even in the case where objections intended to have an 'intermediary effect' remain in these strict limits and aim at excluding only provisions which have a particular link with the provision to which the reservation relates, it can be questioned whether this effect can result only from the objection or whether the reserving state needs to consent. It has been suggested that 'these extended objections are, in fact, reservations (limited *ratione personae*)';[58] this finds some support in the fact that certain states have chosen to formulate reservations so as to achieve the same result.[59] Professor Gaja also wrote:

> As a partial rejection modifies the content of the treaty in relation to the reserving State to an extent that exceeds the intended effect of the reservation, acceptance or acquiescence on the part of the reserving State appear to be necessary for a partial rejection to take its effect; failing this, no relations under the treaty are established between the reserving State and an objecting State which partially rejects those relations.[60]

After some discussion, the ILC finally considered that at least some kind of acquiescence is necessary in order for an 'intermediary effect' objection to produce its full effects.[61]

However, even with these limitations, these objections 'of the third type' confirm that it is possible for an objecting state to modulate the treaty relationship which it is ready to undertake in its relations with the reserving state, a choice which is not open to a state accepting a reservation. And clearly these objections are not tantamount to acceptance. This is also true concerning the objection with 'minimum effect', as envisaged in Article 21(3) of the Vienna Convention.

It is true that, when the 1968–69 Vienna Conference adopted the USSR amendment to Article 20(4)(b), reversing the presumption of the legal effect

[57] *Multilateral Treaties Deposited with the Secretary-General*, available at <http://treaties.un.org/>, Chapter XXIII, 1.

[58] See, *inter alia*, J. Sztucki, 'Some Questions Arising from Reservations to the Vienna Convention on the Law of Treaties'. The author suggests that such declarations should be viewed as 'objections only to the initial reservations and own reservations of the objecting States in the remaining part' (ibid., at 291).

[59] See, in particular, the late reservation formulated by Belgium, *Multilateral Treaties Deposited with the Secretary-General*, available at <http://treaties.un.org>, Chapter XXIII, 1.

[60] 'Unruly Treaty Reservations', *supra* note 2, at 326. See also R. Baratta, *supra* note 55, at 385. *Contra* D. Müller, *supra* note 9, at 923–5, paras 64–66.

[61] Guideline 4.3.6 (Effect of an objection on provisions other than those to which the reservation relates) adopted by the ILC, in 2010, seems to transform an 'intermediary effect' objection into a 'counter-reservation' which, again, is submitted to the consent of the reserving state. Paragraph 2 reads: 'The reserving State or organization may, within a period of twelve months following the notification of such an objection, oppose the entry into force of the treaty between itself and the objecting State or organization. In the absence of such opposition, the treaty shall apply between the author of the reservation and the author of the objection to the extent provided by the reservation and the objection' (*GAOR, Sixty-fifth Session, Supplement No.10* (A/65/10) at 65–6).

of an objection on the entry into force of the treaty,[62] the Drafting Committee changed not only the introductory words of Article 21(3) but also the final part. Article 21(3), as proposed by the Drafting Committee and provisionally adopted by the Conference,[63] read: 'When a State objecting to a reservation has not opposed the entry into force of the treaty between itself and the reserving State, *the reservation has the effects provided for in paragraphs 1 and 2*.'[64]

This provision left no doubt about the legal effect of an objection with regard to those produced by an accepted reservation: they were identical. Indeed, the issue had already given rise to some debate within the ILC: Yasseen, who also chaired the Drafting Committee during the Conference, had drawn the attention of his colleagues to the fact that, '[i]n the text before the Commission... objection to a reservation and acceptance thereof seemed to produce the same effect, and objection was therefore made tantamount to acceptance'.[65] The view expressed by Castrén,[66] who considered that the case of a reservation in respect of which a simple objection had been raised was already covered by draft Article 21(1)(b), was not shared by the other members of the ILC. Most members[67] considered it necessary, if not 'indispensable',[68] to have a distinct provision 'in order to forestall ambiguous situations'.[69]

A joint amendment introduced by India, Japan, the Netherlands, and the USSR only a few days before the end of the Conference,[70] in order to replace the end of the provision by the text initially proposed in the ILC draft, brought things back to order. As the Dutch representative rightly explained:

> What has been overlooked, however, was another category of reservations, where the reserving State declared that an article of a treaty was acceptable provided it was interpreted in a particular way; in such a case, a State which objected to that interpretation could not hold the opinion that the legal effects of its objection should be the same as they would be if it accepted the special interpretation.[71]

The amendment was finally adopted by the Conference.[72] Yasseen, chairman of the Drafting Committee, indicated that '[i]t was necessary to distinguish between cases where a State objected to a reservation but agreed that the treaty should

[62] See *supra* pp. 41–2.

[63] United Nations Conference on the Law of Treaties, *supra* note 8, at 36, para. 10 (94 votes to none).

[64] Ibid., at 36 (emphasis added).

[65] *YILC* (1965), vol. I, at 271, para. 5. See also ibid., at 174, para. 40 (Tsuruoka).

[66] Ibid., at 172, para. 15.

[67] Ruda (ibid., para. 13); Ago (ibid., at 271–2, paras 7 and 11); Tunkin (ibid., at 271, para 8), and Briggs (ibid., at 272, para. 14).

[68] See the statement made by Ago (ibid., at 271, para. 7).

[69] Ibid.

[70] A/CONF.39/L.49, United Nations Conference on the Law of Treaties, *supra* note 29 at 273.

[71] United Nations Conference on the Law of Treaties, *supra* note 8, at 179–80, para. 55. The Dutch representative had in mind the case of an objection by which its author did not purport to exclude the application of a treaty provision, but only to modify its application. See also the intervention made by the Soviet representative (ibid., at 180, para. 60).

[72] Ibid., at 181, para. 12.

nevertheless come into force, and cases in which the reservation was accepted'.[73] As Horn puts it, '[t]he view that the institution of objections is in the end void of any special effect is discomforting as it was intended by the framers of the Vienna Convention to be the means by which the parties to a treaty safeguarded themselves against unwelcome reservations'.[74]

This late restoration of the text grants to objections their real object in endowing them with legal effects different from those of an established (ie accepted) reservation. This is particularly clear when considering the case of a reservation whereby its author purports to modify the legal effect of one or several provisions of the treaty, as pointed out by the Dutch representative at the Conference: whereas, once established, such a reservation fully effective and modifies the legal effect of the provision(s) concerned in the bilateral relationship between the reserving state and the accepting state, is Article 21(3) excludes the application of these provisions 'to the extent of the reservation' in the case an objection has been made. The legal effect of an established reservation—which, by definition, has been accepted[75]—and those of an objection to a reservation are thus diametrically opposed. This solution has been confirmed by the decision of the Arbitral Tribunal in the *Anglo-French Continental Shelf* case, which makes clear that an objection does not necessarily exclude the application of the entire provision concerned between the objecting and reserving states, as had been argued by France.[76] Consequently, the objection excludes or modifies the application of the relevant provision only to the extent of the reservation.

In the case of France and the United Kingdom, that meant accepting that Article 6 of the Geneva Convention on the Continental Shelf remained applicable as between the parties, apart from the matters covered by the French reservation. This is what must be understood by the expression 'to the extent of the reservation'. The effect sought by Article 21(3) is to preserve the agreement between the parties to the extent possible by reducing the application of the treaty to the provisions on which there is agreement and excluding the others, or, as J.K. Koh explains: 'Here the Vienna Convention seems to be overtly seeking to preserve as much of the treaty as possible even when parties disagree about a reservation. … The Vienna Convention tries to salvage as much as is uncontroversial about the relations between reserving and opposing states.'[77]

But this cannot mean that, under the Vienna régime of reservations, acceptances and objections are identical and that the Vienna Convention 'threatens to

[73] Ibid., para. 2.

[74] F. Horn, *Reservations and Interpretative Declarations to Multilateral Treaties* (The Hague: T.M.C. Asser Institute, 1988) at 173–4.

[75] See *supra* note 48.

[76] *Delimitation of the Continental Shelf between the United Kingdom of Great Britain and Northern Ireland and the French Republic*, 18 *RIAA* (1977), 42, para. 61.

[77] J.K. Koh, 'Reservations to Multilateral Treaties: How International Legal Doctrine Reflects World Vision', 23 *Harv. Int'l LJ* (1982) at 102.

obliterate the difference between an accepted and an opposed reservation, and renders objection to the reservation a fruitless endeavor'.[78]

However, it is true that there is one circumstance in which the concrete effect of Articles 21(1) and 21(3) happens to be identical. This is the case when a reservation does not purport to modify the legal effect of a provision of the treaty, but purely and simply to exclude the provision under the treaty régime. In such a case, and only in such a case, an objection produces the same effects as an acceptance: the exclusion of the legal effect, or of the application, of the provision to which the reservation relates 'to the extent of the reservation'. An acceptance and a simple objection therefore result in the same treaty relations between the author of the reservation and the author of the acceptance or of the objection with minimum effect. On this point authors agree, including Professor Gaja, who wrote: 'Whenever a reservation, as is normally the case, intends to restrict, either totally or in part, the content of an obligation under a treaty, it is difficult to see any difference between the effects of a reservation to which an objection has been made and those of a reservation which has been accepted.'[79]

Guidelines 4.3.5 (Effects of an objection on treaty relations), paragraph 2, and 4.2.4 (Effect of an established reservation on treaty relations), paragraph 2, of the Guide to Practice[80] reflect this hypothesis where an objection and an acceptance produce concretely the same outcome in the relations between the two states concerned. Paragraph 2 of Guideline 4.3.5 provides that:

> ... [t]o the extent that a valid reservation purports to exclude the legal effect of certain provisions of the treaty, when a contracting State or a contracting organization has raised an objection to it but has not opposed the entry into force of the treaty between itself and the author of the reservation, the objecting State or organization and the author of the reservation are not bound, in their treaty relations, by the provisions to which the reservation relates.

Paragraph 2 of Guideline 4.2.4 specifies:

> To the extent that an established reservation excludes the legal effect of certain provisions of a treaty, the author of that reservation has neither rights nor obligations under those provisions in its relations with the other parties with regard to which the reservation is established. Those other parties shall likewise have neither rights nor obligations under those provisions in their relations with the author of the reservation.

[78] Ibid.

[79] 'Unruly Treaty Reservations', *supra* note 2, at 327. See also B. Clark, 'The Vienna Convention Reservations Regime and the Convention on Discrimination against Women', 85 *AJIL* (1991) at 308; M. Coccia, 'Reservations to Multilateral Treaties on Human Rights', 15 *California Western International Law Journal* (1985) at 36; P.-H. Imbert, *supra* note 20, at 157; J.-M. Ruda, 'Reservations to Treaties', 146 *Recueil des Cours* (1975-III) at 199; Sir I. Sinclair, *The Vienna Convention on the Law of Treaties* (Manchester: Manchester University Press, 2nd edn, 1984) at 76; F. Horn, *supra* note 74, at 173; J. Klabbers, *supra* note 5, at 186–7. See also the explanations of the representative of the Netherlands in respect of the four-state amendment, United Nations Conference on the Law of Treaties, *supra* note 8, at 179, para. 55.

[80] *GAOR, Sixty-fifth Session, Supplement No.10* (A/65/10) at 64–5.

Concretely, even if the intention is different, the content of the legal relationship between the reserving state and an accepting state is the same as the relation between an objecting state and the reserving state.

However, the similarity in the effects of an acceptance and a minimum-effect objection does not mean that the two reactions are identical and that the author of the reservation 'would get what it desired'.[81] The reserving state cannot 'get it' if its reservation only calls for objections with minimum effect; it also needs at least one acceptance. Moreover, while an acceptance is tantamount to an agreement, or at least implies the absence of opposition to a reservation, an objection cannot be considered mere 'wishful thinking';[82] it expresses disagreement and purports to protect the rights of its author as much as a unilateral declaration (ie unilateral protest) does.[83]

Furthermore, this similarity is only observed in the very specific case of excluding reservations, and not when the reserving state purports to modify the legal effects of a treaty provision. In that case, the difference between an objection and an acceptance is very clear. Whereas the establishment of such a reservation modifies the legal obligations between the author of the reservation and the contracting parties with regard to which the reservation is established, Article 21(3) excludes the application of all the provisions that potentially would be modified by the reservation, to the extent of the reservation. If a state makes a reservation purporting to replace one treaty obligation with another, Article 21(3) requires that the obligation potentially replaced by the reservation be excised from the treaty relations between the author of the reservation and the author of the objection with minimum effect. Neither the initial obligation nor the modified obligation proposed by the reservation apply: the former because the author of the reservation has not agreed to it and the latter because the author of the objection has not agreed to it.

The difference between the legal relationships established by a modifying reservation is made apparent by a comparison between Guidelines 4.2.4 (Effect of an established reservation on treaty relations), paragraph 3,[84] and 4.3.5 (Effects of an objection on treaty relations), paragraph 3 of the Guide to Practice.[85] The

[81] J. Klabbers, *supra* note 5, at 179.

[82] '*Un vœu pieux*' (our translation)—P.-H. Imbert, *supra* note 20, at 157 quoting J. Dehaussy, *Jurisclasseur de Droit international*, fasc. 11, mise à jour 8, 1975, n° 97ter.

[83] K. Zemanek, 'Some Unresolved Questions Concerning Reservations in the Vienna Convention on the Law of Treaties', in J. Makarczyk (ed.), *Essays in International Law in Honour of Judge Manfred Lachs* (The Hague-Boston: Martinus Nijhoff, 1984) at 332.

[84] 'To the extent that an established reservation modifies the legal effect of certain provisions of a treaty, the author of that reservation has rights and obligations under those provisions, as modified by the reservation, in its relations with the other parties with regard to which the reservation is established. Those other parties shall have rights and obligations under those provisions, as modified by the reservation, in their relations with the author of the reservation' (*GAOR, Sixty-fifth Session, Supplement No. 10* (A/65/10) at 64).

[85] 'To the extent that a valid reservation purports to modify the legal effect of certain provisions of the treaty, when a contracting State or a contracting organization has raised an objection to it but has not opposed the entry into force of the treaty between itself and the author of the reservation, the objecting State or organization and the author of the reservation are not bound, in their

content between the two relationships is clearly different: on the one hand, the accepted reservation modifies the treaty relationship as provided for under the reservation; on the other hand, the treaty relationship is amputated by the provisions which the reservation purports to modify. In this case, not only is the specificity of an objection with regard to the acceptance appreciable, but, more importantly, the reserving state does not get what it desires: clearly, it gets less.

2.2. Acceptance of, and objection to, an impermissible reservation

The Vienna Convention does not address the issue of the legal effects of impermissible reservations,[86] and this is one of its most serious lacunae which had to be filled by the ILC in the framework of the preparation of the Guide to Practice. To this effect, the Special Rapporteur proposed in its tenth Report to include the following guideline:

> 3.3.2 Nullity of invalid reservations
> A reservation that does not fulfil the conditions for validity laid down in guideline 3.1 [which is reproducing Article 19 of the Vienna Conventions] is null and void.

This nullity entails, as explained in the Special Rapporteur's fifteenth Report, that the impermissible[87] reservation produces no legal effect at all.[88]

Consequently, acceptances and objections do not play any role in determining the legal effect to be attached to an impermissible reservation, contrary to what is provided for by the Vienna Convention concerning permissible reservations. The absence of any reference to impermissible reservations in the Convention suggests that the acceptance/objection mechanism, which is provided for in Article 20, cannot be transposed to impermissible reservations. This may seem surprising if one keeps in mind that objections are, in practice, usually motivated by the fact that the objecting state considers the reservation to be incompatible with the object and purpose of the treaty. But the terms of Article 19 of the Vienna Convention are unambiguous: in the three cases mentioned in that provision, a reservation cannot be formulated.

However, even if the Vienna Convention does not make any allusion to the effect of an acceptance or of an objection to an impermissible reservation, they

treaty relations, by the provisions of the treaty as intended to be modified by the reservation' (ibid., at 65).

[86] A. Pellet, 'Fifteenth Report on the Law of Treaties' (2010), A/CN.4/624/Add.1, para. 398.

[87] And, more widely, any non-valid reservation. The ILC retained the term 'permissibility' (in French '*validité substantielle*') 'to denote the substantive validity of reservations that fulfilled the requirements of article 19 of the Vienna Conventions' (*GAOR, Sixty-first Session, Supplement No. 10* (A/61/10) at 327, para. 7 of the General Commentary to section 3 of the Guide to Practice). The term 'validity' denotes the fulfilment of permissibility requirements *and* of the formal requirements concerning the formulation of a reservation (Article 23 of the Vienna Convention).

[88] A. Pellet, 'Fifteenth Report on the Law of Treaties' (2010), A/CN.4/624/Add.1, paras 416–427.

are not automatically devoid of any effect. Interestingly, even in this case, a clear distinction between acceptance and objection appears.

Accepting a non-valid reservation may appear to be a paradox. One may wonder what might be the intention of a state when accepting an impermissible reservation which, in any event, cannot be established within the meaning of Article 21(1) of the Vienna Convention. At the Vienna Conference, Sir Humphrey Waldock noted without any ambiguity: '[A] contracting State could not purport, under article [20], to accept a reservation prohibited under article [19], paragraph (*a*) or paragraph (*b*), because, by prohibiting the reservation, the contracting States would expressly have excluded such acceptance.'[89]

This is also true concerning paragraph (c). There is no reason to distinguish between these three provisions because

> ... nothing, either in the text of Article 19 or in the *travaux préparatoires*, gives grounds for thinking that a distinction should be made between the different cases: *ubi lex non distinguit, nec nos distinguere debemus*. In all three cases, as clearly emerges from the *chapeau* of article 19, a state is prevented from formulating a reservation and, once it is accepted that a reservation prohibited by the treaty is null and void by virtue of subparagraphs (a) and (b) of article 19, there is no reason to draw different conclusions from subparagraph (c).[90]

It is thus impossible to accept an impermissible reservation, whatever the reason for this impermissibility may be, and any such acceptance would be deprived of legal effect. The ILC confirmed this point of view, in 2010, by adopting Guideline 3.4.1 (Permissibility of the acceptance of a reservation): 'The express acceptance of an impermissible reservation is itself impermissible.'

However, even if a single isolated acceptance expressed by a state to an impermissible reservation cannot 'validate' the reservation[91]—validity (or permissibility)[92] being an objective criterion—the situation may differ in the case where all contracting states accept a reservation which, objectively, is impermissible. As masters of the treaty, and in accordance with the consent principle underlying the law of treaties,[93] 'the Parties always have a right to amend the

[89] United Nations Conference on the Law of Treaties, *supra* note 49, at 133, para. 2.

[90] *GAOR, Sixty-fourth Session, Supplement No. 10* (A/64/10) at 305, para. 4 of the Commentary of Guideline 3.3 (Consequences of the non-permissibility of a reservation).

[91] In its tenth report, the Special Rapporteur proposed draft Guideline 3.3.3 (Effect of unilateral acceptance of an invalid reservation) which highlighted this absence of effect: 'Acceptance of a reservation by a contracting State or by a contracting international organization shall not change the nullity of the reservation.' ('Tenth Report on Reservations to Treaties' (2005), A/CN.4/558/Add.2, para. 202). See also the 'Fifteenth Report on Reservations to Treaties' (2010), A/CN.4/624/Add.1, paras 477–483.

[92] See *supra* note 87.

[93] In this connection, the ICJ specified in its Advisory Opinion of 1951 on *Reservations to the Genocide Convention* that 'it is well established that in its treaty relations a State cannot be bound without its consent, and that consequently no reservation can be effective against any State without its agreement thereto' (*supra* note 11, at 21). The authors of the joint Dissenting Opinion accompanying the Advisory Opinion express this idea even more strongly: 'The consent of the parties is the basis of treaty obligations. The law governing reservations is only a particular application of this fundamental principle, whether the consent of the parties to a reservation is given in advance

treaty by general agreement *inter se* in accordance with Article 39 of the Vienna Conventions and... nothing prevents them from adopting a unanimous agreement to that end on the subject of reservations'.[94] This idea finds some support in practice[95] and, in its tenth Report, the Special Rapporteur proposed a draft Guideline 3.3.4 which takes account of this possible effect of collective acceptance of an invalid reservation:

> A reservation that is explicitly or implicitly prohibited by the treaty or which is incompatible with its object and purpose may be formulated by a State or an international organization if none of the other contracting parties objects to it after having been expressly consulted by the depositary.
>
> During such consultation, the depositary shall draw the attention of the signatory States and international organizations and of the contracting States and international organizations and, where appropriate, the competent organ of the international organization concerned, to the nature of legal problems raised by the reservation.[96]

In such a case, an acceptance becomes an instrument to express its author's agreement with the proposed reservation—independently of the question of whether it is valid or not; and it re-introduces, by the keyhole, the very traditional system of unanimity under which only the consent of other states could 'establish' a reservation.

Similarly, like acceptances, objections to impermissible reservations have no concrete legal effect as such. It is true that Article 21(3) of the Vienna Convention does not limit the application of the rules contained therein to permissible reservations only, as is the case for Article 21(1) in relation to acceptances. However, Article 21(3) cannot operate if the reserving state has not become a party to the

of the proposal of the reservation or at the same time or later.' (ibid., at 32) See also PCIJ, *S.S. Wimbledon (United Kingdom, France, Italy, Japan/Germany, Poland intervening)*, Judgment of 17 August 1923, 1923, Series A, No. 1, at 25; ICJ, *International Status of South-West Africa*, Advisory Opinion of 11 July 1950, *ICJ Reports* (1950) at 139; *Delimitation of the Continental Shelf between the United Kingdom of Great Britain and Northern Ireland and the French Republic*, *supra* note 76, at 41–2, paras 60–61. See also P. Reuter, *supra* note 22, at 20–1; Ch. Tomuschat, 'Admissibility and Legal Effects of Reservations to Multilateral Treaties', 27 *ZaöRV* (1967) at 466.

[94] A. Pellet, 'Tenth Report on Reservations to Treaties' (2005), A/CN.4/558/Add.2, para. 205 (footnotes omitted). This position is supported by D.W. Greig, 'Reservations: Equity as a Balancing Factor?', 16 *Australian YIL* (1995) at 56–7, and L. Sucharipa-Behrmann, 'The Legal Effects of Reservations to Multilateral Treaties', 1 *ARIEL* (1996), at 78. However, D.W. Bowett, who shares this point of view, notes that this possibility is not part of the law of reservations ('Reservations to Non-Restricted Multilateral Treaties', 48 *BYIL* (1976–77) at 84; see also C. Redgwell, 'Universality or Integrity? Some Reflections on Reservations to General Multilateral Treaties', 64 *BYIL* (1993) at 269).

[95] Although it is not, strictly speaking, a unanimous acceptance of the parties to the treaties, the example of the neutrality reservation made by Switzerland upon its accession to the Covenant of the League of Nations remains a prominent example where, despite the prohibition of reservations by the treaty (the Covenant in that case), the author of the reservation was accepted as a member of the League, that is, in the circle of state parties to the Covenant; see M.H. Mendelson, 'Reservations to the Constitutions of International Organizations', 45 *BYIL* (1971) at 140–1.

[96] A. Pellet, 'Tenth Report on Reservations to Treaties' (2005), A/CN.4/558/Add.2, para. 207.

treaty, ie if its reservation has not been accepted by at least one other party; only in that case would it be necessary to determine the concrete legal relationship between the reserving state and the objecting state but, as has been shown, the acceptance of a non-valid reservation is not legally possible.[97] More importantly, an impermissible reservation is simply not open to the consent of other states parties; its effect (or absence of any effect) is based exclusively on the nullity of the reservation, and this is the end of the matter.

Nevertheless, objecting to non-valid reservation is not necessarily a futile gesture. Although an objection to a reservation does not produce any specific legal effect of its own and cannot determine as such the validity of the reservation, it constitutes a significant element of appreciation for all interested parties, ie the author of the reservation, the states and contracting organizations, and any court or competent body, in order to determine the validity of a reservation.

In this respect, it can be noted that, in its 1951 Advisory Opinion, the ICJ considered that: 'each State which is a party to the Convention is entitled to appraise the validity of the reservation and it exercises this right individually and from its own standpoint'.[98]

However, this approach, which rests on a distinction between the validity of a reservation and consent thereto, would hardly be compatible with the contemporary Vienna régime. Thus, in its orders on the request for the indication of provisional measures in the *Use of force* cases between former Yugoslavia, on the one hand, and the United States of America and Spain on the other hand, the Court only noted that: 'the Genocide Convention does not prohibit reservations; [that] Yugoslavia did not object to the United States reservation to Article IX; and [that] the said reservation had the effect of excluding that Article from the provisions of the Convention in force between the Parties'.[99]

The Court did not resort to any test of validity of the reservation; the mere fact that no objection was made to it seemed to imply that it was valid.

However, as Professor Gaja has noted in his latest article on reservations,[100] the Court subsequently changed its mind. In its judgment on jurisdiction and admissibility in the *Armed Activities on the Territory of the Congo* case between

[97] See *supra* p. 55.

[98] ICJ, *Reservations to the Convention on the Prevention and Punishment of the Crime of Genocide*, *supra* note 11, at 26. See also Inter-American Court of Human Rights, *The Effect of Reservations on the Entry into Force of the American Convention on Human Rights (Arts 74 and 75)*, Advisory Opinion, 24 September 1982, Series A No. 2, para. 38 ('The States Parties have a legitimate interest, of course, in barring reservations incompatible with the object and purpose of the Convention. They are free to assert that interest through the adjudicatory and advisory machinery established by the Convention').

[99] ICJ, *Legality of Use of Force (Yugoslavia v United States of America)*, Provisional Measures, Order of 2 June 1999, *ICJ Reports* (1999) at 924, para. 24; and ICJ, *Legality of Use of Force (Yugoslavia v Spain)*, Provisional Measures, Discontinuance, Order of 2 June 1999, *ICJ Reports* (1999) at 772, para. 32.

[100] 'Il regime della Convenzione di Vienna concernente le riserve inammissibili', *supra* note 2, at 354.

the Democratic Republic of the Congo and Rwanda, the Court determined objectively the validity of Rwanda's reservation to the Genocide Convention and, as noted in a Joint Separate Opinion, 'added its own assessment as to the compatibility of [that] reservation with the object and purpose of the Genocide Convention':[101]

Rwanda's reservation to Article IX of the Genocide Convention bears on the jurisdiction of the Court, and does not affect substantive obligations relating to acts of genocide themselves under that Convention. In the circumstances of the present case, the Court cannot conclude that the reservation of Rwanda in question, which is meant to exclude a particular method of settling a dispute relating to the interpretation, application or fulfilment of the Convention, is to be regarded as being incompatible with the object and purpose of the Convention.[102]

However, the absence of any objection was not entirely disregarded. The Court indeed 'strengthened its own conclusion with an *ad hominem* argument',[103] adding: 'as a matter of the law of treaties, when Rwanda acceded to the Genocide Convention and made the reservation in question, the DRC made no objection to it'.[104]

The Strasbourg Court has also given an important place to objections in order to confirm its proper assessment of the validity of Turkey's reservation in the *Loizidou* case.[105] The Human Rights Committee explained in its General Comment No. 24:

The absence of protest by States cannot imply that a reservation is either compatible or incompatible with the object and purpose of the Covenant. Objections have been occasional, made by some States but not others, and on grounds not always specified [...]. However, an objection to a reservation made by States may provide some guidance to the Committee in its interpretation as to its compatibility with the object and purpose of the Covenant.[106]

The Swedish representative at the Sixth Committee also confirmed that:

... [t]heoretically, an objection was not necessary in order to establish that fact but was merely a way of calling attention to it. The objection therefore had no real legal effect of its

[101] ICJ, *Armed Activities on the Territory of the Congo (New Application: 2002) (Democratic Republic of the Congo v Rwanda)*, Jurisdiction of the Court and Admissibility of the Application, Joint Separate Opinion by Judges Higgins, Kooijmans, Elaraby, Owada, and Simma, *ICJ Reports* (2006) at 70, para. 20.

[102] ICJ, *Armed Activities on the Territory of the Congo (New Application: 2002) (Democratic Republic of the Congo v Rwanda)*, Jurisdiction of the Court and Admissibility of the Application, Judgment of 3 February 2006, *ICJ Reports* (2006) at 32, para. 67.

[103] '*Rafforzare la propria conclusione con un argomento* ad hominem' (our translation) G. Gaja, 'Il regime della Convenzione di Vienna concernente le riserve inammissibili', *supra* note 2, at 354.

[104] ICJ, *Armed Activities on the Territory of the Congo (New Application: 2002) (Democratic Republic of the Congo v Rwanda)*, *supra* note 102, at 33, para. 68.

[105] ECHR, *Loizidou v Turkey*, Preliminary Objections, Judgment of 23 March 1995, Series A, No. 310, para. 95.

[106] *GAOR, Fiftieth Session, Supplement No. 40* (A/50/40) at 123–4, para 17.

own and did not even have to be seen as an objection per se; [...] However, in the absence of a body that could authoritatively classify a reservation as invalid, such as the European Court of Human Rights, such 'objections' still served an important purpose.[107]

An objection thus serves not only the consent function expressly envisaged under the Vienna Convention régime; it is also an instrument that permits other states to express their point of view on the validity of a reservation. Whereas an objection to an impermissible reservation is deprived of its first function—because there is no possibility to consent—it retains the second one.

In the specific case of impermissible reservations, an objection and an acceptance are both as such devoid of any legal effect. In this respect, they are comparable. However, they are entirely different in their significance, for the author of the reservation on the one hand, and for states that have reacted to the reservation on the other.

There can be no doubt that the rather improvised reversion of the presumption triggered by the formulation of an objection to a reservation is a source of ambiguity and might have created the impression of an assimilation between the effects of an acceptance of the reservation and an objection with 'minimum effect'. However, in spite of some troubling similarities in specific circumstances, a closer look at the effects and implications of an acceptance of a reservation and of an objection to a reservation shows that there are still some important differences. Indeed, these differences are quite easy to overlook, especially if one considers Articles 21(1) and 21(3) of the Vienna Convention in isolation. Nevertheless, there can be no doubt that these differences do exist, a most fortunate conclusion which confirms, definitively, that an objection is not an acceptance, and that law is not always incompatible with common sense.

107 A/C.6/60/SR.14, para. 22.

4

Legal Consequences of an Impermissible Reservation to a Human Rights Treaty: Where Do We Stand?

*Bruno Simma and Gleider I. Hernández**

1. Introduction

Giorgio Gaja has written some of the most insightful articles on the topic of reservations to multilateral treaties.[1] We therefore take the opportunity of contributing to this book in his honour to trace and critically analyse the latest developments concerning a particularly controversial aspect of the law on reservations, situated at the interface of the law of treaties and international human rights law. Twelve years ago, at what was probably the peak of literary attention to the topic of reservations in general, in another *Festschrift* (on that occasion for Ignaz Seidl-Hohenveldern), the first-named of the present authors (hereinafter 'the first Author') took a critical view of the state of the law and practice on reservations to human rights treaties as it had then developed, particularly at the first reaction in 1997 of the United Nations (UN) International Law Commission (of which the first Author was at the time a member) to the approach taken by its Special Rapporteur on the topic of reservations, Professor Alain Pellet, to what he called 'normative treaties'.[2] In a certain sense, then, our present contribution is a follow-up to the 1998 piece.

* The authors wish to thank Mr. Thomas Liefländer for his proofreading and valuable research assistance in the preparation of this manuscript.

[1] G. Gaja, 'Unruly Treaty Reservations', in *Le droit international à l'heure de sa codification, Études en l'honneur de Roberto Ago* (Milano: Giuffrè, 1987) 313; Id., 'Il regime della Convenzione di Vienna concernente le riserve inammissibili', in *Studi in onore di Vincenzo Starace* (Napoli: Editoriale Scientifica, 2008) 349.

[2] B. Simma, 'Reservations to Human Rights Treaties: Some Recent Developments', in G. Hafner, G. Loibl, A. Rest, L. Sucharipa-Behrmann, and K. Zemanek (eds), *Liber Amicorum Professor Ignaz Seidl-Hohenveldern in Honour of his 80th birthday* (The Hague: Kluwer Law International, 1998) 659–80.

Human rights treaties represent the area of international treaty law where reservations are most popular and numerous. This might suggest that the desire of states parties to these treaties fully to implement internationally agreed-upon human rights standards on the domestic plane is somewhat less than sincere. In this regard, some academic commentary has focused on dubious reservations and the concomitant 'almost universal' failure to object concertedly to such reservations.[3] However, in our view, there are good reasons to adopt a somewhat more balanced position, as set out by the first Author in his 1998 contribution. First, international human rights law is essentially 'inward-targeted': it turns states' insides out almost in a literal sense, and exposes them to international scrutiny. Even governments 'firmly committed to the rule of law will frequently discover that treaty obligations in the field of human rights may assume a weight and a degree of nuisance which they never expected or, at least, grossly underestimated at the time of the conclusion of the treaty'.[4] This will be particularly true when the performance of states parties to a human rights instrument falls under the supervision of international monitoring bodies or even judicial organs adopting an 'evolutionary' or 'dynamic' approach to the interpretation of the obligations arising from such treaties.[5] Thus, the lodging of carefully tailored reservations may also be taken as a sign that the reserving state takes the respective human rights treaty seriously. This is, of course, not to deny that some reservations do offend the very core and essence of a treaty; one can be particularly critical, in this regard, of reservations formulated in such broad, sweeping language that they make a mockery out of a state's adhesion to a treaty instrument. It is therefore not the *practice* of making reservations to human rights treaties *per se*, but the *substance* of such reservations which is of concern.

For this reason, in the present article, we wish to revisit the central issue in the area of reservations to human rights treaties: the legal consequences of a reservation to a human rights treaty which is considered incompatible with that treaty's object and purpose and therefore impermissible. Already in his First Report on the law and practice relating to reservations to treaties, Special

[3] See, eg, I. Boerefijn, 'Impact of the Law on Treaty Reservations', in M.T. Kamminga and M. Scheinin (eds), *The Impact of Human Rights on International Law* (Oxford: Oxford University Press, 2009) 63, at 93; E. Swaine, 'Reserving', 31 *Yale Journal of International Law* (2006) 307, at 324. In relation to the International Covenant on Civil and Political Rights, R. Higgins, 'Human Rights: Some Questions of Integrity', [due to an editorial error entitled 'The United Nations: Still a Force for Peace'], 52 *Modern Law Review* (1989) 1, at 12, has been even more critical: 'one might almost say that there is a collusion to allow penetrating and disturbing reservations to go unchallenged'.

[4] B. Simma, 'Reservations to Human Rights Treaties', *supra* note 2, 660.

[5] R. Higgins, 'Human Rights: Some Questions of Integrity', *supra* note 3, 5–8, argued to the effect that the special nature of human rights treaties also favours the authoritative interpretation by monitoring bodies of such human rights obligations to provide a safeguard for the integrity of the treaty instrument. See also C. Redgwell, 'Reservations to Treaties and Human Rights Committee, General Comment No 24', 46 *ICLQ* (1997) 390, 408–9, who has characterized the existence of such authoritative interpretation by a monitoring organ as the *sine qua non* of any system grappling with the incompatibility of reservations with human rights treaties.

Rapporteur Pellet recognized that the regime on reservations established by the 1969 Vienna Convention on the Law of Treaties[6] does not provide an answer to the fundamental question of whether the provisions of the Convention are to be applied to all reservations, or only to permissible ones.[7] Already in the 1970s, two views had been developed in the literature. One of them, well represented by Ruda in his Hague Lectures of 1975, favoured the application of the Convention regime (Article 20 *et seq.*) to all reservations, even if contrary to the object and purpose of a treaty, and defended an 'opposability doctrine' according to which the permissibility of a reservation can only play out through the process of objections.[8] Following this process on the basis of the view expressed by Ruda would entail that manifestly impermissible reservations may remain valid if other states do not object in sufficient numbers; if a reservation is not reciprocal in nature, it would practically remain unaffected. Obviously, this conclusion leads to grave problems, most prominently in the context of human rights treaties, which are of a special nature (to be discussed in Section 2.2 *infra*). As the first Author explained already in 1998, 'if we decided to follow the "opposability" doctrine and thus viewed the inadmissibility of a reservation as only becoming operational through objections raised by other States, the Vienna Convention regime on consequences of such objections will hardly have any "bite" in case of our human rights treaties'.[9] Our firm position is that the Vienna Convention regime on the acceptance of and objection to reservations as well as on the legal effects of reservations, their acceptance, and objections thereto *does not* apply to impermissible reservations, and *should* not apply to impermissible reservations to human rights treaties by analogy in unmodified terms either. We find unacceptable, both in logic and policy, that the regiome of a codification convention could first declare certain reservations impermissible and then simply continue to regulate the ways in which such impermissible reservations (also) can be made and become effective, without distinguishing them in any way from permissible ones. In other words, we endorse the position articulated by Bowett (the so-called 'admissibility doctrine'), who rejected the idea that the concept of reciprocity had any part to play in so far as the effect of impermissible reservations was concerned, argued that 'if it can be objectively, and preferably judicially, determined that the State's paramount intention was to accept the treaty, as evidenced by the ratification or accession, then an impermissible reservation which is not fundamentally opposed to the object and purpose of the treaty can be struck out and disregarded as a nullity'.[10]

[6] 1969 Vienna Convention on the Law of Treaties (VCLT), 1155 *UNTS*, 331.

[7] First Report on the Law and Practice relating to Reservations to Treaties by Mr Alain Pellet, Special Rapporteur, *YILC* (1995), vol. II(1), 145, paras 119–120.

[8] J.-M. Ruda, 'Reservations to Treaties', 146 *Recueil des Cours* (1975-III) 179, at 190. He considered the object and purpose test embodied in Article 19(c) VCLT 'a mere doctrinal assertion'.

[9] B. Simma, 'Reservations to Human Rights Treaties', *supra* note 2, 663.

[10] D.W. Bowett, 'Reservations to Non-Restricted Multilateral Treaties', 48 *BYIL* (1976–77) 67, at 77.

Up until extremely recently,[11] Special Rapporteur Pellet had demurred in taking a clear position with regard to the effect of impermissible reservations, particularly to human rights treaties. It is true that multilateral treaties rarely specify the consequences of what should happen if a reservation is found invalid,[12] and state practice has remained glaringly inconsistent on the issue. This has given increased importance to the practice of monitoring bodies and international judicial institutions. Against this background, our present essay therefore constitutes an exercise in 'progressive development' in the broadest sense: we propose to analyse Pellet's various reports, including especially various draft Guidelines that he submitted to the ILC with the view that these would help 'clarify' the Vienna Convention regime, in the light of both the Vienna Convention and the particular nature of human rights treaties. For reasons that will be explained below, and building upon the position taken by the first Author 12 years ago, we take the position that the legal consequence of a reservation to a human rights treaty that is found impermissible because it is contrary to the object and purpose of a treaty should be that the reservation is severed from the reserving state's consent, and that the reserving state should remain bound to the obligations contained in the treaty in full. It is heartening that in his most recent report, Pellet seems to have arrived at the same conclusions. We wish to emphasize, however, that our following analysis is confined exclusively to the question of the adequacy of the Special Rapporteur's latest proposals with regard to human rights treaties. We will thus not pass judgment on whether the severability doctrine he has eventually endorsed is suitable for other multilateral treaties.

2. The Continued Relevance of the Vienna Convention on the Law of Treaties

2.1. Operation of the Vienna Convention framework

Article 19 of the Vienna Convention remains the starting-point of any meaningful analysis of the regime governing reservations to treaties. It stipulates that reservations are impermissible in three sets of circumstances: first, where they are expressly prohibited by the treaty; secondly, where the treaty provides that only specified reservations may be made and these do not include the reservation in question; and thirdly, where in case of silence of the treaty text the reservation is incompatible with the object and purpose of the treaty. It is this last situation, set out in Article 19(c), which squarely puts into focus how little, if any, help the

[11] See A. Pellet, 'First Addendum to the Fifteenth Report on Reservations to Treaties', A/CN.4/624/Add.1 (26 May 2010), directly addressing the legal effects of an impermissible reservation to treaties. It will be discussed *in extenso* in Section 3.4 below.

[12] As commented upon by R. Baratta, 'Should Invalid Reservations to Human Rights Treaties be Disregarded?' 11 *EJIL* (2000) 413, at 414.

Convention turns out to be when it comes to establishing the admissibility *vel non* of a reservation or when looking for guidance regarding the manner in which a contracting party, unwilling to accept an impermissible reservation, could react in an effective way, going beyond essentially empty gestures.[13]

From the outset, the Vienna Convention regime proved difficult to operate in this regard, given that Article 19 sheds no light on how a treaty's object and purpose is to be discerned and in fact borders on the self-referential.[14] As regards the compatibility of reservations with the object and purpose of human rights instruments, this shortcoming has major practical repercussions. Representing essentially a codification of the *Reservations to the Genocide Convention* Opinion,[15] the Convention left major gaps, both by failing to provide a means to measure a reservation against the object and purpose of the relevant treaty, and by leaving open the consequences to be attached to a reservation considered impermissible under this test.[16] Further, the Convention is silent as to whether its rules concerning the making of objections against reservations are applicable to *all* reservations, even those which violate the treaty's object and purpose, or whether different rules apply to such reservations, especially—and importantly—when relating to provisions of a universalist character.

To counter this gap, various human rights supervisory bodies turned to adopting a practice of their own regarding the admissibility and effect of reservations to human rights treaties. In a series of cases beginning with *Temeltasch*[17] in 1982, and through *Belilos*,[18] *Chrysostomos*,[19] and *Loizidou*,[20] the European Commission

[13] B. Simma, 'Reservations to Human Rights Treaties', *supra* note 2, 662.

[14] As W.A. Schabas, 'Reservations to Human Rights Treaties: Time for Innovation and Reform', 32 *Canadian Yearbook of International Law* (1994) 39, at 48, suggests, an application of Article 31 of the Vienna Convention leads to the circular conclusion that a treaty's object and purpose is to be determined in the light of its object and purpose. See also K. Zemanek and I. Buffard, 'The "Object and Purpose" of a Treaty: An Enigma?' 3 *ARIEL* (1998) 311, at 333.

[15] ICJ, *Reservations to the Convention on the Prevention and Punishment of the Crime of Genocide*, Advisory Opinion of 28 May 1951, *ICJ Reports* (1951) 15, at 23, first observing that the Genocide Convention 'was manifestly adopted for a purely humanitarian and civilizing purpose' and that '[i]n such a convention the contracting States do not have any interests of their own; they merely have, one and all, a common interest, namely, the accomplishment of these high purposes which are the *raison d'être* of the convention'. The drafting history of Article 19 demonstrates the ambiguities inherent in the 'object and purpose' test and the attempts of the Commission to reconcile the twin purposes of securing the unity of a convention and ensuring maximum accession to the obligations contained therein. See, in this regard, ILC, Draft Articles on the Law of Treaties, Commentary to Articles 16 and 17, *YILC* (1966), vol. II, 205, paras 10–11; and H. Waldock, 'First Report on the Law of Treaties', *YILC* (1962), vol. II, 65–6, para. 10.

[16] B. Simma, 'Reservations to Human Rights Treaties', *supra* note 2, 662–3.

[17] European Commission of Human Rights, *Temeltasch v Switzerland*, Case 9116/80, 5 May 1982, 5 *European Human Rights Reports* (1982) 417.

[18] ECHR, *Belilos v Switzerland*, Judgment of 24 April 1988, Series A, No. 132, 10 *European Human Rights Reports* (1988) 466.

[19] European Commission of Human Rights, *Chrysostomos et al v Turkey*, Cases 15299-15300-15318/89, comm. 68/216, 4 March 1991, reprinted in 12 *HRLJ* (1991) 113.

[20] ECHR, *Loizidou v Turkey*, Preliminary Objections, Judgment of 23 March 1995, Series A, No. 310, 20 *Essex Human Rights Review* (1995) 99.

and European Court of Human Rights developed what in 1998 the first Author termed the 'Strasbourg approach',[21] arrogating to themselves the competence to determine whether so-called 'interpretative declarations' were in fact reservations proper, as well as the power to determine the admissibility of what they found to be reservations. By finding that inadmissible reservations could lead to the reserving state remaining fully bound to the European Convention on Human Rights, the Strasbourg approach gave life to the 'severability doctrine', which, albeit somewhat grudgingly, became accepted by the states parties to the Convention.

On the plane of universal human rights law, the 'severability' approach came to be adopted by the Human Rights Committee in its General Comment No. 24 (52) of 2 November 1994.[22] General Comment No. 24 was highly controversial at the time because it concluded from the specific character of human rights treaty obligations, in this case those of the International Covenant on Civil and Political Rights,[23] that the classic rules on reservations embodied in the Vienna Convention, although applicable in principle, were inadequate in case of treaties such as the Covenant. Particularly striking was the manner in which the Human Rights Committee maintained that it 'necessarily' had the power to determine whether a specific reservation is compatible with the object and purpose of the Covenant:

> This is in part because... it is an inappropriate task for States parties in relation to human rights treaties, and in part because it is a task that the Committee cannot avoid in the performance of its functions. In order to know the scope of its duty to examine a State's compliance under article 40 or a communication under the first Optional Protocol, the Committee has necessarily to take a view on the compatibility of a reservation with the object and purpose of the Covenant and with general international law. Because of the special character of a human rights treaty, the compatibility of a reservation with the object and purpose of the Covenant must be established objectively, by reference to legal principles, and the Committee is particularly well placed to perform this task.[24]

What has reverberated most is the Committee's endorsement of the 'Strasbourg approach', concluding that the legal consequence of a reservation being found incompatible with the object and purpose of a treaty is severance, 'in the sense that the Covenant will be operative for the reserving party without benefit of the reservation'.[25]

[21] B. Simma, 'Reservations to Human Rights Treaties', *supra* note 2, 670–1. See also G. Cohen-Jonathan, 'Les réserves dans les traités institutionnels relatifs aux droits de l'homme', 4 *RGDIP* (1996) 915, at 940.

[22] Human Rights Committee, General Comment No. 24, CCPR/C/21/Rev.1/Add.6, reprinted in 15 *HRLJ* (1994) 464.

[23] 1966 International Covenant on Civil and Political Rights, 999 *UNTS*, 171.

[24] General Comment No. 24, *supra* note 22, para. 18. [25] Ibid.

2.2. Beyond the Vienna Convention, without leaving it behind

In what regard are human rights treaties qualitatively different from other types of treaties? Certainly, what distinguishes them is the universalist character of the substantive norms embodied therein. To use the words of Rosalyn Higgins, human rights treaties 'reflect rights inherent in human beings, not dependent upon grant by the state'.[26] Hence, as she emphasized, given the heterogeneity of states and their differing legal systems, not to mention the diversity of cultures and religions, arriving at an understanding of the rights embodied in human rights conventions is a challenge.[27]

The argument that human rights are not just voluntary concessions made by enlightened states for the benefit of their subjects has been used by theory to justify abandoning a purely bilateralist and subjective method of analysing reservations to human rights treaties. Indeed, reciprocity, as underlying the rules on reservations in the Vienna Convention, does not adapt easily to the structure of, and the sociology behind, human rights treaties,[28] whose essential characteristic remains that such treaties do not define inter-state relationships, but are 'inward-targeted',[29] as states commit to a certain behaviour above all vis-à-vis their own nationals.[30] The Vienna Convention regime governing the rejection of reservations relies on the process of objections; yet, the objection-based system has not been designed to account for the special nature of treaties protecting human rights, to which it seems unsuited as regards impermissible reservations. This conclusion is shared by Pellet, in that, when a treaty is not itself based on reciprocity of rights and obligations between the parties, as is the case with human rights treaties, a reservation cannot produce such reciprocal

[26] R. Higgins, 'Human Rights: Some Questions of Integrity', *supra* note 3, 11.

[27] Ibid., 2.

[28] A recurring *leitmotif* in Strasbourg: see ECHR, *Ireland v United Kingdom,* Judgment of 18 January 1978, Series A, No. 25, 2 *European Human Rights Reports* (1978) 256, reprinted in 59 *ILR* 199, para. 239; *Loizidou v Turkey* (1995), *supra* note 20, para. 93.

[29] B. Simma, 'Reservations to Human Rights Treaties', *supra* note 2, 660.

[30] A. Pellet, Second Addendum to the Fourteenth Report on Reservations to Treaties (2009), A/CN.4/614/Add.2, at 40, para. 285, referring to General Comment No. 24, *supra* note 22, para. 8, at 17. See also W. Schabas, 'Reservations to Human Rights Treaties: Time for Innovation and Reform', *supra* note 14, at 72, citing ICCPR, *supra* note 23, Article 2, para. 1. Draft Guideline 4.2.5, entitled 'Non-reciprocal application of obligations to which a reservation relates', reads as follows: 'in so far as the obligations under the provisions to which the reservation relates are not subject to reciprocal application in view of the nature of the obligation or the object and purpose of the treaty, the content of the obligations of the parties other than the author of the reservation remains unaffected. The content of the obligations of those parties likewise remains unaffected when reciprocal application is not possible because of the content of the reservation.' The authors note that many of the draft Guidelines on the legal effects of reservations and interpretative declarations proposed by Pellet were provisionally adopted, with amendments, by the Drafting Committee during the 2010 session of the Commission. See ILC, 'Draft Guidelines', provisionally adopted by the Drafting Committee on 2010, A/CN.4/L.760/Add.1.

effect either.[31] This is surely accurate: when following the familiar pattern of reciprocity, a reservation, once accepted, has the effect of releasing the reserving state from compliance with the treaty obligations the subject of the reservation; reciprocally that state also loses the right to require the other states parties to fulfil their treaty obligations covered by the reservation.[32] In other words, both reserving and objecting/accepting states are exempted from the reserved provisions in their treaty relations, as their mutual consent is confined to the narrower limits indicated by the reservation.[33] Hence, it comes as no surprise that the protagonists of a 'human rights approach' to our topic attempt to move beyond this bilateralist and reciprocity-based system in the case of impermissible reservations to human rights treaties.

One clarification is in order. We emphatically do not argue here that the Vienna Convention regime on reservations is incompatible with the particular structure of performance of human rights treaties. Rather, because of this particular structure and in the light of the object and purpose pursued by these treaties, the Vienna Convention regime on the effects of reservations is to operate differently with respect to them.[34] Returning for a moment to the structure of their obligations, from a strictly legal point of view, human rights treaties are 'built' like all other multilateral treaties. Their parties promise each other to respect and ensure the rights set out in the treaty vis-à-vis all individuals within their jurisdiction.[35] Human rights treaties, too, create rights and obligations between their parties to the effect that any state party is obliged as against any other state party to perform its obligations, and that, conversely, any party has a correlative right to integral performance by all the other contracting states. The obligations arising from such treaties can be considered obligations *erga omnes partes*, that is, the *omnes* here being limited to the circle of the other contracting parties. The performance of obligations arising from such treaties cannot be split up into pairs of bilateral interactions, like, for instance, in the application of the two Vienna

[31] A. Pellet, Fourteenth Report on Reservations to Treaties, Second Addendum, *supra* note 30, at 40, paras 284–285.

[32] Ibid., at 36, paras 273–274. This is further developed in draft Guideline 4.2.4, para. 2, as provisionally adopted by the Drafting Committee in 2010, *supra* note 30, 4.

[33] H. Waldock, First Report on the Law of Treaties, *supra* note 15, 68, para. 21; and ICJ, *Certain Norwegian Loans (France v Norway)*, Judgment of 6 July 1957, *ICJ Reports* (1957) 9, at 23, where the Court confined its jurisdiction within the narrower limits indicated by the French reservation, on the basis of reciprocity.

[34] See F. Coulée, 'À propos d'une controverse autour d'une codification en cours: les réactions aux réserves incompatibles avec l'objet et le but des traités de protection des droits de l'homme,' in L. Condorelli *et al.* (eds), *Libertés, Justice, Tolérance: Mélanges en hommage au Doyen Gérard Cohen-Jonathan* (Brussels: Bruylant, 2004) 500, 507 *et seq.*

[35] B. Simma, 'From Bilateralism to Community Interest', 250 *Recueil des Cours* (1994-VI) 229, at 335; G. Cohen-Jonathan, 'Les réserves dans les traités institutionnels relatifs aux droits de l'homme', *supra* note 21, 940.

Conventions on diplomatic and consular relations; rather, such performance is inseparable, or integral.

Since we are of the view that the Vienna Convention regime on reservations as it stands neither regulates the courses of action which may be followed by states in their reactions to impermissible or intolerable reservations nor the consequences that these states might attach thereto, we suggest that one must look beyond a restrictive reading of the Vienna Convention and consider an application of its rules which balances the consent of the reserving state with the consent of the other states parties to a treaty instrument. Moreover, we consider that certain rules of customary international law which were not expressly restated in the Vienna Convention may yet provide guidance in this regard, especially in the light of more recent practice.[36]

For these reasons, we agree with the following conclusions arrived at during the joint meeting of 15–16 May 2007 of certain members of the International Law Commission and representatives of United Nations human rights treaty bodies and regional human rights bodies.[37]

> The special nature of human rights treaties was reflected in the test provided for in article 19(c) of the Vienna Convention on the Law of Treaties, which concerned the incompatibility of a reservation with the object and purpose of the treaty. It was nevertheless pointed out that that specific feature was not unique and that environmental protection treaties and disarmament treaties also presented particular features that could have an impact in terms of reservations. The reason that human rights treaties were of special interest to the Commission was that they had treaty monitoring bodies. The representatives of the human rights bodies stressed the fact that it was not necessary to establish a separate regime governing reservations to human rights treaties. However, they did feel that the general regime should be applied in an appropriate and suitably adapted manner.[38]

It is from that vantage point that we will now turn to the recent work of the International Law Commission on the issue of reservations to treaties, and explore whether it may inspire further reflection on the consequences of an impermissible reservation contrary to the object and purpose of a treaty.

[36] G. Gaja, 'Il regime della Convenzione di Vienna concernente le riserve inammissibili', *supra* note 1, 350, pursues a different approach by attempting to establish a regime for impermissible reservations whilst remaining within the confines of the Vienna Convention.

[37] The minutes are annexed to A. Pellet, 'Fourteenth Report on Reservations to Treaties' (2009), A/CN.4/614.

[38] Ibid., 32, para. 27. The analysis here reflects the findings in International Law Commission, A. Pellet, 'Second Report on Reservations to Treaties', A/CN.4/477 and Add.1 (10 May and 13 June 1996), *YILC* (1996), vol. II(1), 56, paras 85–87.

3. The Work of the International Law Commission, 1996–2010

3.1. From the Second Report (1996) to the Tenth Report (2005)

3.1.1. The continued applicability of the Vienna Convention regime

The work of the International Law Commission on the topic of reservations to treaties dates back to 1993, when it was first included in the Commission's agenda.[39] Using the relevant rules embodied in the Vienna Conventions of 1969, 1978, and 1986 as a starting-point, the Commission's project aimed to fill the gaps and clarify the ambiguities left in the existing law.[40] One major question taken up by Special Rapporteur Pellet from the outset was that of the applicability of the Vienna Convention regime on reservations, without modification, also to so-called 'normative treaties', and especially to human rights treaties, in the light of the challenge posed by the jurisprudence of the Strasbourg court and, particularly, by the then-recent adoption of General Comment 24 by the Human Rights Committee. Thus, in his Second Report (1996), and in a markedly pugnacious spirit, Pellet took issue with the assertion of competence by treaty bodies definitively to determine the admissibility of reservations. Demanding that the 'voice of international law' be heard,[41] Chapter II of the Second Report affirmed that the Vienna Convention regime in its present form was sufficient, that consent remained the governing principle in a treaty regime which also extended, in unmodified form, to human rights treaties, that it was primarily for the states parties to these treaties to determine the permissibility *vel non* of reservations and how to deal with impermissible ones and that, consequently, human rights treaty monitoring bodies could not have more competences in these matters than those specifically granted to them by states parties to the respective treaties.[42] After a lively debate during the 1997 session of the International Law Commission, in which an alternative view made itself heard (amongst others, by the first Author) to the effect that the Vienna Convention regime on reservations had only a very limited grip on human rights treaties not premised on reciprocity (and that the paramount consideration for these treaties was unity of substance rather than universality of participation), the Commission adopted a set of 'Preliminary Conclusions' which were based on a 'draft resolution' proposed by the Special Rapporteur in his Second Report,[43] but worded in somewhat more restrained language.[44] The first Author criticized this state of discourse on the matter in

[39] See *YILC* (1993), vol. II(2), 96, paras 427–430, at 440.

[40] A. Pellet, 'Second Report on Reservations to Treaties', Chapter I, *supra* note 38. In the following, only the rules of the 1969 Convention will be considered.

[41] Ibid., 53, para. 62, and in the Preamble of the draft resolution Pellet submitted on the topic and which was appended to the Second Report, ibid., 83, immediately following para. 260.

[42] Ibid., 82, para. 252(d).

[43] Ibid., 83, immediately following para. 260.

[44] *YILC* (1997), vol. II(2), 57, immediately following para. 157.

1998, arguing that the Commission had neglected the 'progressive development' aspects of its mandate and taken a 'conservative, pronouncedly statist' stand on the issue of the consequences of reservations to human rights treaties;[45] he considered that, in abstracting the Vienna Convention rules to be applicable as general rules and thus to accept them as also governing reservations to human rights instruments, the Commission's position in its 1997 Preliminary Conclusions was only correct on the most formalistic level.[46]

3.1.2. A cautious step towards a new approach to normative treaties

It seems that on some level, Pellet has taken to heart criticism like that to which reference has just been made. In his Tenth Report,[47] released in 2005, Pellet explored the conditions for the validity of reservations to treaties. After some justification for the choice of the term 'validity' over that of 'permissibility' of reservations (to his mind, the former term better taking into account both the concepts of opposability and permissibility),[48] Pellet explained how the principle of freedom to formulate reservations entails a presumption that they are valid,[49] thus implying both the possible existence of invalid reservations and that the consequences attached to such invalid reservations might be different from those attaching to valid reservations.

The First and Second Addenda to the Tenth Report[50] presented a series of draft Guidelines dealing with the validity of reservations. Several of these Guidelines are designed to assist in discerning whether a certain reservation is compatible with the object and purpose of a treaty,[51] although these general guidelines do not stipulate the consequences of incompatibility. Other guidelines consider reservations 'worded in vague, general language which does not allow [their] scope to be determined', as being incompatible *per se* with a treaty's object and purpose;[52] reservations relating to customary norms as not being invariably contrary to a treaty's object and purpose;[53] and reservations relating to peremptory norms as invariably being null and void.[54]

[45] B. Simma, 'Reservations to Human Rights Treaties', *supra* note 2, 678. [46] Ibid.

[47] A. Pellet, Tenth Report on Reservations to Treaties (2005), A/CN.4/558.

[48] Ibid., 2–4. [49] Ibid., 5–9.

[50] A. Pellet, First Addendum to the Tenth Report on Reservations to Treaties (2005), A/CN.4/558/Add.1; Ibid., Second Addendum to the Tenth Report on Reservations to Treaties (2005), A/CN.4/558/Add.2.

[51] Ibid., First Addendum to Tenth Report on Reservations to Treaties, *supra* note 50, 8–14, paras 75–92 (draft Guidelines 3.1.5 and 3.1.6).

[52] Ibid., 26, para. 115 (draft Guideline 3.1.7). This draft Guideline in large part reflects 'General Comment No. 24' (1994), *supra* note 22, para. 19.

[53] Ibid., 29–30, para. 120: because a reservation may be limited only to treaty-specific aspects of a customary norm, leaving unaffected the norm's binding force under customary international law. Cf. 'General Comment No. 24' (1994), *supra* note 22, para. 8, which stated that ICCPR provisions that also embody rules of customary international law may not be the subject of reservations.

[54] Ibid., 36, paras 136–137. The Drafting Committee did not agree with Pellet's conclusion on this point, instead adopting draft Guideline 4.4.3, in which an invalid reservation 'does not affect

Whilst the draft Guidelines discussed thus far are conceptually interesting but do not illuminate much as regards the consequences of incompatibility, another one of Pellet's 2005 proposals is closer to our point. Already in 1996, Pellet had termed the competence of the supervisory organs of human rights treaties to determine not only compatibility, but also the legal consequences of a determination, the 'determination function'.[55] In draft Guideline 3.1.12 of 2005, he attempted to provide further guidance to monitoring bodies and states parties in discerning the object and purpose of general human rights treaties, and highlighted their particular nature:

> To assess the compatibility of a reservation with the object and purpose of a general treaty for the protection of human rights, account shall be taken of the indivisibility, interdependence and interrelatedness of the rights set out in the treaty as well as the importance that the right or provision which is the subject of the reservation has within the general thrust of the treaty, and the gravity of the impact the reservation has upon it.[56]

It is the focus on the manner in which such rights are set out within human rights treaties which is pertinent. By offering a specific interpretative rule which applies only to them, this draft Guideline is significant in that it marks a shift away from the general, bilateralist framework of the Vienna Convention regime and constitutes cautious recognition by the Special Rapporteur of the limitations of that regime in so far as normative treaties are concerned.

3.2. ILC work on effects of reservations, Fourteenth Report (2009)

3.2.1. Valid and invalid reservations

Because the Tenth Report's approach was limited to the validity of reservations as regards their form or their compatibility with the object and purpose of the treaty, it was only with the Fourteenth Report of the Special Rapporteur, submitted in 2009, that the legal effects of a finding of impermissibility were considered anew, albeit through the lens of the effects of reservations and interpretative declarations.[57] However, from the outset, Pellet concentrated his analysis on the nature and effect of *valid* reservations, in that regard confirming the Vienna Convention principle that the legal effect of reservations is to modify the relations

the binding nature' of a peremptory norm, thus applying the same rule as with regard to customary international law. See *supra* note 30, 8.

[55] A. Pellet, Second Report on Reservations to Treaties, *supra* note 38, 83, at fifth operative clause of the draft resolution following para. 260.

[56] ILC, Report on the Work of its Fifty-ninth Session (2007), *GAOR, Sixty-second Session, Supplement No. 10*, (A/62/10) at 113–16.

[57] A. Pellet, Second Addendum to the Fourteenth Report on Reservations to Treaties Part IV, *supra* note 30; Id., 'Fourteenth Report on Reservations to Treaties', *supra* note 37, 4, para. 12, it was noted that some delegations felt that the question of reservations incompatible with the object and purpose of a treaty was the most important aspect of the topic.

between the reserving state and other states with regard to which the reservation was entered.[58]

Pellet's analysis expressly relied on the assumption that Articles 20 and 21 of the Vienna Convention contain an important gap, in that they only purport to regulate the effects of a reservation whose permissibility is not called into question, and neither set out the consequences of a reservation being found impermissible under Article 19 (or formally so under Articles 23 and elsewhere), nor resolve the question whether the application of Article 21, paragraph 3, on the combined effect of a reservation and an objection, is limited to cases of permissible reservations.[59]

In this respect, Pellet highlighted some recent developments with regard to reservations and interpretative declarations, focusing notably on practice concerning human rights. Figuring prominently was the product of a 'Working Group on Reservations', established jointly by the Chairpersons of the human rights treaty bodies and the Inter-Committee Meeting of these bodies.[60] The Working Group examined the practice of human rights treaty bodies with respect to reservations to 'their' treaties, concluding that the specific nature of human rights treaties was that they 'do not constitute a simple exchange of obligations between States but are the legal expression of the essential rights that each individual must be able to exercise as a human being', although it also explained that 'general treaty law remains applicable to human rights instruments', even if such law can only be applied 'taking fully into account their specific nature, including their content and monitoring mechanisms'.[61] This led the Working Group to draw the following important conclusions:

> As to the consequences of invalidity, the Working Group agrees with the proposal of the Special Rapporteur of the International Law Commission according to which an invalid reservation is to be considered null and void. It follows that a State will not be able to rely on such a reservation and, unless its contrary intention is *incontrovertibly* established, will remain a party to the treaty.[62]

[58] Ibid., 29, para. 253 *et seq.*, relying upon the wording of Article 21, para. 1(a) of the 1969 Vienna Convention.

[59] Ibid., 8, para. 195. G. Gaja, 'Unruly Treaty Reservations', *supra* note 1, 330, calls Article 21 'rather obscure'. In his 2008 piece, the same author considers that more recent practice of states and treaty organs has tended to leave the path prescribed by 1969 Vienna Convention Articles 20 and 21: cf. *supra* note 1, 353, at 356.

[60] Report on the Practice of Human Rights Treaty Bodies with respect to Reservations to International Human Rights Treaties, submitted to the seventeenth meeting of chairpersons of the human rights treaty bodies and the fourth Inter-Committee Meeting of the human rights treaty bodies, (2005) HRI/MC/2005/5.

[61] Report of the Meeting of the Working Group on Reservations of the Sixth Inter-Committee Meeting of the human rights treaty bodies, (2007) HRI/MC/2007/5, 6–7, para. 19 [due to an editorial error; listed as para. 16 in the Report], sub-para. 8, quoted in A. Pellet, Fourteenth Report on Reservations to Treaties, *supra* note 37, 16–18.

[62] Ibid., para. 19, sub-para. 7 (emphasis added).

Special Rapporteur Pellet embraced this position, but only to a certain extent. He explained that the Working Group's conclusions placed the emphasis solely on the presumption that the state entering an invalid reservation has the intention to remain bound by the treaty without the benefit of the reservation as long as its contrary intention has not been *incontrovertibly* established. Pellet considered that the test thus articulated 'perhaps goes a little far'.[63] He did not disagree, however, that there was room for treaty bodies to express their concern as regards reservations formulated to certain provisions, in line with the Working Group's recommendations in this regard.[64] Of further interest is the fact that the Working Group recommended that treaty monitoring bodies can ask states why a given reservation was considered necessary and was maintained, and enquire about its effect and projected longevity.[65] These aspects may eventually be of use in determining the essential nature of a reservation and ultimately its permissibility.

3.2.2. *The consequence of invalid reservations: nullity*

Pellet's first step in addressing the problem of the consequences of the non-validity of a reservation is taken in draft Guideline 3.3 of his Fourteenth Report: 'A reservation formulated in spite of a prohibition arising from the provisions of the treaty or in spite of its incompatibility with the object and purpose of the treaty is impermissible, without there being any need to distinguish between these grounds for non-permissibility.'[66]

The effect of draft Guideline 3.3 is to establish a common approach for the three types of invalid reservations defined in Article 19, although it does not address the actual consequences of the invalidity of a reservation except to state that such a reservation is not valid. Because the draft Guideline and the commentaries thereto do not elaborate what those specific consequences will be, its scope therefore seems to be confined to the conclusion that an impermissible reservation, even if validly formed, will still be impermissible. No elaboration is given as to whether the nullity of the reservation invalidates the reserving state's consent to be bound,[67] which is at the heart of the question presently at hand. A hint at another (non-) consequence of impermissibility can be found in draft Guideline 3.3.1, however: '[t]he formulation of an impermissible reservation

[63] A. Pellet, Fourteenth Report on Reservations to Treaties, *supra* note 37, 18, para. 54.

[64] Report of the Meeting of the Working Group on Reservations, *supra* note 61, para. 19, sub-para. 9.

[65] Ibid.

[66] ILC, Report on the Work of its Sixty-first Session (2009), *GAOR Sixty-fourth Session, Supplement No. 10* (A/64/10) at Chapter V, Section C.2, at 302 *et seq.*, draft Guidelines 3.3 and 3.3.1. These draft Guidelines were reformulated somewhat and provisionally adopted by the Commission at its 3025th meeting of 22 July 2009, ibid., para. 61; all quotations are to the reformulated guidelines.

[67] A. Pellet seems to have gone to certain lengths to avoid this point; in 'Second Addendum to the Tenth Report on Reservations to Treaties', *supra* note 50, 25, para. 200, he expressly deferred consideration of the topic to future meetings.

produces its consequences pursuant to the law of treaties and does not, in itself, engage the responsibility of the State or international organization which has formulated it.'[68]

Draft Guideline 3.3.1 thus clarifies the nature of the act of formulating a reservation, confining it strictly to the law of treaties, and in this sense settles in the negative the question of whether formulating a reservation could entail a breach of an international obligation.[69] More directly related to the effects of an invalid reservation is the nullity attached thereto in what was originally draft Guideline 3.3.2: 'A reservation that does not fulfil the conditions for validity laid down in Guideline 3.1 [which repeats the conditions set out in Article 19 of the Vienna Convention] is null and void.'[70] While what is now draft Guideline 3.3.2 [formerly 3.3.3], by providing that '[a]cceptance of a reservation by a contracting State or by a contracting international organization shall not change the nullity of the reservation'[71] is in keeping with the general spirit of the Fourteenth Report as it also confirms that the reservation has no legal effect, the following proposal (draft Guideline 3.3.3 [formerly 3.3.4]) on the possibility of a collective acceptance of an invalid reservation, deserves a closer look. It reads as follows:

> A reservation that is explicitly or implicitly prohibited by the treaty or which is incompatible with its object and its purpose may be formulated by a State or an international organization if none of the other contracting parties object to it after having been expressly consulted by the depositary.
>
> During such consultation, the depositary shall draw the attention of the signatory states and international organizations and of the contracting states and international organizations and where appropriate, the competent organ of the international organization concerned, to the nature of the legal problems raised by the reservation.[72]

On the one hand, the approach embodied in this proposal may be regarded as pragmatically sound: it does not do away with the rule that, even after a process

[68] ILC, Report on the Work of its Sixty-first Session, *supra* note 66, 309, draft Guideline 3.3.1. In the Commentary thereto, Pellet refers to the ICJ's decision in *Gabčíkovo-Nagymaros Project (Hungary/Slovakia)*, Judgment of 25 September 1997, *ICJ Reports* (1997) 7, at 38, para. 47, as lending support to the formula employed in this guideline.

[69] G. Gaja, 'Unruly Treaty Reservations', *supra* note 1, 317, had already, in 1987, given a negative answer to that question.

[70] Second Addendum to the Tenth Report on Reservations to Treaties, *supra* note 50, 25, para. 200. In his 2010 First Addendum to the Fifteenth Report on Reservations to Treaties, *supra* note 11, 15, paras 416–419, the Special Rapporteur suggested that the principle of nullity found in draft Guideline 3.3.2 should instead be mentioned in Part IV of the Guide to practice. Thus, in the Draft Report of the International Law Commission on the Work of its Sixty-second session, UN Doc A/CN.4/L.764/Add.2 (30 July 2010), Ch. IV, what was draft Guideline 3.3.2 was deleted and the idea of nullity was incorporated within what is now draft Guideline 4.5.1. It should also be noted that draft Guidelines 3.3.3 and 3.3.4 were subsequently renumbered as draft Guidelines 3.3.2 and 3.3.3, respectively. In the present chapter we will, when relevant, refer to the numbering provisionally adopted by the Commission in July 2010, with the old numbers previously used by the Special Rapporteur following in square brackets.

[71] Second Addendum to the Tenth Report on Reservations to Treaties, *supra* note 50, 26, draft Guideline 3.3.2 [formerly 3.3.3].

[72] Ibid., 28, draft Guideline 3.3.3 [formerly 3.3.4].

of extensive consultation, a single objection suffices to nullify an impermissible reservation. That said, as a matter both of legal dogmatics and, maybe more importantly, of policy, we do not consider this approach to be opportune, since it leaves open the possibility, even if slight, that a reservation which is incompatible with the object and purpose of a convention may ultimately serve its (illegitimate) purpose due to some collective acceptance, however it may have been achieved. We maintain that no such collective acceptance, even if unanimous, can serve to cure an offending reservation of its incompatibility with the object and purpose of a treaty and the consequences entailed by such an incompatibility. This appears particularly important in the case of an impermissible reservation to a human rights treaty, in view of the fundamental premise that such rights do not constitute more or less generous concessions granted by states but derive from the dignity inherent in all human beings.[73]

3.3. ILC work on objections, Fifteenth Report (2010)

It is only in Professor Pellet's Fifteenth Report, which is in substance a continuation of the Fourteenth Report,[74] that the Special Rapporteur finally deals with the effect of objections made to reservations, although the Report limits its analysis to objections to valid reservations, which *a fortiori* are those compatible with the object and purpose of a treaty. Its utility for our purposes lies, *inter alia*, in the fact that, in articulating the relationship between objections and reservations, the bilateralist conception which underlies the Vienna Convention regime on reservations becomes once again apparent in order to be overcome subsequently in regard to human rights treaties (*infra* Section 4 *et seq*.).

The Fifteenth Report outlines that a state objecting to a reservation has several choices as to the effect which its objection may have. The objecting state may choose not to have the treaty enter into force between it and the reserving state, on condition that such intent be expressed *definitively*.[75] It may also elect not to oppose the entry into force of the treaty between itself and the reserving state (or refrain from saying anything on the matter), in essence reserving its rights as regards the extent to which its treaty relations with the reserving state are modified in accordance with Article 21(3) of the Vienna Convention. This is consonant with Pellet's view that reservations are 'consubstantial' with a state's consent to be bound, and as such, objections constitute the objecting state's expression of its refusal to consent to that reservation.[76]

[73] See again R. Higgins, 'Human Rights: Some Questions of Integrity', *supra* note 3, 11.

[74] A. Pellet, Fifteenth Report on Reservations to Treaties (2010), A/CN.4/624, 3.

[75] Ibid., 4 *et seq*., para. 296 *et seq*. explain this in more detail. The respective guidelines were provisionally adopted on 28 May 2010, see *supra* note 30, 4–7.

[76] A. Pellet, Fifteenth Report on Reservations to Treaties, *supra* note 74, 3–4, paras 292–293, where the Special Rapporteur draws upon the Commentary to Guideline 2.6.1, found in ILC, Report on the Work of its Fifty-seventh Session (2005), *GAOR Sixtieth Session, Supplement No. 10*

The effect of an objection, therefore, is to make a valid reservation *inapplicable* against an objecting state, as draft Guideline 4.3 suggests,[77] but the objection does not preclude the entry into force of a treaty between the two states in question, except in cases where the objecting state goes one step further and declares definitively that it does not intend to apply the treaty vis-à-vis the author of the reservation and thus does not want a treaty relationship with the reserving state to come about.[78] In state practice, this option, described by the Special Rapporteur as 'maximum effect' given to the objection and consisting in a definitive expression of the intention not to apply the treaty vis-à-vis the author of the reservation,[79] has, again according to Pellet, fallen into desuetude; now, there exists the new practice of objecting states attempting to modify the treaty relations by adapting them to their own position.[80] Basing themselves on the finding that the reservation is incompatible with the object and purpose of a treaty, states have taken the 'super-maximum' position: severability; the treaty applies without modification to the reserving state.

Pellet excludes the applicability of a 'super-maximum' outcome in the case of permissible reservations with vehemence. He does so in draft Guideline 4.3.9, which establishes clearly that the author of a permissible reservation cannot be compelled to comply with the provisions of a treaty without the benefit of the reservation.[81] He considers that to apply the severability solution in the case of permissible reservations would be 'clearly incompatible with the principle of mutual consent': '[t]he objecting State... cannot impose on the reserving State... that has validly exercised its right to formulate a reservation any obligations which the latter has not expressly agreed to assume'.[82] This seems surely unobjectionable in the case of valid reservations, but cannot extend to reservations which are not considered valid (a point which the Special Rapporteur himself highlights)[83] because the 'super-maximum' effect of severance has been developed by state practice precisely within the context of objections made to reservations that are incompatible with the object and purpose of a treaty.[84]

(A/60/10) at 191, para. 13, and ICJ, *Reservations to the Convention on the Prevention and Punishment of the Crime of Genocide, supra* note 15, at 26.

[77] Ibid., 4 *et seq.*, para. 296 *et seq.* The wording of draft Guideline 4.3 is all consonant with the shift from unanimity which took place between 1951 and 1969 at the Commission, see ibid., 5–7, paras 300–305 for the brief drafting history behind this curious compromise. As adopted on 28 May 2010, see *supra* note 30, 4, the word 'inapplicable' has disappeared, replaced instead with the idea that 'the formulation of an objection to a valid reservation precludes the reservation from having its intended effects as against' the reserving state or international organization.

[78] Ibid., 7, para. 306.

[79] Ibid., 8, paras 307–308, draft Guideline 4.3.3. As provisionally adopted by the Drafting Committee on 28 May 2010, *supra* note 30, the formulation is somewhat changed, from the negative 'unless a contrary intention has been definitely expressed' to the positive 'if the objecting State... has definitely expressed'.

[80] Ibid., 12, para. 320.

[81] Ibid., 27, para. 367, draft Guideline 4.3.9, which was provisionally adopted by the Drafting Committee on 28 May 2010, *supra* note 30, 7, as draft Guideline 4.3.7.

[82] Ibid., 27, para. 366, in what now is draft Guideline 4.3.7.

[83] Ibid., 16, para. 335.

[84] Ibid., 26, para. 365.

One last observation on this point: despite the fact that it is dogmatically sound, the traditional method used for accepting or objecting to reservations remains entrenched in the bilateralist framework embodied in the Vienna Convention regime. Because the effectiveness and deterrent effect of an objection remains contingent on the follow-up conduct of an objecting party and other parties to a treaty after the filing of an objection, to focus narrowly on objections in identifying impermissible reservations frames the question of the admissibility of reservations subjectively. Determination of the permissibility of a reservation remains vested in states parties rather than in any objective decision-maker.[85] For this reason, even if objections are raised in a concerted manner, and despite the fact that objections by states can constitute evidence as to the incompatibility of a reservation with the object and purpose of a treaty,[86] when determining the compatibility of a reservation with the object and purpose of a treaty, reliance upon objections is not particularly well-suited to the human rights framework.

3.4. The Addendum to the Fifteenth Report of 26 May 2010

Just before our contribution went to press, the Special Rapporteur submitted the First Addendum to his Fifteenth Report (circulated in June 2010),[87] in which he confirmed the idea that a presumption of severability was to apply in the case of impermissible reservations to human rights treaties, leaving the reserving state's consent to be bound untouched. The Addendum finally focuses on impermissible reservations, highlighting concerns such as those raised in the present chapter and by the first Author in 1998, as well as the impact which the practice of the various treaty monitoring bodies has had on the development of the law. Pellet's recommendations on these issues merit close review, since they also constitute a synthesis of his earlier reports and represent the logical culmination of his work on our subject of concern in the Tenth, Fourteenth, and Fifteenth Reports.

3.4.1. The nullity of an invalid reservation and the consequences thereof

As highlighted above and introduced in Pellet's Tenth Report, draft Guideline 3.3.2 provided for the nullity of a reservation that does not fulfil the conditions for validity; however, as the Special Rapporteur now recalls, the nullity of a

[85] See Ago's intervention on this point in the *YILC* (1962), vol. I, 163, paras 25–27. But cf. the International Convention on the Elimination of All Forms of Racial Discrimination (CERD), 660 *UNTS*, 195, Article 20(2), which provides that if at least two-thirds of the states parties to the Convention object to the reservation, it is considered incompatible with the object and purpose of CERD; the reserving state must either withdraw the reservation or it cannot become a party to the Convention.

[86] G. Cohen-Jonathan, 'Les réserves dans les traités institutionnels relatifs aux droits de l'homme', *supra* note 21, 942.

[87] A. Pellet, First Addendum to Fifteenth Report on Reservations to Treaties, *supra* note 11.

reservation and the consequences and effects of such nullity remain two separate matters. Pellet describes the nullity of an act as merely one of the characteristics which influence the capacity of that act to produce or modify a legal situation.[88] He then identifies the very problem with the bilateralist framework embodied in the Vienna Convention regime, namely, that placing the power of determining the permissibility of a reservation solely with the other contracting parties has the effect of denying 'any useful effect' to Article 19 of the Vienna Convention, in so far as states could accept reservations which are not valid under the Convention regime.[89] The state practice of objecting to impermissible reservations surveyed in the Report concords with Bowett's view that objections need not, and indeed cannot, be made against impermissible reservations; whilst objections may assist in *identifying* impermissible reservations by flagging them, they do not in and of themselves do much to determine their validity: 'the test of permissibility is the treaty itself'.[90]

From this starting-point, Pellet's draft Guideline 4.5 covers the effect of invalid reservations, in the sense that they are to be considered 'null and void'.[91] In the commentary thereto, Pellet reviews state practice, as well as the experience of treaty-monitoring bodies, to demonstrate that reservations found incompatible with a treaty's object and purpose do not prevent that treaty from entering into force between objecting and reserving states, not withstanding the conclusion by the objecting states and monitoring bodies that the reservation itself is deprived of any legal effect.[92] He therefore confirms this important development based on the practice of human rights monitoring bodies.

[88] Ibid., 11, para. 407. In para. 408 *et seq.* he describes the consequences of nullity at some length.

[89] Ibid., 12–13, paras 410–413.

[90] D.W. Bowett, 'Reservations to Non-Restricted Multilateral Treaties', *supra* note 10, at 81. See also J. Klabbers, 'Accepting the Unacceptable? A New Nordic Approach to Reservations to Multilateral Treaties', 69 *Nordic JIL* (2000) 179, at 187, who surveys the practice of the European Nordic states in asserting a super-maximum effect of their objections to reservations: 'such objections have the aim of seeing to it that the reserving state does not get what it wants'. But rather than endorsing their practice, he views the Nordic approach to severability as 'an attempt to influence the development of the law on reservations', ibid., 190. E. Swaine, 'Reserving', *supra* note 3, at 359 considers these innovative objections as liberating non-reserving states to choose amongst a spectrum of alternatives in their reaction to reserving states, so that reserving states no longer unilaterally manage the risks of treaty-making.

[91] A. Pellet, First Addendum to the Fifteenth Report on Reservations to Treaties, *supra* note 11, 16, draft Guideline 4.5.1. In the Fifth Report of the Drafting Committee on Reservations to Treaties (UN Doc A/CN.4/L.760/Add.3 (23 July 2010)), it was suggested that draft Guidelines 4.5.1 and 4.5.2 be merged. The Drafting Committee's proposed reformulation was provisionally adopted by the Commission at its 3069th meeting on 27 July 2010, as can be seen in the Draft Report of the International Law Commission on the Work of its Sixty-second session, *supra* note 70, 32.

[92] Ibid., 18–22, paras 426–433. Draft Guideline 4.5.2 was meant to codify this widespread acceptance; the idea that an invalid reservation is deprived of legal effect has been provisionally adopted by the Commission in what is now draft Guideline 4.5.1: see Draft Report of the International Law Commission on the Work of its Sixty-second session, *supra* note 70, 32.

3.4.2. Effects of the nullity of a reservation on the consent of its author to be bound

The consequences of the nullity of a reservation are at the heart of our present study, and Pellet now finally turns to addressing this question.[93] For decades, various options had been debated in international legal doctrine. Sir Hersch Lauterpacht's classic Separate Opinions in *Norwegian Loans* and *Interhandel* maintained that, if a provision is invalid, then the entire instrument in which it is contained is invalid, for one must operate on the assumption that the consent in that instrument is made *on the basis* of its containing the problematic provision.[94] This position against severability, or in favour of 'maximum effect', has elicited much support in doctrine;[95] nonetheless, Pellet attempts to bridge the gap, in his own words, 'to find a middle ground', between such a theory of 'integral' consent and that of the 'super-maximum' effect of severability, according to which the invalid reservation is considered null but leaving the consent to be bound untouched.[96] He cites recent practice in favour of the severability doctrine of 'super-maximum effect',[97] as well as the Strasbourg approach and the effect of General Comment No. 24 described above, but nevertheless notes the difficulties inherent in a presumption of severability. He also emphasizes the view that it should be the author of a reservation that should take the final decisions to 'cure' the nullity of a reservation, and should not be considered a party to a treaty so long as that nullity persists.[98]

[93] Ibid., 22 *et seq.*, paras 435 *et seq.*

[94] ICJ, *Certain Norwegian Loans (France v Norway), supra* note 33, Separate Opinion of Judge Lauterpacht, at 55–9; *Interhandel (Switzerland v United States),* Preliminary Objections, Judgment of 21 March 1959, *ICJ Reports* (1959), 6, Separate Opinion of Judge Lauterpacht, at 117.

[95] This view was endorsed, *inter alia,* by D.W. Bowett, 'Reservations to Non-Restricted Multilateral Treaties', *supra* note 10, 89; R. Jennings and A. Watts (eds), *Oppenheim's International Law* (London: Longmans, 9th edn, 1992) vol. I, 1247; C. Redgwell, 'Universality or Integrity? Some Reflections on Reservations to General Multilateral Treaties', 64 *BYIL* (1993) 245, 267; C.A. Bradley, J.L. Goldsmith, 'Treaties, Human Rights, and Conditional Consent', 149 *University of Pennsylvania Law Review* (2000) 399, 429–39; L. Helfer, 'Not Fully Committed? Reservations, Risk and Treaty Design', 31 *Yale Journal of International Law* (2006) 367, at 380. However, G. Gaja, 'Il regime della Convenzione di Vienna concernente le riserve inammissibili', *supra* note 1, at 361, rightly regards this theory as 'una soluzione che non pare conciliabile con il fondamento consensuale dei vincoli derivanti di trattati'.

[96] A. Pellet, First Addendum to the Fifteenth Report on Reservations to Treaties, *supra* note 11, 22, para. 435.

[97] Ibid., 23–24, paras 437–439, citing the recent practice of the Nordic states as reviewed by J. Klabbers, 'Accepting the Unacceptable?', *supra* note 90, at 183–6, and B. Simma, 'Reservations to Human Rights Treaties', *supra* note 2, at 667–8. A. Pellet also cited the 2010 practice of several European states objecting to the reservation by the United States to the Third Protocol on the Convention on Certain Conventional Weapons, 1342 *UNTS*, 137, and to Qatar's reservations to the Convention on the Elimination of Discrimination against Women, 1249 *UNTS*,13.

[98] Ibid., 28, para. 448. A. Pellet cites the practice of the Secretary-General and some state practice in this regard, ibid., paras 449–452, but recognizes that the 'immense majority' of states objecting to reservations have nevertheless considered that their objection should not prevent the entry into force of the treaty between objecting and reserving states.

3.4.3. The presumption of the will of the author of the invalid reservation

Faced with these two conflicting viewpoints, Pellet explains that both positions may be reconciled with the basic principle governing the law of treaties, that is, consent.[99] Examining both Lauterpacht's *Interhandel* and *Norwegian Loans* Opinions on the one hand, and the relevant work of the various human rights courts (the European Court of Human Rights' practice in *Belilos* and *Loizidou* and the Inter-American Court of Human Rights' finding in *Hilaire*)[100] on the other, he concludes (correctly, in our view) that the paramount consideration in all of these decisions remains the reserving state's consent to be bound.[101] After considering the solution embodied in General Comment No. 24, according to which the 'normal consequence'[102] of an invalid reservation was the entry into force of a treaty for the reserving state without the benefit of the reservation, Pellet returns to the recommendation of the Working Group in 2007 referred to above,[103] whereby a reserving state faced with an assessment by another party, a monitoring body, or a court to the effect that its reservation is invalid, must '*establish incontrovertibly*' that the reservation was a *conditio sine qua non* of its consent to be bound by the treaty, and that it does not want to remain a party without the benefit of the reservation.[104] Although in 2007, Pellet considered that establishing 'incontrovertibility' as the relevant test went 'a little too far', he now seems to have come to the conclusion that a presumption of severability can, and does, give adequate consideration to the reserving state's consent to be bound. This point had already been made by the first Author in 1998:

> At first glance, it is not easy to square [a presumption of severability] with the principle of consent governing the law of treaties. It can be reconciled, however, if the reserving State is presumed as having tacitly agreed—accepted the risk—that, if its reservation were found unacceptable and therefore invalid and thus severed from its consent to be bound, it might find itself bound by the treaty in its entirety.[105]

[99] Ibid., 31, para. 455.

[100] IACHR, *Hilaire v Trinidad and Tobago,* Preliminary Objections, Judgment of 1 September 2001, Series C, No. 80, *IACHR Reports* (2001), paras 93–94.

[101] A. Pellet, First Addendum to the Fifteenth Report on Reservations to Treaties, *supra* note 11, 31–32, paras 456–460.

[102] General Comment No. 24 (1994), *supra* note 22, para. 18.

[103] *Supra* note 60.

[104] Examples include the US reservations to the ICCPR: see United States, Senate Committee Foreign Relations Report on the International Convention on Civil and Political Rights, 31 *ILM* (1992) 645, at 658–9; United States practice in relation to the United Nations Convention Against Torture and Other Cruel, Inhuman, or Degrading Treatment or Punishment, 1465 *UNTS,* 85, is also pertinent, see Multilateral Treaties Deposited with the Secretary-General, Status of 31 December 1994, ST/LEG/SER.E/13, 179. See also D.W. Bowett, 'Reservations to Non-Restricted Multilateral Treaties', *supra* note 10, at 77.

[105] B. Simma, 'Reservations to Human Rights Treaties', *supra* note 2, at 666–7. G. Gaja, 'Il regime della Convenzione di Vienna concernente le riserve inammissibili', *supra* note 1, at 360, remains sceptical towards this solution; according to him 'sarebbe difficile giustificare l'esistenza di una presunzione in tal senso'. While he regards the approach of 'maximum effect' as even more problematic than that of the 'super-maximum' effect/presumption of severability, he appears to consider these developments at least helpful in the sense that they might lead the reserving state

Similarly, Pellet considers that a presumption of severability can validly be established, and should be seriously taken into consideration by the Guide to Practice, 'since it offers a reasonable compromise between the underlying principle of treaty law—consent—and the potential to consider that the author of the impermissible reservation is bound by the Treaty without benefit of the reservation'.[106] He lays out several additional policy considerations which privilege a presumption of severability. First, the author of a reservation has by definition wished to become a contracting party to the relevant treaty; reservations thereto, whilst playing an important part in a state's consent, do not necessarily reflect the essential conditions for a state to consent to be bound.[107] Secondly, to his mind, the practical implications of keeping a reserving state within the treaty regime during the process of resolving the difficulties posed by an impermissible reservation outweigh the disadvantages of keeping a recalcitrant state inside the treaty framework.[108] Thirdly, Pellet argues that a presumption of severability privileges legal certainty, in that under such a presumption, there is no 'legal vacuum' between the point in time at which the reservation is made and the (later) point in time at which it is found impermissible and therefore null; the reserving state is bound as a state party to the treaty.[109]

4. The Advantages of a Presumption of Severability

The Special Rapporteur's considerations in the Addendum to his Fifteenth Report being in line with what we have maintained throughout this chapter and what the first Author suggested 12 years ago, we wish to conclude with some final observations on the advantages of a presumption of the severability of impermissible reservations to human rights treaties, which we believe confirm rather than undermine the importance and seriousness of consent.

The first advantage is the transparency that would undoubtedly result from a state knowing *ex ante* that its reservation runs the risk of being found incompatible with the object and purpose of a treaty. Although the ambiguity in the Vienna Convention regime as to the effects of incompatibility does also have a certain advantage, in that it may 'engender the flexibility necessary to enable

either to withdraw its impermissible reservation or acquiesce 'rispetto alla considerazione che la volontà di tale Stato di essere parte del trattato sia considerata prevalente rispetto a quella espressa nella riserva', ibid., at 361. G. Gaja thus seems to accept a solution which comes very close to that presented by Special Rapporteur A. Pellet and supported by the present authors.

[106] A. Pellet, First Addendum to the Fifteenth Report on Reservations to Treaties, *supra* note 11, 35, para. 465.

[107] Ibid., 35–36, para. 469.

[108] Ibid., 36, para. 470. It is true that there can be high costs of re-accession associated with the 'maximum effect' of a reserving state no longer being bound to the treaty: see, eg, the enormously complex treaty ratification process in the United States Senate, as described by C.A. Bradley and J.L. Goldsmith, 'Treaties, Human Rights, and Conditional Consent', *supra* note 95, 404–10.

[109] Ibid., 36, para. 471.

states party to a convention to adjust gradually and progressively to rules which may not be precise in their application nor interpreted consistently over time',[110] we consider that the time has come to resolve such ambiguity at least with regard to human rights treaties. Pellet's call for the Commission to endorse a presumption of severability is therefore most welcome.

Secondly, a presumption of severability is justified by the very nature of a state's consent to be bound by a human rights treaty of a universal character. By consenting to the obligations embodied in a treaty of that kind, a state *ipso facto* expresses its consent to be bound by the essential purposes of the treaty, its very core and *raison d'être.* In other words, the reserving state consents to the 'common core' of the consent of all states parties and consents to be bound by all provisions central thereto. Thus, in case of an impermissible reservation, assuming that it is made in good faith, the severability solution tacitly holds the reserving state to agreeing that a reservation cannot infringe upon the fundamental consent to be bound by the treaty's object and purpose and all provisions central thereto. A determination that a given reservation goes against the object and purpose of the treaty will necessarily entail a determination that the provision against which the reservation has been entered constitutes part of the treaty's object and purpose, and a state making a reservation must accordingly have foreseen the possibility that its reservation might conceivably be found to be invalid. In the face of a situation in which a state has expressed its consent to be bound by the treaty's object and purpose, while at the same time desiring to exclude a provision that is central to that object and purpose, it must be presumed that the fundamental consent to be bound, expressed in the act of ratification, is paramount and takes primacy over the reservation.[111] This holds true unless, as outlined above, the reserving state incontrovertibly (or definitively) rebuts the presumption and instead establishes that its consent was premised on the effectiveness, the 'success', of the reservation.[112]

Thirdly, to oblige a reserving state to establish that it considered its reservation to be an essential condition for it to be bound *at the time* the reservation was

[110] C. Redgwell, 'Universality or Integrity? Some Reflections on Reservations to General Multilateral Treaties', *supra* note 95, 279; E. Swaine, 'Reserving', *supra* note 3, 345. A. Pellet also recognized the deliberate normative gap in the Vienna Convention regime, see A. Pellet, Second Addendum to the Tenth Report on Reservations to Treaties, *supra* note 50, para. 181.

[111] Cf. R. Goodman, 'Human Rights Treaties, Invalid Reservations, and State Consent', 96 *AJIL* (1992) 531, at 536; the opposite presumption assumes that a state would have preferred not to be part of the treaty without the reservation, and further unravels what can be a complicated series of interrelated guarantees.

[112] B. Simma, 'Reservations to Human Rights Treaties', *supra* note 2, 667. From the outset A. Pellet foresaw a relaxation of the rules governing the time limits for the formulation or re-formulation of reservations for precisely these reasons. See A. Pellet, Second Report on Reservations to Treaties, *supra* note 38, 81, paras 247–251. Any comprehensive treatment of the time element as regards the process of reservations and objections thereto exceeds the scope of this chapter. See, eg, the Commentary to draft Guideline 2.6.15 (on late objections to reservations) in ILC, Report on the Work of its Sixtieth session (2008), *GAOR, Sixty-third Session, Supplement* 10 (A/63/10) at 221–5.

made, would also facilitate the task of a third-party monitor or adjudicator by providing it with the freedom to honour a state's definitively expressed consent to be bound. Where parties to a treaty have established their own monitoring or judicial machinery, as under the European and Inter-American human rights conventions, they have already accepted a 'primarily objective standard for the assessment of the validity of reservations and the effect that such invalidity might eventually entail'.[113] Even if such monitoring or judicial machinery is not a special creation of the treaty, from a strong human rights viewpoint it would be highly problematic if a state were to make a reservation excluding recourse thereto, especially if such recourse constitutes the only option available to have questionable reservations evaluated in an 'objective' manner. This point was central to the Joint Separate Opinion of Judges Higgins, Kooijmans, Elaraby, Owada, and Simma in *Armed Activities in the Territory of the Congo,*[114] which noted the importance of the role of the International Court of Justice for the achievement of the purposes of a treaty such as the Genocide Convention, where, in the absence of a treaty body exercising supervisory functions, states are the only monitors of each other's compliance with their treaty obligations.[115] The five judges concluded that it is 'thus not self-evident that a reservation to Article IX [the Convention's compromissory clause] could not be regarded as incompatible with the object and purpose of the Convention'.[116] We maintain that the monitoring of human rights obligations is a central element in the protection of the overarching object and purpose of human rights treaty instruments,[117] and we contend that the permissibility of a reservation excluding the competence of a treaty body or a judicial institution over the monitoring of a human rights treaty is far from established.

Fourthly, a presumption of severability finds its root in the consent of states taken as a whole. Because a reservation incompatible with the object and purpose of a human rights treaty would, if successful, *ipso facto* constitute a fundamental change to the treaty,[118] it follows logically that the ability of states to restrict the scope of their consent relating to the core purposes of that treaty would do violence to the consent of all other states parties. As was recognized in the Advisory Opinion on *Reservations to the Genocide Convention*, '[i]t is well established that

[113] D.W. Greig, 'Reservations: Equity as a Balancing Factor?' 16 *Australian YIL* (1995) 21, at 108.

[114] ICJ, *Armed Activities in the Congo (Democratic Republic of the Congo v Rwanda),* Judgment of 3 February 2006, *ICJ Reports* (2006) 3, Joint Separate Opinion of Judges Higgins, Kooijmans, Buergenthal, Elaraby, and Simma, at 65.

[115] The Joint Separate Opinion also noted, ibid., at 70, para. 21, that, in the case of human rights treaties, a reservation to a procedural provision excluding the role of treaty monitoring bodies could be contrary to a treaty's object and purpose.

[116] Ibid., at 72, para. 29.

[117] In his Second Report on Reservations to Treaties, *supra* note 38, 75, para. 209, A. Pellet emphasizes the special role of human rights monitoring bodies because of the 'ordinariness' of these bodies: 'Being established by treaties, they derive their competence from those instruments and must verify the extent of that competence on the basis of the consent of the States parties and of the general rules of the law of treaties.'

[118] R. Goodman, 'Human Rights Treaties, Invalid Reservations, and State Consent', *supra* note 111, at 534.

in its treaty relations a State cannot be bound without its consent. [...] none of the contracting parties is entitled to frustrate or impair, by means of unilateral decisions or particular agreements, the purpose and *raison d'être* of the convention'.[119]

The essential purpose of a treaty concluded between states therefore may be considered as a common core of the states parties' consent, a core which other states may not freely modify or change. For this reason, then, objections based on incompatibility with the object and purpose of a treaty acquire heightened importance in so far as the validity of reservations may be considered. A presumption of severability serves to accommodate the values of universality and integrity,[120] the hallmarks of human rights treaties; it accepts the view that such treaties constitute a set of fundamental normative propositions whilst simultaneously deriving the normative aspect of these treaties from the intention of the parties which drafted them.

A final word: we see the great appeal of a presumption of severability in the fact that it removes human rights instruments from the grip of the bilateralist paradigm and places them into an objective, but equally consensualist, framework. In adopting this solution states will not agree to severability *simpliciter*: they agree in advance to the assessment of the compatibility of their reservations with the object and purpose of the treaty, and they agree in advance to abide by the effect which might be ascribed to their reservations. A presumption of severability is far more subtle than a presumption of 'maximum effect', whereby the impermissible reservation 'poisons' the consent to be bound as a whole. It takes into account a state's consent to be bound *at the time* of the definitive expression of such consent, not at a subsequent point in time.

Of course, a presumption of severability will carry with it certain challenges. It will sometimes be difficult in practice to discern the intention of the author of a reservation, and there will be problems in distinguishing between reservations which are essential to the consent to be bound and those which are dispensable in order to secure the benefits of treaty participation in any eventual severability test. Our presumption could moreover exacerbate future difficulties in that expressions of consent could be subjected to a practice of 'overclaiming' whereby a state might declare that every one of its reservations is indispensable for its consent to be bound, thus distorting the ability of other states to object to reservations and diminishing their discretion to do so.[121] However, it remains clear that a presumption of severability introduces transparency into the treaty-making

[119] ICJ, *Reservations to the Convention on the Prevention and Punishment of the Crime of Genocide*, *supra* note 15, at 21.

[120] R. Goodman, 'Human Rights Treaties, Invalid Reservations, and State Consent', *supra* note 111, at 535.

[121] L. Helfer, 'Not Fully Committed? Reservations, Risk and Treaty Design', *supra* note 95, at 381; R. Goodman, 'Human Rights Treaties, Invalid Reservations, and State Consent', *supra* note 111, at 537.

process as a whole, thus elevating a state's genuine consent to be bound over a narrow, cautious approach to consent that the application of 'maximum effect' would entail. For this reason, we welcome the step towards a presumption of severability taken by Special Rapporteur Pellet, and hope that the Commission's future—and concluding—debate will pay due regard to what is an important development in the field of reservations to treaties.

5

Provisional Application of Treaties in International Law: The Energy Charter Treaty Awards

Mahnoush H. Arsanjani and W. Michael Reisman

1. Parties to a treaty may craft their agreement as they wish, subject only to the constraints of *jus cogens*.[1] But because of the importance of the moment from which a state is bound by a treaty, the Vienna Convention on the Law of Treaties sets forth a detailed code of the modes by which a state may express its consent to be bound; these include 'signature, exchange of instruments constituting a treaty, ratification, acceptance, approval or accession, or... any other means if so agreed'.[2] Whatever the mode by which a state expresses its consent to be bound, the 'treaty enters into force in such manner and upon such date as it may provide or as the negotiating states may agree'.[3]

In addition to the forms of expression to be bound by a treaty, the Vienna Convention also provides for consent to provisional application of treaties. Article 25 of the Vienna Convention establishes the basic principles governing the provisional application of a treaty pending its entry into force. It provides, in relevant part, that '[a] treaty or a part of a treaty is applied provisionally pending its entry into force if... the treaty itself so provides' or 'the negotiating States have in some other manner so agreed'.[4] The Commentary to what became Article 25 clarifies its purpose:

(1) This article recognizes a practice which occurs with some frequency to-day and requires notice in the draft articles. Owing to the urgency of the matters dealt with

[1] 1969 Vienna Convention on the Law of Treaties, Article 53 ('A treaty is void if, at the time of its conclusion, it conflicts with a peremptory norm of general international law. For purposes of the present Convention, a peremptory norm of general international law is a norm accepted and recognized by the international community of States as a whole as a norm from which no derogation is permitted and which can be modified only by a subsequent norm of general international law having the same character'); see I. Brownlie, *Principles of Public International Law* (Oxford: Oxford University Press, 6th edn, 2003) 488–9 (enumerating the 'least controversial examples' of *jus cogens* norms: 'the prohibition of the use of force, the law of genocide, the principle of racial non-discrimination, crimes against humanity, and the rules prohibiting trade in slaves and piracy') (footnotes omitted).

[2] Ibid., Article 11.

[3] Ibid., Article 24.

[4] Ibid., Article 25(1).

in the treaty or for other reasons the States concerned may specify in a treaty, which it is necessary for them to bring before their constitutional authorities for ratification or approval, that it shall come into force provisionally. Whether in these cases the treaty is to be considered as entering into force in virtue of the treaty or of a subsidiary agreement concluded between the States concerned in adopting the text may be a question. But *there can be no doubt that such clauses have legal effect and bring the treaty into force on a provisional basis.* (italics supplied)

(2) An alternative procedure having the same effect is for the States concerned, without inserting such a clause in the treaty, to enter into an agreement in a separate protocol or exchange of letters, or in some other manner, to bring the treaty into force provisionally. Paragraph 1 of the article provides for these two contingencies.[5]

While provisional application does not mean provisional 'entry into force', '[w]hen the treaty has a provisional application clause', it imposes obligations on a state by virtue of that state's 'participation in the adoption of the treaty... Even after entry into force, provisional application may continue among those states which have not by then ratified. The date from which a treaty is to be applied provisionally can be the date of adoption or signature or whatever the negotiating states can agree on.'[6]

Provisional application of treaties was not a central issue in the design of the regime of the law treaties. Neither was it an object of major discussions in the deliberations of the International Law Commission or the Vienna Conference which adopted the Convention on the Law of Treaties. Both the Commission and the Conference intended to maintain an existing practice, even if uncommon, without expressing any particular view on it. This was explicitly stated by Professor Virally, then a French delegate at the Vienna Conference:

[T]he existence of a well-established practice, the value of which had been fully demonstrated, made it necessary for the convention to safeguard the freedom of States to agree that the treaty could enter into force provisionally until such time as they were able to give final confirmation.... It would be preferable to recognize existing practice rather than adopt a particular position on the point.[7]

Professors Brierly and Lauterpacht, the first and second Special Rapporteurs of the International Law Commission on the Law of Treaties listed examples as early as 1880 of treaties which were subject to ratifications but took effect, by the consent of the parties, at the time of signature of the treaty.[8]

[5] United Nations Conference on the Law of Treaties, *Official Records*, vol. III, at 30.

[6] See A. Aust, *Modern Treaty Law and Practice* (Cambridge: Cambridge University Press, 2000) 139–40 (footnotes omitted).

[7] Vienna Conference, *supra* note 5, at 142.

[8] Professor Brierly provided the following as examples: 'Some treaties provide for ratification, but specify that they shall come into force from the date of signature. The Treaty of Madrid (1880), which was subject to ratification, and concerned the protection of the nationals of the High Contracting Parties in Morocco, provided that, by exceptional agreement of the parties, the provisions of the treaty should enter into force as from the date of signature. The Balkan Pact of Non Aggression (1934), although subject to ratification, took effect from the date of signature, as did the Soviet–Czech–Slovak Treaty of Friendship and Mutual Assistance (1943). Instances of particular clauses of a treaty coming into force from the date of signature are as follows: Treaty of

Peace treaties were good candidates for provisional application for obvious reasons.[9] But the urgent need for provisional application of more contemporary treaties soon expanded to other matters. Provisional applications were effected either by a provision in the treaty itself, or through an agreement separate from the treaty itself, for example, by a protocol. The most important international constitutional agreement, the Charter of the United Nations, was accompanied by the Interim Agreement establishing the Preparatory Commission. The Interim Agreement provided that it was effective as of the date of signature, 26 June 1945.[10] The Preparatory Commission, among others, was charged with making 'provisional arrangements for the first session of the General Assembly, the Security Council, the Economic and Social Council, and the Trusteeship Council, for the establishment of the Secretariat, and for the convening of the International Court of Justice'.[11]

The General Agreement on Tariffs and Trade[12] is the most comprehensive and far-reaching agreement that has been applied provisionally for an extended period of time, from 1947 when it was concluded until 1994 when it was replaced by the World Trade Organization. But it is hardly the sole modern use of this technique. Following the oil crisis of 1973 and in response to it, the OECD members concluded the Agreement on an International Energy Program establishing the International Energy Agency in order to cooperate and take measures to meet oil supply emergencies and to develop an emergency

Peace, Amity, Commerce and Navigation (1893) between Japan and Peru (1893); Treaty of Rapallo between Germany and Russia (1922); Agreement between the Union of South Africa and Portugal (1928).' See *YILC* (1962), vol. II, at 53. Professor Lauterpacht, who took over from Brierly as Special Rapporteur of the International Law Commission on the law of treaties, also provided examples of treaties while subject to ratification but by agreement of the parties entered into force earlier: they included, the Trade and Payments Agreement between Denmark and Argentina of 14 December 1948, which after providing, in Article 41, that it 'shall be approved in conformity with the constitutional procedure of each of the High Contracting Parties', lays down that 'without prejudice to its final approval, this Agreement shall enter into force provisionally fifteen days from the date of signature and shall remain in force for five years' subject to a right of denunciation after the first year. Similarly, the Franco-Belgian Convention for the Avoidance of Double Taxation signed on 29 December 1947 provided, in Article 10, that it shall be ratified and the instruments of ratification exchanged as soon as possible, but that it shall enter into force provisionally on the date of its signature (46 *UNTS,* 117). See *YILC* (1953), vol. II, at 90, 114.

9 See, for example, Pact of Balkan Entente between Greece, Romania, Turkey, and Yugoslavia. Signed at Athens on 9 February 1934. Article 3 of the Pact provides: 'Le présent accord entrera en vigueur dès sa signature par toutes les Puissances contractantes, et sera ratifié le plus rapidement possible. Il sera ouvert à tout pays balkanique dont l'adhésion fera l'objet d'un examen favorable de la part des Parties contractantes et prendra effet dès que les autres pays signataires auront notifié leur accord.' 153 *League of Nations Treaty Series*, 154.

10 It was done in the United States as an executive agreement. See Congressional Research Service, Law of the Sea Treaty: Alternative Approaches to Provisional Application, prepared for the Subcommittee on International Organizations and Movements of the House Committee on Foreign Affairs, 93D CONG., 2D Sess. (Committee Print 1974) at 3 and 10.

11 59 Stat.1411, E.S.A. No. 461.

12 The Agreement was concluded on October 30, 1947. 55 *UNTS*, 187.

self-sufficiency in oil supply.[13] Article 68 of the Agreement provides for provisional application.

Concerns for safety accounted for provisional application of two treaties under the auspices of the IAEA. The meltdown of the Chernobyl Nuclear Power Plant on 26 April 1986, the worst nuclear power plant disaster in history, resulted in a radioactive cloud detected over almost all of Europe.[14] Dealing with the crisis required speedy drafting and identical provisional application clauses in two IAEA treaties: the Convention on Early Notification of a Nuclear Incident[15] and the Convention on Assistance in the Case of a Nuclear Incident.[16]

The need for taking early steps for the establishment of international organizations responsible for implementation of specific treaties has also led to the use of provisional application of agreements for preparatory commissions. A Report prepared by the Secretary-General of the United Nations in connection with the Law of the Sea Convention provides examples of provisional application of multilateral treaties. The Report lists the United Nations, the United Nations Educational, Scientific and Cultural Organization (UNESCO), the International Civil Aviation Organization (ICAO), the Inter-Governmental Maritime Consultative Organization (IMCO), the International Refugee Organization (IRO), and the World Health Organizations (WHO).[17] While some preparatory commissions were simply of an administrative nature, only empowered to set up the organization in question, others were assigned more substantive powers, performing some of the functions of the organization to be established.[18]

Commodity agreements have been applied provisionally pending ratification for economic reasons. Commodity agreements maintain a balance between demand and supply through a quota system and facilitate and coordinate market policies. Since commodity agreements are usually concluded to apply for a limited duration and are then replaced by subsequent agreements, it is important to ensure that the succeeding treaties become operational, even provisionally, before the preceding treaties terminate so that there are no timegaps between the two treaties.[19] Because of their nature and purpose, then, commodity agreements include complex arrangements for provisional application. In general, states are allowed a limited time to pursue their domestic constitutional requirements for becoming party. Those states that cannot comply with their constitutional requirements within the given time are entitled to declare that they will apply the treaty provisionally pending ratification, accession, etc.[20] Such provisional

[13] 14 *ILM* (1975) 1.

[14] Except for Spain, Portugal, and Andorra.

[15] 25 *ILM* (1986) 1370, Article 13.

[16] 25 *ILM* (1986) 1377, Article 15.

[17] Examples of Precedents of Provisional Application, Pending Their Entry into Force, of Multilateral Treaties, Especially Treaties which have Established International Organizations, Report of the Secretary-General, A/AC.138/88, (1973), para. 4. A similar pattern was followed for the establishment of the International Atomic Energy Agency. Ibid.

[18] Ibid., para. 5.

[19] See para. 72 and note 56 in ibid.

[20] For example the International Sugar Agreement of 24 October 1968 (654 *UNTS*, 3) provides for speedy ratification within a specified time in Article 60. Those governments that cannot

application of commodity agreements is, normally, for a specified time that can be extended subject to approval by the governing councils of the agreements.[21] States that apply these treaties provisionally are nevertheless regarded as 'contracting parties'.[22] In order for commodity agreements to enter into force either definitively or provisionally, however, a certain number of states are required to become party or to notify that they will apply the agreement provisionally.[23]

2. The Energy Charter Treaty (ECT) is a multilateral arrangement designed to promote energy security through the operation of more open and competitive energy markets. Signed in December 1994, it entered into force in 1998. In order to attract and stimulate foreign investment development as soon as possible, a provisional application scheme was also incorporated in the ECT.[24] The ECT's provisional application regime is of particular interest, since it has been the subject of important international arbitral awards.

Article 45 of the ECT provides:

(1) Each signatory agrees to apply this Treaty provisionally pending its entry into force for such signatory in accordance with Article 44, *to the extent that such provisional application is not inconsistent with its constitution, laws or regulations.*

(2) (a) Notwithstanding paragraph (1) any signatory may, when signing, deliver to the Depository a declaration that it is not able to accept provisional application. The obligation contained in paragraph (1) shall not apply to a signatory making such a declaration. Any such signatory may at any time withdraw that declaration by written notification to the Depository.

(b) Neither a signatory which makes a declaration in accordance with subparagraph (a) nor Investors of that signatory may claim the benefits of provisional application under paragraph (1).

(c) Notwithstanding subparagraph (a), any signatory making a declaration referred to in subparagraph (a) shall apply Part VII provisionally pending the entry into force of the Treaty for such signatory in accordance with Article 44, *to the extent that such provisional application is not inconsistent with its laws or regulations.*

(3) (a) Any signatory may terminate its provisional application of this Treaty by written notification to the Depository of its intention not to become a Contracting Party to the Treaty. Termination of provisional application for any signatory shall take

meet the deadline for submission of their instrument of ratification may request an extension in accordance with Article 61. Those governments asking for an extension are entitled to apply the Treaty provisionally. Article 62 provides for an indication to apply the agreement provisionally and provides in paragraph 1; 'Any Government which gives a notification pursuant to Article 61 may also indicate in its notification, or any time thereafter, that it will apply the Agreement provisionally.' See ibid., paras 73–74. Other commodity agreements have similar provisions such as: the International Coffee Agreement of 1968 (647 *UNTS*, 3) and the International Agreement on Olive Oil of 1956 (336 *UNTS*, 177) cited in ibid., note 56.

[21] See Sugar Agreement, ibid., Article 62, para. 2.

[22] For example, para. 3 of Article 62 of the 1968 International Sugar Agreement provides: 'A provisional Member of the Agreement shall, pending ratification, acceptance or approval of, or accession to the Agreement, be regarded as being a Contracting Party thereto.' Ibid.

[23] Article 63 of the International Sugar Agreement makes this distinction between the entry into force of the Agreement 'definitively' and 'provisionally'. See ibid.

[24] 2080 *UNTS*, 95.

effect upon the expiration of 60 days from the date on which such signatory's written notification is received by the Depository.

(b) In the event that a signatory terminates provisional application under subparagraph (a), the obligation of the signatory under paragraph (1) to apply Parts III and V with respect to any Investments made in its Area during such provisional application by Investors of other signatories shall nevertheless remain in effect with respect to those Investments for twenty years following the effective date of termination, except as otherwise provided in subparagraph (c).

(c) Subparagraph (b) shall not apply to any signatory listed in Annex PA. A signatory shall be removed from the list in Annex PA effective upon delivery to the Depository of its request therefore.[25]

Article 45 establishes different regimes with respect to provisional application for different parts of the Treaty; each regime provides for a different scope of operation and a different critical date for the relevance and role of the domestic law of a signatory state. One provisional application regime is for the Treaty as a whole; Article 45(1), (2)(a), (2)(b), (3)(a), (3)(b), and (3)(c) prescribe the law for this regime, which we will call the 'Treaty provisional application regime'. Nesting within it is a slightly different provisional application regime which applies exclusively to Part VII of the Treaty; Article 45(2)(c) prescribes the law for this regime, which we will call the 'Part VII provisional application regime'.

The 'Treaty provisional application regime' applies automatically to every signatory, without possibility of reservation,[26] subject 'to the extent that such provisional application is not inconsistent with its constitution, laws or regulations' or what we will call the 'to the extent' clause. Under Article 45 paragraph 2(c), even if a signatory state submits a declaration in accordance with paragraph 2(a) refusing provisional application, it is nevertheless obliged to apply Part VII of the ECT provisionally pending entry into force of the Treaty for such a signatory, again subject to the 'to the extent clause'. Part VII of the ECT deals with institutional aspects of the Treaty, further negotiations on protocols and voting rules of such negotiations, the Secretariat, and funding issues. The 'to the extent clause' in Article 45(2)(c) does not include the 'constitution' of a state, referring only to 'laws and regulations' of the state.

Article 45(1) provides for the provisional application of the ECT for each signatory subject to a condition: 'to the extent that such provisional application is not inconsistent with its [that state's] constitution, laws or regulations'. The 'to the extent clause' in Article 45 of the ECT is not a paragon of drafting clarity. Not only does it pose problems of interpretation, as we will see; it also creates an anomaly in the relationship between the parties and signatories to the Treaty.

3. To what do the words 'such provisional application' refer? The permissibility of provisional application of a treaty, as a whole, under a state's constitution, laws, or regulations? Or the consistency of specific obligations, specified in

[25] Ibid., Article 45. Emphasis added. [26] Article 46.

various provisions of the Treaty, with a state's constitution, laws, or regulations? In response to this question, the tribunals in *Kardassopoulos*[27] and *Hulley, Yukos,* and *Veteran Petroleum*[28] (herineafter referred to as the *Yukos* cases) held that the words 'such provisional application' referred to the permissibility of provisional application of the whole Treaty under the constitution, laws, or regulations of signatory states and not to the obligations specified in various provisions of the Treaty.[29] In the tribunals' view, this conclusion is consistent with the object and purpose of the ECT, viz., that 'it be possible for the ECT as a whole to apply immediately on signature'.[30] In the *Yukos* cases 'Interim Awards on Jurisdiction', the tribunal also undertook a textual analysis, concluding that the word 'such' in the phrase '*such* provisional application' referred to 'this Treaty'.[31] This reading supported the Tribunal's view that 'such provisional application' was intended to apply to the *whole* of the Treaty in the sense of whether 'provisional application of a treaty', as such, was allowed under a signatory's constitution, laws, or regulations.[32]

The tribunals' interpretation[33] of the provisional application regime of the ECT is not without problems. While we agree that the object and purpose of the ECT is to provide certainty for its provisional application as of the date of signature, the language of Article 45(1) is more supportive of the view that the reference to 'such provisional application' does not refer to the *whole* of the Treaty but to specific obligations of the Treaty. Recall that Article 45(1) includes: '*to the extent* that such provisional application is not inconsistent with *its constitution, laws or regulations*'. If Article 45(1) had been intended to refer to the notion of the permissibility of the provisional application of a treaty as such, it would not have been necessary to introduce the phrase '*to the extent*'. Domestic law either permits or does not permit provisional application of treaties; there would be no function for the words '*to the extent*'. If the intention in Article 45(1) had been to refer to permissibility of provisional application of a treaty as such, the phrase, 'to the extent', would have been replaced with words such as 'if' or 'where'. The phrase, 'to the extent', is meaningful only if it refers to the various obligations in the ECT.

[27] *Ioannis Kardassopoulos and Georgia*, Decision on Jurisdiction, ICSID Case No. ARB/05/18.

[28] These are a series of three cases against the Russian Federation based on the provisional application of the ECT. *Hulley Enterprises Limited (Cyprus) and The Russian Federation*, Interim Award on Jurisdiction and Admissibility of 30 November 2009, PCA Case No. AA 226, available at <http://ita.law.uvic.ca/>. *Yukos Universal Limited (Isle of Man) v The Russian Federation*, Interim Award on Jurisdiction and Admissibility of 30 November 2009, PCA Case No. AA 227, in ibid. *Veteran Petroleum Limited (Cyprus) v The Russian Federation*, Interim Award on Jurisdiction and Admissibility of 30 November 2009, PCA Case No. AA 228, in ibid.

[29] See *Kardassopoulos, supra* note 27, paras 205–211 and 219; *Hulley, Yukos,* in ibid., paras 304–312.

[30] *Kardassopoulos, supra* note 27, para. 214.

[31] *Hulley, supra* note 28, para. 304. See also paras 305–329.

[32] Ibid.

[33] The three cases of *Hulley, Yukos,* and *Veteran Petroleum* were examined by the same Tribunal.

The last phrase in Article 45(1), namely '*its constitution, laws and regulations*', also compels the conclusion that Article 45(1) refers to provisional application of various obligations of the Treaty. The capacity of a state to provisionally apply a treaty is of such importance that it would normally be settled by the highest authoritative law of the land, the constitution. Exceptionally, it is possible that such authorization might be effected by an act of legislation, so there would be a reason to include 'laws'. But Article 45(1) refers also to '*regulations*'. Now '*regulations*' generally refer to secondary prescriptions that are made, by delegation to lower levels of the chain of authority, for example in administrative codes by government agencies or municipalities.[34] It is, to say the least, difficult to imagine how an issue as important as the authority of a state to provisionally apply a treaty would be decided by '*regulation*'. By contrast, arrangements for specific matters covered by the ECT would normally be effected within a state not only by authorizations, or prohibitions expressed in the constitution and laws of a state, but also in regulations dealing with particular issues addressed in the Treaty.

This particular interpretation is supported by the language of Article 45(2)(c). Under this provision, even where a state makes a declaration under Article 45(2)(a) namely that it is unable to apply the Treaty provisionally, that state is nevertheless bound to apply Part VII of the Treaty provisionally 'to the extent that such provisional application is not inconsistent with its laws and regulations'. As we explained earlier, Part VII of the Treaty deals with institutional aspects of the Treaty, further negotiations on protocols and voting rules of such negotiations, Secretariat, and funding issues. Clearly, the reference 'to the extent' here could not have meant the capacity of a state to apply a treaty provisionally. If that were the case, the answer would have already been given by the state in making its declaration under Article 45(2)(a). The reference 'to the extent' could only refer to specific obligations in Part VII of the Treaty. There is no reference to the 'constitution' of a state in Article 45(2)(c), because we would infer that the issues addressed in Part VII of the Treaty are mostly administrative issues which are dealt with by laws or regulations.

[34] 'Regulations' are defined as: 'Rules and administrative codes issued by governmental agencies at all levels, municipal, county, state and federal. Although they are not laws, regulations have the force of law, since they are adopted under authority granted by statutes, and often include penalties for violations. One problem is that regulations are not generally included in volumes containing state statutes or federal laws but often must be obtained from the agency or located in volumes in law libraries and not widely distributed. The regulation-making process involves hearings, publication in governmental journals which supposedly give public notice, and adoption by the agency. The process is best known to industries and special interests concerned with the subject matter, but only occasionally to the general public. Federal regulations are adopted in the manner designated in the Administrative Procedure Act (A.P.A.) and states usually have similar procedures', available at <http://dictionary.law.com/Default.aspx?selected=1771>. *Black's Law Dictionary* (9th ed) defines 'regulation' as: '1. The act or process of controlling by rule or restriction <the federal regulation of the airline industry>. self regulation. [...] 2. BYLAW (1) <the CEO referred to the corporate regulation>. 3. A rule or order, having legal force, usu. issued by an administrative agency <Treasury regulations explain and interpret the Internal Revenue Code>. —...Also termed (in sense 3) *agency regulation; subordinate legislation; delegated legislation...*' Ibid., at 1398.

4. We agree with the interpretations of the tribunals to the effect that provisional application under Article 45(1) begins at the time of signature of the Treaty. It is at the moment of signature that a state that wants to exercise the option provided for it under Article 45(2)(a), namely that it shall not accept its provisional application, must so declare. This interpretation is consistent with the structure of the ECT and the specific formulation of other parts of Article 45 which provide the 'context', in the sense of Article 31 of the Vienna Convention.

First, a signatory which did not invoke Article 45(2)(a) is bound by the provisional application regime of the Treaty until submission of its 'written notification to the Depository of its intention not to become a Contracting Party'. Even then, the termination does not become effective according to Article 45(3)(a), until 'the expiration of 60 days from the date on which such signatory's written notification is received by the Depository'.[35] But if Article 45(1) is not read in the light of Article 45(2)(a), then claims under Article 45(1) would be immediately effective, if not retroactive, depriving Article 45(3)(a) and (b) of all effect.

Secondly, the provisional application obligation applies automatically upon signature and continues until either termination or ratification. Indeed, in specific reference to Article 45(1), a scholarly analysis which recommends itself for its cogency concludes that

> ... if a treaty enters into force while not all States that apply the treaty provisionally have expressed their consent to be bound, it is equally self-evident that provisional application by those States does not come to an end. This situation has been anticipated in treaty practice as it often provided that a state should apply a treaty provisionally pending its entry into force *for that State*.[36]

Thirdly, by contrast to the limited obligation to apply Part VII provisionally in accordance with Article 45(2)(c) subject to a rolling application of the 'to the extent' clause, any qualification of the obligation which Article 45(1) imposes by operation of the 'to the extent' clause is subject to an advance notification requirement. Notification in the prescribed form is required because, unlike Part VII, whose application only involves the state, many other parts of the ECT invite reliance by investors and other states parties; they must know precisely which entities are subject to the ECT regime.

A key objective of the ECT regime—encouragement and facilitation of investment in energy—depends on potential investors' ability to know the legal situation with certainty. Clarity with respect to provisional application is clearly indispensable to the essential purposes of the ECT. As it is, a state is given ample

[35] Ibid., Article 45(3)(a).

[36] R. Lefeber, 'The Provisional Application of Treaties', in J. Klabbers and R. Lefeber (eds), *Essays on the Law of Treaties* (The Hague: Kluwer Law International, 1998) 81, at 86. See also C.S. Bamberger, J. Linehan, and T. Wälde, 'Energy Charter Treaty in 2000: in a New Phase', 18 *Journal of Energy and Natural Resources Law* (2000) 331, where the authors affirm: 'following entry into force, the ECT is applied provisionally by a number of signatories, including the Russian Federation', at 349.

opportunity to opt out of the provisional application regime. First, the state need not sign the ECT. Second, if it does, it can avoid the provisional application regime because of an inability arising from its domestic law by a declaration issued upon signature. But it must duly notify in advance that its constitution, laws, or regulations disable it from provisional application, a requirement which puts prospective foreign investors as well as other states parties on notice. If the relevant time is not considered the time of signature and is left to the discretion of the state, then the balance of interests which is fundamental to all agreements, and was designed for protection by the ECT, no longer exists. A state could then simply assert, at any time, even years after the signature of the ECT, with regard to a particular investor with a long-standing investment in its territory and a possible reliance claim, that it is unable to comply with the provisional application regime of the ECT because of its constitution, laws, or regulations.

Alternatively, a state, subsequent to its signature, could change its laws and regulations so that it could not comply with the ECT provisional application. This would change the regime which an investor in that state reasonably assumed when it made its investment. The ECT provides explicitly for the legitimate interest of a signatory state in case of subsequent change of constitution, laws, and regulations. It has the right to terminate its obligation of provisional application under Article 45(3)(a) and (b), by notifying the depository that it does not intend to become a contracting party to the ECT. Termination of the Treaty's provisional application takes place 60 days after notification. For those investors that had already invested in that state, however, Parts III and V of the ECT remain in force for 20 years with regard to any investments made in that state during the provisional application, unless a declaration rejecting the 'tail' is made at the time of signature.[37]

For the tribunals in the *Kardassopoulos* and *Yukos* cases, however, the question of whether a signatory state is under an obligation to apply the ECT is not determined by the Treaty but by reference to the legal order of each state party on a case-by-case basis, ie whether, in fact, provisional application is not inconsistent with each state's constitution, laws, or regulations at the time of signature. This is, in the tribunals' view, a verifiable matter, so obvious on its face that it need not be declared. Indeed, under the tribunals' reasoning, a state need not make a declaration. The tribunals do not indicate who is competent to make such a factual determination, if it is not the signatory state and, indeed, in each of these cases, the tribunal itself examined the constitution, laws, or regulations of the relevant states to determine whether there was any inconsistency at the time of signature.

Under the tribunals' reasoning, the burden of examining the domestic constitution, laws, and regulations of another signatory state that has not made any

[37] A state may declare that it will not accept the obligation to apply Parts III and V of the ECT with respect to investments for 20 years (the so-called 'tail') should that state terminate its provisional application. These states are listed in Annex PA of the ECT. We assume that the declaration must be made at the time of signature.

declaration is on every other signatory state or any investor relying on the ECT. Is this not an undue burden? Is it reasonable to expect an investor to examine the whole range of a host state's domestic regulatory regime, its constitution, laws, and regulations (and its case law illuminating it) to determine whether a state is barred from provisionally applying the ECT with respect to which it has not made a declaration under Article 45(2)(a)? Is it reasonable to impose the same burden on all other signatory states who might have to decide whether they are bound to apply the ECT with respect to the investors of states which made no declaration under Article 45(2)(a)? Are such individual determinations of the law of a non-declaring state likely to coincide, given the uncertainty of constitutional law? Individual determinations by either the investors or other signatory states are, of course, subject to challenge by that state, but only at the time of a dispute!

The possibilities of uncertainty are great, since domestic laws are not always crystal clear and much constitutional law is notoriously controversial, subject to exceptions, special circumstances, etc., none of which can be divined with assurance by a third party. The tribunals' approach creates an uncertain environment for an investor or another signatory state, which can only be resolved when a dispute erupts and is referred to a tribunal. If one of the functions of investment treaties is to clarify and stabilize expectations as a way of managing risk, the tribunals' reading of Article 45 would seem to do quite the opposite.

There is yet a further problem with the premise which the tribunals applied. If the determination of the 'to the extent' clause is factual as of the moment of signature, regardless of any declaration by a state, how does one deal with subsequent changes of law in a host state which remove barriers to the provisional application of a treaty? Should that state be required to make a declaration that *it will apply* the ECT provisionally, a procedure not provided for under the Treaty? Assume that state A, a signatory to the ECT, does not make a declaration under Article 45(2)(a). Assume further that state A has a provision in its constitution or has legislation requiring the consent of the legislature for the provisional application of treaties. The executive of state A plans to seek a waiver of the legislation for that particular treaty and secures it a few years later. Under the logic of the Tribunals in the cases under discussion, state A is not subject to provisional application of the ECT, because under its laws at the time of signature, it and its investors would not be entitled to benefit from the provisional application of the ECT in other signatory states.

Is an interpretation that creates so much uncertainty consistent with the essential purposes of the ECT? We would think that, considering the objects and purposes of the ECT and the text of Article 45(1) and (2), the more reasonable interpretation is that the determination of the 'extent to which' the provisional application of the ECT is consistent with the 'constitution, laws and regulations' of a state is assigned to the individual signatory states, who must declare the matter at the moment of signature. After all, who other than that state is in a better position to make such a determination, especially bearing in mind other domestic strategies that the executive may be contemplating to deal with the issue? If the state determines that 'it is not able' to accept the ECT provisional application, it should say so publicly by making a declaration under Article 45(2)(a). A state always has the option of withdrawing its declaration. But it is, in our view, impermissible for a signatory state, which had not exercised the option of making a declaration at the critical date, *subsequently* to invoke 'its constitution, laws or regulations', as a justification for and defence against dishonouring all or some part of its commitment to apply the Treaty provisionally.

5. A further question relates to the nature of the option available to a signatory state, under Article 45(2)(a). In addressing this issue, the tribunal in *Kardassopoulos* concluded that the option of a declaration of non-compliance with provisional application provided for a signatory state in Article 45(2)(a) is unrelated to the 'to the extent' clause in Article 45(1). In other words, a signatory state may choose not to comply with provisional application of the ECT even if, in fact, there is no inconsistency with its constitution, laws, or regulations. As the tribunal put it, 'There is no necessary link between paragraphs (1) and (2) of Article 45. A declaration made under paragraph (2) may be, but does not have to be, motivated by an inconsistency between provisional application and something in the State's domestic law; there may be other reasons which prompt a State to make such a declaration.'[38]

With respect, we find the tribunal's interpretation unpersuasive. As will be recalled, Article 45(2)(a) provides: 'Notwithstanding paragraph (1) any signatory may, when signing, deliver to the Depository a declaration that it *is not able* to accept provisional application. The obligation contained in paragraph (1) shall not apply to a signatory making such a declaration. Any such signatory may at any time withdraw that declaration by written notification to the Depository.'

The words 'not able' are important and indicate that the 'to the extent' clause of Article 45(1) is a qualified legal and not an unqualified political power; it may only be exercised in the case of a specific type of inability. Although the ECT allows a signatory state to declare, in *good faith*, that it is unable to accept provisional application—which is the only means for such a state to the evade provisional application of the entire treaty—Article 45(2)(a) does *not* give a signatory an absolute and legally unqualified discretion to decide that it does not want to assume the obligations of provisional application of the ECT as a whole or, to put it differently, to take a 'reservation' to Article 45. Indeed, the ECT explicitly *prohibits* reservations. In other words, it does not create an optional or facultative regime under which each signatory enjoys an unfettered discretion to accept or reject provisional application of the ECT. The ECT applies *simpliciter* provisionally, because Article 45(2)(a) only permits a signatory to avoid undertaking

[38] *Kardassopoulos*, *supra* note 27, para. 228.

provisional application by declaring at the time of signature 'that it [the signatory State] is not *able* to accept provisional application'.[39]

If the exception to provisional application under Article 45(2) were a simple option, amounting to a reservation to paragraph (1) of the same Article, it should have been drafted as such to say 'that it [the signatory state] does *not wish* or *decides not* to accept provisional application'. The provision does not say 'that it [the signatory State] finds it *politically inconvenient* to accept provisional application'. Nor does it use any other verb indicating or implying a facultative power. It says 'it is not *able* to accept provisional application' and it is clear from the preceding paragraph (1) which establishes the framework for the rest of Article 45, that the inability in Article 45(2)(a) refers to an inability arising from an inconsistency between the provisional application regime and its 'constitution, laws or regulations'.

Rather than a discretionary political power, this is a legally defined power which may only be exercised on account of a real inability, determined in *good faith* by the signatory state, which is caused by an inconsistency between the obligations imposed by provisional application and the state's 'constitution, laws or regulations'. And, of course, it must be exercised at the time of signature, lest the balance of interests in this instance between potential host states and potential investors, which is at the heart of any investment agreement, be disturbed.

The inexorability of this interpretation may be shown most economically by setting out Article 45(1) and (2)(a) and overstriking the final clause of Article 45(1):

(1) Each signatory agrees to apply this Treaty provisionally pending its entry into force for such signatory in accordance with Article 44~~, to the extent that such provisional application is not inconsistent with its constitution, laws or regulations~~.

(2) (a) Notwithstanding paragraph (1) any signatory may, when signing, deliver to the Depository a declaration that it is not able to accept provisional application. The obligation contained in paragraph (1) shall not apply to a signatory making such a declaration…

It is clear that if Article 45(1) did not include the final clause which is overstruck in the above quotation, then the power assigned to a signatory state in Article 45(2)(a) might be construed as an unlimited political power, for there would be no 'context' in the sense of Article 31 of the Vienna Convention in which the notion of inability could be put or to which it could refer. But in fact the final clause *is* included, making clear that the power in Article 45(1) may only be exercised if, at the time of signature, provisional application would be inconsistent with the signing state's constitution, laws, or regulations.

This requirement, which enables reliance by investors, is surely central to the object and purpose of the ECT and distinguishes it from similar 'to the extent'

[39] Emphasis added.

clauses in other treaties with provisional application regimes. Investors, as defined by Article 1(7), must be able to determine whether they can rely on the ECT's protections and benefits with respect to each signatory. Likewise, a signatory state must know to the investors of which states it must grant the protection under the ECT. Otherwise, it might grant treaty benefits to investors of a signatory, while its own investors would be deprived of those same benefits in the territory of that other state.

The scenario we have constructed would be unfair even to the investors of the state that has not made a declaration under Article 45(2)(a) but later claimed that it was not bound by the ECT. These investors may have made significant investments in the territory of another signatory state on the assumption that they qualify as investors of a signatory state bound by the provisional application regime and therefore entitled to benefit from ECT protection in the territory of another signatory state. Only after several years will they discover that that is not so. Such a situation could not have been the intention of the drafters of the ECT. Indeed, Article 45(2)(b) clarifies the implications of a declaration of inconsistency: 'Neither a signatory which makes a declaration in accordance with subparagraph (a) nor Investors of that signatory may claim the benefits of provisional application under paragraph (1).'[40]

It is possible that a state's constitution, laws, and regulations may permit provisional application of some of the obligations of the ECT, but not all; in that case, the state should make a declaration under Article 45(2)(a). A declaration in such a case is necessary in order to provide certainty with regard to the applicability or lack thereof of the ECT. In addition, the ECT does not provide for partial application. Therefore, as noted above, any *good faith* determination by a state that certain parts of its laws or regulations do not allow provisional application of some of the obligations under the ECT will require that state to make a declaration. That declaration puts other states and potential investors on notice. Absent such a declaration, the ECT binds the state to provisional application of the entire ECT.

6. This brings us to the issue of the 'critical date', the significant temporal limit on the power to exercise the notification power. Once that critical date for signature passes, states may not make declarations or otherwise benefit from the provisions of Article 45(2)(a); thereafter, the only way to terminate the provisional application of the ECT is to withdraw from the Treaty, in accordance with Article 45(3)(a). Article 45(3)(a) establishes the mode for terminating provisional application: written notification of the intention not to become a contracting party. But, even then, investment-related obligations continue in force for 20 years, for all states other than for publicly noticed Annex PA signatories. The obligations of a signatory to apply the ECT provisionally terminate '60 days from the date on which such signatory's written notification is received by the depository', but the effect

[40] ECT, Article 45(2)(b).

of termination by declaration is limited *ratione materiae* and *ratione temporis*. Article 45(3)(b) provides:

In the event that a signatory terminates provisional application under subparagraph (a), the obligation of the signatory under paragraph (1) to apply Parts III and V [concerning, respectively, 'Investment Promotion and Protection' and 'Dispute Settlement'] with respect to any Investments made in its Area during such provisional application by Investors of other signatories shall nevertheless remain in effect with respect to those Investments for *twenty years* following the effective date of termination, except as otherwise provided in subparagraph (c).[41]

Because provisional application of the ECT is so central to the timely achievement of its objects and purposes, the ECT requires, as the sole means for a signatory to end its provisional-application obligations, the submission of written notification to the depository of the state's intention not to become a contracting party.[42] By virtue of the depositary's publication, this constitutes notice—in a meaningful sense—to all other states parties, not to speak of the universe of potential investors.

Moreover, the binding character of the ECT's provisional application regime is confirmed by Article 45(3)(a), which provides a written mode for termination of the provisional application regime. Why would a treaty provide for a precise mode of terminating something that was not binding?

Our textual analysis is supported by an Award rendered by a tribunal sitting in Stockholm in application of the ECT. In *Petrobart Limited v The Kyrgyz Republic*,[43] the claimant, a legal entity incorporated in Gibraltar, argued that the Treaty became provisionally applicable on 17 December 1994, the day upon which the United Kingdom signed the Treaty and stated that it intended to apply it provisionally *inter alios* to Gibraltar under Article 45(1) of the Treaty.[44] The respondent argued that the Treaty no longer applied to Gibraltar because the United Kingdom's instrument of ratification of 13 December 1996 referred to the United Kingdom, the Bailiwick of Jersey, and the Isle of Man, but did not refer to Gibraltar.[45]

Hence the tribunal was constrained to examine the question of provisional applicability of the Treaty to Gibraltar. The tribunal reasoned that:

It is obvious that Article 45(1) envisages, at least primarily, the simple case where a signatory first accepts provisional application and subsequently ratifies the Treaty in respect of the same territory with the effect that upon its entry into force the provisional application ceases and is succeeded and replaced by the direct application resulting from the

[41] Emphasis added. Subparagraph (c) permits signatories to refuse the continuation of obligations under Article 45(3)(b) by listing themselves in Annex PA.

[42] Ibid., Article 45(3)(a).

[43] *Petrobart Limited v Kyrgyz Republic*, Arb. No. 126/2003, Arbitration Institute of the Stockholm Chamber of Commerce (Energy Charter Treaty), Arbitral Award of 29 March 2005, available at <http://ita.law.uvic.ca/about.htm>.

[44] Ibid., at 22.

[45] Ibid., at 42.

ratification. As regards the unusual situation where the territory accepted for provisional application and for application upon ratification does not coincide, no rule is to be found in the Treaty, and a problem of interpretation therefore arises.

The Arbitral Tribunal considers that in principle, on matters of this kind, a rather formal approach based on the wording of the Treaty is appropriate. It is then to be noted that according to the text of the Treaty provisional application ceases if it is terminated either by a special notification under Article 45(3)(a) of the Treaty or by transition from provisional application to a corresponding and final legal commitment resulting from the entry into force of the Treaty. It could indeed be expected that the United Kingdom, if it wished the provisional application of the Treaty to Gibraltar to be terminated as a result of a ratification not including Gibraltar, should have made this clear by making a notification in line with Article 45(3)(a) or a declaration in some other form in connection with the ratification.[46]

The tribunal thus concluded that:

. . . the fact that the ratification, for political or other reasons, did not include Gibraltar does not justify the conclusion that the United Kingdom intended to revoke the application of the Treaty to Gibraltar on a provisional basis. It may be observed that what is at issue here is not only the rights of investors from Gibraltar in other states but also the protection of foreign investors in Gibraltar.

The Arbitral Tribunal therefore finds that the Treaty continues to apply on a provisional basis to Gibraltar despite the fact that the United Kingdom's ratification does not cover Gibraltar.[47]

7. Unless clearly indicated in a treaty, provisional applications are not aspirational nor are they left to the political discretion of parties. To begin with, all agreements concluded between states with the possible exception of a *modus vivendi* are subject to the rule of *pacta sunt servanda*. Plainly, the ECT was a solemn agreement, replete with imperative language, a compulsory dispute resolution mechanism, a Secretariat, and a designated depository. Indeed, it was registered as a treaty, under Article 102 of the UN Charter, with the Secretariat of the United Nations on 30 April 1999.[48] One of the modes by which parties concluding an instrument which they do not wish to be binding may indicate this intention is by explicitly precluding registration with the United Nations Secretariat under Article 102 of the Charter; thus the Helsinki Final Act was, by its own terms, 'not eligible for registration under Article 102'.[49]

While states are free to devise a treaty by mutual consent, the language in a treaty for the benefit of third parties must be clear. In case of ambiguity, in accordance with the *contra proferentem* rule, the treaty is to be interpreted for the benefit of the third parties who relied on it, lest parties to a treaty avoid, at will, compliance with their obligation. This is not to say that states may not create

[46] Ibid., at 62. [47] Ibid., at 62–3.

[48] Registration No. 1-36116, 2080 *UNTS*. The Energy Protocol was registered on the same date, No. 1-36117, 2081 *UNTS*. [49] 14 *ILM* (1975) 1293, at 1325.

an entirely discretionary provisional application regime where third parties are involved, but the plain language of such provisions must be clear. Treaties are too important to be left in a normative limbo.

Lefeber explains that it is to be expected that 'the competent organ *should* abstain from expressing its consent to be bound to an agreement on provisional application. If it does not, it will either have to comply with the treaty, or have to face its liability for an internationally wrongful act.'[50]

That, in our view, says it all.

[50] R. Lefeber, 'The Provisional Application of Treaties', *supra* note 36, at 90 (emphasis supplied). See also C.S. Bamberger, J. Linehan, and T. Wälde, 'Energy Charter Treaty in 2000: in a New Phase', *supra* note 36, at 349–51.

PART II

INTERPRETATION OF TREATIES

6

The Rules on Interpretation: Misgivings, Misunderstandings, Miscarriage? The 'Crucible' Intended by the International Law Commission

Mark E. Villiger

1. Introduction

Since 1963,[1] Giorgio Gaja has published extensively on international law and in particular on the law of treaties of international law with a special emphasis on *jus cogens* and reservations.[2] In his publications, Gaja has also addressed the topic of interpretation.[3] The following contribution concentrates on this last mentioned issue. It is prepared in honour of Gaja's life-long devotion to, and considerable influence on, the doctrine of international law. It is proposed in particular to look more closely at the provisions on the interpretation of the 1969 Vienna

[1] Gaja's earliest publication on international law which this author could find was: 'Legislazione siciliana e obblighi internazionali', *Giurisprudenza Italiana* (1963) 1359 *et seq.*

[2] For a selection of Gaja's publications on the law of treaties, see in chronological order: 'Reservations to Treaties and the Newly Independent States', 1 *Ital. Yb. Int'l L* (1975) 52 *et seq.*; '*Jus Cogens* beyond the Vienna Convention', 172 *Recueil des Cours* (1981) 271 *et seq.*; 'Unruly Treaty Reservations', in *International Law at the Time of its Codification. Essays in Honour of Roberto Ago* (Milan: Giuffrè, 1987) vol. I, 307 *et seq.*; ' "Italy", The Effects of Treaties in Domestic Law', in F.G. Jacobs and S. Roberts (eds), *The Effects of Treaties in Domestic Law* (London: Sweet and Maxwell, 1987) 87 *et seq.;* 'A "New" Vienna Convention on Treaties between States and International Organizations or between International Organizations: A Critical Commentary', 58 *BYIL* (1987) 253 *et seq.*; 'Modalità singolari per la revoca di una riserva', 72 *Riv. di Diritto Internaz.* (1989) 905 *et seq.*; 'Trattati internazionali', *Digesto delle Discipline Pubblicistiche* (Torino: UTET, 1999) vol. XV, 344 *et seq.*; 'Le riserve tardive ai trattati: un fenomeno a molti inviso (ma non sempre visto bene)', 86 *Riv. di Diritto Internaz.* (2003) 463 *et seq.*; 'Convention de Vienne de 1969—Article 38', in O. Corten and P. Klein (eds), *Les Conventions de Vienne sur le droit des traités* (Bruxelles: Bruylant, 2006) 1505 *et seq.*; 'Convention de Vienne de 1986—Article 38', ibid., 1521 *et seq.*; 'Il regime della Convenzione di Vienna concernente le riserve inammissibili', *Studi in onore di Vincenzo Starace* (Napoli: Editoriale scientifica, 2008) 349 *et seq.*

[3] See, *inter alia*: 'The Perspective of International Law', in G. Maisto (ed), *Multilingual Texts and Interpretation of Tax Treaties and EC Tax Law* (Amsterdam: IBFD, 2005) 91 *et seq.*

Convention on the Law of Treaties, in particular Articles 31 and 32. Due not least to their special position in a 'treaty on treaties',[4] over the years, numerous misgivings and misunderstandings have arisen and the criticism has even been voiced that these provisions amounted to a failure.[5]

2. Misgivings on Rules on Interpretation

To interpret a rule is to assign a meaning to the words contained therein. The meanings of words are not ironclad; words can mean many things to many people. This is confirmed in Article 31, which deals in paragraph 4 with 'special' meanings of a term.[6] So the process of eliciting the different meanings—and in particular the 'correct' meaning—from the terms of a treaty is altogether a creative process leaving room for extralegal considerations such as one's personal and cultural background. It is in this context that the International Law Commission (ILC) wrote in its commentary on the articles of interpretation that 'the interpretation of documents is to some extent an art, not an exact science'.[7] Naturally, misgivings will arise whether such a process can be cast into rules at all—and whether it is indeed necessary to have a rule on the interpretation of treaties in a 'treaty on treaties'. Confirmation for such misgivings can be found in the domestic sphere. Thus, in most domestic legal orders rules on interpretation on national legislation will not be found in the legislation itself; rather, they have been developed and formulated over the years in judicial practice. It is with these misgivings in mind that we must now examine Articles 31 and 32 more closely.

3. The *Travaux Préparatoires* of Articles 31 and 32

It is telling how the ILC hesitated for many years to take up the interpretation of treaties as a subject of the codification and progressive development of international law. The ILC began discussing the topic of the law of treaties in 1950; the fourth Special Rapporteur, Sir Humphrey Waldock, took up his functions in 1962, but only in 1964 did he prepare a first preliminary draft on the interpretation of treaties. These early provisions were clearly inspired by the 1957 Articles on interpretation of the *Institut de Droit International*.[8] They proceeded from the primacy of the text and granted certain discretion in

[4] See R.D. Kearney and R.E. Dalton, 'The Treaty on Treaties', 64 *AJIL* (1970) 495 *et seq.*

[5] See *infra* note 16.

[6] See *infra* note 28.

[7] See *YILC* (1966), at 218, para. 4, *mutatis mutandis*, in the context of the usefulness of rational techniques of interpretation, *supra* note 5.

[8] 46 *Annu. de l'Inst. de Droit Internat.* (1956) 317 *et seq.*

the choice of approach to interpretation.[9] In the opinion of most Commission members in 1964, these rules found support in international law and embodied the contextual approach to interpretation. The Draft Articles of the ILC of 1964 (then Articles 69–71) contained the nucleus of the present Articles 31 and 32. It was only now that the 'objects and purposes' and the 'subsequent practice' came to constitute integral parts of the 'General Rule'.[10] In 1966 there was a consensus in the ILC that the ordinary meaning of terms was relevant, but constituted only the starting point of a wider inquiry.[11] The discussion focused on the arrangement of means listed in the 'General Rule', and on questions of context and the special meaning of terms.[12] The ILC then adopted Articles 27 and 28 of the ILC Draft 1966.[13]

At the 1968/1969 Vienna Conference, altogether 38 delegations commented on the ILC Draft on the interpretation of treaties (Articles 27 and 28). Of these, 31 favoured these Articles, and seven criticized them. Most delegations endorsed the legal quality of rules of interpretation, their remarks concentrating principally on the merits of various approaches to interpretation. Seven delegations deemed the Articles to reflect international law, while five regarded them as being new. Seven delegations concurred with the ILC that Article 27 established a parity of all means of interpretation, whereas 19 delegations viewed the article as entrenching the classical textual approach. Similar patterns can be detected with regard to Article 28, where eight delegations supported the ILC's intention to admit liberal recourse to the 'supplementary means', whereas for 15 delegations the use of these means was restricted.[14]

At the Vienna Conference, the United States delegation tabled an amendment suggesting eight 'relevant factors' to be considered in the interpretation of treaty terms.[15] Myres McDougal of the delegation directed trenchant criticism towards the alleged textuality of Articles 27 and 28 of the ILC Draft 1966, which in

[9] *YILC* (1964), vol. II, at 8 *et seq.* and at 52 *et seq.*; ie draft Article 70 on the 'General Rule'; Article 71 on the Application of General Rules; Article 72 on the Effective Interpretation of the Terms; Article 56 on Intertemporal Law; and Article 73 on the Effects of a Later Customary Rule or a Later Agreement on Interpretation of a Treaty. The preliminary debate is reproduced at *YILC* (1964), vol. I, at 20 *et seq.*

[10] Ibid., at 275 *et seq.*

[11] The ILC Report 1964 is reproduced at *YILC* (1964), vol. II, at 199 *et seq.*

[12] *YILC* (1966), vol. I(2), at 183 *et seq.*, 267 *et seq.*, 328 *et seq.*, and 346–7.

[13] Ibid., at 270; Article 27 was adopted by 16 votes to none; Article 28 by 15 votes to none. The articles are reproduced at *YILC* (1966), vol. II, at 217 *et seq.*

[14] See on this section M.E. Villiger, *Customary International Law and Treaties. A Study of Their Interactions and Interrelations with Special Consideration of the 1969 Vienna Convention on the Law of Treaties* (Dordrecht: Martinus Nijhoff Publishers, 1985) at 482. The minutes of the deliberations are reproduced in Vienna Conference on the Law of Treaties, *Official Records*, vol. I, 166 *et seq.*, and 441–2; and *Official Records*, vol. II, at 57–8.

[15] Reproduced in *Official Records*, vol. III, at 149–50. Altogether 15 states submitted amendments, ibid.

his view 'would prove totally unworkable',[16] whereas the US amendment would restore a well-established process of interpretation, permitting recourse to factors extrinsic to the treaty text. The amendment was rejected by 66 votes to eight, with 10 abstentions.[17]

In 1969 the Conference adopted today's Articles 31 and 32 (which had remained unchanged in Vienna), respectively, by 97 votes to none, and 101 votes to none.[18]

We can draw the following conclusions from these materials. The ILC texts on the rules of interpretation disclose that the ILC clearly acknowledged the legal quality of rules on interpretation.[19]

It found substantial support for this in case law, at least for some means of interpretation.[20] Also, the ILC materials indicate considerable uncertainty on the part of the ILC, at least originally, about other means such as the position and function of subsequent practice; the treaty's object and purpose; and the equal value and interrelation of all the means of the 'General Rule'.

As regards the Vienna Conference, it is significant that no state proposed the deletion of the ILC Draft Articles on interpretation. In fact, a substantial majority of states endorsed the ILC Draft Articles, though it may be noted that claims emphasizing the customary nature of these rules were balanced by statements that the rules were innovatory.

4. The Means of Interpretation in Articles 31 and 32—An Overview

This is not the place to assess the various means of interpretation in Articles 31 and 32—there are nine of them—though it appears important to highlight them briefly.

1. *Good faith* is given pride of place in the opening sentence of Article 31(1), and indeed, it lies at the centre of the application of interpretation throughout which it prevails. *Bona fides*, which is also mentioned in the Preamble and in Article 26 on *pacta sunt servanda*, prevents an excessively literal interpretation of a term, instead requiring consideration of its context and of other means of interpretation.[21] Good faith implies consideration of the object and purpose of a treaty and

[16] *Official Records*, vol. I, at 167, para. 44, and ibid. para. 38 *et seq*. But see the statement by the *United Kingdom* Delegation in Vienna, ibid. 178, para. 10, for whom the United States text 'actually placed primary emphasis on the text of the treaty'.

[17] Ibid. 185, para. 75.

[18] *Official Records*, vol. II, at 57–8. See the statement by the Chairman of the Vienna Conference, Roberto Ago, ibid. 59, para. 7 ('the Conference had successfully disposed of the most controversial and difficult subject in the whole field of the law of treaties').

[19] eg, the statement by A. Verdross in the ILC, *YILC* (1964), vol. I, at 21, para. 15.

[20] eg, Sir H. Waldock in the ILC, *YILC* (1966), vol. I (2), at 206, para. 38; the sixth Waldock Report, *ibid.*, vol. II, at 95, para. 5.

[21] ILC Report, ibid., at 211, para. 2.

plays a part in establishing the 'acceptance' in subparagraph 2(b) of Article 31 and in evaluating subsequent practice as in subparagraph 3(b). Finally, good faith assists in determining recourse to the supplementary means of interpretation as set forth in Article 32. When interpreting a treaty, good faith raises at the outset the presumption that the treaty terms were intended to mean something, rather than nothing.[22] Furthermore, good faith requires the parties to a treaty to act honestly, fairly, and reasonably, and to refrain from taking unfair advantage.[23] Legitimate expectations raised in other parties are to be honoured.[24] A right which has been forfeited may no longer be claimed (*venire contra factum proprium*). The prohibition of the abuse of rights, flowing from good faith, prevents a party from evading its obligations and from exercising its rights in such a way as to cause injury to the other party.[25]

2. The ordinary meaning of a term, as in Article 31(1), is the starting point of the process of interpretation. This is its current and normal, regular and usual meaning. A term may have a number of ordinary meanings, which may even change over time.[26] This relativist view of hermeneutics underlies Article 31, which in paragraph 1 requires the ordinary meaning 'to be given' by the interpreter in good faith to the terms of the treaty.[27] In other words, *that* particular ordinary meaning will be established which is the common intention of the parties.[28] The relativity of the meaning of a term is confirmed by paragraph 4, which envisages the possibility of a 'special' meaning going beyond the ordinary meaning of terms. As the Court stated in the *South West Africa Cases*, Preliminary Objections, the limits of this means of interpretation lie 'in a meaning incompatible with the spirit, purpose and context of the clause or instrument in which the words are contained'.[29]

3. The *context of a treaty term* is essential for the establishment of its meaning and term, since treaty terms are not drafted in isolation, and their meaning can only be determined by considering the entire treaty text. The context will include the

[22] See the Minority Opinion in the *Iran–United States Claims Arbitration* (1981), 62 *ILR* (1982) at 603 *et seq*.

[23] See the 1981 *Interpretation of the Algerian Declarations of 19 January 1981* by the Iran–United States Claims Tribunal, ibid., at 605–6 ('spirit of honesty and respect for law').

[24] J.P. Müller, *Vertrauensschutz im Völkerrecht* (Köln-Berlin: Heymanns, 1971) at 128 '(good faith) fordert ein an objektiven Massstäben gegenseitiger Rücksichtnahme orientiertes Verhalten'.

[25] See the *avis de droit* of the Swiss Federal Department of Foreign Affairs, 32 *Stanford Journal of International Relations* (1976), at 79 *et seq*. and 82; the Swiss Federal Court, ibid. 28 (1972) at 214.

[26] This intertemporal aspect is essentially a matter of good faith, depending on the intentions of the parties; see H. Waldock, 'Sixth Report', *YILC* (1966), vol. II, at 96, para. 7 and 97, para. 13; *per contra* the 1980 *Young Loan Arbitration*, 59 *ILR* (1980) at 530 *et seq*., para. 19; M.K. Yasseen, 'L'interprétation des traités d'après la Convention de Vienne sur le droit des traités', 151 *Recueil des Cours* (1976-III) at 27, para. 7 (but see para. 9).

[27] See H. Waldock, 'Sixth Report', *YILC* (1966), vol. II, at 94, paras 2–3.

[28] See the ILC Report 1966, ibid., at 220, para. 11.

[29] ICJ, *South West Africa (Ethiopia v South Africa; Liberia v South Africa)*, Preliminary Objections, Judgment of 21 December 1962, *ICJ Reports* (1962) at 335–6.

remaining terms of the sentence and of the paragraph; the entire article at issue; and the remainder of the treaty, ie its text, including its preamble, and the other means mentioned in paragraphs 2 and 3 of Article 31 thus embody the contextual or systematic means of interpretation which aim to avoid inconsistencies between the individual term and its textual surroundings.

4. A treaty's *object and purpose* equally serves to determine the ordinary meaning of a term (Article 31(1)). A treaty may indeed have many objects and purposes.[30] One of them will be to maintain the balance of rights and obligations created by the treaty.[31] Where is a treaty's object and purpose to be sought? Traditionally, the preamble is resorted to, or a general clause at the beginning of the treaty. The structure of Article 31 as a 'General Rule' leaves no doubt that all the elements of Article 31 as well as the supplementary means of interpretation in Article 32 contribute to this end.[32] Consideration of a treaty's object and purpose ensures the effectiveness of its terms (*ut res magis valeat quam pereat,* the *effet utile*). Nevertheless, interpretation in the light of a treaty's object and purpose finds its limits in the treaty text itself. One of the (originally many possible) ordinary meanings will eventually prevail. In other words, Article 31 avoids an extreme functional interpretation which may, in fact, lead to 'legislation' or the revision of a treaty.[33]

5–7. Paragraph 2 and subparagraphs 3(a) and (b) of Article 31 list three means of *authentic interpretation*, in particular, agreements reached between the parties, 'instruments' which are acquiesced in by the other parties, and practice subsequent to the treaty. They serve, together with paragraph 1, to establish the meaning of a particular treaty term. The means in paragraphs 2 and 3 can only be invoked if all the parties to the treaty have been involved in the interpretation of a particular meaning of a treaty term by means of an agreement, or if one or more of the parties have been involved by means of an instrument or subsequent practice[34] to which the other parties have agreed. Article 31,

[30] See the statement by Y. Tusuruoka in the ILC 1966, *YILC* (1966), vol. I, at 326, para. 91 ('both singular and plural had the same meaning').

[31] H.-D. Treviranus, 'Vorbehalte zu mehrseitigen Verträgen: Wohltat oder Plage?', 25 *GYIL* (1982) 520 *et seq.*

[32] In the *Sovereignty Over Pulau Ligitan and Pulau Sipadan (Indonesia/Malaysia),* Merits, Judgment of the 17 December 2002, *ICJ Reports* (2002) at 652, para. 51, the ICJ had recourse to the 'very scheme' of the Convention at issue. See also (but with emphasis on the text), M.K. Yasseen, 'L'interprétation des traités d'après la Convention de Vienne sur le droit des traités', *supra* note 26, at 57, para. 6, and the comment by A. Verdross in the ILC, *YILC* (1966), vol. I (2), at 186, para. 14.

[33] ILC Report 1966, ibid., vol. II, at 219, para. 6 and 220, para. 11; ICJ, *Interpretation of Peace Treaties with Bulgaria, Hungary and Romania*, Advisory Opinion of 30 March 1950, *ICJ Reports* (1950) at 229; also the statement in Vienna by J. de Aréchaga of the *Uruguayan* delegation, *Official Records*, vol. I, at 170, para. 67; M.K. Yasseen, 'L'interprétation des traités d'après la Convention de Vienne sur le droit des traités', *supra* note 26, para 4.

[34] See recently ICJ, *Dispute Regarding Navigational and Related Rights (Costa Rica v Nicaragua),* not yet reported, para. 70, available at <http://www.icj-cij.org>, where the Court had reference

paragraphs 2 and 3, thus envisage a uniform interpretation of the treaty by the parties and for the parties. All parties agree on (or at least tacitly accept) the interpretation of treaty terms by means extrinsic to the treaty. This means of interpretation is not only particularly reliable, it is also endowed with binding force. It provides *ex hypothesi* the 'correct' interpretation among the parties in that it determines which of the various ordinary meanings shall apply. Indeed, the parties to the treaty are their own masters; they may by means of the instruments, agreements, or practice mentioned in paragraph 2 and subparagraphs 3(a) and (b) not only give a special meaning to the term at issue but also amend, extend, or delete a text. Importantly, authentic interpretation in subparagraph 3(b) is of a dynamic nature in that it may alter the original ordinary meaning of a term in two ways: (i) subsequent practice may modify a treaty provision contractually *qua* authoritative interpretation (there is no preconceived delimitation between the old and the new rule);[35] and (*ii*) parties may in their practice gradually wander from interpretation (as in subparagraph 3[b]) to customary modification of the treaty.

8. Subparagraph 3(c) of Article 31 mentions '*other rules of international law*'. Thus, it envisages treaty interpretation against the whole background of international law. The meaning of a treaty term shall correspond with any relevant rules of international law applicable in the relations between the parties. These rules need have no particular relationship with the treaty other than assisting in the interpretation of its terms. On the whole, they will provide a contemporary interpretation of the ordinary meaning of a term.[36] The 'rules' correspond with the notion of the sources of international law as in Article 38(1) of the International Court of

to this means of interpretation as a result of which it concluded that 'the notion of "commerce"' does not have the same meaning today as it did in the mid-nineteenth century: it is the present meaning which must be accepted for purposes of applying the treaty'. Note that the application of a treaty always presupposes its interpretation. See G. Distefano, 'La pratique subséquente des parties à un traité', 40 *AFDI* (1994) 41 *et seq.*; A. Aust, *Modern Treaty Law and Practice* (Cambridge: Cambridge University Press, 2nd edn, 2007) at 242–3 refers to the well-known example of subsequent practice in respect of Article 27, para. 3 of the UN Charter. See also R. Kolb, 'La modification d'un traité par la pratique subséquente des parties. Note sur l'affaire relative au régime fiscal des pensions versées aux fonctionnaires retraités de l'UNESCO résidant en France; sentence du 14 janvier 2003', 14 *SZIR* (2004) 9 *et seq.*

[35] R. Bernhardt, 'Interpretation and Implied (Tacit) Modification of Treaties. Comments on Arts. 27, 28, 29 and 38 of the ILC's 1966 Draft Articles on the Law of Treaties', 27 *ZaöRV* (1967) 499 *et seq.* See the German Federal Constitutional Court in the 1994 *International Military Operations Case*, 106 *ILR* (1997) at 338–9 ('[i]n practice, international law is characterized by a fluid transition from treaty interpretation to treaty amendment [...] [I]n certain cases this practice can have the same effect on a treaty as a proper amendment'); see also the 1982 *Aminoil Arbitration*, 21 *ILM* (1982) at 1023, para. 97 *et seq.*

[36] On the subject, see also the Report of the ILC Study Group on the Fragmentation of International Law, which includes a section on Article 31, subpara. 3(c), *YILC* (2006), vol. II, at 413 *et seq.*, para. 251 and subpara. 17 *et seq.*

Justice (ICJ) Statute.[37] Furthermore, they are applicable in the relations between the parties, ie, binding on all the parties to the treaty at issue.[38] The term 'applicable' leaves no room for doubt: *non*-binding rules cannot be relied upon. The rules to be resorted to may be general, regional, or local customary rules, as well as bilateral or multilateral treaties, and even general principles of international law.[39] It is assumed that in entering treaty obligations, the parties did not intend to act inconsistently with other previous obligations.[40] The applicable rules are those in force at the time of the interpretation of the treaty.[41] Furthermore, the rules will have to be relevant, ie concern the subject-matter of the treaty term at issue.[42]

9. Article 32 refers to supplementary means of interpretation, *inter alia*, to a treaty's *travaux préparatoires*, which are the most important supplementary means. The preparatory work includes all documents relevant to the forthcoming treaty and generated by the parties during the treaty's preparation up to its conclusion.[43] Among other supplementary means 'included' but not listed in Article 32, the following may be mentioned:[44] *travaux préparatoires* of an earlier version of the treaty; interpretative declarations made by treaty parties which do not qualify as reservations; rational techniques of interpretation (such as *per analogiam, e contrario, contra proferentem, eiusdem generis, expressio unius est exclusio alterius, lex posterior derogat legi priori; lex specialis derogat legi speciali, in dubio mitis, interpretatio in favorem debitoris*, etc.);[45] and, finally, any non-authentic

[37] See H. Waldock, 'Sixth Report', *ibid.* (1966), vol. II, at 97, para. 10; H. Waldock in the ILC, ibid. (1964), vol. I, at 310, para. 10; 316, paras 13 and 17.

[38] See the position of the delegation of the Federal Republic of Germany in Vienna. United Nations Conference on the Law of Treaties, *Official Records*, vol. I, at 172, para. 395. In the *Interpretation of the Agreement of 25 March 1951 between the WHO and Egypt,* Advisory Opinion of 20 December 1980, *ICJ Reports* (1980) at 126 Judge Mosler considered in his Separate Opinion other agreements which shared with the WHO/Egypt Agreement of 1951 the same, or a similar, object and purpose.

[39] ILC Report 1964, *YILC* (1964), vol. II, at 202–3, para. 11 ('General Rule'); statement by E. Castren, ibid. (1966), vol. I(2), at 188, para. 49; M.K. Yasseen, 'L'interprétation des traités d'après la Convention de Vienne sur le droit des traités', *supra* note 26, at 62 *et seq.* and 66 *et seq.*

[40] C. McLachlan, 'The principle of systemic interpretation and Article 31(3)(c) of the Vienna Convention', 54 *ICLQ* (2005) 290 *et seq.*

[41] In 1966 the ILC deleted the words 'in force at the time of its conclusion' previously included in its 1964 draft, *YILC* (1966), vol. II, at 222, para. 167; see the Declaration by Judge Robinson in the Judgment of 21 July 2000, *The Prosecutor v Anto Furundžija*, Case No. IT-95-17/1-A, of the International Criminal Tribunal for the former Yugoslavia, 121 *ILR* (2002) at 360 *et seq.*

[42] See the statements in the ILC by G.I. Tunkin, *YILC* (1964), vol. I, at 310; H. Waldock, ibid. para. 10; *versus* P. Reuter, ibid. (1966), vol. I (2), at 195, para. 22; by the *German* delegation in Vienna, *Official Records*, vol. I, at 172, para. 10. In 1977, the German Federal Constitutional Court stated that, in doubt, a treaty text had to be interpreted in the light of the relevant rules and principles of international law, 46 *Entscheidungen des Bundesverfassungsgerichts (BVerfGE)*, at 342 *et seq.*

[43] M.K. Yasseen, 'L'interprétation des traités d'après la Convention de Vienne sur le droit des traités', *supra* note 26, at 84; the example given by A. Aust, *Modern Treaty Law and Practice, supra* note 34, at 245 *et seq.*

[44] See ILC Report 1964, *YILC* (1964), vol. II, at 204; the statement by H. Waldock in ILC, ibid. (1966), vol. I(2) at 347, para. 173.

[45] S. Torres Bernárdez, 'Interpretation of Treaties by the International Court of Justice Following the Adoption of the 1969 Vienna Convention on the Law of Treaties', in G. Hafner *et al.* (eds), *Liber Amicorum Professor Ignaz Seidl-Hohenveldern in Honour of his 80th Birthday* (The

translations of the authenticated text. These supplementary means of interpretation are by their very nature notoriously heterogeneous, different documents at times even contradicting each other. They can only serve as means to aid the process of interpretation.[46] The extent to which they are able to do so will depend on their cogency, in particular on their accessibility,[47] their direct relevance to the treaty terms at issue, the consistency among the means found, the number of parties involved in the evolution of the particular means,[48] and the reactions of the other parties thereto. Article 32 envisages three cases when recourse may be had to these supplementary means, ie (i) in order to confirm the meaning resulting from the application of Article 31; (ii) where the various means of Article 31 do not lead to a clear result and leave the meaning ambiguous or obscure (paragraph [a]);[49] and (iii) in the unlikely event that the General Rule in Article 31 leads to a result which is manifestly absurd or unreasonable (paragraph [b]). In fact, in the light of these conditions, it is indeed difficult to imagine situations where the means of Article 32 may not be employed.[50]

5. The 'Crucible'—How Are Articles 31 and 32 Intended to Be Applied?

Having examined the various means of interpretation in Articles 31 and 32, the question arises how they are to be applied in the process of interpretation. The text of Article 31 gives the following indications as to the manner in which they are to be employed. Its title speaks of the 'General Rule of interpretation'. Paragraph 1 states that 'a treaty shall be interpreted [. . .] in accordance with [. . .] and in the light of [. . .]'. According to paragraph 2, 'the context shall comprise [. . .]'. According to paragraph 3, 'there shall be taken into account together with the context [. . .]'.

Thus, it transpires from these formulations that the various means mentioned in Article 31, on the one hand, are all to be employed and, on the other, are all

Hague: Kluwer Law International, 1998) 726 *et seq*. Nevertheless, to the extent that these techniques amount to rules of international law, they would have to be considered as part of the General Rule in Article 31 and in particular its para. 3(c); and agreements and practice among a subgroup of parties to a treaty not falling within the ambit of authentic interpretation in Article 31, para. 2 and subparas 3(a) and (b).

[46] See ILC Report 1966, *YILC* (1966), vol. II, at 223, para. 19.

[47] *Young Loan Arbitration*, *supra* note 26, at 544 *et seq*., para. 34.

[48] See here the ILC Report 1966, *YILC* (1966), vol. II, at 223, para. 20.

[49] See the ILC Report 1966, *YILC* (1966), vol. II, at 222–3, especially 223, para. 19; the *Commonwealth of Australia et al. v Tasmania et al.*, case of the High Court of Australia (Gibbs C.J.), 68 *ILR* (1985) at 304 ('[i]f there is an ambiguity, the *travaux préparatoires* may help to resolve it').

[50] S. Torres Bernárdez, 'Interpretation of Treaties by the International Court of Justice Following the Adoption of the 1969 Vienna Convention on the Law of Treaties', *supra* note 45, at 739; differently I. Sinclair, *The Vienna Convention on the Law of Treaties* (Manchester: Manchester University Press, 2nd edn, 1984) at 142 ('recourse is permissible in carefully controlled circumstances').

of equal value; none is of an inferior character.[51] As the singular in the heading 'General Rule' indicates, all means will be considered in one and the same, single process of application. No one particular means mentioned in Article 31 dominates the others.[52] There is no hierarchy of rules in Article 31. In particular, it does not entrench the '*in claris non fit interpretatio*' or textual method of interpretation.[53]

This interpretation of Article 31 is confirmed by the ILC Report 1966, which stated:

> ... [t]he application of the means of interpretation in the article would be a single combined operation. All the elements, as they were present in any given case, would be thrown into the crucible, and their interaction would give the legally relevant interpretation... [T]he article, when read as a whole, cannot properly be regarded as laying down a legal hierarchy of norms for the interpretation of treaties.[54]

In what order should the various means be considered for the process of interpretation? The ordinary meaning of a term serves as a natural starting point, since interpretation turns on the meaning and scope of written words.[55] Following on from this, on an equal level, are the consideration of the context; the object and purpose; any authentic means of interpretation; and any relevant rules of international law. All means in Article 31 should be considered. However, not every means will necessarily yield a result as to the interpretation of the treaty term. The order chosen in Article 31 among the various means therefore appears to be that of logic, proceeding from the intrinsic to the extrinsic, from the immediate to the remote.[56] A majority of means in Article 31 are in fact extrinsic to the treaty text.

Of course, states parties to a treaty are free to agree in the treaty or subsequently to select only some of the means of interpretation mentioned in Articles 31 and 32 and/or to employ different means of interpretation.

6. Misunderstandings—Articles 31 and 32 in Practice and Their Alleged Textual Nature

While Article 31 envisages the equal and balanced consideration of all means of interpretation stated therein, the practice of courts and states discloses different

[51] R.Y. Jennings and A. Watts (eds), *Oppenheim's International Law* (London: Longman, 9th edn, 1992) n. 632.

[52] ILC Report 1966, *YILC* (1966), vol. II, at 219–20, para. 8 and at 220, para. 9.

[53] S. Torres Bernárdez, 'Interpretation of Treaties by the International Court of Justice Following the Adoption of the 1969 Vienna Convention on the Law of Treaties', *supra* note 45, at 733.

[54] ILC Report 1966, *YILC* (1966), vol. II, at 219, para, 8 and 220, para. 9, respectively.

[55] Ibid., at 220, para. 9.

[56] Ibid.; see A. Aust, *Modern Law of Treaties*, *supra* note 35, at 234.

approaches as to the relative position of these means.[57] As the list below indicates, only some instances of practice confirm the single process of application of all the means of the 'General Rule'. Other instances of state practice, and even the practice of the ICJ, are ambivalent. At times, the 'General Rule' in Article 31 is reduced to its paragraph 1, occasionally even to the ordinary meaning of a term, the other means being regarded as discretionary or supplementary.

Thus, the ICJ held in the *Territorial Dispute* (Libya/Chad) that '(according to Article 31) a treaty must be interpreted in good faith in accordance with the ordinary meaning to be given to its terms in their context and in the light of its object and purpose. Interpretation must be based above all upon the text of the treaty.'[58] A similar statement can be found in the *Maritime Delimitation and Territorial Questions, Jurisdiction and Admissibility* (Qatar/Bahrain).[59] In the *Nuclear Weapons Advisory Opinion*, the Court examined subsequent practice as in subparagraph 3(b).[60] In the *Oil Platforms Case* (Iran/United States of America), Preliminary Objections, the Court resorted again to paragraph 1: 'a treaty must be interpreted in good faith in accordance with the ordinary meaning to be given to its terms in their context and in the light of its object and purpose'.[61] In the *Kasikili/Sedudu Island Case* (Botswana/Namibia), the Court invoked paragraphs 1 and 2 and then examined subparagraphs 3(a) and (b).[62] But in the *Legality of Use of Force Case* (Serbia and Montenegro/Belgium), Preliminary Objections, the Court again considered that 'interpretation must be based above all upon the text of the treaty'.[63]

Among other international courts, the European Court of Human Rights has consistently employed all means of interpretation in Articles 31 and 32.[64]

[57] Similarly, S. Torres Bernárdez, 'Interpretation of Treaties by the International Court of Justice Following the Adoption of the 1969 Vienna Convention on the Law of Treaties', *supra* note 45, at 721 *et seq.*

[58] ICJ, *Territorial Dispute (Libyan Arab Jamahirya/Chad),* Judgment of 3 February 1994, *ICJ Reports* (1994) at 21, para. 41. On the development of the Court's case law on Article 31, see generally S. Torres Bernárdez, *supra* note 45, *passim*, for whom the Court's judgments indicate a development from a textually oriented interpretation to one of 'unreserved recognition' of Articles 31 and 32.

[59] ICJ, *Maritime Delimitation and Territorial Questions between Qatar and Bahrain (Qatar/Bahrain), Jurisdiction and Admissibility*, Judgment of 15 February 1995, *ICJ Reports* (1995) at 18, para. 33.

[60] ICJ, *Legality of the Threat or Use of Nuclear Weapons in Armed Conflict*, Advisory Opinion of 8 July 1996, *ICJ Reports* (1996) at 75, para. 19.

[61] ICJ, *Oil Platforms (Islamic Republic of Iran v United States of America)*, Preliminary Objections, Judgment of 12 December 1996, *ICJ Reports* (1996) at 812, para. 23.

[62] ICJ, *Kasikili/Sedudu Island (Botswana/Namibia),* Judgment of 13 December 1999, *ICJ Reports* (1999) at 1059 *et seq.*

[63] ICJ, *Legality of Use of Force (Serbia and Montenegro v Belgium),* Preliminary Objections, Judgment of 15 December 2004, *ICJ Reports* (2004) at 318, para. 100.

[64] M.E. Villiger, 'Articles 31 and 32 of the Vienna Convention on the Law of Treaties in the Case-Law of the European Court of Human Rights', in J. Bröhmer *et al.* (eds), *Internationale Gemeinschaft und Menschenrechte. Festschrift für G. Ress* (Köln–Berlin–München: Heymanns, 2005) 317 *et seq*. See, eg, the 1975 *Golder v United Kingdom judgment*, Series A, No. 18, para. 30, in which the European Court referred to the means of interpretation in Article 31 as constituting a 'unity'.

Conversely, the Inter-American Human Rights Court has traditionally referred solely to the means of Article 31(1).[65] Similarly, the Court of Arbitration in the 1977 *Beagle Channel Arbitration (Argentina v Chile)* resorted 'in the first place (to) an analysis of the text',[66] and the Arbitral Tribunal in the 1986 *La Bretagne Arbitration (Canada v France)* referred to the means in Article 31(1).[67] In the 1985 *Maritime Delimitation Arbitral Award (Guinea v Guinea-Bissau)*, the Court of Arbitration found that: '(the text) must be interpreted in good faith, with each word being given its ordinary meaning within the context and in the light of the object and purpose of the Convention'.[68]

State practice is inconsistent.[69] Some examples—eg the courts of *Canada*[70]—seem to confirm a broad use of all means of interpretation in Article 31. Other examples—eg practice from Israel,[71] Italy,[72] Switzerland,[73] the UK,[74] and apparently also the US[75]—appear to indicate that domestic courts frequently rely on Article 31(1).

Indeed, the predominance of the treaty text would appear to be confirmed by the comparatively small number of cases on interpretation reported in the compilations of domestic practice. Since every treaty application presupposes treaty

[65] See, eg, the 1984 *Costa Rica Naturalization Provisions*, Advisory Opinion, 79 *ILR* (1989) at 292, para. 22; the 1986 *Right to Reply*, Advisory Opinion, ibid. at 342; the 1985 *Meaning of 'Laws'*, Advisory Opinion, ibid. at 329, para. 13; the 1987 *Velasquez Rodriguez Case*, Preliminary Objections, ibid. 95 (1994) at 243–4, para. 30; and the 1987 *Habeas Corpus in Emergency Situations*, Advisory Opinion, ibid. 96 (1994) at 396–7, para. 14.

[66] Ibid. 52 (1977) 127; see also M.E. Villiger, *Customary International Law and Treaties. A Study of Their Interactions and Interrelations with Special Consideration of the 1969 Vienna Convention on the Law of Treaties*, *supra* note 14, n. 503.

[67] 82 *ILR* (1990) at 620, para. 37.

[68] 77 *ILR* (1988) at 658, para. 46; see ibid. para. 57, the reference to paras 2 and 3.

[69] See M.E. Villiger, *Customary International Law and Treaties. A Study of Their Interactions and Interrelations with Special Consideration of the 1969 Vienna Convention on the Law of Treaties*, nn. 484–98, *supra*, note 14.

[70] See, eg, the 1990 *Hagermann v US and Others Case*, Canadian Court of Appeal, 92 *ILR* (1993) at 725; C.C. Emmanuelli and S. Slosar, 'L'application et l'interprétation des traités internationaux par le juge canadien', 13 *Revue Juridique Thémis* (1978) at 69 *et seq.* ('le juge canadien [...] tient compte de la pratique des Etats qui a trait au texte interprété, conformément aux dispositions de l'Article 31 al. 2 et 3').

[71] See, eg, the 1988 Judgment of the Israel Supreme Court, 83 *ILR* (1990) at 131–2.

[72] See, eg, the 1987 Judgment of the Italian Court of Cassation, 101 *ILR* (1995) at 377 and 379.

[73] See, eg, the 1986 and 1997 Judgments of the Swiss Federal Court, *Schweizerisches Bundesgericht* 112 V 341, and 123 I 121, respectively. While the latter judgment refers to the means in subparas 3(b) and (c), it qualifies them (only) as 'd'importants moyens auxiliaries d'interprétation'.

[74] See, eg, the statement of the UK Minister of State, Foreign and Commonwealth Office in Parliament, 57 *BYIL* (1986) at 559–60; the UK government's Memorandum of 31 May 1990 in the *US/UK Arbitration Concerning Heathrow Airport User Charges*, 63 *BYIL* (1992) at 709, referred to the 'object and purpose of a treaty (as) a secondary or ancillary process in the application of the general rule'.

[75] See D.J. Bederman, *Classical Canons: Rhetoric, Classicism and Treaty Interpretation* (London: Ashgate Publishing, 2001); Ibid., 'Revivalist Canons and Treaty Interpretation', 41 *University of California at Los Angeles Law Review* (1994) at 972, for whom '[t]here is greater conflict today than ever before between U.S. practice and more international approaches to treaty interpretation'; see also ibid., at 973: 'resort to extrinsic evidence of the parties' intent [...] is meant to be only an exceptional occurrence'.

interpretation, reported cases should actually be abundant. The fact that they are not suggests that, in most cases, courts view the treaty terms as 'clear' and, in the light of the clear (ie ordinary) meaning rule, do not consider that the case in question calls for interpretation.

Three reasons appear to account for these developments. First, various approaches can be read into Articles 31 and 32 precisely because the ILC intended them to serve as a compromise to satisfy textualists, subjectivists, and teleologists. Secondly, the original Waldock Report III did indeed have a certain textual predisposition. Thirdly, somewhat unfortunately—and here indeed lies a misunderstanding—the forceful United States campaign in Vienna most likely led to this conclusion: because its delegation criticized the alleged textuality of Articles 31 and 32, a *rejection* of the US amendment appeared to imply that the articles were textual.

7. Miscarriage? Articles 31 and 32 *Qua* Customary International Law and *Qua* Contractual Obligation

So far, the intended meaning and scope of Articles 31 and 32 have been analysed, and it has been shown how these provisions have been applied in practice. The apparent discrepancy leads to the question whether these provisions were in any way a success—or indeed a miscarriage. Thus, in 1970, shortly after the Vienna Convention's adoption, Professor D.P. O'Connell was quite pessimistic when he made a somewhat stark prediction:

> [T]he priorities inherent in the application of (Articles 31 to 33) are not clearly indicated and the rules themselves are in part so general that it is necessary to review traditional methods whenever interpreting a treaty. The danger in these rules is that States will argue that they are comprehensive of the canons of interpretation, whereas they are selective and themselves ambiguous. More controversy is likely to be aroused by them than allayed.[76]

The 'success' of Articles 31 and 32 can be appreciated in various respects. The first means is to assess their nature as customary international law. For if Articles 31 and 32 were to apply even without a contractual obligation, on the basis of unwritten law, surely this would demonstrate a measure of 'success'. The second means is to look at the contractual significance of the 1969 Vienna Convention, ie at the number of states which have accepted to be bound, *inter alia*, by Articles 31 and 32.

7.1. Basis of customary international law

In view of the unsettled pre-1969 situation, in particular the various methods of interpretation, a customary rule on interpretation could not have arisen before the ILC took up the matter. The ILC, while attempting to 'isolate and codify

[76] D.P. O'Connell, *International Law* (London: Stevens, 2nd edn, 1970) at 253.

the basic rules of interpretation', reached consensus only at an advanced stage on the (hence originally innovative) structure of the 'General Rule' in Article 31.[77] At the Vienna Conference in 1968 and 1969 these provisions were adopted unanimously. Since 1969 there has been a growing conviction among states and courts[78] that Article 31 is declaratory of customary law. The Court has been adamant in its view that Articles 31 and 32 reflect customary international law.[79] Authors differ in their views.[80]

It can, therefore, be said that, based on state and court practice, there is indeed emerging customary law on the means of interpretation in Articles 31 and 32 which originated in Vienna in 1968/69 on the basis of the 1966 ILC Draft Articles. This customary basis of Articles 31 and 32 implies that states will use these means of interpretation on the basis of unwritten rules—and even if they have not ratified the 1969 Vienna Convention. However, the picture is not sufficiently unequivocal, particularly since these provisions leave considerable flexibility to the interpreting agency.

As pointed out above, a different conclusion may be drawn in respect of the customary nature of the *structure* of the 'General Rule'. The ILC intended the 'General Rule' to be a 'crucible' in which the text served as a starting point, and all means were of equal value and had to be equally employed. As regards Article 32,

[77] *YILC* (1966), vol. II, at 219, para. 7.

[78] See, in addition to the references in M.E. Villiger, *Customary International Law and Treaties. A Study of Their Interactions and Interrelations with Special Consideration of the 1969 Vienna Convention on the Law of Treaties*, *supra* note 14, nn. 484–506; the 1987 *Habeas Corpus in Emergency Situations* of the Inter-American Court of Human Rights, *supra* note 65, at 3967–98, para. 14 ('rules of interpretation set out in the [Convention] may be deemed to state the relevant international law principles'); the Australian High Court in the *Commonwealth of Australia et al. v Tasmania et al. Case* (Gibbs C.J.), *supra* note 49, at 304 ('[Articles 31 and 32] do no more than endorse or confirm the existing practice'); and the Swiss Federal Court, *Schweizerisches Bundesgericht* 122 II 238, for whom Article 31 is codificatory. According to R. Gardiner, 'Treaty Interpretation in the English Courts since *Fothergill v Monarch Airlines* (1980)', 44 *ICLQ* (1995) at 622, British court practice accepts Articles 31 and 32 as customary. *Contra* K.J. Vandevelde, 'Treaty Interpretation From a Negotiator's Perspective', 21 *Vanderbilt Journal of Trade Law* (1988) at 296 ('it is unclear that courts in practice really adhere to international law as codified in Articles 31 and 32').

[79] See, eg, ICJ, *Legality of Use of Force Case (Serbia and Montenegro v Belgium)*, *supra* note 63, at 318, para. 100 ('customary international law, reflected in Article 31'); *LaGrand (Germany v United States of America)*, Judgment of 27 June 2001, *ICJ Reports* (2001) at 501, para. 99 ('customary international law [...] reflected in Article 31'); *Kasikili/Sedudu Island* (Botswana/Namibia), *supra* note 62, at 1059, para. 18 ('neither Botswana nor Namibia are parties to the [Convention], but [...] both of them consider that Article 31 [...] is applicable inasmuch as it reflects customary international law'); the 1991 *Arbitral Award of 31 July 1989* (Guinea-Bissau/Senegal), Judgment of 12 November 1991, *ICJ Reports* (1991) at 69–70, para. 48 ('Articles 31 and 32 [...] may in many respects be considered a codification of existing customary international law on the point').

[80] For instance, H.F. Köck, *Vertragsinterpretation und Vertragsrechtskonvention* (Berlin: Dunker and Humboldt, 1976) *passim*, and G. Barile, 'La structure de l'ordre juridique international: règles générales et règles conventionnelles', 161 *Recueil des Cours* (1978-III), at 86, regard Article 31 as customary. G. Schwarzenberger, 'Myths and Realities of Treaty Interpretation. Articles 27–29 of the Vienna Draft Convention on the Law of Treaties', 9 *Va. J Int'l L* (1968) at 8 *et seq.* and at 19, para. 1, sees therein a departure from customary concepts; M.K. Yasseen, *supra* note 26, at 16, para. 24, sees progressive development in Article 31.

the ILC envisaged automatic resort to the supplementary means. In actual fact, states and courts have at times come to see Article 31 as entrenching a predominance of the text and a relatively subsidiary position of other means; and Article 32 as providing only limited recourse to its means. Hence, the important qualification is that the emerging customary rule does not appear to conform to the text of Articles 31 and 32. If and when such a customary rule will have developed, there is even the possibility that it may actually have modified the original provision.

On the whole, this evolving customary nature of Articles 31 and 32 at least confirms that states and courts concentrate in their practice on these provisions and indeed have come to consider that they are obliged by law—*opinio juris*—to apply these provisions. That in itself would appear to be a wonderful compliment to the provisions and confirm their acceptance in international law. Nevertheless, the picture is troubled by the fact that there are different interpretations of the structure of the 'General Rule' in Article 31. Still, this would at least appear to suffice to call in question the success of these provisions.

7.2. Contractual basis

After the Vienna Convention was adopted on 22 May 1969, 79 votes to one (*France*), with 19 abstentions, it was opened for signature the next day, on 23 May 1969.[81] Forty-five states signed the Convention, and of these 29 states ratified it. Clearly, this cannot be considered a success. The low number can be explained by the differences transpiring between states as to the settlement of disputes in Articles 65 *et seq.*;[82] some states indeed wished to introduce, by way of a convention on the law of treaties, a compulsory settlement of disputes in international law.

However, with the fall of the Berlin Wall and a certain distance from differences in Vienna, states have warmed to the Convention. In the meantime, 73 states have acceded to the Convention (a further eight states succeeded to it following the dissolution of the former Yugoslavia, and the former Czechoslovakia). Currently, the Convention counts 110 member states. It appears that among these member states all continents are equally reflected.

Since 1969, states have made various declarations to the Convention of which some are expressly declared as reservations, aiming to exclude or modify the legal effect of certain provisions, as in Article 2, subparagraph 1(d) of the Convention; others are stated to be declarations (often amounting in fact to interpretative declarations), while others again amount to objections to reservations, and of a fourth group it is not entirely clear what their purpose is.

[81] See on these statistics M.E. Villiger, 'Final Act Of The United Nations Conference On The Law Of Treaties' and 'Status Of The Convention', in *Commentary on the 1969 Vienna Convention on the Law of Treaties* (Netherlands: Martinus Nijhoff Publishers, 2009) at 999 *et seq.* and 1003 *et seq.*, respectively.

[82] See here M.E. Villiger, 'Article 65', ibid., n. 4.

It suffices here to point out that most reservations, declarations, and other instruments were directed against the Convention's provisions concerning dispute settlement and *jus cogens* (in particular Article 53). The others concerned Article 11 on the 'Means of expressing consent to be bound by a treaty', Article 25 on 'Provisional application', Article 38 on 'Rules in a treaty becoming binding on third states through international custom', Article 52 on the 'Coercion of a state by the threat or use of force', and Article 62 concerning the *clausula rebus sic stantibus*. In other words, no reservations or declarations were directed at Articles 31 and 32 on the means of interpretation.

In this context, it can further be pointed out that the 1969 Vienna Convention has served as a 'model' for the Vienna Convention on the Law of Treaties between States and International Organisations or Between International Organisations of 1986. (The 1986 Convention fills the gap left open in the 1969 Convention in Article 3 according to which that convention does not apply to international agreements concluded between states and other subjects of international law or between such other subjects of international law.) Here, it can be noted that the 1986 Convention takes over virtually *verbatim* the text of Articles 31 and 32.

Finally, one may wonder whether there have been any attempts at reforming Articles 31 and 32 of the Convention. For example, the International Law Commission has been aiming at presenting a draft on reservations to treaty, though the purpose is in fact to complement Articles 19–23 of the Convention. In respect of Articles 31 and 32, no such attempts—at least no official attempts[83]—have been made. The topics which have been or are currently being studied by the ILC only marginally concern the interpretation of treaties.[84]

On the whole, we are left with the picture that the Convention as a whole has attracted widespread support and is now applicable *qua* contractual obligation to 110 states. Whilst some reservations have been filed to the Convention, none of them concern Articles 31 and 32. Moreover, these provisions have been taken over by the 1986 Vienna Convention. Finally, there have been no attempts to reform or revise Articles 31 and 32. As a result, it can be said that also on the

[83] But see M. Ris, 'Treaty Interpretation and ICJ Recourse to *travaux préparatoires*: Towards a Proposed Amendment of Articles 31 and 32 of the Vienna Convention on the Law of Treaties', 14 *Boston College of International and Comparative Law Review* (1991) 111 *et seq.*, who at 135 proposes amendments to Article 32, in particular postulating that the International Court of Justice should determine which *travaux préparatoires* of a treaty may be employed.

[84] The ILC took up the following topics: (i) 'fragmentation of international law: difficulties arising from the diversification and expansion of international law'. In this respect, the ILC adopted the final Report in 2006, containing some remarks on Articles 30 and 31 subpara. 3(c) of the Convention without, however, calling them into question. See *YILC* (2004), vol. II (2), at 294 *et seq.* and ibid. (2006), vol. II (2), at 413 *et seq.*, respectively; (ii) 'treaties over time' which was included in the ILC's programme of work in 2008. The topic appears to relate to subsequent agreements and subsequent practice as in Article 31(3)(a) and (b); see *YILC* (2008), vol. II (2), at 355, para. 353; finally (iii) 'effects of armed conflicts on treaties', taken up by the ILC in 2008, aims to fill the gap Article 73 of the Convention left open, namely that it does not intend to prejudge any question that may arise in regard to a treaty, *inter alia*, following the outbreak of hostilities.

contractual level Articles 31 and 32 have come to be accepted by states and can, therefore, be considered a success.

Still, by way of comparison, it can be pointed out that other conventions have proved to be even more successful. The 1961 Vienna Convention on Diplomatic Relations has 186 parties, while the more recent 1982 UN Convention on the Law of the Sea has 158 parties. Of course, the comparatively low number of 110 parties to the 1969 Vienna Convention can be explained by the fact that non-states parties are aware that the latter has to a large extent become binding *qua* customary law (which, it is argued, is in itself an element of success),[85] and they do not, therefore, find it necessary formally to be bound by the instrument.

8. Conclusion

Some 70 years ago, the eminent Danish jurist Max Sørensen wrote in the context of the 1928 Havana Convention that:

> ... [t]he question, whether Article 18 can be applied to the convention of which it is itself a part [...] must probably be answered in the negative in conformity with the general principle of logic that a statement as to the validity or invalidity of a logical proposition cannot be applied to itself—a principle which like all other principles of logic must be interpreted in all legal interpretation.[86]

This question—the application of the various rules on the law of treaties (and in particular the rules of interpretation) to themselves—has subsequently occupied each new generation of international lawyers. Most recently, J. Kammerhofer has explained:

> ... [i]t is not a tautology that rules of interpretation also need to be interpreted—by their nature as norms rules on interpretation actually change the text to be interpreted and thus become part of the norm to be interpreted. Interpretation properly speaking is always beyond the reach of norms, for it is the connection between the human being and the text.[87]

It is hoped that this article served to demonstrate that Articles 31 and 32 of the Vienna Convention are successfully applied in daily practice in international law and can hardly be considered a failure. The misgivings would therefore appear unfounded. It may well be that international courts have occasionally employed these provisions as a 'fig leaf' behind which they have hidden whatever result of interpretation they wished to achieve in the first place. But this cannot call into question the value of Articles 31 and 32.

[85] See *supra* Section 7.1.

[86] 'The Modification of Collective Treaties Without the Consent of all the Contracting Parties', 9 *Acta Scandinavica Juris Gentium* (1938) at 153.

[87] J. Kammerhofer, 'Book Review on A. Orakhelashvili, The Interpretation of Acts and Rules in Public International Law', 20 *EJIL* (2008) at 1284.

To the contrary, courts and in particular states have accepted these provisions as constituting established norms of general international law and have duly and conscientiously applied them. Of course, it should immediately be added that courts in particular have only accepted with difficulty the full list of means of interpretation enshrined in Articles 31 and 32 as embodying the mandatory rule of interpretation.[88] The interesting development that courts may come to regard the 'General Rule' as corresponding with Article 31(1), or even to regard Article 31 as embodying solely the textual approach, goes back to the US delegation's forceful intervention in Vienna and can only be explained, as Briggs has noted, by an overly textual interpretation of Article 31 itself.[89]

On the whole, the ILC can be commended for its courage in devising norms on interpretation the codification of which remains unknown even to many domestic legal orders. Articles 31 and 32 lie at the centre of the Convention; arguably, they are its most important provisions. Thanks to Articles 31 and 32, 'the doctrinal discussion on the utility and even the existence of rules of international law governing the interpretation of treaties is now a thing of the past'.[90] Article 31 comes over as a masterpiece of precise drafting,[91] combining the various important means of interpretation. States remain free to agree to employ other means of interpretation. Article 32 provides for a valuable complement to the means in Article 31. It further offers welcome clarification as to the conditions and circumstances of resorting to the *travaux préparatoires* and other supplementary means of interpretation.

The 'General Rule' provides the interpreting agency with considerable flexibility, enabling it in particular to adapt the various means of interpretation to the type of treaty (bi- and multilateral treaties, human rights treaties, etc.).[92] This flexibility would nevertheless not appear to erode the legal certainty which *jus scriptum* is intended to provide.

[88] On the ICJ, see S. Torres Bernárdez, 'Interpretation of Treaties by the International Court of Justice Following the Adoption of the 1969 Vienna Convention on the Law of Treaties', *supra* note 45, at 722 ('initial silence'); J.I. Johnstone, 'Treaty Interpretation: The Authority of Interpretive Communities, who in a learned article in 1991 on the interpretation of international treaties did not appear to refer to Articles 31 and 32', 12 *Mich. J Int'l L* (1991) 371 *et seq.*

[89] A. Briggs, 'The *travaux préparatoires* of the Vienna Convention on the Law of Treaties', 65 *AJIL* (1971) at 709–10.

[90] S. Torres Bernárdez, 'Interpretation of Treaties by the International Court of Justice Following the Adoption of the 1969 Vienna Convention on the Law of Treaties', *supra* note 45, at 721.

[91] See the UK government's Memorandum of 31 May 1990 in the *US/UK Arbitration Concerning Heathrow Airport User Charges*, *supra* note 74, at 707 ('lapidary formula').

[92] C. McLachlan, 'The principle of systemic interpretation and Article 31(3)(c) of the Vienna Convention', *supra* note 40, at 291.

7

Evolutionary Interpretation of Treaties: Between Memory and Prophecy

Pierre-Marie Dupuy

'Every legal order is a challenge in time, an effort to conserve the social order that it establishes.'[1] This opinion by a great internationalist and legal philosopher, Michel Virally, appears to echo an observation made by Georges Ripert, who considered 'man to require guidance from a set of general and *permanent* rules'.[2] Both authors consider a quest for stability to be an inherent characteristic of Law, written here with a capital L! The Ten Commandments were already written in stone.[3]

However, to place too much emphasis on stability, albeit an essential component of every legal order, would neglect the temporal dimension of law. Moreover, stability presupposes adaptability; durability requires change. The Darwinian theory of evolution also applies to norms, which as Serge Sur has aptly noted have an almost organic life: 'they develop and survive if they are adapted to their environment and they are able to evolve with it'.[4] As a consequence, in addition to the structural solidity necessary for its longevity, law is made up of a series of adjustable variables, i.e. normative devices that serve to provide the flexibility necessary for the survival of law.

Although the notion of time is sometimes presented at conferences as posing difficulties for the law,[5] the legal scholar need not feel at a loss with the notion of time on the basis that it is one of the most fundamental philosophical problems. Time is a special subject of inquiry in legal philosophy because it is everywhere,

[1] M. Virally, *La pensée juridique* (Paris: Editions Panthéon-Assas, collection Les introuvables, 2nd edn, 1998; Paris: LGDJ, 1st ed., 1960).

[2] (Unofficial translation) 'la direction des hommes exige un ensemble des règles générales et *permanentes*', G. Ripert, *Les forces créatrices du droit* (Paris: LGDJ, 1955).

[3] M. Bretone, *Diritto e tempo nella tradizione europea* (Bari-Roma: Laterza, 2004) 1–329.

[4] S. Sur, *L'interprétation en droit international public* (Paris: LGDJ, 1974) at 81.

[5] J. Verhoeven, 'Les conséquences et les implications du temps en droit international', in *Le droit et le temps* (Paris: Pedone, Colloque SFDI, 2001) at 9 *et seq.*

including *in* the law. It permeates legal structures and relentlessly impacts upon them.[6]

Legal thinking and legal practice in contentious cases bring this to light on a daily basis. Two examples may be cited in this respect. First, the rule that sometimes reflects the 'fundamental norm' in a Kelsenian sense, *pacta sunt servanda*, can neither be understood nor applied except on the basis of a restrictive condition: *rebus sic stantibus*! Treaty obligations are maintained only to the extent that the facts upon which they are premised remain sufficiently constant. However, even if the preceding rule still remains difficult to plead in international proceedings, what is sure is that, as already asserted by Heraclitus of Ephesus, things *never* remain as they were. Secondly, facts—and internationally wrongful acts in particular—are notably categorized on the basis that they are either 'immediate' or 'continuing'. Furthermore, international practice demonstrates that there are few tribunals the jurisdiction of which is not challenged on the basis of its *ratione temporis*.

Of course, no norm can escape the notion of time! However, not all norms are affected by time in quite the same way. Custom follows its own ancient rhythm. For custom, time is of long duration if not always an eternal yesterday, to which it looks in order to establish a tradition by degrees of mimicry. In common law countries, the tradition of accumulating precedents creates law in conjunction with legislation. By contrast, legislation alone may be qualified as being temporally 'Promethean'. From the moment of its promulgation, a legislative act manifests an intention to change existing law, to establish a new set of rules to fulfil the desired objective. These same temporal characteristics are shared by the Constitution, the Law of all laws, and are accentuated by its greater pomp and solemnity. By formalizing an alliance between Nation and Law, a Constitution encompasses a foundational element that is derived from an account of its origins.[7] The Charter of the United Nations shares this characteristic to some extent, which is not, however, sufficient to consider it to be the 'Constitution of the international legal order'.[8] With respect to all these norms, it would be vain to ask whether they represent a future choice, or are a product of the past. Laetitia Gianformaggio is right to observe that they are, by definition, both, as will be discussed below.[9]

What about treaties? An intuitive response is that a treaty should be understood in contradistinction to custom, and by analogy with legislation. The date

[6] See in particular F. Ost and M. Van Hoecke, *Temps et droit. Le droit a-t-il pour vocation de durer? Time and law. Is it the Nature of Law to Last?* (Brussels: Bruylant, 1998) (hereinafter Ost and Van Hoecke, *Time and Law*). See also J. Combacau, 'L'écoulement du temps', in *Le droit et le temps*, *supra* note 5, at 77 *et seq.*; F. Ost and M. Van de Kerchove, 'Pluralisme temporel et changement. Les jeux du droit', in *Nouveaux itinéraires en droit. Hommages à François Rigaux* (Brussels: Bruylant, 1993) at 392.

[7] L. Gianformaggio, 'Temps de la constitution, temps de la consolidation', in Ost and Van Hoecke, *Time and Law*, *supra* note 6, at 339 *et seq.*

[8] P.M. Dupuy, 'L'unité de l'ordre juridique international—Cours général de droit international public', 297 *Recueil des Cours* (2002) at 215 *et seq.*

[9] *Supra* note 7.

of its entry into force marks the coming into being of a new intention, defined by reference to its provisions, its objectives to fulfil, and by the rights and obligations that it thereby sets in motion. However, one immediately perceives that an analogy between treaties and legislation cannot be stretched too far. Although it is somewhat risky to generalize in relation to treaties, time seems to be more brittle, its duration more precarious, for treaties than for municipal legislation. The reason lies in the necessity of maintaining a continuing concordance of all parties who are each, at least formally, bestowed with sovereign equality. Now, a treaty is subject to many interpretations, and each party consequently strives to protect itself, its own interests, from the ulterior motives of other parties underlining the reasons for their consent to be bound.

Indeed, a treaty is never etched in stone because sovereigns refuse to be bound in perpetuity.[10] If a treaty no longer responds adequately to the situation for which it was designed to apply, at least according to one party, it may, of course, be revised. Nevertheless, to counter the possibility of a treaty being too easily modified, the process of revision frequently stipulates more or less demanding procedural requirements, depending on the treaty in question, with the end result that modification is not actually possible or remains at least uneasy to perform. Permissible modifications to a treaty that take into account the passing of time thus often require a new interpretation of its terms. To this end, a judge is often requested to redefine the meaning of a treaty without altering its nature. Such a manner of interpreting treaties, sometimes called an *evolutionary* interpretation, is no mean feat. In many cases the very survival of the agreement and its applicability to present-day concerns are at stake.[11]

Although judges are not alone in undertaking an evolutionary interpretation of a text, they will form the focus of the discussion that follows. Judges are not always in the same legal and political position to undertake a dynamic reading of the agreement before them. Certain cases bring into sharp relief what René-Jean Dupuy termed the '*ordre relationnel*' (relational order), namely the classical horizontal relationship that exists between equal sovereigns. This will be the case where the judge is exercising jurisdiction based solely on the consent of the parties. In such cases, the international judge will take particular care in ensuring that his interpretation is based on the will of the parties as manifested in the past, in order to breathe new life into the terms of the treaty without changing them. A more or less new reading of the treaty will thus be driven by the memory of the intention of the parties.

Conversely, in other cases, a judge will be emboldened to undertake a more dynamic interpretation of a treaty where he does not simply act as an arbitrator between the parties, but rather occupies the role of a guardian of a common

[10] A. Wijffels, 'La validité *rebus sic stantibus* des conventions: quelques étapes de développement historique', in Ost and M. Van Oecke, *Time and Law, supra* note 6, at 247.

[11] T. Georgopoulos, 'Le droit intertemporel et les dispositions conventionnelles évolutives', 108 *RGDIP* (2004) 123–47.

institution. In such cases, the institutional mandate conferred upon the judge will provide him with the necessary authority and legitimacy to demonstrate the preferred approach to adopt for the furtherance of a collective plan. The judge does not act in such cases as a mere instrument of the parties. He exercises an institutionalized judicial power the purpose of which is to ensure the continuing existence of objectives articulated by a community, and he will thus interpret meaning pursuant to these communal interests. To use the words of Chief Justice Wendell Holmes, in such a case evolutionary interpretation is not simply an exercise of memory; it tends towards prophecy.[12]

1. Evolutionary Interpretation Supported by Memory

Evolutionary interpretation may be said to be supported by memory to the extent that it is based on the will of the parties, as manifested in the past, and often expressed in the very terms of the treaty. It is not a matter of giving a meaning to the text that was unintended by its authors; rather, it is the task of the judge to ensure that a new reading is undertaken in such a way as to reflect the common desire of the parties as if they had renegotiated the same agreement taking into account the circumstances that have since evolved. This first form of evolutionary interpretation is considered by its supporters to amount to a loyal translation of the will of the parties, as opposed to a deliberate betrayal of this will.

This form of evolutionary interpretation raises two questions which will each be examined in turn: first, the question of the choice of methods to adopt, which is to a large extent codified under Article 31 of the Vienna Convention of the Law of Treaties; second, the question of determining the point in time with respect to which the applicable law for the interpretation of the treaty provisions may be established. These two issues are interwoven, and although pedagogical reasons require them to be addressed separately, it is important to stress that they constitute two sides of the same coin.

1.1. In his celebrated book on the law of treaties in light of the Vienna Convention, Sir Ian Sinclair explains why the codifiers were quickly confronted with questions of 'intertemporal law' particularly in relation to how to define the 'ordinary meaning to be given to the terms of the treaty' pursuant to Article 31(1) of the Convention.[13] During a second reading, the International Law Commission (ILC) members chose to address this thorny question in the third paragraph of the said article, which for the purpose of interpretation envisages the applicability of 'any relevant rules of international law applicable on the relations between

[12] W. Holmes, 'The Path of the Law', 10 *Harv. L Rev.* (1897) at 458.

[13] Sir I. Sinclair, *The Vienna Convention on the Law of Treaties* (Manchester: Manchester University Press, 2nd edn, 1984) at 138.

parties'. Sir Ian explained that this *renvoi* served to ensure that 'every treaty provision [...] be read not only in its context, but in the wider context of general international law'.

The explanation provided by Sir Ian is particularly enlightening given that he was a member of the Commission. It does not, however, provide an entirely satisfactory answer to why Articles 31 and 32 remain silent on the question of evolutionary interpretation. Other paragraphs also refer to a temporal dimension in the interpretation of a treaty, such as Article 31(3)(b), which provides that 'any subsequent practice in the application of the treaty which establishes the agreement of the parties regarding its interpretation' may be taken into account. Nevertheless, the Vienna Convention remains largely mute on how temporal considerations should operate in determining the meaning of treaty provisions and, as will be discussed later, for determining the relevant period for a determination of the applicable international law. There is thus a lacuna in the rules of the Convention that provides some room to manoeuvre for those wishing to adopt an evolutionary interpretative approach.

In reality, there is a solid tradition of viewing dynamic interpretation with some suspicion on the basis that it risks giving the judge too much licence not to scrupulously respect the will of the parties as expressed in the treaty instrument. Two opinions may be cited in support of this attitude, and although these opinions are now quite dated, they warrant consideration given that they were expressed by two particularly eminent legal counsel: Charles de Visscher and Sir Gerald Fitzmaurice.

Charles de Visscher noted in *Problèmes d'interprétation judiciare en droit international public* that '[t]he purpose of interpretation is not to perfect an instrument, to adapt it more or less to achieve what may be deemed to be the logically postulated objective, but to shed light on the real intention of the parties'.[14]

Sir Gerald appears to add to the chorus:

> The objectives of a treaty do not exist in the abstract; they derive from the intention of the parties and expressed in the terms of the treaty or as evidenced by them and are closely in relation to them as they are their only source [...]. They (the intentions of the parties) cannot be introduced afterwards in the guise of objectives which were not contemplated at the time.[15]

According to the approach expressed in these two opinions, the appropriate method of interpretation of treaties is that which is set out in the first paragraph

[14] C. De Visscher, *Problèmes d'interprétation judiciaire en droit international public* (Paris: Pedone, 1963), the English translation of which is found in F. Ost, 'The Original Canons of Interpretation of the European Court of Human Rights', in M. Delmas-Marty (ed.), *The European Convention for the Protection of Human Rights: International Protection Versus National Restrictions* (Dordrecht: Martinus Nijhoff Publishers, 1992) at 288.

[15] Cited by F. Ost, 'The Original Canons of Interpretation of the European Court of Human Rights', *supra* note 14. Commentary by Sir Gerald on the European Court of Human Rights case of *National Union of Belgian Police*, Judgment of 27 October 1975, Series A, No. 19, at 33.

of Article 31: to read the text by giving its terms their ordinary meaning at the moment of the conclusion of the treaty. Consequently, it is argued, the judge should not inopportunely intervene by attempting to determine the meaning to be attributed to a treaty through the use of the incontrollable criterion of the object and purpose of the treaty. Such a Praetorian interpretative exercise is too dynamic and insufficiently respectful to the original will of the parties. The treaty's object and purpose is at risk of being changed by the judge. Memory must remain loyal and not serve to rewrite history; a treaty belongs to its authors and not to the judge.

In line with this approach, 'good faith' under Article 31(1) not only refers to the good faith of the parties, but also to the good faith of the judge. The judge must reflect upon the true meaning and scope of the terms employed at the time of the drafting of the treaty by taking into account the will of the parties, and he must not be guided by ulterior motives. Even leaving aside the notion of 'ordinary meaning', which remains debatable, this approach would require the judge to take on the role of a historian, particularly if the treaty to be applied is quite old. According to the same approach, resort should not be had to the 'context' under paragraph 2 of Article 31, and to the 'preparatory work' of the treaty under Article 32, unless necessary in order to determine the original intention of the parties to the agreement.

Does this mean that an evolutionary interpretation of a treaty will always be prohibited because it does not assist in determining the will of the parties? Case law has attempted to provide an answer to this question, and in so doing, cases have adopted successive responses to the question: what is the relevant point in time for determining the applicable law for the interpretation of a treaty?

1.2. The traditional position taken to answering this question was first articulated in the arbitral award handed down by Max Huber in the celebrated case of the *Island of Palmas*, in which he stated that 'a juridical fact must be appreciated in the light of the law contemporary with it, and not of the law in force at the time when a dispute in regard to it arises or falls to be settled'.[16] This approach was adopted by the Permanent Court of International Justice (PCIJ) in the *S.S. Wimbledon Case*, and was also taken up by the International Court of Justice (ICJ), notably in the *Case concerning rights of nationals of the United States of America in Morocco*.[17] As will be discussed below, the approach of the Court is different in the context of advisory proceedings, where it exercises a much more dynamic approach to interpretation.

It is thus unsurprising that it was precisely in an Advisory Opinion, namely the *Legal Consequences for States of the Continued Presence of South Africa in Namibia,*

[16] *Island of Palmas case*, I *RIAA* (1928), 829 *et seq.*, at 845.

[17] ICJ, *Rights of Nationals of the United States of America in Morocco (France v United States of America)*, Judgment of 27 August 1952, *ICJ Reports* (1952) at 189.

notwithstanding Security Council Resolution 276 (1970), that the Court changed its approach to the question. In this Advisory Opinion, the Court recalled that it was 'mindful [...] of the primary necessity of interpreting an instrument in accordance with the intentions of the parties at the time of its conclusion'; however, the Court also noted that 'the concepts embodied in Article 22 of the Covenant—the strenuous conditions of the modern world and the well-being and development of the people concerned—were not static, but were by definition evolutionary, as also, therefore, was the concept of the "sacred trust" (of civilisation). The parties to the Covenant must consequently be deemed to have accepted them as such.'[18]

The Court concluded a little later in the generalized form of an *obiter dictum* as follows: 'Moreover, an international instrument has to be interpreted and applied within the framework of the entire legal system prevailing at the time of the interpretation.'

The passage above prompts the following three reflections:

- First, the Court took great care in recalling the requirement of respect for the will of the parties—in the case at hand, the parties to the Covenant of the League of Nations—as limiting the scope of its interpretation;
- Secondly, the Court noted that the parties themselves had chosen to incorporate concepts and notions in the text of the Covenant that were of an evolving character open to political and social transformation;
- Thirdly, in the form of an *obiter dictum* as mentioned above, the Court set out a rule of interpretation of universal application that was by no means limited to certain types of treaty instruments (such as constitutive documents of a new international system or an international institution), but which applies to all types of 'international instruments'.

The Court has adopted a similar interpretative approach in subsequent cases, not only in advisory proceedings but also in contentious cases. In the *Case concerning the Gabčíkovo-Nagymaros Project* the Court had to interpret in 1997 the terms of a bilateral treaty concluded 20 years earlier, in 1977, between two Socialist countries concerning the construction of an integrated system of hydroelectric dams. The Court observed in relation to the bilateral treaty that the subsequent practice of the parties manifested that the terms of the instrument were open to renegotiation (para. 138). This case is generally cited as a step in the direction of a dynamic interpretation of treaties. It is important, however, to emphasize a point that commentators—no doubt influenced by the Separate Opinion of Judge Bedjaoui—sometimes neglect: the Court did not itself undertake an evolutionary interpretation of the terms of the 1977 treaty. Rather, the Court recommended

[18] ICJ, *Legal Consequences for States of the Continued Presence of South Africa in Namibia (South West Africa) notwithstanding SC Resolution 276 (1970)*, Advisory Opinion of 21 June 1971, *ICJ Reports* (1971) at 31, para. 53.

that the parties, when renegotiating the terms of the treaty in conformity with its Article 5, take into account the significant normative developments and new standards of the law governing the protection of the international environment that had developed during the period from the conclusion of the bilateral treaty in 1977 to the moment of its revision (after September 1997). It is in this limited context that the Court's statements must be read, namely that

> ... in order to evaluate the environmental risk, current standards must be taken into consideration. This is not only allowed by the wording of Articles 15 and 19, but even prescribed, to the extent that these articles impose a continuing—and thus necessarily evolving—obligation on the parties to maintain the quality of the water of the Danube and to protect nature.[19]

Later in its judgment the Court explains the evolutionary approach which it invites the parties to adopt in the renegotiation of the treaty terms, and not in the interpretation of the treaty, as follows:

> Owing to new scientific insights and to a growing awareness of the risks for mankind—for present and for future generations—of pursuit of such interventions at an unconsidered and unabated pace, new norms and standards have been developed, set forth in a great number of instruments during the last two decades. Such new norms have to be taken into consideration, and such standards given weight, not only when States contemplate new activities but also when continuing with activities begun in the past.[20]

This strong position taken by the Court with respect to the necessity of taking into account the particularly abundant normative developments in environmental law is not, however, imposed upon third parties. Paying attention to the evolution in progress was an issue to govern the behaviour of the parties during the renegotiation of the Treaty. It would be erroneous to view the *Case concerning the Gabčíkovo-Nagymaros Project* as a break with previous case law, which maintained a link with the will of the parties. Rather, it was the negotiable character of the Treaty provisions in that case that the Court drew upon in order to situate the subsequent practice of the parties. Earlier in the judgment, at para. 104, the Court noted that it was 'the formulation of Articles 15, 19 and 20, designed to accommodate change (which) made it possible for the parties to take account of such developments and to apply them when implementing these treaty provisions'.

The ICJ clarified the will of the parties; it did not substitute its own will for theirs. There is a link with the approach adopted in this case, with the position the Court took in the *Namibia Case* insofar as the Court refers to the law at the moment of interpreting a treaty.

The same approach is again followed in a recent case where the Court took an evolutionary interpretative approach to a treaty text the adaptability of which was brought into question by the parties. In the *Case concerning the River San Juan* of

[19] ICJ, *Gabčíkovo-Nagymaros Project* (*Hungary/Slovakia*), Judgment of 25 September 1997, *ICJ Reports* (1997) at 78, para. 140.

[20] Ibid.

13 July 2009, the Court was called upon to interpret the term 'commerce' in the 1858 treaty concluded between the two parties to the dispute. In so doing, the Court stated:

> Though adopted in connection with the interpretation of a reservation to a treaty, the Court's reasoning in that case is fully transposable for purposes of interpreting the terms themselves of a treaty. It is founded on the idea that, where the parties have used generic terms in a treaty, the parties necessarily having been aware that the meaning of the terms was likely to evolve over time, and where the treaty has been entered into for a very long period or is 'of continuing duration', the parties must be presumed, as a general rule, to have intended those terms to have an evolving meaning.[21]

In this case, the Court verified the existence of such a situation and concluded that the intention manifested by the parties was that the Treaty 'was entered into for an unlimited duration'. This implies an evolutionary interpretation of the term 'commerce', and thus an interpretation contrary to the position taken by Nicaragua, who favoured a traditional interpretative approach that takes into account the applicable law and the meaning of the terms at the moment of the conclusion of the Treaty.

Where evolutionary interpretation is not undertaken in a clearly defined institutional context, it will be characterized by a levelheaded audacity. In such cases, the following rule will apply: bearing in mind the legal context in which the treaty was drafted, there is a presumption in favour of the applicable law for treaty interpretation being the law that prevailed not only at the time of conclusion of the treaty, but also the law that prevails at the time of the interpretation of the treaty. It will be left to each jurisdiction to decide in each particular case which law to apply. According to the current state of positive international law, the ICJ only allows for a dynamic interpretation of a treaty where justified by notions and concepts in the terms of the treaty from which it may be inferred that the text is open to considerations of factual or legal evolution after the conclusion of the treaty. International jurisdictions may act more boldly when they are called upon to interpret treaties the object of which is to establish new international institutions with a view to promoting a collective project.

2. Evolutionary Interpretation towards Prophecy

An international judge charged with the task of interpreting a treaty that establishes an organization designed to achieve a shared purpose, must respect the will of all the parties. It generally transpires that in such cases the judge is less bound by the consent of each individual party. The judge is the depositary of a

[21] ICJ, *Case concerning the Dispute Regarding Navigational and Related Rights (Costa Rica v Nicaragua)*, Judgment of 13 July 2009, paras 66–67, not yet reported, available at <http://www.icj-cij.org>.

common finality, the outcome of which he is there to assist. The collective institution thus overrides individual consent. The Court thus uses individualized disputes to remind all parties of the route that each one of them must follow in order to achieve the collective goal.

In this vein, the international judge brings to mind the constitutional judge in domestic legal orders, and one thinks of Oliver Wendell Homes, judge of the Supreme Court of the United States of America, who affirmed in 1897 that 'the primary rights and duties with which jurisprudence busies itself again are nothing but prophesies'.[22] Such an attitude often generates, as a side-effect, allegations of 'judicial activism', and leads one to question how far a dynamic interpretation should be taken.

2.1. The ICJ has already evinced a tendency to act less like a loyal servant to the individual intention of the parties, and more like an artisan with a dynamic vision of the common design. This is particularly the case where the Court is exercising its advisory jurisdiction. In this role, the Court acts as the 'principal judicial organ of the United Nations', pursuant to the Charter. The first Advisory Opinions that the ICJ handed down during the life of the United Nations (UN) are in this respect emblematic. The most audacious of these undoubtedly remains the 1949 Advisory Opinion concerning *Reparations for Injuries Suffered in the Service of the United Nations*.[23] It will be recalled that in this case, the Court did not hesitate in deducing from the terms of the Charter, and particularly from its aims, that the Organization possessed an international legal personality.[24]

Although it is important to distinguish the one from the other, it may be noted that much of the time a dynamic interpretation amounts to a teleological interpretation, the aim of which is a quest for practical effect, as that approach has been borrowed from the Supreme Court of the United States of America.[25] At this point, an interpretation of the object and purpose assigned to a treaty does not elicit in the judge the same care advocated by Charles de Visscher and Sir Gerald Fitzmaurice in the context of a classic bilateral context.[26] To take the case of the 1970 Advisory Opinion concerning *Namibia*, the Court noted in an *obiter dictum* that 'an international instrument has to be interpreted and applied within the framework of the entire legal system prevailing at the time of the interpretation', which in turn contributes to the popularity of the dynamic interpretation

[22] *Supra* note 12.

[23] ICJ, *Reparation for Injuries Suffered in the Service of the United Nations*, Advisory Opinion of 11 April 1949, *ICJ Reports* (1949) 174 *et seq.*

[24] See the author's commentary in 'L'unité de l'ordre juridique international', *supra* note 8, at 107 *et seq.*, in relation to the conclusions that may be drawn from this fundamental opinion with respect to the general theory of subjects in international law.

[25] In the celebrated case of *Marbury v Madison*, 5 U.S. (1 Cranch) (1803) at 137.

[26] Charles de Visscher himself noted: 'C'est dans l'interprétation des traités normatifs et des traités d'organisations internationales que la notion de l'objet et du but revêt toute son ampleur.' C. de Visscher, *Problèmes d'interprétation judiciaire en droit international public, supra* note 14, at 65.

of ordinary treaties (that is, treaties which are not the constitutive instruments of organizations). It is worth recalling that it was in relation to the end of mandates established under the League of Nations, a system that was inherited by the UN, that the Court made its findings concerning the contemporary meaning to be given to this institution.

The move towards a prophetic designation of the treaty purposes to be achieved has particular force in the context of certain regional international organizations. In this respect, the role of the European Court of Justice (ECJ) is of particular importance. As the ECJ noted in 1982 in the case of *CILFIT*,[27] 'every provision of Community law must be placed in its context and interpreted in the light of the provisions of Community law as a whole, regard being had to the objectives thereof and to its state of evolution at the date on which the provision in question is to be applied'. The Court seated in Luxembourg made clear in its earliest cases that it would take a particularly bold approach to interpretation based on the radical specificity of the legal order of the European Community. Although the ECJ is itself international, and integrated into the international legal order, it distinguishes itself by a number of different traits. The celebrated cases concerning the direct applicability and the primacy of community law remain emblematic in this respect.[28] The case law of the European Community will not be the focus here precisely because of its unique character. Indeed, the purpose of the European Community treaties is quasi-federal, insofar as they are means toward the progressive realization of an organization of integration based on the partial, but very real, transfer of powers by each member state to the communitarian executive. The focus here will instead be the case law of the European Court of Human Rights (ECHR) which demonstrates both the application and the limits of evolutionary interpretation.

The preamble to the European Convention on Human Rights of 4 November 1950 recalls that 'the aim of the Council of Europe is the achievement of greater unity between its members and that one of the methods by which the aim is to be pursued is the maintenance and *further realization* of Human Rights and Fundamental Freedoms'. It is noteworthy that from the very beginning, particular emphasis has been placed on the progressive and evolutionary character of the 'collective enforcement of certain of the Rights stated in the Universal Declaration'. The ECHR[29] remains loyal in its application of the methods of interpretation set out in Articles 31 and 32 of the 1969 Vienna Convention, to which the Court explicitly has made reference, for example in the case of *Golder*

[27] Case No. 283/81 *Srl CILFIT and Lanificio di Gavardo SpA v Ministry of Health*, [1982] ECR 3415; G. Gaja, *Introduzione al Diritto Communitario* (Roma-Bari: Laterza 2007); D. Simon, *Le système juridique communautaire* (Paris: PUF, 3rd edn, 2001) at 376.

[28] Case C-34/89 *Van Gend en Loos* [1963] ECR 1; Case C-6/64 *Costa v ENEL* [1964] ECR 1127; see G. Gaja, *Introduzione al Diritto Communitario, supra* note 27.

[29] The purpose of the ECHR is to settle disputes between a state and individuals under that state's jurisdiction who ground their claims of human rights violations on the basis of the Convention and its Protocols.

of 21 December 1975.[30] Equally, the ECHR has been assisted by the preamble of the Convention to look towards the future. The Court has referred to the purposes to be achieved and the efforts to be made by states, who are viewed by the ECHR both as parties to the Convention and as members of the Council of Europe, in order for their acts and internal legislation to conform with their international obligations.[31]

This led the Strasbourg bench to affirm in 1978, in the case of *Ireland v the United Kingdom*, that: '[u]nlike international treaties of the classic kind, the Convention comprises more than mere reciprocal engagements between contracting states. It creates, over and above a network of mutual, bilateral undertakings, objective obligations which, in the words of the Preamble benefit from a "collective enforcement".'[32]

The case at hand concerned the promotion of the application of human rights in accordance with a treaty that establishes 'objective obligations', namely obligations to which the logic of reciprocity does not apply. This in turn reinforces the 'objective' character of the interpretative approach adopted by the ECHR according to which the Court moved away from too literal an understanding of the will of each of the parties. The ECHR is confronted by a double dynamic which must be taken into account in its case law: on the one hand, the rights affirmed in the 1950 Convention and in the internal legislation of member states, including their constitutions, and which appear open to evolutionary interpretation; on the other hand, what is in reality the cause and effect of the first dynamic, namely the evolution of ethical concepts embedded in the social fabric of the different member states which produce a number of practices.

In particular, the European case law has tried to take into account different ways of living, including by reference to developments in scientific and social research. For example, this has been the case with the difficult question of transexuality, as the cases of *Rees v the United Kingdom*[33] and *Sheffield and Horsham v the United Kingdom*,[34] illustrate. At the crossroads of these two dynamics are 'legal standards' which vary from one country to the next, and which progressively change. The Court has made reference to the need to consider such standards in the cases that come before it, for example, in the case of *Guzzardi v Italy*.[35]

Despite this double necessity for flexibility, recourse to evolutionary interpretation is not unproblematic, nor is it the only option open to the ECHR. The

[30] *Golder v United Kingdom*, Judgment of 21 December 1975, Series A, No.18, para. 29 *et seq.*

[31] R. Bernhardt, 'Evolutive Treaty Interpretation, Especially of the European Convention of Human Rights', 42 *GYIL* (1999) 11–25; F. Rigaux, 'Interprétation consensuelle et interpretation évolutive', in *L'interprétation de la Convention européenne des droits de l'homme* (Brussels: Nemesis-Bruylant, 1998) 41–62; F. Ost, 'The Original Canons of Interpretation of the European Court of Human Rights', *supra* note 14.

[32] *Ireland v United Kingdom*, Judgment of 18 January 1978, Series A, No. 25, at 90, para. 239.

[33] *Rees v the United Kingdom*, Judgment of 17 October 1986, Series A, No. 106, para. 47.

[34] *Sheffield and Horsham v the United Kingdom*, Judgment of 30 July 1998, *RJD* 1998-V, paras 1–4.

[35] *Guzzardi v Italy*, Judgment of 6 November 1980, Series A, No. 39, para. 95.

Court disposes of other 'adjustable variables', including the 'margin of appreciation' which leaves it to each state party to determine the concrete application of certain issues, such as at what moment a foetus may be considered a 'human being'. The use of this margin of appreciation in many cases serves to do away with the need for the Court to provide a radical evolutionary interpretation of certain freedoms, as the case of *Rasmussen v Denmark,*[36] and the abovementioned case of *Sheffield and Horsham v the United Kingdom*, attest.[37]

However, if there is a statement that has become a sort of 'leitmotiv' in the case law of the ECHR, it must be that 'the convention is a living instrument which [...] must be interpreted in the light of present day conditions'. The Strasbourg Court applies what has become an adage to different areas in the protection of human rights among which may be mentioned patrimonial rights of children, as in the case of *Marckx v Belgium,*[38] conceptions of marriage (*Johnston and others v Ireland*),[39] and the penal policy of member states, such as in the cases of *Tyrer v the United Kingdom*[40] and *Soering v the United Kingdom,*[41] or the right to property in the celebrated case of *Loizidou v Turkey*.[42]

In having recourse to a dynamic interpretation of the terms of the European Convention in accordance with the development of social and legal standards that surface and transform in different member states, the Court does not, however, forget to maintain a link with the original intention of the parties. Similarly, the ECHR does not lose sight of the requirement for a degree of coherence with its earlier decisions. The ECHR thus attempts to establish a measure of equilibrium among these different considerations. In this vein, in the 2002 case of *Goodwin v the United Kingdom*, the Court stated:

> While the Court is not formally bound to follow its previous judgments, it is in the interest of legal certainty, foreseeability and equality before the law that it should not depart, without good reason, from precedents laid down in previous cases (see, for example, *Chapman v UK*, n° 27238/95, ECHR-I, para. 70). However, since the Convention is first and foremost a system for the protection of human rights, the Court must have regard to the changing conditions within the respondent state and within contracting states generally and respond, for example, to any evolving convergence as to the standards to be achieved (see, amongst other authorities, *the Cossey judgment*, para. 35, and *Stafford v UK*, n° 46295/99, paras 67–68). It is of crucial importance that the Convention is interpreted and applied in a manner which renders its rights practical and effective, not theoretical and illusory.[43]

[36] *Rasmussen v Denmark*, Judgment of 28 November 1984, Series A, No. 87, para. 40.

[37] *Supra* note 34.

[38] *Marckx v Belgium*, Judgment of 13 June 1979, Series A, No. 31, para. 58.

[39] *Johnston and others v Ireland*, Judgment of 18 December 1986, Series A, No. 112, para. 53.

[40] *Tyrer v the United Kingdom*, Judgment of 25 April 1978, Series A, No. 26, para. 31.

[41] *Soering v the United Kingdom*, Judgment of 7 July 1989, Series A, No. 161, paras 102–104.

[42] *Loizidou v Turkey*, Preliminary Objections, Judgment of 23 March 1995, Series A, No. 310, paras 70–71.

[43] *Goodwin v the United Kingdom*, Judgment of 11 July 2002, *RJD* 2002-VI, para. 6.

This concern for efficacy leading to a flexible interpretation of the Convention warrants particular attention as it constitutes a recurring theme in the case law of the ECHR, as the cases of *Airey v Ireland*[44] and *Stafford*[45] attest. It may be noted that the concern driving the ECHR to use its judgments in order to balance out a range of diverse factors which it must take into consideration, demonstrates the Court's awareness of the possible excesses, and the limit beyond which dynamic interpretation risks degenerating through an abuse of power.

2.2. Allegations of 'judicial activism', often invoked by states and sometimes supported to a lesser or greater extent by legal scholarship, like the allegations made in relation to some of the reports emanating from the Word Trade Organization (WTO) Appellate Body, should be treated with care.[46] It is often the case that such allegations demonstrate the political reluctance of some states to engage in the institutional and normative framework which they voluntarily agreed to be part of, but which they now view as an international jurisdiction behaving on the international stage like a constitutional judge. In this vein, it is worth recalling the sometimes uneasy relationship that has existed between the European Court of Justice and its member states.[47]

The issue of an abuse of power by the international judge that may surface in relation to a lack of legal reasoning in certain decisions, may also arise with respect to the inherent risks of an overly systematic use of evolutionary interpretation. This was the concern expressed by President Judge Bedjaoui in his Individual Opinion to the ICJ judgment in the *Case concerning the Gabcikovo-Nagymaros Project*.[48] In particular, Judge Bedjaoui stressed what appears incontrovertible, that 'the "evolutionary interpretation" can only be applied if the general rule of interpretation in Article 31 of the Vienna Convention on the law of treaties is respected'.

It should be recalled that the ICJ invoked the classic rule according to which 'the interpretation of the treaty must comply with the intentions of the parties expressed at the time of its conclusion', in its Advisory Opinion of 1970 on *Namibia*. In order to justify a return to a traditional position—which is not, however, as a general rule, the approach taken by the author—Judge Bedjaoui added that 'the intentions of the parties are presumed to have been influenced by the law in force at the time the treaty was concluded, the law which they were supposed to know, and not by future law, as yet unknown'. A literal reading of this statement appears to allow an evolutionary interpretation of a treaty only in exceptional cases.

[44] *Airey v Ireland*, Judgment of 9 October 1979, Series A, No. 32, para. 24.

[45] *Stafford v United Kingdom*, Judgment of 28 May 2002, *RJD* 2002-IV, para. 5.

[46] D.S. Beckford, *Power and Judicial Activism in the WTO, The Appellate Body's Interpretation of Trade Remedy Agreements* (London: VDM Verlag, 2008).

[47] D. Simon, *L'interprétation judiciaire des traités d'organisations internationales, Morphologie des Conventions et fonction juridictionnelle* (Paris: Pedone, 1981).

[48] ICJ, *Gabčíkovo-Nagymaros Project, supra* note 19, at 117–21.

Judge Bedjaoui thus considered that the '"definition" of a concept [is] not to be confused with the "law" applicable to that concept'.[49] This seems to be a pertinent distinction to draw, even if Judge Bedjaoui himself in the case at hand appears to have been in error in stating that the notion of the 'environment' 'is not evolutionary'. In reality, a number of areas covered by international law require frequent adaptation that is of growing importance. This is particularly the case where the law regulates a particular area of human activity at a given moment based on the scientific and technological knowledge available at that time, as the successive treaties codifying the law of the sea concluded in Geneva in 1958, and then in Montego Bay in 1982, attest.

It appears incontestable that, in a general sense, the interpretation of a treaty by a judge should not be confused with its revision, which can only be undertaken by the parties themselves.[50] The terms in which the treaty provisions to be interpreted are drafted provide a solid indication of whether the text is open to an evolutionary interpretation. This is the case, even though in reality the reconstruction of the initial will of the parties remains an exercise requiring almost as much imagination as skill on the part of the judge in finding reliable indices that point to what the parties really wanted. The practice of evolutionary interpretation is another expression of the art of judging, which is constantly balanced between providing for stability based on respect for the principle of autonomy of the will of the parties, and a quest for the necessary flexibility to keep a treaty afloat by meeting the objectives it was designed to address.

In addition to these considerations, it is also important to note that the survival of unrevised treaty obligations, which are particularly exposed to erosion by time, presupposes that the judge or arbitrator is in a position to follow the political, economic, and social evolutions which transform more and more the scope, if not the very nature, of the agreed upon obligations. This brings to mind the opening dialogue between the Poet and the Painter in Shakespeare's *Timon of Athens*: 'Poet: I have not seen you long. How goes the world? Painter: It wears, sir, as it grows.'

[49] Ibid., 119. [50] Ibid., 120.

8

Subsequent Practice as a Means of Interpretation in the Jurisprudence of the WTO Appellate Body*

Georg Nolte

1.1. While interpretation is the main task of the Appellate Body under the WTO Dispute Settlement Understanding, the same is not true for the ILC. The ILC mostly acts as a body which formulates and articulates rules. But, of course, the formulation and articulation of rules often implies interpretation. And sometimes the ILC even selects topics which directly address the question of how to interpret international rules. The best-known example is the preparation by the ILC of the Vienna Convention of the Law of Treaties and in particular its provisions on interpretation.

In 2009, the Commission decided to include the topic 'Treaties over time' in its active programme of work.[1] Elucidating the role of 'subsequent agreement and subsequent practice' as a means of interpretation will be part of the work of the Commission under this topic. The ILC works on 'subsequent agreements' and 'subsequent practice' because the question of how to use these means of interpretation may become more relevant as major treaties age and their context changes.[2] International treaties cannot be amended easily, but they must remain capable of fulfilling their purposes. Subsequent agreements and subsequent practice are means of interpretation which are characteristic for international law. The way in

* Giorgio Gaja is not only an eminent and gracious colleague, he is also a leading member of the International Law Commission (ILC). One could even say that he embodies certain aspects of the Commission. Being sensitive to institutional identities, he may be interested to read about how one of the major quasi-judicial international bodies conceives and applies an important element of the ILC-inspired Vienna Convention on the Law of Treaties (VCLT).

An earlier version of this contribution was delivered in the presence of Giorgio Gaja in July 2009 to the members of the WTO Appellate Body at a 'retreat session' to which members of the ILC were invited to discuss 'Approaches to Treaty Interpretation'. I thank Robert Howse, NYU, for constructive comments and Christian Djeffal, Humboldt University, for technical help.

[1] *GAOR, Sixty-fourth Session, Supplement No. 10* (A/64/10), at 360, para. 217.

[2] Ibid., *Sixty-third Session, Supplement No. 10* (A/63/10), Annex A, at 365, para. 3; H. Thirlway, *International Customary Law and Codification* (Leiden: A. W. Sijthoff, 1972) 1–125.

which they are to be used, in particular in relation to other means of interpretation, has not been sufficiently explored, and they are used differently by different dispute settlement bodies.

1.2. The Appellate Body of the WTO has dealt on several occasions with invocations of 'subsequent agreements' and 'subsequent practice' by different parties and panels. The most relevant cases are:

- In *Japan—Alcoholic Beverages* the Appellate Body rejected the finding of the Panel according to which an adopted Panel report constituted a determinative 'subsequent practice' with respect to the provisions which were interpreted in the report.[3]
- In *EC—Computer Equipment* the Appellate Body rejected the finding of the Panel according to which the classification practice of a few main importers constituted a determinative 'subsequent practice', despite the fact that certain other importers and the main exporter did not follow the same practice.[4]
- In *Chile—Price Band System* the Appellate Body rejected the finding of the Panel according to which the lack of objection against a specific form of determination of customs duties was sufficient to constitute relevant 'subsequent practice'.[5]
- In *US—Gambling* the Appellate Body rejected the finding of the Panel that certain Scheduling Guidelines constituted 'subsequent practice' for the purpose of interpreting the commitment of the US regarding 'other recreational services'.[6]
- In *EC—Chicken Cuts* the Appellate Body rejected the finding of the Panel according to which a classification of certain chicken parts by the EC which had remained unopposed for six years constituted relevant 'subsequent practice'.[7]
- In *EC—Bananas III* the Appellate Body rejected the finding of the Panel according to which a waiver could constitute relevant 'subsequent practice' for the purposes of prolonging a related agreement by way of interpretation.[8]

These cases seem to suggest that the Appellate Body seeks to limit or even largely to exclude subsequent agreement and subsequent practice as means of

[3] *Japan—Alcoholic Beverages*, Report of the Appellate Body, WT/DS8/AB/R, WT/DS10/AB/R and WT/DS11/AB/R.

[4] *EC—Computer Equipment*, Report of the Appellate Body, WT/DS62/AB/R, WT/DS67/AB/R, WT/DS68/AB/R, para. 92.

[5] *Chile—Price Band System*, Report of the Appellate Body, WT/DS207/AB/R, para. 212.

[6] *US—Gambling*, Report of the Appellate Body, WT/DS285/AB/R, para. 193.

[7] *EC—Chicken Cuts*, Report of the Appellate Body, WT/DS269/AB/R, WT/DS286/AB/R, paras 272 and 276.

[8] *EC—Bananas III*, Report of the Appellate Body, WT/DS27/AB/RW2/ECU, WT/DS27/AB/RW/USA, para. 389.

interpretation within the WTO system. However, a closer look at the reasoning of the Reports of the Appellate Body, in particular the one in *EC—Chicken Cuts*,[9] and at unopposed Panel Reports[10] suggests that the question of the role of subsequent agreement and subsequent practice as means of interpretation remains a relevant issue within the WTO system.[11]

Why should this aspect of the process of interpretation be a worthwhile question for the ILC, and why should it be significant for the WTO dispute settlement system?

For the ILC, the jurisprudence of the WTO Dispute Settlement Body is not merely one of many different regimes. This jurisprudence makes an influential contribution to the methods of interpretation of international norms. Indeed, the Appellate Body claims to faithfully follow and to articulate the rules of interpretation as they are formulated in the Vienna Convention on the Law of Treaties.[12] This invites the question of whether the jurisprudence of the Appellate Body is in line with that of other dispute settlement bodies, in particular with that of the International Court of Justice.

Articles 31–33 VCLT do not set up a rigid system, or method, of interpretation, but rather offer a range of means of interpretation whose relative importance must be assessed in a holistic fashion in the light of the particular circumstances of the case and of the treaty concerned.[13] The style of reasoning of different dispute settlement bodies may differ depending on their respective environments and in particular the expectations of their audiences.[14] But these insights should not lead to an excessively critical, relativistic 'anything goes' approach. Reasoning and openly acknowledged methods of interpretation are important, not least because they impose pressure on the interpreters to be consistent and because they reveal much about their self-understanding.

The best-known example for the importance, and the revelatory nature, of the respective interpretative styles, is the difference between the jurisprudence of the European Court of Justice and European Court of Human Rights on the one hand, and of the WTO Dispute Settlement Body on the other. In Europe we can observe an emphasis on object and purpose as means of interpretation, or if

[9] *EC—Chicken Cuts*, *supra* note 7, para. 251.

[10] *United States—Section 110(5) of the US Copyright Act*, Panel Report, WT/DS160/R, para. 6.55; *Brazil—Measures affecting desiccated Coconut*, Panel Report, WT/DS22/R, para. 255; *United States—Zeroing*, Panel Report, WT/DS294/R, para. 7.218.

[11] See I. Van Damme, *infra* n. 16, at 338–50, A.M. Feldman, 'Evolving Treaty Obligations: A Proposal for A, at nalyzing Subsequent Practice Derived from WTO Dispute Settlement', 41 *NYUJ of Int'l L & Pol.* (2009) 655–706, at 676 *et seq.*

[12] *United States—Gasoline*, Report of the Appellate Body, WT/DS2/AB/R, at 16; *Japan—Alcoholic Beverages*, *supra* note 3, at 10.

[13] *YILC* (1966), vol. II, at 218, para. 4 and 219, para. 8.

[14] G. Abi-Saab, The Appellate Body and Treaty Interpretation', in M. Fitzmaurice, O. Elias, and P. Merkouris (eds), *Treaty Interpretation and the Vienna Convention on the Law of Treaties: Thirty Years On* (Leiden: Martinus Nijhoff, 2010) at 105–7.

you will, on *effet utile*, and on the topos of the 'living instrument',[15] while in the WTO world it is the textual meaning which is the professed guiding star.[16] Here, I only want to tentatively explore whether the use of 'subsequent agreement' and 'subsequent practice' as means of interpretation sheds any light on the different approaches.

1.3. The Appellate Body underpins its use of subsequent agreement and subsequent practice as means of interpretation with references to general international law. It has sometimes quoted the ILC Commentary on Article 31(3)(a) and (b) VCLT,[17] and since *Japan—Alcoholic Beverages* it uses like a mantra a definition of subsequent practice which is taken from the context of the VCLT. According to this definition, subsequent practice requires a '"concordant, common and consistent" sequence of acts and pronouncements which is sufficient to establish a discernable pattern implying the agreement of the parties regarding its implementation'.[18]

While this approach sounds intuitively plausible, it is in fact somewhat less authoritative than it appears at first sight. The adopted definition of 'subsequent practice' has been formulated by Sir Ian Sinclair,[19] who represented the United Kingdom at the Vienna Conference on the Law of Treaties and who drew on a similar formulation in French by Mustafa Kamil Yasseen,[20] using elements from the work of the ILC and the jurisprudence of the International Court of Justice (ICJ).

Also, in substance, the approach of the ICJ is rather more liberal and less rigorous than the one so far adopted by the Appellate Body. The ICJ quite often considers whether a treaty provision must be interpreted in the light of a subsequent agreement or of a subsequent practice between the parties. Its jurisprudence is rich and subtle. The Court does not limit itself to considering what may be seen as subsequent practice in the narrower consensual sense, but it also recasts practice of one side as an element of context, as in its 1999 judgment in the *Kasikili/Sedudu Island* dispute between Namibia and

[15] An early example of the principle of *effet utile* is provided by European Court of Justice, Case No. C-9/70 *Grad v Finanzamt Traunstein* [1970] ECR 825, para. 5; for an example for the topic of living instrument see European Court of Human Rights, *Tyrer v United Kingdom*, Judgment of 25 April 1978, Series A, No. 26, para. 31.

[16] C.-D. Ehlermann, 'Six Years on the Bench of the World Trade Court', 36 *Journal of World Trade Law* (2002) at 615; I. Van Damme, *Treaty Interpretation by the WTO Appellate Body* (Oxford: Oxford University Press, 2009) at 221; G. Abi-Saab, *supra* note 14, at 106–107.

[17] See, eg, Report of the Appellate Body, WT/DS269/AB/R, WT/DS286/AB/R, 12 September 2005, paras 255 and 390. Report of the Appellate Body, WT/DS27/AB/RW2/ECU, WT/DS27/AB/RW/USA, 26 November 2008.

[18] *Japan—Alcoholic Beverages, supra* note 3, para. 2.

[19] I. Sinclair, *The Vienna Convention on the Law of Treaties* (Manchester: Manchester University Press, 2nd edn, 1984) at 137.

[20] M.K. Yasseen, 'L'interprétation des traités d'après la Convention de Vienne sur le droit des traités', 151 *Recueil des Cours* (1976-III) at 48.

Botswana.[21] The Court also does not limit its use of subsequent practice to serving as a means of interpretation, but also as a way of recognizing modifications of treaty obligations over time. This has happened not only in cases which involved the delimitation of borders, as in the well-known *Temple at Preah Vihear* case of 1962,[22] but also in cases concerning the functions and powers of international organizations and their organs, in particular with respect to the United Nations, such as in the *Wall Opinion* of 2004,[23] or in the *Certain Expenses case* of 1962.[24]

There are different possible explanations for the difference between the approaches of the WTO Appellate Body and of the ICJ concerning the use of the subsequent practice element of interpretation. The most obvious is the fact that the ICJ, as a body of general jurisdiction with the first and final say, should remain more flexible concerning its methods of interpretation, while the WTO Appellate Body, as a body of special jurisdiction, may have a stronger interest in developing a jurisprudence which serves legal certainty and systemic coherence.[25] Another possible explanation is that the subject-matter of the WTO treaty system lends itself more easily to more formal methods of interpretation.

Be this as it may, the picture changes if the jurisprudence of the Appellate Body is compared to that of the European Courts. The ECJ, although it administers a body of rules which is in some ways similar to that of the WTO, rarely refers to the subsequent practice of the parties to the treaties, but uses its all-encompassing purposive interpretation to take account of changing contexts and subsequent developments.[26] The European Court of Human Rights in Strasbourg more explicitly refers to changing circumstances, but these circumstances are not usually the subsequent practice of the parties to the Convention, but rather the changing conditions in the different European societies which require an evolving interpretation.[27]

Sure enough, both the Appellate Body and the ICJ have on occasion recognized that certain terms have an evolutive meaning. In *US—Shrimp*, the

[21] ICJ, *Kasikili/Sedudu Island* (*Botswana/Namibia*), Judgment of 13 December 1999, *ICJ Reports* (1999) at 1045–76, para. 50.

[22] ICJ, *Temple of Preah Vihear* (*Cambodia v Thailand*), Judgment of 15 June 1962, *ICJ Reports* (1962) at 6 and 22.

[23] ICJ, *Legal Consequences of the Construction of a Wall in the Occupied Palestinian Territory*, Advisory Opinion of 9 July 2004, *ICJ Reports* (2004) at 136 and 148, para. 24.

[24] ICJ, *Certain Expenses of the United Nations (Article 17, paragraph 2, of the Charter)*, Advisory Opinion of 20 July 1962, *ICJ Reports* (1962) at 151 and 160.

[25] G. Abi-Saab, *supra* note 14, at 106–7.

[26] Case No. C-6/90 and C-9/90 *Francovich and Others v Italy* [1991] ECR I-5357, para. 32; Case No. C-213/89 *Factortame and Others* [1990] ECR I-2433, para. 20.

[27] *Tyrer v United Kingdom*, *supra* note 15; R. Bernhardt, 'Evolutive Treaty Interpretation, Especially of the European Convention on Human Rights', 42 *GYIL* (1999) 11 *et seq.*; M. Fitzmaurice, 'Dynamic Evolutive Interpretation of Treaties', 21 *Hague Yearbook of International Law* (2008) 101 *et seq.*

Appellate Body has famously recognized that the expression 'natural resources' in Article XX(g) GATT is 'by definition, evolutionary' so as to also cover living resources,[28] and the ICJ, in a judgment concerning a dispute between Costa Rica and Nicaragua, has recently done the same with respect to the words 'articles of trade' (*objetos de comercio*) to cover not only goods but also services.[29] But such 'evolutionary interpretations' are (still?) comparatively rare both for the Appellate Body and for the ICJ.

And they can be contested. In the *Costa Rica v Nicaragua* case, two judges dissented from the evolutionary interpretation given to the term '*objetos de comercio*'. While they did not contest the result, Judge Skotnikov expressly suggested that the Court should rather have based its reasoning on the 'subsequent practice' of the parties which in his opinion showed that the agreed freedom of commerce covered not only goods but also services.[30] Judge Guillaume seems to have implied such reasoning. I do not want to argue whether one or the other approach was correct. What is interesting is the choice of reasoning and the choice of the means of interpretation which are considered to be most relevant for the legitimacy of the decision. The agreement of the parties, as evidenced by their subsequent practice, can sometimes provide a higher legitimacy than the invocation of an inherently evolutionary meaning.

1.4. The question is whether the comparison of the jurisprudence of the Appellate Body with that of the ICJ on the one hand, and with that of the European Courts on the other, suggests that the WTO Appellate Body is least open to any forms of evolutionary interpretation, be it on the basis of the object and purpose of the treaty, or on the basis of subsequent agreement and practice of the parties. While it is understandable that the Appellate Body is reluctant to engage in purposive interpretation which is not warranted by the stated intentions of the parties,[31] the same reluctance is intuitively less plausible with respect to interpretations which are based on the actual practice of the parties themselves.

The reluctance of the Appellate Body to engage in more openly purposive interpretation may have to do with the attitude of a young institution which must establish its authority and with the reciprocal nature of the undertakings. Both reasons do not, however, affect subsequent agreement and subsequent practice as means of interpretation. Subsequent practice is based on the authority of the parties to the treaty. The reciprocal nature of the obligations remains the same whether or not the parties engage in what is ultimately a reciprocal practice. Therefore the restrictive attitude of the Appellate Body with respect to subsequent

[28] *United States—Importation of Certain Shrimp and Shrimp Products*, Report of the Appellate Body, WT/DS58/AB/R, para. 130.

[29] ICJ, *Case Concerning the Dispute Regarding Navigational and Related Rights* (*Costa Rica v Nicaragua*), not yet reported, available at <http://www.icj-cij.org>, para. 64.

[30] Separate Opinion of Judge Skotnikov, para. 8; Déclaration de M. le Juge *ad hoc* Guillaume, para. 16.

[31] G. Abi-Saab, *supra* note 14, at 106–7.

agreement and subsequent practice as means of interpretation must have other reasons. Perhaps the following two reasons play a role.

The first reason may be the specific nature of certain undertakings within the WTO system. This would seem to be true in particular for Schedules of commitments. It is unclear whose practice and whose agreement in which form would be sufficient to establish agreement about them. Only those states between whom trade in a particular product actually takes place, or also states with a potential trading interest? Such questions deserve to be explored and the *EC—Chicken Cuts case* is perhaps just a point of departure for a coming line of cases.

The second reason may be just inertia. Perhaps the restrictive attitude of the Appellate Body to subsequent agreement and practice as a means of interpretation is a consequence of its generally restrictive attitude towards interpretation which does not go significantly beyond the common intention of the parties as derived from the textual meaning of a provision or a treaty. Should the Appellate Body one day consider that the time has come to move from a rather exegetic approach to a more liberal approach to interpretation, without however yet taking interpretative liberties which the European Courts permit themselves, the Appellate Body might want to consider making greater use of a means of interpretation which continues to rest on the will of the parties and still permits some flexibility. Such a means of interpretation would obviously be the subsequent agreement and subsequent practice of the parties.

9

Supplementary Means of Interpretation

Luigi Sbolci

1. Introduction

The interpretation of international treaties raises specific questions that cannot be resolved on the basis of general theories of interpretation, which frequently reflect the principles of national legislation. An interpreter who is not aware of these specific questions might be tempted to interpret a treaty in line with the rules of interpretation pertaining to his or her own legal system. Examples of this attitude are to be found, for instance, in Italian case law. Certain judgments of the Court of Cassation have expressly confirmed that international agreements, enacted through national law, should be subject to the same interpretative criteria as those used to interpret national legislation.[1] This position has subsequently evolved. In judgments issued in 1995 and 2007, the Court of Cassation accepted that 'the interpretation of international treaties transposed into national legislation should be conducted on the basis of the criteria of context, object and purpose as laid down in Articles 31 and 32 of the Vienna Convention on the Law of Treaties of 1969'.[2]

The interpretation of treaties calls for the adoption of standard criteria, applicable by all the contracting states. To achieve this end, a number of different theories were developed, especially prior to the 1969 Vienna Convention on the Law of Treaties. Some of these upheld the use of purely logical and not legally binding criteria of interpretation, leaving considerable discretion to the interpreter.[3]

[1] *Oleificio Bestetti v Can Grain Ltd* (1979), 63 *Riv. di Diritto Internaz.* (1980) 529 *et seq.*; *Parzinger e Nowak v Provincia autonoma di Bolzano e Comune di Renon* (1986), 71 *Riv. di Diritto Internaz.* (1988) 426 *et seq.*

[2] *Messina & C spa v Setramar spa* (2007), available at <http://dejure.giuffre.it>, making reference to the *Di Lazzaro* judgment (1995), 118 *Foro italiano* (1995), at 3409.

[3] H. Lauterpacht, 'Rapport à l'Institut de droit international', 43 *Annu. de l'Inst. de Droit Internat.* (1950) at 336–74; G. Barile, *La rilevazione e l'integrazione del diritto internazionale non scritto e la libertà di apprezzamento del giudice,* (Milano: Giuffrè, 1953) at 194 *et seq.*; D. Anzilotti, *Corso di diritto internazionale* (Padova: CEDAM, 4th edn, 1955) at 102 *et seq.*; A. McNair, *The Law of Treaties* (Oxford: Clarendon Press, 1961) at 366 *et seq.*; J.L. Brierly, *The Law of Nations* (Oxford: Clarendon Press, 1966) at 325.

However, the views that supported the existence of specific legal rules of treaty interpretation under international law were more numerous.[4]

Prior to the Vienna Convention, the debate on the general rules of treaty interpretation revolved around the identification of material criteria of interpretation that could be used to determine the precise content of a treaty rule. Treaty rules could be interpreted in an extensive or restrictive sense, and could be regarded as having an effective or, at times, a *contra proferentem* meaning.[5] However, the debate mainly focused on methodology, and above all on whether preference was to be accorded to a subjective or an objective method of treaty interpretation.

The arguments of those in favour of a subjective method stressed the need to interpret a treaty according to the common intention of the contracting parties, as it had emerged at the time the treaty was concluded.[6] From this perspective, reference to the preparatory works, and any other appropriate means for ascertaining the real intentions of the parties, was considered decisive.

By contrast, the supporters of an objective approach considered that the interpreter should seek the common intent of the parties as expressed and declared in the text of the treaty itself.[7]

The debate on these and other problematic aspects of treaty interpretation continued until the Vienna Conference, when states codified in Article 31 the objective method as the general rule of treaty interpretation. The main elements characterizing the subjective method were then incorporated, as supplementary means of interpretation, within the framework of Article 32.[8]

[4] R. Phillimore, *Commentaries upon International Law* (London: Butterworths, 3rd edn, 1882) at 95 *et seq.*; Ch. Rousseau, *Principes généraux de droit international public* (Paris: Pedone, 1944) at 676 *et seq.*; Ch. de Visscher, *Problèmes d'interprétation judiciaire en droit international public* (Paris: Pedone, 1963) at 50 *et seq.*

[5] L. Ehrlich, 'L'interprétation des traités', 24 *Recueil des Cours* (1928-IV) at 30 *et seq.*; G. Fitzmaurice, 'The Law and Procedure of the International Court of Justice: Treaty Interpretation and Certain Other Points', 28 *BYIL* (1951) at 8 *et seq.*; J. Touscoz, *Le principe d'effectivité dans l'ordre international* (Paris: LGDJ, 1964) at 167 *et seq.*; H. Gutierrez Posse, 'La maxime ut res magis valeat quam pereat (Interprétation en fonction de l'effet utile). Les interprétations "extensives" et "restrictive"', 23 *Österreichische Zeitschrift für öffentliches Recht (und Völkerrecht)* (1972) at 229 *et seq.*

[6] L. Ehrlich, 'L'interprétation des traités', *supra* note 5, at 30; H. Lauterpacht, 'Rapport à l'Institut de droit international', *supra* note 3, at 377–402.

[7] G. Fitzmaurice, 'The Law and Procedure of the International Court of Justice: Treaty Interpretation and Certain Other Points', *supra* note 5, at 8 *et seq.*; ibid. 33 (1957), at 203 *et seq.*; S. Neri, *Sull'interpretazione dei trattati nel diritto internazionale* (Milano: Giuffré, 1958) at 135 *et seq.*; V.D. Degan, *L'interprétation des accords en droit international* (The Hague: Martinus Nijhoff, 1963) at 76 *et seq.*; Ch. de Visscher, *Problèmes d'interprétation judiciaire en droit international public*, *supra* note 4, at 84 *et seq.*

[8] Paragraph 4 of Article 31 of the Vienna Convention, according to which '[a] special meaning shall be given to a term if it is established that the parties so intended', also implies the application of a subjective criterion, since the intent of the parties to which it refers is not an element that can be reconstructed purely on the basis of objective elements (G. Gaja, 'Trattati internazionali', *Digesto delle Discipline Pubblicistiche* (Torino: UTET, 1999) vol. XV, at 356).

2. The General Rule of Interpretation and Supplementary Means

The regime established by the Vienna Convention through Articles 31 and 32 settled many controversial issues. The Convention sets out specific legal rules of treaty interpretation, in particular a general rule and supplementary means of interpretation.

The preparatory works of the International Law Commission (ILC), which preceded the Vienna Conference, illustrate the main reasons behind this approach. In the first place, it emerges that the interpretation of treaties 'according to law is essential if the *pacta sunt servanda* rule is to have any real meaning'.[9] Thus, the need to define clear legal rules excluded the codification of interpretational criteria such as, for example, *ut res magis valeat quam pereat, contra proferentem*, since 'they are, for the most part, principles of logic and good sense'.[10] The works of the ILC also shed light on the reasons underlying the relationship established in the Convention between the general rule of interpretation and supplementary means. This relationship is characterized by a distinct hierarchy.

According to Special Rapporteur Waldock, supplementary means of interpretation, which, as codified under Article 32 of the Vienna Convention, refers to the preparatory work of the treaty and the circumstances of its conclusion, were intended to be used in a manner subordinate to the general rule, now set out in Article 31, and under specific circumstances, that is, if the natural and ordinary meaning of a term leads to an interpretation which is manifestly absurd or unreasonable, or if the meaning of the term is not clear.[11] Supplementary means might also be used, he suggested, for the purpose of confirming the meaning of a textual interpretation.[12] The report of the ILC commenting on the drafts of Articles 69 (general rule of interpretation) and 70 (further means of interpretation), provisionally adopted in its 1964 session, confirmed this approach.[13]

The preparatory works of the Vienna Conference that took place in the first session of 1968 appear to indicate that, in reality, some states were not willing to accept the hierarchical relation between the general rule and supplementary means as formulated by the ILC. Undoubtedly they considered that no fixed hierarchy should be established among the rules of treaty interpretation.[14]

9 ILC Report (1964), *YILC* (1964), vol. II, at 200, para. 6.

10 See H. Waldock, 'Third Report on the Law of Treaties', ibid. at 54, para. 6. In the same sense, ILC Report (1964), ibid., at 200, paras 4–5.

11 Ibid., vol. II, at 52.

12 Ibid.

13 ILC Report (1964), ibid., at 204, para. 15.

14 The amendment proposed by the United States (A/CONF.39/C.1./L.156), supported by Switzerland (United Nations Conference on the Law of Treaties, *Official Records*, vol. I, at 180, para. 27) and rejected by the Conference (by 66 votes to 8, with 10 abstentions; see ibid., at 184–5, para. 75) aimed to eliminate the rigidities, restrictions, and hierarchical distinctions in draft Articles 27 and 28. In the US delegation's opinion, the text of a treaty should be made the point of departure of interpretation but it should not be the end of the inquiry. The text would thus be treated as one important indication, among many, of the common intent of the parties.

International jurisprudence prior to the Vienna Convention reflects state practice, which was at the time ambiguous regarding the hierarchical relation between the subjective and objective means of the treaty.[15] Certain arbitral awards and several rulings by the Permanent Court of International Justice (PCIJ) have relied on subjective means of interpretation without—at least apparently—subordinating them to the textual and objective criteria.[16]

However, a large part of international case law was mainly oriented towards subordinating the use of the subjective method to the textual method of interpretation. Evidence of this approach is illustrated in the 1932 Judgment of the PCIJ in the *Interpretation of the Statute of the Memel Territory* case.[17] The Court adopted a similar approach in its Opinion on the *Interpretation of the Convention of 1919 Concerning Employment of Women during the Night*[18] and in the Judgment on the *Lighthouses Case between France and Greece.*[19] The same position was then confirmed by the International Court of Justice in its Advisory Opinion of 1948 on the *Conditions of Admission of a State to Membership in the United Nations.*[20]

The elements of international practice prior to the Vienna Convention of 1969 indicated the existence of a general trend towards attributing priority to the objective method of treaty interpretation based on the text of the treaty, while subjective means were used in a subsidiary manner. This was the majority trend, although it cannot be said that it was universally accepted.

Based on a global evaluation of such practice, we can reasonably deduce that the Vienna Convention did not codify well-established rules of general international law on treaty interpretation. On the other hand, it seems reasonable to assume that the consensus reached in Vienna generated the crystallization of a rule *in fieri* on the hierarchical relationship between the objective and the subjective method of treaty interpretation, a rule to which the ICJ has routinely referred.[21]

[15] See G. Gaja, 'Trattati internazionali', *supra* note 8, at 355.

[16] See arbitrations: *Aroa Mines Case*, IX *RIAA* (1903) at 402 *et seq.*; *The North Atlantic Coast Fisheries Case*, XI *RIAA* (1910), at 167. See also: PCIJ, *S.S. Wimbledon (United Kingdom, France, Italy, Japan v Germany, Poland intervening)*, Judgment of 17 August 1923, Series A, No. 1, at 23; ICJ, *Anglo-Iranian Oil Co. (United Kingdom v Iran)*, Preliminary Objections, Judgment of 22 July 1952, *ICJ Reports* (1952) at 93 and 104.

[17] PCIJ, *Interpretation of the Statute of the Memel Territory (United Kingdom, France, Italy, Japan v Lithuania)*, Preliminary Objections, Judgment of 24 June 1932, Series A/B, No. 47, at 249.

[18] PCIJ, *Interpretation of the Convention of 1919 concerning Employment of Women during the Night*, Advisory Opinion of 15 November 1932, Series A/B, No. 50, at 378.

[19] PCIJ, *Lighthouses Case Between France and Greece (France v Greece)*, Judgment of 17 March 1934, Series A/B, No. 62, at 13.

[20] ICJ, *Conditions of Admission of a State to Membership in the United Nations (Article 4 of the Charter)*, Advisory Opinion of 28 May 1948, *ICJ Reports* (1948) at 63.

[21] ICJ, *North Sea Continental Shelf* (*Federal Republic of Germany/Denmark; Federal Republic of Germany/Netherlands*), Judgment of 20 February 1969, *ICJ Reports* (1969) at 41, para. 69. For the theory in favour of codification, see P. Reuter, *La Convention de Vienne sur le droit des traités* (Paris: A. Colin, 1970), at 7; I. Sinclair, *The Vienna Convention on the Law of Treaties* (Manchester: Manchester University Press, 2nd edn, 1984) at 153.

International practice subsequent to the Vienna Convention confirms the general perception of a correspondence between the discipline of the Vienna Convention and general international law.[22]

3. Conditions of Admissibility of Supplementary Means of Interpretation

The hierarchical relationship established in the Vienna Convention between the general rule of treaty interpretation and recourse to supplementary means is better clarified by the conditions of admissibility of such means. Article 32 of the Convention subordinates the use of preparatory works and other supplementary means to various assumptions connected with the outcome of the interpretation made on the basis of the general rule contained in Article 31.

Article 32 considers first and foremost the case in which the interpreter deems it necessary to have a confirmation of the interpretation obtained by using the objective method. Secondly,[23] supplementary means can be used when reliance on Article 31 leaves the meaning ambiguous or obscure, or when it leads to a result which is manifestly absurd or unreasonable.

The formulation of Article 32 largely reflects the proposals Special Rapporteur Waldock advanced in his Third Report.[24] In this way, the Commission sought to avoid drawing a rigid line between the supplementary means of interpretation and the means included in the general rule.[25] The same reasons would also appear to confirm the idea that the method of interpretation accepted by the Vienna Convention can be construed as an objective method, mitigated by several significant corrective devices.[26]

The conditions of admissibility of the supplementary means of interpretation, which are functional to the definition of the hierarchical relation between the general rule and reliance on supplementary means, were drawn from prevailing

[22] The pertinent rules of the Convention have been generally accepted as rules that reflect the general international law in force. More specifically, the jurisprudence of the ICJ has repeatedly confirmed that Articles 31 and 32 of the Convention correspond to general international law. In this regard, it is sufficient to mention, among the most recent cases, the judgment issued in the case concerning the *Application of the Convention on the Prevention and Punishment of the Crime of Genocide* (*Bosnia and Herzegovina v Serbia and Montenegro*), not yet reported, available at <http://www.icj-cij.org>, at 60, para. 160. See also the judgment of 13 July 2009 issued by the ICJ on the *Case Concerning the Dispute Regarding Navigational and Related Rights* (*Costa Rica v Nicaragua*), not yet reported, para. 47.

[23] For this breakdown into two scenarios, see G. Gaja, 'Trattati internazionali', *supra* note 8, at 356; Arbitral Tribunal for German External Debts, Judgment in the *Young Case* (1980), *ILM* (1980), at 1379, para. 32.

[24] H. Waldock, 'Third Report on the Law of Treaties', *YILC* (1964), vol. II, at 58, para. 20.

[25] ILC Report (1966), *YILC* 1966, vol. II, at 220, para. 10.

[26] S. Bariatti, *L'interpretazione delle convenzioni internazionali di diritto uniforme* (Padova: CEDAM, 1986) at 185.

international jurisprudence which, prior to the Vienna Convention, had favoured the objective method of treaty interpretation. The condition of admissibility most frequently referred to was the lack of clarity of the treaty, that is, the persistence of aspects of obscurity or ambiguity following the objective interpretation of the treaty's text. The contents of the Draft Articles of the ILC that were embodied in Article 32 of the Vienna Convention drew on rulings issued by both the PCIJ and the ICJ.[27]

The Vienna Conference of 1969, which approved the text of the Convention on the Law of Treaties, expressed a general acceptance of the conditions of admissibility of the supplementary means of interpretation previously affirmed in international case law and accepted by the ILC. Since certain states did not agree with the relation between the objective method and subjective method proposed by the ILC,[28] we can assume that this acceptance within the framework of the Conference brought about the crystallization of a general rule of international law of corresponding content, including in particular the conditions of admissibility. This would indicate that the nature of the hierarchical subordination of the supplementary means to the general rule of interpretation is not a rigid hierarchy.[29]

International jurisprudence subsequent to the Vienna Convention authoritatively confirms that the rule establishing the conditions of admissibility of the supplementary means of interpretation of the treaties corresponds to the general international law currently in force. Also emerging from this case law is the tendency to favour the supplementary means, particularly the preparatory works, with a view to confirming the meaning derived from application of the

[27] See PCIJ, *S.S. Lotus* (*France v Turkey*), Judgment of 7 September 1927, Series A, No. 10, at 16. See also the judgment in the *Interpretation of the Statute of the Memel Territory, supra* note 17, at 249; the Advisory Opinion of 4 February 1932 on the *Treatment of Polish Nationals and Other Persons of Polish Origin or Speech in the Danzig Territory* (PCIJ, Series A/B, No. 44, at 33); PCIJ, *Payment of Various Serbian Loans issued in France* (*France v Kingdom of the Serbs, Croats and Slovenes*), Judgment of 12 July 1929, Series A, No. 20, at 30; the *Lighthouses Case between France and Greece, supra* note 19, at 13. For the case law of the ICJ, see the ICJ Advisory Opinion on the *Conditions of Admission of a State to Membership in the United Nations, supra* note 20, at 63 and the ICJ Advisory Opinion of 3 March 1950 on the *Competence of the General Assembly for the Admission of a State to the United Nations, ICJ Reports* (1950) at 8. More rarely, jurisprudence prior to the Vienna Convention mentioned as a requisite for admissibility of the supplementary means of interpretation the need to confirm the meaning derived from the textual interpretation of the treaty. The clearest statement in this regard can be found in the 1932 Opinion on the *Interpretation of the Convention of 1919 concerning Employment of Women during the Night, supra* note 18, according to which 'the preparatory work thus confirms the conclusion reached on a study of the text of the Convention that there is no good reason for interpreting Article 3 otherwise than in accordance with the natural meaning of the words'. See also the 1963 judgment of the Arbitral Tribunal on the *Interpretation of the Air Transport Services Agreement between the United States of America and France,* XVI *RIAA* (2006) at 51–2.

[28] H. Waldock, 'Third Report on the Law of Treaties', *supra* note 24, at 205, para. 16; ILC Report (1966), *YILC* (1966), vol. II, at 223, para. 19.

[29] Ibid., at 220, para. 10. See also I. Sinclair, *The Vienna Convention on the Law of Treaties, supra* note 21, at 117.

general rule of interpretation. In this regard, we note an inversion of trends in comparison with the period prior to the Vienna Convention. In the international jurisprudence of this period, the supplementary means were taken into consideration principally for the purpose of interpreting a treaty that continued to be ambiguous or obscure following a textual interpretation. Yet an ambiguous text frequently stems from preparatory works that are equally ambiguous and hence of little utility.[30] Possibly for this reason too, after the Vienna Convention the tendency was to resort to the supplementary means principally for the purpose of confirmation. Evidence of this trend can be seen in arbitral awards,[31] and above all in the case law of the ICJ.[32]

However, the fact that supplementary means are used for the purpose of confirming the meaning derived from the application of the general rule of interpretation of the treaties does not alter the conclusion that the content of Article 32 of the Vienna Convention is, taken as a whole, considered to correspond to the general international law currently in force.

4. The Preparatory Works of a Treaty

The concept of supplementary means for the interpretation of treaties principally relates to the preparatory works. Indeed, in listing the supplementary means in a non-exhaustive manner, Article 32 of the Vienna Convention mentions the preparatory works first.

Article 32 does not offer any further details. The Vienna Convention says nothing about the concept of preparatory works, or about the direct and immediate purpose of using them to confirm the meaning derived from the application

[30] See I. Sinclair, *The Vienna Convention on the Law of Treaties, supra* note 21, at 142; B. Conforti, *Diritto internazionale* (Napoli: Editoriale Scientifica, 7th edn, 2006) at 95.

[31] See Arbitral Tribunal for German External Debts, judgment in the *Young Case, supra* note 23, para. 32.

[32] See ICJ, *Border and Transborder Armed Actions* (*Nicaragua v Honduras*), Judgment of 20 December 1988, *ICJ Reports* (1988) at 85, para. 37; *Territorial Dispute (Libyan Arab Jamahiriya/Chad)*, Judgment of 3 February 1994, ibid. (1994) at 27, para. 55; *Maritime Delimitation and Territorial Questions between Qatar and Bahrain* (*Qatar v Bahrain*), *Jurisdiction and Admissibility*, Judgment of 15 February 1995, ibid. (1995) at 21, para. 40; *Kasikili/Sedudu Island (Botswana/Namibia)*, Judgment of 13 December 1999, ibid. (1999) at 1074, para. 46; *Legal Consequences of the Construction of a Wall in the Occupied Palestinian Territory*, Advisory Opinion of 9 July 2004, ibid. (2004) at 179, para. 109; *Legality of the Use of Force* (*Serbia and Montenegro v Italy*), Preliminary Objections, Judgment of 15 December 2004, ibid. (2004) at 904–5, para. 102; *Application of the Convention on the Prevention and Punishment of the Crime of Genocide, supra* note 22, at 63, para. 165. Jurisprudence subsequent to the Vienna Convention has similarly—albeit rarely—considered the use of the supplementary means of interpretation with a view to overcoming obscure or unreasonable meanings deriving from the application of the general rule established by Article 31 of the Convention (see ICJ, *Arbitral Award of 31 July 1989* (*Guinea-Bissau v Senegal*), Judgment of 12 November 1991, ibid. (1991) at 69, para. 48, with reference to the 1950 Opinion on the *Competence of the General Assembly for the Admission of a State to the United Nations, supra* note 27.

of Article 31, or to determine the meaning of a treaty that proves to be obscure or ambiguous. Nor does Article 32 specify the conditions in which preparatory works may be enforceable against states that have not taken part in the negotiations and accede to the treaty at a later date. Consequently, the contents of Article 32 of the Vienna Convention regarding the preparatory works do not appear sufficient to dispel the numerous criticisms concerning the significance of the preparatory works in the theory of treaty interpretation.

In this regard, we should recall that reservations regarding preparatory works are long-standing and constant.[33] The most frequent criticism stresses the lack of homogeneity, which prevents any form of classification or delimitation.[34] It has also been noted that the most complex problems in treaty negotiations are not discussed in the official reports, but rather are dealt with in confidential negotiations.[35] Moreover, it has also been observed that the positions of the states as they appear from the preparatory works can frequently change over time and that the reports are merely brief summaries.[36] At times, it emerges that a state could be led to bring forth in the preparatory works a pre-established position to be used subsequently for the purpose of interpretation.[37] There are also suspicions that the statements of the negotiators could be influenced by personal convictions,[38] while others consider that, in terms of relevance, a distinction ought to be made between *traités-contrats* and *traités-lois*.[39] The notion of preparatory works is defined as an *omnibus* concept, which comprises a multitude of elements,[40] including the drafts of the treaty, the notes and the diplomatic letters relating to the negotiations, the memoranda, and the reports of the meetings.[41] According to a more restrictive conception, the preparatory works comprise only the diplomatic negotiations that have led to the conclusion of the treaty.[42]

These and other critical observations can be resolved—at least partially—or in any case reduced, by reference to various indications from the comments of the ILC and from international case law. The ILC, though it was aware of the

[33] See E. Canal-Forgues, 'Remarques sur le recours aux travaux préparatoires dans le contentieux international', 97 *RGDIP* (1993) at 902.

[34] Ibid.

[35] G. Strozzi, *Il diritto dei trattati* (Padova: Giappichelli, 1999) at 61.

[36] M.K. Yasseen, 'L'interprétation des traités d'après la Convention de Vienne sur le droit des traités', 151 *Recueil des Cours* (1976-III) at 85.

[37] G. Strozzi, *Il diritto dei trattati*, *supra* note 35, at 56.

[38] R. Quadri, *Diritto internazionale pubblico* (Napoli: Liguori, 1968) at 186.

[39] Ch. Rousseau, *Principes généraux de droit international public*, *supra* note 4, at 727 *et seq*.; id., *Droit international public* (Paris: Sirey, 1970) at 292 *et seq*.

[40] A. McNair, *The Law of Treaties*, *supra* note 3, at 411; E. Canal-Forgues, 'Remarques sur le recours aux travaux préparatoires dans le contentieux international', *supra* note 33, at 904.

[41] Ibid., at 905; M.K. Yasseen, 'L'interprétation des traités d'après la Convention de Vienne sur le droit des traités', *supra* note 36, at 83; A. Briggs, 'The *travaux préparatoires* of the Vienna Convention on the Law of Treaties', 65 *AJIL* (1971) at 705; S. Bariatti, *L'interpretazione delle convenzioni internazionali di diritto uniforme*, *supra* note 26, at 210.

[42] Ch. de Visscher, *Problèmes d'interprétation judiciaire en droit international public*, *supra* note 4, at 115.

debate regarding precisely what preparatory works consist of, opted to use the generic and all-inclusive formula of 'preparatory works', as the *Institut de droit international* had done before it with reference to the '*travaux préparatoires*' in its resolution on the interpretation of treaties adopted in the Granada session of 1956.[43] After Special Rapporteur Waldock had noted that 'it is the constant practice of states and tribunals to examine any relevant travaux préparatoires',[44] in commenting on draft Article 70 as provisionally adopted in the 1964 session, the ILC confirmed that it did not think that anything would be gained by trying to define *travaux préparatoires*; 'indeed, to do so might only lead to the possible exclusion of relevant evidence'.[45]

The Vienna Conference did not alter the standpoint expressed in this regard by the Commission, despite the fact that this had been prompted by the questions raised by various states.[46]

Elements useful for constructing a plausible response to this question could be drawn from international case law. The case law preceding the Vienna Convention makes it possible to map out a broad notion of preparatory work, in harmony with the understanding of the ILC. For example, the PCIJ made fairly frequent reference to generic concepts of 'documents preparatory',[47] 'various and preliminary drafts',[48] to the notion of 'amendment to the relevant article of the draft'[49] and to that of the 'text submitted by the Drafting Committee'.[50]

However, the *omnibus* notion of preparatory works that emerges from the observations of the ILC and from jurisprudence prior to the Vienna Convention appears to have been curtailed by certain indications of jurisprudence subsequent to the Convention. It was above all the Arbitral Tribunal for German External Debts, in the 1980 judgment in the *Young Case*, that set limits to the notion of preparatory works. In the opinion of the Arbitral Tribunal:

A few words seem necessary at this point to define the concept of *travaux préparatoires*. It must first be stressed that the term must normally be restricted to material set down in writing—and thereby actually available at a later date. This means that oral statements and opinions not recorded in minutes or conference papers can apparently be regarded as a component of *travaux préparatoires* only in exceptional cases [. . .]. A further

[43] Cf. Article 2, para. 2, of the resolution of 19 April 1956, 46 *Annu. De l'Ist. De Droit Internat.* (1956) at 358–9.

[44] 'Third Report on the Law of Treaties', *YILC* (1964), vol. II, at 58, para. 20.

[45] ILC Report (1964), ibid., at 205, para. 17.

[46] For example, in the point raised by Tanzania that 'it might also be asked what was meant by preparatory work' (United Nations Conference on the Law of Treaties, *Official Records,* vol. I, at 173, para. 18). See also the remarks of Poland (ibid., at 174, para 24) and the United Kingdom (ibid., at 178, para. 8).

[47] PCIJ, *Case Concerning the Payment of Various Serbian Loans Issued in France*, *supra* note 27, at 30; PCIJ, *Lighthouses Case between France and Greece, supra* note 19, at 13.

[48] PCIJ, *Treatment of Polish Nationals and Other Persons of Polish Origin or Speech in the Danzig Territory*, *supra* note 27, at 33.

[49] PCIJ, *S.S. Lotus*, *supra* note 27, at 16.

[50] PCIJ, *Interpretation of the Convention of 1919 Concerning Employment of Women during the Night*, *supra* note 18, at 378.

prerequisite if material is to be considered as a component of *travaux préparatoires* is that it was actually accessible and known to all the original parties.[51]

A restrictive notion of preparatory works was also adopted by the Arbitral Tribunal for the *Delimitation of the Maritime Boundary between Guinea and Guinea-Bissau* in the award of 14 February 1985.[52] The ICJ appears to be less rigorous. With respect to the preparatory works for its Statute and for that of the PCIJ, it referred to the need to 'examine the drafting history of both Statutes'.[53] A similar line emerged when the Court included, among the preparatory works for the 1963 Convention on consular relations, the explanations to the delegates made by the Conference's expert, a former Special Rapporteur of the ILC.[54]

The restrictive notion adopted by arbitral jurisprudence following the Vienna Convention appears to indicate a new trend that would expediently restrict preparatory works to the elements contained in written documents and accessible to all the contracting parties. This is a significant trend that could become consolidated in international practice.

As regards the immediate and direct objective pursued by the examination of the preparatory works, there is a convergence of trends. The interpreter draws upon the preparatory works to reconstruct the real and actual intent of the contracting parties at the time of the conclusion of the treaty.[55] The reconstruction of this common intent can be used by the interpreter both to confirm the meaning of the text and to clarify a text that remains obscure or ambiguous after a textual interpretation. Special Rapporteur Waldock proposed to the ILC that the role of preparatory works should be to 'furnish proof of the *common* understanding of the parties as to the meaning attached to the terms of the treaty'.[56]

[51] Arbitral Tribunal for German External Debts, judgment in the *Young Case, supra* note 23, para. 34. In this regard, see, *inter alia,* T. Scovazzi, *Corso di diritto internazionale* (Milano: Giuffré, 2006) at 65.

[52] *Delimitation of the Maritime Boundary between Guinea and Guinea*-Bissau, 25 *ILM* (1986) at 283, para. 70.

[53] ICJ, *Legality of the Use of Force, supra* note 32, at 904–5, para. 102. See also ICJ, *Application of the Convention on the Prevention and Punishment of Crime of Genocide, supra* note 22, at 62, para. 164, with reference to the Convention on Genocide.

[54] ICJ, *Avena and Other Mexican Nationals* (*Mexico v United States of America*), Judgment of 31 March 2004, *ICJ Reports* (2004) at 49, para. 86.

[55] Cf. H. Lauterpacht, *Les travaux préparatoires et l'interprétation des traités,* 48 *Recueil des Cours* (1934-II) at 763; L.M. Bentivoglio, *La funzione interpretativa nell'ordinamento internazionale* (Milano: Giuffré, 1958) at 45; S. Neri, *Sull'interpretazione dei trattati nel diritto internazionale, supra* note 7, at 243; W. Lang, 'Les règles d'interprétation codifiées par la Convention de Vienne sur le droit des traités et les divers types de traités', 24 *Österreichische Zeitschrift für öffentliches Recht (und Völkerrecht)* (1973) at 155; E. Canal-Forgues, 'Remarques sur le recours aux travaux préparatoires dans le contentieux international', *supra* note 33, at 907; B. Conforti, *Diritto internazionale, supra* note 30, at 95; M. Valenti, *Gli standard di trattamento nell'interpretazione dei trattati in materia di investimenti stranieri* (Torino: Giappichelli, 2009) at 110.

[56] H. Waldock, 'Third Report on the Law of Treaties', *YILC* (1964), vol. II, at 58, para. 21.

In the Reports of the ILC and in the debate that took place during the Vienna Conference, the argument was not analysed, providing implicit proof of the convergence of approaches. Indeed, the PCIJ confirmed that 'the Court, in accordance with its practice, has to consult the documents preparatory to the Special Agreement, in order to satisfy itself as to the true intention of the parties'.[57]

In the jurisprudence subsequent to the Vienna Convention we can observe a similar indication formulated by the ICJ. This takes into consideration the works of the San Francisco Conference regarding the drafting of the Statute of the Court to reconstruct the 'intention to widen the scope of Article 36 paragraph 5'.[58]

The possibility of attributing to the preparatory works of a bilateral treaty a meaning that is different from that of the preparatory works of a multilateral treaty[59] was considered in practice largely with reference to their enforcement against the states that did not take part in the negotiations for the adoption of the multilateral treaty but later acceded to it. A clear indication comes from the 1929 order of the PCIJ in the case relating to the *Territorial Jurisdiction of the International Commission of the River Oder*.[60] Three of the parties concerned in this case had not participated in the work of the Conference which prepared the Treaty of Versailles, and, 'accordingly, the record of this work [could not] be used to determine, in so far as they are concerned, the import of the Treaty'.[61] The Vienna Convention, however, does not formally condition the use of preparatory works on participation in the conference or publication of documents. A similar view was expressed by Special Rapporteur Waldock[62] and by the comments of the ILC. More specifically, in its comment on the Draft Articles adopted in the session of 1966, the Commission 'doubted, however, whether this ruling (of the Permanent Court) reflects the actual practice regarding the use of *travaux préparatoires* in the case of multilateral treaties that are open to accession by states which did not attend the conference at which they were drawn up'.[63] In the opinion of the ILC, a state acceding to a treaty without having participated in its drafting is perfectly entitled to request to see the *travaux préparatoires*, if it so wishes, before acceding. The Commission also applies these considerations to unpublished but accessible preparatory works. Accordingly, it decided not to

[57] PCIJ, *Lighthouses Case between France and Greece, supra* note 19, at 13. See also the ICJ Advisory Opinion on the *Competence for the General Assembly for the Admission of a State to the United Nations, supra* note 27, at 8.

[58] ICJ, *Military and Paramilitary Activities in and against Nicaragua* (*Nicaragua v United States of America*), *Jurisdiction and Admissibility*, Judgment of 26 November 1984, *ICJ Reports* (1984) at 406, para. 31.

[59] L.M. Bentivoglio, *La funzione interpretativa nell'ordinamento internazionale, supra* note 55, at 45; Ch. Rousseau, *Droit international public* (Paris: Sirey, 1980) at 293 *et seq.*

[60] PCIJ, *Territorial Jurisdiction of the International Commission of the River Oder* (United Kingdom, Czechoslovakia, Denmark, France, Germany, Sweden/Poland), Order of 15 August 1929, Series A, No. 23, at 41.

[61] Ibid., at 42.

[62] 'Third Report on the Law of Treaties', *YILC* (1964), vol. II, at 58, para. 21.

[63] ILC Report (1966), *YILC* (1966), vol. II, at 223, para. 20.

include any special provision regarding the use of preparatory works in the case of multilateral treaties.[64]

The Vienna Conference confirmed this position, creating a gap that legal theory has sought to fill. For some it would be reasonable to confirm that preparatory works can be invoked against a state that has acceded to a multilateral treaty only if the state has had an opportunity to take cognizance of them.[65] A state that accedes to a multilateral treaty could be expected to be familiar with the published preparatory works and could request to consult all materials that have not been published but are accessible. On the other hand, the principle of good faith would exclude the enforceability of unpublished preparatory works against a state if it was unable to take cognizance of those works.[66] These opinions would appear to be supported by the findings of the Arbitral Tribunal for German External Debts in the *Young Case*.[67] To restrict the scope of the preparatory works, the Arbitral Tribunal relied, *inter alia,* upon the criterion of the possibility of accessing their documentation. This limitation could provide a clue for resolving the question of the enforceability of the preparatory works against states acceding to a multilateral treaty when they have not taken part in its negotiation.

5. The Circumstances Surrounding the Conclusion of a Treaty

The supplementary means of interpretation of treaties expressly mentioned in Article 32 of the Vienna Convention include, after the reference to the preparatory works of the treaty, 'the circumstances of (the treaty's) conclusion'. There is no apparent hierarchical order among the supplementary means. Recourse to preparatory works is more frequent, but this does not mean that it prevails over the other supplementary means, including the circumstances characterizing the conclusion of the treaty. Indeed, Article 32 establishes that recourse may be had to supplementary means of interpretation, 'including the preparatory work of the treaty and the circumstances of its conclusion'. This additional category of supplementary means could overlap, at least partially, with the preparatory works. More specifically, the circumstances of conclusion could be included within the notion of preparatory works because they may reflect the intent of the contracting parties as determined by these circumstances.[68] Generally, however, preparatory

[64] Ibid.

[65] G. Gaja, 'Trattati internazionali', *supra* note 8, at 356.

[66] M.K.Yasseen, 'L'interprétation des traités d'après la Convention de Vienne sur le droit des traités', *supra* note 36, at 89; I. Sinclair, *The Vienna Convention on the Law of Treaties*, *supra* note 21, at 144; S. Bariatti, *L'interpretazione delle convenzioni internazionali di diritto uniforme*, *supra* note 26, at 212.

[67] Arbitral Tribunal for German External Debts, judgment in the *Young Case*, *supra* note 23, para. 34.

[68] W. Lang, *Les règles d'interprétation codifiées par la Convention de Vienne sur le droit des traités et les divers types de traités*, *supra* note 55, at 155.

works can reflect only some of the circumstances in which a treaty is concluded.[69] Consequently, the use of this further category of supplementary means can be considered independently.[70]

For some time, even before the Vienna Convention, it was stressed that a treaty must also be interpreted on the basis of the circumstances surrounding its conclusion.[71] Undoubtedly, an appraisal of the *de facto* and *de jure* situation existing at the time of conclusion of the treaty enables the interpreter to identify the common intent of the parties. This intent is always influenced by the historical context in which it has emerged.[72] In this regard, we can note a convergence of approaches.[73]

The position adopted by the ILC reflected this consensus. No objection was made to the proposal of Special Rapporteur Waldock when, in presenting draft Article 71, he declared that paragraph 2 'also makes special reference to the circumstances surrounding the conclusion of the treaty. This broad phrase is intended to cover both the contemporary circumstances and the historical context in which the treaty was concluded.'[74] The Draft Articles definitively adopted by the ILC in 1966 confirmed the proposal made by the Rapporteur without any significant debate. During the Vienna Conference the national delegations rarely, and only in passing, mentioned the circumstances in which a treaty had been concluded, and always in conformity with the proposal developed by the ILC.[75]

The initial proposal of Special Rapporteur Waldock drew upon an explicit reference to the opinion of the PCIJ in the case *Jurisdiction of the European Commission of the Danube between Galatz and Braila*. In order to interpret Article 6 of the Definitive Statute of Danube, the Court made reference 'to the conditions which existed in fact before the war in the contested sector' and to 'the historical facts' at the origin of that Statute.[76]

After the Vienna Convention of 1969, the case law of the ICJ specified, above all, the role of this means of interpretation of treaties as compared to the textual method. Confirming the rule crystallized by Article 32 of the Convention, the

[69] M.K. Yasseen, 'L'interprétation des traités d'après la Convention de Vienne sur le droit des traités', *supra* note 36, at 90.

[70] Ibid.

[71] L. Ehrlich, 'L'interprétation des traités', *supra* note 5, at 130.

[72] S. Neri, *Sull'interpretazione dei trattati nel diritto internazionale*, *supra* note 7, at 229; Ch. de Visscher, *Problèmes d'interprétation judiciaire en droit international public*, *supra* note 4, at 74.

[73] I. Sinclair, *The Vienna Convention on the Law of Treaties*, *supra* note 21, at 141. See also M.K. Yasseen, 'L'interprétation des traités d'après la Convention de Vienne sur le droit des traités', *supra* note 36, at 90; S. Bariatti, *L'interpretazione delle convenzioni internazionali di diritto uniforme*, *supra* note 26, at 221; G. Gaja, 'Trattati internazionali', *supra* note 8, at 356.

[74] 'Third Report on the Law of Treaties', *YILC* (1964), vol. II, at 59, para. 22.

[75] See the declarations made by the delegations from Viet-Nam (United Nations Conference on the Law of Treaties, *Official Records*, vol. I, at 168, para. 51), Tanzania (ibid., at 173, para.14), France (ibid., at 175, para. 46); Mexico (ibid., at 181, para. 38) and Portugal (ibid., at 183, para. 56).

[76] PCIJ, *Jurisdiction of the European Commission of the Danube between Galatz and Braila*, Advisory Opinion of 8 December 1927, Series B, No. 14, at 28.

Court regarded the circumstances surrounding the conclusion of the treaty as merely supplementary evidence. Significantly, in the case concerning the *Land, Island and Maritime Frontier Dispute*,[77] the Court held that, 'what Honduras is proposing is recourse to the "circumstances of the conclusion" of the Special Agreement, but these, it is generally recognized, constitute no more than a supplementary means of interpretation'.[78]

The method of interpretation established by Article 32 of the Vienna Convention appears to be confirmed by subsequent international practice. The rank of supplementary means of interpretation which is attributed to it by Article 32 has been adopted by recent case law. This tends to highlight the fact that this interpretative instrument has to be used within the framework of a hierarchical relation between the principal and supplementary means of interpretation of the treaties.[79]

6. Other Supplementary Means of Interpretation

Article 32 of the Vienna Convention of 1969 contains a formula that grants the interpreter the possibility of using, as supplementary means, other criteria in addition to those expressly mentioned. The significant formula in this context is the incidental phrase 'including the preparatory work of treaty and [. . .]'. Hence, the list laid down in Article 32 is not exhaustive.[80] The possibility of considering further supplementary means may permit the application of material criteria of interpretation, and it may permit reliance on approaches that emerged prior to the Vienna Convention with reference to the maxims *ut res magis valeat quam pereat, in dubio mitius, contra proferentem,* etc.[81] The unilateral behaviour of the parties following the conclusion of a treaty was also considered a useful means of interpretation, as it was deemed to be indicative of the manner in which each of the contracting parties understood the treaty.[82]

[77] ICJ, *Land, Island and Maritime Frontier Dispute (El Salvador/Honduras: Nicaragua intervening)*, Judgment of 11 September 1992, *ICJ Reports* (1992) at 351.

[78] Ibid., at 584, para. 376.

[79] See *supra* para. 2.

[80] M.K. Yasseen, 'L'interprétation des traités d'après la Convention de Vienne sur le droit des traités', *supra* note 36, at 79; S. Bariatti, *L'interpretazione delle convenzioni internazionali di diritto uniforme, supra* note 26, at 212 *et seq.*; M. Valenti, *Gli standard di trattamento nell'interpretazione dei trattati in materia di investimenti stranieri, supra* note 55, at 132.

[81] L. Oppenheim, *International Law. A Treatise* (London: Longmans, Green & Co, 1928) at 759 *et seq.*; M. Jokl, *De l'interprétation des traités normatifs par la doctrine et la jurisprudence internationale* (Paris: Pedone, 1936) at 109 *et seq.*; S. Neri, *Sull'interpretazione dei trattati nel diritto internazionale, supra* note 7, at 285 *et seq.*; A. McNair, *The Law of Treaties, supra* note 3, at 393 *et seq.*; G. Harastzi, *Some Fundamental Problems of the Law of Treaties* (Budapest: Akademiai Kiadó, 1973) at 187; Ch. Rousseau, *Droit international public, supra* note 59, at 275 *et seq.*

[82] S. Neri, *Sull'interpretazione dei trattati nel diritto internazionale, supra* note 7, at 274 *et seq.*; J.P. Cot, 'La conduite subséquente des parties à un traité', 70 *RGDIP* (1966) at 632.

International case law preceding the Vienna Convention referred to these interpretative criteria with the utmost caution.[83] The criterion of effectiveness expressed by the maxim *ut res magis valeat quam pereat* was mentioned, and then rejected, by the ICJ in its 1950 Advisory Opinion on the *Interpretation of Peace Treaties with Bulgaria, Hungary and Romania*.[84] A similar reference was later made by the same court in the 1966 judgment on the *South West Africa Cases*.[85]

Abundant caution was applied by the Arbitral Tribunal in the judgment on the *Interpretation of the Air Transport Services Agreement between the United States of America and Italy* as far as the principle of *contra proferentem* is concerned. The Tribunal suggested that a treaty should be interpreted in such a way as to set the fewest limitations on state sovereignty.[86] Supporting this prudent position on the principle of restrictive interpretation, the Tribunal recalled previous international decisions, and in particular the judgment of the PCIJ in 1929 in the case relating to the *Territorial Jurisdiction of the International Commission of the River Oder*.[87]

The unilateral behaviour of the parties subsequent to the treaty was instead taken into account in the case law in order to establish their respective intentions. Indeed, the manner in which each state party applies the treaty, even when it does not give rise to a practice that 'establishes the agreement of the parties regarding its interpretation' pursuant to Article 31 of the Vienna Convention, may be useful for indicating that party's intent at the time the treaty was concluded. In other words, it is presumed that a state will apply a treaty in conformity with its original intent.[88] This was the position of the Arbitral Tribunal in the judgment on the *Interpretation of the Air Transport Services Agreement between the United States of America and Italy*, according to which 'the conduct of the parties [...] can however serve as additional evidence as regards the meaning to be attributed to the text'.[89] This was not the first time that an international judge applied this interpretative criterion; the PCIJ and the ICJ had already appraised the subsequent practice of a contracting state as a means of interpreting treaties.[90]

[83] See G. Gaja, 'Trattati internazionali', *supra* note 8, at 354.

[84] ICJ, *Interpretation of Peace Treaties with Bulgaria, Hungary and Romania*, Advisory Opinion of 30 March 1950, *ICJ Reports* (1950) at 229.

[85] ICJ, *South West Africa* (*Ethiopia v South Africa*; *Liberia v South Africa*), *Second Phase*, Judgment of 18 July 1966, *ICJ Reports* (1966) at 48, para. 91.

[86] *Interpretation of the Air Transport Services Agreement between the United States of America and Italy*, XVI *RIAA* (2006) at 94, para. 3.

[87] PCIJ, *Territorial Jurisdiction of the International Commission of the River Oder*, *supra* note 60, at 26, where the Court stated that it could not 'accept the Polish Government's contention that, the text being doubtful, the solution should be adopted which imposes the least restriction on the freedom of States. This argument, though sound in itself, must be employed with greatest caution.'

[88] J.P. Cot, 'La conduite subséquente des parties à un traité', *supra* note 82, at 639 observes that 'la conduite subséquente des Parties est retenue tantôt comme indice de la volonté originale des Parties, tantôt comme indice de la volonté ultérieure de celles-ci'.

[89] *Arbitral Award of 17 July 1965*, *supra* note 86, at 99, para. 6.

[90] See PCIJ, *Competence of the ILO in Regard to International Regulations of the Conditions of Labour of Persons Employed in Agriculture*, Advisory Opinion of 12 August 1922, Series B, No. 2,

The ILC and the Vienna Conference only partially assimilated the guidelines previously offered by international theory and case law regarding supplementary means in addition to the preparatory works and the circumstances of conclusion. The Draft Articles and the Vienna Convention authorized the use of such means but did not formulate a rule that attached explicit relevance to them. This decision reflects the uncertainty regarding the legal value of such additional supplementary means. The Third Report submitted to the ILC by Special Rapporteur Waldock recalls that the jurisprudence of international tribunals is rich in references to principles and maxims of interpretation used in national systems of law; 'for example, those frequently referred to in their Latin form, *ut res magis valeat quam pereat, contra proferentem* [...]'.[91] This international practice should justify their inclusion in a codification of the law of treaties. But the question posed by the Special Rapporteur relates, rather, to the non-obligatory character of these maxims. They are principles of logic which can guide the interpreter, and so, 'in other words, recourse to many of these principles is discretionary'.[92] With particular reference to the principle of effective interpretation, Waldock underlines, first, a tendency to confuse 'effective' with 'extensive' or 'teleological' interpretation, and secondly, the 'effective' interpretation may be said to be implied in an interpretation made in good faith.[93]

In the opinion expressed by Third Report on the law of treaties, the probative value of subsequent practice varies according to whether it shows the common understanding of the parties as to the meaning of the terms. The practice of an individual state may, however, have special cogency when it relates to the performance of an obligation which particularly concerns that state.[94] The ILC, which in 1964 and in 1966 adopted its Draft Articles, confirmed the position of the Special Rapporteur.

As regards the general principles and the maxims of interpretation, the Commission considered that 'they are, for the most part, principles of logic and good sense'[95] and that the principle of effective interpretation ought to be included in the principle of good faith.[96] However, the Commission also tended to attach importance—within the ambit of the supplementary means of interpretation—to the behaviour of states following the conclusion of the treaty, although it did not derive from this a consequential *ad hoc* rule. In the opinion of

at 39; ICJ, *International Status of South-West Africa*, Advisory Opinion of 11 July 1950, *ICJ Reports* (1950) at 135–6; ICJ, *Anglo-Iranian Oil Co.*, *supra* note 16, at 107.

[91] 'Third Report on the Law of Treaties', *YILC* (1964), vol. II, at 54, para. 5.

[92] Ibid., para. 6.

[93] Ibid., at 60, para. 27. For the inclusion of this principle in the ambit of the objective interpretation of treaties, see T. Treves, *Diritto internazionale—Problemi fondamentali* (Milano: Giuffré, 2005) at 393; A. Cassese, *Diritto internazionale,* P. Gaeta (ed.), (Bologna: Il Mulino, 2006) at 254.

[94] 'Third Report on the Law of Treaties', *YILC* (1964), vol. II, at 59, para. 24.

[95] 1964 Report, ibid. (1964) at 200, para. 5. See also 1966 Report, ibid. (1966) at 218, para. 4.

[96] 1964 Report, ibid. (1964) at 201, para. 8. See also 1966 Report, ibid. (1966) at 219, para. 6.

the Commission, 'the practice of individual states in the application of a treaty, on the other hand, may be taken into account only as one of the "further" means of interpretation'.[97]

The Vienna Conference did not devote particular attention to the issue of the relevance of the principles and maxims of interpretation,[98] but the question was taken up again in the case law subsequent to the 1969 Convention. The criterion of *contra proferentem* interpretation was mentioned both by the Arbitral Tribunal for German External Debts in the *Young Case* and by the ICJ in the *Fisheries Jurisdiction* case. In both cases the criterion was deemed inapplicable, but the Tribunal did recall that 'the Respondent has referred repeatedly and with particular emphasis'[99] to the principle, and the Court admitted that 'the *contra proferentem* rule may have a role to play in the interpretation of contractual provisions'.[100]

The principle of effectiveness has had a greater impact. Mentioned by the ICJ in the judgment on the *Fisheries Jurisdiction* case ('this principle has an important role in the law of treaties'),[101] the principle of effectiveness was applied by the Iran–United States Claims Tribunal in the case concerning the *Balance Remaining in the Fund Held by the Federal Reserve Bank of New York pursuant to the Algiers Award*.[102] The ICJ also recognized its value as a fundamental principle in its judgment in the *Territorial Dispute* case.[103]

International practice subsequent to the Vienna Convention appears to confirm the rule expressed in Article 32 whereby the interpretation of treaties on the basis of supplementary means is open to the use of criteria that are not expressly laid down. Many of these criteria appear to lack the solid juridical foundation in general international law which would be necessary for them to be regarded as obligatory. The extreme caution with which they are used in international jurisprudence would appear to confirm this conclusion. They correspond to principles of logic and good sense, in line with the meaning attributed to them by the ILC.[104] The principle of effectiveness is different, in that it is upheld by

[97] 1964 Report, ibid. (1964) at 204, para. 13. See also H. Waldock, 'Sixth Report on the Law of Treaties', ibid. (1966) at 98, para. 18.

[98] For a significant contribution on 'general notions and Latin maxims', see the declarations of the Ghana delegation, United Nations Conference on the Law of Treaties, *Official Records*, vol. I, at 170, para. 69.

[99] Arbitral Tribunal for German External Debts, judgment in the *Young Case, supra* note 23, at 1383, para. 40.

[100] ICJ, *Fisheries Jurisdiction* (*Spain v Canada*), Judgment of 4 December 1998, *ICJ Reports* (1998) at 454, para. 51.

[101] Ibid., para. 52.

[102] In this judgment of 20 August 1986, the Tribunal declares: '[...] accordingly, it would be difficult to admit that they are deprived of any legal effects. This would be inconsistent with the ordinary meaning to be given to the term of this provision, as prescribed by Article 31, para. 1, of the Vienna Convention on the Law of Treaties, as well as with the principle of effectiveness (*ut res magis valeat quam pereat*), generally accepted as one of the main principles of treaty interpretation' (26 *ILM* (1987) at 1568, para. 17).

[103] ICJ, *Territorial Dispute, supra* note 32, at 25, para. 51.

[104] Third Report on the Law of Treaties, *YILC* (1964), vol. II, at 54, para. 6.

international jurisprudence as a fundamental principle. With respect to effectiveness, we may assume that the necessary prerequisites exist to make it operative in the international community as a general principle of law pursuant to Article 38(1)(c) of the Statute of the International Court of Justice.

7. Conclusion

The approach described in Article 32 of the Vienna Convention of 1969 regarding the supplementary means of interpretation of treaties can be considered to correspond to the international law in force. A consistent practice has upheld this position. Consequently, at the time of the Vienna Conference of 1969—with respect to the hierarchical relationship between the means envisaged in the general rule of interpretation and the supplementary means—Article 32 represented the crystallization of an emerging rule, rather than the codification of a general rule.

The use of supplementary means of interpretation of treaties is important when the application of the general rule established in Article 31 leaves the meaning 'ambiguous or obscure', or 'manifestly absurd or unreasonable'.

However, the reasons that can lead the interpreter to find, in the supplementary means contemplated by Article 32, a confirmation of the meaning emerging from the application of the general rule expressed in Article 31 should not be overlooked. Recent international jurisprudence appears to authoritatively illustrate this. Both the interpreter who sets out to defend the rights of a contracting party to an international treaty, and the interpreter with the *super partes* function of judge or arbitrator, may derive benefits from the use of supplementary means for the purpose of confirmation. A state which, on the basis of a treaty rule, intends to bring a claim or to challenge the claim of another contracting state to the treaty, may, in both legal and out-of-court proceedings, find useful support in an interpretation which, primarily on the basis of the criteria laid down in Article 31, is confirmed, for example, in the preparatory works. The state's claim may have a greater chance of success in light of such a supporting interpretation, which could extend to the use of supplementary means that are not expressly specified in Article 32, and among which there is no hierarchical relationship.

Furthermore, such an interpretation could contribute to the diplomatic settlement of the dispute.

The judge or international arbitrator can avail itself of supplementary means of interpretation to confirm the meaning already derived on the basis of the textual criteria. Indeed, an international judgment in which the reasons for interpreting a treaty rule in a certain way are based not only on the means provided under Article 31 but also on the preparatory work and other supplementary means will be more convincing for the parties in dispute. More specifically, the states will be more easily led to spontaneously respect the international ruling.

Similar observations should also hold, *mutatis mutandis*, for national judges and for domestic agents who are called upon to interpret the provisions of an international treaty. A national judge who also draws upon supplementary means in order to confirm the interpretation of a treaty rule may issue a judgment that the parties are more likely to accept.

10

Treaty Interpretation by the WTO Appellate Body: The Conundrum of Article 17(6) of the WTO Antidumping Agreement*

Donald McRae[**]

1. Introduction

One of the more controversial issues in World Trade Organization (WTO) dispute settlement goes by the name of 'zeroing', an arcane matter relating to the way in which margins of dumping (the amount by which a product is being undersold in a foreign market by comparison with the home market price) are calculated in antidumping disputes.[1] The issue is complex and one on which even many international trade lawyers plead ignorance. But, integral to the 'zeroing' issue is a generic question of treaty interpretation. It involves the meaning of a particular, and unusual, provision of the WTO Antidumping Agreement, Article 17(6)(ii), which directs how WTO panels and the Appellate Body are to act in the event of two or more 'permissible' interpretations of a provision of the Antidumping Agreement.[2] Thus, there is more to the zeroing issue than how dumping margins are to be calculated. There is a much more fundamental question about how

* Among Giorgio Gaja's many contributions as a member of the International Law Commission is his attention to language, its precision, and clarity. Not only is this epitomized by his successive reports as Special Rapporteur on the Responsibility of International Organizations, but also by his work as a key member of the Drafting Committee of the Commission. When the Committee is stuck, it is invariably Giorgio Gaja who comes up with the apposite word or the felicitous phrase that enables the work of the Drafting Committee to move ahead. It is with Giorgio Gaja's insight and commitment to the importance of language and meaning in mind that this chapter, on precision in treaty interpretation in international trade law, has been written. International trade law is not an area on which Professor Gaja has focused in his career, but it is one that could benefit immeasurably from his approach.

** I wish to thank John Siwiec for his research assistance and Amanda Turnbull for her editorial assistance.

[1] See P. Van den Bossche, *The Law and Policy of the World Trade Organization, Text, Cases and Materials* (Cambridge: Cambridge University Press, 2005) at 524–6.

[2] Agreement on Implementation of Article VI of the General Agreement on Tariffs and Trade 1994, 15 April 1994 (hereafter Antidumping Agreement), Marrakesh Agreement Establishing the

treaties are to be interpreted, which calls into question the interpretative methodology of the WTO Appellate Body and the way in which it goes about applying Articles 31 and 32 of the Vienna Convention on the Law of Treaties.[3]

2. The Article 17(6)(ii) Problem

International trade law involves a tension between liberal notions of a free trade regime and sovereigntist, or protectionist, instincts of states. The liberal international trade regime embodied in the General Agreement on Tariffs and Trade (GATT), and now generalized beyond goods to services under the WTO, consists of a series of 'disciplines' designed to ensure that states are limited in their ability to restrict the flow of goods or services across their borders and that they do not discriminate between domestic and foreign goods within their markets. However, states want the ability to take measures that will protect their domestic producers from competition that is seen as 'unfair'. So, alongside the rules relating to market access and non-discrimination are rules allowing states to take protective measures against what is seen as 'unfair' trade. One form of unfairness is perceived to be the 'dumping' of goods, which refers to selling goods in a foreign market at a price that is lower than the price at which they are sold in their home market.

Such 'unfair' trade is counteracted by antidumping measures, whereby a state imposes duties on imported goods designed to offset the amount by which goods are being sold at an 'unfair' price, measured by the difference between the price of the goods in their home market and the price they are being (under)sold in the market of the country applying the antidumping duties. Antidumping measures are long-standing, and they are controversial.[4] The way the GATT sought to deal with this was to accept the legitimacy of antidumping measures but surround them with procedural guarantees to ensure that there was due process in their imposition, and this approach was further refined in the Tokyo Round Antidumping Code[5] and the WTO Antidumping Agreement.[6]

These guarantees include defining the 'normal' value of goods and what constitutes the domestic market, as well as requiring that there be a finding of a margin of dumping and a finding of material injury before duties are imposed and stipulating the procedures under which such findings are to be made. All of this is

World Trade Organization (hereafter WTO Agreement), Annex 1A, Legal Instruments—Results of the Uruguay Round, 33 *ILM* (1994) 1133.

[3] Vienna Convention on the Law of Treaties, 1155 *UNTS*, 331.

[4] See J.H. Jackson, *The World Trading System: Law and Policy of International Economic Relations* (Cambridge, MA: MIT Press, 2nd edn, 1997) at 251–61.

[5] Agreement on Implementation of Article VI of the General Agreement on Tariffs and Trade, LT/TR/A/1, 12 April 1979, available at <http://www.wto.org/english/docs_e/legal_e/tokyo_adp_e.pdf>.

[6] Antidumping Agreement, *supra* note 2.

set out in the Antidumping Agreement and non-compliance by a WTO Member can lead to the invocation of WTO dispute settlement.

It is in dispute settlement that the problem arises. Antidumping determinations are made within states by domestic agencies, and complaints of non-compliance with the Antidumping Agreement are complaints about the decisions of these agencies. Thus, when a complaint that the determination of a domestic agency is not in compliance with the provisions of the Antidumping Agreement comes before a WTO panel, or the Appellate Body, what is the standard of review to be applied in respect of that agency's determination?

Article 17(6) of the Antidumping Agreement purports to deal with this question. It does so in two parts: first, it indicates how factual matters are to be dealt with by a WTO panel, and secondly, it deals with questions of legal interpretation.

Article 17(6)(i) provides:

> [I]n its assessment of the facts of the matter, the panel shall determine whether the authorities' establishment of the facts was proper and whether their evaluation of those facts was unbiased and objective. If the establishment of the facts was proper and the evaluation was unbiased and objective, even though the panel might have reached a different conclusion, the evaluation shall not be overturned...

This is a direction to WTO panels on how they are to review the facts of a case and review the appraisal of the facts by the domestic authorities. As the Appellate Body pointed out in *US-Hot-Rolled Steel*,[7] Article 17(6)(i) defines the role of a WTO panel in examining the way in which an investigating authority has established and evaluated the facts. Although paragraph (i) has its own interpretative difficulties and has some relevance to the interpretation of the rest of Article 17(6), it is paragraph (ii) of this Article that is of principal concern in this paper.

Article 17(6)(ii) provides:

> [T]he panel shall interpret the relevant provisions of the Agreement in accordance with customary rules of interpretation of public international law. Where the panel finds that a relevant provision of the Agreement admits of more than one permissible interpretation, the panel shall find the authorities' measure to be in conformity with the Agreement if it rests upon one of those permissible interpretations.

The wording of this paragraph has been described as 'the compromise language of the Uruguay Round negotiators'.[8] It is useful, then, to look briefly at the history of its inclusion in the Antidumping Agreement.

[7] WTO Appellate Body Report, *United States—Anti-Dumping Measures on Certain Hot-Rolled Steel Products from Japan*, WT/DS184/AB/R, adopted 23 August 2001, paras 55–56 (hereafter *US—Hot-Rolled Steel*).

[8] S.P. Croley and J.H. Jackson, 'WTO Dispute Procedures, Standard of Review, and Deference to National Governments', 90 *AJIL* (1996) 193, at 200 (hereafter Croley and Jackson).

3. The Background to Article 17(6)(ii)

There are no formal *travaux préparatoires* for the Uruguay Round negotiations. Nevertheless, some knowledge exists of the negotiation of this provision and it has been well chronicled by Matthias Oesch.[9] There were two basic issues. Should panels generally give a degree of deference to national authorities? How deferential should this deference be? The matter ultimately became critical in the Uruguay Round and was regarded as a 'deal-breaker'.[10]

The strongest advocate of deference was the United States. It wanted deference to apply across the board in all matters under the WTO Agreements covered by dispute settlement and it advocated a standard of 'reasonableness'.[11] If the actions of a Member constituted a 'reasonable' interpretation of a covered agreement then a panel was to defer to them. However, neither the breadth of application of deference nor 'reasonableness' as a standard was acceptable to other states. The ultimate compromise was that a standard of deference was included only in respect of disputes relating to antidumping matters, but it was to be deference to a 'permissible' interpretation, not to a 'reasonable' interpretation. This accounts for the specific wording of Article 17(6)(ii).

On the basis of interviews with negotiators, Croley and Jackson state that there were two parts to the compromise; one was the change of the word 'reasonable' to the word 'permissible', the other was the inclusion of the first sentence of Article 17(6)(ii): 'the panel shall interpret the relevant provisions of the Agreement in accordance with customary rules of interpretation of public international law'.[12] The question of a possible broader application of a notion of deference beyond the area of antidumping to other disputes under the WTO Agreements was left open. At the conclusion of the Uruguay Round, a 'Ministerial Decision' provided that the standard of review in Article 17(6) was to be reviewed after a period of three years 'with a view to considering the question of whether it is capable of general application'.[13]

In fact, there was no obvious 'standard of review' provision elsewhere in the WTO Agreements applicable to dispute settlement. Article 11 of the Dispute

[9] See M. Oesch, *Standards of Review in WTO Dispute Settlement* (Oxford: Oxford University Press, 2003) at 88–104. See also Croley and Jackson, *supra* note 8.

[10] Croley and Jackson, *supra* note 8, at 194.

[11] Based apparently on US domestic law 'Chevron' test: *Chevron U.S.A., Inc. v Natural Res. Def. Council, Inc.* 467 U.S. 837, 842–3 (1984). See Croley and Jackson, *supra* note 8, at 202–6.

[12] J. Klabbers, 'On Rationalism in Politics: Interpretation of Treaties and the World Trade Organization', 24 *Nordic JIL* (2005) 405–28, at 412, argues that this type of wording, as used in DSU Article 3(2), 'makes fairly little sense from an instrumental–legal perspective' since even in its absence the customary rules of treaty interpretation would apply. In the abstract, Klabbers' point is correct, but given the particular history of GATT where the international legal status of the General Agreement was always unclear, the inclusion of such a provision is less surprising.

[13] WTO Agreement, *Decision on Review of Article 17.6 of the Agreement on Implementation of Article VI of the General Agreement on Tariffs and Trade 1994*, available at <http://www.wto.org/english/docs/legal_e/40-dadp2_e.htm>.

Settlement Understanding (DSU),[14] titled 'Functions of Panels' provides: 'a panel should make an objective assessment of the matter before it, including an objective assessment of the facts of the case and the applicability of and conformity with the relevant covered agreements...' However, while this clearly relates to the way in which a panel is to assess the facts of a case (and has its parallel in paragraph (i) of Article 17(6)), it says nothing about how 'conformity with the relevant covered agreements' is to be assessed—the question of standard of review and the substance of paragraph (ii) of Article 17(6). As Oesch points out, 'The issue of standard of review is one of those legal concepts which are not governed by the DSU.'[15]

The special nature of Article 17(6) is noted in the DSU. It is included in the provisions mentioned in Appendix 2 to the DSU of 'Special or Additional Rules and Procedures contained in the Covered Agreements'. According to Article 1(2) of the DSU, the provisions of the DSU are to be applied 'subject to' the special or additional rules and procedures set out in Appendix 2.[16] Article 1(2) goes on to say that in the event of a conflict between the DSU and the Appendix 2 provisions, the Appendix 2 provisions are to prevail.

In interpreting the relationship between the specific provisions relating to dispute settlement of the Antidumping Agreement included in Appendix 2 and the general provisions relating to dispute settlement in the DSU, the Appellate Body took the view that the specific provisions were not intended to be a wholesale replacement of the DSU. Instead, it said, it is 'only where the provisions of the DSU and the special or additional rules and procedures of a covered agreement *cannot* be read as *complementing* each other that the special or additional provisions are to *prevail*'.[17] In the view of the Appellate Body, the only circumstance where the special provisions would prevail is where there is 'an *inconsistency* or a *difference* between a provision of the DSU and a special or additional provision of a covered agreement'.[18] As we shall see, this approach has had implications for the way in which Article 17(6)(ii) has been interpreted.

4. The Reaction to Article 17(6)

Academic reaction to the deference standard of Article 17(6) was generally unfavourable. Antidumping laws are frequently viewed with disfavour and deference

[14] WTO Agreements, *Understanding on Rules and Procedures Governing the Settlement of Disputes*, Annex 2 to WTO Agreement, 33 *ILM* (1994) 1226 (hereinafter DSU).

[15] M. Oesch, *Standards of Review in WTO Dispute Settlement*, *supra* note 9, at 6.

[16] Articles 17(4)–(7) of the Antidumping Agreement, all of which relate to dispute settlement in antidumping disputes, are included in Appendix 2.

[17] WTO Appellate Body Report, *Guatemala—Anti-Dumping Investigation Regarding Portland Cement from Mexico*, WT/DS60/AB/R, adopted 25 November 1998, para. 65 (emphasis in the original), (hereafter *Guatemala—Cement*).

[18] Ibid.

to domestic authorities on decisions on antidumping matters was seen as retrogressive.[19] The specific focus of the concern was on the language and structure of Article 17(6)(ii). The parameters for the debate over Article 17(6)(ii) were set by Steve Croley and John Jackson in an article published shortly after the WTO Agreements came into effect.[20] They made two points that are central to any thinking about the interpretation and application of this paragraph.

First, they stated that Article 17(6)(ii) involved a 'two-step' process: determining whether a provision admitted of two interpretations, and then, if it did, whether the national interpretation in question fell within one of the 'permissible interpretations'.[21] Secondly, Croley and Jackson queried whether the application of the 'customary rules of interpretation of public international law' would ever admit of more than one interpretation. In their view, the interpretative rules of the Vienna Convention on the Law of Treaties, which provide the customary rules of interpretation of public international law, were themselves capable of resolving any ambiguities in texts. As a result, they said, 'it is not clear in the light of that Convention, whether or how a panel could ever reach the conclusion that provisions of an agreement admit of more than one interpretation'.[22]

The Croley and Jackson analysis was picked up by other scholars as well, who reiterated the conundrum of finding more than one permissible interpretation by application of rules of treaty interpretation that are designed to provide a single interpretation of the treaty.[23] Matthias Oesch sees the relationship between the first and second sentences of Article 17(6)(ii) as 'ambiguous, to say the least',[24] but points out that unless the possibility of two interpretations existing side by side is admitted, then the second sentence of Article 17(6) is rendered 'redundant or inutile', a conclusion that itself is contrary to established principles of treaty interpretation.[25]

5. Article 17.6 and the WTO Appellate Body

The interpretative approach of the WTO Appellate Body has been frequently described in the literature.[26] From the outset, the Appellate Body made clear that the mandate provided in Article 3(2) of the DSU to clarify the provisions of the WTO Agreements in accordance with the customary rules of interpretation of public international law, involves applying Article 31 and 32 of the Vienna Convention on the Law of Treaties as an expression of those customary rules of

[19] See J.H. Jackson, *The World Trading System: Law and Policy of International Economic Relations*, *supra* note 4, at 272–4.

[20] Croley and Jackson, *supra* note 8.

[21] Ibid., at 200.

[22] Ibid.

[23] M. Oesch, *Standards of Review in WTO Dispute Settlement*, *supra* note 9, at 93–5.

[24] Ibid., at 94.

[25] Ibid., at 95.

[26] For a comprehensive account, see I. Van Damme, *Treaty Interpretation by the WTO Appellate Body* (Oxford: Oxford University Press, 2009).

interpretation.[27] Focusing on the words of Article 31, that treaties are to be interpreted in good faith 'in accordance with their ordinary meaning in context and in the light of the object and purpose of the treaty as a whole', the early approach of the Appellate Body was to give primacy to ordinary meaning, although it came to give more weight to context.[28] Yet, as Isabelle Van Damme has demonstrated, the interpretative approach of the WTO Appellate Body is rich and varied, utilizing the principles of the Vienna Convention as well as other customary rules of interpretation of public international law.[29] Against this background, it is useful to consider how in fact the Appellate Body has gone about the interpretation of Article 17(6)(ii).

5.1. The initial approach of the Appellate Body

The first case in which Article 17(6)(ii) was raised was *EC—Bed Linen*,[30] which involved the compatibility of the practice of 'zeroing' with the Antidumping Agreement. The panel said that its task under Article 17(6)(ii) was to interpret the provision in question in accordance with customary principles of interpretation of public international law, and then ask the question whether the interpretation placed on the provision by the EC was 'permissible'.[31] The Appellate Body endorsed this approach, stating,[32]

> ... the emphatic and unqualified nature of this finding of inconsistency that the Panel did not view the interpretation given by the European Communities of Article 2(4)(2) of the *Anti-Dumping Agreement* as a 'permissible interpretation' within the meaning of Article 17(6)(ii) of the *Anti-Dumping Agreement*.

It is clear, however, from an examination of the panel report, that the panel had simply interpreted Article 2(4)(2) of the Antidumping Agreement, and reached a conclusion about its meaning. Having reached its conclusion, there was no scope for the panel to consider the possibility that there were two or more possible 'permissible interpretations'. Indeed, the panel had not specifically addressed the question of whether there were two 'permissible' interpretations of Article 2(4)(2) of the Antidumping Agreement.

On the basis then of the *EC—Bed Linen* case, it appeared that the second of Croley and Jackson's predictions was being borne out. Application of the first sentence of Article 17(6)(ii)—'the panel shall interpret the relevant provisions

[27] WTO Appellate Body Report, *United States—Standards for Reformulated and Conventional* Gasoline, WT/DS2/AB/R, adopted 20 May 1996, at 17.

[28] C.-D. Ehlermann, 'Reflections on the Appellate Body of the WTO', 6 *Journal of International Economic Law* (2003) 695.

[29] I. Van Damme, *Treaty Interpretation by the WTO Appellate Body, supra* note 26, Part II.

[30] WTO Panel Report, *European Communities—Anti-Dumping Duties on Imports of Cotton-Type Bed Linen from India*, WT/DS141/R, 30 October 2000; Appellate Body Report, WT/DS141/AB/R, adopted 12 March 2001 (hereinafter *EC—Bed Linen*).

[31] Ibid., Panel Report, para. 4.46.

[32] Ibid., Appellate Body Report, para. 65.

of the Agreement in accordance with customary rules of interpretation of public international law'—was trumping the second sentence. Interpretation in accordance with the customary rules of interpretation of public international law produced a single interpretation, not two or more 'permissible' interpretations.

By contrast, the first of Croley and Jackson's points was being ignored. The panel had not been required to determine whether there were two permissible interpretations of Article 2(4)(2) of the Antidumping Agreement. Its 'emphatic and unqualified' finding led to a presumption that there was no other permissible interpretation. The object then was to interpret—to produce a single meaning—not to determine whether there were two or more 'permissible' interpretations.

In *US—Hot-Rolled Steel*,[33] the issue of 'zeroing' with the Antidumping Agreement came back to the Appellate Body. This time the Appellate Body looked at the relationship of Article 17(6) to the general provisions for dispute settlement in the DSU, reiterating the approach it had taken in *Guatemala—Cement*, that the special dispute settlement provisions of the Antidumping Agreement prevailed over those of the DSU only to the extent they could not be seen as complementing the DSU.[34] This had implications for the way in which Article 17(6)(ii) was to be interpreted.

In respect of the first sentence of paragraph (ii), the Appellate Body noted that since that provision required interpretation in accordance with the customary principles of interpretation of customary international law, it reflected the provisions of Article 3(2) of the DSU and hence there was no conflict.[35] Further, the Appellate Body said, the first sentence of Article 17(6)(ii) confirms, 'that the usual rules of treaty interpretation under the DSU also apply to the *Anti-Dumping Agreement*'.[36]

In respect of the second sentence of paragraph (ii), the Appellate Body noted that although there was no parallel to it in the DSU, the provision 'supplemented' rather than conflicted with the DSU.[37] According to the Appellate Body, the effect of the provision was that under the Antidumping Agreement, 'panels are obliged to determine whether a measure rests upon an interpretation of the relevant provisions of the *Anti-Dumping Agreement* which is *permissible under the rules of treaty interpretation* in Articles 31 and 32 of the *Vienna Convention*'.[38] It then went on to say that a permissible interpretation was one that was, 'found to be appropriate *after* the application of the pertinent rules of the *Vienna Convention*'.[39]

When it came to the actual application of Article 17(6)(ii) in that case, the Appellate Body accepted that the panel was correct in saying that the test was whether the provision in question 'admits of' the interpretation found by the United States.[40] Since the panel concluded that the provision could not be interpreted the way the United States argued, a position with which the Appellate

[33] *Supra* note 7. [34] Ibid., paras 51–52. [35] Ibid., para. 57. [36] Ibid.
[37] Ibid., para. 62. [38] Ibid., para. 60. [39] Ibid. [40] Ibid., para. 130.

Body agreed, then the panel had correctly applied Article 17(6)(ii). Yet, when one looks at the panel decision, it is clear that the panel did not ask itself whether the provision admitted of one or more permissible interpretations and, if so, whether the United States position fell within one of those permissible interpretations. Instead, the panel had simply determined what it had considered to be the correct interpretation of the provision in question.

Later in *US—Hot-Rolled Steel*, the Appellate Body overturned the ruling of the panel that use of 'downstream sales' in the calculation of 'normal value' was contrary to Article 2(1) of the Antidumping Agreement.[41] In doing so, the Appellate Body said that the United States approach 'rested upon an interpretation of Article 2.1 of the *Anti-Dumping Agreement* that is, in principle, "permissible" following application of the rules of treaty interpretation in the *Vienna Convention*'.[42] This statement was made without any reference to Article 17(6)(ii) and when one looks at how the Appellate Body went about reaching this conclusion, it is clear that the interpretation was 'permissible' because the Appellate Body had concluded that it was the correct interpretation of Article 2(1), not because it had found it to be one of two or more 'permissible' interpretations.[43]

Arguably, then, the Appellate Body was not in fact applying the second sentence of Article 17(6)(ii) when it reached the conclusion that the United States had based itself on a permissible interpretation of Article 2(1) of the Antidumping Agreement. In its earlier discussion of Article 17(6)(ii), it had stated that the second sentence '*presupposes* that application of the rules of treaty interpretation in Articles 31 and 32 of the *Vienna Convention* could give rise to, at least, two interpretations of some provisions of the *Anti-Dumping Agreement*...'.[44] But, in its discussion of Article 2(1) the Appellate Body made no mention of two interpretations of that provision. As a result, it is unclear why the Appellate Body was using the language of 'permissible interpretation'—language that presumably has reference only to the second sentence of Article 17(6)(ii).

The approach of the Appellate Body in the cases that followed was to admit the possibility that there might be two permissible interpretations of provisions of the Antidumping Agreement, but never to find them. Indeed, it can be argued that the Appellate Body had never in fact looked. The question always addressed by the Appellate Body was how the provision in question was to be interpreted in accordance with the customary rules of interpretation, that is to say the Vienna Convention rules. Having established the interpretation of the provision in question, the Appellate Body would then conclude that alternative interpretations

[41] Ibid., paras 159–173. [42] Ibid., para. 172.

[43] See R.O. Cunningham and T.H. Cribb, 'Dispute Settlement Through the Lens of "Free Flow of Trade": A Review of WTO Dispute Settlement of US Anti-Dumping and Countervailing Duty Measures', 6 *Journal of International Economic Law* (2003) 155, at 163, where the authors see the Appellate Body as reserving itself the right to find only one permissible interpretation.

[44] *US—Hot-Rolled Steel*, *supra* note 7, para. 59.

were not 'permissible'.[45] In effect, the way in which the first sentence of Article 17(6)(ii) was applied ensured that the Appellate Body never got to the situation contemplated in the second sentence. In doing so, they appear to have affirmed the Croley and Jackson proposition that interpretation in accordance with the Vienna Convention produced a single interpretation of the provision, not one or more permissible interpretations. As Isabelle Van Damme has pointed out, 'The Appellate Body seeks the "proper" or "correct" interpretation, not any "permissible" interpretation.'[46]

There was widespread opposition, particularly in the United States, to the Appellate Body's treatment of the zeroing issue, much of which focused on the way in which the Appellate Body has approached Article 17(6). A common theme is that Article 17(6)(ii) was intended to incorporate a notion of deference, but the Appellate Body has patently failed to show any deference to national authorities in the use of zeroing. The US *Chevron* doctrine, it has been argued, was the model intended to be followed[47] and there has been a suggestion that the European Court of Human Rights doctrine of 'margin of appreciation' should also guide the Appellate Body in its application of Article 17(6).[48] One commentator suggested that the Article 17(6) had become a dead letter.[49]

5.2. Clarification by the Appellate Body

More recently, the Appellate Body has sought to restate its approach to Article 17(6)(ii). In *US—Stainless Steel (Mexico)*,[50] a panel had upheld the validity of zeroing on the basis of an interpretation of the Antidumping Agreement that differed from that of the Appellate Body in previous cases. The panel also argued that it was not bound by previous rulings of the Appellate Body.[51] Not surprisingly, the panel decision was overturned on appeal and the Appellate Body's rejection of zeroing re-affirmed.[52]

[45] WTO Appellate Body Report, *United States—Final Anti-Dumping Measures on Stainless Steel from Mexico*, WT/DS344/AB/R, adopted 20 May 2008, para. 136 (hereinafter *US—Stainless Steel (Mexico)*).

[46] I. Van Damme, *Treaty Interpretation by the WTO Appellate Body*, *supra* note 26, at 70.

[47] See S. Choi, 'The WTO Appellate Body Strikes Down the U.S. Zeroing Methodology Used in Antidumping Investigations', *ASIL Insights* (4 May 2006), available at <http://www.asil.org/insights060504.cfm>; and, R.P. Alford, 'Reflections on *U.S.—Zeroing*: A Study in Judicial Overreaching by the WTO Appellate Body', 45 *Columb. J of Transnat'l L* (2006) 196.

[48] R.P. Alford, ibid., at 202.

[49] J. Greenwald, 'WTO Dispute Settlement: An Exercise in Trade Law Legislation?', 6 *Journal of International Economic Law* (2003) 113, at 117.

[50] WTO Panel Report, *United States—Final Anti-Dumping Measures on Stainless Steel from Mexico*, WT/DS344/R, 20 December 2007.

[51] Ibid., paras 7.102–7.106. There is no formal doctrine of *stare decisis* in relation to decisions of the WTO Appellate Body. In practice, however, panels have followed the Appellate Body's rulings, and if they have not, then they are overturned in appeal.

[52] *US—Stainless Steel (Mexico)*, *supra* note 45.

But the use of zeroing by US domestic authorities continued and the matter came back to the Appellate Body in *US—Continued Zeroing*.[53] There the panel had stated that it agreed with the interpretation of the panel in *US—Stainless Steel (Mexico)* that zeroing was in conformity with the Antidumping Agreement even though that position had been overturned on appeal. However, the panel said, it would nevertheless follow what the Appellate Body had decided in *US—Stainless Steel (Mexico)* and find zeroing incompatible with the provisions of the Antidumping Agreement.[54] In light of this approach, the United States argued on appeal that the panel had failed to apply Article 17(6)(ii) correctly. In the view of the United States, having identified another interpretation that it preferred (the interpretation of the panel in *US—Stainless Steel (Mexico)*), the panel in *US—Continued Zeroing* had essentially found that there was more than one permissible interpretation. Since the approach of the United States domestic authorities had been consistent with one of those interpretations, a proper application of Article 17(6)(ii), the United States argued, required that the approach of the domestic authorities be upheld.[55] These were precisely the circumstances where Article 17(6)(ii) called for deference to be given.

The Appellate Body in *US—Continued Zeroing* did not address the question whether the panel had applied Article 17(6)(ii) correctly; it considered that all it had to do was to determine whether the panel's ultimate finding—that by application of zeroing methodology the United States was in violation of the provisions of the Antidumping Agreement—should be upheld.[56] However, in doing so it set out its views on the interpretation and application of Article 17(6)(ii).[57]

The essence of the Appellate Body's view was that the second sentence of Article 17(6)(ii)—that where two permissible interpretations exist, deference must be given to the national authorities—must be read in the light of the first sentence—that interpretation had to be in accordance with the customary principles of interpretation of public international law.[58] Application of the provision, said the Appellate Body, was sequential; only after interpretation had occurred under the first sentence could the question of two or more permissible interpretations be raised in accordance with the second sentence.[59]

The Appellate Body then went on to explain the second sentence of Article 17(6)(ii) in a way that differed from its earlier statements about Article 17(6)(ii). Whereas previously the Appellate Body had said that Article 17(6)(ii) presupposed that application of the principles of treaty interpretation could give rise to two interpretations of some of the provisions of the Antidumping Agreement, the Appellate Body now appeared to go further. It said:[60]

> ... the second sentence allows for the possibility that the application of the rules of the *Vienna Convention* may give rise to an interpretative range and, if it does, an interpretation

[53] WTO Appellate Body Report, *United States—Continued Existence and Application of Zeroing Methodology*, WT/DS350/AB/R, adopted 19 February 2009 (hereinafter *US—Continued Zeroing*).
[54] Ibid., paras 245–258.
[55] Ibid., para. 265.
[56] Ibid., para. 275.
[57] Ibid., paras 267–273.
[58] Ibid., para. 271.
[59] Ibid.
[60] Ibid., para. 272.

falling within that range is permissible and must be given effect by holding the measure to be in conformity with the covered agreement. The function of the second sentence is thus to give effect to the interpretative range rather than to require the interpreter to pursue further the interpretative exercise to the point where only one interpretation within that range may prevail.

This seemed to imply that the application of the first sentence would not necessarily result in a final interpretation of the provision in question. In saying that interpretation may result in a range of meanings and that if it does there is no need to make any final determination of meaning, the Appellate Body appeared to be implying that the application of the first sentence does not necessarily resolve the question of interpretation. This seemed to give a substance to the second sentence that had not been obvious from the Appellate Body's earlier treatment of Article 17(6)(ii).

What did the Appellate Body mean by an 'interpretative range'? On its face, it might suggest that the Appellate Body was contemplating the possibility of a range of interpretations for particular provisions of the Antidumping Agreement that could be regarded as 'permissible'. But, in the following paragraph the Appellate Body says: 'We further note that the rules and principles of the *Vienna Convention* cannot contemplate interpretations with mutually contradictory results. Instead, the enterprise of interpretation is intended to ascertain the proper meaning of a provision...'[61] This seems to imply that an interpretative range cannot extend to include interpretations that are contrary to one another.

This conclusion is reinforced by what the Appellate Body says after analysing whether zeroing is consistent with Article 9(3) of the Antidumping Agreement:[62]

> We have found, by the application of those rules, that zeroing is inconsistent with Article 9(3). A holding that zeroing is also consistent with Article 9(3) would be flatly contradictory. Such contradiction would be repugnant to the customary rules of treaty interpretation referred to in the first sentence of Article 17(6)(ii). Consequently, it is not a permissible interpretation within the meaning of Article 17(6)(ii), second sentence.

What this suggests is that the Appellate Body was not focusing on any interpretative range, and deciding on permissibility within that range. Rather, it was trying to determine the meaning of the provision. Having determined that meaning, then, by definition, any other meaning was not permissible. In short, application of the first sentence of Article 17(6)(ii) trumped the second sentence, and thus, the second sentence had no application.

On this basis, the 'interpretative range', if any, would seem to be quite narrow. All competing interpretations are in some way contrary or contradictory. It makes no sense to suggest that 'permissible' interpretations are only those that are consistent with each other. If they are consistent then there is no need to defer to one over the other. If 'permissible' interpretations within the meaning of Article 17(6)(ii) cover only those interpretations that are in substance no different from each

[61] Ibid., para. 273. [62] Ibid., para. 317.

other, then Article 17(6)(ii) has essentially no meaning. In short, notwithstanding the apparent shift in the approach of the Appellate Body in *US—Continued Zeroing*, in fact there seems to be no fundamental change.

6. The Failure of the Appellate Body's Interpretative Methodology

There have been many attempts to explain the approach of the Appellate Body to Article 17(6)(ii). The Appellate Body has been seen as imposing its own 'free trade' ideology;[63] it has been seen as hostile to the idea of deference: it has been seen as consciously developing a constitutional approach to the hierarchy of WTO dispute settlement over national authorities.[64] At heart, however, the problem over the interpretation and application of Article 17(6)(ii) comes down to a question of interpretative methodology.

One of the hallmarks of the work of the Appellate Body in WTO dispute settlement has been to develop and generally follow an identifiable approach to the use of the interpretative principles set out in Articles 31 and 32 of the Vienna Convention on the Law of Treaties. The Appellate Body has applied the Vienna Convention rules in quite a structured or formalistic way. This has in fact been an important, positive contribution of the Appellate Body to dispute settlement under the WTO. It has guided counsel in arguing cases and contributed to 'security and predictability'.[65] Initially there was considerable reliance on ordinary meaning, later on context, and then object and purpose came to play a greater role. Now, as is made clear in *US—Continued Zeroing*, the approach is a more 'holistic' one,[66] which takes into account all aspects, thereby putting less emphasis on ordinary meaning.

It is not clear, however, what interpretative methodology has been applied by the Appellate Body to determine the meaning of Article 17(6)(ii) itself. There has been no search for the ordinary meaning of key terms, such as the word 'permissible'.[67] In *US—Hot-Rolled Steel*, the Appellate Body said, 'a permissible interpretation is one which is found to be appropriate *after* application of the pertinent rules of the *Vienna Convention*'.[68] 'Permissible' seems here to be equated with 'appropriate', a definition not found in the Shorter Oxford English

[63] R.O. Cunningham and T.H. Cribb, 'Dispute Settlement Through the Lens of "Free Flow of Trade": A Review of WTO Dispute Settlement of US Anti-Dumping and Countervailing Duty Measures', *supra* note 43.

[64] S. Choi, 'Global Constitutional Lawmaking', Expresso (2009), available at <http://works.bepress.com/sungjoon_cho/51>.

[65] Article 3(2) of the DSU, *supra* note 15.

[66] *US—Continued Zeroing*, *supra* note 53 at para. 268.

[67] The use by the Appellate Body of the Shorter Oxford English Dictionary to find the meaning of terms used in the WTO Agreements is legendary.

[68] *Supra* note 7, para. 60.

Dictionary.[69] The qualifier 'after the application of the pertinent rules of the Vienna Convention', appears to be based on the conclusion of the Appellate Body, later articulated clearly in *US—Continued Zeroing*, that the second sentence of paragraph (ii) has to be read in the light of the first sentence.[70]

The failure of the Appellate Body to approach the interpretation of Article 17(6)(ii) in the systematic way in which it has approached the interpretation of other provisions of the Convention—considering the ordinary meaning of the words, the surrounding context, and where appropriate the object and purpose of the treaty as a whole—leads to the impression that the approach of the Appellate Body has been to treat the meaning of Article 17(6)(ii) as essentially self-evident. This has resulted in some gaps in its analysis.

An important example of such a gap is found in the statement of the Appellate Body in *US—Continued Zeroing* that the second sentence of Article 17(6)(ii) is to be read in the light of the first.[71] Although there is no specific mention of Article 31 of the Vienna Convention, this is clearly contextual interpretation and seems fully in accord with that provision. And, the conclusion is in fact critical because it is central to the Appellate Body's approach under which there has to be interpretation in accordance with the rules of the Vienna Convention before any question of two permissible interpretations can arise. And, then, having reached an interpretation of the provision in question, there is no scope for any other permissible interpretation that would contradict the interpretation the Appellate Body has already reached. In effect, the conclusion that the second sentence of Article 17(6)(ii) has to be read in the light of the first sentence is the foundation for the first sentence trumping the second.

However, if the second sentence is to be read in the light of the first, why is the first sentence not to be read in the light of the second? Obviously the interpretative process has to be sequential; you cannot decide whether there are two permissible meanings unless you have engaged in interpretation. But is interpretation under the first sentence not to be done in light of the fact that the question under Article 17(6)(ii) is not 'what is the final meaning', but rather, 'are there two permissible interpretations' of the provision in question?

In other words, the first sentence of Article 17(6)(ii) cannot be treated just as a restatement of Article 3(2) of the DSU, that interpretation is to be in accordance with the customary rules of interpretation of public international law, and thus panels and the Appellate Body simply have to search for the meaning of the provision in question. The second sentence is just as much part of the context for the first sentence as the first sentence is part of the context for the second. But

[69] 'Permissible' is defined as 'That can or ought to be permitted allowable'; whereas 'appropriate' is defined as 'Attached or belonging (*to*) as an attribute, quality, or right; peculiar (*to*); inherent, characteristic; specially suitable (*for, to*); proper, fitting.' The respective definitions have not changed from the 1993 edition to the most recent 2007 edition. See *Shorter Oxford English Dictionary*, 6th edn, *s.v.* 'permissible' and 'appropriate'.

[70] *US—Continued Zeroing, supra* note 53, para. 271.

[71] Ibid.

while the Appellate Body acknowledges that the second sentence is qualified by the first sentence, it ignores the fact that the first sentence is equally qualified by the second.

Failure to recognize that the influence of the two sentences is reciprocal rather than one way is at the heart of the problem with the Appellate Body's application of Article 17(6)(ii). Under the Appellate Body's approach, the question of two permissible interpretations can only arise once the provision has been interpreted in accordance with the Vienna Convention rules. The first sentence has to be applied before the second sentence. But application of the Vienna rules produces a result—an interpretation—and so after the application of the first sentence to the provision in question there is no room for the second sentence to have any effect. This is illustrated by the statement of the Appellate Body in *US—Continued Zeroing*: 'We have found, by the application of those rules, that zeroing is inconsistent with Article 9(3). A holding that zeroing is also consistent with Article 9(3) would be flatly contradictory.'[72]

In part, such reasoning is a consequence of the Appellate Body's early attempt to integrate Article 17(6) within the general dispute settlement provisions of the DSU, following its approach to reading the WTO Agreements together set out in *Guatemala—Cement*.[73] Article 17(6), it said, was not intended to replace the general dispute settlement provisions. The only circumstances where the special provision, Article 17(6), would prevail over the general provisions would be where there was an 'inconsistency or difference'.[74] This, then, is the basis for treating the first sentence of Article 17(6)(ii) precisely the same as Article 3(2) of the DSU, ignoring the fact that the first sentence cannot be read in isolation from the second sentence, which contains a qualification that does not exist in the case of Article 3(2) of the DSU.

If the Appellate Body had not tried to integrate Article 17(6) with the general dispute settlement provisions of the WTO, but had treated it as a form of *lex specialis,* the consequences might have been different. The first sentence of paragraph (ii) might have been viewed on its own terms and in the context of the second sentence, and not tied so rigidly to Article 3(2) of the DSU. Indeed, the inclusion of Article 17(6) in Appendix 2 of the Antidumping Agreement among the 'special and additional rules and procedures' that took priority over the general dispute settlement rules might well have been seen as a mandate to do precisely this.

Equally, there has been a failure by the Appellate Body to consider the meaning of paragraph (ii) of Article 17(6) within the broader context of paragraph (i). That paragraph clearly limits the way in which panels deal with factual matters in disputes under the Antidumping Agreement. Paragraph (ii) equally is concerned with limiting what panels and the Appellate Body can do when interpreting the Antidumping Agreement. This makes it difficult to conceive of the first

[72] *US—Continued Zeroing, supra* note 53, para. 317.

[73] *Guatemala—Cement, supra* note 17. [74] Ibid., para. 65.

sentence of paragraph (ii) as nothing more than a reiteration of the normal rules of interpretation.

Furthermore, underlying the approach of the Appellate Body is the belief that the Vienna Convention rules are binding rules that dictate a result in any interpretative exercise. This is evident in the terminology used by the Appellate Body to describe the Vienna Convention rules. They are referred to as 'disciplines', language used in the field of trade law to refer to the substantive obligations placed on states under GATT and the other WTO Agreements.[75]

But, as George Abi-Saab has pointed out,[76] the Vienna Convention rules are not primary rules of obligation; they are secondary rules telling states and adjudicators how to go about the process of interpretation. They do contain obligations within them, for example, not to resort to preparatory work unless the result is ambiguous or manifestly absurd. They do not, however, dictate any particular result. They are facilitative not disciplinary and do not 'instruct the treaty interpreter to find a single meaning of the treaty' as a former Appellate Body member has written.[77]

This approach that sees the rules on treaty interpretation as imposing obligations resulting in violation of the Vienna Convention if not complied with is somewhat unique to the field of international trade law and the work of the Appellate Body. Elsewhere in international law, the Vienna Convention provisions are seen as 'principles' not rules intended to guide treaty interpreters. In his recent 14th Report to the International Law Commission (ILC) on the Reservations to Treaties, the Special Rapporteur, Alain Pellet, referred to the Article 31 rule as a 'guideline' and spoke about the multiple possible interpretations of any provision that can be derived from the application of the Article 31 rule.[78] Under this view, an interpretation is authoritative not because of the application of the Vienna Convention, but rather because of the authority of the tribunal that made the choice amongst the various possible interpretations. In this light, the existence of one or more permissible interpretations in any interpretative exercise is the norm rather than the exception. It is based on the view that the core of interpretation is choice.

Moreover, as Giorgio Gaja has pointed out when speaking about treaty interpretation under the European Court of Human Rights,[79] the Vienna Convention

[75] *US—Hot-Rolled Steel*, *supra* note 7, para. 60; *US—Continued Zeroing*, *supra* note 53, para. 273. This, too, was the error in the Croley and Jackson approach; the implication that any use of the rules of the Vienna Convention meant that a final, single interpretation must be reached.

[76] G. Abi-Saab, 'Appellate Body and Treaty Interpretation', in G. Sacerdoti, A. Yanovich, and J. Bohanes (eds), *The WTO at Ten: The Contribution of the Dispute Settlement System* (Cambridge: Cambridge University Press, 2006) 453, at 458.

[77] C.- D. Ehlermann and N. Lockhart, 'Standard of Review in WTO Law', 7 *Journal of International Economic Law* (2004) 491, at 500.

[78] ILC, *Fourteenth Report on Reservations to Treaties* by Alain Pellet, Special Rapporteur, A/CN.4/614, 2 April 2009, available at <http://untreaty.un.org/ilc/sessions/61/61docs.htm>.

[79] G. Gaja, 'Does the European Court of Human Rights Use its Stated Methods of Interpretation?', in *Divenire Sociale e Adeguamento del Diritto: Studi in Onore di Francesco Capotorti* (Milano: Giuffrè, 1999) vol. 1, 213, at 213.

rules on interpretation were not developed with a view to being applied in the context of a treaty regime, which had a binding system of interpretation. The European Court, he argues, pays lip service to the Vienna Convention rules but arguably does not take them seriously. Indeed, by contrast with the WTO Appellate Body, which has placed more emphasis on the text, the European Court has tended to focus more on what it sees as the object and purpose of human rights provisions, rather than their textual formulation.[80]

Based on an exhaustive examination of WTO dispute settlement, Isabelle Van Damme argues that in fact the WTO Appellate Body has 'approached treaty interpretation as a matter governed by principles not rules', although she concedes that justifications offered have sometimes been 'excessive'.[81] Yet in respect of Article 17(6)(ii), the Appellate Body is caught in a conundrum: it considers that it is bound by rules of treaty interpretation which direct it to find a single result, an interpretation that cannot admit of any contrary or contradictory position. Applying a sequential approach, it considers that it is directed by the first sentence to interpret the provision in question. And that interpretation results in a single meaning. Thus, although lip service is paid to the possibility that there may be a number of permissible interpretations, effectively that result can never occur.

7. A Suggested Approach for the Interpretation of Article 17(6)(ii)

What is needed in the interpretation of Article 17(6)(ii) is for the Appellate Body to distinguish between process and result. The first sentence of paragraph (ii) is concerned with process. It directs the treaty interpreter on the way to go about interpreting the Antidumping Agreement. By using the same terminology as that of DSU Article 3(2), it indicates that the approach to interpreting the Antidumping Agreement is no different from that for interpreting the other WTO Agreements. But, the first sentence, which indicates the methodological approach, has to be read in the light of the second sentence, which directs deference in the event of there being two 'permissible' interpretations of the provision in question.

In other words, although the method for going about the interpretation of the Antidumping Agreement is the same as that for interpreting any other WTO Agreement, in the case of the other agreements interpretation must reach a result. In the case of the Antidumping Agreement, the purpose of the interpretation is to determine whether there are two or more 'permissible' interpretations of

[80] D. McRae, 'Approaches to the Interpretation of Treaties: The European Court of Human Rights and the WTO Appellate Body', in S. Breitenmoser and B. Ehrenzeller *et al.* (eds), *Liber Amicorum Luzius Wildhaber* (Baden-Baden: Nomos Verlagsgesellschaft, 2007) 1407–22.

[81] I. Van Damme, *Treaty Interpretation by the WTO Appellate Body*, *supra* note 26, at 56.

a provision. This turns the focus of attention onto the meaning of the word 'permissible'.

The Appellate Body has never engaged in a rigorous analysis of the meaning of the term 'permissible'. As pointed out earlier, in *US—Hot-Rolled Steel* it oddly equates 'permissible' with 'appropriate'.[82] Yet the starting point for any analysis of Article 17(6)(ii) has to be the meaning of the word 'permissible'. Obviously, the term cannot signify any claim to meaning put forward by a party. But equally, it cannot mean the correct answer as finally determined by a tribunal. That would mean that there could never be two permissible interpretations. The answer must lie somewhere between these extremes. It certainly cannot be that a 'permissible' interpretation is simply one that is not expressly excluded by the words of the provision in question, a position that Choi characterizes[83] as akin to the approach of the famous *Lotus* case.[84]

If the purpose of Article 17(6)(ii) was to provide for deference in circumstances where there can be legitimate dispute over the meaning of a provision of the Antidumping Agreement, the task of the Appellate Body is to determine at what point a proposed interpretation has the necessary degree of legitimacy so that deference should occur, even though that interpretation might not have been chosen by the Appellate Body itself if it had continued the interpretative process in order to reach a final result. Thus, the Appellate Body should focus more directly on the question of the interpretative range that it referred to in *US—Continued Zeroing*[85] and be explicit about the factors that prevent a proposed interpretation from being a 'permissible' interpretation. And this has to be more than saying that since one interpretation is the correct interpretation the other, essentially by definition, cannot be permissible.

In other words, what is required is an analysis of the interpretations put forward by both parties to the dispute indicating the arguments for and against each, and ultimately indicating why one interpretation is not a permissible interpretation. Obviously there is a continuum between the competing arguments of the parties about the interpretation of a provision of the Agreement and the final result, but at some point along that continuum, one interpretation loses analytical support. The further it is from the final result, the less likely it is to be treated as 'permissible', but the greater the balance between the different approaches, the greater the likelihood that there can be said to be two permissible interpretations, even though if the process went further, one would be chosen. This may mean that 'permissible' interpretations will be discovered by application of Article 31 alone, without going further and applying the supplementary interpretative principles of Article 32. What needs to be articulated is where this happens and why.

[82] *Supra* note 69, and accompanying text.

[83] S. Choi, 'Global Constitutional Lawmaking', *supra* note 64, at 39–40.

[84] PCIJ, *S.S. Lotus (France v Turkey)*, Judgment of 7 September 1927, Series A, No. 10, at 18–19 (whereby sovereign states enjoy 'a wide measure of discretion which is only limited in certain cases by prohibitive rules').

[85] *Supra* note 53.

It may be that in fact this was the process in which the Appellate Body was mentally engaged in *US—Continued Zeroing*.[86] The hint that this might have been so is found in the concurring opinion of a member of the Division, who stated: 'The range of meanings that may constitute a permissible interpretation does not encompass meanings of such wide variability...' But the full sentence seems to undermine this initial thought as it reads as follows: 'The range of meanings that may constitute a permissible interpretation does not encompass meanings of such wide variability and even contradiction, so as to accommodate the two rival interpretations. One must prevail.'[87]

This simply reiterates the problem that exists with the decision of the Appellate Body as a whole. Applying the normal rules of treaty interpretation to any of the other WTO Agreements, one view must prevail. But the point of Article 17(6)(ii) is that in the application of that provision one interpretation need not prevail. The question is whether one of the rival interpretative approaches lacks sufficient analytical support for it to be regarded as a 'permissible' interpretation. And, what is needed from the Appellate Body's analysis is the threshold for determining that permissibility.

8. Conclusion

Article 17(6)(ii) is an unusual provision. It results from a compromise in the Uruguay Round that was not popular, and it appears to favour rather than diminish national applications of antidumping laws. It is not surprising therefore that it has engendered controversy. That controversy is enhanced by the failure of the Appellate Body to indicate convincingly that it is in fact applying Article 17(6)(ii) in a way that does not involve the first sentence automatically trumping the second. Under the present approach, it appears that applying the first sentence of Article 17(6)(ii) leads to a single permissible interpretation and that excludes any other possible permissible interpretation, thus voiding Article 17(6)(ii) of any substantive content.

In some respects, the Appellate Body is a victim of its own success. Its structured approach to treaty interpretation has led to an expectation that its conclusions on the meaning of a treaty provision will always be impeccably reasoned and the result will flow almost inevitably from the treaty language. In this respect, Article 17(6)(ii) by its very nature poses a particular challenge. It is also unfortunate that this challenge has had to be met in the context of the controversial practice of 'zeroing' where whatever approach is taken to treaty interpretation, the outcome will evoke partisan response.

In her study of treaty interpretation by the WTO Appellate Body, Isabelle Van Damme notes that 'excessive justification of findings on the basis of

[86] *Supra* note 53. [87] Ibid., para. 312.

principles of treaty interpretation can make an interpretation less convincing'[88] and perhaps the Appellate Body has been guilty of this.[89] But the problem in the case of Article 17(6)(ii) of the Antidumping Agreement is different. Here the Appellate Body has articulated a process of interpretation whose application leads to the denial of the very object of Article 17(6)(ii)—the search to determine whether there are two permissible interpretations of a provision of the Antidumping Act.

Ultimately what is needed from the Appellate Body is a variation in the methodology for approaching the interpretation and application of Article 17(6)(ii). This may not lead to a different result on the hotly debated question of zeroing, but at least the outcome would be based on a more defensible application of Article 17(6)(ii).

[88] I. Van Damme, *Treaty Interpretation by the WTO Appellate Body, supra* note 26, at 53–4.

[89] See WTO Appellate Body Report, *European Communities—Customs Classification of Frozen Boneless Chicken Cuts*, WT/DS269/AB/R; WT/DS286/AB/R, adopted 27 September 2005.

PART III

OBSERVANCE AND APPLICATION OF TREATIES

11

Consistency among Treaty Obligations

Benedetto Conforti

1. Article 30 of the Vienna Convention on the Law of Treaties

The international law regime of consistency among treaties, or, in the negative sense, of conflicts between treaties,[1] is obtained by combining the principles of the succession of treaties over time and those concerning the effects of treaties on third-party states. Here, as far as succession is concerned, I will start from the principle that the later treaty abrogates the earlier one,[2] and regarding the effects on third-party states, from the principle of the lack of effectiveness of the treaties in their regard (*pacta tertiis neque nocent neque prosunt*).

Article 30 of the Vienna Convention, which deals with this issue, confirms the point I have just made. It states that:

1. Subject to Article 103 of the Charter of the United Nations, the rights and obligations of States parties to successive treaties relating to the same subject-matter shall be determined in accordance with the following paragraphs.

   [...]

[1] H. Lauterpacht, 'The Chinn Case', 16 *BYIL* (1935), 162 *et seq.*; F. Capotorti, 'L'extinction et la suspension des traités', 134 *Recueil des Cours* (1971-III), 504 *et seq.*; H. Pazarci, 'Problèmes d'incompatibilité des accords conclus par la CEE', in *Mélanges offerts à Paul Reuter. Le droit international: unité et diversité* (Paris: Pedone, 1981) 391 *et seq.*; E. Sciso, *Gli accordi internazionali confliggenti* (Bari: Cacucci, 1986); E. Roucounas, 'Engagements parallèles et contradictoires', 206 *Recueil des Cours* (1987-VI) 9 *et seq.*; J.B. Mus, 'Conflicts between Treaties in International Law', 45 *NILR* (1998) 208 *et seq.*; E. Cannizzaro, 'Accordi confliggenti nel diritto comunitario?', 83 *Riv. di Diritto Internaz.* (2000) 154 *et seq.*; A. Sadat-Akhavi, *Methods of Resolving Conflicts Between Treaties* (Leiden: Martinus Nijhoff, 2003); A. Schulz, 'The Relationship Between the Judgements Project and Other International Instruments', *Hague Conference on Private International Law, General Affairs and Policy, Prel. Doc. N° 14, December 2003,* para. 10, p. 6; J. Pauwelyn, *Conflicts of Norms in Public International Law* (Cambridge: Cambridge University Press, 2003) in particular Chapters 5, 6, and 7; E. Roucounas, 'The Biomedicine Convention in Relation to Other International Instruments', in J. Gevers, E. Hondius, and J. Hubben (eds), *Health Law, Human Rights and the Biomedicine Convention. Essays in Honour of H.R. Abbing* (Leiden: Martinus Nijhoff, 2003) 23 *et seq.*; C. Borgen, 'Resolving Treaty Conflicts', 37 *George Washington International Law Review* (2005) 573 *et seq.*

[2] I do not feel, however, that the practice regarding conflicts between treaties also favours the application of the principle according to which special law, even if earlier, prevails over general law. For an opposing view, see A. Schultz, 'The Relationship between the Judgements Project and Other International Instruments', *supra* note 1, para.10, at 6.

3. When all the parties to the earlier treaty are parties also to the later treaty [...] the earlier treaty applies only to the extent that its provisions are compatible with those of the later treaty.
4. When the parties to the later treaty do not include all the parties to the earlier one: a) as between a State party to both treaties the same rule applies as in paragraph 3; b) as between a State parties to treaties and a State party to only one of the treaties, the treaty to which both States are parties governs their mutual rights and obligations.
5. Paragraph 4 is without prejudice [...] to any question of responsibility which may arise for a State from the conclusion or application the provisions of which are incompatible with its obligations towards another State under another treaty.

Article 30 therefore fully sanctions the validity and effectiveness of both incompatible treaties. Of course, the responsibility of a state which concluded both treaties remains and it will have to choose whether to execute one, violating the other, or vice versa. Practice generally points in this direction: suffice it to mention the case law of the Commission and the European Court of Human Rights, which have always refused to justify failure to comply with the European Convention on Human Rights by states claiming that the violations they committed arose from their commitment to earlier treaties.

It has been said that Article 30 is neither an accurate description of the practice nor a sure guide for those who have to solve conflicts between treaties.[3] In particular, the expression 'the same subject matter' has been criticized because it is allegedly ambiguous. For example, it has been said that it is not clear whether it is a question of two treaties which generally and precisely deal with the same matter, or treaties which deal with different matters, such as, for instance, in the case of international trade agreements and agreements concerning the environment or human rights.[4] In my opinion, this criticism is mere pedantry since it is evident that if Article 30 is to be interpreted according to common sense, whatever the treaty, conflict only arises when the *behaviour* required by a rule of one entails the violation of a rule of the other. Establishing precisely which behaviour can give rise to conflict is, on the other hand, a problem of how the two treaties are interpreted.

It has also been stated that Article 30 does not address a particularly frequent case, ie when states negotiate in order to avoid the later treaty conflicting with the earlier one.[5] It would seem to me that, if states negotiate, no conflicts arise and the provisions of Article 30 on the matter will have nothing to say.

All that remains to be said is that Article 30 is rarely applied precisely because states attempt to avoid conflicts when drawing up treaties.

[3] See C. Borgen, 'Resolving Treaty Conflicts', *supra* note 1, at 578. [4] Ibid., at 579–80.

[5] Ibid., at 634–5, and A. Schulz, 'The Relationship Between the Judgements Project and Other International Instruments', *supra* note 1.

2. Article 103 of the UN Charter. Apart from the Charter, Are There Treaties which Prevail over Other Treaties?

I turn now to Article 103 of the United Nations Charter, which sanctions the primacy of obligations deriving from the Charter over obligations arising from any other international treaty. Also Article 30(1) of the Vienna Convention embodies a saving clause with regard to Article 103.

From a strictly formal point of view, ie looking at the Charter as a treaty, it is not to be ruled out, in this case too, that two or more states may agree that, in the case of certain obligations laid down by the Charter, this priority must be waived. However, the principle contained in Article 103 is considered by the whole international community as a principle going beyond the law of treaties and it has come to be regarded as a customary rule. Internal case law also tends to follow this line, for example, with regard to the binding decisions of the Security Council concerning individual sanctions adopted within the framework of the fight against terrorism.[6]

For the sake of argument, one could also say that the customary rule corresponding to Article 103 can be derogated from by special agreement, given that there is no hierarchy between custom and treaties. In my opinion, and precisely because in practice the obligations deriving from the Charter are considered to be inderogable and binding, the customary rule in question may be classified as *jus cogens*.

Apart from Article 103 there do not seem to be any other cases where the obligations of one treaty have to prevail over later ones. In my opinion, primacy cannot be accorded to some multilateral treaties of great importance, such as, for example, those on human rights or those which are concluded in the context of the World Trade Organization, since there is no significant practice on the matter.[7] Of course, if a multilateral treaty contains rules which reproduce norms of *jus cogens*, such norms will take priority.

I do not think that the opposite view may be drawn from Article 30(5) of the Vienna Convention in particular where it is stated that 'Paragraph 4 is without prejudice to Article 41'.

According to Article 41, two or more of the parties to a multilateral treaty 'may conclude' an agreement to modify the treaty as between themselves if the modification in question is not prohibited by the treaty and does not affect the rights of

[6] See the case law cited by P. De Sena, 'Sanzioni individuali del Consiglio di Sicurezza, art. 103 della Carta delle Nazioni Unite e rapporti fra sistemi normativi', in F. Salerno (ed.), *Sanzioni 'individuali' del Consiglio di Sicurezza e garanzie processuali fondamentali* (Padova: CEDAM, 2010) 55 *et seq.*

[7] On the contrary, according to E. Roucounas, 'The Biomedicine Convention in Relation to Other International Instruments', at 25, in the specific field of human rights, instead of applying the principles on priority between treaties, a choice should be made in favour of the rules of treaties which are 'more beneficial to the individual concerned'.

the other states and does not relate to provisions from which derogation would be incompatible with the object and purpose of the treaty as a whole.

What does the expression 'may conclude' mean? Or rather, what happens if two or more parties conclude and implement an agreement which they 'may not conclude' because they do not comply with the conditions set out in Article 41? In my opinion, the answer can only be framed in terms of responsibility towards the other contracting parties of the multilateral treaty arising from its violation. Otherwise it would have to be said that the partial agreement is void. Such an excessive interpretation is belied by both the preparatory work, and the fact that the alleged invalidity in the cases indicated in Article 41 is not one of the causes of invalidity of treaties listed in the part of the Vienna Convention (Articles 46 *et seq.*) dealing with this matter.[8]

3. Treaties Clauses of Compatibility or Subordination

As we have said above, conflicts between treaties are not frequent as states prefer to negotiate in order to avoid them. Most of the time, negotiations lead to the inclusion in a treaty of declarations of 'compatibility' with or 'subordination' to another treaty, or a series of other treaties, for example, all the pre-existing treaties binding on one of the parties. It is clear that by adopting clauses of this kind, the problem is solved from the start. According to Article 30(2) of the Vienna Convention: 'When a treaty specifies that it is subject to, or it is not to be considered as incompatible with, an earlier treaty, the provisions of that other treaty prevail.'

In addition to subordination, there may also be a commitment by the parties to undertake all (legal) steps needed to free themselves of conflicting commitments deriving from pre-existing treaties, such as denunciation upon expiry, or the opening of negotiations for the revision of them.

Treaties claiming to be subordinated to, or considered compatible with, other treaties are numerous and they need not be discussed here, as they present no particular problems. It is worth recalling, however, the example of Article 351 of the Treaty on the Functioning of the European Union (pursuant to Article 307 of the EC Treaty) safeguarding treaties concluded by member states prior to 1 January 1948 or, for acceding states, before the date of their accession. Furthermore, the member states—the article goes on to say—shall take all appropriate steps to eliminate the incompatibility that may exist with previous agreements.[9]

[8] For this interpretation of Article 41, see F. Capotorti, 'L'extinction et la suspension des traités', *supra* note 1.

[9] See on the subject G. Gaja, *Introduzione al diritto comunitario* (Bari: Laterza, 2003) 164 *et seq.*

Unfortunately the European Court has not always taken these norms into consideration, sometimes resorting to not very convincing arguments to get round the issue. An example of this is its case law relating to the relationships between European Union (EU) law and the General Agreement on Trade and Tariffs (GATT).[10] Despite generally affirming that GATT obligations, previously binding on the member states, had to be respected, in practice, the Court circumvented such a general statement by arguing that GATT norms were programmatic, flexible, and 'lacking an unconditional character'. Actually it is well-known that when one does not wish to take a legal principle into consideration, one affirms that it is only a programme. Thus, the attitude of the EU Court with regard to GATT is very similar to that often taken by domestic courts, particularly concerning the rules contained in the Constitutions. But such case law is reprehensible!

[10] See the case law cited in my *Diritto Internazionale* (Napoli: Editoriale scientifica, 7th edn, 2006) 85 *et seq.*

12

Beyond the Vienna Convention: Conflicting Treaty Provisions

Jan Klabbers

1. Usually, when scholars draw up the balance of collective experiences with the Vienna Convention on the Law of Treaties (VCLT), that balance is a positive one. Thus, Marcelo Kohen suggests that the Convention has proved by and large successful,[1] and Anthony Aust too, in his fine textbook, suggests that the Convention works very well—even though the very title of the book in question suggests a disparity between what the law says, and what states actually do.[2] It would indeed seem to be the case that on a number of provisions the Convention is successful not so much because states actually follow those provisions religiously, but rather because they have given them an unexpected meaning. Perhaps the clearest example of this is Article 60 VCLT, dealing with material breach. Contrary to the terms of Article 60, states and tribunals do not focus on the gravity of the provision breached when discussing or analysing material breach—instead, they focus on the gravity of the breach itself.[3]

Yet, on two sets of provisions, there is fairly widespread agreement that the Convention does not really solve much, and may have contributed to the creation of unworkable regimes. This applies most famously perhaps to the provisions on reservations, which have even been sent back to the International Law Commission (ILC) for further study and reflection—and this further study and reflection has already been going on for a decade-and-a-half. The other set of norms to which this may be said to apply are the rules on treaty conflict which, in the guise of the broader topic of the fragmentation of international law, have also

[1] See M. Kohen, 'La codification du droit des traités: quelques éléments pour un bilan global', 106 *RGDIP* (2000) 577–613.

[2] See A. Aust, *Modern Treaty Law and Practice* (Cambridge: Cambridge University Press, 2nd edn, 2007).

[3] As already anticipated in a brilliant piece by a young B. Simma, 'Reflections on Article 60 of the Vienna Convention on the Law of Treaties and its Background in General International Law', 20 *Osterreichische Zeitschrift für öffentliches Recht* (1970) 5–83. For illustration, see J. Klabbers, 'The Substance of Form: The *Case Concerning the Gabcikovo-Nagymaros Project*, Environmental Law, and the Law of Treaties', 8 *Yearbook of International Environmental Law* (1997) 32–40.

demanded renewed attention by the International Law Commission.[4] It is the purpose of this chapter to discuss those rules on treaty conflict, adding to what is rapidly becoming a considerable body of literature.[5] I will do so in a marked Gajan spirit. In his usual mild manner, Giorgio Gaja, in one of his seminal works, chided overly idealistic authors for asserting all sorts of norms protecting the community interest. This was not the way to do it, according to Gaja. Instead, he wrote, 'I believe that an international lawyer's concern for those interests should rather show itself in exposing the reality as it is and the need for improvement—if possible, also in suggesting some ways to this end.'[6]

2. The increase in the number of studies on treaty conflict probably finds its cause in two developments. One is systemic in nature: the growth in the number of treaties brings with it a greater possibility for conflict between those treaties, and thereby adds impetus to the drive to study such conflicts and find practical solutions. The other reason is perhaps rather more mundane, and resides in the academic urge to jump on existing bandwagons: since some treaty conflicts have been given a high profile (shrimp-turtle, anyone?), the topic presents itself as being apparently amenable to external funding, and on which it might not be all that difficult to secure publication.

Treaty conflict is probably best defined as a conflict between provisions of different treaties which cannot be resolved through such mechanisms as 'reconciling interpretation' or even 'balancing' or 'proportionality'.[7] Treaty conflicts are almost by definition conflicts involving different parties to those different treaties, although the Vienna Convention says otherwise when it allows for the possibility of conflicts between treaties having identical parties (Article 30(3)) and treaties abrogating earlier treaties with identical parties (Article 59). While the title of Article 30 of the Vienna Convention suggests a limit to the scope of the

[4] More recently they also form part of the problematique within the mandate of the ILC Study Group on 'Treaties over Time' established in 2009 and chaired by Georg Nolte.

[5] Several monographs have seen the light in recent years. See eg J. Pauwelyn, *Conflict of Norms in International Law: How WTO Law Relates to Other Rules of International Law* (Cambridge: Cambridge University Press, 2003); R. Wolfrum and N. Matz, *Conflicts in International Environmental Law* (Berlin: Springer, 2003); S.A. Sadat-Akhavi, *Methods of Resolving Conflicts between Treaties* (Leiden: Martinus Nijhoff, 2003); M. Koskenniemi, *Fragmentation of International Law: Difficulties Arising from the Diversification and Expansion of International Law. Report of the Study Group of the International Law Commission* (Helsinki: Erik Castrén Institute, 2007), and J. Klabbers, *Treaty Conflict and the European Union* (Cambridge: Cambridge University Press, 2008). Somewhat older are W.H. Wilting, *Vertragskonkurrenz im Völkerrecht* (Cologne: Carl Heymans Verlag, 1996) and, in Dutch, J. Mus, *Verdragsconflicten voor de Nederlandse rechter* (Zwolle: Tjeenk Willink, 1996). Path-breaking is G. Binder, *Treaty Conflict and Political Contradiction: The Dialectic of Duplicity* (New York: Praeger, 1988).

[6] See G. Gaja, '*Jus Cogens* Beyond the Vienna Convention', 172 *Recueil des Cours* (1981-III) 271–316, at 289.

[7] Proportionality is the newest new thing in international legal thought. For undiluted praise, see D. Beatty, *The Ultimate Rule of Law* (Oxford: Oxford University Press, 2004). See also A. Stone Sweet and J. Mathews, 'Proportionality Balancing and Global Constitutionalism', 47 *Columb. J of Transnat'l L* (2008) 72–164.

very notion of treaty conflict (limited to treaties on the same subject-matter), this is usually considered inadequate. Since the most serious conflicts tend to be between provisions from different areas (eg trade versus environment, or investment versus labour, or extradition versus human rights), it makes little sense to limit the Convention's scope in this way: it would mean that the rules on treaty conflict do not apply where they are most needed and, what is more, that this is in accordance with the intentions of the Vienna Convention's drafters.[8]

There seems to be a consensus amongst scholars and practitioners alike that the solutions offered by the Vienna Convention's regime on treaty conflicts are of limited value at best. Things are fairly unproblematic, at least on the level of theory, when there is a conflict between the United Nations (UN) Charter and any other treaty. In such a case, as Article 30(1) VCLT confirms, obligations under the Charter shall prevail. And while the infamous *Kadi* decision of the European Court of Justice (ECJ) may signal a dilution of this idea, nonetheless as a matter of principle it still stands, at least with respect to lawful obligations under the Charter.[9]

There is also little problem when the treaties (or perhaps treaty provisions)[10] at issue comprise identical parties. In that case, the later in time can be said to prevail, as the later in time is to be considered the most recent and therefore most accurate reflection of the intentions of the parties. Paragraph 3 of Article 30 VCLT states as much, and the provision makes eminent sense.

Things get considerably more difficult though when the parties to the treaties concerned are not identical. Here Article 30(4) VCLT governs matters, but this is far from satisfying. It states that in such a case, the newer treaty may be applied by its parties but only by leaving intact the rights of those that are only parties to the earlier treaty. This may work, on occasion, and one may postulate that it works best in cases where multilateral treaties can be reduced to dyads of bilateral relations between the parties,[11] and cases where the treaties belong to, roughly, the same issue areas (regimes, as political scientists are wont to say), where the

[8] See also E.W. Vierdag, 'The Time of the Conclusion of a Multilateral Treaty: Art. 30 of the Vienna Convention on the Law of Treaties and Related Provisions', 59 *BYIL* (1988) 92–111. But see C.J. Borgen, 'Resolving Treaty Conflicts', 37 *George Washington International Law Review* (2005) 573–648, for such a suggestion, following I. Sinclair, *The Vienna Convention on the Law of Treaties* (Manchester: Manchester University Press, 1984).

[9] Many adhere to the thesis that in *Kadi*, the Security Council's sanctions regime was created unlawfully, which would thus release UN members from the obligation to implement those sanctions. It is worth underlining though that at no point did the ECJ suggest that the Security Council had acted unlawfully, and if so, under what legal order. It merely stated that the EU's implementing decision had been unlawful under EU law, but this is without prejudice to the possibility that under international law (or UN law) the Security Council had acted lawfully. See Case C-402/05 P *Kadi v Council and Commission* [2008] ECR I-6351.

[10] There is the nasty hypothetical possibility of an incompatibility not contained in the treaty itself, but arising due to a reservation by one of the parties: without the reservation, the regimes would be compatible. Perhaps it is best to let this slide.

[11] This helps explain Pauwelyn's insistence on the bilateral character of WTO obligations. See J. Pauwelyn, *Conflict of Norms in International Law: How WTO Law Relates to Other Rules of*

conflicts are in the nature of coordination problems rather than clashes of values. But at the end of the day, it would seem that where values clash, the law offers little solace, and can only offer what has become known as the 'principle of political decision': in case of such an unsolvable treaty conflict, the responsible party will eventually have to choose which commitment to honour, and make sure that it compensates the other treaty partner or partners.[12] Essentially, then, this amounts to an admission that any answers need to be found in the law of state responsibility; the law of treaties does not provide them—and this, in turn, is the direct consequence of the choice made by the drafters of the Vienna Convention to focus on treaties as instruments rather than as obligations: form, rather than substance.[13]

While it may be attractive to criticize the Vienna Convention's drafters for failing to solve the problem of treaty conflict, it is perhaps useful to discuss what options they would have had at their disposal, and to sketch a little of the background. For in the drafters' defence, treaty conflicts were not very common then, in the days when the Convention was drafted; the academic literature was fairly scarce and it pointed in different directions;[14] there was no authoritative decision by an international tribunal to fall back on,[15] and the possible solutions all have their own drawbacks, something that became clear only with the rise of multilateral normative instruments after the Second World War.

Before discussing those possible solutions, however, it is also useful to sketch the heuristic problems involved: treaty conflicts do not always present themselves as treaty conflicts pure and simple, but can take on many different guises and, thus, be approached in many different ways.

In much the same way as Rosenne once astutely observed that breach of treaty may well be characterized as a difference of interpretation,[16] so too can treaty conflicts sometimes be cast as interpretative disagreements. In such a case, the application of Article 30 VCLT might be overdone, and the parties might be better off concentrating on Article 31 VCLT. This may apply, for instance, when a

International Law, *supra* note 5 and J. Pauwelyn, 'A Typology of Multilateral Treaty Obligations: Are WTO Obligations Bilateral or Collective in Nature?', 14 *EJIL* (2003) 907–52.

[12] This was first formulated by M. Zuleeg, 'Vertragskonkurrenz im Völkerrecht. Teil I: Verträge zwischen souveränen Staaten', 20 *GYIL* (1977) 246–76.

[13] See generally S. Rosenne, 'Bilateralism and Community Interest in the Codified Law of Treaties', in W. Friedmann, L. Henkin, and O. Lissitzyn (eds), *Transnational Law in a Changing Society: Essays in Honor of Philip C. Jessup* (New York: Columbia University Press, 1972) 202–27.

[14] The leading studies, pre-Vienna Convention, include C. Rousseau, 'De la compatibilité des normes juridiques contradictoires dans l'ordre international', 39 *RGDIP* (1932) 133–92; H. Aufricht, 'Supersession of Treaties in International Law', 37 *Cornell Law Quarterly* (1951–52) 655–700, and C.W. Jenks, 'The Conflict of Law-making Treaties', 30 *BYIL* (1953) 401–53.

[15] The closest to an authoritative decision was the decision in *Oscar Chinn*, or rather, the joint dissent by Van Eysinga and Schücking, holding that an earlier multilateral treaty had created a constitutional regime from which no modification *inter se* would be possible—at least not without further action. See PCIJ, *Oscar Chinn (United Kingdom v Belgium)*, Judgment of 12 December 1934, Series A/B, No. 63.

[16] See S. Rosenne, *Breach of Treaty* (Cambridge: Grotius, 1985).

later agreement can be characterized as a subsequent agreement between some of the parties, or even as subsequent practice of the parties (or some of them).

Conversely, it is by no means excluded that a later treaty involving non-identical parties would be construed as a breach of the original treaty. Unlikely as it may be, it is still a possibility: a bilateral treaty to derogate from a human rights convention, for example, can be seen as subsequent agreement for purposes of interpretation; as a later, irreconcilable treaty; or simply as a breach of treaty.[17]

Finally, such a treaty can also be construed as a modification between some of the parties. While the VCLT places strict restrictions on such modifications, it does allow them if they do not affect the rights of parties to the original treaties or conflict with the original treaty's object and purpose. In short, the VCLT recognizes that treaty conflicts can be, and are, construed in different ways. It offers a smorgasbord of possibilities, without exactly stipulating which one to follow in which circumstances. Put thus, a meta-rule to indicate whether there is a treaty conflict to begin with is absent.[18]

3. In the absence of any possible hierarchy in international law (save the position of the UN Charter) and accepting the proposition that a simply reconciliatory interpretation might not always be available, the Vienna Convention's drafters had, essentially, three classic maxims at their disposal when contemplating how to solve treaty conflicts: the *lex prior*, *lex posterior*, and *lex specialis* principles.

The *lex prior* principle received some attention in the early stages of the International Law Commission's work, especially in the work of Lauterpacht,[19] and found some support in the Opinion of Judges Van Eysinga and Schücking in the *Oscar Chinn* case. Under this principle, earlier law shall prevail over later law, and good policy arguments can be advanced in support. Thus, as Lauterpacht already observed, if states A and B conclude a treaty, and B later concludes a conflicting one with C, then B's behaviour can be regarded as a breach of its commitment towards A: B should have known better, and cannot escape from earlier commitments by entering into new ones. Legal certainty would demand that A can count on B once B has committed: the *pacta sunt servanda* principle would be undermined by anything else.

[17] See, eg, G. Noll, 'Diplomatic Assurances and the Silence of Human Rights Law', 7 *Melbourne Journal of International Law* (2006) 104–26.

[18] Matters are made more complicated still by the emergence of all sorts of instruments that claim not to have legally binding force but nonetheless aim at changing or influencing the behaviour of actors: what to do if a high-level 'declaration' conflicts with earlier treaty commitments? For a brief discussion, see J. Klabbers, *Treaty Conflict and the European Union*, *supra* note 5.

[19] See in particular the first paragraph of draft Article 16 as contained in H. Lauterpacht, 'Report on the Law of Treaties', *YILC* (1953), vol. II, 90–162, at 156: 'A treaty is void if its performance involves a breach of a treaty obligation previously undertaken by one or more of the contracting parties.' Note that Lauterpacht was of the opinion that the later treaty would not just be left inapplicable, but would constitute a nullity.

The problem with this view is often thought to be threefold.[20] First, it presupposes that B at all times knows what it is doing. While this is a desirable state of affairs, it is probably not very accurate: treaties are concluded by different people representing different ministries or branches of government of one and the same state. More often than not, the trade people in state B may not be aware what their brethren at the Ministry of the Environment agreed with their counterparts yesterday, and these problems of coordination are aggravated by the increase in the conclusion of so-called informal agreements. As even the biggest advocate thereof, Tony Aust, has to concede, sometimes the widespread conclusion of informal agreements creates 'retrieval problems'.[21] Hence, the presumption underlying the *lex prior* principle is bound to remain unsatisfied in most cases.

Second, Lauterpacht himself immediately had to soften his stance in realization of the fact that it might result in minor violations rendering important treaties void and, perhaps more pointedly, upon realizing that an insistence on the *lex prior* would make the future progressive development of international law well nigh impossible. The very same draft article that posits the *lex prior* in no uncertain terms in its first paragraph, posits something of a *de minimis* rule in its third paragraph and carves out a large exception with respect to legislative treaties in its fourth paragraph.[22]

Third, there is also the normative concern that an insistence on the *lex prior* is difficult to reconcile with the fluid, not to say anarchic, nature of international politics. Some might think that in order to be responsive to changing political circumstances, the law should not be too rigid; yet, prioritizing the *lex prior* might create precisely such rigidity, stifling responsiveness, and stifling the progressive development of international law. For the law to remain responsive, so the argument goes, it should allow states to act with some flexibility, and conclude new treaties wherever necessary, even if these create problems with respect to existing treaties.

This idea that law should be flexible and responsive is no doubt a sensible course of action when the parties to the earlier and the later treaty are identical, and it is for this reason that Article 59 VCLT allows for new treaties to abrogate

20 Leaving aside the problem of trying to determine which one is actually the earlier in time, and which the later. On this, see E.W. Vierdag, 'The Time of the Conclusion of a Multilateral Treaty: Art. 30 of the Vienna Convention on the Law of Treaties and Related Provisions', *supra* note 8, who feels there cannot be a simple one-size-fits-all solution.

21 See A. Aust, 'The Theory and Practice of Informal International Instruments', 35 *ICLQ* (1986) 787–812.

22 Paragraph 3 reads: 'The above provisions apply only if the departure from the terms of the prior treaty is such as to interfere seriously with the interests of the other parties to that treaty or seriously impair the original purpose of the treaty.' And para. 4 provides: 'The rule formulated under paragraphs (1) and (2) does not apply to subsequent multilateral treaties, such as the Charter of the United Nations, partaking of a degree of generality which imparts to them the character of legislative enactments properly affecting all members of the international community or which must be deemed to have been concluded in the international interest.' See H. Lauterpacht, 'Report on the Law of Treaties', *supra* note 19, at 156.

older treaties. It applies less clearly though to circumstances where the parties are not identical: in such situations, it remains the case that the position of state A (which does not go along with the new treaty) suggests that perhaps the change of circumstances is less dramatic than states B and C may want to convey. If there is a strong objective need to change the regime, no doubt A would happily participate; the fact that A does not participate might suggest not so much that A wants to play hardball, but simply that there is political disagreement about the desirability of the new regime; and if that is the case, then allowing for the new treaty to prevail is a political choice for B and C, and against A—a choice which cannot be dictated by the existence of more or less objective circumstances. And in such a case A may indeed want to insist on its legal right to have its expectations and rights honoured by B.

If the *lex prior* principle comes with drawbacks, so does the *lex posterior* principle. Here, the idea is that in case of conflict the later in time shall prevail, and as noted, this is sensible when it concerns treaties with identical parties. The main justification for seeing the *lex posterior* prevail is, after all, that it is the most recent, and thus most accurate, reflection of the relevant political actors (well, some of them, at any rate), and in a legal order based on individual consent where order and stability are intimately related to whatever it is the main actors desire, it makes political sense to have law mirror politics as closely as possible. A law that becomes too lofty and too detached from political configurations, after all, will not be of great practical use, as Max Huber already knew.[23]

Yet, the *lex posterior* principle is less useful when it comes to conflicts between treaties with non-identical parties, and largely for the same reason: in a legal order based on sovereign consent and on the intentional creation of commitments by the relevant actors, the later treaty between B and C is of no concern to state A. Treaties are, in the international legal order, best seen as so many specimens of *res inter alios acta*, of things between the parties, with no radiating effects on other parties (save in exceptional circumstances, for instance with respect to so-called objective regimes).[24] In other words: A does not have to accept in any way the situation where B, through B's own acts, is not in a position to honour its commitments towards A. There is considerable irony in the circumstance that the same horizontal structure of international law which might make it desirable to sponsor the *lex posterior* also militates against it.

[23] See M. Huber, *Die soziologischen Grundlagen des Völkerrechts* (Berlin: Rothschild, 1928). What Huber did not yet realize is that the reverse is also true: a law that merely reflects what states are willing to do at any rate is not terribly normative, and thus of little independent use either. The point is forcefully made by M. Koskenniemi, *From Apology to Utopia: The Structure of International Legal Argument* (Helsinki: Finnish Lawyers' Publishing Company, 1989).

[24] See, eg, B. Simma, 'The Antarctic Treaty as a treaty providing for an "objective regime"', 19 *Cornell International Law Journal* (1986) 189–209; J. Klabbers, 'Les cimétières marins sont-ils établis comme des régimes objectifs? À propos de l'accord sur l'épave du M/S Estonia', 11 *Espaces et Ressources Maritimes* (1997) 121–33.

In recognition of the problems surrounding the application in practice and theory of both the *lex prior* and *lex posterior* principles, it is sometimes posited that maybe the *lex specialis* principle could offer a useful way out.[25] And indeed, at first blush, it would seem attractive to focus not so much on a formal criterion (whether a treaty was concluded later or earlier in time), but rather on a substantive criterion: special law should prevail over general law. The attraction follows, it would seem, from the same source which upholds such notions as subsidiarity in international legal thought:[26] political decision-making (of which treaty-making is a species) should ideally stay close to the relevant actors, and not take place in some faraway capital, far removed from any understanding of the concerns of those actors. Hence, while it might be useful to have general regimes, it is also desirable to have the possibility of adapting these to local circumstances, or adapting them to cases in which states boast special relations, *et cetera*.

Still, the *lex specialis* principle comes with a number of methodological issues, none of them solvable without more. First, it is by no means self-evident how to determine, in most ordinary cases, which treaty is the special one and which is the general one. Essentially, there are two ways of approaching the matter. First, one can look at the number of parties, and then conclude that the one with the smaller number must by definition represent the special law. This, however, falls back to a formalism of the same kind that the resort to *lex specialis* was meant to prevent: instead of counting dates of conclusion, one counts numbers of parties, but either way, the result might be unsatisfactory. It might lead, for example, to the morally unpleasant situation that a bilateral extradition treaty between A and B might represent the *lex specialis* against the background of a general human rights agreement, and therewith justify the extradition of individuals even if violations of their human rights are to be expected.[27]

Alternatively, one can look not at the number of parties, but at the substance of the agreement, but this stumbles at the formidable hurdle that it is well-nigh impossible to decide substantively which agreement will represent general law, and which will represent special law, and where this is possible at all, again the result may be unpalatable. Thus, one might postulate that against the background of universal regimes, regional regimes on the same topic represent the special law, but this would mean (in a nutshell, and in the abstract, disregarding other considerations) prioritizing NATO over the UN, and the European Union (EU) over the World Trade Organization (WTO) (and Benelux over the EU,

[25] See, eg, A. Lindroos, 'Addressing Norm Conflicts in a Fragmented Legal System: The Doctrine of *Lex Specialis*', 74 *Nordic JIL* (2005) 27–66.

[26] See P.G. Carozza, 'Subsidiarity as a Structural Principle of Human Rights Law', 97 *AJIL* (2003) 38–79.

[27] Recent emanations may well be formed by, in euphemistic language, the so-called 'extraordinary rendition agreements', handing over individuals to countries where torture can reasonably be expected. See, eg, G. Noll, 'Diplomatic Assurances and the Silence of Human Rights Law', *supra* note 17 and M. Jones, 'Lies, Damned Lies and Diplomatic Assurances: The Misuse of Diplomatic Assurances in Removal Proceedings', 8 *European Journal of Migration and Law* (2006) 9–39.

for that matter). It would go against the grain of international law, where often enough the universal is seen as somehow morally superior to the local or regional. The very substance of the *lex specialis* maxim is difficult to reconcile with the universalist ambitions of international law.

Of greater practical relevance though is that whatever the drafters of the Vienna Convention may have felt about *lex specialis*, they could not insert it into the Vienna Convention precisely because of its prima facie substantive orientation. The Vienna Convention, as noted, is built around a conception of the treaty as form, not substance (the treaty as instrument, not as obligation), and eschews all considerations of substance, with two possible exceptions: the introduction of the *jus cogens* idea, and (less obviously) the repeated references to the object and purpose of treaties.[28] Other than these, however, all considerations of substance are barred, which helps explain why there are no provisions on breach of treaty (other than material breach, which is problematically defined in purely formal terms),[29] and why such problematic topics as reservations to multilateral treaties are approached not by invoking the substance of reservations, but by reference to the number of objections they provoke.[30]

4. In light of the above, it is surely no accident that the Vienna Convention fails to come up with any ready-made, one-size-fits-all solutions to solve treaty conflicts. As a result, practice and theory demonstrate a number of ways in which states and other actors aim to mitigate the worst effects of being confronted with unsolvable treaty conflicts. Perhaps the most obvious one is to set up negotiating fora for further discussion and reflection. This is said to occur in particular in the field of environmental relations which, indeed, often serves as international law's laboratory:[31] it has a history of finding creative, smooth solutions to resolve or gloss over often difficult diplomatic issues. International environmental law arguably formed the cradle of the soft law discussion and pioneered the idea of creating treaty regimes complete with broadly phrased framework agreements and more detailed implementing agreements and even more flexible adjustment procedures; in international environmental law, the idea of settling disputes by means of soft non-compliance procedures (those 'gentle pressurizers')[32] first came to the fore, and it is in international environmental law that parties may aspire to commit to 'common, but differentiated responsibilities'.

[28] On the latter, see J. Klabbers, 'Some Problems Regarding the Object and Purpose of Treaties', 8 *Finnish YIL* (1997) 138–60.

[29] See *supra* note 3.

[30] See, eg, L. Lijnzaad, *Reservations to UN Human Rights Treaties: Ratify and Ruin?* (Leiden: Martinus Nijhoff, 1995).

[31] R. Wolfrum and N. Matz, *Conflicts in International Environmental Law*, *supra* note 5.

[32] This evocative term is borrowed from T. Kuokkanen, 'Putting Gentle Pressure on Parties: Recent Trends in the Practice of the Implementation Committee under the Convention on Long-range Transboundary Air Pollution', in J. Petman and J. Klabbers (eds), *Nordic Cosmopolitanism: Essays in International Law for Martti Koskenniemi* (Leiden: Martinus Nijhoff, 2003) 315–26.

Useful as this may be to settle conflicts between various environmental commitments, it does little to alleviate conflicts based on different values: conflicts between commitments in a single field may be relatively easy to solve, insofar as the individuals concerned at least will be able to communicate with each other and will, roughly, share a similar outlook and background assumptions; this will play out rather differently though when treaty conflict involves conflicts between different value systems; environmentalists and the trade community rarely speak the same language.[33]

Some theorists look to systems theory for a solution.[34] According to this line of thought, distinct regimes (trade, environment, etc) are self-contained and self-referential systems which are, however, able to communicate with one another, and they tend to do so in particular through their courts. Conflict-solving takes place through such means as mutual recognition and cooperation between regimes. This version of systems theory scores high on diagnostics (in that a depiction of the world in terms of functional regimes strikes one as eminently plausible), but has problems with involving human agency: it seems to suggest that systems do what they do, regardless of who is directing them (or, more strongly still, that those systems go undirected to begin with). Moreover, the systems approach tends to ignore the political aspects: it is by no means a given that certain topics belong to certain regimes. The discussion on genetically modified foods, for example, can be cast as a trade issue, but also as a health issue, a human rights issue, an environmental issue, or even a security issue. Systems theory has no readily available answer to the question of how such a topic comes to be seen as belonging to one regime rather than the other.

Yet another approach (or cluster of approaches, really) posits some form of hierarchy in international law. This is partly inspired no doubt by the existence of Article 103 UN (confirmed in Article 30 VCLT),[35] which holds that in case of a conflict between an obligation under the Charter and obligations arising out of other agreements, those under the Charter shall prevail. While Article 103 is a logical component in any treaty aiming to establish a universalist global governance organization (the UN's predecessor, the League of Nations, had a similar clause in its Covenant), it might not be quite as easy with other norms or regimes: indeed, by the very nature of things, only one regime can be supreme.

Some have posited *jus cogens* norms at the pinnacle of the international legal order.[36] While plausible, though, there is still widespread disagreement as to

[33] This builds on J. Klabbers, *Treaty Conflict and the European Union*, *supra* note 5, which points out that the truly difficult class of problems consists of clashing values.

[34] See especially A. Fischer-Lescano and G. Teubner, *Regime-Kollisionen: Zur Fragmentierung des Globalen Rechts* (Frankfurt am Main: Suhrkamp, 2006).

[35] Useful on Article 103 UN is R. Liivoja, 'The Scope of the Supremacy Clause of the United Nations Charter', 57 *ICLQ* (2008) 583–612.

[36] This often is done in the framework of the discussion on the constitutionalization of international law. See generally J. Klabbers, A. Peters, and G. Ulfstein, *The Constitutionalization of International Law* (Oxford: Oxford University Press, 2009).

which norms qualify as *jus cogens* and, more importantly for present purposes, the category of *jus cogens* will do little to settle most treaty conflicts. The very concept of *jus cogens* would suggest that it can only comprise a small group of norms (such as the prohibitions on genocide, torture, slavery, and aggression), which renders it fairly useless in solving conflicts involving, say, freedom of expression and wildlife protection, or freedom to trade versus the protection of endangered species. An obvious response might be to broaden the circle of *jus cogens* norms, but this cannot be done as long as such conflicts exist (their very existence, after all, suggests that the norm at issue has not been unconditionally accepted as a *jus cogens* norm) and, what is more, it might undermine the very idea of *jus cogens*: if everything is *jus cogens*, then the category loses its analytical sharpness, and any treaty conflict will then continue in the form of a conflict between two conflicting *jus cogens* norms.[37]

A variation on the same theme is the upgrading, by authorial fiat, of certain norms as hierarchically superior. This has the great benefit, of course, of being able to solve conflicts (at least those pitting such a superior norm against an inferior one), but much hinges on the plausibility of the upgrading itself. Here then problems typically come in, with authors proposing their preferred lists of values but usually with little to back these up; equally typically then, they end up having to tone things down: the circle turns out to be resistant to squaring.[38]

A variation on this variation, even more dependent on authorial fiat, is to elevate some norms to superior status while at the same time maintaining that they form part of the antagonist regime. Its main exponent, following the Court of Justice of the European Union, is Petersmann, who in a series of articles proclaimed the positive existence of certain human rights not only as classical human rights but also as trade-related rights (eg the freedom to contract), and therein found these to be part of the world trade regime, with the consequence that conflicts between trade norms and human rights norms would quickly dissipate: instead, trade norms are human rights norms, and hence there either is no conflict, or there is only a coordination conflict, solvable within the regime precisely because it does not start from different values. Those underlying values have become one.[39]

Ingenious as the approach is, it is vulnerable to the critique that the existence of trading rules as human rights norms is not uncontroversial. While many accept the right to property as a human right (even though it is not mentioned in the International Covenant on Civil and Political Rights, and was absent from the

[37] See generally G. Gaja, 'Jus Cogens Beyond the Vienna Convention', *supra* note 6.

[38] As good an example as any is provided by Fitzmaurice and Elias, proclaiming that within environmental law a norm such as that referring to the common heritage of mankind is of higher status than ordinary norms, but later acknowledging that such a norm may be useful as an aid to interpretation, regardless of its substantive legal status. See M. Fitzmaurice and O. Elias, *Contemporary Issues in the Law of Treaties* (Utrecht: Eleven, 2005), especially at 341, and at 345.

[39] See, eg, E.-U. Petersmann, 'Time for a United Nations "Global Compact" for Integrating Human Rights into the Law of Worldwide Organizations: Lessons from European Integration', 13 *EJIL* (2002) 621–50.

original European Convention on Human Rights as well), other norms are less warmly embraced as human rights norms: while it is one thing to construe the prohibition on torture as a human right, it is quite another to think of the freedom to contract or the right to trade as human rights, especially perhaps when many still die of poverty and malnutrition as a (possible) result of the very same freedom to contract and right to trade.

Among the more sensible suggestions is to allow conflicting norms in through the interpretative process: a principle of systemic integration, as the International Law Commission came to refer to it.[40] Article 31(3)(c) VCLT provides the technical support for this approach, urging interpreters to take all relevant rules of international law between the parties into account when interpreting a treaty provision.[41] Sensible as it is, though, it sometimes stumbles on tricky hurdles, the most tricky one possibly being the question how those 'parties' should be defined: parties to a dispute? Or parties to the antagonist agreement? In the latter case, it might prove impossible to find treaties with fully overlapping parties, as the European Community (EC) found out to its dismay in a dispute before the WTO concerning biotechnological products. The WTO panel held that the rule of the VCLT meant that all WTO member states also had to be parties to the environmental agreement invoked by the EU—quite an insurmountable hurdle.[42]

A final approach to settle treaty conflicts is to grant priority to other regimes, an idea pioneered by the EU. Article 307 EC Treaty (pre-Lisbon) provides that treaties concluded by EC member states before the EC was created, or before they joined, shall remain unaffected by EC law. That said though, paragraph 2 of the same article stipulates that the member states should eliminate all incompatibilities. The Court of Justice of the EC has been less than generous in applying the rule: while ostensibly safeguarding anterior member state agreements, the clause has always been more about achieving a balance between the protection of those earlier treaties and the protection of the autonomy of the EC's legal order—and that is a charitable reading.[43] Less charitably, there is ample ground for interpreting the case law of the ECJ as simply protecting the EC legal order without aiming to achieve any balance—full stop.[44]

[40] See M. Koskenniemi, *Fragmentation of International Law: Difficulties Arising from the Diversification and Expansion of International Law. Report of the Study Group of the International Law Commission*, *supra* note 5. See also C. McLachlan, 'The Principle of Systemic Integration and Article 31(3)(c) of the Vienna Convention', 54 *ICLQ* (2005) 279–320.

[41] See also J. Klabbers, 'Reluctant *Grundnormen*: Articles 31(3)(c) and 42 of the Vienna Convention on the Law of Treaties and the Fragmentation of International Law', in M. Craven, M. Fitzmaurice, and M. Vogiatzi (eds), *Time, History and International Law* (Leiden: Martinus Nijhoff, 2007) 141–61.

[42] See *European Communities—Measures Affecting the Approval and Marketing of Biotech Products*, WT/DS291.292.293, 29 September 2006.

[43] See, eg, P. Koutrakos, *EU International Relations Law* (Oxford: Hart, 2006).

[44] See J. Klabbers, *Treaty Conflict and the European Union*, *supra* note 5. For more general reflection on the EU courts' attitude towards international law, see J. Klabbers, '*Völkerrechtsfreundlich*?

5. Clearly, in a horizontal legal order, the solution of treaty conflicts is bound to remain problematic. As long as states remain sovereign equals, as long as treaties are based on the consent of those sovereign equals, and as long as those treaties cannot be regarded as anything other than *res inter alios acta*, the law lacks the instruments to settle treaty conflicts in a simple and straightforward way. If anything, discussing treaty conflict demonstrates how far removed international law still is from being a legal order containing public elements—only in such an order can notions of hierarchy, for example, be fruitfully developed, or would it be possible to break through the *res inter alios acta* paradigm.

In such a setting, it is no coincidence that the drafters of the Vienna Convention (the special rapporteurs, the other ILC members, and the diplomats present at Vienna in 1968 and 1969) could not find a way to deal satisfactorily with treaty conflicts: after all, one cannot place square pegs into round holes. The best the discipline has to offer, then, is the so-called principle of political decision. While this cannot be regarded as a legal principle in any Dworkinian sense, it is nonetheless more useful than it might appear, as it is precisely the inconclusive nature of treaty conflicts that allows for the participation of the formerly excluded: where the law fails to provide a clear-cut answer, activists and lobbyists may come in to try and influence the outcome.

Put thus, situations of treaty conflict call out for proper guarantees concerning participation and representation. In a situation where the outcome of a dispute can be influenced on the strength of political argument, there is a premium on ensuring that all relevant arguments may be heard. Courts and tribunals should liberally interpret their own rules, including jurisdictional clauses, so as to allow intervention by all possible 'stakeholders', and individual judges and arbitrators should be open to accept views from across the political spectrum. Judicial values should include openness, modesty and humility, and candour about the reasons why they reach their decisions. In an intensely pluralist world, where sometimes deeply conflicting values need to coexist, much will come to depend on the virtue of individual judges and arbitrators.[45]

Much the same will hold true with respect to the individual activists and lobbyists who benefit from the law's indeterminacy. This, admittedly, opens up possibilities for abuse: it is not too difficult to imagine industrial lobbyists spending a great deal of money on campaigning in favour of industry-friendly solutions to conflicts setting up trade values and environmental values, for example. But even so, the alternative may be worse: the above discussion of the *lex prior, lex posterior,*

International Law and the Union Legal Order', in P. Koutrakos (ed.), *European Foreign Policy: Legal and Political Perspectives* (Cheltenham: Edward Elgar, forthcoming).

[45] See generally C. Farrell and L.B. Solum (eds), *Virtue Jurisprudence* (Basingstoke: Palgrave MacMillan, 2008); H.J. Powell, *Constitutional Conscience: The Moral Dimension of Judicial Decision* (Chicago: University of Chicago Press, 2008). More specifically referring to international law is J. Klabbers, 'Virtuous Interpretation', in M. Fitzmaurice, O. Elias, and P. Merkouris (eds), *Treaty Interpretation and the Vienna Convention: 30 Years On* (Leiden: Martinus Nijhoff,) 17–37.

and *lex specialis* maxims suggests that all three may come to work against the community interest, and that one of them (*lex specialis*) even seems structurally tilted against the community interest. In such circumstances, it is arguable that a simple adversarial model of judicial decision-making breaks down, and tribunals assume the duty, *ex officio*, to make sure that all interests are accurately represented before them.

This is not, admittedly, an accurate description of judicial practice just yet: tribunals confronted with conflicts between regimes have thus far been keen to apply narrow conceptions of their own jurisdiction, despite occasional protestations to the contrary.[46] The WTO may signal that its law should not be read 'in clinical isolation' from public international law,[47] but its narrow reading of Article 31(3)(c) VCLT, as mentioned above, effectively guarantees such clinical isolation. Likewise, the ECJ's attitude in the infamous *Mox Plant* dispute[48] can hardly be referred to as 'broad-minded', and has even been likened to a Soviet-style attitude.[49]

6. To conclude: the Vienna Convention on the Law of Treaties is less than fully successful when it comes to resolving treaty conflicts, but this should come as no surprise. Given the largely horizontal structure of international law, things could hardly be otherwise. In order to settle complex disputes then, much hinges on the attitudes—nay, virtues—of the actors involved: from community activists and lobbyists to diplomats and members of international tribunals. Honest deliberation, taking into account all affected interests, may result in relatively painless global governance; prioritizing partisan or sectoral interests, by contrast, is bound to remain unsatisfactory.

[46] Even then, however, it is possible to do justice to external concerns. A good example is the *Arbitration regarding the Iron Rhine (Ijzeren Rijn') Railway*, between Belgium and the Netherlands, decision of 24 May 2005, in *RIAA*, vol. XXVII, 127–31.

[47] See WTO Appellate Body Report, *United States—Standards for Reformulated and Conventional Gasoline*, WT/DS2/AB/R, adopted 20 May 1996.

[48] See Case C-459/03 *Commission v Ireland (Mox Plant)* [2006] ECR I-4653.

[49] See M. Koskenniemi, 'International Law: Constitutionalism, Managerialism and the Ethos of Legal Education', 1 *European Journal of Legal Studies* (2007) (no page numbers indicated).

13

International Organizations as Third Parties under the Law of International Treaties

Christian Tomuschat

1. Introduction

It is a well-established rule under international treaty law that treaties do not create either obligations or rights for a third party without its consent. Already in Roman law, this proposition was generally accepted: *pacta tertiis nec prosunt nec nocent*. The basic premise of consent does not allow anyone to produce legal effects for other persons who do not participate in the legal transaction concerned. Contracts as well as treaties are instruments of self-commitment. In a society of equals, no one is able to impose his/her will on others. In the case of states, the legal basis of this rule is provided—and strengthened—by the principle of sovereign equality (United Nations [UN] Charter, Article 2(1)).[1] States decide under their own responsibility what policy decisions to take. In particular, they are not prepared to be coerced into obligations which they have not freely accepted. Accordingly, the 1969 Vienna Convention on the Law of Treaties (VCLT I) has codified this classic principle of treaty law[2] in Articles 34 to 36.

One of the reasons why the VCLT remained confined to treaties between states (Article 1) was doubt as to the suitability of the regime governing the third-party effect of treaties for international organizations. When, shortly after the successful conclusion of the 1969 Vienna Conference on the Law of Treaties (Vienna I) the topic of international treaties involving international organizations was placed on the agenda of the International Law Commission (ILC)

[1] Y. Dinstein, 'The Interaction Between Customary International Law and Treaties', 322 *Recueil des Cours* (2006) 243, at 331; M.E. Villiger, *Commentary on the 1969 Vienna Convention on the Law of Treaties* (Leiden–Boston: Martinus Nijhoff, 2009) 467, Commentary on Art 34, margin number 1.

[2] A. McNair, *The Law of Treaties* (Oxford: Clarendon Press, 1961) 309–21; C. Tomuschat, 'Völkerrechtlicher Vertrag und Drittstaaten', 28 *DGVR Berichte* (1988) 9, at 10.

(1970), the Special Rapporteur, Paul Reuter, raised in his reports many issues that to him in fact distinguished inter-state treaties from treaties to which international organizations were parties.[3] In particular, he felt that treaties concluded by an international organization could not be regarded as *res inter alios actae* by the members of that organization. Following the model of Article 228(2) of the Treaty Establishing the European Economic Community,[4] he proposed an Article 36*bis* that was designed to extend the effects of such treaties to the members of the organization concerned.[5] From the very outset, this proposal proved extremely controversial. Eventually, it was adopted by the ILC as part of its final draft[6] and sent to the 1986 Vienna Diplomatic Conference (Vienna II). At that Conference, it did not survive. For most of the states attending the Conference, Article 36*bis* was a novelty that had too many unknown characteristics to be easily agreeable.[7]

Diplomatic history also provides examples of the opposite configuration where treaties concluded between states intend to impose obligations on an international organization. One of the most interesting cases in point would be the provisions of the Peace Treaty of Versailles,[8] which set forth that the German territory of the *Saar* was to be administered by the League of Nations (Article 49(1)).[9] Politically, the imposition of this burden on the League was no great problem, since the League was essentially a creation of the victorious powers of World War I. All the signatories of the Treaty of Versailles were to become the original members of the League,[10] and 13 other states individualized by name were explicitly invited to join the new organization. However, in legal terms the victorious powers of World War I were unable to make determinations on behalf

[3] First report, *YILC* (1972), vol. II, 171, at 189; Second report, *YILC* (1973), vol. II, 75, at 89–93.

[4] 'Agreements concluded under the conditions laid down above shall be binding on the institutions of the Community and on Member States.'

[5] Sixth report, *YILC* (1977), vol. II(1), 119, at 128.

[6] *YILC* (1982), vol. II(2), 43.

[7] See C. Brölmann, 'The 1986 Vienna Convention on the Law of Treaties—The History of Draft Article 36bis', in *Essays on the Law of Treaties. A Collection of Essays in Honour of Bert Vierdag* (The Hague *et al.*: Martinus Nijhoff, 1998) 127–34, at 121; P. Reuter, *Introduction au droit des traités* (Paris: Presses Universitaires de France, 3rd edn, reviewed by P Cahier, 1995) 107; K. Zemanek, 'The United Nations Conference on the Law of Treaties Between States and International Organizations or Between International Organizations: the Unrecorded History of its "General Agreement"', in *Law of Nations—Law of International Organizations—World Economic Law* (Köln *et al.*: Carl Heymanns, 1988) 665, at 675.

[8] Of 28 June 1919, *Reichsgesetzblatt* (German Imperial Gazette) 1919, 700, reprinted also in W.G. Grewe, *Fontes Historiae Juris Gentium—Sources Relating to the History of the Law of Nations* (Berlin: Walter de Gruyter, 1992) vol. 3/2, 682.

[9] 'Germany renounces in favour of the League of Nations, in the capacity of trustee, the government of the territory defined above.'

[10] In fact, the Covenant of the League of Nations was the first part of the Treaty of Versailles (Articles 1–26). However, it is well known that in particular the United States neither ratified the Treaty of Versailles nor joined the League.

of the League. Consent by the League was a requirement for the implementation of the relevant stipulations.[11,12]

2. The 1986 Vienna Convention

With the adoption of the Vienna Convention on the Law of Treaties between States and International Organizations or between International Organizations (VCLT II) in March 1986 the codification of the international law of treaties came to completion.[13] Generally, the Vienna II Conference opted for remaining as close as possible to the text adopted 17 years earlier. Accordingly, most of the innovations which the Special Rapporteur had hoped to introduce were put aside.[14] Apart from the changes rendered necessary by the altered scope *ratione materiae* and consequently also *ratione personae*, since treaties between states and international organizations or between international organizations necessarily imply dealing with this supplementary class of subjects of international law, the text remained essentially unaltered. The ILC felt that the intellectual bases of the VCLT I should not be abandoned as consensualism amply justified the rejection of treaties designed to produce legal effects for third parties. Paul Reuter had alerted his colleagues to the fact that the main pillar of Articles 34 to 36 VCLT I was lacking in the project under review since international organizations were neither sovereign nor equal.[15] This *avertissement* was essentially ignored, however. The two Vienna Conventions run largely parallel to one another, also with regard to the rules on third-party effect of international treaties.

The perfection of this parallelism is not self-evident. A simple example may suffice to show that some reflection is necessary to accommodate theory and practice. Article 83 VCLT I determines that the relevant instruments of accession to the Convention itself 'shall be deposited with the Secretary-General of the United Nations'. This instruction constitutes not only a reminder of Article 102 United Nations (UN) Charter pursuant to which '[e]very treaty and every international agreement' shall be registered with the UN Secretariat and published by it. The tasks of a depositary go far beyond the simple operation of receiving the texts of international instruments and publishing them in due form. The preceding provisions of the VCLT I, namely Articles 76 to 79, provide abundant evidence

[11] See K. Schmalenbach, *Die Haftung Internationaler Organisationen im Rahmen von Militäreinsätzen und Territorialverwaltungen* (Frankfurt *et al.*: Peter Lang, 2004) 148–52.

[12] The submission of a report on Kosovo by UNMIK, the UN Interim Administration in Kosovo, to the Human Rights Committee under the ICCPR (CCPR/C/UNK/1) is to be seen in a different light. UNMIK acted functionally on behalf of Serbia which, under Security Council resolution 1244 (1999), could not exercise its sovereign rights over Kosovo.

[13] United Nations (ed.), *The Work of the International Law Commission* (New York: United Nations Publications, 7th edn, 2007) vol. II, 228. The Convention has not yet entered into force. Currently (19 November 2010), it has 29 states parties. The threshold requires 35 states parties.

[14] See C. Brölmann, *supra* note 7, 123.

[15] *Supra* note 5, 120, para. 6.

of the breadth of the functions which the depositary of a multilateral treaty has to perform. One cannot deny that the VCLT I, like any other treaty, has a life of its own. It is an agreement to which 111 states have by now adhered—certainly a considerable number, but far fewer than the number of members of the United Nations (192). In other words, Article 83 VCLT I, a treaty concluded between states only, supported by slightly more than half of the UN membership, imposes an obligation on an organ of the United Nations, ie the United Nations itself. How can this be justified? The subsequent considerations will show that there are different ways to explain a configuration which is simple only at first glance but which has never attracted great attention in legal writings since it is generally deemed to be 'natural' that the Secretaries General of international organizations discharge certain responsibilities for their organizations outside the field proper of the organization concerned.

The example chosen demonstrates at the same time that there is a gap between the two Vienna Conventions. Clearly, the VCLT I deals only with treaties concluded between states (Article 1). However, the VCLT II specifies in Article 1 that it applies first to treaties between, on the one hand, one or more states and, on the other hand, one or more international organizations, and second, to treaties between international organizations. This limitation does not cause any difficulties as long as the legal problem to be settled remains confined to the formal parties to such treaties. Precisely with regard to treaties that purport to bring into being legal relationships with third parties, however, the legal space to be covered must be wider. Since international organizations have been put on a par with states, a rule is required that excludes a third-party effect to their detriment. Articles 34 and 35 VCLT I, the provisions that deal with inter-state treaties, protect only third states, not third international organizations. On the other hand, initially the texts of Article 34 and 35 of the VCLT II prepared by the drafting committee of the ILC did not take account of the necessity also to shield international organizations from burdens which states might attempt to impose on them. Draft Article 34 read:

1. A treaty between international organizations does not create either obligations or rights for a third state or a third organization without the consent of that State or that organization.
2. A treaty between one or more States and one or more international organizations does not create either obligations or rights for a third state or a third organization without the consent of that State or that organization.[16]

Article 35 of the draft was framed more broadly,[17] but it was conceived as the logical elaboration of Article 34 and pursuant to its purpose did not, therefore,

[16] *YILC* (1977), vol. II(2), 105, at 123.

[17] '1. [Subject to article 36bis,] an obligation arises for a third State from a provision of a treaty if the parties to the treaty intend the provision to be the means of establishing the obligation and the third State expressly accepts that obligation in writing.'

cover the case of an inter-state treaty providing for obligations to be borne by third organizations.

Through an ingenious trick, the Special Rapporteur avoided the unfortunate inference that states are free to bring into being obligations for international organizations. Claiming that he only wanted a simplification of the text of Article 34, he replaced the cumbersome formula framed by the drafting committee by the straightforward words: 'A treaty does not create either obligations or rights for a third State or a third organization without the consent of that State or that organization.'[18]

This text, which clearly goes beyond the scope of VCLT II, also covers inter-state treaties and thus closes the gap just noted—if it is construed in accordance with its plain literal meaning. It was not changed by the Vienna Conference II and hence constitutes the final outcome of the efforts to establish a coherent system applicable to treaties that intend to deploy legal effects outside the circle of their parties.

3. Different Axiomatic Premises

When inquiring into the intellectual foundations of the legal rules applicable to treaties involving international organizations either as active formal parties or as negatively affected non-parties, one must always bear in mind that international organizations are subjects of international law of a specific nature. As rightly pointed out by the Special Rapporteur of the ILC, they are neither sovereign nor equal. Their recognition as subjects of international law first by the International Court of Justice (ICJ),[19] which dealt only with the United Nations, and thereafter more generally in international practice,[20] cannot detract from certain features which distinguish them profoundly from states. On the one hand, notwithstanding their autonomy, functionally international organizations are agencies of their member states for the pursuit of common objectives. In a certain sense, states 'pool' their sovereignties by establishing

2. An obligation arises for a third international organization from a provision of a treaty if the parties to the treaty intend the provision to be the means of establishing the obligation in the sphere of its activities and the third organization expressly accepts that obligation.'

[18] 'Tenth Report', *YILC* (1981), vol. II(1), 65, para. 91. He thereby returned essentially to the wording he had suggested in his 'Sixth report', *YILC* (1977), vol. II(1), 119, at 127.

[19] ICJ, *Reparation for Injuries Suffered in the Service of the United Nations*, Advisory Opinion of 11 April 1949, *ICJ Reports* (1949) 174, at 179.

[20] While the drafters of the Charter of the United Nations had simply overlooked the necessity to explicitly address the issue of international personality of the UN and while the Statute of the Council of Europe has the same lacuna, in the contemporary world almost no statute lacks a provision to that effect: European Union, Article 47 TEU; World Trade Organization, Agreement, Article VIII.

an entity able to perform transboundary activities which an individual state would not be capable of carrying out, being confined by the general rules on state jurisdiction. This first aspect means that an international organization exists in a 'classic' relationship of non-interference with truly third states, states non-members of the organization. These states must respect the area of jurisdiction of an international organization to which they do not belong in the same way as they are bound to respect the areas of jurisdiction of third states.[21]

However, the members of an international organization find themselves in a much closer relationship to that organization. The organization is to some extent 'their child'. They act within the organization, they use the organization for the furtherance of their interests, and they cooperate with the other members in the pursuit of common goals. Accordingly, if they entrust the organization with certain tasks this has all the appearances of legitimacy, contrary to what a true outsider could do. This basic differentiation is not reflected in the VCLT II. Proceeding pursuant to formal criteria, it acknowledges only one type of third organization, namely an organization which is not a party to the treaty concerned (Article 2(1)(h)).

As already mentioned, the attention of the Special Rapporteur of the ILC was focused primarily on the legal effects which a third-party treaty concluded by an international organization could possibly produce for the members of the organization.[22] On the other hand, however, he failed to inquire into the opposite phenomenon, the question of whether the members of an organization may impose on the organization legal commitments through a treaty to which the organization itself does not become a party. He was aware of the fact that the founding of an international organization is a distinct phenomenon.[23] It would indeed be awkward to classify the treaty establishing an organization as a treaty producing third-party effects vis-à-vis the organization.[24] But neither the Special Rapporteur nor the ILC looked into the legal regime of treaties drawn up within an organization, which almost unavoidably keep some links with the organization which gave birth to them.[25] This issue deserves closer consideration.

[21] C. Brölmann, *The Institutional Veil in Public International Law. International Organisations and the Law of Treaties* (Oxford and Portland: Hart Publishing, 2007) 253.

[22] Likewise, this is the only issue discussed by E. Klimis, 'Article 34', in O. Corten and P. Klein (eds), *La Convention de Vienne sur le droit des traités* (Bruxelles: Bruylant, 2006) vol. II, 1417–23.

[23] First Report, *YILC* (1972), vol. II, 171, at 197, paras 84–85; Second Report, *YILC* (1973), vol. II, 90, para. 92. Acknowledged also by C. Chinkin, *Third Parties in International Law* (Oxford: Clarendon Press, 1993) 12, 95 *et seq.*

[24] This observation applies also to the Convention on the Privileges and Immunities of the United Nations, adopted by GA resolution 22 (I), 13 February 1946, 1 *UNTS*, 15, which particularizes Art. 104 UN Charter.

[25] C. Chinkin, *supra* note 23, 89 confines herself to observing that an international organization 'may also be an interested third party to a treaty between States'.

4. The Practice

The first relevant example has already been mentioned. It consists of charging the Secretary-General of an international organization with acting as the depositary for all the treaties elaborated within the organization. Such treaties, after their adoption, leave the house of the organization and become autonomous instruments. Rarely does the circle of members of the organization coincide with the circle of the states parties having ratified the treaty concerned. Some of the treaties that came about under the roof of the United Nations were extremely successful. But even the most successful one of all of them, the Convention on the Rights of the Child,[26] notwithstanding a participation of 193 states, has not yet obtained acceptance by Somalia and the United States. Logically, even if eventually all members of the organization should accept becoming bound, there is always an intermediate period where a discrepancy in the status *ratione personae* may be noted since the ratification process invariably extends over a certain period of time.

Concerning the Secretary-General of the United Nations, there is no explicit rule in the Charter advising or instructing him to perform the duties of a depositary. By resolution 24 (I) of 12 February 1946 the General Assembly (GA) declared that the United Nations was willing to continue the functions of depositary which had been entrusted to the League of Nations under treaties concluded during the time of existence of the League.[27] But no such authorization with regard to future treaties has ever been given to the Secretary-General.[28] In the French Commentary on the UN Charter, the depositary functions of the Secretary-General are not even mentioned,[29] and in the German Commentary, edited by Bruno Simma, the commentator of Article 98, Wilfried Fiedler, simply states: 'A multitude of multilateral conventions assign to the SG depositary or other functions. Many of these conventions were concluded under the auspices of the UN, in which case the UN organs involved have often encouraged and supported entrusting the SG with the duties assigned to him by the convention.'[30]

No need is seen by him to comment on this practice, which he apparently acknowledges as a fact of life which by its massive presence renders any further reflection futile.

[26] Adopted by GA resolution 44/25, 20 November 1989, without vote, 1577 *UNTS*, 3.

[27] GA resolution 172 (II), 14 November 1947, deals only with the registration function of the Secretary-General.

[28] See generally S. Rosenne, 'The Depositary of International Treaties', 61 *AJIL* (1967) 923–45; Id., 'More on the Depositary of International Treaties', 64 *AJIL* (1970) 838–52.

[29] A.L. Vaurs-Chaumette, 'Commentary on Article 98', in J.P. Cot, A. Pellet, and M. Forteau (eds), *La Charte des Nations Unies. Commentaire article par article*, (Paris: Economica, 3rd edn, 2005) vol. II, 2035–50.

[30] 'Commentary on Article 98', in B. Simma *et al.* (eds), *The Charter of the United Nations. A Commentary*, (Oxford: Oxford University Press, 2nd edn, 2002) vol. II, 1214 marginal number 48.

Neither is the legal position less ambiguous in the Council of Europe, the second example chosen to illustrate this examination of the legal issues surrounding the depositary functions. The Statute of the Council of Europe is silent on those functions. It limits itself to stating that the Secretary-General of the Organization shall 'provide such secretariat and other assistance as the Consultative Assembly may require' (Article 37(b)).[31] Before the entry into force of the Statute, the Secretary-General could obviously not exist as an organ of the Council of Europe. Therefore, one of the governments participating in the founding conference, the UK Government, was entrusted with acting as the depositary (Article 42(1)). Immediately after the coming into force of the Statute on 3 August 1949, the General Agreement on Privileges and Immunities of the Council of Europe[32] provided (Article 22(1)): 'The present Agreement shall be ratified. Instruments of ratification shall be deposited with the Secretary General.'

This practice has continued up to this date. In an explanation provided by the Council of Europe itself, one can read:

> The Treaty Office exercises, for the Secretary General, depositary functions with respect to more than 200 Council of Europe treaties. It keeps the originals of all treaties and registers signatures and ratifications, as well as declarations and reservations, and any withdrawals or modifications thereof. It notifies all legal acts relating to the treaties to all the member States and any other States or Organisations mentioned in the treaty concerned.[33]

As it emerges from this enlightening passage, a constant practice has developed and has continued its unbroken course until today.

One might assume that the Secretaries General of the two organizations are prepared to offer their help to any group of states that requires a depositary for the administrative business entailed by the manifold tasks of a depositary. This is not the case, however. With regard to the United Nations, an internal memorandum of 27 March 1984[34] specifies that the Secretary-General should not automatically accept depositary functions in respect of multilateral treaties other than those providing for universal participation. Four main grounds for this cautious attitude are advanced. Primarily, it is argued that the task of the Secretary-General would become exceedingly burdensome if he were to act as depositary for the numerous multilateral treaties being concluded every year. The memorandum shows very clearly that performance of the functions of a depositary is indeed an activity that carries with it many onerous responsibilities. Accordingly, the Secretary-General suggests that his authority as depositary

[31] The legal personality of the Council of Europe under international law is derived from its power to conclude a headquarters agreement with France (Statute, Article 40(b)); see H.G. Schermers and N.M. Blokker, *International Institutional Law* (Boston–Leiden: Martinus Nijhoff, 4th edn, 2003) 988, para. 1564.

[32] Council of Europe, *European Treaty Series* No. 2, 2 September 1949.

[33] Available at <http://www.coe.int/t/dlapil/default_en.asp.>

[34] *UN Juridical Yearbook* (1984), 181.

should be confined to treaties with universal participation, very exceptionally with regional participation only, and treaties drawn up under the auspices of the United Nations, either by UN institutions or by diplomatic conferences convened by the United Nations. The inference can quite easily be drawn that the relationship between the member states of an international organization and 'their' organization is a special one, making it necessary to differentiate when one speaks of 'third' states or 'third' organizations. Giorgio Gaja has indeed cogently observed that

> ... there is some incongruity in considering the member States totally as 'third States' when often the international organization only acts under the member States' direct control.[35]

Another, even more striking, example are the clauses in the international conventions for the protection of human rights pursuant to which the Secretary-General of the United Nations is instructed to provide the necessary staff and facilities for the performance of the work to be discharged by the different monitoring bodies. The relevant provisions of the International Covenant on Civil and Political Rights (ICCPR)[36] may serve as a representative embodiment of the model which one finds also almost everywhere else. Article 36 provides: 'The Secretary-General of the United Nations shall provide the necessary staff and facilities for the effective performance of the functions of the Committee under the present Covenant.'

Similar provisions can also be found in most other treaties, including the most recent ones, the Convention on the Rights of Persons with Disabilities (Article 34(11))[37] and the International Convention on the Protection of All Persons from Forced Disappearance (Article 26(7)).[38]

In addition, some of the relevant conventions provide that the members of the supervisory bodies shall receive emoluments from United Nations resources 'on such terms and conditions as the General Assembly may decide' (Article 35 ICCPR). Precisely with regard to the expenditure caused by the work of the individual members of the monitoring bodies, however, considerable discrepancies can be perceived. Under Article 8(6) of the International Convention on the Elimination of All Forms of Racial Discrimination (CERD)[39] states were burdened with the responsibility for the expenses of the members of the Committee on the Elimination of Racial Discrimination while in the discharge of their functions. In other words, the expenditure was split up. While the United Nations had to bear the general costs for the operation of

[35] 'A "New" Vienna Convention on Treaties Between States and International Organizations or Between International Organizations: A Critical Commentary', 58 *BYIL* (1987) 253, at 264.

[36] Adopted by GA resolution 2200 A (XXI), 16 December 1966, 999 *UNTS*, 171.

[37] Adopted by GA resolution 61/106, 13 December 2006.

[38] Adopted by GA resolution 61/177, 20 December 2006 (not yet in force).

[39] Adopted by GA resolution 1904 (XVIII), 20 November 1963, 660 *UNTS*, 195.

the monitoring machinery, it was felt that the experts were to be funded by the community of the participating states. This arrangement was abandoned one year later when the ICCPR was adopted by the General Assembly, but it came back again with renewed strength in 1984 in connection with the establishment of the Convention against Torture and Other Cruel, Inhuman or Degrading Treatment of Punishment (CAT). The CAT was approved without a vote. Yet many states were intimately convinced that the time was not yet ripe for a conventional instrument that essentially sought to strengthen the prohibition on torture by stringent procedural mechanisms. Thus, although they did not want formally to oppose the adoption of an instrument combating torture, they placed little rocks onto its path. One of these obstacles was the provisions according to which states parties not only had to bear the expenses of the experts members of the Committee against Torture (Article 17(7)), but were furthermore obligated to reimburse the United Nations for the staff and facilities put at the disposal of the Committee in order to enable it to hold its sessions. One year later, the Convention against Apartheid in Sports[40] again took up the CERD formula by stating that the states parties had to defray the costs for the individual members of the Committee against Apartheid in Sports while they were discharging their duties (Article 11(7)).

The question of whether the United Nations was to—or should—bear the costs of all monitoring bodies in the field of human rights was generally not seen as a legal, but instead as a political issue. Australia took the initiative to align both the CERD and the CAT with the regime applicable to the Human Rights Committee and all the other expert bodies in the same area. It proposed amendments which were both approved by the respective Conference of the states parties and then also endorsed by the General Assembly.[41] According to the amendment provisions applicable both to the CERD[42] and the CAT (Article 29(2)), each time two-thirds of the states parties have eventually to give their consent. Unfortunately, to date the requisite minimum number of ratifications has not been attained. Accordingly, both the CERD and the CAT remain applicable in their original versions. Nonetheless, the General Assembly has granted the requisite financial means for the operation of the Committee against Torture.[43] From the very outset, the 2002 Optional Protocol to the CAT, which established a new Subcommittee on Prevention, also provided for complete financing by the United Nations.[44] Given the fact that the costs entailed by the operation of the Subcommittee may be considerable, some states expressed reservations

[40] Adopted by GA resolution 40/64, 10 December 1985, 1500 *UNTS*, 161.

[41] Resolution 47/111, 16 December 1992.

[42] The CERD has no specific stipulations on how suggestions for revision should be handled. It was the decision of the Conference of the states parties which determined the threshold of two-thirds.

[43] GA resolution 63/166, 18 December 2008, para. 36.

[44] Adopted by GA resolution 57/199, 18 December 2002, by 127 to four votes (Nigeria, Marshall Islands, Palau, USA), with 42 abstentions.

concerning the financial regime chosen, hinting that the General Assembly was not authorized under Article 17 UN Charter to subsidize activities outside the jurisdictional purview of the world organization.[45]

As far as the Convention against Apartheid in Sports is concerned, no effort has been undertaken with a view to amending the rule on the allocation of costs to the states parties. Since the abolition of apartheid in South Africa, the Convention has lost its relevance. The number of states parties has remained stuck at a threshold of 60 states. After its liberation from the yoke of apartheid, not even the 'new' Republic of South Africa has found it useful to proceed to the ratification of the Convention. The Committee against Apartheid in Sports has not been convened for many years.

In this connection, it is worth recalling a 'declaration' made by the former German Democratic Republic (GDR) on the occasion of its ratification of the CAT on 9 September 1987 with regard to the activities of the Committee against Torture. Article 20 CAT authorizes the Committee to carry out measures of inquiry with the cooperation of the state concerned. This power does not have to be accepted by the states parties; they can declare that they do not recognize it (Article 28). To recognize the competence of the Committee to receive and consider individual communications is likewise optional (Article 22). In accordance with its general position that the international monitoring bodies should not get directly involved in the implementation of human rights at the domestic level, the GDR also distanced itself, as to their financial implications, from these procedures which, on principle, it rejected: 'The German Democratic Republic declares that it will bear its share only of those expenses in accordance with article 17, paragraph 7, and article 18, paragraph 5, of the Convention arising from activities under the competence of the Committee as recognized by the German Democratic Republic.'[46]

The logic underlying this declaration was explained by Manfred Mohr, an international lawyer from the GDR. In a commentary on the declaration, he wrote that it was 'derived from the principles of sovereign equality as well as from general organizational law'.[47] Many states from the Western European and Others Group raised objections against the declaration.[48] In strict legal terms, this controversy has nothing to do with the problematique of the impact of treaties on international organizations, but is linked to it by the peculiar clauses of the CAT which imposed the burden of all the activities of the Committee against

[45] GA, plenary meeting, 18 December 2002, A/57/PV.77: Bahrain, 15; Japan, 16.

[46] See electronic version of *UNTS*, available at <http://treaties.un.org/Pages/ViewDetails.aspx?src=TREATY&mtdsg_no=IV-9&chapter=4&lang=en>; also reprinted by M. Coccia, 'A Controversial Declaration on the U.N. Convention Against Torture', 1 *EJIL* (1990) 314, at 315. The declaration was withdrawn on 13 September 1990, a few days before German reunification.

[47] 'The GDR's Declaration on the Anti-Torture Convention and its Consequences: an Attempt at Evaluation', 1 *EJIL* (1990) 328, at 333.

[48] France, Luxembourg, Sweden, Austria, Norway, Canada, Greece, Spain, Switzerland, Italy, Portugal, Australia, Finland, New Zealand, Netherlands.

Torture on the states parties. The GDR felt that those components from the procedural tool box of the Committee which it had not accepted should not be financially imputable to it.

It is not easy to give a clear-cut answer as to the lawfulness of the declaration. The objecting states generally argued that the declaration, to be understood as a true reservation, was incompatible with the object and purpose of the CAT. The question may be asked, however, whether the withholding of financial contributions by just one contracting party, amounting to a small percentage of the amounts required for visits as envisaged in Article 20 CAT and for the examination of individual communications under Article 22, can be seen as a measure threatening to paralyse the discharge by the Committee against Torture of its functions. Clearly missing the point was the view by Massimo Coccia who spoke of an infringement of *jus cogens* where a state does not support the entire array of procedural instruments in the service of combating torture.[49] It is true, however, that acceptance of the reservation would have led to extremely complex calculations gravely hampering legal certainty.[50] In any event, however, this was a dispute about the lawfulness of reservations to an inter-state treaty. Precisely because of the peculiarity of the two clauses contained in Articles 17(7) and 18(5) CAT the United Nations was not involved.

5. Assessment

The practice referred to above is relatively uncontroversial. On the other hand, it seems to lack a consistent theoretical framework. I shall attempt to shed more light on the issues involved.

5.1. Secondary law

International organizations may be authorized by their statutes to establish new legal obligations both for the organization itself and for the states parties. The culmination point of this development has been reached in the European Union, where in many fields the European institutions act not unlike the organs of a state. To an ever-growing extent, the United Nations has also embarked on this path. From the very outset, the General Assembly was endowed with the power to establish financial obligations on the strength of its budgetary powers (Article 17 UN Charter), whereas generally its decision-making power is confined to the internal sphere of the United Nations. The bulk of the decision-making powers of the United Nations, however, rests with the Security Council

[49] *Supra* note 46, 321–4.

[50] See G. Gornig and M. Ney, 'Die Erklärungen der DDR zur UN-Antifolterkonvention aus völkerrechtlicher Sicht', 43 *Juristenzeitung* (1988) 1048, at 1050.

under Chapter VII of the Charter. The acts issued under such authorizations are, by their very nature, unilateral acts and do not come within the scope of the law of treaties. Accordingly, the two Vienna Conventions are not to be consulted with regard to their provisions on the third-party effect of international treaties when the need arises to examine whether a decision or resolution relies on unchallengeable legal foundations. Proper interpretation will, of course, always be necessary.

5.2. Treaties drawn up within an international organization

It is one of the tasks of most international organizations to advance the process of codification and progressive development of the law. Article 13(1)(a) UN Charter explicitly directs the General Assembly to work in that direction. The ILC is the most prominent body established for assisting the General Assembly in this endeavour. In a similar manner, the regional organizations have also been entrusted with conceiving of and formulating legal answers to the pressing problems of our contemporary world.[51] Accordingly, the elaboration of international treaties is one of the core functions of all of these organizations. As is well known, different techniques can be used when framing legal rules that may eventually end up as multilateral conventions. On the one hand, such texts can be elaborated by the standing organs of the organization which, in order to be properly assisted, may set up auxiliary expert bodies, among which the ILC and UNCITRAL are the most prominent ones at UN level. Or else, if topics of major complexity are to be addressed, the preferable option may be to call a diplomatic conference.

There can be no doubt that the expenses entailed by the work of an institution of an international organization duly mandated to frame new legal rules are expenses of that organization. In the case of the United Nations, the legal opinion of the ICJ of 1962 on *Certain Expenses of the United Nations* has shed some light on the demarcation of the scope of Article 17(2) UN Charter.[52] There cannot be the faintest doubt that all the costs of any conference until the very last minute are to be borne by the relevant organization. As from the adoption of the final text and the closure of the conference, however, the new treaty, if it is to be put into force by the usual route of ratification and accession, becomes a legal instrument of its own. The authority of the founders still supports the provisions on how the treaty may come into force, how and where it requires to be ratified, and how many instruments of acceptance are needed before it can take its full effect.

[51] Charter of the Organization of American States, A-41, 30 April 1948, Article 2; Statute of the Council of Europe, 5 May 1949, Article 1; Constitutive Act of the African Union, 11 July 2000, Article 3.

[52] ICJ, *Certain Expenses of the United Nations (Article 17, paragraph 2, of the Charter)*, Advisory Opinion of 20 July 1962, *ICJ Reports* (1962) 151. It is common knowledge that the deliberations of this Opinion were overshadowed by heavy political pressures.

Eventually, however, when all the requirements are fulfilled, the treaty concerned will definitively have become a separate legal instrument, being governed by one of the two Vienna Conventions.

Accordingly, it becomes necessary to find legal grounds why it is generally found acceptable that many multilateral treaties set forth provisions which continue to impose on the Secretary-General of the 'mother institutions' obligations which have no temporal limit but are meant to remain applicable forever.[53]

Consent provides the most plausible explanation. In particular, when the text of a treaty is adopted 'without vote', ie by *consensus*, the relevant clauses which provide for certain responsibilities of the United Nations under that treaty are obviously approved together with all the other provisions. One could thus speak of a case of application of Article 35 VCLT II. However, not all treaties are adopted in such a harmonious way. Thus, the final vote on the VCLT I took place against one negative vote (France),[54] and, as already noted, there were no less than four no votes when the CAT was adopted. It is true that acceptance by an organization generally does not require the unanimous consent of all of its members. International organizations would be paralysed if every one of its members had a veto right.

However, a new difficulty arises. First of all, it needs to be determined who can be deemed authorized to express the required consent. A diplomatic conference convened under the auspices of the United Nations is not a body of the United Nations in the strict sense of the term. The organization is certainly obligated to defray the costs of such a conference initiated by it. But a conference on its part has no mandate to engage the United Nations in permanent financial or other obligations. Therefore, a conference resolution is a shaky basis for the claim that the burden must be borne by the United Nations. This issue was hotly debated with regard to the Preparatory Commission for the Authority under the Law of the Sea Convention.[55] Resolution I of the UN Conference on the Law of the Sea, adopted together with the Law of the Sea Convention provisionally on 30 April 1982 and definitively on 10 December 1982,[56] provided that the expenses of the Commission shall be met from the regular budget of the United Nations,

[53] ILC member *Kearney* stated during the discussion on the drafts of the VCLT II that acceptance by an organization of the effects of a treaty to which it was not a party should be governed by 'a less restrictive set of rules than those of the Vienna Convention', 1241st meeting, 4 July 1973, *YILC* (1973), vol. I, 201, para. 28. But he did not detail what specific solution he favoured.

[54] See S. Verosta, 'Die Vertragsrechts-Konferenz der Vereinten Nationen 1968/69 und die Wiener Konvention über das Recht der Verträge', 29 *Heidelberg Journal of International Law* (1969) 654, at 671.

[55] See P.J. Hynes, 'United Nations Financing of the Law of the Sea Preparatory Commission: May the United States Withhold Payment?', 6 *Fordham Int'l L J* (1982–83) 472, commenting on President Reagan's statement of 30 December 1982 that the United States would not pay its assessed share of the expenses of the Law of the Sea Preparatory Commission; see E. Zoller, 'The "Corporate Will" of the United Nations and the Rights of the Minority', 81 *AJIL* (1987) 610.

[56] Annex I to the Final Act, adopted by 130 votes to 4, 17 countries abstaining.

subject to the approval of the General Assembly.[57] The same problems arose with regard to the Preparatory Commission for the International Criminal Court.[58] It is inconceivable that a treaty establishing a new international organization purely and simply allocates the ensuing financial implications to the budget of the United Nations. Only the General Assembly has clear statutory budgetary powers (Article 17). Its vote is therefore determinative.

The General Assembly, on its part, must respect the limits restricting its powers under Article 17. It cannot according to free discretion make decisions as to activities anywhere in the world deserving financial assistance. Operational activities outside the institutional framework of the United Nations on the basis of an international treaty subscribed to by only a part of the UN membership are not expenses of the United Nations. Rightly, therefore, a specific financing mechanism was found for the Law of the Sea Authority as well as for the International Criminal Court as soon as the two entities had taken their definitive legal shape through the entry into force of the relevant agreements, the Law of the Sea Convention, and the Rome Statute.

It emerges from the preceding considerations that some kind of customary practice has developed in the United Nations. On the one hand, to provide minor services to a conventional regime that has its roots in the organization is considered to be covered by the general object and purpose of the Charter. Appointing the Secretary-General as the depositary of a treaty elaborated under UN auspices has therefore become a matter of routine. The assignment of this function is not seen as the imposition of a duty which requires a formal act on the part of the world organization. Accordingly, the formalities prescribed by Article 35 VCLT II are considered to be out of place. The origin of the treaty concerned constitutes a link which obviates the need to engage in formal procedures. Metaphorically speaking, the United Nations remains the home of a treaty which was given birth there.

It is more difficult to find a consistent formula for instances where a treaty requires far more extensive services, in particular the provision of staff and facilities for the performance of the duties of a committee of experts under a separate treaty. It stands to reason that through such clauses the financial burden is shifted from the states parties to the treaty to the entire membership of the United Nations, comprehending also states which deliberately have abstained from accepting the treaty. It is for this reason that originally the CERD and the CAT

[57] The requisite approval was indeed given by resolution 37/66, 3 December 1982, adopted by 135 votes to 2, with 8 abstentions.

[58] Conference resolution F, adopted by a majority of 120 to 7 with 21 abstentions, determined: '10. The Commission shall meet at the Headquarters of the United Nations. The Secretary-General of the United Nations is requested to provide to the Commission such secretariat services as it may require, subject to the approval of the General Assembly of the United Nations', UN Diplomatic Conference of Plenipotentiaries on the Establishment of an International Criminal Court, *Official Records*, A/CONF.183/13 (vol. I) 72. The GA responded positively to this invitation; see resolution 53/105, 8 December 1998. This time, there was no opposition in the final vote.

and still today the Convention against Apartheid in Sports have devised formulae which leave the financial responsibility with the states parties. The departure from this logical construction is explained by the desire of the majority of states in the General Assembly not to 'punish' the states that have had the courage to join the relevant human rights instruments. As long as human rights activities are carried out within the institutional structures of the United Nations the financial responsibility of the world organization cannot give rise to any doubts. When such activities are transferred to the firmer foundations of a multilateral treaty the intention is of course to provide them with better support. If, however, the states parties had to shoulder the ensuing economic burden, there would be a great risk that some governments might be deterred from joining the relevant treaty systems. For that reason, an extensive reading of Article 17 UN Charter has gained ground and is no longer seriously contested.

A further step is taken when the United Nations declares itself ready to finance the Preparatory Commission of a future international organization in the period between the adoption of the treaty concerned and its entry into force. Such instances permit of no easy classification. Neither of the two Vienna Conventions deals explicitly with treaties in their embryonic status before their entry into force, except for setting forth that a state that has signed an agreement is bound not to frustrate its object and purpose (Article 18 VCLT I and II). Indeed, in the two cases taken into account, the UN Law of the Sea Convention and the Rome Statute, the allocation of expenses to the United Nations was the result of a resolution of a conference of states parties. The relevant treaties themselves were not yet able to deploy their full legal effects. Under such circumstances, it can hardly be denied that the General Assembly, by assuming the financial responsibility, exceeds the limits inherent in Article 17 UN Charter. This infringement may be justifiable as a temporary bridging operation, seeking to ensure start-up financing which otherwise could not be obtained. However, this is a borderline situation which may easily go awry. If an operation receives its own structural mechanism under a multilateral treaty, states members of the mother organization which oppose that mechanism cannot be compelled, under the budgetary powers of the organization, to finance the new entity which they do not approve. Such attempts display all the features of a circumvention of the *pacta tertiis* rule. Not only direct, but also indirect methods of circumventing this rule are forbidden.

Within the European Union, an interesting example is provided by the European Schools. The original treaties on European integration did not contemplate the establishment of schools for the children of the staff in the service of the European institutions. However, fairly soon the need was felt to establish such schools in the main towns and cities where a considerable number of European civil servants had their workplace. Given the absence of any specific authorization in the Treaty Establishing the European Coal and Steel Community (ECSC), the six original founding members concluded an agreement under which they themselves provided for the creation of a European School in Luxemburg.[59] But they expected, of course, that the ECSC would participate in financing the budget of the School.[60] In order to put the financial regime on secure foundations, the School concluded, some months later, an agreement with the ECSC under which the ECSC pledged to make an annual contribution to the budget.[61] This was juridically an unchallengeable method to obtain the desired results.

5.3. Human rights as limits of the authority of the United Nations

A heated, sometimes emotional, debate has taken place on the question of whether the United Nations is bound by human international human rights when adopting resolutions or taking factual measures.[62] This debate, which has drawn a lot of inspiration from the *Kadi* judgments of the two Luxemburg courts of the European Community (now: European Union),[63] cannot be taken up here to its full extent. Only one specific issue will be addressed.

There is no need to explain at length that again many differentiations are necessary in examining the effect of human rights on the competences of the United Nations organs. In this chapter, issues related to the concept of *jus cogens* are not addressed. Nor does the chapter probe into the concept of general international law. The focus will be exclusively on the question of whether human rights treaties elaborated within the United Nations are susceptible of producing a binding effect for the institutions of the United Nations. In this connection, the CERD, the ICCPR, and the CEDAW are the most relevant treaties. Fortunately, there is no danger that torture or forced disappearance might be committed by personnel of the United Nations although the relevant treaties might also have repercussions for the authorities established under the UN Charter.

To date, the clauses on signature and ratification of the ICCPR have remained unchanged (Article 48). Only states are entitled to become parties to it. In Europe, a revision of this classic approach is beginning to take shape. The Treaty

59 Statute of the European School, 12 April 1957, 443 *UNTS*, 128.

60 Article 26 provided that the budgetary needs were to be covered, *inter alia*, by 'des subventions des institutions avec lesquelles l'Ecole a conclu des contrats'.

61 Agreement of 11 December 1957.

62 See, for instance, J. Klabbers, 'The Security Council and Human Rights', in *International Human Rights Monitoring Mechanisms: Essays in Honour of Jakob Th. Möller* (Leiden: Nijhoff, 2nd edn, 2009) 241–7; A. Reinisch, 'Developing Human Rights and Humanitarian Law Accountability of the Security Council for the Imposition of Economic Sanctions', 95 *AJIL* (2001) 851–72; G. Thallinger, 'Sense and Sensibility of the Human Rights Obligations of the United Nations Security Council', 67 *Heidelberg Journal of International Law* (2007) 1015–40; C. Tomuschat, *Human Rights. Between Idealism and Realism* (Oxford: Oxford University Press, 2nd edn, 2008) 101.

63 In *Kadi*, the ECJ affirmed the autonomy of the European legal order (Case C-402/05 P *Kadi v Council and Commission* [2008] ECR I-6351), whereas the Court of First Instance saw the European legal order as part and parcel of the universal legal order which today has its centrepiece in the UN Charter (Case T-315/01, *Kadi v Council and Commission* [2005] ECR II-3649).

on the European Union establishes that the European Union shall accede to the European Convention on Human Rights.[64] It is thus trivial to note that, to date, the United Nations is not a party to any of the human rights conventions which it has sponsored. Consequently, the ICCPR cannot be binding on the United Nations *qua* treaty.

However, an argument can be derived from the imperative of consistency, which is related to the classic concept of estoppel. Since its fresh start with the Human Rights Council, the United Nations has introduced a new procedure, Universal Periodic Review.[65] All states members of the United Nations have to undergo this specific type of examination, in the course of which little account is taken of the formalities of legal positivism. The practice is very generous in determining the applicable yardstick.[66] Frequently, reference is made to the Universal Declaration of Human Rights. However, the background of most of the questions is the relevant treaties, in particular the two treaties on non-discrimination, as well as the ICCPR.[67] Given this state of affairs, it would be extremely inconsistent to argue that the examiners, the nations acting through the Human Rights Council—a body of the United Nations—are entitled to make use of a yardstick which the United Nations itself is not obligated to comply with. It must be acknowledged, however, that this indirect application of the human rights standards enshrined in UN-sponsored human rights treaties does not fit neatly into the framework of the rules governing the third-party effect of international treaties.

6. Concluding Observations

The most interesting result of the preceding observations is the discovery that the VCLT II, more by accident than by intentional strategy, has closed the gap left open by the lack of a rule denying any directly binding force to treaties

[64] A corresponding revision of the European Convention on Human Rights is, of course, necessary to determine the rights and obligations of the European Union. One of the key issues will be whether the European Union is entitled to nominate a 'national' judge—who would almost unavoidably have the nationality of one of the states parties. Thereby, the traditional prohibition on two judges of the same nationality would be set aside.

[65] Human Rights Council, resolution 5/1, 18 June 2007, Annex, s I.

[66] Formally, resolution 5/1, s. I., para. 1(c), determines as the yardstick of review 'human rights instruments to which a State is party', but in fact the reviewers generally refer to a more general concept of human rights.

[67] Just recently, during the 7th session on 11 February 2010, critical questions were put to Fiji, a non-party to the ICCPR, by Canada, Denmark, Latvia, Norway, Sweden, and the United Kingdom. Just one sample may be provided (Sweden), available at <http://lib.ohchr.org/HRBodies/UPR/Documents/Session7/FJ/Fiji.pdf>: 'What measures is the Government of Fiji taking to ensure all persons' right to participate in the government of their country and to a fair trial? Reports indicate extensive restrictions on freedom of expression with wide media censorship, prohibitions to print, publish or broadcast anything that portrays the government in a negative light, attacks, harassment, intimidation and detention of journalists, critics and human rights activists.'

purporting to impose obligations on international organizations. The second relevant result is that the practice has developed patterns of conduct which differ widely from the theoretical mechanisms imagined by the authors of the VCLT II. Almost imperceptibly, the debate on the binding force of treaties for international organizations flows over into the debate on the limits of the budgetary powers of the General Assembly under Article 17 UN Charter. In any event, it becomes clear that the concept of a 'third' state or a 'third organization' is much too generic to be helpful in trying to identify the legal rights and obligations in the relationship between an international organization and its members.

14

Treaties Establishing Objective Regimes

Francesco Salerno

1. Introduction

The conclusion of a codification treaty like the Vienna Convention on the Law of Treaties (VCLT) is not a simple task: previous international practice is rarely entirely consistent, and political difficulties often arise, hindering the negotiations. The text of the VCLT, finalized in 1969, is the outcome of a compromise between different readings of previous practice, and it is therefore 'flexible' enough to allow for the development of further interpretations, which could take into account the subsequent evolution of international practice. This should be taken into consideration when studying the issue of the so-called 'treaties establishing objective regimes'.

'Treaties establishing objective regimes' are international agreements setting up 'objective rules' whose effects spread *erga omnes*, even if the number of states parties is limited.[1] The issue was considered by the International Law Commission (ILC) when dealing with the effects of treaties on third states. The definition of objective regimes given by Special Rapporteur Waldock, in his 1964 Report to the ILC,[2] included only treaties defining the status of a particular territory, area of the sea or airspace, with the intent of establishing, in the general interest, a set of treaty rules universally valid, representing the only international regime applicable to the situation.[3] According to Waldock's definition, international agreements through

[1] H. Kelsen, 'Contribution à la théorie du traité international', *Revue internationale de la théorie du droit* (1936) 265 *et seq.*; A. McNair, *The Law of Treaties* (Oxford: Clarendon Press, 1961) 259 *et seq.*; J.-F. Prevost, *Les effets des traités conclus entre Etats à l'égard des Etats tiers,* thèse doctorale (Paris, 1973) 378 *et seq.*; H. Mosler, 'The international society as a legal community', 140 *Recueil des Cours* (1974) 234 *et seq.*; P. Cahier, 'Le problème des effets des traités à l'égard des États tiers', 143 *Recueil des Cours* (1974) 660 *et seq.*; S. Bastid, *Les traités dans la vie internationale. Conclusion et effets* (Paris: Economica, 1985) 143 *et seq.*; P. Subedi, 'The Doctrine of Objective Regimes in International Law and the Competence of the United Nations to Impose Territorial or Peace Settlements on States', 37 *GYIL (*1994) 174.

[2] *YILC* (1964), vol. II, 26.

[3] E. David, 'Article 34', in O. Corten and P. Klein (eds), *Les Conventions de Vienne sur le droit des traités. Commentaire article par article* (Bruxelles: Bruylant, 2006) 1408–9 (hereinafter *Commentaire*).

which states parties dispose of their real rights do not establish objective regimes if no general interest of the international community is involved.[4] Treaties establishing objective regimes must affect situations or rights that are not (or not any more) considered disposable due to the existence of a prevailing general interest in the certainty of the law. As the objective regime established by the treaty needs to be unique and indivisible, it necessarily affects third states.[5]

Waldock's proposal was built on elements of previous international practice. The Special Rapporteur considered, *inter alia*, the 1920 Report of the Committee of Jurists created by the League of Nations to establish whether Sweden, which was not a party to the 1856 Treaty of Paris providing for the demilitarization of the Åland Islands, was nevertheless entitled to invoke the provisions of the latter Treaty against Finland.[6] The Special Rapporteur also took into consideration treaties concerning protected and neutral states[7] and the agreements establishing international servitudes, such as those providing for the free navigation of international canals.[8] The *erga omnes* effect of such treaties was first recognized by Article 109 of the Final Act of the Vienna Congress,[9] and it was later confirmed by the Permanent Court of International Justice (PCIJ) in the *Wimbledon* case.[10] The latter concerned the *erga omnes* effects of Article 380 of the 1919 Treaty of Versailles, according to which Germany was to allow for the free navigation of the Kiel Canal. After World War II, reference to the general interest of mankind was made, in order to ensure *erga omnes* effects to the qualification of a state as an aggressor,[11] in the International Court of Justice (ICJ)

[4] A. McNair, 'Treaties Producing Effects "erga omnes"', in *Scritti di diritto internazionale in onore di Tomaso Perassi* (Milano: Giuffrè, 1957) vol. II, 23. These kinds of treaties produce *erga omnes* effects only because they involve real rights, and not because they serve a common interest of the international community (A. McNair, *The Law of Treaties*, *supra* note 1, 256–7).

[5] P. Braud, 'Recherches sur l'État tiers en droit international public', 72 *RGDIP* (1968) 82.

[6] See P. Cahier, 'Le problème des effets des traités à l'égard des États tiers', *supra* note 1, 665; C. Chinkin, *Third Parties in International Law* (Oxford: Clarendon Press, 1993) 29.

[7] J.-F. Prevost, *Les effets des traités conclus entre Etats à l'égard des Etats tiers, supra* note 1, 430 *et seq*. Thus, the neutrality of Switzerland was established during the Congress of Vienna (1815). See also, more recently, the Declaration of 1962 (Article 5) establishing the neutrality of Laos and the Agreements of 23 October 1991 on a Comprehensive Political Settlement of the Cambodia Conflict, and in particular the Agreement concerning the Sovereignty, Independence, Territorial Integrity and Inviolability, Neutrality and National Unity of Cambodia (see S.R. Ratner, 'The Cambodian Settlement Agreements', 87 *AJIL* (1993) 31 *et seq*.

[8] J. Hostie, 'Le statut international du Rhin', 28 *Recueil des Cours* (1929) 105 *et seq*.; J.-F. Prevost, *Les effets des traités conclus entre Etats à l'égard des Etats tiers, supra* note 1, at 399 and 447.

[9] P. Cahier, 'Le problème des effets des traités à l'égard des États tiers', *supra* note 1, 680 *et seq*.; see, however, the critique of M. Giuliano, 'L'ordinamento internazionale e i fiumi navigabili d'interesse internazionale', *Riv. di Diritto Internaz.* (1959) 212.

[10] *S.S. 'Wimbledon' (United Kingdom, France, Italy, Japan/Germany, Poland intervening)*, Judgment of 17 August 1923, PCIJ, Series A No. 1 (1923) 21, especially at 28.

[11] This position was sustained by Soviet scholars: T. Schweisfurth, 'International Treaties and Third States', 45 *ZaöRV* (1985) 669, and R.G. Wetzel, *The Vienna Convention on the Law of Treaties: travaux préparatoires* (Frankfurt am Main: Alfred Metzner Verlag, 1978) 269. See also Article 75 of the VCLT (*infra*).

case law concerning the international status of South-West Africa,[12] and in the preamble of the Washington Treaty concerning Antarctica. The intention of the 12 states that concluded the Antarctic Treaty was not only to freeze the respective claims of sovereignty, but also to establish a particular and unique regime for the continent.[13]

Waldock's proposal, however, was rejected by the ILC, which feared that it could boost the hegemonic position of the Great Powers, thus compromising the egalitarian structure of the international community.[14] Article 34 of the VCLT provides that: 'a treaty does not create either obligations or rights for a third State without its consent'. This rule is consistent with the general principle of relativity (of autonomy) of the treaties, laid down in Article 26.[15] The latter principle, according to which a treaty is binding only upon states parties, precluded the inclusion in the Vienna Convention of a rule concerning treaties establishing objective regimes, regardless of whether they provide for *erga omnes* rights or obligations.

The model laid down in the 1969 VCLT was somehow altered by the 1978 Convention on Succession of States in Respect of Treaties. According to Articles 11 and 12 of the Convention, the successor state is bound by treaties establishing the regime of a boundary or 'other territorial regimes'.[16] Under general international law, the principle of continuity of treaty obligations is sometimes applied to other categories of agreements (eg to human rights treaties).[17]

The developments of international practice just described impinge upon the principle of relativity of treaties in the case of newly independent states: the latter may acquire conventional rights or obligations simply by establishing their sovereignty over the territory of a state which was a party to the relevant treaty. On the other hand, such developments have little to do with the issue of treaties

[12] ICJ, *International Status of South-West Africa,* Advisory Opinion of 11 July 1950, *ICJ Reports* (1950) 128, at 131–2; ICJ, *South West Africa (Ethiopia v South Africa)*, Judgment of 21 December 1962, *ICJ Reports* (1962) 319, at 329 and 331; ICJ, *Legal Consequences for States of the Continued Presence of South Africa in Namibia (South West Africa) notwithstanding Security Council Resolution 276 (1970)*, Advisory Opinion of 21 June 1971, *ICJ Reports* (1971) 16, at 56, para. 126.

[13] R.E. Guyer, 'The Antarctic System', 139 *Recueil des Cours* (1973) 149 *et seq.*; D.R. Rothwell, *The Polar Regions and the Development of International Law* (Cambridge: Cambridge University Press, 1996).

[14] P. Cahier, 'Le problème des effets des traités à l'égard des États tiers', *supra* note 1, 615–16; S.P. Subedi, 'The Doctrine of Objective Regimes in International Law and the Competence of the United Nations to Impose Territorial or Peace Settlements on States', *supra* note 1, 171.

[15] See, among others, P. Cahier, 'Le problème des effets des traités à l'égard des États tiers', *supra* note 1, 611 *et seq.* The PCIJ was very sensitive to the principle of relativity of treaties: *Certain German Interests in Upper Silesia*, Merits, *(Germany v Poland)*, Judgment of 26 May 1926, PCIJ, Series A No.7 (1926) 28–9.

[16] A treaty, however, 'cannot be interpreted as disposing of the rights of independent third Powers' (*The Island of Palmas Case*, Arbitrator M. Huber, 4 April 1928, available at <http://www.pca-cpa.org>).

[17] Human Rights Committee, *General comment No. 26 on Issues relating to the Continuity of Obligations to the International Covenant on Civil and Political Rights*, 29 October 1997, CCPR/C/21/Rev.1/Add.8/Rev.1, para. 4.

establishing objective regimes, as the latter potentially affect any third state, and not only successor states.

Meanwhile, moreover, the phenomenon of treaties establishing objective regimes has evolved, taking into account new international interests. The international regime of the 'Area'—subject to the International Sea-Bed Authority within the provisions of the 1982 Montego Bay Convention as modified by the 1994 Agreement—easily fits into the original model of objective regimes established by treaties.[18] *Erga omnes* effects may also arise from treaties for the preservation of certain fish stocks, such as the 1995 Agreement for the Conservation and Management of Straddling Fish Stocks and Highly Migratory Fish Stocks.[19] Other international agreements establish objective regimes, in the interest of the international community, for the protection of certain species of fauna[20] or of the environment,[21] to ensure international peace or disarmament,[22] to address drug trafficking,[23] to regulate international communications,[24] or to define the status of the so-called 'maritime cemeteries'.[25] The ICJ implicitly acknowledged that the United Nations (UN) Charter establishes an objective regime when it recognized that the UN is a subject of international law, capable of raising claims against third states.[26] The regime established by a treaty may affect individuals and, in general, non-state actors, even though the latter could never become a party thereto.[27] This happens, in particular, when states parties conclude a treaty defining the *status* of a non-state actor and assume the obligation to ensure the *erga omnes* respect of that legal regime. This is the case, for example, of the 1951 Refugee Convention and of other similar treaties. The state where the refugee has sought protection issues the refugee's identity papers and travel documents, and it may exercise diplomatic protection on

[18] H. Mosler, 'The international society as a legal community', *supra* note 1, page 252.

[19] J.A. (De) Yturriaga, *The International Regime of Fisheries. From Unclos 1982 to the Presential Sea* (The Hague: Martinus Nijhoff Publishers, 1997) 164 *et seq.*

[20] See, in particular, the International Convention for the Regulation of Whaling of 2 December 1946, the customary nature of which is expressly excluded by C.L. Carr and G.L. Scott, 'Multilateral Treaties and the Environment: a Case Study in the Formation of Customary International Law', 27 *Den. J Int'l L & Pol.* (1998–99) 323.

[21] See D.M. Ong, 'International Environmental Law's "Customary" Dilemma: Betwixt General Principles and Treaty Rules', 1 *Irish Yearbook of International Law* (2006) 29.

[22] See, in this respect, some Soviet scholars: T. Schweisfurth, 'International Treaties and Third States', *supra* note 11, 663.

[23] P. Cahier, 'Le problème des effets des traités à l'égard des États tiers', *supra* note 1, 654–5.

[24] J.-F. Prevost, *Les effets des traités conclus entre Etats à l'égard des Etats tiers, supra* note 1, 424 *et seq.*

[25] See the remarks of J. Klabbers, 'Les cimetières marins sont-ils établis comme des régimes objectifs? A propos de l'accord sur l'épave du *M/S Estonia*', 11 *Espaces et Ressources Maritimes* (1997), 121–33, concerning the so-called '*Estonia Agreement*' of 23 February 1995.

[26] ICJ, *Reparation for Injuries Suffered in the Service of the United Nations*, Advisory Opinion of 11 April 1949, *ICJ Reports* (1949) 174, at 185.

[27] P. Reuter, *Introduction to the Law of Treaties* (translated by J. Mico and P. Haggenmacher) (London–New York: Pinter Publishers, 1989) 78.

behalf of the refugee, raising claims even against a state which is not a party to the Geneva Convention.[28]

It is not easy to lump all these different types of treaties establishing objective regimes into a single category.[29] As the ILC itself recognized, the VCLT is deficient in this respect.[30] In order to fill this gap, reference has to be made to the existing customary rules governing the issue.[31] The ILC, however, did not entirely exclude the relevance of the rules governing the effects of treaties on third states.[32] According to the VCLT, though, a treaty may affect third states only with their consent. For the ILC,[33] this principle stems directly from the Latin maxim *pacta tertiis nec nocent nec prosunt*.[34] This maxim, however, cannot be considered to be a general principle of law, and thus it cannot be regarded as a source of international law.[35] Firstly, the maxim developed in a private law context, where *pacta* are divested of any law-making function.[36] Even if considered in its strictly private law characterization, moreover, the maxim cannot be regarded as common to a large number of systems of municipal law. The stipulation of a contract for the benefit of a third party was admitted, albeit on an exceptional basis, already under Roman Law,[37] and it is nowadays well known by several systems of municipal law.[38] Although the maxim *pacta tertiis nec nocent nec prosunt* was unknown in Roman scholarship and case law,[39] positivistic international scholars did not hesitate to exploit it, considering it 'a self-evident proposition' of international law.[40] The principle of autonomy, upon which the maxim relies, perfectly suits

[28] See Article 8 of the Draft ILC Articles on Diplomatic Protection with commentaries (A/61/10).

[29] See, for some attempts at a definition (such as 'service public international' or 'droit territorial d'intérêt général'): J.-F. Prevost, *Les effets des traités conclus entre Etats à l'égard des Etats tiers, supra* note 1, 420.

[30] Draft Articles on the Law of Treaties with commentaries–hereinafter ILC Commentaries—*sub* Article 34, *YILC* (1966), vol. I(2), 232.

[31] See also the Preamble of the VCLT: '*Affirming* that the rules of customary international law will continue to govern questions not regulated by the provisions of the present Convention'.

[32] ILC Commentaries, at 232.

[33] See also Article 34 of the 1986 Vienna Convention on the Law of Treaties between States and International Organizations or between International Organizations (hereinafter VCLTSIO).

[34] R.G. Wetzel, *The Vienna Convention on the Law of Treaties: travaux préparatoires, supra* note 11, 266.

[35] R. Roxburgh, *International Conventions and Third States* (London: Longmans, 1917) 6.

[36] See H. Kelsen, *Contribution à la théorie du traité international, supra* note 1, 254; see also I. Detter, *Essays on the Law of Treaties* (London: Sweet and Maxwell, 1967) 100.

[37] See, in particular, G. Pacchioni, *I contratti a favore di terzi*, (Padova: Cedam, 3rd edn, 1933) 8 *et seq.*

[38] See E. Jimenez de Arechaga, 'Treaty Stipulations in Favour of Third States', 50 *AJIL* (1956) 346 *et seq.*; I. Detter, *Essays on the Law of Treaties, supra* note 36, 114; P. Braud, 'Recherches sur l'État tiers en droit international public', *supra* note 5, 52.

[39] No traces of the maxim could be found on *Bibliotheca Iuris Antiqui (BIA)*, edited by N. Palazzolo, and on *Bibliotheca Teubneriana Latina (BTL)*. For a similar glossary see L. Meriggi, *I trattati ed i terzi* (Torino: UTET, 1939) 9–10.

[40] R. Roxburgh, *International Conventions and Third States* (London: Longmans, 1917) 23; M. Lachs, 'Le développement et les fonctions des traités multilatéraux', 92 *Recueil des Cours* (1957) 313 *et seq.*

the traditional inter-individual conception of the international legal order, based on the principles of independence and sovereign equality of states.[41] This idea of the international legal order, however, is not completely in line with international practice, not only in relation to treaties establishing objective regimes, but also in relation to conventions establishing uniform private international rules which may compel states parties to apply the laws of a third state.[42]

Treaties establishing objective regimes would not require a specific regulation if the rules enshrined in such treaties were to be considered customary rules. In this case, the rules would apply 'potenzialmente all'intera società internazionale'.[43] This possibility is admitted by Article 38 of the VCLT, according to which a rule set forth in a treaty may become binding upon a third state as a customary rule of international law, recognized as such.[44] In a situation of particular urgency, a treaty establishing an objective regime may well serve as a means to provide a clear set of rules in the interest of the international community as a whole. The intention of the parties is to endow the treaty with *erga omnes* effects, thus affecting third states as well. This claim could be more easily upheld if the regime established by the treaty were 'functionally' linked with an already-existing customary rule. This link, however, is often very feeble. The legal regime established by the treaty, moreover, rarely develops into new customary rules soon after the entry into force of the treaty.[45]

This process is hindered, first of all, by certain peculiarities of the law of treaties, such as the possibility to formulate reservations or to include subordination clauses.[46] Even when some of the norms enshrined in the treaty become binding as customary rules,[47] it is difficult to admit that the entire objective regime established by the treaty has become a part of general international law.[48] Treaties establishing objective regimes often establish permanent collective organs between the states parties. Through such mechanisms, the objective regime created by the treaty can be refined over time, sometimes

[41] P. Braud, 'Recherches sur l'État tiers en droit international public', *supra* note 5, 19; P. Reuter, 'Du consentement des tiers aux normes d'un traité', in A. Bos and H. Siblesz (eds), *Realism in Law-Making. Essays on International Law in Honour of Willem Riphagen* (Dordrecht: Martinus Nijhoff Publishers, 1986) 155; C. Chinkin, *Third Parties in International Law, supra* note 6, 26.

[42] J. Kropholler, in C. Tomuschat, H. Neuhold, and J. Kropholler, *Völkerrechtlicher Vertrag und Drittstaaten* (Heidelberg: Muller, 1988) 105 *et seq.*

[43] G. Gaja, 'Trattati internazionali', in *Digesto delle Discipline Pubblicistiche* (Torino: UTET, 1999) vol. XV, 354.

[44] See, extensively, J.-F. Prevost, *Les effets des traités conclus entre Etats à l'égard des Etats tiers, supra* note 1, 486 *et seq.*

[45] For a similar approach, see C.L. Carr and G.L. Scott, 'Multilateral Treaties and the Environment: a Case Study in the Formation of Customary International Law', *supra* note 20, *passim*.

[46] See Article VI of the Convention on the Conservation of Antarctic Marine Living Resources (22 May 1980).

[47] See R. Quadri, *Lezioni di diritto internazionale* (Padova, 1946) 111.

[48] See E. Zamuner, 'I trattati che creano regimi obiettivi nel diritto internazionale', XXIII *Comun. e Stud.* (2007) 941.

becoming extremely detailed;[49] the rules thus adopted, however, are subject to the authority of the treaty, and cannot become a part of international custom.[50] Finally, treaty rules establishing a clear hierarchy among states, such as those enshrined in the Antarctic Treaty, are unlikely to evolve into international custom.[51]

The main obstacle to the codification of treaties establishing objective regimes is the principle of the relativity of treaties. The impact of this principle on the rules enshrined in the VCLT must be ascertained. It is also necessary to assess whether (and to what extent) the relevance of consent for the conclusion of the effects of a treaty has diminished in subsequent practice.

The phenomenon of groups of states claiming to act *uti universi* for the fulfilment of some public interest is not new in international law.[52] Thus, for example, when a violation of an *erga omnes* obligation is at stake, and especially when this involves a serious breach of a peremptory norm, the sanction regime established against the responsible state is generally defined by a group of Great Powers.[53] A group of Great Powers, or a large number of states, may also play a leading role in the creation of new customary and *jus cogens* rules. Particularly relevant here is not only the ability of a treaty concluded by such states to influence subsequent practice, but also the intention of the parties thereto to consider the legal regime established by the treaty as customary, and to ensure that the agreement is considered a part 'of the International order of things'.[54] In this case, the principle of sovereign equality is somehow superseded by that of effectivity.[55] However, this does not affect the position of states that have consistently objected to the

[49] On the relationship between the 'material' and the 'organizational' aspects of treaties establishing objective regimes, see: PCIJ, *Territorial Jurisdiction of the International Commission of the River Oder (United Kingdom, Czechoslovakia, Denmark, France, Germany, Sweden/Poland)*, Judgment of 10 September 1929, PCIJ, Series A, No. 23 (1929) 23–4.

[50] See C. Tomuschat, 'Treaties under International Law and Third States', 41 *Law and State* (1990) 7, at 9; *contra* G. Gaja, *Article 38*, in *Commentaire*, 1519.

[51] See B. Simma, 'The Antarctic Treaty as a Treaty providing for an "objective regime"', 19 *Cornell Journal of International Law* (1986) 195; F. Aumond, 'La "convergence antarctique". Radioscopie, de l'actuel consensus concernant la gestion du continent blanc', 136 *Clunet* (2009) vol. 4, 1213 *et seq.*

[52] See G. Balladore Pallieri, *Diritto internazionale pubblico* (Milano: Giuffrè, 6th edn, 1952) 77 *et seq.*, and especially A. McNair, Separate Opinion to the ICJ, Advisory Opinion of 11 July 1950 (*supra* note 12, 153). Rozakis, however, contests the very possibility for states parties to manifest the intention 'to produce law for third States outside the scope of the participants' (see C. Rozakis, 'Treaties and Third States: a Study in the Reinforcement of the Consensual Standards in International Law', 35 *ZaöRV* (1975) 11.

[53] P. Picone, 'Obblighi *erga omnes* e codificazione della responsabilità degli Stati', 88 *Riv. di Diritto Internaz.* (2005) 893 *et seq.*, especially at 907 *et seq.*

[54] See R. Roxburgh, *International Conventions and Third States, supra* note 40, at 81; R. Quadri, *Diritto internazionale pubblico* (Napoli: Liguori, 5th edn, 1968) 141 *et seq.*

[55] This process of creation of customary rules is what Giuseppe Barile considered to be an expression of the so-called 'volontà atipiche': ibid., *Lezioni di diritto internazionale* (Padova: CEDAM, 2nd edn, 1983) 82 *et seq.*

development of the treaty rules into generally applicable rules of customary law (so-called 'persistent objectors').[56]

The principles of independence and sovereign equality of states still play a decisive role in contemporary international law, preventing the formation of a general rule allowing for treaties to affect third parties without their consent.[57] This limit, however, may only operate within the framework of a structurally non-organic international legal order. Different considerations apply with respect to the increasing law-making activity of international organizations,[58] especially as concerns the resolutions the Security Council may adopt under Chapter VII of the Charter in order to react to a breach of the peace, a threat to the peace, or an act of aggression. The maxim *pacta tertiis nec nocent nec prosunt* does not prevent the Security Council from imposing resolutions with binding effects upon third states (and other subjects of international law), according to Article 2(6) of the UN Charter.[59] In this framework, the Security Council may also compel a third state to respect a particular treaty it never ratified. Article 75 of the VCLT confirms the peculiar role of the UN collective security system, affirming that '[t]he provisions of the [...] Convention are without prejudice to any obligation in relation to a treaty which may arise for an aggressor State in consequence of measures taken in conformity with the Charter of the United Nations with reference to that State's aggression'. As pointed out by Lachs, 'l'intérêt de la paix et de la sécurité internationale peut rendre nécessaire d'imposer à un tel Etat des restrictions et devoirs spéciaux'.[60]

2. The Effects of Treaties on Third States under the Vienna Convention on the Law of Treaties

A simple consideration confirms that the maxim *pacta tertiis nec nocent nec prosunt* is often wrongly invoked to justify the principle of relativity of treaties. Under Roman law, contracts stipulated for the benefit of a third party (and, even more

[56] See ICJ, *Fisheries Case (United Kingdom v Norway)*, Judgment of 18 December 1951, *ICJ Reports* (1951) 116, at 131; see also E. David, *Article 34*, *supra* note 3, 1410.

[57] See the succinct remarks of Cyprus: *YILC* (1966), vol. II, 285: 'The primary rule... is that the parties to a treaty cannot impose an obligation on a third State without its consent. The rule is one of the bulwarks of the independence and equality of States.' See also L.N. Mathur, 'Treaties and Third States', in S.K. Agrawala (ed.), *Essays on the Law of Treaties* (Bombay: Orient Longman, 1972) 41; T.O. Elias, *The Modern Law of Treaties* (New York-Leiden: Oceana-Sijthoff, 1974) 59 *et seq.*

[58] See J. Alvarez, 'The new Treaty Makers', 25 *Boston College International and Comparative Law Review* (2002) 213 *et seq.*; M.E. Villiger, *Commentary on the 1969 Vienna Convention on the Law of Treaties* (Leiden: Martinus Nijhoff Publishers, 2009) 473.

[59] C. Chinkin, *Third Parties in International Law*, *supra* note 6, at 108; but see already H. Kelsen, *The Law of the United Nations* (London: Stevens & Sons Ltd, 1951) 85–6 and 108.

[60] M. Lachs, 'Le développement et les fonctions des traités multilatéraux', *supra* note 40, 315.

so, contracts imposing obligations on a third party) were considered null and void.[61] No such rule emerges in international practice, with respect to treaties providing for rights for third states.[62] The VCLT, as we shall see, only regulates the effects of treaties providing for rights (or obligations) for third states,[63] leaving unaffected the validity of such agreements, which may only be contested on the grounds of Articles 46–53.[64] The validity of a treaty affecting third states is thus uncontroversial, and relies on the binding effects of the agreement in respect of states parties that have validly expressed their consent thereto.[65] In order to justify the effects of the treaty in respect of third states, the VCLT relies on the classical positivistic view according to which treaty rules may affect states only with their consent. In this framework, the will of the states which ratified the treaty is supplemented by a sort of 'collateral agreement' between the states parties and the third state, concerning exclusively the rules affecting the latter.[66] This 'collateral agreement' remains distinct from the 'main treaty',[67] to which the third state is not a party.[68]

According to Article 35 of the VCLT, an obligation arises for a third state from a provision of a treaty only if 'the third State expressly accepts that obligation in writing'. This rule is built on the authority of the PCIJ judgment in the *Free Zones of Upper Savoy and District of Gex* case.[69] As pointed out by Gaja, '(si tratta) di un'ipotesi di importanza limitata',[70] but it is in line with the object of the VCLT, whose rules only apply to international agreement concluded in written form (Article 2(1)(a)).[71] Doubts have been raised, however, on the customary

[61] P. Bonfante, 'Contratti a favore di terzi', in P. Ciapessoni (ed.), *Studi di diritto pubblicati dalla Facoltà di giurisprudenza della Università di Pavia* (Pavia: Facoltà di giurisprudenza, 1934) 218 and 222.

[62] L. Oppenheim, *Editorial Introduction to R. Roxburgh, International Conventions and Third States, supra* note 40, underlined the methodological mistake of applying principles derived from municipal law to international law.

[63] It is instructive, in this respect, that the Algerian proposal—according to which Article 34 of VCLT should have declared 'absolutely null and void any obligation imposed by a treaty upon a third State without the latter's assent' (in R.G. Wetzel, *The Vienna Convention on the Law of Treaties: travaux préparatoires, supra* note 11, 264)—was rejected.

[64] See Article 42, para. 1.

[65] ICJ, *Aerial Incident of 27 July 1955 (Israel v Bulgaria)*, Judgment of 26 May 1959, *ICJ Reports* (1959) 127, at 138–9.

[66] P. Reuter, *Introduction, supra* note 27, 80; *YILC* (1966), vol. II, 226–7. The 'collateral agreement' however, can hardly be considered as an autonomous, registrable treaty: C. Chinkin, *Third Parties in International Law, supra* note 6, 41.

[67] M. Fitzmaurice, 'Third Parties and the Law of Treaties', 6 *Max Planck UNYB* (2002) 47.

[68] According to Article 2(1)(h) of the VCLT: '"third State" means a State not a party to the treaty'. This definition should be coordinated with that provided by Article 2(1)(g), according to which: '"party" means a State which has consented to be bound by the treaty and for which the treaty is in force'.

[69] PCIJ, *Free Zones of Upper Savoy and District of Gex (Switzerland/France)*, Judgment of 7 June 1932, PCIJ, Series A/B, No. 46 (1932) 141.

[70] G. Gaja, *Trattati internazionali, supra* note 43, 353.

[71] See also M.E. Villiger, *Commentary on the 1969 Vienna Convention, supra* note 58, 478.

nature of the rule imposing the written consent of the third state.[72] Such a rule, first of all, would conflict with the general principle of the freedom of form in the conclusion of a treaty.[73] According to international practice, moreover, the third state is not required to express its consent using one of the forms commonly admitted by diplomatic practice,[74] as tacit or presumed assent may also be considered sufficient. In other words, the content of the customary rule on treaties providing for obligations for third states is similar to that of the rule concerning treaties providing for rights for third states enshrined in Article 36 of the VCLT.[75] Furthermore, although under Article 37 of the VCLT the consent of the third state is required to revoke or modify an obligation already accepted by it, no formal condition has to be fulfilled in order to re-establish the pre-existing regime of freedom. A similar 'flexible' approach informs the VCLT's rule concerning treaties providing for rights of third states: according to Article 36, in this case the assent of the third state 'shall be presumed so long as the contrary is not indicated'.[76] The reason behind the different formulations of Articles 35 and 36 of the VCLT is rather obvious: the will of the third state to accept a right provided by a treaty may be presumed, because the third state's sovereignty itself would benefit from such a provision.[77] No indication can be found in the VCLT concerning the case in which a treaty provides both for rights and obligations for a third state. According to most scholars, the rule provided by Article 36 should apply in order to better guarantee the sovereignty of the third state.[78] However, this solution does not seem appropriate for treaties establishing objective regimes.

On the other hand, some of the other rules of the VCLT may well be suitable for such treaties. Thus, for example, both Articles 35 and 36 attach great importance to the 'intent' of the parties.

This is a choice that is rather unusual for the VCLT, which generally favours the objective element of the treaty over the subjective one. 'Intent' is decisive for determining the content of the right or obligation provided for third states (Articles 35 and 36 (1)), as well as the form through which the third state

[72] C. Laly-Chevalier, F. Rezek, 'Article 35', in *Commentaire*, 1430–1.

[73] See P. Cahier, 'Le problème des effets des traités à l'égard des États tiers', *supra* note 1, 646.

[74] P. Braud, 'Recherches sur l'État tiers en droit international public', *supra* note 5, 58; P. Reuter, *Du consentement des tiers aux normes d'un traité*, *supra* note 41, 164–5; M.E. Villiger, *Commentary on the 1969 Vienna Convention*, *supra* note 58, 478.

[75] See S. Forlati, *Diritto dei trattati e responsabilità internazionale* (Milano: Giuffrè, 2003) 117.

[76] According to the PCIJ, Judgment of 26 May 1926, *supra* note 15, 29, however, 'in case of doubt, no rights can be deduced from [the treaty] in favour of [third State]'.

[77] The consent of the third state should be expressed—but not necessarily in writing—if the parties decide to revoke or modify the juridical situation established in favour of the third state, and that situation was intended not to be revocable or subject to modification without the consent of the third state (Article 37(2) VCLT).

[78] P. D'Argent, 'Article 36', in *Commentaire*, 1473. This argument loses importance, however, if the stricter rules of the VCLT are not regarded as an expression of general international law.

is to express its consent (Article 37(2) and, albeit more ambiguously, Article 37(1)). Due to the central importance accorded to 'intent', the preparatory work of the treaty becomes a primary means of interpretation of the relevant provisions, whereas under Article 32 it should only be used to supplement the means of interpretation provided by Article 31.[79] The relevance accorded to 'intent' moreover, makes it possible to assess the intention of states parties to act *uti universi* when concluding a treaty establishing an objective regime. This element had already been highlighted by the PCIJ in its judgment of 10 September 1929 concerning the *Territorial Jurisdiction of the International Commission of the River Oder* case. According to the Court, international practice recognized the existence of treaties establishing objective regimes 'in the idea of a community of interest' already in 1815, at the time of the Congress of Vienna.[80] The traditional synallagmatic model—according to which an agreement is a source of reciprocal obligations between the parties[81] but may not create absolute rights with *erga omnes* effects[82]—therefore cannot be considered exhaustive. That model was based on the Roman idea according to which the sole purpose of an agreement is to solve a conflict of interests among the parties.[83] By contrast, international practice from the beginning of the nineteenth century led international scholars to distinguish between 'law-making treaties' (*traités-lois* or *Vereinbarungen*) and 'treaty-contracts' (*traités-contrats* or *Rechtsgeschäftiliche Verträge*),[84] depending on the nature of the interests involved.[85] Although these categories are not taken into consideration by the VCLT,[86] their relevance in contemporary international practice was recently confirmed by the Eritrea–Ethiopia Claims Commission, according to which the Geneva Conventions of 1949 'are concluded for the purpose of creating a treaty law for the parties to the convention and for the related purpose of codifying and developing customary international law that is applicable to all nations'.[87]

79 The PCIJ struggled to identify specific principles for the interpretation of treaties establishing objective regimes: PCIJ, Judgment of 10 September 1929, *supra* note 49, 27 *et seq.*; see also E. Brown Weiss, 'The Evolution of International Water Law', 331 *Recueil des Cours* (2007) 195–6.

80 PCIJ, Judgment of 10 September 1929, *supra* note 49, 27–8.

81 See A. Schiavone, *Studi sulle logiche dei giuristi romani.* Nova negotia e transactio *da Labeone a Ulpiano*, (Napoli: Jovene, 1971) especially 59; for a re-examination of this model from an international law perspective, see A. Pietrobon, *Il sinallagma negli accordi internazionali* (Padova: CEDAM, 1999).

82 A. Guarino, *Diritto privato romano* (Napoli: Jovene, 12th edn, 2001) 878.

83 Ibid., 937.

84 See H. Kelsen, *Contribution à la théorie du traité international, supra* note 1, 258 *et seq.* For a very peculiar exploitation of the model of the 'traités-lois' see G. Scelle, *Précis de droit des gens* (Paris: Sirey, 1934) especially 345 *et seq.* In this regard, see also the discussion *infra*.

85 *Infra.*

86 C. Chinkin, *Third Parties in International Law, supra* note 6, 39.

87 Eritrea–Ethiopia Claims Commission, 1 July 2003, *Partial Award, Prisoners of War, Eritrea's claim, 17*, para. 39, avalaible at <http://www.pca-cpa.org>.

3. The Relevance of Consent in the Conclusion of Treaties Establishing Objective Regimes

In order to clarify the normative implications of treaties establishing objective regimes and their impact on the system of the sources of international law, the relevance of consent within the VCLT has to be reassessed in light of subsequent practice.

Treaties establishing objective regimes enjoy the same normative authority that scholars attached to law-making treaties. To use the words of Special Rapporteur Waldock, the effects of treaties establishing objective regimes upon third states find their justification in the intention of the parties to create 'in general interest general obligations and rights'.[88] The principle of consent does not prevent a treaty from producing *erga omnes* effects[89] because the relevance of that principle is not absolute in the framework of the law of treaties. Thus, for example, whenever a treaty requires a minimum number of ratifications in order to enter into force, the treaty may be deemed to be in force even if it is not in force between two of the states parties due to a qualified objection lodged by one of them to a reservation formulated by the other. Through this mechanism, a state may be regarded as a party from an objective point of view, although it is still considered a third state for some of the parties.[90]

The relevance of consent must also be reassessed in the light of the so-called *vacuum doctrine*. The latter is only partially justified by Article 31(3)(c) of the VCLT, according to which a treaty shall be interpreted in the light, *inter alia*, of any relevant rules of international law applicable in the relations between the parties. The 'vacuum doctrine' has often been invoked by the European Court of Human Rights in order to coordinate the European Convention of Human Rights with other rules of international law, and has sometimes led the Court to compress the material field of application of the former.[91]

The tendency of the 'positive' sources of international law to depart from the principles of independence and sovereign equality of states is even clearer in respect of unilateral acts of states. In its judgment of 20 December 1974 concerning the *Nuclear Tests* case, the ICJ recognized that a unilateral promise may produce *erga omnes* effects even if its content does not reflect a rule of customary international law.[92] The Court thus supported the idea that a rule may provide

[88] *YILC* (1964), vol. II, 26–7.

[89] Such effects were not excluded by the previous *Rapporteur* G. Fitzmaurice, *infra* note 136.

[90] P. Braud, 'Recherches sur l'État tiers en droit international public', *supra* note 5, 26; see also L.N. Mathur, 'Treaties and Third States', *supra* note 57, 45.

[91] See, among others, ECHR, Judgment of 21 November 2001, *Fogarty*, Application. No. 37112/97, para. 35; Judgment of 31 May 2007, *Behrami* and *Saramati*, Application no. 71412/01, para. 144 *et seq.*

[92] ICJ, *Nuclear Tests (New Zealand v France)*, Judgment of 20 December 1974, *ICJ Reports* (1974), 457 *et seq.*, para. 59.

for rights for a state even if the latter has not consented to its adoption.[93] This conclusion was subsequently upheld by the Court in the order of 22 September 1995 concerning the same case.[94]

The relevance of the maxim *pacta tertiis nec nocent nec prosunt* in international law having been so reappraised,[95] the interpretation of the rules of the VCLT concerning the effects of treaties on third states can also be reconsidered and adapted to the characteristics of the treaties establishing objective regimes.[96] This evolutionary interpretation of the VCLT is possible because, in the framework of Articles 35–37, consent is not as paramount as it seems.[97] Moreover, although the VCLT takes into consideration only the case of a treaty specifically identifying the third state (or the third states) which would benefit from the provisions thereto,[98] nothing prevents the states parties, acting *uti universi*, from conferring rights or obligations *erga omnes*.[99] This possibility can only be excluded when a treaty establishing an objective regime explicitly derogates from the model defined by the VCLT.[100]

The scheme of the 'stipulation pour autrui' may apply to treaties establishing objective regimes conferring rights *erga omnes*, if the accent is put on the intention of the states parties[101] and on the acquiescence of the third states.[102] Retaining the formulation of Article 35, the acquiescence of the third states would not serve as a constitutive element of the right which the treaty confers to them, as such right would find its sole source in the treaty, and would thus become fully operative as soon as the treaty enters into force:[103] whenever the treaty provides a third state with a right, states parties assume, jointly and severally, the obligation to respect such a right.[104] On the other hand, if the application of Article 36 were to be excluded, the consent eventually manifested by the third states would have a

[93] See P. Braud, 'Recherches sur l'État tiers en droit international public', *supra* note 5, 17 *et seq*.

[94] ICJ, *Request for an Examination of the Situation in Accordance with Paragraph 63 of the Court's Judgment of 20 December 1974 in the Nuclear Tests (New Zealand v France)*, Order of 22 September 1995, *ICJ Reports* (1995) 288, paras 60–62.

[95] C. Chinkin, *Third Parties in International Law*, *supra* note 6, 26.

[96] P. Reuter, *Introduction*, *supra* note 27, 82.

[97] See C. Rozakis, 'Treaties and Third States: a Study in the Reinforcement of the Consensual Standards in International Law', *supra* note 52, 8–9.

[98] Although Article 35 of the VCLT (unlike Article 36) does not mention the possibility that the treaty provision may be addressed to more than one third state, this possibility should not be excluded: C. Laly-Chevalier and F. Rezek, 'Article 35', *supra* note 72, 1430.

[99] See P. Cahier, 'Le problème des effets des traités à l'égard des États tiers', *supra* note 1, 637–8; see also P. D'Argent, 'Article 36', *supra* note 78, 1475.

[100] C. Laly-Chevalier and F. Rezek, 'Article 35', *supra* note 72, 1433.

[101] See PCIJ, Judgment of 7 June 1932, *supra* note 69, 147–8.

[102] See C. Chinkin, *Third Parties in International Law*, *supra* note 6, 30.

[103] See, in this sense: Article18(*b*) of the Harvard Research Draft Convention on Treaties (in A. McNair, *The Law of Treaties*, *supra* note 1, 309); P. Cahier, 'Le problème des effets des traités à l'égard des États tiers', *supra* note 1, 632.

[104] G. Salvioli, 'Les règles générales de la paix', 46 *Recueil des Cours* (1933) 9–10.

constitutive effect, modifying, albeit retroactively, their legal status.[105] The first solution better fulfils the quest for certainty of the law,[106] also as concerns the direct enforcement of the treaty in the third states' municipal legal orders.[107] Just like unilateral promises, treaties establishing objective regimes which provide third states with a right are immediately effective, once they enter into force, even without the consent of the third states.

According to Article 36, the third state does not become a party to the treaty even if it assents to the right provided thereto:[108] its position remains distinct from that of the states parties which have ratified or adhered to the treaty as a whole. This peculiarity should be borne in mind when analysing the nature of the consent through which, according to the VCLT, the third state 'adheres' to the favourable juridical situation designed by the treaty.[109]

Firstly, the provision introducing a right for the third state is a sort of unilateral promise through which the states parties jointly and severally assume the obligation to respect the right they intend to confer on the third state.[110] The parties, in other words, consider that the provision cannot be disposed of *inter se*.[111] The VCLT does not specify the *erga omnes* nature of the commitment undertaken by the parties with respect to the third state. This is in line with the limited consideration given by the VCLT to *erga omnes* obligations in general: the ILC clearly privileged the conceptual model of bilateral or multilateral treaties concluded according to the traditional synallagmatic scheme, according to which the agreement is a source of reciprocal obligations among the parties.[112]

For the same reason, third states' interests do not need to match perfectly those of the parties to the treaty.[113] By assenting (explicitly or implicitly) to a treaty provision granting it a right, the third state does not express its consent to the treaty as a whole, and cannot formulate reservations in order to modify

[105] See E. Jimenez de Arechaga, 'Treaty Stipulations in Favour of Third States', *supra* note 38, 352–3. See also J. Charpentier, *La reconnaissance internationale et l'évolution du droit des gens* (Paris: Pedone, 1956) 315.

[106] This idea underlies the comments of the Dutch government before the Commission (in R.G. Wetzel, *The Vienna Convention on the Law of Treaties: travaux préparatoires, supra* note 11, 273).

[107] See H. Kelsen, 'Théorie du droit international public', 84 *Recueil des Cours* (1953) 155; P. D'Argent, 'Article 36', *supra* note 78, 1471–2 and note 16.

[108] See M. Lachs, 'Le développement et les fonctions des traités multilatéraux', *supra* note 40, 314; P. Cahier, 'Le problème des effets des traités à l'égard des États tiers', *supra* note 1, 602.

[109] For the divergent evaluation of state practice, see P. Cahier, 'Le problème des effets des traités à l'égard des États tiers', *supra* note 1, 621 *et seq*.

[110] For similar remarks: I. Detter, *Essays on the Law of Treaties, supra* note 36, 115 *et seq*.; P. D'Argent, 'Article 36', *supra* note 78, 1470.

[111] D. Anzilotti, 'Intorno agli effetti delle modificazioni del corso di un fiume sul confine fra due Stati', 8 *Riv. di Diritto Internaz.* (1914) 78.

[112] See C. Chinkin, *Third Parties in International Law, supra* note 6, 35.

[113] The late-imperial doctrine of Roman law and the doctrine in the tradition of Giustinian are oriented in the same sense as concerns contracts stipulated for the benefit of a third party: H. Ankum, 'Une nouvelle hypothèse sur l'origine de la règle *alteri dari stipulari nemo potest*', in *Études offertes à Jean Macqueron* (Aix-en-Provence: Faculté de droit et des sciences économiques d'Aix-en-Provence, 1970) 27.

the scope of the latter.[114] Furthermore, and notwithstanding the silence of the VCLT in this respect, under general international law the third state is always free to waive the right provided for it in the treaty, even after having formally accepted it.[115]

Treaties establishing objective regimes imposing obligations *erga omnes* also involve the joint and several responsibility of the states parties.[116]

Thus, according to Article 3 of the Washington Treaty of 6 February 1922 relating to the Use of Submarines, the parties undertake to punish any attack upon merchant ships, even when perpetrated by a third state. Under Article X of the Convention on International Trade in Endangered Species of Wild Fauna and Flora,[117] states parties exporting to or importing from a third state must obtain 'comparable documentation issued by the competent authorities in that State which substantially conforms with the requirements of the present Convention for permits and certificates'. According to Common Article 1 to the 1949 Geneva Conventions, 'the High Contracting Parties undertake to respect and to ensure respect for the present Convention in all circumstances',[118] whereas common Article 2(3) adds that 'the Powers who are parties [...] shall [...] furthermore be bound by the Convention in relation to [a Power in conflict which is not a party to the Convention], if the latter accepts and applies the provisions thereof'.[119]

In the framework of Article 35 of the CVLT, if the third state formally accepts the obligations arising from the treaty 'the third party remains just that: it does not become a party to the entire treaty'.[120] In order to become a party to the entire treaty, the third state would need to accede to it. By expressing its consent to the 'collateral agreement'[121] concerning the provision affecting it, the third state does not become a party to the 'main treaty' to which that provision belongs.[122]

[114] See also P. Reuter, *Du consentement des tiers aux normes d'un traité*, *supra* note 41, 156.

[115] J.E. de Arechaga, 'Treaty Stipulations in Favour of Third States', *supra* note 38, 353.

[116] The same PCIJ, very sensitive to the principle of relativity of treaties (see *supra* note 15), was reluctant to apply to treaties establishing objective regimes the traditional rule according to which, in case of doubt, a treaty should always be interpreted restrictively, as imposing 'the least restriction on the freedom of States': PCIJ, Judgment of 10 September 1929, *supra*, note 49, 26; but see also, earlier, PCIJ, Judgment of 26 May 1926, *supra* note 15, 29.

[117] Washington, 3 March 1973.

[118] The clause '*si omnes*' of the XIV 1907 Hague Convention (Article 2) is thus superseded. See also ICJ, *Military and Paramilitary Activities in and against Nicaragua (Nicaragua v United States of America)* Merits, Judgment of 27 June 1986, *ICJ Reports* (1986), 169, para. 220.

[119] Unlike Article 35 of the VCLT (above), this rule does not expressly require the consent of the third state to be written.

[120] See C. Chinkin, *Third Parties in International Law*, *supra* note 6, 41.

[121] See *Report of the International Law Commission on the work of its eighteenth session*, *YILC* (1966), vol. II, 226–7; P. Reuter, *Introduction*, *supra* note 27, 80.

[122] H. Waldock, *YILC* (1964), vol. II, 21–2; M. Fitzmaurice, 'Third Parties and the Law of Treaties', *supra* note 67, 47; P. Braud, 'Recherches sur l'État tiers en droit international public', *supra* note 5, 31; T.O. Elias, *The Modern Law of Treaties*, *supra* note 57, 65.

According to Article 36(2) of the VCLT: 'a State exercising a right in accordance with paragraph 1 shall comply with the conditions for its exercise provided for in the treaty or established in conformity with the treaty'. This rule applies, in particular, to the interpretation of the treaty clause which provides the third state with a right. According to Articles 31(3)(a) and 31(3)(b), the only practice which is relevant for the interpretation of a similar provision is that of the parties to the 'main treaty'.

The issue arises only insofar as the third state formally rejects the treaty provision which affects it, following the procedure defined by the VCLT or other analogous procedures. This could give rise to an international dispute, which could lead the states parties to modify the text of the treaty,[123] or even to terminate it.[124]

The termination of the treaty by consent of all the parties would necessarily affect the provision providing for a right for the third state. According to the VCLT (and just as happens with unilateral promises), the states parties to a treaty establishing an *erga omnes* regime could not unilaterally modify the right they have granted to the third state;[125] however, the parties may invoke one of the other grounds for termination provided under general international law, such as the emergence of a new peremptory norm of general international law conflicting with the treaty. Treaties establishing an objective regime may also specify other autonomous grounds for their termination or define specific procedures through which the provisions affecting third states may be modified or even revoked.[126] This explains why a treaty creating an international organization may be modified without the formal consent of those third states.[127]

4. The Significance of Objective Regimes for the International Legal Order

As already pointed out, the intention of the group of states which concludes a treaty establishing an objective regime is to define a general and unique international regime for a situation affecting the international community, thus granting the treaty provisions with *erga omnes* effects. Due to the structural deficiencies of the international law-making process,[128] only partially overcome by the law-making activity of international organizations, treaties establishing objective

[123] C. Laly-Chevalier and F. Reziek, 'Article 35', *supra* note 72, 1430.

[124] In any case, the third state would not be subjected to the judicial dispute settlement mechanism provided for by that treaty, as such mechanisms always depend on the consent of the parties (see *Status of Eastern Carelia*, Advisory Opinion of 23 July 1923, PCIJ, Series B No. 5 (1923) 27).

[125] C. Laly-Chevalier and F. Rezek, 'Article 35', *supra* note 72, 1432.

[126] See A. Aust, *Modern Treaty Law and Practice* (Cambridge: Cambridge University Press, 2nd edn, 2000) 259; see also E. Jimenez de Arechaga, 'Treaty Stipulations in Favour of Third States', *supra* note 38, 349.

[127] P. Reuter, *Introduction*, *supra* note 27, 78.

[128] C. Tomuschat, 'Treaties under International Law and Third States', *supra* note 50, 8.

regimes are the only 'tool' available to fill the normative gaps of the international legal order, responding to a need perceived across the international community, though not necessarily by all of its members.

That is why the rules provided in such treaties affect third states, especially by imposing duties on them. However, following the traditional inter-individual model of classical international law, a treaty establishing an objective regime could not impose obligations on a third state without its formal consent, or, *a fortiori*, if the treaty does not provide the third state with the possibility to accede to it or to otherwise accept its provisions. Yet even in these circumstances the *erga omnes* relevance of a treaty establishing an objective regime cannot be excluded completely.

Due to the relevance for the international legal order of the unique international objective regime created by the treaty, the situation regulated by it can no longer fall within the scope of the absolute 'freedom' previously accorded to third states. In order to ensure the consistency of the international legal order, it is for the latter to establish the conditions for the coordination of the previous regime of freedom and the regime established by the treaty. Since treaties establishing objective regimes do not give rise to instant customary rules, the means by which such coordination is established need to be consistent with the traditional non-organic structure of the international legal order. Thus, the group of states which concluded the treaty cannot be considered an 'organ' of the international legal order, as was affirmed, albeit from different perspectives, by Kelsen,[129] Quadri,[130] and Scelle.[131] The model of the 'dédoublement fonctionnel' discussed by Scelle and others[132] cannot even be adopted in respect to the law-making activities of the Security Council. Nevertheless, the choice made by a group of states willing to identify, regulate, and protect a general interest of the international community inevitably impinges upon the regime of freedom enjoyed by third states. The initiative of the group of states that concluded the treaty establishing the objective regime has an impact on the international legal order as a whole. After recognizing both the first and the second regime, the international legal order needs to coordinate them in a consistent way.

The impact of a treaty establishing an objective regime over the other sources of international law is less relevant if the treaty is nothing but a means to 'concretize, and elaborate on, principles which on their part are constituent elements of

[129] See H. Kelsen, *Contribution à la théorie du traité international*, *supra* note 1, 262 *et seq.*

[130] R. Quadri, *Diritto internazionale pubblico*, *supra* note 54, 27 *et seq.*, who spoke of an 'Autorità sociale'.

[131] G. Scelle, *Précis* de *droit des gens. Principes et systématique* (Paris: Sirey, 1932) 43.

[132] Ibid.; C. Guillien, 'Un cas de dédoublement fonctionnel et de législation de fait internationale: le statut du Canal du Suez', in *La technique et les principes du droit public. Etudes en l'honneur de Georges Scelle* (Paris: LGDJ, 1950) tome II, 735 *et seq.* Although subordinated to a form of state consent, the thesis is indirectly shared by E. Klein, *Statusvertrage im Volkerrecht: Rechtsfragen territorialer Sonderregime* (Berlin–Heidelberg–New York: Springer, 1980) 209 *et seq.*, and 356.

international legal order'.[133] However, treaties establishing objective regimes are not all functional to the implementation of general principles of international law; even when this is the case, the treaty still needs to be coordinated with all the other international rules that coexist with that principle or affect its scope of application.

In order to assess the impact of a treaty establishing an objective regime over previous treaties concerning the same matter, the intention of the parties must be taken into account. The intention of the states which conclude a treaty establishing an objective regime is to elaborate a unique regime for the protection of an interest which is perceived as common to the international community. Thus, under Article 103 of the UN Charter, the obligations under the Charter prevail over conflicting obligations arising from any other treaty. The peculiar competences attributed to the UN for the maintenance of global peace explain why the international community never contested this rule but rather enlarged its scope of application to encompass the Security Council's binding resolutions.

Notwithstanding the intention of the parties, analogous solutions are unlikely to develop in the context of treaties concluded during the present stage of development of international law. In any case, third states would not be compelled to respect the rules provided by a treaty establishing an objective regime if such rules were inconsistent with those of a treaty they had ratified. Moreover, disputes may arise in case of conflict between a claim based on the regime of freedom previously in force with respect to a given situation and the subjective legal situations established by the treaty. Leaving aside the possibility that the treaty establishing an objective regime becomes, with time, a part of general international law, the conflict, *de lege lata*, concerns rules established by two different treaties. In such cases, the only solution that the international legal order can provide relies on the rule concerning the abuse of rights. According to that rule, although the states parties to a treaty establishing an objective regime cannot compel third states to respect the provisions of that treaty, third states must take into consideration the reasons that led the states parties to establish such a regime acting *uti universi*. In other words, a treaty establishing an objective regime may not create specific obligations for third states without their consent, but the international freedom of third states must confront the general interest underlying the objective regime. Since both values belong to the same international legal order, it is for the latter to coordinate them: the closer the connection of the treaty establishing the objective regime with generally recognized international principles, the greater the limits imposed upon the freedom of third states. Through this coordination, the state which is not a party to a treaty establishing an objective regime may nevertheless indirectly be affected by it,[134] as the regime defined by the treaty interferes

[133] C. Tomuschat, 'Obligations arising for states without or against their will', 241 *Recueil des Cours* (1993) 269.

[134] On the 'indirect' effects of treaties establishing objective regimes on third states, see also C. Tomuschat, *Treaties under International Law and Third States*, *supra* note 50, 18.

with the freedom previously enjoyed by that state.[135] The abuse of rights doctrine can be applied to this issue, insofar as the subjective legal situations involved are considered to belong to the same legal order rather than to two distinct inter-individual relationships. The abuse of rights doctrine has no relevance under the 2001 Draft Articles on State Responsibility,[136] as the latter are based on the traditional positivistic approach according to which the international legal order is made of reciprocal relationships established among pairs of states, one of which has assumed an obligation towards the other which has thus acquired a right in respect to the former.[137] The present chapter serves to highlight the limits of such a model.

[135] See also P. Vigni, *Concorrenza fra norme internazionali: il regime giuridico dell'Antartide nel contesto globale* (Milano: Giuffrè, 2005) 63–4 and 316–17. This is the reason why nowadays it would not be possible to uphold the claim of a third state considering Antarctica 'terra nullius': in this sense, see already H. Waldock, *YILC* (1964), vol. I, 105.

[136] The ILC invokes it indirectly in Draft Articles on the Responsibility of States for Internationally Wrongful Acts. General Commentary, *sub* Article 2, para. 8, *YILC* (2001), vol. II(2), 35.

[137] R. Ago, *YILC* (1970), vol. I, 191–2.

15

The Law of Treaties and the UN Security Council: Some Reflections

Michael Wood

In a short piece published in 2009, Giorgio Gaja dealt masterfully with the impact of United Nations (UN) Security Council resolutions on state responsibility.[1] The aim of the present contribution is to offer some thoughts on the Security Council's impact on another area of 'secondary rules': the law of treaties.[2]

A comprehensive treatment of the subject could follow the framework and terminology of the Vienna Conventions of 1969 and 1986. It could deal systematically with the Security Council's role in relation to the conclusion and entry into force of treaties; the observance, application, and interpretation of treaties; the amendment and modification of treaties; the invalidity, termination, and suspension of the operation of treaties; the miscellaneous matters dealt with in Articles 73, 74, and 75 of the Vienna Convention of 1969;[3] and matters not dealt with directly in the Conventions, such as the breach or threatened breach of a treaty as a threat to international peace and security, and the enforcement of treaty obligations as a measure to be taken by the Security Council. Each of these topics could make a chapter of its own, for over the years the Security Council (like the other principal organs of the United Nations, not least the International Court of Justice) has dealt extensively with treaties, reflecting the central role that treaties play in contemporary international relations. In addition to the effect of Council action on treaties, a comprehensive account would also consider the impact of treaties on the Council. For example, treaties may make express provision for

[1] G. Gaja, 'The Impact of Security Council Resolutions on State Responsibility', in G. Nolte (ed.), *Peace through International Law: The Role of the International Law Commission* (Heidelberg: Springer Verlag, 2009) 53–60.

[2] There is an important terminological distinction between 'the law of treaties' and 'treaty law'. The former refers to the secondary rules set forth, for the most part, in the Vienna Conventions on the Law of Treaties of 1969 and 1986; the latter refers chiefly to those primary rules to be found in treaties, sometimes known as 'conventional international law' as opposed to customary international law.

[3] Articles 74, 75, and 76 of the Vienna Convention of 1986 on the Law of Treaties between States and International Organizations or between International Organizations.

Council action, as does Article 16 of the Rome Statute of the International Criminal Court; or even appear to encroach upon the prerogatives of the Council, as with the 2010 Kampala amendments to the Rome Statute (concerning the crime of aggression).

One important preliminary point is that many agreements that the Security Council has to deal with are of uncertain status. They are not treaties between states, but take other forms, in particular agreements with non-state actors and with states the legal nature of which is obscure.[4] It would be interesting to consider how far Council action affects or at least clarifies the status of such agreements. On a more general level, it would be interesting to study how far the practice of the Security Council has clarified the legal issues surrounding such agreements. But this is beyond the scope of the present contribution.

Much of the case law and the literature has concentrated on the effect of Article 103 of the UN Charter. But the Security Council's role in respect of treaty obligations is by no means confined to the creation of Charter obligations that prevail over all other obligations. Treaties of various kinds play an important part in the work of the Council. This is an aspect of the Security Council's wider relationship to international law. Indeed, in many respects there is no difference in principle between Council action in respect of rules of conventional international law (treaty law) and Council action in respect of rules of customary international law. They often overlap, as with the Hague Regulations of 1907 and the Fourth Geneva Convention of 1949, or the law of the sea.

1. Beyond the Vienna Convention

The Vienna Convention on the Law of Treaties of 1969 ('Vienna Convention') mentions the Charter of the United Nations in three places: the preamble; article 30(1); and article 75.[5] The preamble, in addition to recalling the principles of international law embodied in the Charter, expresses the belief that 'the codification and progressive development of the law of treaties achieved in the present Convention will promote the purposes of the United Nations set forth in the Charter, namely the maintenance of international peace and security [...]'. The provisions of article 30 (successive treaties) are '[s]ubject to Article 103 of the Charter'; and Article 75 is the somewhat obscure provision entitled 'Case of an aggressor State'.

[4] A prime example are the so-called 'Dayton Accords', implemented by Security Council resolution 1031 (1995) of 15 December 1995 and subsequent resolutions.

[5] The corresponding provisions of the Vienna Convention of 1986 on the Law of Treaties between States and International Organizations or between International Organizations are the preamble, Article 30, para. 6 (reflecting the relationship of international organizations to the UN Charter, which is not the same as that of states) and Article 76.

Sir Arthur Watts noted that the Vienna Convention on the Law of Treaties 'is [...] in a number of important respects a less comprehensive treatment of the subject than might appear at first sight'.[6] He did not list compliance and enforcement among the omissions, perhaps with good reason, since such matters may be thought to fall outside the law of treaties *stricto sensu*, being more a matter of international responsibility,[7] though it is not possible to divide international law into watertight compartments. In any event, compliance and enforcement are of central importance for the practical effectiveness of treaties, and it is in this sphere that—when international peace and security are threatened by a breach of treaty—the Security Council has a special role to play.

Part V of Rosalyn Higgins's book *The Development of International Law through the Political Organs of the United Nations*, published in 1963, is entitled 'The Law of Treaties: United Nations Practice'. It is the longest part of the book. The author concluded, even then, that '[t]he contribution being made by the political organs is of enormous significance to the development of the law of treaties'.[8] It is striking that, when dealing with the law of treaties, she focused largely on the practice of the Secretariat: 'United Nations treaty practice differs from the subject-matter of the previous parts in several respects. The political organs most concerned with all the other subjects discussed have been the Security Council and the General Assembly; in the case of treaties, however, the Secretariat has played a vital role.'[9] There are only a few passages in which she refers to the Security Council, but these are interesting and indicate that its practice in this field is not entirely new. The cases she considered include, for example, Egypt's request in 1947 that the Council find the Anglo-Egyptian Treaty of 1936 obsolete,[10] and Tunisia's similar request in 1958 concerning the Franco-Tunisian Conventions of 1955.[11] Were she writing today, the emphasis of Part V might well be on the Security Council, rather than on the Secretariat.

Some 45 years later, in an article in the *Revue Hellénique*, Stefan Talmon examined the way in which the Security Council had used its powers under the Charter 'to take certain treaty actions'.[12] In particular, he asked 'whether there are any legal limits to the Security Council adapting existing treaties to a particular

[6] Sir A. Watts, *The International Law Commission 1949–1998, Volume II: The Treaties* (New York: Oxford University Press, 1999) at 612.

[7] See Article 73 ('shall not prejudice any question that may arise in regard to a treaty [...] from the international responsibility of a State') and Article 30(5) of the Vienna Convention. See also Article 12 (and Commentary) of the Articles on State Responsibility ('regardless of its origin or character') and the corresponding provision of the draft on the responsibility of international organizations (ILC Report 2009, at 77–80, draft Article 9, available at <http://www.un.org/law/ilc>).

[8] R. Higgins, *The Development of International Law through the Political Organs of the United Nations* (London: Oxford University Press, 1963) at 346. [9] Ibid., at 241.

[10] Ibid., at 344–5. [11] Ibid., at 345.

[12] S. Talmon, 'Security Council Treaty Action', 62 *Revue Hellénique de Droit International* (2009) 65-116, at 66; E. Papastavridis, 'Security Council Resolutions and the Law of Treaties: Lessons of Iraq', 18 *Public Law Applications* (2005) 405–56 [in Greek].

situation, and whether it can prescribe pre-existing treaty provisions to non-state parties'. He also examined 'the consequences if the Security Council formally endorses a certain treaty, and the role it plays in the enforcement and interpretation of treaties'.[13]

The present contribution seeks not to duplicate Professor Talmon's article, which (given the scope attributed by the writer to the notion of 'adapting' treaties) covers much of the field, but rather to offer a few reflections that may usefully be borne in mind when approaching the important topic of the Security Council and treaties.

2. 'Demonization' of the Council

Much of the writing about the Security Council by international lawyers has an air of unreality. It is based neither on the practice of states nor on the practice of the organs of the United Nations, nor yet on decisions of courts and tribunals. It reflects the authors' dogmatic reading of the text of the United Nations Charter, and often attempts, unrealistically, to apply domestic or 'European' constitutional principles to the field of international relations.[14] It seems to be asserted that much that the Council has done since the end of the Cold War is *ultra vires*, beyond its powers under the Charter, or otherwise unlawful. This is not, of course, the case. But if such efforts to 'demonize' the Council were taken seriously, they might eventually harm its standing, weaken the collective security system to which it is central, and thus set back efforts to promote multilateral approaches to international relations.

It is not only writers who tilt at windmills in this way. A major complaint of those states that fear the Council, and wish to see its powers constrained, is that it plays fast and loose with international law. One such accusation is that it ignores or overrides the law of treaties. Not all go as far as Cuba, which in 2002 described the draft that became Security Council resolution 1422 (2002) as 'an

[13] Ibid., at 66.

[14] M. Wood, '"Constitutionalization" of International Law: A Sceptical Voice', in K.H. Kaikabad and M. Bohlinder (eds), *International Law and Power. Perspectives on Legal Order and Justice. Essays in Honour of Colin Warbrick* (Dordrecht: Martinus Nijhoff, 2009) 85–97. These somewhat harsh strictures are not aimed at Talmon, though even he sometimes adopts a rather negative tone (for example at 67 in the paragraph following the Bellinger quotation). His assertion (at 68) that 'the Council's actions are subject to the principle of proportionality' seems to be conjured out of thin air. He does then try to put the genie back in the bottle by immediately adding that, given the Council's wide discretion, there is little scope for it being found to have contravened the principle. And his digression on 'the rule of law' (at 94–96)—essentially a domestic law concept—is of doubtful relevance to a discussion of the Security Council, notwithstanding references to the rule of law at the international level in certain resolutions of the General Assembly (most notably resolution 60/1 of 16 September 2005 [World Summit Outcome] and resolution 61/39 of 4 December 2006 and subsequent annual resolutions on 'The rule of law at the national and international levels').

armed assault on the law of treaties'.[15] Certain *causes célèbres* before the Council, such as resolutions 1373 (2001) (counter-terrorism),[16] 1422 (2002) (International Criminal Court),[17] and 1540 (2004) (counter-proliferation),[18] have led to somewhat less colourful criticisms. But even these should not be taken at face value. Rather than being based on considered opinions of the law, such criticisms mostly reflect strong political feelings, for example, in the case of resolution 1422 (2002) exasperation at the then US Administration's attitude towards the International Criminal Court.[19]

3. Obligations Set Forth in Treaties

The reality is otherwise; just as treaties are an important tool of international relations, so the Security Council is an important actor in relation to treaties. The latest Security Council resolution on Iran, resolution 1929 (2010), adopted on 9 June 2010 with 12 votes in favour, two against (Brazil, Turkey), and one abstention (Lebanon), illustrates this well. In addition to broadening and strengthening the implementation of sanctions targeted at Iran's nuclear programme, the resolution contains a number of provisions directed specifically at Iran's treaty relations (provisions which do not seem to have been controversial, unlike the strengthened sanctions). In the preamble, the Security Council reaffirmed 'its commitment to the Treaty on the Non-Proliferation of Nuclear Weapons, the need for all States Party to that Treaty to comply fully with all their obligations ...'.[20]

The Council then offered an interpretation of Iran's Safeguards Agreement, when it emphasized that in accordance with Article 39 thereof: 'Code 3.1 cannot be modified nor suspended unilaterally and that the IAEA's right to verify design information provided to it is a continuing right, which is not dependent on the stage of construction of, or the presence of nuclear material at, a facility'.[21]

[15] S/PV.4568 (Resumption I), 10 July 2002, at 14 (cited in S. Talmon, 'Security Council Treaty Action', *supra* note 12, at 65).

[16] Seen as the highpoint of Council 'legislation'.

[17] Followed, one year later, by resolution 1487 (2003) of 12 June 2003. The United States refrained from presenting a third resolution in 2004. Even more controversial were grants of immunity not based on Article 16 of the Rome Statute: see resolutions 1497 (2003) and 1593 (2005). See W. Schabas, *The International Criminal Court: A Commentary on the Rome Statute* (Oxford: Oxford University Press, 2010) at 325–34 (with further references).

[18] See D. Guilfoyle, *Shipping Interdiction and the Law of the Sea* (Cambridge: Cambridge University Press, 2009) at 238–43.

[19] The citations given by S. Talmon, 'Security Council Treaty Action', *supra* note 12, at 65–66, illustrate this all too clearly, as does the letter from Brazil, Canada, New Zealand, and South Africa, challenging the Council's authority to interpret and change the meaning of treaties (S/2002/754).

[20] Security Council resolution 1929 (2010), second preambular paragraph.

[21] Ibid., tenth preambular paragraph.

In support of the operative provisions concerning inspections at sea, the Council recalled 'that the law of the sea, as reflected in the United Nations Convention on the Law of the Sea (1982), sets out the legal framework applicable to ocean activities'.[22] And it called for 'the ratification of the Comprehensive Nuclear-Test-Ban Treaty by Iran at an early date'.[23]

From the point of view of the law of treaties, the most interesting provision of resolution 1929 (2010) is paragraph 5, in which the Council:

> *[d]ecides* that Iran shall without delay comply fully and without qualification with its IAEA Safeguards Agreement, including through the application of modified Code 3.1 of the Subsidiary Arrangement to its Safeguards Agreement, *calls upon* Iran to act strictly in accordance with the provisions of the Additional Protocol to its IAEA Safeguards Agreement that it signed on 18 December 2003, *calls upon* Iran to ratify promptly the Additional Protocol, and *reaffirms* that, in accordance with Articles 24 and 39 of Iran's Safeguards Agreement, Iran's Safeguards Agreement and its Subsidiary Arrangement, including modified Code 3.1, cannot be amended or changed unilaterally by Iran, and *notes* that there is no mechanism in the Agreement for the suspension of any of the provisions in the Subsidiary Arrangement.

This operative paragraph illustrates an elementary but crucial distinction, observed in the practice of the Council, as regards obligations set forth in a treaty.[24] On the one hand, the obligations set forth in a treaty are binding on the parties to the treaty by virtue of their participation in the treaty; on the other hand, the obligations set forth in a treaty may be binding on states and others for some reason outside the treaty,[25] including because they are made so by mandatory action of the Security Council. In paragraph 5 of resolution 1929 (2010), the Council called upon Iran to act strictly in accordance with *the provisions of* the Additional Protocol to its Safeguards Agreement, which it had signed but not yet ratified. In doing so, the Council did not imply that Iran was already bound by the Additional Protocol as a matter of treaty law, still less did it 'make' Iran a party to the Additional Protocol.

[22] Ibid., nineteenth preambular paragraph.

[23] Ibid., twentieth preambular paragraph.

[24] For a similar analysis, see S. Talmon, 'Security Council Treaty Action', *supra* note 12, at 97–108.

[25] A similar point could be made about the 'separate existence' of rules set forth in a treaty and the corresponding rules of customary international law: see ICJ, *Military and Paramilitary Activities in and against Nicaragua (Nicaragua v United States of America)*, Merits, Judgment of 27 June 1986, *ICJ Reports* (1986) 14, at 95, para. 178. See also provisions such as Article 3(b) of the Vienna Convention on the Law of Treaties of 1969, which provides that the fact that the Convention does not apply to certain international agreements 'shall not affect [...] the application to them of any of the rules set forth in the present Convention to which they would be subject under international law independently of the Convention'. And see the guidelines in cluster 4.4 (effects of a reservation on rights and obligations outside of the treaty) of the Guide to Practice on Reservations to Treaties, provisionally adopted by the International Law Commission in 2010 (Report of the International Law Commission for 2010, A/65/10, XX–XX, at 170–5).

An earlier example of a similar approach may be found in Security Council resolution 1757 (2007) of 30 May 2007 concerning the Special Tribunal for Lebanon. In that resolution, the Council decided that '[t]he provisions of the annexed document, including its attachment, on the establishment of a Special Tribunal for Lebanon shall enter into force on 10 June 2007'. The 'annexed document' was the Agreement between the United Nations and the Lebanese Republic on the establishment of a Special Tribunal for Lebanon, which had been signed by the government of Lebanon and the United Nations, but which had not entered into force in accordance with its terms because the Lebanese government had been unable to notify the United Nations that the legal requirements for its entry into force had been complied with. Once again, we see the Council referring to *the provisions of* a treaty, rather than the treaty itself.[26]

In its resolution 1593 (2005) of 31 March 2005, referring 'the situation in Darfur since 1 July 2002' to the Prosecutor of the International Criminal Court, the Security Council decided 'that the Government of Sudan [...] shall cooperate fully with and provide any necessary assistance to the Court and the Prosecutor'. Sudan had signed but not ratified the Rome Statute, but the Council nevertheless imposed upon it obligations to cooperate at least as comprehensive as those it would have if it had been a party.

Perhaps the clearest case of the distinction is to be found in resolution 1718 (2006) of 14 October 2006, in which, following the claim to have conducted a nuclear test made by the Democratic People's Republic of Korea (DPRK), the Council demanded that the DPRK 'immediately retract its announcement of withdrawal' from the Non-Proliferation Treaty (NPT) and that it 'return to the Treaty'; and at the same time decided that 'the DPRK [...] shall act strictly in accordance with the obligations applicable to parties under the Treaty on the Non-Proliferation of Nuclear Weapons and the terms and conditions of its International Atomic Energy Agency (IAEA) Safeguards Agreement', which agreement had also ceased to be in force assuming the DPRK's withdrawal from the NPT was effective.

An example where the Council imposed upon states the terms of a treaty, this time without any mention the treaty itself, is resolution 1373 (2001) of 28 September 2001. Paragraph 1 required all states to comply with provisions corresponding to those in the International Convention for the Suppression of Terrorist Financing of 1999.[27]

[26] B. Fassbender, 'Reflections on the International Legality of the Special Tribunal for Lebanon', 5 *Journal of International Criminal Justice* (2007) 1091–105; 'Current Legal Developments, The Special Tribunal for Lebanon' (with articles by F. Mégret, W.A. Schabas, and B. Elberling), 21 *Leiden J Int'l L* (2008) 483–538; S. Talmon, 'Security Council Treaty Action', *supra* note 12, at 105.

[27] At the time of the adoption of Security Council resolution 1373 (2001), the 1999 Convention had not entered into force. It did so only on 10 April 2002. As of 21 November 2010, it had 173 parties. Security Council resolution 1373 (2001) was to an extent controversial, especially

4. Particular Aspects of Security Council Treaty Action

4.1. The Security Council's role in relation to the conclusion and entry into force of treaties

The negotiation and entry into force of treaties can be slow. The principle of 'free consent'[28] means that key states may stand aside. For these and other reasons, it is sometimes suggested that treaties are not a satisfactory basis for solving pressing problems. But these fears can also be exaggerated, as was shown, for example, in the case of the relatively rapid negotiation and entry into force of the Rome Statute of the International Criminal Court. And treaties undoubtedly have advantages over other methods in terms of clarity and legitimacy.

The perceived need for speed has led some to look for ways of improving the multilateral treaty-making process,[29] and even to seek other ways of developing rules of international law and imposing obligations on states. For some, acting through the Security Council has seemed an attractive option, at least in certain fields such as counter-terrorism, non-proliferation, and piracy. The then Legal Adviser to the State Department expressed it well:

> [T]he Council has invoked its Chapter VII authorities to create specific legal frameworks to address threats to international peace and security. While these frameworks typically incorporate specialized bodies of law as part of the legal foundation of the Council's response, there are cases in which the Council has adapted these bodies of international law in order to meet the threat. [...] Council action can have the effect of tailoring a specialized body of law to better work in a specific set of circumstances.[30]

The Security Council, like any other political organ, may encourage the negotiation of a treaty. This it did, for example, in resolution 635 (1989) of 14 June 1989, which was a joint Czechoslovak–United Kingdom initiative following the Lockerbie incident. The Council urged the International Civil Aviation Organization 'to intensify its work [...] on devising an international regime for the marking of plastic or sheet explosives for the purpose of detection'.[31]

In another field, the Council has requested states to enter into Status of Forces/Mission Agreements (SOFAs, SOMAs), and has sometimes required them to

among some authors; it was seen as a primary example of the Council asserting a 'legislative' function.

[28] 1969 Vienna Convention on the Law of Treaties, preamble.

[29] See the activity of the United Nations General Assembly and the International Law Commission in 1978–79 on the item 'Review of the multilateral treaty-making process': General Assembly resolution 32/48 of 8 December 1977, *YILC* (1979), vol. II(2), 187–8.

[30] Cited by S. Talmon, 'Security Council Treaty Action', *supra* note 12, at 67. See also M. Matheson, *Council Unbound: The Growth of UN Decision Making on Conflict and Post conflict Issues after the Cold War* (Washington D.C.: United States Institute of Peace Press, 2006).

[31] The Convention on the Marking of Plastic Explosives for Detection was opened for signature on 1 March 1991, and entered into force on 21 June 1998.

apply the UN Model Agreement provisionally, pending the conclusion of such agreements.[32]

The question is sometimes asked whether the Security Council can impose an obligation upon a state to become party to a treaty—or even make a state party to a treaty. This has remained a largely theoretical question, since—perhaps out of respect for the principle of consent that underlies the law of treaties—the Council has refrained from doing this.[33] But it is difficult to see that it would necessarily be acting *ultra vires* if it did. The Council has frequently called upon states generally,[34] and in some cases individually,[35] to become or consider becoming parties to particular treaties, for example, the counter-terrorism conventions. But it has avoided imposing an obligation to do so, probably for policy reasons rather than out of conviction that it lacked the power. Whether this is because '[t]he Council can impose obligations, it cannot impose treaties'[36] remains an open question. In any event, the Council has not shied away from imposing the obligations set forth in a treaty.

4.2 Breach or threatened breach of treaty as a threat to international peace and security, and the enforcement of treaty obligations as a measure to be taken by the Security Council

The importance of the performance of treaties in good faith (*pacta sunt servanda*) for the maintenance of international peace and security hardly needs restating.[37] It is reflected in the preambles to the United Nations Charter ('respect for the obligations arising from treaties') and the Vienna Convention itself. It is, of course, those treaties that are most sensitive for states that are most likely to be relevant for the maintenance of international peace and security, such as

[32] See, for example, Security Council resolutions 1626 (2005) of 19 September 2005, para. 9 (Liberia); 1671 (2006) of 25 April 2006, para. 4 (DRC); 1769 (2007) of 31 July 2007, para.15(b) (Sudan).

[33] It is misleading to suggest that the Special Court for Lebanon was 'established by Agreement whose entry into force was imposed by a Chapter VII resolution': D. Shraga, 'Mixed or internationalized courts', in A. Cassese (ed.), *The Oxford Companion to International Criminal Justice* (Oxford: Oxford University Press, 2009) at 424.

[34] As in its many resolutions in the field of terrorism: see, for example, resolution 1377 (2001), annex (Ministerial Declaration on the Global Effort to Combat Terrorism), in which the Council 'called on all states to become parties as soon as possible to the relevant international conventions and protocols relating to terrorism'. More generally, see the resolutions listed by S. Talmon, 'Security Council Treaty Action', *supra* note 12, at 96.

[35] In resolution 687 (1991), para. 7, the Council invited Iraq to ratify the Biological Weapons Convention of 1972; in resolution 1029 (1995), preamble, the Council called for Iran to ratify the Additional Protocol to its Safeguards Agreement at an early date.

[36] S. Talmon, 'Security Council Treaty Action', *supra* note 12, at 98.

[37] See the contributions by A. Vermeer-Künzli, P. Escarameia, and G. Hafner, in G. Nolte (ed.), *Peace through International Law: The Role of the International Law Commission*, *supra* note 1, 67–121.

boundary treaties and those in the fields of arms control and non-proliferation, immunities, and international criminal law.

Ensuring compliance with treaties, and their enforcement, are not matters dealt with in the Vienna Convention, except peripherally in article 60 (Termination as a consequence of breach) and article 73 (State responsibility). The Security Council naturally has an important role (though so far more potential than actual) in securing compliance with treaties, and where necessary their enforcement. This is so not only in those cases, largely in the arms control and non-proliferation fields, where the Council's role is expressly or implicitly recognized in the treaty.[38]

4.3 Article 103 of the Charter

Article 103 of the Charter has a direct bearing on treaty obligations. It reads as follows: 'In the event of a conflict between the obligations of the Members of the United Nations under the present Charter and their obligations under any other international agreement, their obligations under the present Charter shall prevail.'

In recent years, this key provision of the Charter has assumed increasing importance, and has been much discussed in the courts[39] and in the literature. It is not intended, on this occasion, to re-examine in detail the many interesting issues to which this provision gives rise. My own conclusions were set out, a few years ago, as follows:[40]

51. [...] Overall, it may be said that [Article 103] should not be interpreted narrowly if it is to have the effect intended by the drafters of the Charter [...].

52. *First,* the effect of the Article is not to invalidate the conflicting obligation, but merely to set it aside to the extent of the conflict. The analysis in the Report of the International Law Commission's Study Group[41] is impeccable. Any other position,

[38] For example, Treaty on the Non-Proliferation of Nuclear Weapons, Article 10; Convention on the Prohibition of the Development, Production and Stockpiling of Bacteriological (Biological) and Toxin Weapons and on their Destruction 1972, Article VI; Chemical Weapons Convention 1993, Article XII(4); Comprehensive Test Ban Treaty 1996, Article V(4). See also Convention on the Prevention and Punishment of the Crime of Genocide, Article VIII.

[39] See, for example, House of Lords, *R (on the Application of Al-Jedda) v Secretary of State for Defence* [2007] UKHL 58; Grand Chamber of the European Court of Human Rights, *Al-Jedda v United Kingdom*, hearing of 9 June 2010. See also M. Wood, 'Detention During International Military Operations: Article 103 of the UN Charter and the *Al-Jedda* Case', 47 *Military Law and the Law of War Review* (2008), vol. 1-2.

[40] Hersch Lauterpacht Memorial Lectures 2006, 'The UN Security Council and International Law', First Lecture ('The Legal Framework of the Security Council'). The lectures are available on the website of the Lauterpacht Centre for International Law, University of Cambridge. An expanded version of the lectures will be published by Cambridge University Press as a book within the *Hersch Lauterpacht Memorial Lectures* series.

[41] *Fragmentation of International Law: Difficulties arising from the Diversification and Expansion of International Law: Report of the Study Group of the International Law Commission*, A/CN.4/L.682 and Add.1, reproduced in A. Pronto and M. Wood, *The International Law Commission 1999–2009: Volume IV* (Oxford: Oxford University Press, 2010) 626–814.

for example, that the conflicting obligation is or becomes void, is not borne out in practice and in most cases would make no sense. Thus, if a sanctions regime is incompatible with rights of navigation under the Danube Convention, it is obvious that the effect of Article 103 is not to void provisions of the Danube Convention, even for the target state, but merely to give priority to the Charter obligations while they subsist.

53. *Second,* the Article applies also to obligations imposed by mandatory resolutions of the Security Council, since by virtue of Article 25 (and Article 48) such obligations are 'obligations [...] under the present Charter'. *Lockerbie* is authority for this, and has been followed in the European and English cases [...].
54. *Third,* in order to be effective Article 103 must apply equally to action taken under authorizations of the Council. This question was canvassed at length in the *Al-Jedda* case [...].
55. *Fourth,* it is generally accepted that the priority which Article 103 affords to the Charter over international agreements is equally applicable to rules of customary international law (general international law). This is indeed essential if the purposes of the Charter in the field of the maintenance of international peace and security are to be achieved, for example where obligations under customary international law subsist in parallel with obligations under treaties [...].
56. *Fifth,* there are no exceptions to the obligations under treaty and customary law over which Charter obligations prevail, other than (according to a widely held view) *jus cogens* norms (peremptory norms of general international law). Any such exception is, I believe, more theoretical than real [...].

The effect of Article 103 is sometimes described as 'adapting' treaties, sometimes as justifying a breach of treaty. This distinction, drawn by Talmon,[42] seems somewhat unreal. Talmon gives as examples of 'adaptation' the resolutions on Lockerbie, those in 2003–2004 on Iraq concerning the Hague Regulations and the Fourth Geneva Convention, those on the International Criminal Court, and on the United Nations Convention on the Law of the Sea. As examples of resolutions justifying a breach he cites resolution 820 (1993) of 17 April 1993, which requires states to prevent Serbian shipping on the Danube notwithstanding the Danube Convention, and resolution 1333 (2000) of 19 December 2000 concerning Afghanistan, under which all states were required to deny certain aircraft landing, taking off, or overflight.

5. Conclusion

As suggested above, those who would 'demonize' the Security Council have, among other things, picked on what they see as the Council's disregard for both the law of treaties and treaty law. It is hoped that enough has been said to

[42] S. Talmon, 'Security Council Treaty Action', *supra* note 12, at 86–9.

show that such accusations are largely unfounded. The Council has shown self-restraint, as indeed it should, in its approach to treaties, only 'interfering' to the extent necessary for the maintenance of international peace and security (as in the fields of terrorism and non-proliferation). And most such 'interference' can be readily explained and analysed by having regard to the distinction between Council action that affects treaty obligations as such (as is the case under Article 103, though even then only to a limited extent), and Council action that imposes obligations set forth in a treaty (*the provisions of* a treaty), but not the treaty itself. In reality, 'Security Council treaty action' can be a useful tool in the challenging task of maintaining and restoring international peace and security, and should not be seen as an attack on the law.

16

The European Courts and the Law of Treaties: The Continuing Story

Pieter Jan Kuijper

1. Introduction

It seems fitting on this occasion to pay homage to Giorgio Gaja[1] by returning to some issues related to the way in which the European Courts, the European Court of Justice (ECJ), and the (then) Court of First Instance (CFI)[2], deal with the law of treaties as embodied in the Vienna Convention on the Law of Treaties 1969 (VCLT I).[3] This question has been analysed

[1] Professor Giorgio Gaja and the writer of this contribution have always shared a practical and academic interest for the boundary zone between general international law and the law of what is now called the European Union. Perhaps Professor Gaja's interest in the matter originated in the period in the eighties when, together with a number of other distinguished University professors from different member states, he was asked to sit on a committee of international lawyers with a view to advising the Legal Service of the European Commission on international legal matters. This advisory committee—which sometimes took on the aspect of a supervisory committee—was created because the number of questions of international law with which the Legal Service was confronted was rising fast, while the number of lawyers with expertise in this area of the law was very limited at that time in the Legal Service (the number started to increase only with the influx of some Spanish international lawyers after the accession of their country and since then has grown in a more regular way so as to ensure that the Service could deal in a professional fashion with international law questions and with specialized domains such as WTO law and litigation). It was thus that Professor Gaja oversaw some of my activities in the Legal Service at that time, only for us to meet again as (friendly) adversaries in recent times on the matter of the responsibility of international organizations, on which he is the International Law Commission (ILC) Rapporteur.

[2] This chapter will generally refer to the European Union and Union law, as is appropriate after the entry into force of the Treaty of Lisbon; sometimes, when it is necessary to do so for historical reasons, however, the old terms European Community and Community law will be used. For G. Gaja's interest in the matter, see his 'Restraints imposed by European Community Law in the Treaty-making Power of the Member States', in I. Cameron and A. Simoni (eds), *Dealing with Integration: Perspectives from Seminars on European Law* (Uppsala: Iustus, 1998) and 'A "new" Vienna Convention on Treaties between States and International Organizations or between International Organizations: a Critical Commentary', 58 *BYIL* (1987) 253–69.

[3] There is, of course, the so-called second Vienna Convention of 1986, the Vienna Convention on Treaties between States and International Organizations or between International Organizations, but the European Courts and other European Institutions hardly ever refer to this Convention. It has not yet entered into force and it is highly unlikely that the EU will ever

earlier, in 1998,[4] but it would seem worthwhile to look into it again on the basis of new case law. Is there any change in the way the European Courts resort to the Vienna Convention and in the occasions when and the reasons why the Courts do so?

This chapter will essentially follow an inductive approach to the cases.[5] However, within the framework of a necessarily limited contribution the most important strands of case law will have to be reserved for analysis and others left out. It will thus concentrate first on the question on what basis the European Courts have recourse to the Vienna Convention and to which Vienna Convention, that of 1969 (VCLT I) or that of 1986 (VCLT II). Secondly, the Courts have recourse to the Vienna Convention most frequently for matters of interpretation, and specifically with a view to justifying an interpretation which goes beyond the text alone. The question of what is being interpreted is an important one here: international agreements concluded by the EU, the EU treaties themselves, or even secondary Union law? Of all the questions that require interpretation, the question of self-executingness or direct effect of international agreements is the most frequent and the most important; commensurate attention will be devoted to it. Thirdly, special attention will be paid to the importance of good faith, not only in the interpretation, but also in the application and implementation of international agreements. Finally, a number of more technical issues stand out in our sample, such as the territorial reach of treaties,[6] error in treaty-making,[7] 'illegally concluded treaties',[8] and succession between treaties. Of these, the last

conclude it, after the unhappy episode of first the inclusion and finally the rejection of Article 36 bis. See C. Brölmann, *The Institutional Veil in Public International Law* (Oxford: Hart Publishing, 2007) 212–25.

[4] P.J. Kuijper, 'The Court and the Tribunal of the EC and the Vienna Convention on the Law of Treaties 1969', 25 *Legal Issues of European Integration* (1998) 1–23. This chapter is based on study of all the relevant cases between 1998 and 2010. There are roughly 40 cases in which the Courts make explicit reference to the Vienna Convention in this period. There are also a few cases included in the discussion, in which the principles of the Vienna Convention are used without explicit reference, but one cannot be sure to have found all of them. Dramatic cases that have been extensively discussed in the literature, such as the *Kadi* case and the *MOX Plant* case, have been left out on purpose. Advocates-General have referred to the Vienna Convention 1969 in more, and other, cases than those in which the Court has explicitly referred to it; their views are used here mainly in an illustrative manner.

[5] For an example of this approach, see G. Schwarzenberger, *International Law as Applied by International Courts and Tribunals* (London: Stevens, 1957 and 1968) vols I–II; (London: Sweet & Maxwell, 1976) vol. III.

[6] Case C-37/00 *Weber v Universal Ogden Services* [2002] ECR I-2013, point 29 *et seq*. This case concerned the application of Community law on the continental shelf and also contained references to the UNCLOS Convention.

[7] Case C-347/03 *Regione autonoma Friuli-Venezia Giulia (Tocai Friulano)* [2005] ECR I-3785, in which the Italian Court asking preliminary questions seemed to intimate that there was a case of error in treaty-making, but the Italian Court believed that the error was on the part of the Court, which had not realized that Tocai friulano was not a protected geographical indication; see points 99–101 of the judgment.

[8] Joined Cases C-317–318 *European Parliament v Council and Commission (PNR Agreement)* [2007] ECR I-4721. See in particular points 71–74 on the limitation of the effects of the judgment

mentioned group is the most interesting, since it raises the issue of the special character of EU law as compared to international law. Therefore it will be discussed in greater detail later.

2. The Trends in the Case Law

2.1. Why the Vienna Convention of 1969?

The older case law simply refers to the rules of interpretation of VCLT I, as laid down in Articles 31–33, without giving much in the way of further justification. The maximum the Courts say is that, insofar as the Vienna Convention of 1969 contains customary rules of international law, these rules also bind the Community.[9] It is only in the very recent *Brita* case that the ECJ explicitly explains, with reference to the Vienna Convention itself, why the Court has recourse to VCLT I in interpreting the EC–Israel Association Agreement with a view to deciding whether imports from the Israeli-occupied territories of the West Bank can profit from the free-trade provisions of that agreement.[10]

The ECJ first states that the answer to this question depends first and foremost on the interpretation of the territorial clause of Article 83 of the EC–Israel Association Agreement. It next recalls that an international agreement concluded by the Council with a non-member state, according to standing case law, constitutes an act of one of the institutions of the Union and therefore can be interpreted by the EU Courts. However, it also remains an international instrument that is subject to international law and therefore this interpretation must follow the rules of the international law of treaties.[11] The Court proceeds to recall that:

> ... [t]he international law of treaties was consolidated, essentially, in the Vienna Convention. Under Article 1 thereof, the Vienna Convention applies to Treaties between States. However, under Article 3(b) of the Vienna Convention, the fact that the Vienna Convention does not apply to international agreements between States and other subjects of international law is not to affect the application to them of any of the rules set forth in that convention to which they would be subject under international law independently of the convention.
>
> It follows that the rules laid down in the Vienna Convention apply to an agreement concluded between a State and an international organization, such as the EC–Israel Association Agreement, insofar as the rules are an expression of general customary law...[12]

which are entirely in conformity with Article 46 of the Vienna Convention. See also P.J. Kuijper, *supra* note 4, 12–13.

[9] See P.J. Kuijper, *supra* note 4, 1.

[10] Case C-386/08 *Brita GmbH v Hauptzollamt Hamburg Hafen*, Judgment of 25 February 2010, not yet reported.

[11] *Brita* case, *supra* note 10, points 38–39.

[12] See *Brita* case, *supra* note 10, points 40–41.

It is quite likely that the Court was inspired to clarify the basis for its earlier recourse to the maxims of interpretation of Articles 31–33 of the Vienna Convention so clearly, because there were two other agreements with a non-State entity that were indirectly at issue in this case. They were the EC–PLO Agreement of 1997 and the so-called Israel–PLO Interim Agreement of 1995, both concluded with the Palestinian Authority as represented by the PLO in the wake of the Clinton Administration's 1995 efforts for peace in the Middle East.[13]

It is these other agreements that were of considerable importance in this case in bringing the ECJ to refer to another rule of customary law in the Vienna Convention, namely the rule of relative effect of treaties, also known as the *pactum tertiis* rule, laid down in Article 34 of the Vienna Convention. In the view of the Court it was incumbent upon it to use the rules of interpretation of Articles 31–33 of the Vienna Convention 1969 in the light of the rule of Article 34. The ECJ quite rightly did not want to give an interpretation to the phrase 'the territory of the State of Israel' that was used in Article 83 of the EC–Israel Agreement so as to influence in any way these other agreements and their provisions relating to territory and authority over territory. In particular, the EC–PLO Agreement stated that it applied to 'territories of the West Bank and the Gaza Strip',[14] whereas the Israel–PLO Interim Agreement, as the Advocate-General pointed out but the Court did not mention, recognized the authority of the Palestinian Authority to govern commerce inside the West Bank and Gaza and with other countries, including the exercise of customs authority.[15] Thus the Court arrived at the core conclusion of its preliminary ruling that the West Bank and Gaza were not part of the territory of the State of Israel. Hence goods imported from these territories could not profit from free access to the Union on the strength of a declaration of Israeli origin issued by Israeli custom authorities.

2.2. Resort to the Vienna Convention's Rules of Interpretation

The first crucial question to ask is: which instruments of Union law are to be interpreted by the rules of interpretation of the Vienna Convention? Only the treaties concluded by the Union, the Union treaties themselves and what is comprised in them, or also instruments of secondary Community and Union law? This question is strongly related to the special character of Union law and the well-known transition between the *Van Gend en Loos* case, where the Community legal order was described as 'a new legal order of international law',[16] and *Costa/ENEL* less than two years later, where the words 'of international law' were omitted.[17] There

[13] Advocate-General Bot produced an excellent opinion that gives a very good overview of the facts; see Opinion of Advocate-General Bot of 29 October 2009, not yet reported.

[14] See *Brita* case, *supra* note 10, point 23, referring to Article 73 of the EC-PLO Association Agreement.

[15] Opinion of Advocate-General Bot, points 44–48.

[16] See Case 26/62 *Van Gend en Loos* [1963] ECR English special edition 1.

[17] See Case 6/64 *Costa v ENEL* [1964] ECR English special edition 585.

has always been a tendency at the Court to argue that the special character of the Community legal order required special, more teleologically oriented, interpretation methods than was usual in international law. At the same time the Court, in Opinion 1/91, has already made a not quite convincing attempt at founding the special character of the Community legal order by applying the normal rules of interpretation.[18] As we will see in this chapter, both approaches are still alive.

2.2.1. The Vienna Convention of 1969 and international agreements concluded by the EU

There is no doubt that the Vienna Convention's rules of interpretation are resorted to most often for the interpretation of the international agreements of the Union. This is as it should be. In most cases the principles of Articles 31 and 32, and occasionally Article 33, are put forward in order to go beyond the textual interpretation and imply not only the context, but also the object and purpose of the agreement in the interpretation of the treaty clauses that are placed before the Courts for interpretation. In many cases the rules of interpretation of the Vienna Convention are used to decide the question of direct effect of the provisions of the international agreement at issue.

It is important to realize that the Courts apply the object and purpose of the agreement, not merely as an aid to interpretation of a specific provision of an international agreement, but they also have recourse to this technique when applying a kind of preliminary test of the nature and structure of the agreement, which will determine whether the agreement *as such* is capable of being given direct effect. This approach is best known for initially having been applied to the GATT and later to the WTO.[19] In those cases, however, as has often been pointed out, this interpretation technique was heavily mixed with separation of powers concerns. The Courts, seeing that, even long after panel and Appellate Body reports had become definitive and had been partially implemented, negotiations were still going on between the EC and its adversaries in the WTO dispute settlement procedure, while WTO-authorized sanctions were also being applied, clearly did not want to sit down in the chair of the negotiators, the Commission, or of the legislator, the Council.

A purer application of the preliminary interpretation of the object and purpose of an international agreement can be found in the *Intertanko* case.[20] In that case the ECJ, looking at the overall structure and purpose of UNCLOS, decided that the agreement was primarily intended to lay down rights and duties between states as to the various uses of the seas, within different zones agreed in the Convention.

[18] See P.J. Kuijper, *supra* note 4, 4.

[19] Cases 21–24/72 *International Fruit* [1972] ECR 1219 and Case C 377/02 *Van Parijs* [2005] ECR I-1465.

[20] Case 308/06 *Intertanko* [2008] ECR I-4057.

Even insofar as these provisions seemed to grant rights to ships, in the view of the Court, such rights were primarily derived from states who granted their flag to ships and thus had assumed an obligation to supervise these ships and their crew and to ensure the application and enforcement of certain (agreed) rules on board the vessels flying their flag.[21]

When the object and purpose approach to treaty interpretation is applied by the Courts, the result is often that direct effect is indeed granted to certain provisions of the agreement concerned, in any case as long as the *prima facie* textual interpretation is not contradicted by an object and purpose analysis. This is the approach followed in the case of *Sema Sürül,* which concerned the possible direct effect of Article 3 of Decision 3/80 of the EC–Turkey Association Council in the field of social security of migrating workers, laying down a rule of non-discrimination in the application of that Decision.[22] The Court in that ruling first recalled the settled case law in respect of the requirements for direct effect of provisions of an agreement concluded by the Community with non-member countries. They were considered 'directly applicable'[23] when, 'regard being had to its wording and to the purpose and nature of the agreement itself, the provision contains a clear and precise obligation which is not subject, in its implementation or effects, to the adoption of any subsequent measure'.[24] The Court had no difficulty deciding that, as far as the textual aspect was concerned, Article 3 of Decision 3/80 satisfied those conditions, as it was a directly and straightforwardly drafted complete prohibition on discrimination on the basis of nationality. Interestingly enough, the Court carried out the test of the 'purpose and nature' of the Agreement, of which the provision formed part, only afterwards in order to verify whether it did not 'contradict the finding that the principle of non-discrimination embodied in Article 3 [...] is capable of directly governing the situation of individuals'. Basing itself on the relevant provisions of the Association Agreement with Turkey and its 1970 Protocol, the Court found that there is no such contradiction.[25]

However, object and purpose as important criteria for interpretation often lead to rather nuanced outcomes. The Court has pointed out on numerous occasions that the interpretation of near-identical provisions can vary greatly between two treaties that have wholly different purposes.[26] This insight was

[21] Case 308/06 *Intertanko, supra* note 20, point 61.

[22] Case C-262/96 *Sema Sürül v Bundesanstalt für Arbeit* [1999] ECR I-2685, point 60 *et seq.*

[23] As is also the case with the direct effect of pure Community law, the Court is weak in making a proper distinction between 'direct applicability' and 'direct effect', the first being the question of the law of the land, the second being that of invocability by private parties. See J. Winter, 'Direct Applicability and Direct Effect, Two Different and Distinct Concepts of Community Law', 9 *Common Market Law Review* (1972) 425.

[24] See Case C-262/96, *supra* note 23, point 60.

[25] See Case C-262/96, *supra* note 23, points 69–72.

[26] See P.J. Kuijper, *supra* note 4, 2–3, referring in this context to Case 270/80 *Polydor* [1982] ECR 329 and Opinion 1/91 [1991] ECR I-6079.

applied, for instance, in the case of *Barkoci and Malik*.[27] In that case two service providers from Czechia invoked the *Sürül* precedent in relation to the interpretation of Article 45(3) of the EC–Czechia Association Agreement that was, moreover, virtually identical to Article 49 of the EC Treaty (now 56 of the TFEU), laying down, as it did, the freedom to provide services in terms of non-discrimination on the grounds of nationality. Therefore, this provision of the agreement ought to be given direct effect in the same way as Article 49 of the EC Treaty and the non-discrimination provision in the field of social security in *Sürül* had been granted direct effect. The ECJ could go along with this without much of a problem. However, it could not but point out that the consequences of such direct effect would necessarily be much more limited, especially in respect of the rights to entry and residence, which in the context respectively of the EC Treaty and the EC–Turkey Association, because of the objective of a single internal market underlying the EC Treaty and, though perhaps to a lesser extent, the EC–Turkey Association, had always been considered subordinate to the right to provide services or the admission to the labour market, respectively. The objective of the EC–Czechia Association being merely to establish a gradual integration with a view to a possible future accession, its Article 59(1) in particular made it clear, however, that no such subordination existed in that context, since the Community member states remained free to apply their *normal* rules for entry and residence, even though Article 45(3) of the Association Agreement had direct effect. The scope of such direct effect therefore was severely restricted, compared to the *Sürül* case,[28] though abuse of the rules for entry and residence that would nullify the right to provide services as an independent was prohibited.

The same approach to direct effect combined with a similar approach based on the distinction between the object and purpose of an internal market and a slow approximation towards accession was applied by the Court in the *Glosczuk* case concerning a Polish building contractor wanting to offer his services in the UK and invoking a similar provision of the EC–Poland Association Agreement.[29] Similarly, in *El-Yassini,* a Moroccan worker in the UK invoked Article 40 of the EC–Morocco Agreement, an equal treatment clause for workers in respect of remuneration and working conditions, to argue that his residence permit ought to be extended in order to guarantee his equal treatment with Turkish nationals.[30] In both cases the Court came to the conclusion that the provision on non-discrimination on the basis of nationality for service providers had direct effect, but that deriving a right of entry, stay, or residence from that was a bridge too far. Moreover, in the case of *El-Yassini* the Court probably had in mind a

[27] See Case C-257/99 *Barkoci and Malik* [2001] ECR I-6557.

[28] See Case C-257/99, *supra* note 27, points 55–59.

[29] Case C-63/99 *Gloszczuk* [2001] ECR I-6369.

[30] Case C-416/96 *El-Yassini v Secretary of State for the Home Department* [1999] ECR I-1209, points 33–35.

joint declaration in the Final Act of the new, 1996 Mediterranean Agreement with Morocco, which stated that the non-discrimination clause, in particular with respect to redundancy, could not be invoked to obtain a renewal of a residence permit.[31] As Advocate-General Colomer pointed out in his later Opinion in *Gattousi*, such declarations are to be taken into account for the purposes of interpreting international agreements under Article 31 of the Vienna Convention 1969.[32]

An extra twist was added by a case brought by a number of Polish and Czech 'ladies of the night' plying their trade in the Netherlands under the protection of the status of self-employed service providers.[33] They claimed that under the relevant EC agreements with Poland and Czechia they had a right to remain, given that their financial administrations showed that they were *bona fide* self-employed persons paying taxes. Certain Dutch authorities sought to remove the ladies back to their home country on the basis that their trade was 'illegal' and 'immoral' and hence stood in the way of regarding them as exercising an economic activity in a self-employed capacity. With an almost audible chuckle the Court wrote: 'Far from being prohibited in all Member States, prostitution is tolerated, even regulated, by most of those states, notably the Member State concerned in the present case.'[34] However, as in the cases mentioned earlier, the Netherlands formally retained the right to apply normally its law on entry, stay, and residence to the ladies in question, though an important weapon for applying it to them had been taken from it. This case is the only one of our sample in which implicitly the good faith required in any interpretation pursuant to the criteria of Article 31 plays, at least implicitly, a role.

One might sometimes tend to forget it, but there are still cases in which the ECJ simply interprets an international agreement in order to find out whether a given piece of EU legislation can be interpreted in conformity with it. A good example is the *IATA* case,[35] in which the organization of airline companies attempted to sow doubt before the High Court of Justice of England and Wales about the question of whether the new Regulation on compensation and assistance to airline passengers who had been denied boarding and had suffered long delays and cancellation of flights[36] was fully compatible with the so-called

[31] Advocate-General Léger mentioned this declaration in point 57 of his Opinion in *El-Yassini*, *supra* note 30. However, since the case was about the interpretation of the old 1976 EC-Morocco Agreement, which had not been accompanied by such a declaration, the Court preferred not to use the declaration openly. The 1996 EC-Morocco Agreement was finally concluded by Council and Commission Decision 2000/204, [2000] OJ L70/1.

[32] Opinion of Advocate-General Ruiz-Jarabo Colomer in Case C-97/05 *Gattoussi v Stadt Rüsselsheim* [2006] ECR I-11917.

[33] Case C-268/99 *Jany and Others v Staatssecretaris van Justitie* [2001] ECR I-8615.

[34] Case C-268/99 *Jany*, *supra* note 33, point 57.

[35] Case C-344/04 *IATA* [2006] ECR I-403.

[36] Regulation (EC) 261/2004 establishing common rules on compensation and assistance to passengers in the event of denied boarding and of cancellation or long delay of flights, [2004] OJ L46/1.

Montreal Convention to which the EC and its member states had become parties.[37] Invoking for once not just Article 31 of the Vienna Convention 1969, but also the same article from the 1986 Vienna Convention, the Court sets out to analyse the object and purpose of the Montreal Convention on the basis of its preamble and thus to come to a conclusion about its scope. The idea behind the Montreal Convention is thus seen to be the protection of the interest of consumers by providing equitable compensation based on the principle of restitution. This indicates that the Montreal Convention is intended to take care of the individual damage that a passenger may suffer and that is connected to each passenger's individual situation and can only be calculated and determined after the fact on the basis of an individual claim. The Court points out, however, that the EU Regulation aims to deal with the immediate damage and inconvenience that is near-identical for all passengers (food, drink, lodging, need to communicate, etc).

> Since the assistance and taking care of passengers envisaged by Article 6 [of the EU Regulation] in the event of a long delay to a flight constitute such standardized and immediate compensatory measures, they are not among those whose institution is regulated by the Convention. The system prescribed in Article 6 simply operates at an earlier stage than the system which results from the Montreal Convention.[38]

The standardized and immediate assistance and care provided by the EC Regulation would not prevent passengers who are victims of a long delay from making individualized claims under the Montreal Convention. In the view of the Court, the measures instituted by the EC Regulation are merely an addition to the regime of the Montreal Convention and in line with its objective to protect the passengers' interest, even improving the conditions under which the Convention's system of restitution functions. Therefore, there can be no question of inconsistency.[39]

A new and highly interesting category of cases which, because of the text of the EC Treaty (now TFEU), may need to be constantly informed by the interpretation of a specific international agreement is formed by the cases concerning the implementation and application of the Directive on minimum standards for the granting of refugee status or of other international protection status. Article 63(1)

[37] Convention for the Unification of Certain Rules for International Carriage by Air (the Montreal Convention) was approved by Decision of the Council of 5 April 2001, [2001] OJ L194/38. Actually, as Advocate-General Geelhoed pointed out, Reg. No. 261/2004 was adopted before the Montreal Convention entered into force for the EC. He argued, however, entirely in keeping with Article 18 of the Vienna Convention, that 'the institutions were obliged, as from 9 December 1999, the date of signature, to refrain from acts which would defeat the object and purpose of the Convention. Thus there was an obligation to refrain from adopting Community legislation which could be incompatible with the Montreal Convention.' Opinion of Advocate-General Geelhoed in Case 344/04 *IATA* [2006], *supra* note 35, point 32.

[38] Case C-344/04 *IATA*, *supra* note 35, point 46.

[39] Ibid., points 47–8.

EC Treaty (now Article 78(1) TFEU) refers explicitly to the Geneva 1951 Refugees Convention and its 1967 Protocol as a yardstick for EU legislation in this area. This has led Advocate-General Sharpston recently to delve deeply into the Geneva Convention and the instruments relevant to the status of Palestinians in order to advise the Court of Justice on the status of a Palestinian woman who had demanded asylum in Hungary.[40] Many more such cases can be expected in future.

2.2.2. *The Vienna Convention of 1969 and the EU/EC Treaties*

The preceding section already demonstrated, insofar as it referred to the cases where comparisons were made between the EC Treaty and international agreements concluded by the EC as to their object and purpose in order to differentiate between quasi-identical provisions included in both agreements, that the Courts are ready to apply the Vienna Convention 1969 to the Union Treaties themselves. That is not surprising, since the Vienna Convention itself states explicitly that it applies to the constituent treaties of international organizations as well as to agreements adopted within an international organization.[41]

In an earlier analysis, it was shown that an international agreement that the Commission had 'concluded' as a kind of administrative agreement with the two US anti-trust authorities, the US Attorney-General, and the Federal Trade Commission on cooperation and exchange of information in anti-trust matters was regarded by the ECJ as a 'treaty' within the meaning of Article 2 of VCLT I.[42] An important consideration for the Court was that the instrument in question on the basis of its wording was binding and could engage the Community's responsibility. Hence the Commission had no power under the Treaty to 'conclude' the agreement, since the notion of 'treaty' under the Vienna Convention and the notion of agreement under Article 228 (later 300 EC Treaty and 218 TFEU) were coterminous in this case and hence only the Council could conclude it, according to the system of the EC Treaty.

Some 10 years later the Commission again agreed an instrument with the US, the so-called Trans-Atlantic Regulatory Agenda, and this time both parties took great pains to characterize 'the arrangement' as non-binding in international law in the run-up to and during the negotiations themselves. This was considered acceptable by the Council committee that followed these negotiations

[40] Opinion of Advocate-General Sharpston in Case C-31/09 *Bolbol v BAH*, 4 March 2010, not yet reported.

[41] Article 5 of the Vienna Convention 1969. The category of agreements adopted within an international organization has become inapplicable to the EU ever since the so-called third pillar, where this kind of agreement was used, was removed from that sector by the Treaty of Amsterdam.

[42] P.J. Kuijper, *supra* note 4, 11–12, discussing Case C-327/91 *France v Commission* [1994] ECR I-3641.

very closely under the commercial policy provisions of the EC Treaty. France, however, again started an action for annulment against the so-called 'conclusion' of this arrangement, once more taking the view that this was in fact a 'treaty' within the meaning of the Vienna Convention's Article 2, which could not be legally concluded by the Commission. However, this time the ECJ sided with the Commission and recognized the document as truly non-binding and thus not a treaty either under the Vienna Convention or the EC Treaty. Under some conditions the Court accepted that the Commission could agree such a text with a foreign administration.[43]

This line of cases also showed that the ECJ had a great aversion to having recourse to later practice within the EC's institutions as an aid to interpretation of the EC Treaty in line with Article 31(3)(b) of VCLT I.[44] 'Mere practice cannot override the provisions of the Treaty' used to be the Court's brutal response to any attempt in this direction.[45] There may now be a slight opening visible in the Court's position on this issue.

In the landmark *Ecowas* case,[46] also called the small arms and light weapons case, the ECJ was asked to determine the boundary line between the Common Foreign and Security Policy and Community Development Co-operation in the light of the formers Article 47 TEU. In order to find the appropriate answer the ECJ made reference to various non-binding policy documents adopted by the Council and by different institutions jointly. Thus it mentioned a 1999 resolution of the Development Council on small arms, it referred to the 'European Union Strategy to combat illicit accumulation and trafficking of small arms and light weapons', adopted by the Council on 15–16 December 2005, and it highlighted the 'European Consensus on Development' of 2006, which was a joint statement by the Council, the representatives of the governments of the member states meeting within the Council, the European Parliament, and the European Commission.[47] All these references point to a greater willingness on the part of the Court than hitherto to pay attention to the practice of the institutions and the member states in the interpretation of the founding Treaties, in line with Article 31(3)(b) VCLT I. A distinctive feature of 'Community' treaty interpretation is thus perhaps being changed.

[43] Case C-233/02 *France v Commission* [2004] ECR I-2759, points 42–46. Nevertheless, this does not imply that the Commission can 'conclude' any non-binding arrangement, at least not from the point of view of EC/EU law. For the Court it was important that this arrangement was agreed between the EC and the US within the sphere of the common commercial policy, where the Commission has considerable management power under the oversight of a Council Committee and that the Commission had respected the normal procedures in this respect; see point 40 of the judgment.

[44] Article 31(3)(b) reads as follows: 'There shall be taken into account together with the context... (b) any subsequent practice in the application of the treaty which establishes the agreement of the parties regarding its interpretation.'

[45] See Case C-327/91 *France v Commission*, *supra* note 42, point 36.

[46] Case C-91/05 *Commission v Council* [2008] ECR I-3651.

[47] See Case C-91/05, *supra* note 46, points 66–69.

Another problem of treaty interpretation is the question of which instruments connected to the founding Treaties and other primary law, such as Treaties of Accession, may be used, when interpreting the latter. For Community lawyers this is clear with respect to Protocols, since the founding Treaties themselves state that they form an integral part thereof. The position with respect to declarations is much less clear to them, since the founding Treaties say nothing about the status of declarations, whether they are unilateral or shared by all member states. The general tendency among Community lawyers is, therefore, to attach very little importance to them.[48] Indeed, the Vienna Convention too says nothing explicit about the status of declarations to international agreements, including the constituent instruments of international organizations. It is, however, a simple question of getting your categories right. As Advocate-General Trstenjak pointed out in another context: '[d]eclarations adopted by an inter-governmental conference do not form part of the founding Treaties, but may be relevant in interpreting such Treaties in accordance with Article 31(2)(b) of the Vienna Convention on the Law of Treaties.'[49]

Without explicitly referring to this provision of the Vienna Convention, the Court of First Instance (CFI, now the General Court) acted in conformity with its approach when it attached a certain interpretative weight to joint declaration 31 to the Act of Accession of Austria, Finland, and Sweden, which stated that in respect of state aids to the agricultural processing industry in Finland and Austria 'flexibility [should be granted to] transitional national aid schemes designed to facilitate restructuring'. The CFI indeed attached importance to this declaration, saying that the Commission should show such flexibility, but in the end did not require that the Commission give preponderant importance to it in its decision on state aid granted by Austria to a sugar-processing industry. The CFI's approach was upheld on appeal.[50]

What one could call a category mistake within the framework of the Vienna Convention was made by a number of Advocates-General who, during a certain period (1999–2003), resisted the ECJ's case law, which declined to give direct effect to unconditionally formulated provisions of the WTO Agreement, in particular Articles XI and XIII of the GATT on the prohibition on quantitative restrictions and the non-discriminatory administration of tariff quotas, respectively. The opponents of direct effect of the WTO often referred to recital 11 of Decision 94/800, the decision by which the WTO Agreements were

[48] In his Opinion in Case C-64/05 P *Sweden v Commission* [2007] ECR I-11389 (a case on access to documents) Advocate-General Poiares Maduro refers to a number of writings by such authors as Toth, Constantinesco, and Simon, who all have concluded in this sense.

[49] Article 31(2)(b) reads as follows: 'The context for the purpose of the interpretation of a treaty shall comprise, in addition to the text, including its preamble and annexes:... (b) any instrument which was made by one or more parties in connection with the conclusion of a treaty and accepted by the other parties as an instrument related to the treaty.'

[50] Case T-187/99 *Agrana Zucker v Commission* [2001] ECR II-1587, point 51 *et seq.* and Case C-321/01 P *Agrana Zucker v Commission,* [2002] ECR I-10027.

approved by the Council.[51] This paragraph stated that '... by its nature, the Agreement establishing the World Trade Organization, including the Annexes thereto, is not susceptible to be directly invoked in Community or Member State courts'.

Some Advocates-General characterized this paragraph as being governed by the rules on reservations to treaties laid down in Articles 19–23 of the Vienna Convention 1969 and as such being invalid, since not made in conformity with the prescribed procedures.[52] This would seem to be a complete miscategorization: the preambular paragraph was intended to express the view of the legislator, nothing more and nothing less, and could never have more than an internal effect. Because it was not in the operative part of the decision, contrary to the way in which the US legislator bound the Courts by denying any *self-executingness* to the WTO Agreement and its Annexes,[53] the Courts retained their autonomy and could listen or not. In the end, the ECJ openly referred to the clause.[54] This in no way undermined its much older statement in *Kupferberg* to the effect that, whatever the internal system—monist or dualist, direct or no direct effect—in the end any party to a treaty is bound, under Article 26 of the Vienna Convention 1969, to perform the obligations of a treaty in good faith.[55]

2.2.3. The Vienna Convention of 1969 and secondary EU law

Normally one would not expect that the rules of interpretation of treaties of the Vienna Convention 1969 should be applied to secondary Community law. Community law constitutes its own legal order (no longer 'of international law', at least not in the perception of the Court of Justice) and there is no indication in the Vienna Convention itself that its rules apply to any act of international organizations that is not a 'convention adopted within an international organization'.[56] Obviously, the Court of Justice has applied the rules of treaty law and notably the rules of interpretation to 'decisions' of Association Councils.[57] These, however, in reality are a kind of '*traités en forme simplifiée*'. For normal regulations and directives there is no reason to apply international law rules of interpretation and

[51] Council Decision (EC) 94/800 concerning the conclusion on behalf of the European Community, as regards matters within its competence, of the agreements reached in the Uruguay Round multilateral negotiations (1986–94) [1994] OJ L336/1.

[52] Advocate-General A. Saggio in his Opinion in Case C-149/96 *Portugal v Council* [1999] ECR I-8395, point 20. He also seemed to characterize the recital as being part of the 'travaux préparatoires'. Advocate-General Alber in his Opinion in Case C-94/02 P *Biret v Council* [2003] ECR I-10565, point 99 *et seq.*

[53] See Section 102(c) of the Uruguay Round Agreements Act.

[54] See Case 377/02 *Van Parijs, supra* note 19.

[55] See Case 104/81 *Kupferberg* [1982] ECR 3641, point 18.

[56] See Article 5 of the 1969 Vienna Convention.

[57] *Inter alia* Case C-192/89 *Sevince* [1990] ECR I-3461, point 14.

although the Court often invokes object and purpose also in the interpretation of these typical Community acts, this is precisely because these elements of interpretation are relatively more important as a Community interpretation method than text and context. The Union Courts will not tend to start their interpretation of provisions of regulations or directives with a reference to the New Shorter Oxford Dictionary (or to the Larousse), as the Appellate Body of the WTO was wont to do.

The few instances that have been found of a reference to the rules of interpretation of the Vienna Convention 1969 to texts of secondary Community law are mostly advanced by private parties, are usually contradicted by the Commission, if it is a party or an intervener, and frankly ignored by the Court.[58] There is only one deviant case in which the CFI itself asserts that the rules of interpretation of secondary Community law, in that particular case the Anti-dumping Regulation, are identical to the rules of Article 31 of the Vienna Convention 1969. Perhaps not by coincidence, in that case the CFI also refers to the New Shorter Oxford Dictionary, when interpreting the word 'date'.[59] The probable explanation for this deviance is the fact that, though the WTO Anti-dumping Agreement, in contrast to other WTO Agreements, can be granted direct effect by the CFI in the exceptional situation of the so-called *Nakajima* doctrine,[60] the CFI also wishes to maintain as much as possible a harmonious interpretation between the Anti-dumping Agreement and the EU Anti-dumping Regulation, the texts of which are very close. Since the Anti-dumping Agreement must be interpreted in conformity with the principles of Article 31 of the Vienna Convention, applying the same standards of interpretation to the Anti-dumping Regulation may be helpful to this end. One wonders, however, whether the mimicry of the Appellate Body of the WTO needs to go so far as to include recourse to the New Shorter Oxford Dictionary.

There is one peculiar case, where the Vienna Convention's rule of interpretation supporting equal authenticity of different language versions of treaties (Article 33) was mobilized by an individual complainant to give greater weight to the same provision in the EC Treaty (Article 314 EC now Article 55 TEU) and to argue that Article 1 of Regulation 1 on the EC's language regime[61] is somehow immutable, which in turn is used to argue that provisions which establish selected 'working languages' for institutions or agencies, especially in contacts with the

[58] An example is Case C-500/99 P *Conserve Italia v Commission* [2002] ECR I-867, point 73 *et seq.*

[59] Case T-45/06 *Reliance Industries v Council & Commission* [2008] ECR II-2399, points 101 and 102.

[60] See Case C-69/89 *Nakajima All Precision Co. v Council* [1991] ECR I-2069. In this case the ECJ allowed a direct invocation of the WTO Anti-Dumping Agreement by private parties on the strength of the fact that the EC Anti-Dumping Regulation stated in its preamble that it had been taken specifically with a view to implementing the WTO Anti-dumping Agreement.

[61] This article lists the official languages of the European Community.

public, are impermissible.[62] The CFI simply points out that Regulation 1 is based on Article 290 EC (now 342 TFEU) which does not constrain the Council in establishing special language regimes; any claim of the immutability of Article 1 of Regulation 1 lifts it to a status of primary law, which it simply does not have. The misguided claim that Article 33 of the Vienna Convention somehow gives a fundamental rights colouring to a simple article of a simple Regulation is thus implicitly dismissed by the CFI.

2.3. The rule of good faith in treaty law

Good faith plays different roles in the law of treaties as codified by the Vienna Convention 1969. First of all there is the notion of good faith in interpretation (Article 31). Secondly, there is the good faith performance of treaties (*Pacta sunt servanda* Article 26). Finally, there is the special rule of good faith to the effect that states shall not nullify the object and purpose of a treaty during the period between signature and entry into force (Article 18). All of these aspects of good faith appear in the case law of the Courts. In analysing the case law of the Courts during the selected period, attention will be fixed on the last two manifestations of good faith, since the question of good faith in the interpretation of treaties is hardly ever raised as an independent element and, as we saw in the cases analysed so far, only played an implicit role in the one brought by the Polish and Czech 'ladies of the night' working as self-employed service providers in the Netherlands.[63]

2.3.1. Good faith performance of treaties

The rule of *pacta sunt servanda* was used by some Advocates-General in the later stages of the various banana litigations as a kind of crowbar to pry loose the Court from its entrenched conviction that the WTO Agreement as a whole was not invocable by individuals before Community and national courts and that this could not be changed by judgments of the dispute settlement organs of the WTO. In the case of *Merck Genéricos* Advocate-General Colomer stated that, in particular, turning the cold shoulder on the judgments of Panels and the Appellate Body was contrary to the performance of international agreements in good faith.[64] Moreover, he made an impassioned plea for the member states and the Union to base their approach to international agreements on the principle of good faith 'in accordance with Articles 26 and 31 of the Vienna Convention'. In his view, this

[62] This argument was launched by Ms Kik, a Dutch trade mark attorney in her quest, supported by the Greek government, for equality of all EC languages in the procedure for trade mark registration in OHIM, see Case T-120/99 *Kik v OHIM* [2001] ECR II-2235 confirmed by the Court in Case C-361/01 P. [2003] ECR I-8283.

[63] See *supra* notes 33–34 and accompanying text above.

[64] Conclusions of Advocate-General Ruiz-Jarabo Colomer in Case C-431/05 *Merck Genéricos v Merck* [2007] ECR I-7001, point 71.

entailed that provisions of international agreements which according to the rules of interpretation of the Vienna Convention contained clear and precise obligations ought to be given direct effect. However, after the judgment in *Van Parijs* he could see 'no chance of abandoning the dualistic system by which, on an uncertain legal basis, the Court of Justice has transformed the implementation in the Community of the *jus gentium*, and of the WTO Agreements, into a means of evading its obligations'.[65] Nevertheless, he went on to argue that the Court should treat the TRIPS Agreement differently from the rest of the WTO, insofar as direct effect was concerned, given that TRIPS is largely about intellectual property rights accruing to individuals.[66] The Court left these arguments to one side, simply deciding that, since there was no Community legislation in respect of the duration of patent protection laid down in TRIPS' Article 33, national courts were free to decide for themselves whether or not the term of 20 years mentioned in Article 33 should have direct effect or not.[67]

It is to be noted that the CFI, in an earlier case, had already rejected the argument that denying direct effect to clear and precise provisions in the GATT on the basis of a systemic argument based on the inherent nature of the WTO and its annexed agreements was contrary to the requirements of good faith performance of treaties. In *Chiquita Brands* the CFI argued that insofar as the argument of good faith was bound up with other arguments advanced by the complainant, the rejection of these arguments also served to dismiss the good faith argument. Insofar as this argument intended to say that, even without infringing its WTO obligations, the Community nevertheless acted without good faith, the CFI stated that, given that the agreement of which the complainant questioned the good faith performance did not have direct effect, the complainant could not rely on it.[68]

2.3.2. Good faith between signature and ratification of an international agreement

Ever since the CFI in *Opel Austria* feigned application of the rule of Article 18 of the Vienna Convention directly in favour of the car producer who saw its right to import transmissions from its plant in Austria free of duty for assembly

[65] Ibid., points 77–78. The present author does not agree with these characterizations and takes a more nuanced approach to whether or not the Court's approach implies dualism 'à la carte' and to how the Courts of the Union should deal with the judgments of international courts, which bind the Union; see P.J. Kuijper, 'La jurisprudence usine MOX, est-elle symptomatique d'un dialogue de sourds entre la CJCE et les autres jurisdictions internationals?', in Y. Kerbrat (ed.), *Forum Shopping et concurrence des procédures dans le contentieux international* (Brussels: Bruylant, forthcoming 2011).

[66] Ibid., points 82–83.

[67] Case C-431/05 *Merck Genéricos v Merck*, *supra* note 64, point 34 *et seq*.

[68] Case T-19/01 *Chiquita Brands v Commission* [2005] ECR II-315, points 246–48. The argument is somewhat circular, but it must also be said that the complainant's case was marred by advancing cases like *Opel Austria* and *Racke,* which were not relevant in this context.

into its cars in Germany under the new EEA Agreement nullified by the imposition of compensating anti-subsidy levies imposed under the old EC–Austria FTA a few days before the EEA was about to come into force, there have been inventive lawyers who have sought to apply the principle in many more cases.[69]

In the end the CFI did not dare to base its judgment on the rule of Article 18 alone and declared that the same principles were at the basis of the Community principle of legitimate expectations. However, it is possible to say that the new awareness of this rule has probably helped the ECJ to apply it shortly afterwards to the period between the adoption of a Community directive and the deadline for its implementation. According to the Court, which knew better than to base itself on a principle of international law and referred to the Community loyalty that member states had to observe under (then) Article 5 EC Treaty (now Article 4(3) TFEU) as well as to the fact that directives under Article 189 EC Treaty (now Article 288 TFEU) are binding as to the result to be achieved, the member states during this period are barred from taking any measure that may seriously compromise the result prescribed by the directive.[70]

A rather curious recourse to Article 18 was had by Eurocontrol, the European Organization for air traffic control in the upper atmosphere, when it intervened in the *Selex Sistemi* case.[71] This company, active in the field of air traffic management systems, had accused Eurocontrol of abuse of a dominant position. During the appeals procedure Eurocontrol, intervening on the side of the Commission, suddenly advanced the argument that the Commission should recognize its immunity in the exercise of its official activities. The Commission was bound to recognize Eurocontrol's immunity, since it had signed the Protocol on the accession of the European Community to Eurocontrol, though that Protocol had not, at the time of the procedure before the Court, as yet entered into force.

It was highly doubtful whether this argument could be advanced by a party intervening on the side of the Commission and even whether it could be advanced at all in the appeals procedure, given that it had never been considered during earlier stages of the procedure. The ECJ elegantly side-stepped both issues by recalling earlier case law to the effect that Eurocontrol had been considered to be subject to the Community competition rules, insofar as it appeared from the substance of the case that Eurocontrol had acted in its capacity *jure gestionis* rather

[69] Case T-115/94 *Opel Austria v Council* [1997] ECR II-39. This case has already been commented. A case in which the application of the rule of Article 18 was argued to be applicable to a new Swedish levy on sugar being held in stock in Sweden on the eve of the Swedish accession and was rejected by the ECJ is Case C-27/96 *Danisco Sugar* [1997] ECR I-6653, points 20 and 31.

[70] Case C-129/96 *Inter-Environnement Wallonie* [1997] ECR I-7411.

[71] Case C-113/07 P *Selex Sistemi Integrati SpA v Commission* [2009] ECR I-2207.

than in its official capacity.[72] In short, this case should be seen more as an example of too great an eagerness to have recourse to the good faith principle than as an actual application of the principle.

A case where the application of the good faith principle of Article 18 of the Vienna Convention 1969 was applied in an exemplary way was the drama of the *Abuja II* project. When Nigeria decided to move its capital from Lagos to Abuja, the European Commission provisionally rented an office building for its delegation in the new capital, in which several member states also had their embassies (*Abuja I* project). Later the idea surfaced to commission a completely new building in which not just the Commission delegation but also 10 (later 13) member states' embassies would have their offices. This was called the *Abuja II* project. A Memorandum of Understanding was drawn up in April of 1994 with the member states concerned and the Commission as signatories. This so-called initial memorandum was drawn up on the basis of Article 20 TEU (now Article 35 TEU) on the cooperation between diplomatic representations of the member states. According to this Memorandum the project was to be financed by contributions from all the participating partners reflecting their individual share of the project. Expenses were advanced by the Commission, which sent payment orders from time to time, as the project progressed, to the various participating member states. Gradually member states started withdrawing from the project. At a certain stage (1998) an additional memorandum was agreed between the Commission and six remaining member states in the project. This additional memorandum was signed by Greece, but Greece never ratified it and later claimed to have withdrawn from the project. However, as the CFI pointed out in its judgment, Greece never objected to the payment orders it received between 1998 and September 2000 and never showed any intention to withdraw from the project or not to ratify the additional memorandum, whereas a party that wishes to withdraw from an international agreement must notify the other parties of that intention.[73]

The CFI stated very explicitly at the outset of its legal findings that it was to base its judgment on the rule of good faith in treaty relations, as first recognized by the PCIJ in the case of *Certain German Interests in Polish Upper Silesia*,[74] later codified in Article 18 of the Vienna Convention 1969 and interpreted by the CFI itself as the corollary in public international law of the principle of legitimate expectations in the Community legal order.[75] Its later conclusion in the *Abuja II* case to the effect that Greece had not acted in good faith by refusing to pay the

[72] Case C-113/07 P *Selex Sistemi*, *supra* note 71, points 59–64. This approach, as the Court pointed out itself, was in conformity with the earlier Case C-364/92 *SAT Fluggesellschaft* [1994] ECR I-43.

[73] Case T-231/04 *Greece v Commission* [2007] ECR II-63, point 98.

[74] PCIJ, Judgment of 25 August 1925, Series A No. 7, 30, and 39.

[75] Case T-115/94 *Opel Austria v Council*, *supra* note 69, point 93.

Commission's payment orders for the *Abuja I* and *II* projects, given its earlier actions of signing the additional memorandum and its actual conduct thereafter, seems to be exactly in line with a proper application of Article 18.[76] This approach by the CFI was completely upheld by the ECJ on appeal.[77]

2.4. Succession between treaties

The CFI had no difficulty whatsoever in following Advocate-General Elmer and in applying the rule of the extinction of an earlier treaty by a subsequent treaty relating to the same subject-matter (Article 59(1)(a) of the Vienna Convention 1969) to the succession between the GATT 1947 and the GATT 1994. In light of the fact that Article II:4 of the WTO Agreement explicitly declared that the latter was legally distinct from the former, it was easy to arrive at the conclusion that the latter had replaced the former.[78]

Things were slightly more difficult, when the Community treaties themselves were involved, as was the case when the European Coal and Steel Community (ECSC) Treaty expired on 23 July 2002[79] and a succession between ECSC and the EC Treaties was only partially regulated by explicit Community acts such as decisions on the taking over of the ECSC's treaty rights and obligations by the EC[80] and the transfer of funds from the ECSC to the EC.[81] The Commission had expressed certain opinions with respect to the exercise of its powers in competition and state aids cases in respect of coal and steel companies after the expiry of the ECSC Treaty, but these were not binding.[82] It thus became possible for companies which were addressees of Commission decisions on practices that straddled the expiration date of the ECSC Treaty to argue that Article 65 ECSC could no longer be relied on after expiry of the Treaty, while the relevant EC Treaty articles could not be used with respect to matters having taken place before the date of expiry. Article 70 of VCLT I stated after all that parties were liberated

[76] Case T-231/04 *Greece v Commission*, *supra* note 73, points 96–99. Note that the case was brought as a case from Greece against the Commission, since the Commission, given Greece's stubborn refusal to pay its contributions, had resorted to an offset of these payments due against transfers to Greece on the basis of the Regional Fund. It was this offset that was contested by Greece.

[77] Case C-203/07 P *Greece v Commission* [2008] ECR I-8161, point 64 *et seq.*

[78] Case T-2/99 *T. Port* [2001] ECR II-2093, point 80 *et seq.*

[79] This was in conformity with the 50-year life-span of the ECSC Treaty laid down in Article 97 of that Treaty.

[80] See Decision of the Representatives of the Governments of the Member States meeting within the Council of 19 July 2002 on the consequences of the expiry of the European Coal and Steel Community Treaty on international agreements concluded by the ECSC, [2002] OJ L194/35 (transfer from ECSC to EC) and Council Decision of 19 July 2002 on the consequences of the expiry of the ECSC Treaty on the international agreements concluded by the ECSC, [2002] OJ L194/36 (acceptance by EC of ECSC rights and obligations).

[81] See Decision of the Representatives of the Governments of the Member States meeting within the Council of 19 July 2002 on the consequences of the expiry of the European Coal and Steel Community Treaty on international agreements concluded by the ECSC, *supra* note 80.

[82] Commission Communication of 18 June 2002, [2002] OJ C152/5.

from their obligations after expiry, unless parties had agreed otherwise (which was not the case).

In response to this challenge, the CFI climbed on its high horse, declaring that

> ... [t]he Community Treaties put in place a unique [in the sense of 'single' PJK] legal order in the context of which, as is reflected in Article 305(1) EC Treaty, the ECSC Treaty constituted a specific regime derogating from the general rules established by the EC Treaty. Consequently, on 24 July 2002, the scope of the general regime resulting from the EC Treaty was extended to the sectors which were initially covered by the ECSC Treaty.[83]

The Court then pointed out that, though the rules on state aid under the ECSC Treaty differ somewhat from those under the EC Treaty, aid granted under the ECSC Treaty falls under the meaning of aid as laid down under the EC Treaty. Thus the pursuit of the aim of undistorted competition in the coal and steel sector is not suspended because of the expiry of the ECSC Treaty, since that objective is also pursued in the context of the EC Treaty.[84] 'The continuity of the Community legal order and the objectives which govern its functioning thus require' that the EC ensures compliance of individuals and member states with ECSC norms in the field of competition and state aid that applied *eo tempore* under the ECSC Treaty.[85]

On this basis the Court develops the approach that the Commission can use its power under the EC Treaty in respect of state aids after the expiry of the ECSC Treaty in order to rule on matters that occurred before the expiry of the ECSC Treaty, as long as it does so in conformity with the substantive rules of the ECSC Treaty (ie Article 65(1) and (2) ECSC Treaty) instead of the criteria of the EC Treaty in respect of state aids.[86] This is derived from 'settled case law that, although procedural rules are generally held to apply to all disputes pending at the time when they enter into force, this is not the case with substantive rules'.[87]

It is interesting to signal that the Court of First Instance in this case purports to base itself on the special character as a single legal order and the specific important objectives of that legal order, such as undistorted competition. The same result could have been arrived at by a normal international law approach, signalling that Article 305(1) of the EC Treaty concluded between the same parties as the ECSC Treaty contracted out of the normal (international law) consequences of the expiry of the ECSC Treaty. Obviously, Article 305 is being invoked in this and similar cases, but placed in a wholly different context of Community

[83] Case T-25/04 *Gonzalez y Diez v Commission* [2007] ECR II-3121, points 53–54.

[84] Ibid., point 55.

[85] Ibid., point 56.

[86] Ibid., points 58–60. This was strongly confirmed in Joined Cases T-27/03 *SP SpA et al v Commission* [2007] ECR II-4331, where the Commission had followed a demarche that was incompatible with this approach and its decision was annulled. In yet another case, namely T-24/07 *ThyssenKrupp v Commission* [2009] ECR II-2309, the Commission had done it right.

[87] Case T-25/04, *supra* note 83, point 58.

uniqueness in order to give a greater sense of the inevitable to the interpretation reached.

3. Some Conclusions

From the foregoing it can be concluded that after many years of invoking the provisions of VCLT I, and in particular its rules of interpretation, the Court only very recently gave a full explanation of what in its view justifies this longstanding practice, namely Article 3(b) of the Convention itself.

Where it concerns the interpretation of international agreements concluded by the Union (and its member states) the question of determining direct effect is still the most important and most frequently invoked issue for which the rules of interpretation of the Vienna Convention of 1969 are called upon by the Courts. Over the past 10 years there has been an evolution in the level of sophistication in the recourse to the object and purpose test in order to determine whether direct effect should or should not be excluded for the agreement as a whole or, though accepted, should be limited or circumscribed. The *Intertanko* case is a new example of the exclusion of direct effect on this basis for the UNCLOS Convention as a whole. The cases concerning the free access of service providers from Eastern Europe before accession are an example of direct effect being circumscribed in its effect because of the context and the object and purpose of the agreements concerned. They are a further development of the old *Polydor* line of cases that developed on the basis of the Western European Free Trade Agreements of the 1970s.

Apart from the question of direct effect, text-based and contextual interpretation techniques are used to distinguish Community legislation from, and thus to reconcile it with, international agreements. The *IATA* case forms a good example of such conflict avoidance techniques sometimes used by the Union courts.

Insofar as the interpretation of the EU and EC Treaties themselves with help of the interpretation techniques of the Vienna Convention is concerned, the Court has refined its analysis of what is a treaty for the purpose of the Vienna Convention and of the EU and EC Treaties. Non-binding instruments are not treaties, but it has to be extremely clear from the actions of the 'parties' that the absence of binding effect was intended. Even then, institutions that are normally not equipped with treaty-making power, such as the Commission, can only agree to non-binding instruments, if they stay clearly within established EC Treaty procedures, for example as set out in the field of commercial policy.

Another marked tendency in the Courts' case law is the increased willingness to take account of declarations made at the time of the conclusion or revision of the founding Treaties as part of the context of the relevant treaty provisions, in accordance with Article 31(2)(b) of the Vienna Convention. Similarly, the

ECJ has shown its first inclination to take notice of practice within the institutions and of member states, when interpreting fundamental notions used in the founding Treaties, such as development cooperation—which thus far was almost a taboo.

The two last-mentioned tendencies, in particular, may have something to do with the constant treaty reform over the past two decades, which has increased the feeling that, after all, the founding Treaties are still treaties and can be treated as such.

As to the role of good faith in the law of treaties, it is only very occasionally invoked in the framework of treaty interpretation; it is almost imperceptibly bound up with the application of the different techniques of interpretation. In connection with good faith application, the Court has even said explicitly that good faith cannot be independent from the performance of the treaty itself: it is unimaginable that there is full performance and that good faith is nevertheless considered absent. Since full performance of a treaty is possible without granting direct effect to certain treaty provisions, in the view of the ECJ, the requirement of good faith performance of treaties cannot be a bar to the denial of direct effect to such treaty provisions. Good faith within the meaning of Article 18 of the Vienna Convention has become almost too popular in litigation after the *Opel Austria* case, but that case seems to have had the salutary effect of introducing the basic principle of Article 18 also into the period when a directive is waiting for its implementation after its adoption.

As to the succession between the different founding Treaties, as exemplified by the succession of the ECSC Treaty by the EC Treaty upon the former's expiry, suddenly the reflexes of the CFI go back to 'Community uniqueness' and the continuity of the application of the competition and state aid rules as between the two treaties, precisely in the absence of explicit binding EC rules on this part of the succession. One cannot say that the CFI ignores the relevant rules of treaty law, but they are served with a heavy Community sauce, whereas the *lex specialis* character of the ECSC Treaty and the general fall-back character of the EC Treaty could have been based on pure international law interpretation of the relevant treaties.

For most of the readers and critics of the recent big, dramatic cases involving international law, such as *Kadi* or *MOX-Plant*, the position of the EU Courts in respect of international law seems to have been one of withdrawal and estrangement. For this reader of the cases, which show the month-to-month engagement of the EU Courts with the law of treaties, a different picture is emerging that is much more mixed. What is striking is that the Courts are intensively occupied almost constantly with using the law of treaties in connection with more and more detailed Union law and thus become ever more nuanced and sophisticated in their dealings with it. Thus they give expression to the way Union law is truly interwoven with many international agreements. There is little doubt that the

Courts continue to see international agreements as 'the law of the land', as the US Constitution puts it, and as being of higher rank than secondary Union law, but the consequences of these principles are expressed by the Union's judges in much more nuanced ways than in the past, precisely because of their greater exposure to the law of treaties (and other rules of international law) than that of their predecessors on the bench.

17

Some Remarks on the Continuity of Human Rights and International Humanitarian Law Treaties

Fausto Pocar

1. Recent developments in international relations as well as significant changes in the constitutional structure of some states have brought about the existence of an increased number of new independent states which had previously been constituent parts of other states.[1]

Several problems of state succession in respect of treaties have arisen under international law as a result of such fragmentation of, or separation from, state entities. Since the beginning of the last decade of the twentieth century, several international fora, including international courts and other international bodies, have given special consideration to the treatment of international obligations entered into by the predecessor state under human rights and humanitarian law treaties.[2] In particular, they have expressed concern that such events might lead to a decrease in the existing level of adherence to these types of treaties and respect for the standards enshrined therein on the territory of the newly independent states. The need arose, therefore, to determine whether the people living in the successor states would continue to benefit from the protections afforded to them.

It is important to recall, in this context, that the question of whether successor states succeed multilateral treaty obligations entered into by the predecessor state is not entirely settled in international law; however, the United Nations has deployed laudable efforts to codify this delicate field and to promote the

[1] For a thorough analysis of these situations see in particular B. Stern, 'La succession d'Etats', 262 *Recueil des Cours* (1996) 9-438. See also J. Crawford, 'State Practice and International Law in Relation to State Succession', *BYIL* (1998) 85–117.

[2] Among them the Human Rights Committee established under the International Covenant on Civil and Political Rights, has played a significant role, as will be shown later. On the Committee and its function, in particular on the consideration of state reports, see D. McGoldrick, *The Human Rights Committee. Its Role in the Development of the International Covenant on Civil and Political Rights* (Oxford: Clarendon Press, 1991) 62–119; F. Pocar, 'The International Covenant on Civil and Political Rights', in *Manual on Human Rights Reporting* (Geneva: United Nations, 1997) 171–266.

adoption of a coherent body of rules, with a view to supplementing the codified law of treaties[3] and ensuring greater legal security. These efforts have led to the elaboration, within the framework of the International Law Commission (ILC), of the Convention on Succession of States in respect of Treaties, concluded in Vienna on 23 August 1978,[4] which lays down some principles on this matter. The Convention, however, is the result of a compromise which had to take into account the positions of newly independent states emerging from colonial domination. It therefore reflects to a large extent the practice followed within the context of the decolonization process, whereby newly independent states claimed that the colonial powers formerly responsible for their territories did not necessarily act in their interest. Accordingly, international obligations entered into by the colonial powers regarding such territories could not automatically bind newly independent states and remained in force only subject to a unilateral assessment of that interest by each successor state followed by a declaration of succession.

Thus, according to the general rule set forth in Part III of the Convention, 'a newly independent State is not bound to maintain in force, or to become a party to, any treaty by reason only of the fact that at the date of the succession of States the treaty was in force in respect of the territory to which the succession of States relates'.[5] It is therefore, in principle, for a newly independent state to decide, by a notification of succession, whether to continue to be a party to a treaty which was in force in respect of the territory to which the succession of states relates, unless it appears that a continuing application of the treaty would be incompatible with the object and purpose of the treaty or would require the consent of all parties.[6]

However, this general rule is surrounded by a number of precisions and derogations, as well as by other rules which hardly concur to form a coherent framework providing legal certainty in all situations.[7] In particular, different rules apply to uniting and separation of states,[8] with special reference to the case of dissolution of the predecessor state or of separation of a part of that state to form a new state.

By virtue of Article 34(1) of the Convention,

> ...when a part or parts of the territory of a State separate to form one or more States, whether or not the predecessor State continues to exist: *(a)* any treaty in force at the date

[3] As reflected in the 1969 Vienna Convention on the Law of Treaties, 1155 *UNTS*, 331.

[4] 1946 *UNTS*, 3.

[5] See Article 16 of the Convention, first provision of Part III, titled 'Newly Independent States'.

[6] See Article 17 of the Convention. The consent of the other party would in any event be required in the case of bilateral treaties.

[7] For a discussion of the Convention's solutions, also in relation to the American Law Institute's Restatement (Third) on the Foreign Relations Law of the United States (1987), see D. F. Vagts, 'State Succession: The Codifiers' View', 33 *Va J Int'l. L* (1993) 275–97.

[8] See Part IV of the Convention. This difference of treatment between newly independent states because of decolonization and following uniting or separation of states has sometimes been severely criticized in legal doctrine, though with arguments which do not appear persuasive in light of state practice. See B. Conforti, *Diritto Internazionale* (Napoli: Editoriale Scientifica, 7th edn, 2006) 106, who maintains, however, that the affirmation of the principle of continuity of treaties in Article 34 of the Convention does not reflect customary international law.

of the succession of States in respect of the entire territory of the predecessor State continues in force in respect of each successor State so formed; (*b*) any treaty in force at the date of the succession of States in respect only of that part of the territory of the predecessor State which has become a successor State continues in force in respect of that successor State alone.

Although Article 34(2) makes the succession dependent upon the absence of a different agreement between the states concerned and the compatibility of the application of the treaty in respect of the successor state with the object and purpose of the treaty, the provision appears to sustain the position that in principle treaty obligations entered into by the predecessor state pass automatically on to the successor states. Furthermore, according to the *chapeau* of para. 1, the principle applies both in the case of new states arising out of the dissolution of a state and in the case of separation of parts of a state, which continues to exist.[9]

This provision, if applicable, would provide a basis for a solution to the question referred to above, in support of the continuity of treaty obligations on successor states. The Vienna Convention, however, only received a limited number of ratifications and accessions, which delayed its entry into force until 6 November 1996, between only a limited number of states.[10] The problem of the continuity of treaties following the dissolution or the separation of parts of a state to form new states arose before that date, however; in particular, in relation to the formation of the new states which succeeded to the former Yugoslavia or separated from the Soviet Union at the beginning of the nineties.[11] The Convention could not therefore be applied, as such, to issues arising out of the latter situations.

Thus, the more appropriate question to address is whether the rule enshrined in Article 34 of the Convention should be regarded as a codification of principles reflecting customary rules of international law relating to the succession of states in respect of treaties or, rather, as an innovative provision aimed at further developing international law in this field.[12] Additionally, should one conclude that Article 34 did not reflect customary international law when it was drafted,[13] the

[9] For the reasons that justify the same treatment of 'dissolution of a state' and 'separation of part of a state' see *YILC* (1974), vol. II(1), 265, paras 21–24.

[10] On 4 May 2010, there were 22 states parties to the Convention, among them the successor states of the former Yugoslavia, which declared to succeed to the Convention as ratified by their predecessor state. Another 15 states had signed the Convention, but not ratified it.

[11] In the case of the former Yugoslavia, which had ratified the Vienna Convention on 28 April 1980, the Convention was therefore not in force at the time when it dissolved into new states, at the beginning of the 1990s. Likewise, it was not in force for the Soviet Union, which had neither signed nor ratified it.

[12] The Conference where the Convention was drafted was indeed 'convinced... of the need for the codification and progressive development of the rules relating to succession of States in respect of treaties as a means for ensuring greater juridical security in international relations': see the third preambular paragraph of the Convention.

[13] See, among others, B. Conforti, *Diritto internazionale*, *supra* note 8; R. Mullerson, 'New Developments in the Former USSR and Yugoslavia', 33 *Va. J Int'l L* (1993) 316.

question would still remain whether it had developed into a customary rule by the time the abovementioned events occurred or has done so since.

Admittedly, this issue is of general scope and may arise in the context of any kind of treaty and, thus, affords specific solutions for different categories of treaties.[14] However, it is submitted that this issue is particularly significant for human rights and humanitarian law treaties. The brief remarks that follow will address the debate only insofar as these treaties are concerned.

2. State practice on the abovementioned issue is not very rich, though largely concordant, and it is undeniable that it has been influenced to a great extent by the position maintained by the Human Rights Committee on the matter. When faced with the question,[15] the Committee expressed the view that, so far as human rights treaties are concerned—and without prejudice to the position that may be taken in relation to other categories of treaties—their provisions should be regarded as applying, on a continuing basis, to the people within the territories of the new states. Various indicators pointed in this direction, including the nature of the conventions striving to protect human rights and fundamental freedoms, whose purpose was not to provide individual advantages to the contracting states, but rather to reflect their common interest—ie, an interest of all mankind—in protecting human values. The intended universal application of such conventions provided an additional reason to conclude that, once the people living in a territory find themselves under the protection of an international instrument, this protection cannot be denied to them by virtue of the mere dismembering of that territory and its subsequent re-emerging within the jurisdiction of more than one state.

It is worth recalling, in this regard, that the Human Rights Committee affirmed the continuing applicability of the International Covenant on Civil and Political Rights to successor states of a former state having been party to the Covenant even before any declaration confirming their succession. Indeed, the Committee based its authority to request an urgent report from the governments of Bosnia and Herzegovina, Croatia, and the Federal Republic of Yugoslavia (Serbia and Montenegro) on 7 October 1992—as successor states of the Socialist Federal Republic of Yugoslavia—on the consideration that 'all the peoples within the territory of the former Yugoslavia are entitled to the guarantees of the Covenant'.[16]

[14] D.F. Vagts, 'State Succession: The Codifiers' View', *supra* note 7, 289–97.

[15] The first occasion on which the Committee was seized with this issue was in 1992, in relation to the continuity of human rights treaties entered into by the former Socialist Federal Republic of Yugoslavia.

[16] See the second preambular paragraph of the request. This position was initially taken by the Chairman of the Committee in a letter sent to the other Committee members on 18 September 1992. As the Committee was not in session when information of the grave violations of the Covenant's protected rights reached Geneva in the summer of 1992, its Chairman took the initiative of asking the members of the Committee to authorize him, by fax or telegram and in derogation from the Rules, to request the successor states to the Republic of Yugoslavia to submit an urgent

This statement was subsequently confirmed unanimously in a public meeting of the Committee, when its members had an opportunity to publicly express their views before considering the urgent reports submitted by the three successor states.[17] During the debate, it was reaffirmed that the Committee's attitude had been made clear in the request,[18] that this attitude 'could assist in clarifying the uncertainty in international law over th[e] question'[19] of state succession in respect of treaties, and 'was helping international law in such a way that the Covenant would remain in force despite the division of a State',[20] or even that the Committee 'had already begun to make law, and in a revolutionary manner'.[21] As recalled above, the rationale for maintaining that the obligations of human rights treaties would pass automatically on to successor states appears to reside in the consideration that, once a population is under the protection of such a treaty, it cannot be denied the rights enshrined therein. As one member of the Committee put it: 'the international instruments relating to human rights, besides being inter-State instruments, conferred rights on individuals, who could not be deprived of those rights in the event of State succession'.[22] Similarly, another member expressed the view that 'State succession should be viewed as a matter of the acquired rights of the population of the State that had ratified the Covenant, which were not diluted when a State was divided'.[23]

This debate clearly shows a firm general position on the principle affirmed in the decision adopted after the special reports submission request, although it also reveals some concern by members that the reports might not be submitted as requested or that the principle of automatic succession might be openly challenged by the successor states.[24] This concern was later alleviated by the actual submission of the special reports within the deadline assigned by the Committee.

Upon consideration of the reports of the abovementioned states at its forty-sixth session,[25] the Committee further explained (with the exception of Croatia,

report limited to measures taken to prevent and repress violations of Articles 6, 7, 9, 10, 12, and 20 of the Covenant. The subsequent endorsement of the Chairman's proposal by all Committee members resulted in the issuance of a formal request by the Committee 'through its Chairman acting on behalf of and in consultation with the members of the Committee'. For the text of the request see CCPR/C/SR.1178/Add.1, and CCPR/12/Add.1 (*Official Records of the Human Rights Committee*, 1992/93, vol. II, 1997, 504–5). The adoption of this exceptional procedure led later on to an amendment of the Committee's Rules, whereby, by derogation from the rule that a request for a report must be made by the Committee, 'in the case of an exceptional situation when the Committee is not in session, a request may be made through the Chairman, acting in consultation with the members of the Committee'. See the new version of Rule 66, adopted on 8 April 1993, in CCPR/12/Add.1, 506.

[17] See the Summary Record of the 1178th meeting held on 19 November 1992, CCPR/C/SR.1178/Add.1.

[18] Intervention of Nisuke Ando, ibid.

[19] Intervention of Rosalyn Higgins, ibid.

[20] Intervention of Julio Prado Vallejo, ibid.

[21] Intervention of Francisco Aguilar Urbina, ibid.

[22] Intervention of Rein Mullerson, ibid.

[23] Intervention of Alejandro Serrano Caldera, ibid.

[24] See, in particular, the interventions of Andreas Mavrommatis and Kurt Herndl, ibid.

[25] The three reports were considered on 3–4 November 1992: see CCPR/C/SR.1200-1202/Add.1.

whose government had meanwhile declared succession to the Covenant),[26] both in the oral concluding observations of the meeting with the states' delegations[27] and in the written comments issued subsequently on the consideration of each report, that it regarded the submission of the report by the government of each state and the presence of the delegation as a mere 'confirmation' that the new state 'had succeeded, in respect of its territory, to the obligations undertaken under the International Covenant on Civil and Political Rights by the former Socialist Federal Republic of Yugoslavia'.[28]

3. The same approach was subsequently followed by all treaty monitoring bodies established under the United Nations Conventions on human rights. When their chairpersons convened, as they regularly did, to discuss issues of common interest, they jointly reiterated that obligations under human rights treaties automatically bind successor states as of the date of their independence, and that observance of such obligations should not depend on a declaration of confirmation to that effect.[29]

Notwithstanding these firm statements by human rights treaty bodies, it cannot be overlooked that a confirmation was always regarded as desirable, following the position taken by the Human Rights Committee itself when it first took an initiative in this field. It is not surprising, therefore, that a confirmation was desirable to another United Nations human rights body, the Commission on Human Rights, whose membership—comprised of states' delegations—inevitably devotes more attention to political implications of issues on the agenda, than is the case of bodies comprised of independent experts. When dealing with state succession to human rights treaties, the Commission considered it necessary to make a 'call to successor States, who have not yet done so, to confirm to appropriate depositaries that they continue to be bound by obligations under human rights treaties',[30] to reiterate such a call,[31] and subsequently to 'welcome the progress made in the confirmation by some successor States of their obligations under human rights treaties'.[32]

This language clearly suggests that a treaty obligation continues *ipso jure* irrespective of a declaration of succession to the treaty, although the emphasis placed

[26] Croatia's declaration of succession to the International Covenant was made on 12 October 1992, with the indication to succeed 'as of the date of independence' (8 October 1991).

[27] See the Chairman's statements respectively in CCPR/C/SR.1200, para. 52 (Bosnia and Herzegovina), and CCPR/C/SR.1202/Add.1, para. 33 (Federal Republic of Yugoslavia/Serbia and Montenegro).

[28] See the concluding Comments of the Committee in CCPR/C/79/Add.14 to 16, and in *Report of the Committee, Seventeenth Report, GAOR, Forty-eighth Session*, Supplement No. 40 (A/48/40), vol. I (1993), paras 328 (Bosnia and Herzegovina) and 384 (Federal Republic of Yugoslavia/Serbia and Montenegro); also in CCPR/12/Add.1, *supra* note 16, 427 and 434.

[29] See the report of the meeting of 19–23 September 1994, Doc. E/CN.4/1995/80, 28 November 1994, 3.

[30] Resolution 1993/23 of 5 March 1993.

[31] Resolution 1994/16 of 25 February 1994 and 1995/18 of 24 February 1995.

[32] Resolution 1995/18, *supra* note 31.

on the call for confirmation may also give way to a different and more ambiguous interpretation. The latter, however, would not be justified. If the resolutions are taken in their entirety, the framework they refer to is that of a continuity of human rights treaties, rather than that of a *tabula rasa* where succession depends on a formal confirmation, as is the case for the succession to treaties concluded by a former colonial power. Indeed, each resolution begins by '*bearing in mind* relevant decisions of the Human Rights Committee and the Committee on the Elimination of Racial Discrimination on succession issues, in respect of international obligations in the field of human rights', '*emphasizes* the special nature of the human rights treaties aimed at the protection of human rights and fundamental freedoms', '*requests* the human rights treaty bodies to consider further the issue of the *continuing applicability* of relevant international human rights treaties with regard to successor States with the aim of assisting them in meeting their obligations', and '*requests* the Secretary-General to inform successor States that they should confirm their obligations under the international human rights treaties to which their predecessors were a party, *as from the date of their independence*'.[33] A consideration of the context of the resolutions makes it clear that they were adopted on the assumption that human rights treaties, because of their special nature, are automatically binding on the successor states.

4. The principle of automatic state succession to treaties, as affirmed by the Human Rights Committee with respect to the dissolution of the former Yugoslavia, has been consistently reaffirmed by the Committee with respect to the new states which became independent following their secession from the USSR.[34] Most of these states deposited with the Secretary-General of the United Nations a declaration of accession to the Covenant, on different dates after their independence.[35] The Committee stressed that, in its opinion, the entry into force reverted back to the date when each state became independent,[36] notwithstanding that the declaration of accession did not specify that it had such retroactive effect.

[33] The quotations are taken from resolution 1994/16, *supra* note 31 (last emphasis added).

[34] The continuity of the USSR with the Russian Federation was recognized on 27 December 1991. On the issue of the succession or continuity of Russia in respect of the USSR, see R. Mullerson, 'New Developments in the Former USSR and Yugoslavia', *supra* note 13, 302.

[35] That was the case for Armenia (23 June 1993), Azerbaijan (13 August 1992), Estonia (21 October 1991), Georgia (3 May 1994), Kyrgyzstan (7 October 1994), Latvia (14 April 1992), Lithuania (20 November 1991), Republic of Moldova (26 January 1993), andTurkmenistan (1 May 1997). With respect to these countries, the Human Rights Committee reiterated in 1993 that 'all the people within the territory of a former State party to the Covenant remained entitled to the guarantees of the Covenant and that, in particular, Armenia, Georgia, Kazakhstan, Kirghizstan, Tadzikistan, the former Federal Republic of Macedonia, Turkmenistan and Uzbekistan, were bound by the obligations of the Covenant as from the date of their independence': see *Report of the Human Rights Committee, GAOR, Forty-ninth Session*, Supplement No. 40 (A/49/40), vol. I (1994), para. 49.

[36] Ftn (b) appended to each of these states in the list of states parties to the Covenant as published annually by the Committee in its report, clarifies that, irrespective of the date of accession,

This position does not appear to have been challenged by the interested countries, either in general or during the consideration of their reports under Article 40 of the Covenant. The deposit of an instrument of accession instead of a declaration of succession appears to have been chosen by these newly independent states in order to stress that they did not regard themselves as successors to the USSR within the meaning of Article 34 of the Vienna Convention, rather than to challenge the continuity of their obligations under the Covenant.[37] And indeed, when they submitted their reports, their delegations did not raise any objection to questions asked of them by Committee members concerning events that occurred before the date of their accession, thus confirming that they considered that they were bound by the Covenant as of the date of their independence.[38]

But the Committee went even further, and regarded a successor state as bound by the Covenant even when the state had not made a declaration of accession or succession. Such was the case of Kazakhstan, which was listed in the Committee's report to the General Assembly as a state party, although no declaration of accession or succession had been received.[39] Accordingly, on 24 July 2000, the Committee decided to request that Kazakhstan submit its initial report by 31 July

the entry into force goes back to the date of independence: see eg *Report of the Human Rights Committee, GAOR, Fifty-sixth Session*, Supplement No. 40 (A/56/40), vol. I (2001), Annex I.

[37] See also F. Lattanzi, 'Brevi osservazioni su successione fra Stati e accordi internazionali in materia di diritti dell'uomo', in A. Del Vecchio (ed.), *La successione degli Stati nel diritto internazionale* (Milano: Giuffrè, 1999) 65. A special case was that of the Baltic states, which maintained that they had resumed their sovereignty after having been occupied by the Soviet Union in 1940. See M.T. Kamminga, 'State Succession in Respect of Human Rights Treaties', 7 *EJIL* (1996) 479, reporting that '[t]he Baltic States therefore do not regard themselves as new States but as States re-exercising the sovereignty of which they had been illegally deprived'; R. Mullerson, 'New Developments in the Former USSR and Yugoslavia', *supra* note 13, 309, stating that these states 'restored their independence lost in 1940'.

[38] See eg, as to Azerbaijan, the position taken by the Human Rights Committee by noting 'that Azerbaijan has declared that it is bound by the Covenant through a declaration of accession, though it would have been correct for it to have regarded itself as succeeding to the obligations of the Covenant as a State of the former Soviet Union': *Report of the Human Rights Committee, GAOR, Forty-ninth Session*, Supplement No. 40 (A/49/40), vol. I (1994) 294. During the examination of the report it was pointed out that 'the Azerbaijani delegation must have noticed that members of the Committee had mentioned events occurring before the Government declared its accession to the Covenant', and it was reiterated, recalling the position of the Committee as endorsed by the Commission on Human Rights in its resolution 1994/16 of 25 February 1994, 'that any sovereign successor State was bound by the obligations of the Covenant from the day of its independence'. A distinction was, however, made between substantive obligations to protect the Covenant's rights and obligations of cooperation with monitoring bodies, by noting that 'where the submission of initial reports was concerned, the Committee could accept that the obligation came into force as from the date of accession, but the date of independence should continue to be the starting point for all the other obligations': see the intervention of Fausto Pocar, in Summary Record of the 1332nd meeting held on 12 July 1994, CCPR/C/SR.1332, para. 67.

[39] See *Report of the Human Rights Committee, GAOR, Fifty-fourth Session*, Supplement No. 40 (A/54/40), vol. I (2000) 102, Ftn (d), where the Committee reiterates that 'the people within the territory of the State—which constituted part of a former State party to the Covenant—continue to be entitled to the guarantees enunciated in the Covenant in accordance with the Committee's established jurisprudence'. A more prudent approach was taken by the Secretary-General when publishing the list of states parties to the Covenant, as that list contains no mention of Kazakhstan.

2001, in the absence of an instrument of succession.[40] When the report was not received, the Committee reiterated its invitation to the government to submit the initial report 'at its earliest convenience'.[41]

The practice of the Human Rights Committee on the continuity of human rights treaties therefore seems well established. A further confirmation thereof may be drawn from the rejection of any attempt to move towards a different approach, not only in the field of state succession, but also in related areas, such as reservations[42] to or denunciation of the Covenant. Thus, when a state party declared its withdrawal from the Covenant, the Committee deemed it appropriate to take a formal position thereon[43] through the adoption of a General Comment, whereby it observed that 'the drafters of the Covenant deliberately intended to exclude the possibility of denunciation', and concluded that 'international law does not permit a State which has ratified or acceded or succeeded to the covenant to denounce it or withdraw from it'.[44] In reaching this conclusion the Committee took the opportunity to reiterate its longstanding practice 'that the rights enshrined in the Covenant belong to the people living in the territory of the State party', and that

> ...once the people are accorded the protection of the rights under the Covenant, such protection devolves with territory and continues to belong to them, notwithstanding change in Government of the State party, including dismemberment in more than one

See *Multilateral treaties deposited with the Secretary-General*, Status at 31 December 2000 (ST/LEG/SER.E/19), vol. I, 173.

[40] See CCPR/C/SR.1860, para. 55.

[41] See *Report of the Human Rights Committee, GAOR, Sixtieth Session*, Supplement No. 40 (A/60/40), vol. I (2005) para. 79. The smoother language employed in reiterating the request most likely reflects the fact that in the meantime Kazakhstan had signed the Covenant on 17 November 2003. The Covenant was eventually ratified on 24 January 2006: *Report of the Human Rights Committee, GAOR, Sixty-fourth Session*, Supplement No. 40 (A/64/40), vol. I (2009) 201, Ftn (d), where the Committee explains that 'prior to the receipt by the Secretary-General of the United Nations of the instrument of ratification', the Committee's position was as referred to above in note 35.

[42] See, eg, General Comment No. 24 (52) on 'Issues relating to reservations made upon ratification or accession to the Covenant or the Optional Protocols thereto, or in relation to declarations under article 41 of the Covenant', 4 November 1994, in CCPR/C/21/Rev.1/Add.6, which contains significant clarifications about the object and purpose of the Covenant. Although it does not deal expressly with state succession, the omission of a reference to 'succession' in the title clearly implies that no reservation can be made in a declaration of succession, the latter being automatic as to all the obligations under the Covenant. On the issue of state succession as to reservations made by the predecessor state see G. Gaja, 'Reservations to Treaties and the Newly Independent States', 1 *Ital. Yb. Int'l L.* (1975) 52–68.

[43] On this case, concerning the People's Democratic Republic of Korea, see, also for the relevant documents, F. Pocar, 'Sulla possibilità di ritiro dal Patto internazionale sui diritti civili e politici', *Rivista di diritto internazionale privato e processuale* (1977) 1073–84.

[44] General Comment No. 26 (61) on 'Issues relating to the continuity of obligations to the International Covenant on Civil and Political Rights', 29 October 1997, in CCPR/C/21/Rev.1/Add.8, and *Report of the Committee, GAOR, Fifty-third Session*, Supplement No. 40 (A/53/40), vol. I (1998), Annex VII, 102.

State or State succession or any subsequent action of the State party designed to divest them of the rights guaranteed by the Covenant.[45]

5. Besides human rights bodies, the issue of state succession to human rights and humanitarian law treaties was brought to the attention of international courts in the context of the Balkans. In particular, the International Court of Justice was presented with the question whether Bosnia and Herzegovina had automatically succeeded to the Genocide Convention of 1948—which was denied by Yugoslavia—for the purpose of establishing its competence under Article IX of the Convention. The Court, however, did not address the issue in these terms, as it considered the parties bound by the Convention, in any event, when the application before the Court was filed.[46] However, two judges did so in their separate opinions, and maintained, although with different argument and force, that the Genocide Convention was automatically applicable to the successor states to the former Socialist Federal Republic of Yugoslavia, which was a party thereto.

In particular, Judge Weeramantry conducted a thorough analysis of the theories relating to state succession, including the bases of the clean slate principle and the necessary exceptions thereof. He observed that 'human rights and humanitarian treaties involve no loss of sovereignty or autonomy of the new State, but are merely in line with general principles of protection that flow from the inherent dignity of every human being which is the very foundation of the United Nations Charter', and that 'the international community has a special interest in the continuity of such treaties'.[47] Without taking a firm position on the issue of whether all human rights treaties should be exempted from the clean slate principle, he then brought forward a number of reasons favouring the view of an automatic succession to the Genocide Convention, including those put forward by the Human Rights Committee, and concluded that '[a]ll the foregoing reasons combine to create what seems to me to be a principle of contemporary international law that there is automatic State succession to so vital a human rights convention as the Genocide Convention'.[48]

In turn, Judge Shahabuddeen recalled the special characteristics of the Genocide Convention as identified in the Court's Advisory Opinion on the reservations to the Convention,[49] and pointed to an 'inescapable time-gap in the protection which the Genocide Convention previously afforded to all of the "human groups" comprised in the former Socialist Federal Republic of Yugoslavia' that should occur if the successor states were regarded as not bound by the Convention,

[45] General Comment No. 26 (61), *supra* note 44, para. 4.

[46] ICJ, *Application of the Convention on the Prevention and Punishment of the Crime of Genocide (Bosnia-Herzegovina v Yugoslavia)*, Preliminary Objections, Judgment of 11 July 1996, *ICJ Reports* (1996) 19.

[47] Ibid., 54.

[48] Ibid., 63.

[49] ICJ, *Reservations to the Convention on the Prevention and Punishment of the Crime of Genocide*, Advisory Opinion of 28 May 1951, *ICJ Reports* (1951) 23.

a time-gap which would be inconsistent with the Convention.[50] He therefore concluded that the Convention 'would fall to be construed as implying the expression of a unilateral undertaking by each party to the Convention to treat successor States as continuing as from independence any status which the predecessor State had as a party to the Convention'. In his view, however, the necessary consensual bond would only be completed 'when the successor State decides to avail itself of the undertaking by regarding itself as a party to the treaty'.[51]

The problem of state succession was also raised, in the different context of assessing individual criminal responsibility for grave breaches of the Geneva Conventions of 12 August 1949, before the International Criminal Tribunal for the Former Yugoslavia.[52] Rejecting the appellant's argument that the said Conventions were not in force for Bosnia and Herzegovina between the date of the country's independence (6 March 1992) and the date of the deposit of its declaration of succession (31 December 1992),[53] the Appeals Chamber of the Tribunal expressed the view that 'irrespective of any finding as to formal succession, Bosnia and Herzegovina would in any event have succeeded to the Geneva Conventions under customary law, as this type of conventions entail automatic succession, ie, without the need for any formal confirmation of adherence by the successor State'.[54] It added that 'it may be considered in international law that there is automatic succession to multilateral treaties in the broad sense, ie, treaties of universal character which express fundamental human rights'.

It has to be stressed that the issue of automatic succession was especially significant in this case, as it did not affect only the continuity of the state's obligations to apply the relevant conventions, as was the case discussed before the International Court of Justice, where the gap could be remedied by a declaration of succession taking effect as of the date of independence, but also and more importantly the possibility of characterizing a serious violation of the Conventions attributable to an individual as a crime under international law. A retroactive declaration of succession, as was indeed deposited by the successor state in the case at hand, would not have been sufficient to this effect, in light of the principle of legality, which is imperative in criminal law, and according to which no one can be held criminally responsible for any conduct which did not constitute a criminal offence under

[50] ICJ, *Application of the Convention*, *supra* note 46, 54. [51] Ibid., 45.

[52] *Prosecutor v Delalić et al. ('Čelebići Case')*, Case No. IT-96-21-A, Appeals Chamber, Judgment of 20 February 2001. Article 2 of the Statute of the ICTY, as adopted by Security Council resolution 827 (1993) of 25 May 1993 (S/RES/827 (1993)), establishes that the Tribunal shall have the power to prosecute persons committing or ordering to be committed grave breaches of the 1949 Geneva Conventions, and lists the acts which constitute grave breaches if committed against persons or property protected under the provisions of the relevant Geneva Convention.

[53] *Prosecutor v Delalić et al.*, *supra* note 52, paras 107–115.

[54] As the Judgment notes (*Prosecutor v Delalić et al.*, para. 111 *in fine*), it is noteworthy that Bosnia and Herzegovina itself recognized this principle before the ICJ. In its Judgment of 11 July 1996, the Court noted that Bosnia and Herzegovina 'contended that the Genocide Convention falls within the category of instruments for the protection of human rights, and that consequently, the rule of 'automatic succession' necessarily applies' (*ICJ Reports* (1996), para. 21).

national or international law, at the time it was committed.[55] In this context, therefore, the finding of the Appeals Chamber of the Hague Tribunal that 'there was no gap in the protection afforded by the Geneva Conventions, as they, and the obligations deriving therefrom, were in force for Bosnia and Herzegovina at the time of the acts alleged in the Indictment',[56] acquires a significant value.

6. The recent international practice, as described above, no doubt serves to clarify international law pertaining to the delicate issue of state succession to treaties, and to better understand the solutions put forward in the Vienna Convention of 1978 on this matter. In particular, Article 34 of the Convention finds a substantial confirmation, at least insofar as human rights treaties are concerned, and it would be inaccurate to reject such practice as irrelevant. Likewise, it is inaccurate to maintain that the principle of the continuity of treaties in the case of dismemberment of or separation from a state was adopted by the ILC with the declared intent to contribute to the progressive development of international law, rather than to codify a corresponding rule of customary law.[57] As the Commission manifestly declares, its conclusions were indeed based on a review of the state practice and on an assessment of its sufficient consistency to support the formulation of a rule in favour of continuity.[58]

These conclusions are, of course, a matter for discussion in legal doctrine. In the case of state succession, notwithstanding the declared position of the ILC, it may be disputed whether state practice was 'sufficiently consistent' at the time when the Convention was drafted to justify the adoption of a general rule affirming the continuity of all multilateral treaties as a rule reflecting existing customary law. However, even if a different assessment of the then available state practice were to raise doubt as to whether the provision of Article 34 was grounded on customary international law, the question would still remain whether customary international law evolved in that direction thereafter, if not in respect of all treaties, at least in respect of human rights treaties.

From this perspective, it cannot be overlooked that the Convention itself must be regarded as a significant expression of state practice, as the Convention was charged, within the competency of the General Assembly via the UN Charter,

[55] Cf. Article 15(1) of the ICCPR, from which no derogation can be made even in time of public emergency (see Article 4 thereof). As to para. 2, it permits retroactive domestic legislation for the prosecution of crimes such as war crimes and crimes against humanity, but does not allow for retroactive international law, in particular international treaty law. See M. Nowak, *U.N. Covenant on Civil and Political Rights. CCPR Commentary* (Kehl am Rhein: Engel, 2nd rev. edn, 2005) 368.

[56] Para. 114 of the Judgment.

[57] B. Conforti, *Diritto internazionale*, *supra* note 8, p. 106.

[58] See *YILC* (1974), vol. II(1), 265, No. 25. In answering the question whether the principle of continuity or the clean slate principle should be applied to the situations envisaged, the Commission concluded that 'although some discrepancies might be found in State practice, still that practice was sufficiently consistent to support the formulation of a rule which, with the necessary qualifications, would provide that treaties in force at the date of the dissolution should remain in force *ipso jure* with respect to each State emerging from the dissolution'.

to make recommendations for the development and codification of international law;[59] was adopted by a conference with the participation of the entire international community; and was subsequently accepted by number of states. As shown above with respect to human rights treaties, the rule adopted on that occasion has been subsequently confirmed by international practice without any clear exception. There is, therefore, material evidence of state practice moving towards recognition of the principle of continuity as the principle governing state succession to treaties concerning human rights and humanitarian law. Whether this practice requires further corroboration prior to becoming a firm customary international rule may certainly be questioned,[60] but it cannot be denied that significant arguments, including those of a general nature, can be invoked in favour of the existence of such a rule.

First, it should be recalled that the Vienna Convention, by adopting two distinct legal regimes pertaining to state succession to treaties—the *tabula rasa* regime for newly independent states whose territory was previously subjected to colonial domination and the continuity regime for uniting and separation from states to form new states—does not appear to affirm the first regime as the general one and the second as a derogation thereof. Rather, it simply takes note of the general request from developing countries to accede to independence utterly free from any obligation entered into by colonial powers, and gives priority to the former only because of its special political importance when the Convention was drafted. But, with the end of the decolonization process this part of the Convention will become obsolete, and is arguably already obsolete to a certain extent.[61] It is no surprise that the Convention took the view that the entire issue of state succession to treaties should not be affected and 'contaminated' by a regime aimed at resolving a temporary and transitional situation and, instead, opted for two distinct regimes—the second expected to be the more 'stable', or even to become the general regime.

In addressing this more durable regime, the ILC appears to trace a separation between the practice as developed in the pre-United Nations era and the practice subsequent to the Charter. While it accepts that the former provided support for the clean slate rule, it is guided by the more recent practice in the United

[59] Article 13, para. 1 of the UN Charter.

[60] See, eg, M.N. Shaw, *International Law* (Cambridge: Cambridge University Press, 5th edn, 2003) 885–9. After reviewing most of the practice also considered in the present chapter, he observes that 'the question of continued application of human rights treaties within the territory of a predecessor state irrespective of a succession is clearly under consideration. Whether such a principle has been clearly established is at the present moment unclear' (at 889). In the sense that a customary rule of this kind is developing as an exception from the clean slate principle, see recently S. Bariatti, 'L'accordo nel sistema delle fonti e il diritto dei trattati', in S.M. Carbone, R. Luzzatto, and A. Santa Maria (eds), *Istituzioni di diritto internazionale* (Torino: Giappichelli, 3rd edn, 2006) 121.

[61] This may perhaps explain why only a few 'newly independent states' have become parties to the Convention, notwithstanding the favorable regime provided, which had however already been applied in practice.

Nations period, which would only occasionally support the approach that a territory becoming independent because of the dissolution or the separation from a state might be regarded as a 'newly independent state' to which the clean slate rule should apply.[62] And indeed, the United Nations period is rather characterized by multilateral treaties of a normative nature that are of paramount interest to the international community on account of their continuing application in territories of the states parties, irrespective of dissolution into more states or partial separation to form a new state.

Whether this approach is justified for all multilateral treaties concluded in the United Nations period may be questionable. But this is certainly the case for human rights and humanitarian law treaties, as evidenced by their special nature. Legal doctrine and state practice are in agreement in their corresponding emphasis on the fact that in these kinds of treaties

> ... the contracting States do not have any interest of their own; they merely have, one and all, a common interest, namely, the accomplishment of those high purposes which are the *raison d'être* of the convention. Consequently, in a convention of this type one cannot speak of individual advantages or disadvantages to States, or of the maintenance of a perfect contractual balance between rights and duties.[63]

A similar approach is echoed by legal doctrine, when it writes that 'the special body of international law characterized as human rights law is strikingly different from the rest of international law, in that it stipulates that obligations are owed directly to individuals (and not to the national government of an individual)'.[64] This entails a common interest of the international community to see that the application of human rights treaties continue without any gap due to dismemberment of states or secession of parts of their territories.[65]

Admittedly, international practice supporting continuity of human rights and humanitarian law treaties is not always very clear about the reasons behind this position, which is sometimes accepted as such without any further explanation under the pressure of international human rights bodies, as the experience of the Human Rights Committee abundantly shows. However, on one hand this is a feature common to other rules of customary international law, which, although based on the assessment that certain conduct has to be regarded as legally binding, fail to manifest the reasons for supporting such an assessment. It is clear

[62] The obvious case is that of the separation of West and East Pakistan from India, and the subsequent separation of East Pakistan to form Bangladesh. This case is distinguishable, however, because it can easily be associated with the decolonization process.

[63] See the ICJ, *Reservations to the Convention on the Prevention and Punishment of the Crime of Genocide*, Advisory Opinion of 28 May 1951, *supra* note 49, 23.

[64] R. Higgins, *Problems and Process. International Law and How We Use It* (Oxford: Clarendon Press, 1994) 75.

[65] The need for avoiding any gap in the application of these treaties has been rightly underlined by W. Jenks, 'State Succession in Respect of Law-Making Treaties', 29 *BYIL* (1952) 109; by Judge Weeramantry in his Separate Opinion, *supra* note 47, para. 7, as well as by Judge Shahabuddeen in his Separate Opinion, *supra* note 50.

enough, on the other hand, that an *opinio juris* in favour of continuity manifestly finds its justification in the special nature of these treaties as shown above—ie in the treaties' recognition of state obligations not (or not only) to other states, but to individual human beings—a feature that is self-evident and need not be invoked by a new state when acquiescing to human rights obligations entered into by a predecessor state.

From such recognition international practice appears to draw the inference that the rights enshrined in these treaties, once granted protection over a territory, are vested in the persons living therein, so that their protection cannot be taken away following changes in the legal situation of the territory concerned.[66] Some legal doctrine builds on this practice, by drawing an analogy between a treaty vesting human rights and dispositive treaties vesting property rights, which, according to established practice, cannot be weakened in the case of state succession.[67] Whether such an analogy correctly interprets the legal situation arising out of human rights treaties may be a matter for further discussion, since it would be based on a construction whereby continuity will be established only as an exception to a general rule based on the clean slate principle—a construction which may be debatable in light of the structure of the Vienna Convention of 1978, as described above. However, even assuming that this is still a cogent construction under modern international law, it remains to be considered whether a proper analogy may be drawn between dispositive treaties such as those vesting property rights, and treaties affording protection to rights which are recognized as inherent to human beings. Furthermore, recourse to such an analogy is not strictly necessary. Rather, an approach based on the nature of the obligations entered into by states parties upon the conclusion of human rights and humanitarian law treaties can more appropriately justify an exception from a general rule inspired by the clean slate principle and be better suited to provide the grounds for explaining why such kinds of treaties enjoy continuity under customary international law.

[66] This is the position adopted by the Human Rights Committee in its General Comment 26(61), *supra* note 44, para. 4.

[67] See, eg, R. Mullerson, 'The Continuity and Succession of States, by Reference to the Former USSR and Yugoslavia', 42 *ICLQ* (1993) 490; M.N. Shaw, 'State Succession Revisited', 5 *Finnish YIL* (1994) 82; A. Rasulov, 'Revisiting State Succession to Humanitarian Treaties: Is There a Case for Automaticity?', 14 *EJIL* (2003) 141–70.

PART IV

INVALIDITY AND TERMINATION OF TREATIES

18

Invalidity of Treaties: Anything New in/under the Vienna Conventions?

Joe Verhoeven

Clearly, the 1969 and 1986 Vienna Conventions on the Law of Treaties[1] represented 'new' law in the sense that they constituted the first inter-state codification of the rules governing treaties at a universal level. It does not matter in that respect that the International Law Commission had originally decided that this codification should take the form of an 'expository code', and not of a treaty.[2] Nor does it matter that 'private', ie unofficial, attempts at codifying were previously made (Harvard draft, etc) in a more or less successful manner.

Technically, codifying as such entails only the gathering of various provisions governing a given matter in a single instrument, ie a 'code'. It does not necessarily imply that those rules are pre-existing, and even less that they are of a customary nature. It is surely not disputable that in history many codifications resulted in transforming into written law what were originally practices accepted as law in a given group (nation, society). But codifying still keeps its *raison d'être* even where it is concerned with rules lacking unequivocal support in the practice of a given group (nation, society). Consequently, as far as international treaties are concerned, the conclusions of the 1969 and 1986 Vienna Conventions in themselves neither imply nor exclude that their provisions are declarative of general law, ie are binding on all states and international organizations, even when they are not officially parties to them. Needless to say, it is somewhat puzzling to be worried about the 'novel' character of provisions contained in a treaty adopted more than 40 years ago as regards the states, and 25 years ago as far as international organizations are concerned. But it is still an important issue, until now left largely unanswered... despite blunt assertions of the 'customary' character of most of its articles.

[1] The present paper is mostly concerned with the 1969 Vienna Convention on treaties between states, but the comments should normally be relevant for the 1986 Convention on treaties with or between international organizations.

[2] See I. Sinclair, *The Vienna Convention on The Law of Treaties* (Manchester: Manchester University Press, 2nd edn, 1984) 3.

There is no doubt that up to now 'general' law in international law has mostly been comprised of 'international custom[s]', 'as evidence of a general practice accepted as law' to use the terms of Article 38 of the International Court of Justice (ICJ) Statute. In particular, it means that establishing the customary character of the provisions of the Vienna Convention relating to the invalidity of treaties would normally require that evidence should be given of the existence of both a 'general practice' and a practice 'accepted as law'. At the time the Vienna Conventions were adopted, such exercise was problematical in many respects. Indeed, the cases where the invalidity of a treaty was disputed remained very exceptional, and very ambiguous. The difficulty was not only to distinguish what respectively pertains to law and politics in a given case but also to define what were the specific legal requirements characterizing invalidity (which appeared uncertain). Case law in particular is almost totally silent in this regard.[3]

The customary technique is not, however, the only source of 'general' law. Other techniques could be used to produce 'general' rules. The best known is the technique of general principles of law as referred to in Article 38(1) of the ICJ Statute. Such a principle is undisputable when it establishes that its binding content is accepted as law in the domestic law of most, if not all, of the states forming the so-called international community. Which actually is often difficult to verify adequately... especially since domestic case law should normally be taken into account to determine the exact meaning of a legislative provision. That should explain why such general principles based on domestic practices remain somewhat exceptional. But apart from resting on convergent national practices, general principles should also be claimed on the sole basis of the internal coherence which is to be maintained in a 'system' of law, and which should make clear the necessary articulations existing between the various components of what is constitutive of a legal system. Needless to say, the exact content of such principles could, however, be questionable in many respects, at least to the extent that they do not coincide with general principles accepted as law within the meaning of Article 38 of the ICJ Statute. That should explain why many references to general principles, the exact nature of which remains uncertain, are made in the international legal literature so as to validate the declarative character of the provisions of the Vienna Conventions concerning the invalidity of treaties.[4]

Finally, it should be borne in mind that, apart from the difficulties relating to the technical support (custom, principle, etc) of a rule, the idea of a 'new' law also aims simply at the actual content of a provision which had been modified, no matter whether a 'treaty', a 'custom', or a 'principle' is at stake. And domestic

[3] As emphasized by Mc Nair, there exists 'little diplomatic practice, and almost no judicial authority' (*The Law of Treaties* (Oxford: Clarendon Press, 1961) 207).

[4] Cf. 'the subtle difference between existing customary rules and the rationalization of general principles of law' aimed at by V. Degan, *Sources of International Law* (The Hague: Martinus Nijhoff, 1997) 76, or the 'principles dictated by legal logic' referred to by O.A. Elias and C.L. Lim, *The Paradox of Consensualism in International Law* (The Hague: Kluwer Law International, 1998) 218.

practices should not be excluded in that respect, at least as a matter of principle, in assessing such 'novelty'. Changes in the regulation of contractual relations could indeed be relevant for states' regulations, even if they were originally concerned with individuals only.

It remains therefore rather surprising that commentators of the 1969 Vienna Convention, without clearly identifying the legal technique justifying their conclusion, generally consider that its provisions are declarative of general law, and consequently express rules having a binding effect even on states which are not parties to them (3). In such a perspective, the conclusion should be clear: if 'new' law means law having no previous support in the general practice of states, there was nothing which did basically constitute new law within the provisions of the Vienna Conventions governing the invalidity of treaties, despite the uncertainties relating to its customary basis. Apparently, there is only one important exception in that respect, apart from purely procedural issues: Article 53 of the Conventions affirming the invalidity of a treaty whose provisions are inconsistent with peremptory norms having a *jus cogens* character, which was forcefully opposed during the negotiations at Vienna by states who eventually refused to become parties to the Conventions. Today, the mood could, however, be changing in this respect. Indeed, some states are apparently more prepared to accept, or at least less displeased with, the principle of an *ordre public* in international relations.

The issue is not any longer whether or not to decide on the contractual or general (customary) character of the articles of the Vienna Conventions governing the invalidity of treaties, but rather to determine if, and in the affirmative to what extent, those provisions eventually modify the usual content of the traditionally applicable rules, no matter whether they are of a customary or purely conventional origin. 'New' law in such a perspective aims at rules whose content has changed. In such a perspective, however, the difficulty could be to determine the exact content of the 'previous' rule, ie of the rule by reference to which the 'innovative' character of the Vienna provision is to be appreciated. Since international law is at stake, this rule should be an 'international' one. But there is, as previously emphasized, almost no practice in that respect. As already pointed out, domestic law which sometimes provides the only credible reference should therefore not as a matter of principle be disregarded on the sole basis of its 'national' origin, even if the respective needs of a national and an international community cannot necessarily be considered as similar. Nor should they be considered as necessarily different.

As far as the law on invalidity is concerned, three kinds of issues have to be distinguished. They respectively pertain to the causes, procedure, and effects of invalidity. It has been previously pointed out that traditional practice was very poor on those issues. The Vienna Conventions did not change much from this point of view, apart from the fact that (relatively) clear written provisions now exist. Inevitably, support is consequently to be found in domestic practices to decide on difficulties left unsettled in the Vienna Conventions. Civil and common law traditions should of course both be considered to that end. But the provisions regarding procedure are in any case specific to international law, since there is still no compulsory jurisdiction within the so-called 'international community', whatever those terms, still partly controversial, might exactly mean. Provisions concerning the effects of invalidity also partly reflect some structural characteristics of that community, which *a priori* does disqualify to some extent references made to national practices in constructing them. But grounds of invalidity were directly inspired, at least as far as the defects in consent ('*vices du consentement*') are concerned, by civil law traditions... despite the fact that most of the rapporteurs within the International Law Commission were common law lawyers.

1. Grounds of Invalidity

The very possibility of the invalidity of a legal act is probably axiomatic. How indeed could such an act produce its legal effects if the conditions which are basically required to that end are not satisfied? The difficulty, however, is to agree on the content/nature of such basic conditions, especially in a system still largely rooted in customs, ie in (state) practices as distinguished from mere usages (habits).

Those conditions remained largely uncertain until the adoption of the 1969 Vienna Convention on the Law of (state) Treaties, cases of nullity remaining—as previously emphasized—very much the exception. The basic provision probably was simply that the consent of the state to be bound is null and void when it has not been 'regularly' given. What does the term 'regularly' concretely intend to convey? Basically, firstly that the consent be expressed by a person duly authorized to that end and, secondly, that it be expressed 'freely'.[5] Failing other express provisions, it should depend upon the peculiarities of each case as to whether both requirements are satisfied or not. This conclusion does not express any 'political' choice; it is only evidencing fundamental requirements of a legal transactions theory. That said, the proposition remained largely theoretical till at least the conclusion of the Vienna Conventions—which identified much more specific grounds of invalidity—especially in the absence of a judge before whom the case of invalidity could be brought. Of course, nothing was preventing the parties from agreeing on the validity of 'their' treaty. However, the hypothesis remained apparently exceptional. And in any case the very fact that there was an agreement to nullify would have been muddling what is due respectively to the sovereign will of the parties and to the logic of invalidity.

Those hesitations disappeared with the 1969 Vienna Convention, which listed the admissible grounds of nullity in its Articles 46 to 53 and Article 42;

[5] According to G.F. de Martens, the negotiators of the treaty must have been 'sufficiently authorized' (para. 48), and the consent be 'declared' (para. 49), 'free' (para. 50), and 'mutual' (para. 51) (*Précis du droit des gens moderne de l'Europe* (Göttingen: De Dieterich, 3rd edn, 1820)).

these articles make clear that 'the validity of a treaty or of the consent of a State to be bound... may be impeached only through the application of the present convention'.[6] As previously emphasized, these articles to a large extent reproduce in substance a theory of defects in consent ('*vices de consentement*') very well known in civil law countries whose legal regimes are based, directly or indirectly, on the Napoleonic code. The point is worth emphasizing in a context where common law traditions tend to become the usual reference.

According to the Vienna Convention, six grounds of invalidity are admissible: lack of competence (Articles 46 and 47), error (Article 48), fraud (Article 49), corruption (Article 50), coercion (Articles 51 and 52), and violation of a peremptory norm (Article 53). Such a list probably includes all the defects usually admitted in civil law countries as vitiating the consent, but two of them were not (always) taken into consideration: lack of competence and corruption. Does that imply that the provisions of the Vienna Conventions are 'new' in that regard? Probably not.

1.1. The issue of competence does inevitably arise when a legal person (*personne morale*) is concerned, since it necessarily requires the intervention of a physical person to express its consent, whether orally or in writing. And logically the former could only be validly bound by the consent given by the latter if that physical person was 'competent' in that regard. National and international laws are faced with the same difficulty. At first sight, there should not be important divergences of view in this respect. The difference, however, is still that all subjects of international law—apart from the reservation concerning the present evolution concerning individuals—are legal persons. Consequently, the problem of competence is necessarily raised when an 'international' agreement is entered into, while it remained much more 'exceptional' under domestic laws. This probably explains why the lack of competence is not usually analysed as a specific '*vice de consentement*' in domestic law. As such, it is a problem for the law governing legal persons, and not for the law governing contracts. But there is no difference between national and international law, subject to this remark.

Should there be a difference, it would arise from the fact that, according to Article 46(1), the lack of competence would only result in invalidating the consent when it was 'manifest and concerned a rule of its internal law [regarding competence to conclude treaties] of fundamental importance'. No such restriction normally applies where contracts, as distinguished from treaties, are concerned, even when the process of their conclusion is as complex as the one applicable to treaties. Any lack of competence could normally be invoked to declare the contract null and void, at least when it was not covered in one way or another by

[6] For other possible grounds—largely doubtful—see M. Kohen, 'Article 42', in O. Corten and P. Klein (eds), *Les Conventions de Vienne sur le droit des traités*, vol. II (Bruxelles: Bruylant, 2006) 1603 (hereinafter *Commentaire*).

the contracting party. Does that constitute 'new' law as far as international law is concerned? At the time when the Vienna Conventions were concluded, the answer would probably have been affirmative, no practice—not even doctrine—really supporting the idea that a state could not invoke the incompetence of its legal representative, at least when it was acting in good faith. This is probably also the position in domestic laws, especially since general rules would normally be substituted for the nullified contract, so as to provide clear legal answers when needed. From that point of view, the situation is quite different as far as international law is concerned, at least as long as the customary process remains the only usable process to produce 'general' law. This should explain why only a qualified lack of competence has been accepted as a ground of invalidity in the Vienna Conventions. Does that mean that the restrictions expressed in Article 46 of the Vienna Conventions only apply as a matter of principle in the relations between contracting states? This would be surprising, almost 50 years after the adoption of the 1969 Vienna Convention on the Law of Treaties. Even if practice remains meagre, Article 46 provisions are so widely accepted, at least by legal scholars and other experts, that it would be somewhat amazing if they were characterized as purely conventional, even if intellectual consensus is not enough —thank God!—to create law! Be that as it may, the conclusion is no less artificial than the one affirming that the mere fact of not invoking the invalidity, supposing it to be established, constitutes a kind of acquiescence curing the invalidity.

Should the 'restrictions' of competence, aimed at in Article 47 of the Vienna Convention, be distinguished, when they are ignored by the state agent concerned, from the lack of competence aimed at in Article 46? Probably not; in both cases indeed, the state representative acted outside of its area of competence. According to Article 47, however, ignorance of such a restriction could only invalidate the consent expressed when it was 'specific'—whatever that means exactly—and had been notified to the other contracting parties. The exact purpose of such a provision nevertheless remains uncertain, the difference between both articles being apparently that the restrictions aimed at in Article 47 do not imply a violation of the 'internal law' of the state concerned, as mentioned in Article 46. Which remains problematical... that said, Article 47 has until now remained without any practical interest (applications). Consequently, it does not matter whether it is considered as 'new' law[7] or not.

1.2. Error, fraud, and corruption are admitted as grounds of invalidity according to Articles 48 to 50 of the Vienna Convention, at least when they have, in one way or another, induced the victim state to consent to be bound by the treaty.

Some pre-Vienna Conventions cases of 'error' are established in international practice. The customary character of Article 48 should therefore not be disputed, even if some disagreement may exist concerning the exact conditions which

[7] See P. Martin-Bidou, 'Article 47', in *Commentaire, supra* note 6, at 1728.

must be satisfied to invalidate the consent. Proven cases of fraud and corruption remain exceptional, however. Some commentators are apparently suggesting that they (should) have been rather common business. But such allegations are insufficient to constitute the factual basis of a customary rule. It would therefore be hazardous to affirm the declaratory character of Article 48 and Article 50[8] if it is allegedly based on the existence of a general practice accepted as law.

Could general principles of law support a conclusion which is not validated by customary techniques? Why not, in principle? Domestic laws, however, do not clearly confirm that the contract or at least most of the contracts reached through corruption are void, even when corruption constitutes a legal offence, at least to the extent that it did not either cause an error or constitute a coercion opening the way to an invalidation. As far as Article 49 is concerned, it is still surprising that it should be entitled 'fraud' in the English text and '*dol*' in the French as if both terms were identical,[9] which they are not.[10] A '*dol*' is a kind of qualified 'fraud' unknown, however, in legal systems which are not close heirs of the Napoleonic code and which consequently have serious difficulties in understanding the specificity of that qualification.[11] The precedent of the 1929 Warsaw Convention for the unification of certain rules related to international carriage by air is well known in that respect. To rule out the limitation of the responsibility normally benefiting the aerial carrier, its Article 25 provides indeed that such a limitation does not apply, according to the French text of the Convention, when 'le dommage provient de son dol ou d'une faute [. . .] considérée comme équivalente au dol', which becomes in the English text: 'if the damage is caused by his wilful misconduct or by such default [. . .] considered to be equivalent to wilful misconduct'.[12] But twenty-five years later a specific protocol was needed to explicate the meaning of a term which has remained particularly obscure for the (judicial) authorities of most of the contracting states. In the amending Hague Protocol of 1955, the formula became: 'if the damages resulted from an act or omission [. . .] done with the intent to cause damage or recklessly and with knowledge that damage will probably result' (Article 25 A). In such a context, the reappearance of the '*dol*' in a treaty on the law of treaties between states is rather amazing, especially since the term

[8] For the affirmation that corruption as a ground of invalidity is 'une idée absolument neuve', see J.-P. Cot, 'Article 50', in *Commentaire, supra* note 6, at 1820.

[9] The '*dol*' is rarely mentioned in international doctrine as a ground which could invalidate a legal transaction (a treaty), even among scholars of civil law traditions (*contra*, for instance P. Guggenheim, *Traité de droit international public*, (Genève: Librairie de l'Université, 1953) vol. 1, 92–3).

[10] For a denial of the existence of fraud ('*dol*') as a ground of invalidity, see Judge Gros as quoted by G. Niyungeko, 'Article 49', in *Commentaire, supra* note 6, at 1781.

[11] Cf. the reference to an 'erreur provoquée' by E. Wyler, 'Article 48', in *Commentaire, supra* note 6, at 1763.

[12] Cf. the declaration of the Philippines at the Vienna Conference, according to which 'fraud amounts to deceit or wilful misrepresentation', quoted in M. Villiger, *Commentary on the 1969 Vienna Convention on the Law of Treaties* (Leiden: Martinus Nijhoff, 2009) 617.

'fraud' as used in the English text of Article 49 does exist in French as well, and since 'wilful misconduct' and not 'fraud' was considered as equivalent to '*dol*' in the 1929 text. That said, the important point is still that the substance of the article is identical in both texts. From this point one should be induced not to pay (too) much attention to the titling of the article and the discrepancy in its translation, even if official titles should normally be taken into account when construing their content.

1.3. The two cases of coercion referred to in the Vienna Conventions are widely accepted today, even if they raised much debate at the time they were discussed, first within the International Law Commission and later at the Vienna Conference.[13] The duality of articles is justified by the distinction made between coercion of the state as such and coercion of its representative only. Does it imply that in the absence of a specific provision concerning the state's representative, coercion could not have been taken into account in deciding on the validity of the consent? Clearly not. Having said that, the interest in distinguishing Article 51 from Article 52 still remains that the treaty as such is void when it was generated by the threat or use of force against the state as a whole while its consent to be bound only is 'without any legal effect' when its representative only is concerned. Does 'logic' or 'coherence' support the distinction, in the absence of any consistent practice in that regard? It depends on what 'logic' means. At least, it is coherent to deny any result to the use of armed force when it is illegal, ie when it was exercised in violation of the UN Charter. But could the distinction be based on a general principle of law? Probably. With that reservation in mind, nothing should therefore be considered as constituting 'new' law as far as coercion is concerned. And that should be regretted to a certain extent.

It is well known that economic coercion was, for instance, not admitted as a ground of invalidity at Vienna, despite the demands of many, mostly developing, countries. Accepting such a ground in the absence of any use of military force, however, appeared much too risky to the majority of the participants at the Vienna Conference, including almost all developed countries. Possibly, such caution was wisdom 50 years ago. Is it still? That is at least doubtful. It is interesting to note that national tribunals traditionally reluctant to take into account economic violence now move towards accepting it. And proposals are officially made to modify the civil code so as to give a legislative foundation to a judicial evolution. It is not that economic pressure is now illegal; it is simply

[13] The customary character of Article 52 was not that clear at the time the Vienna Convention was adopted. In any case, very (too) old precedents should be of little significance in that respect (see the concordat between Pope Pascal II and the King of England, Henry I, whose conclusion was obtained through imprisonment of the former by the latter, referred to by G. Distefano, 'Article 51', in *Commentaire*, *supra* note 6, at 1845 (possibly, there was a confusion in that respect between Henri I Beauclerc and Henri V, Emperor of Germany).

that a contract obtained by abusing the weak position of another party to gain advantages it would not have given had it not been in a situation of dependence or necessity is voidable.[14] Contracts under domestic law cannot, of course, be equated with treaties under international law. There is no reason, however, for excluding categorically that treaties obtained through economic coercion might be voidable at the request of the victim state. Everybody knows that at Vienna the compromise solution was to declare in an annex to the Convention that economic violence was illegal but not to mention it explicitly in the articles relating to coercion.[15] Possibly that was a wise solution at the time the Vienna Convention was negotiated. But there is nothing to suggest that it could never constitute a 'violation of the principles of international law embodied in the Charter of the United Nations', to quote the terms of Article 52 of the Vienna Convention.

1.4. There was, and up to a certain point there still is, much debate about Article 53 of the Vienna Convention, and the so-called *jus cogens* it was officializing. Indeed, the article did not rest on any explicit practice existing before its adoption, and it was as such fiercely opposed by some state officials or legal scholars. Why? That remains unclear. The justification apparently was that a state is sovereign, whereas a private contracting entity is not, and consequently the validity of what it has agreed never might be impeached by any general rule of international law, customary or not, 'peremptory' or not. French authorities, or even scholars, were adamant in that respect.[16] This remains rather strange. The *jus cogens* norm is indeed simply a norm, necessarily general, ie normally of a customary character in the present state of international relations, which cannot be derogated from by a treaty (contract) because it was protecting a 'general' interest necessarily surpassing the private (particular) expectations of the contracting parties. As such, that is far from being revolutionary. '*Ordre public*' is very well known in any domestic (national) system.[17] Why should it be outlawed in international law? Of course, few norms could clearly be said to be 'peremptory' because of the present state of disorganization of a 'community'—to use the contemporary terminology (it used to be a 'family' before)—whose members still disagree on many, sometimes very important, issues. That should explain why *jus cogens* has not proven until now to be of a great use, and consequently why its customary support is

[14] See the 'Principes européens du droit des contrats'.

[15] See O. Corten, 'Article 52', in *Commentaire*, *supra* note 6, at 1877–9.

[16] Cf. E. Raftopoulos, sniggering at the 'futile theoretical attempts to identify the *jus cogens* rules in international law' (*The Inadequacy of the Contractual Analogy in the Law of Treaties* (Athens: Alkyon Publishers, 1990) 249).

[17] For a rather unclear distinction between *jus cogens* and *ordre public*, see, for instance, L. Alexidze, 'Legal nature of Jus Cogens in Contemporary International Law', 172 *Recueil des Cours* (1981-III) 241.

rather weak, if not non-existent.[18] But it is still axiomatic[19] in any system of law that private parties may never by contract endanger the essential values and interests of a given 'community'.[20] Customary practice, requiring a certain number of similar cases expressing converging solutions, should not be necessary therefore to validate in international law the specific effects of the violation of the 'peremptory' norms aimed at in Article 53 of the Vienna Convention.[21]

In other words, and contrary to a rather common opinion, *jus cogens* is anything but 'new' law. It could be politically wise to affirm that Article 53 constitutes a 'progressive development' rather than a strict 'codification' of international law. But so-called progressive development does not mean much, from a legal point of view, at least where 'axiomatic' rules are concerned. That said, the concrete usefulness of *jus cogens* is still limited. And it will remain weak as long as the content of the '*intérêt général*' within the community of nations remains poor. But the legal machinery of the '*ordre public*' (*jus cogens*) exists, no matter whether its utilization remains exceptional or not. Unless that conclusion is proved to be ill-founded, it is still strange that some states apparently persist in refusing to become party to the Vienna Convention because of its Article 53, which is probably the only provision that need not be accepted. Needless to say, determining the utility of *jus cogens* outside of contractual matters is another story. Whatever the conclusions in that regard may be, and they may sometimes be rather fanciful—as the assertion that *jus cogens* necessarily entails jurisdiction of the ICJ when its content/existence is disputed—it does not affect Article 53 as such.

If need be, it must be emphasized that this has nothing to do with what is called, according to French terminology, the 'cause' of a contract. In many civil law countries at least, a contract is void when its 'cause' is proved to be illegal (illicit). What such 'cause' exactly entails remains partly (largely?) unclear. The idea, however, is that it is not enough for a contract to be valid that it is expressing the 'sovereign' will of the parties. The reason why or the interest explaining why that was actually the will of those parties also needs to be taken into

[18] See J. Combacau, in J. Combacau and S. Sur, *Droit international public* (Paris: Montchrestien, 7th edn, 2006) 51–2, for whom Article 53, however, is only expressing a conventional rule whose content remains 'indiscernible' ('*insaisissable*').

[19] Which has nothing to do with 'natural law' (see J. Verhoeven, 'Considérations sur ce qui est commun (Cours général de droit international public)', 334 *Recueil des Cours* (2008) 228 *et seq.*), contrary to what had been several times affirmed (see, for instance, G. Danilenko, *Law-Making in the International Community* (Dordrecht: Martinus Nijhoff, 1993) 214 *et seq.*).

[20] It is sometimes suggested that any resort to '*jus cogens*' as a ground of invalidity should be excluded before the entry into force of the 1969 Vienna Convention, in accordance with the adage '*pas de nullité sans texte*' (see G. Robledo, 'Le ius cogens: sa genèse, sa nature, sa fonction', 172 *Recueil des Cours* (1981-III) 148). But that adage is meaningless in a customary system.

[21] The affirmation, however, is often, at least implicitly, denied (see, for instance, G. Tunkin: 'actually the recognition of the existence of jus cogens was an element of a new thinking reflecting the realities of a new era in history'—no less!—the ILC being not fully aware 'that it was a new approach to international law', 'when discussing the problem of jus cogens' ('Law and Force in Interstate System', 219 *Recueil des Cours* (1989-VII) 300).

consideration in that regard, so as to be able to invalidate, for instance, the contract whose specific 'aim' is clearly illicit. There is (was) much debate in (some) civil law countries on the soundness of this rather obscure requirement, the contemporary practice apparently tending towards dismissing such an approach. And in common law countries the so-called 'cause' apparently should not go beyond what 'consideration' implies, which means that the undertaking of one party should be the only 'cause' of the promise of the other party. Apparently the 'cause' of a treaty was never referred to in international (treaty) practice.[22] And it is such a confusing notion that it would certainly be preferable not to make any use of it. But in any case 'cause' is normally unrelated to '*ordre public*', which only invalidates an agreement when its content, ie what the parties agreed, is illicit. And it is all the more difficult in international relations to accept it since states at least will probably strongly oppose any control of what they had in a sovereign manner decided, at least beyond what *jus cogens* provisions require.

1.5. As previously underlined, no other ground of invalidity is in principle admissible according to the Vienna Conventions.

What about 'capacity', which traditionally is a basic requirement? There clearly is no problem as far as states are concerned, Article 6 of the 1969 Vienna Convention affirming that 'every State possesses capacity to conclude treaties'. None should disagree with the conclusion. The only difficulty could be to establish the existence of the state when it remains uncertain. Controversies regarding the validity of treaties concluded by or with unrecognized states are for instance well known, as are the problems relating to federal states when the federated entities are claiming a separate capacity to conclude treaties. There is no problem in this respect as long as those entities are acting as 'organs' of the federation in which the international personality of the state is vested. But in that case the treaty is a treaty of the federal state, no more and no less than the one concluded through a federal organ. Subject to that remark, there is for the time being no international capacity of federated entities to conclude treaties, at least none that is clearly accepted. But the 1969 Vienna Convention is not concerned with the problem, since it deals only with 'state' treaties.

Does that mean that, apart from states, no other international person is vested with a capacity to conclude agreements under international law? Clearly not, quite the contrary. The very fact of enjoying an (international) personality should necessarily entail the capacity to enter into relations with others, and especially to conclude agreements. Affirming the contrary would be inconsistent with the very notion of being a person, no matter whether international law or any other legal order is concerned. Non-state persons remain, however,

[22] Cf., in another context, J. Klabbers, *The Concept of Treaty in International Law* (The Hague: Kluwer Law International, 1996) 86–7.

exceptional in present international law. International organizations possibly constitute the only undisputed non-state legal persons in present practice, excepting the colonial peoples... which possibly no longer exist. It is consequently not surprising that a separate convention was concluded to determine the legal regime of the treaties concluded by or with international organizations (1986 Vienna Convention). Why, however, should a special regime be necessary in that respect, domestic laws making clear that there is substantially no difference in the regime of contracts depending on whether a legal person (*personne morale*) or an individual is a party? That remains unclear, apart from affording the opportunity of checking whether a difference could be justified or not, which actually was the case as far as Article 66 was concerned. The interesting point, however, is that according to Article 6 of the 1986 Vienna Convention 'the capacity of an international organisation to conclude treaties is governed by the rule of that organisation', which contrasts with Article 6 of the 1969 Convention just quoted. The exact significance of that article is however, unclear. Certainly, the capacity of an international organization to conclude treaties is to be exercised in conformity with the rules of that organization, and firstly with its statutory provisions. But it is not for the organization to decide itself whether it has the capacity to conclude treaties or not, at least in the absence of specific rules of general international law in that respect. It is for the states establishing the international organization to decide whether it enjoys a separate personality or not, which in the affirmative should (necessarily) entail an autonomous capacity to conclude treaties. That said, there is clearly a trend in contemporary practice towards affirming that, like states, every international organization is a separate legal person, ie that it enjoys legal personality. The conclusion is possibly well founded from a statistical point of view. Legally speaking, it is not.

2. Procedure

The procedure to be followed with respect to invalidity is determined in Articles 65 to 68 of the Vienna Conventions. Needless to say, procedure is a realy important issue, since the very (valid) existence of contractual obligations is concerned. And it is all the more important since general rules governing settlement of disputes in international law still remain 'elementary', despite the increasing 'internationalization' of social issues and the growing number of states and international organizations. A specific chapter being devoted to those procedural provisions in the present book, a few points only will be dealt with here as regards their 'new' character. Two different issues are to be distinguished in that respect: the first one is related to the technique which should be used, and the second to the persons entitled to make use of them, especially where judicial settlement is concerned.

2.1. Mechanism

The procedural mechanism is quite simple in its principle: should a party to a treaty consider its consent (or the treaty) as invalid, it must notify its claim to the other party (or parties). If the parties agree on the invalidity, any difficulty is removed. In case they do not, the resulting conflict must be peacefully settled through one of the techniques aimed at in Article 33 of the UN Charter if the dispute remains unresolved during the 12 months following the objection to validity. Where *jus cogens* is concerned, any one of the parties may, however, unilaterally submit the dispute to the ICJ unless they agree by common consent to submit it to arbitration. Where others grounds of invalidity are concerned, such recourse to a jurisdictional settlement is not imposed, the only obligation of the parties being to submit their dispute to the special conciliation machinery set out in an annex to the Vienna Convention. Needless to say, the parties are bound by the decision of either the ICJ or the arbitral tribunal as far as the dispute concerning *jus cogens* is concerned, while they remain free not to accept the conciliatory solution.

Clearly, such a device is not very original. When a contracting party to a treaty contests its validity (or at least the validity of its consent), how could it get the benefit of the invalidity without duly informing the other party(ies) of its claim and of the grounds supporting it. Should all contracting parties agree on a common solution to address it, then it does not really matter whether invalidity was concerned or not (excepting in some respects issues relating to *jus cogens*); it is sufficient that they all agree. But if they do not, a dispute will be substituted for a mere divergence of (legal) views, which necessarily needs to be settled peacefully. Independently of the particular dispute settlement mechanism chosen by the states, judicial settlement—like any other mechanism—will rest on the agreement of the parties. And it is worth emphasizing that, apart from judicial ones, special conciliation techniques are organized so as to facilitate as much as possible the search for the necessary compromise between the conflicting expectations of the parties to the dispute.

The solution is surely interesting. Is it related to customary, as opposed to treaty, law, or should it be considered as creating/constituting 'new' law by accepted national or international standards? The question is probably badly posed. The duty of states to remain peaceful in settling a dispute regarding the validity/termination of a treaty need not be validated by a customary rule in order to be binding on them. The issue is one of outlawing resort to armed force, not of deciding on the procedures that must be used to settle disputes concerning the invalidity of conventional provisions. Of course, the outlawing of force has rested up to now on customary prohibitions, at least as long as the UN Charter provisions are not considered as legally binding independently of either a customary or a conventional technique. But neither custom nor treaty is needed, in a system where the unilateral resort to armed force is as a matter of principle prohibited, to validate the conclusion that the settlement of treaty disputes must remain 'peaceful'. That said, there still could, of course, be an interest in imposing specific obligations in that respect, so as to ensure as far as possible the efficiency of a particular technique.

None would contest in that regard the importance of being quite specific in determining either the techniques which should be used in informing other contracting parties or the time limits that should be complied with and the persons habilitated to communicate official information, etc, as provided for in Articles 65 and 67. But as such, those requirements pertain to treaty and not to customary law, important as they might be. The fact that the contracting parties are sovereign states is not relevant—what counts is that the parties to the agreement—whatever their specific quality—are duly informed of elements which could jeopardize its very existence as a binding legal act.

To a certain extent, the same comment should be made about the possible role of the ICJ, or at least of arbitration. As such, there is no arbitration without the consent of both parties, which in domestic law at least constitutes the most basic difference between arbitration and judicial settlement. But in international law consent is also needed in the latter case, even if it is not for the parties to decide on the administrative, statutory, or procedural issues relating to the functioning of the tribunal. It is quite interesting in that respect to notice that, according to Article 66 of the 1969 Vienna Convention, resorting to the ICJ is seen as the 'normal' procedure in case of disputes concerning *jus cogens*. This should remind us that, in many domestic laws, arbitration is not permitted when '*ordre public*' (*jus cogens)* issues are concerned. It should then be clarified that issues concerning public policy (*jus cogens)* are always difficult, and raise questions the interest of which goes beyond the 'private' expectations of the parties. It is fully understandable consequently that the international 'judge' (ICJ) be preferred to the arbitrator as far as *jus cogens* requirements are concerned. But it does not change anything in relation to the fact that judges, just like arbitrators, need to be approved by the states concerned. Article 66 of the Vienna Convention is nothing but a clause by which states agree to accept judicial settlement in matters relating to a dispute raising validity issues involving the *jus cogens*. Clearly, it is immaterial in that regard whether the state concerned should or should not be a party to the Vienna Convention. Quite the contrary. But it helps to affirm that such litigation should one day be reserved for judicial settlement only, independently from any agreement of the parties... simply because it is necessarily questioning the idea of an '*intérêt général*', as uncertain as it might still be, whose determination should be kept within the hands of the most qualified servants of a still stammering international 'community'. Which is not for the immediate future.

Whatever the opinions in that respect may be, it is still important to emphasize that an element of jurisdictional settlement, be it arbitral or judicial, is introduced, which is binding at least on each state party to the 1969 Vienna Convention. A choice is offered between the ICJ and arbitration, but the state could not refuse both. Such a choice is, however, not the classical one, between diplomacy and jurisdictional settlement; both terms of the alternative are jurisdictional: arbitration or judicial settlement, at least as far as *jus cogens* is concerned. Could it nevertheless be refused? In other words, would it be possible for states, when becoming parties to the Vienna Convention, to make a reservation about Article 66 so as to exclude any intervention of the ICJ? Why not, in principle?[23] But accepting such a reservation would result also in greatly weakening the arbitration, since it is, according to Article 66, the only way of avoiding the unilateral submission to the ICJ. In other words, that reservation, even if it is aimed at the ICJ only, will inevitably result in also rendering the recourse to arbitration purely facultative.

That said, the 1969 Vienna Convention remains silent concerning possible reservations to its provisions. Reservations should therefore be admitted as long as they are compatible with the object and purpose of those provisions, according to its Article 19. The provision is indeed considered today, and probably was considered at the time of the adoption of the Vienna Convention, as largely expressing general rules binding on states independently of any formal acceptance on their part.

The question is consequently quite simple: should it be considered incompatible with its object or purpose that a reservation is made with regard to Articles 65 and 66, at least as far as the 1969 Convention is concerned? Clearly no reservation could be made to Article 33 of the UN Charter, as referred to in Article 65(3). But there is nothing to suggest that reservations should be excluded as far as other procedural technicalities are concerned. What about Article 66, which is concerned with methods of settling disputes rather than with procedure as such? Resort to the special conciliation techniques aimed at in Article 66(b) would surely be very useful; but it is still difficult to view it as essential to the object and purpose of the Vienna Convention, so as to invalidate any contradictory reservation. And finally, what about Article 66(a), providing for recourse to the ICJ or to arbitration when the application or interpretation of *jus cogens* (Articles 53 and 64) is at stake? As far as domestic laws are concerned, there is probably a kind of intimacy between invalidity issues and judicial settlement when the parties are in disagreement in that respect, and especially when '*ordre public*' (public policy) is concerned. The point was previously emphasized. Is that sufficient to invalidate such a reservation to Article 66(a), as being incompatible with the object and purpose of the codification of the law on treaties? Probably not. Judicial settlement is surely important, especially when very delicate issues are in dispute—as for instance the existence of a kind of '*intérêt général*' within the community of nations; but it is not as essential as invalidating a refusal to accept

[23] It should be even more readily accepted that Article 66 constitutes 'a formidable deterrent to ratification', as pointed out by G. Gaja ('Jus Cogens beyond the Vienna Convention', 172 *Recueil des Cours* (1981-III) 289), who is, however, concerned not be seen as 'too pessimistic' about the success of the Convention in that regard; see also M. Virally, 'Panorama du droit international contemporain', 183 *Recueil des Cours* (1983-V) 175.

a judicial settlement which is clearly not compulsory under present international law. Regrettably, the role of the judge is still so limited in international relations that it would be difficult to assert, *de lege lata*, the invalidity of a reservation to Article 66 setting aside the ICJ,[24] the arbitration itself being only 'obligatory' within Article 66 to the extent that states agree not to submit their dispute to the ICJ. Should it be recalled in that respect that reservations concerning its very intervention were admitted by the ICJ in relation to such basic issues as preventing and punishing genocide?[25] No doubt, as the case dates back to the immediate post-war period, at the time it was crucial to avoid deepening a fast-growing gap between eastern and western countries. And the attachment to human rights was relatively new, which is not at all to suggest that the ICJ was in any way neglectful at that time of the horror of the crime and the importance of its punishment. Actually, voices within the ICJ have recently been heard affirming, at least implicitly, that the decision could be different, should the issue be brought anew, one way or another, before the Court.[26] Would such a change in the case law of the ICJ in relation to genocide endanger the validity of reservations made to Article 66 of the Vienna Convention? The conclusion is doubtful. Failing at least exceptional circumstances, claims related to the validity of a treaty cannot be equated with problems of application of treaties whose specific purpose is to prevent and punish the most serious international crimes.

But objections to such a reservation should be accepted, in accordance with Article 20(4) of the Vienna Convention. Nothing, indeed, could exclude such objections being made in relation to Article 66, the consequences of which are specified in Article 21 of the Convention. The interesting point, however, is that many contracting states obviously are not satisfied with them. And they consequently declare, even in advance, ie before any reservation was made, that they will not be bound by Article 53 if resort to the ICJ or arbitration is not accepted under Article 66.[27] This kind of counter-reservation clearly emphasizes the importance of judicial settlement when the validity of a treaty is disputed. And it should also be noticed that no reservation to Article 53 was ever made directly, ie independently from Article 66. This point highlights the fact that the problem lies not in the *jus cogens* as such, but only in the decisive role conferred on the judge (arbitrator) when there is a disagreement between the parties as to its actual

[24] 'Doubts' were nevertheless often expressed as regards the validity of such reservation, the justifications for which remain unclear (see, for instance, A. Remiro Bretons *et al.*, *Derecho internacional* (Valencia: Preliminares Editorial Tirant Lo Blanche, 2007) 75).

[25] See the well-known *Reservations to the Convention on the Prevention and Punishment of the Crime of Genocide*, Advisory Opinion of 28 May 1951, *ICJ Reports* (1951) 496.

[26] See the Joint Separate Opinion of Judges Higgins, Kooijmans, Elaraby, Owada, and Simma (para. 6 *et seq.*) in the case concerning *Armed activities on the territory of the Congo (new application: 2002) (Democratic Republic of the Congo v Rwanda), Jurisdiction and Admissibility*, Judgment of 3 February 2006, *ICJ Reports* (2006) at 66 *et seq.*

[27] See M. Villiger, *Commentary on the 1969 Vienna Convention on the Law of Treaties*, *supra* note 12, at 822–3.

content. That said, the fact is still that *jus cogens* cannot be refused either directly, ie via a reservation to Article 53,[28] or indirectly, ie via a reservation to Article 66. Both reservations should be considered as null and void. Affirming the contrary would be misjudging the very nature of a peremptory norm. In other words, a mechanism whose specific aim is to consolidate a rule by prohibiting unilateral or conventional derogation is the first provision to which no reservation could ever be raised.[29]

2.2. *Locus Standi*

Whatever the mechanism that should or could be used to get a decision on validity/nullity might be, it is still to be decided which persons (states) would be entitled to bring a claim in this respect. Politically speaking, any state which feels concerned might raise the case, at its own political risk. But it is clearly another issue to determine who is legally entitled to bring proceedings before a court.

As a far as defaults in consent are concerned, it is normally for the state whose consent was defective to bring the claim. The Vienna Convention is quite clear in that respect as far as lack of competence (Articles 46–47), error (Article 48), fraud (Article 49), corruption (Article 50), and coercion of a representative of a state (Article 51) are concerned. This is elementary law. Indeed, how could a state whose consent was not vitiated assert that such consent to the treaty was invalid? There is nothing 'new' in that regard.

If a difficulty exists, it is in relation to Articles 52 and 53. In both cases, the treaty is said to be 'void', without any indication as to the state entitled to claim the invalidity, which is somewhat surprising.

As far as Article 52 is concerned, the state which was coerced clearly has a claim. The contrary would be surprising. But should it be inferred from the wording of Article 52 ('a treaty is void') that any other contracting party could also bring a claim in invalidity before a judge or an arbitrator, or whatever other body. The conclusion would be sound if that other party was also a victim of the coercion. But if it was not, what could support its assertion that its consent to the treaty should be nullified? A contrary conclusion would be difficult to reconcile with general principles of law regarding the legal consequences of a '*vice du consentement*'.

The difference between Article 52 (coercion by force) and Article 53 (*jus cogens*) is clearly that what was agreed on by the contracting parties is, as such, contrary to peremptory norms, in such a way that all of them should necessarily be allowed

[28] Cf. however B. Conforti, 'Cours général de droit international public', 212 *Recueil des Cours* (1988-V) 134.

[29] See J. Verhoeven, 'Jus Cogens and Reservations or "Counter-Reservations" to the Jurisdiction of the ICJ', in K. Wellens (ed.), *International Law in Theory and Practice—Essays in Honour of Eric Suy* (The Hague: Martinus Nijhoff, 1998) 195 *et seq.*; H. Ruiz-Fabri, 'Article 66', in *Commentaire, supra* note 6, at 2410 *et seq.*

to claim the invalidity of what they agreed in common, and possibly could be blamed for not doing so, ie for maintaining a situation which is incompatible with basic requirements of inter-state relations. The formula 'a treaty is void' is quite correct in that respect. Actually, the real issue would be to decide whether a non-contracting state could have a claim in this respect, ie could bring proceedings so as to obtain the judicial finding that a treaty to which it is not a party is null and void. Until now this has been an open issue. Even if the existence of an *actio popularis* is generally denied,[30] it cannot be categorically excluded.[31] At least, it is not explicitly ruled out either by the Vienna Convention or by the general (judicial) practice, despite the reluctance sometimes expressed by the ICJ in that regard. It would clearly be better to entrust some common body, within the UN or elsewhere, with the task of provoking judicial control of treaties when serious doubts exist about their compatibility with *jus cogens*, at least when the contracting parties remain silent in that respect. However, that eventuality, which would open up new possibilities of controlling the respect of basic requirements, is for the time being too 'new' to have a reasonable chance of being accepted. And as such it is in any case much more concerned with judicial issues, especially the '*locus standi*' (*intérêt pour agir*) requirements than with the law of treaties.

That said, the state, supposing it has a claim, loses its right to invoke 'a ground for invalidating [...] a treaty under article 46 to 50' if either it has expressly agreed to its validity or 'must by reason of its conduct be considered as having acquiesced in' it (Article 45). It has been pointed out that the provision rests on customary practice, which is problematic in the absence of clear cases where the validity of treaties was seriously questioned. But that provision is without doubt expressing general law simply because what is a stake in Article 46 to 50 is only the private interest of the state concerned, which is quite free to take in that respect whatever decision it deems appropriate. It does not matter whether this is explicitly or tacitly expressed, provided it is certain. But it is worth noting that the 'loss' aimed at in Article 45 is excluded when coercion or *jus cogens* (Article 53) is at stake. As far as *jus cogens* is concerned, the conclusion is easily understandable: how could a state indirectly validate—by losing its right to claim the invalidity—a treaty directly conflicting with peremptory norms of international law? This is pure 'logic'. There is no need for customary support to validate the conclusion. But the conclusion is much more doubtful as far as coercion is concerned, whether it is exercised on the representative of the state (Article 51)

[30] *Contra*, for instance, A. Cassese, *International Law* (Oxford: Oxford University Press, 2001) at 133, who refers to 'customary rules corresponding to the Vienna Convention's provisions on invalidity of treaties' whose affirmation is at least doubtful in the absence of any practice in that respect.

[31] As such the *actio popularis* is not at all 'illogical'; it is simply 'dangerous' in the present state of international relations. But there is no logic in admitting that, beyond the states parties to the treaty allegedly inconsistent with *jus cogens*, the parties to the 1969 Vienna Convention be admitted as having *locus standi* in that regard (see A. Orakhelashvili, *Peremptory Norms in International Law* (Oxford: Oxford University Press, 2006) 515).

or directly on the state itself (Article 52). In such a perspective the object of the treaty is as such irrelevant, the consent of the state only being concerned. The difficulty does not result from what was agreed on by the parties, but only from the circumstances under which they had agreed. Why should the confirmation of such consent be excluded, either by an explicit declaration or by unambiguous conduct? It has been said that violence radically corrupts any consent. The point surely is relevant for either the treaty itself, or its direct or indirect acceptance under Article 45.[32] But if such acceptance was not 'coerced' on the basis of either Article 51 or Article 52, why should it be inadmissible? The conclusion is possibly expressing a new and opportune legislative policy; at least for states not parties to the Vienna Convention; it should not, however, constitute binding provisions.

3. Effects

A void treaty is not (validly) binding on its contracting parties. That is the specific effect of invalidity. There should be no disagreement in that regard. But doubts still exist as to the legal meaning of that rule, ie on its exact consequences at law. That is partly due to often rather obscure distinctions between a 'relative' and an 'absolute' nullity, whose exact significance remains partly unclear.[33] Three aspects must be distinguished in that regard.

3.1. *Ratione Personae*

As such, the invalidity of the treaty only concerns the contracting states—all of them. When the consent of the state only is concerned, the nullity has no consequences for the parties who validly consented to the treaty. This goes without saying, as it goes without saying that the bilateral treaty will not even be binding on the state whose consent was valid, since there is no creditor or debtor with which it could still be engaged.

Nothing in the Vienna Convention suggests that the opposability of such nullity, be it of the treaty itself or of the consent of any of the contracting parties, might be restricted. Opposability should be the rule, since it logically results from the retrospective effect of invalidity. Should exceptions be admitted to a principle of opposability? Why not, in principle? At least national laws make clear that such exceptions might be justified, for instance to protect the possessor in good faith of a property. There is no reason to exclude similar exceptions as a matter of principle in public international law. The Vienna Convention is, however, silent in that respect, which makes it difficult to validate a 'creative' interpretation in that regard.

32 See M. Kohen, *supra* note 6, vol. II, at 1680.

33 See generally J. Verhoeven, 'Article 69', in *Commentaire, supra* note 6, vol. III, at 2483 *et seq.*

3.2. *Ratione Materiae*

The 'logic' normally is that the treaty 'disappears' as a whole when its invalidity is established. It would be inconsistent with its very nature if it were construed as an accumulation of separate agreements whose eventual invalidity had no consequences on the validity of the others. But the will of the parties should be decisive in that respect, as well as in relation to any other contractual issue. If the parties so agreed nothing should therefore prevent the treaty from being dismantled in such a way that some of its provisions disappear and the others survive. Such is only partly the approach followed by the Vienna Convention. The 'separability' of treaty provisions indeed appears to be admitted or refused on a mostly 'objective' basis, ie as far as the 'surviving' clauses either are, according to Article 44, 'separable from the remainder of the treaty with regard to their application', or did not constitute 'an essential basis of the consent of the other party or parties to be bound by the treaty as a whole', and provided 'continued performance of the remainder of the treaty would not be unjust' (para. 3). No separation, however, is permitted where coercion (Articles 51 and 52) or *jus cogens* (Article 53) are concerned, the decision to accept or refuse separation being left to the state concerned in case of fraud or corruption (Articles 49 and 50).

Up to now, there has been no customary practice clearly supporting either the principle of separability or the circumstances/conditions under which it could be accepted/refused. And it is doubtful that this rather complex regulation of the separability of treaty provisions as far as invalidity is concerned could be vested in a general principle of law, ie on domestic legal practices. Does this mean that the Vienna Convention is formulating 'new' law in that regard? Possibly, at least to a certain extent. The separability is, as such, justified by the necessity to safeguard, if possible, part of what was agreed upon by the parties. The concern is particularly important in international law, since most of its rules are of a conventional origin. The role of customary (general) law is indeed limited, especially in the divided world inherited from the cold war—apart from any other 'social' considerations— and in a context of growing technicalities which could not easily be regulated by purely customary practices. It is easily understandable in such a context that the parties, and beyond them the international community, are concerned with avoiding the destruction of the whole of what was agreed upon by them, ie to limit the consequences of invalidity to its core effects.[34] Actually, the concern is not specific to the international community. In domestic laws also, such a concern has been manifest. But the decisive factor in that regard is apparently the will of the parties, without any other 'objective' consideration. Consequently, the nullity of a contractual provision does not result in invalidating the whole of the treaty when that provision was not the fundamental basis for consent. Other factors are usually not taken into consideration in that respect, and, in particular,

[34] To that extent, invalidity is still a kind of 'luxury' in international law (see J. Verhoeven, 'Les nullités du droit des gens', in IHEI, *Droit international 1* (Paris: Pedone, 1981) 47).

no reference is made to a requirement of 'justice' as mentioned in Article 44(3)(c) of the Vienna Convention, whose terms are actually rather mysterious, or at least permit a variety of conclusions. With that reservation, separability as a principle could probably be considered as a general principle of law, much more at least than as a customary provision. And it should not consequently be considered as a 'new' law binding only the contracting parties. But it would still be difficult to back up most of its technical specifications, as resulting from paragraphs 3 to 5, with convincing references to either customary practices or the convergent national solutions which are in theory necessary to support the existence of a general principle of law.

3.3. *Ratione Temporis*

It is characteristic of the invalidity that it draws consequences from a defect in the treaty existing at the time of its conclusion. It cannot be confused in that respect with termination or suspension, which rests on factual elements, including the will of the parties, appearing after its conclusion.

Consequently, nullity operates *ex tunc* while termination (suspension) operates *ex nunc*. In other words, the retrospective effect is specific to the invalidity. There should be no disagreement in this regard. True, largely unclear distinctions were made, during the debates of the International Law Commission, between a treaty which is void *ab initio* and one which would become voidable at a certain date, as if it suddenly ceased to be valid although it had originally been so. There does not appear to be any firm basis for such a distinction. And Article 64, according to which 'if a new peremptory norm of general international law emerges, any existing treaty which is in conflict with that norm becomes void and terminates' is highly critical in that respect, the specific effect of such new norm being clearly to put an end to the application of the treaty without questioning as such its validity at the time the new peremptory norm did not yet exist, or at least was not of a (*jus cogens*) character.

Strangely enough, the retrospective (retroactive) effect of the invalidity is not expressly mentioned in Article 69 of the Vienna Convention, dealing with the consequences of the invalidity. However, it results to a certain extent from paragraph 2 thereof, the specific *raison d'être* of which is to limit such retroactivity 'if acts have nevertheless been performed in reliance on a void treaty. That is a classical difficulty, with which every domestic law has been confronted. According to the Vienna Convention, a party must only 'establish as far as possible' the situation which would have existed in its relations with other parties, had such acts not been performed. But such an obligation only exists if the state is so required by a contracting party (Article 69(2)(a)), the situation of other contracting parties remaining unchanged as long as no similar request is made on their part. It does not matter, apparently, whether those acts were performed in good or in bad faith; but if good faith is established, they 'are not rendered unlawful by reason only of the invalidity' (Article 69(2)(b)). Such mitigation of the consequences of the invalidity does not apply, however, in case of fraud, corruption, or coercion as far as the party to which it is imputable is concerned. And apparently it does not apply either when the invalidity results from the violation of *jus cogens*, the parties being only required to 'eliminate as far as possible the consequences of any act performed in reliance on any provision which conflicts with the peremptory norm' (Article 71). No request from another contracting party is needed in such a case; nor is any attention paid to good or bad faith, which has the concrete result that bad faith must always be presumed.

Does such a determination of the consequences of the invalidity of a treaty express existing law or does it constitute 'new' law? Once again, no clear support exists in a practice almost inexistent in that regard. Could the solutions of the articles nevertheless be generalized, ie be considered as binding even to states not being parties to the Vienna Conventions on the basis of either general principles of law or at least some intrinsic 'logic' of law? The difficulty probably is that the provisions of the 1969 Vienna Convention remain largely unclear, apart from certain obvious points, and this makes any attempt to generalize that content problematic. Certainly, any treaty—as a legal act—could only be binding if the basic requirements imposed by law to that end are satisfied. But that does not prejudge the exact consequences resulting from their violation. Article 69 is especially cautious, as is made clear by the repeated reference to 'as far as possible'. No doubt, '*à l'impossible, nul n'est [ne saurait être] tenu*'. But not many impossibilities actually exist as far as states are concerned. When they are of a legal nature, the adoption of a statute (act) or judgment could indeed remedy most of the 'impossible' situations. And the Problem is generally of a purely financial character when it is not a factual one... but the hypothesis cannot be totally excluded. In some cases, it will surely appear that the consequences of an act performed in reliance on a void treaty cannot be 'eliminated', which validates the cautious terms of both articles. It is interesting, however, to notice in that regard that Articles 69 and 71 remain silent on the consequences of such impossibility. That is somewhat disturbing. Should it be admitted that there is no consequence, it would be difficult to distinguish invalidity from termination. In domestic law, some financial compensation at least is ordinarily due in that case. No mention, however, is made of such an obligation—or any other obligation—in the Vienna Conventions.

The point as such does not raise a question of responsibility; it is only to find an acceptable substitute, as far as possible, to the impossibility of re-establishing the situation which would have existed had the relevant acts not been performed in reliance on a (later declared) void treaty. That said, it is quite possible that a question of responsibility may be raised in relation to the invalidity (invalidation) of a treaty. It is certainly the case when the ground of invalidity rests on a breach of international law, as for instance in case of coercion under Article 52 or violation of the *jus cogens* (Article 53). Needless to say, such a violation necessarily entails for its perpetrator a duty to give reparation for the detrimental consequences of its conduct. But invalidity as such is not part of the reparation; it is only a way of limiting the damage for which reparation is due. It does not matter in that respect that, according to Article 69(2)(b) of the Vienna Convention, acts performed in good faith before the invalidity of the treaty was invoked are not 'rendered unlawful by reason only' of that invalidity. As a matter of principle indeed, reparation should be due not only for the illegal conduct on which that invalidity is grounded, but also for all its consequences, even those which are not illegal *per se*, when their detrimental character is established.

19

Coercion as a Ground Affecting the Validity of Peace Treaties

Serena Forlati

1. The Rule on Coercion Established by Article 52 of the Vienna Convention

According to Article 52 of the Vienna Convention on the Law of Treaties, '[a] treaty is void if its conclusion has been procured by the threat or use of force in violation of the principles of international law embodied in the Charter of the United Nations'.

Conflicting views were taken at the Vienna Conference over the precise scope of prohibited coercion: the issue is inextricably linked to the interpretation not only of Article 2(4) of the UN Charter, but also of the customary rules pertaining to the use of force,[1] whose content and relationship to the Charter principles are among the most controversial aspects of contemporary international law. Nevertheless, Article 52 (Article 49 of the draft) was adopted by a broad majority and with no negative vote, since it was seen as a 'logical consequence' of the prohibition of the use of force,[2] based on the principle *ex iniuria ius non oritur*.

The specific regime established by other rules of the Vienna Convention, such as Articles 44 and 45, makes it clear that such a ground of 'absolute invalidity' is seen not only as a means of safeguarding freedom of consent in the conclusion of treaties, but also as a 'sanction',[3] insofar as it aims at ensuring reparation for the unlawful act that is at the origin of the invalid treaty.[4]

[1] See T.O. Elias, 'Problems Concerning the Validity of Treaties', 134 *Recueil des Cours* (1971-III) at 387.

[2] R. Ago, 'Droit des Traités et Convention de Vienne', 134 *Recueil des Cours* (1971-III) at 319.

[3] See M. Bothe, 'Consequences of the Prohibition of the Use of Force', 27 *ZaöRV* (1967) at 508; P. Reuter, *Introduction au droit des traités* (Paris: Librairie Armand Colin, 1972) at 172 and 175; P.M. Dupuy, 'Droit des traités, codification et responsabilité internationale', 43 *AFDI* (1997) at 14; O. Corten, 'Article 52—Convention de 1969', in O. Corten and P. Klein (eds), *Les Conventions de Vienne sur le droit des traités—Commentaire Article par Article* (Bruxelles: Bruylant, 2006) vol. II, at 1869. On the relationship between invalidity and *restitutio in integrum* see also P. Guggenheim, 'La validité et la nullité des actes juridiques internationaux', 74 *Recueil des Cours* (1949-I) at 239.

[4] A number of provisions of the Vienna Convention share the function of ensuring cessation of internationally wrongful acts and reparation. For an overall appraisal see S. Forlati, *Diritto dei trattati e responsabilità internazionale* (Milano: Giuffré, 2005).

Several participants to the Vienna Conference stressed the paramount importance of Article 52. France, for instance, voted against what is now Article 53, abstained on the other articles concerning the invalidity of treaties, and did not sign the Convention. However, it voted in favour of draft Article 49 since 'it attached the highest importance to the principle that there should be no resort to force in international relations'.[5] Furthermore, the abstaining states emphasized their opposition to 'coercion of states by the threat or use of force'.[6] Their decision was explained with reference to the potentially destabilizing effect of Article 52 on treaty relations.[7] Stability of peace treaties was a specific reason of concern,[8] notwithstanding the fact that, according to both the International Law Commission (ILC) and the Vienna Conference, Article 52 could apply to such treaties only under very strict conditions. As to the time element, the ILC acknowledged that 'there is no question of the article having retroactive effects on the validity of treaties concluded prior to the establishment of the modern law' regarding the threat or use of force;[9] while avoiding any precise indication in this respect, the Commission held that the rule concerning coercion on a state 'is applicable at any rate to all treaties concluded since the entry into force of the Charter'.[10] Moreover, the wording of Article 52 and the ILC 1966 Commentary make it clear that only unlawful recourse to force might give rise to this ground of invalidity: peace treaties imposed by the victim of an aggression, or after recourse to force is decided by the Security Council in the exercise of its powers under Chapter VII, do not fall within the scope of Article 52.[11]

[5] See the statement of the French delegate, Hubert, at 18th plenary meeting, 9 May 1969, United Nations Conference on the Law of Treaties, *Official Records*, vol. II, at 92, para. 78. See also the statements of the delegates of Ecuador, Escudero (ibid., at 90, para. 65); Cyprus (ibid., at 91, para. 73); Chile (ibid., at 92, para. 75); Turkey (ibid., at 92, para. 79); and Bolivia (ibid., at 93, para. 2).

[6] See the statement of the Swiss delegate, Bindschedler, ibid., at 91, para. 72.

[7] eg, the Swiss delegate justified as follows the decision to abstain: 'his delegation [...] like the United Kingdom delegation, [...] doubted whether the principle set forth in that article was in accordance with the teachings of history and [...] its adoption might endanger the stability of the entire system of international law'.

[8] See the discussion by the Swiss delegate of the amendment aimed at applying current Article 45 to coerced treaties. The amendment was proposed by Switzerland and rejected by the Conference at the 67th meeting of the Committee of the Whole, 13 May 1968: United Nations Conference on the Law of Treaties, *Official Records*, vol. I, at 395, para. 26, and 401, para. 116.

[9] ILC, 'Report on the work of its eighteenth session', *YILC* (1966), vol. II, at 247, para. 7. Cf. T.O. Elias, 'The Validity of Treaties', *supra* note 1, at 382–3.

[10] ILC, 'Report on the work of its eighteenth session', *supra* note 9, at 247, para. 8. On the caution used by the International Law Commission as regards determination of the scope of the prohibition of the use of force see P. Palchetti, 'The ILC and Customary Rules on the Use of Force', in E. Cannizzaro and P. Palchetti (eds), *Customary International Law on the Use of Force* (The Hague: Brill, 2005) at 237.

[11] See O. Corten, 'Article 52', *supra* note 3, at 1885; A. Aust, *Modern Treaty Law and Practice*, (Cambridge: Cambridge University Press, 2nd edn, 2007) at 256–7; M.E. Villiger, *Commentary on the 1969 Vienna Convention on the Law of Treaties* (Leiden-Boston: Nijhoff, 2009) at 643.

Even beyond these express limits, however, coercion has had virtually no practical role as a ground of invalidity of peace treaties[12] after the adoption of the Vienna Convention. This phenomenon cannot be ascribed only to the overall lack of effectiveness of the rule enshrined in Article 52, or of the prohibition on the use of force upon which it is based.[13] Breaches of the latter rule have often been alleged by states and, in some cases, were the object of third-party assessment, including by international judicial bodies; this has helped to clarify at least some aspects of the relevant legal regime.[14] No comparable developments occurred as regards the 'logical corollary' we are dealing with here.

2. Practice after 1969

Some elements of international practice have confirmed, expressly or by implication, that Article 52 does reflect customary international law. A corresponding text is now incorporated in Article 52 of the 1986 Convention on Treaties concluded by International Organizations, which was adopted without vote; in discussing this provision within the International Law Commission no doubt was cast as to the existence of the principle according to which treaties concluded on grounds of coercion are void.[15]

As regards judicial practice, in the *Fisheries Jurisdiction* cases the International Court of Justice maintained: 'there can be little doubt, as is implied in the Charter of the United Nations and recognized in Article 52 of the Vienna

[12] This wording is used here with reference to international agreements aimed at terminating armed conflicts, even if they are not formally denominated as peace treaties: indeed, the distinction between peace treaties and other agreements on the cessation of hostilities such as ceasefires or armistices has lost much of its relevance after 1945. See C. Greenwood, 'Scope of Application of Humanitarian Law', in D. Fleck (ed.), *The Handbook of International Humanitarian Law* (Oxford: Oxford University Press, 2nd edn, 2009) at 67 *et seq.*; A. Gattini, *Le riparazioni di guerra nel diritto internazionale* (Padova: CEDAM, 2003) at 473 *et seq.*

[13] R.L. Bindschedler, 'Völkerrechtliche Verträge und Zwang', 21 *Rev. Esp.de Derecho Internac.* (1968) 309, at 310 and 313; J. Stone, '*De Victoribus Victis*: The International Law Commission and Imposed Treaties of Peace', 8 *Va. J Int'l. L* (1967–68) at 356. This opinion is shared by G. Gaja, 'Trattati internazionali', *Digesto delle Discipline Pubblicistiche* (Torino: UTET, 1999) vol. XV, at 360.

[14] As regards the last decade, cf. ICJ judgments in the cases of the *Oil Platforms (Islamic Republic of Iran v United States of America)*, Judgment of 6 November 2003, *ICJ Reports* (2003) at 161 and *Armed Activities on the Territory of the Congo (Democratic Republic of the Congo v Uganda)*, Judgment of 19 December 2005, ibid. (2005) at 168, as well as its Advisory Opinion concerning the *Legal Consequences of the Construction of a Wall in the Occupied Palestinian Territory*, of 9 July 2004, *ibid.* (2004) at 136; see also the award issued by the Eritrea–Ethiopia Claims Commission on 19 December 2005, *Partial Award,* Jus ad Bellum, *Ethiopia's Claims 1–8*, para. 17, 45 *ILM* (2006) 430.

[15] The debate focused rather on the practical relevance of this principle for international organizations: see the Commentary to draft Article 52, *YILC* (1982), vol. II(2) 17, at 55–6, paras 2 and 8. See further O. Corten, 'Article 52–Convention de 1986', in O. Corten and P. Klein (eds), *Les Conventions de Vienne*, *supra* note 3, 1901, at 1902.

Convention on the Law of Treaties, that under contemporary international law an agreement concluded under the threat or use of force is void'.[16] More recently, the judgment concerning the *Territorial and Maritime Dispute (Nicaragua v Colombia)*,[17] while not addressing the merits of the contention submitted by Nicaragua as regards the invalidity the 1928 bilateral Treaty concerning Territorial Questions at Issue between Colombia and Nicaragua on grounds of coercion, implicitly confirmed the customary nature of this rule, which is further upheld by some arbitral tribunals. For example, according to the *Dubai-Sharjah Border Arbitration* award, 'Articles 51 and 52 of the Vienna Convention of 1969 reflect [. . .] customary rules of international law which are binding upon States even in the absence of any ratification of that Convention.'[18] Coercion was not held to have actually taken place in the abovementioned cases, but in a few instances states and national courts have assessed the invalidity of treaties on this ground. The main example in this respect concerns the 1938 Munich Agreements and the German–Czechoslovak Nationality Treaty that was concluded on that basis;[19] more recently, a similar stance was taken by the Latvian Constitutional Court as regards the consent given by Latvia to the

[16] ICJ, *Fisheries Jurisdiction (Federal Republic of Germany v Iceland)*, Jurisdiction, Judgment of 2 February 1973, *ICJ Reports* (1973) 49, at 59, para. 24.

[17] *Territorial and Maritime Dispute (Nicaragua v Colombia)*, Preliminary Objections, Judgment of 13 December 2007, *ICJ Reports* (2007) 832. According to the Court, 'Nicaragua cannot today be heard to assert that the 1928 Treaty was not in force in 1948'; furthermore, 'the 1928 Treaty was valid and in force on the date of the conclusion of the Pact of Bogotá', which therefore could not apply as a basis for the Court's jurisdiction (at 859 paras 80–81). This approach is not completely straightforward, since neither the possible role of the rule enshrined in Article 45 of the Vienna Convention nor the moment at which coercion became a ground invalidating consent in international law are discussed in any way. For a critical appraisal in this respect see the Declaration of Judge Simma, at 2, the Separate Opinion of Judge Abraham, paras 45–46, as well as the Dissenting Opinions of Vice-President Al-Khasawneh, paras 5–6, and Judge Bennouna, at 2–5. See F. Vincenzetti, 'Sull'ambito di applicazione *ratione temporis* del vizio di violenza nei trattati', 91 *Riv. di Diritto Internaz.* (2008) 806.

[18] *Dubai-Sharjah Border Arbitration*, Award of 19 October 1981, 91 *ILR* (1981) 543, at 569. See also Iran–US Claims Tribunal, *Amoco International Finance Corporation v Government of the Islamic Republic of Iran, National Iranian Oil Company, National Petrochemical Company and Kharg Chemical Company*, Partial Award of 14 July 1987, n. 310-56-3, 15 *Iran-US CTR* (1987-II) 189, at 215, para. 91.

[19] See, eg, District Court of the Hague, *Amato Narodni Podnik v Julius Keilwerth Musikinstrumentenfabrik*, 31 December 1955-11 November 1956, 24 *ILR* (1957) 437; cf. B. Conforti and A. Labella, 'Invalidity and Termination of Treaties: the Role of National Courts', 1 *EJIL* (1990) 44, at 51. The invalidity of the 1938 Munich Agreement on grounds of coercion was discussed, but not decided upon, by the Supreme Court of Bavaria in *Land Registry of Waldsassen v the Towns of Eger (Cheb) and Waldsassen*, 23 March 1965, 44 *ILR* (1972) 50, at 55; it was, however, formally acknowledged by the Federal Republic of Germany through the Treaty Establishing Normal Relations between Czechoslovakia and the Federal Republic of Germany, Prague, 11 December 1973, 13 *ILM* (1974) 19. See G. Napoletano, *Violenza e trattati nel diritto internazionale* (Milano: Giuffré, 1975) at 310 and 397 *et seq.*; S.S. Malawer, 'Imposed Treaties', 7 *California Western International Law Journal* (1977) 1 *et seq.*, at 100, 152–4.

occupation by USSR forces in 1940.[20] Moreover, the illegality of the military intervention that forced Czechoslovakia to accept the Treaty on the Temporary Sojourn of Soviet Forces in the Territory of the Czechoslovak Socialist Republic of 16 October 1968[21] was acknowledged by the USSR after the abandonment of the 'Breznev doctrine'.[22]

This practice is not widespread, and is qualified by the fact that formal recognition of the illegal coercion could take place only after overcoming the political and military scenario that brought it about.[23] Still, it may be enough in order to conclude that Article 52 of the Vienna Convention is not merely a statement of principle. It should be noted, however, that coercion, sometimes originating from a state that did not take part to the negotiations,[24] has been invoked mostly as regards situations in which the ground of alleged invalidity consisted in the threat of recourse to force,[25] or, in any case, where no military conflict had taken

[20] Latvian Constitutional Court, *Kariņš and Others v Parliament of Latvia and Cabinet of Ministers of Latvia, and joined case, Constitutional review*, Case No. 2007-10-0102, 29 November 2007, *Oxford Reports on International Law (ILDC)* 884, at 25. The Constitutional Court relies on the statement of the relavant facts by the European Court of Human Rights in *Ždanoka v Latvia*, Grand Chamber Judgment of 16 March 2006, Application No. 58278/00, paras 12–13, and thus seems to aim at avoiding allegations as to the biased character of the finding on invalidity. See in this respect B. Conforti and A. Labella, 'Invalidity and Termination of Treaties', *supra* note 19, at 52, especially note 14, quoting the judgment of the People's Court of Germany in the *German Nationality (Alsace-Lorraine)* case, 28 October 1940, *Annual Digest and Reports of Public International Law Cases (AD) (1919–1942)*, to the effect that the Treaty of Versailles was invalid. On this issue, also for further references, see E. Vitta, *La validité des traités* (Leiden: Brill, 1940) at 139 *et seq.*; Lord McNair, *The Law of Treaties*, (Oxford: Clarendon Press, 1961) at 209; G. Napoletano, *Violenza e trattati nel diritto internazionale, supra* note 19, at 321.

[21] 7 *ILM* (1968) 1334.

[22] *Keesing's* (1989) 36982. Upon dissolution of the Warsaw Pact the Soviet Union agreed to pay compensation to Czechoslovakia for the damage done to the country since the 1968 invasion: ibid. (1991) 38365.

[23] Cf. J. Stone, '*De victoribus victis*', *supra* note 13, at 357.

[24] The Vienna Convention clearly envisages this possibility. In the *Nicaragua v Colombia* case, Nicaragua disputed the validity of the 1928 bilateral Treaty *inter alia* because its consent was coerced due to the military occupation of the country by the United States: cf. the memorial of the government of Nicaragua, 28 April 2003, p. 116. Furthermore, coercion by the United Kingdom was alleged by Dubai in the *Dubai/Sharjah* case (*supra* note 18, at 568) and by Iran in connection with the 1937 Frontier Treaty with Iraq (cf. the Statement of the Deputy Minister of Foreign Affairs of Iran in the Senate, 19 April 1969, 8 *ILM* (1969) 481, at 483, which, however, discusses the issue only with reference to the *rebus sic stantibus* principle). See also the Peace Convention between France and Thailand, *infra* note 25.

[25] In this respect cf. the Peace Convention between France and Thailand of 9 May 1941, which was accepted by France because of Japanese threats of recourse to military coercion: see S. Hamamoto, 'Le sort d'un traité imposé: La Convention de paix entre la France et la Thailande conclue en 1941', 102 *RGDIP* (1998) at 958. A threat of recourse to armed force could be construed also with reference to the Rambouillet negotiations of 1999: see Y. Nouvel, 'La position du Conseil de Securité face à l'action militaire engagée par l'OTAN et ses Etats membres contre la République féderale de Yougoslavie', 45 *AFDI* (1999) 292, at 306; E. Decaux, 'La Conférence de Rambouillet: Négotiation de la dernière chanche ou contrainte illicite', in Ch. Tomuschat (ed.), *Kosovo and the International Community. A Legal Assessment.* (The Hague–London–New York: Kluwer, 2001) 45; N. Stürchler, *The Threat of Force in International Law* (Cambridge: Cambridge University Press, 2007) at 150 *et seq.* However, since the proposed Interim Agreement for Peace and Self-Government in Kosovo was not accepted by Serbia, Article 52 of the Vienna Convention does not come into play.

place.[26] As regards treaties aimed at ending armed conflicts, claims of invalidity on grounds of coercion are particularly rare.[27]

Beyond lack of effectiveness, some specific features of contemporary peace agreements are at the basis of this attitude. Peace treaties are governed, in principle, by the same international legal rules applying to other consensual bonds.[28]

Nevertheless, in many cases precisely the status of peace agreements as international legal instruments is doubtful, due to elements such as the presence of non-state entities among the signatories and the drafting of such agreements in terms that may not be legally binding or that place them at the crossroads between national and international law.[29]

Even when peace agreements can be construed as binding international legal instruments, states tend not to cast doubts as to their validity.

3. The Case of the *Armed Activities in the Territory of the Congo*

The case of the *Armed Activities in the Territory of the Congo (Congo v Uganda)* is illuminating in this respect. In that context, the Democratic Republic of the Congo (DRC) did discuss the possible invalidity of the Lusaka Ceasefire Agreement, which was concluded after the occupation of Congolese territory by Uganda. It should be noted, however, that the Congo used the argument in order to plead for a restrictive interpretation of the Ceasefire Agreement, rather than challenging its validity outright:[30] there was clearly an interest in implementing

[26] See the 1968 Treaty between Czechoslovakia and the USSR. Invalidity on grounds of coercion was suggested also as regards the Algiers Agreements, that put an end to the 1979 hostage crisis (cf. J.M. Redwine, 'The Effect of Duress on the Iranian Hostage Settlement Agreement', 14 *Vanderbilt Journal of Transnational Law* (1981) 847, at 859, especially note 94). However, the US administration did not raise the issue of their legally binding character: cf. 81 *Dep't St. Bull* (1981) at 17. In any case, it would be difficult to accept the contention that Iranian behaviour qualifies as 'use of force' within the meaning of the Charter.

[27] Coercion was alleged by Yemen as a ground of invalidity of the 1934 Taif Peace Treaty with Saudi Arabia, but the claim pertained to circumstances which occurred before the establishment of the United Nations, and was not recognized in the final settlement of the dispute concerning the land and maritime border between the two countries: cf. A.H. Al-Enazy, '"The International Boundary Treaty" (Treaty of Jeddah) Concluded Between the Kingdom of Saudi Arabia and the Yemeni Republic on June 12, 2000', 96 *AJIL* (2002) at 166–7.

[28] G. Schwarzenberger, 'Peace Treaties before International Courts and Tribunals', 8 *IJIL* (1968) 1.

[29] C. Bell, 'Peace Agreements: Their Nature and Legal Status', 100 *AJIL* (2006) 379; Ibid., *On the Law of Peace—Peace Agreements and Lex Pacificatoria* (Oxford: Oxford University Press, 2008) at 145. See also M. Starita, *Accordi di riconciliazione nazionale e diritto internazionale*, (Napoli: Jovene, 2003) 281 *et seq*. On non-binding agreeements see also J. Klabbers, *The Concept of Treaty in International Law* (The Hague: Kluwer, 1996) at 157 *et seq*.; H. Hillgenberg, 'A Fresh Look at Soft Law', 10 *EJIL* (1999) 499, at 501.

[30] Cf. the pleading of O. Corten at the hearing of 28 June 2000, CR 2000/24.

an instrument which, in any case, bound Uganda to a progressive disengagement of its troops.

This attitude can be viewed as a 'ratification' of the agreement, as interpreted by the DRC. As noted above, however, Article 45 of the Vienna Convention does not apply to coercion.[31] According to the ILC, acceptance of the content of a coerced treaty would be possible only 'by the conclusion of a new treaty and not by the recognition of the validity of a treaty' procured through coercion.[32]

The Court did not discuss this problem, nor did it hint at the possible invalidity of the agreement. It confined itself to holding that the DRC 'did not thereby recognize the situation on the ground as legal, either before the Lusaka Agreement or in the period that would pass until the fulfillment of its terms'.[33] According to some commentators, this approach implies 'treating the Lusaka Agreement as a political instrument for the settlement of the conflict with no distinct legal consequences for the intervening states'.[34] Nevertheless, both the DRC and Uganda relied on the agreement as a legally binding instrument:[35] this would make it difficult for the Court to consider it as a merely political engagement. Moreover, the Court itself described the Lusaka Agreement as a 'treaty' elsewhere in the judgment,[36] and had qualified it as 'an international agreement binding upon the parties' in the order concerning provisional measures of 1 July 2000.[37] It may therefore be assumed that the Court interpreted the terms of the agreement in a restrictive way, in order to safeguard Congo's freedom of consent,[38] without denying its binding character.

[31] *Supra* note 17.

[32] ILC, 'Report on the work of its eighteenth session', *supra* note 9, at 247, para. 6. This seems to imply the necessity of a formal transposition of the content of the invalid treaty in another treaty, presumably in written form (in the light of Article 2(a) of the Vienna Convention).

[33] *Supra* note 14, para. 99.

[34] P.N. Okowa, 'Congo's War: The Legal Dimension of a Protracted Conflict', 77 *BYIL* (2006) 203, at 236. See also A. Lang, '"Modus Operandi" and the ICJ's Appraisal of the Lusaka Ceasefire Agreement in the *Armed Activities* Case: The Role of Peace Agreements in International Conflict Resolution', 40 *NYUJ of Int'l. L & Pol.* (2008) 107, at 113 and 115 *et seq.* DRC's counsel, O. Corten, does not shed much light on the issue when he states: 'la Cour reprend en substance l'interprétation défendue par le Congo', 'Article 52', *supra* note 3, at 1899, note 177.

[35] Uganda maintained that the Agreement 'establishes a comprehensive system of public order', and filed a counterclaim based on alleged breaches of the Agreement by the DRC. The counterclaim was declared to be inadmissible (*Armed Activities on the Territory of the Congo (Democratic Republic of the Congo v Uganda), Counter-Claims*, Order of 29 November 2001, *ICJ Reports* (2001) 660, at 680, para. 42).

[36] Para. 105 (the term is applied collectively also to the other instruments that subsequently modified the deadlines of the disengagement plan).

[37] ICJ, *Armed Activities on the Territory of the Congo (Democratic Republic of the Congo v Uganda), Provisional Measures*, Order of 1 July 2000, *ICJ Reports* (2000) 111, at 127, para. 37.

[38] Judicial practice concerning interpretation of peace treaties emphasizes the role of the defeated state's consent in this context: cf. G. Schwarzenberger, 'Peace Treaties', *supra* note 28, at 2 *et seq.*; S.S. Malawer, 'Imposed Treaties', *supra* note 19, at 142 *et seq.*

Undoubtedly, this interpretation also allowed the Court to avoid any conflict with the position taken by the Security Council, that had endorsed the Lusaka Agreement as 'the most viable basis for a resolution of the conflict',[39] and, acting under Chapter VII of the Charter, called upon all the parties to fulfil it.[40] Whereas the Security Council's support for the agreement could not, *per se*, preclude a finding of invalidity by the Court,[41] the latter is usually cautious in addressing issues related to the use of force when this may lead to interference with the action of the Security Council.[42]

4. The Role of the Security Council

The Security Council is entrusted with a key role in ensuring respect for the principles underlying Article 52 of the Vienna Convention.[43] As recalled above, the use of force under its authority does not fall within the scope of this provision, nor of the corresponding customary rule. However, the Security Council's action bears a wider influence on their implementation. Article 75 of the Convention stipulates that its provisions 'are without prejudice to any obligation in relation to a treaty which may arise for an aggressor state in consequence of measures taken in conformity with the Charter of the United Nations with reference to that state's aggression'. This prescription confirms that decisions of the Security Council under Chapter VII of the Charter, setting forth peace conditions as regards an aggressor state, are unfettered by Article 52.[44]

Whereas the Security Council often proves unable to react effectively to breaches of Article 2(4) of the Charter, it does play a crucial role in ending armed

[39] Security Council resolution 1279 (1999).

[40] Security Council resolution 1304 (2000).

[41] On the relationship between the Security Council and the International Court of Justice see, among many others, M. Bedjaoui, *Nouvel ordre mondial et contrôle de la légalité des actes du Conseil de sécurité* (Bruylant: Bruxelles, 1994); B. Martenczuk, 'The Security Council, the International Court and Judicial Review: What Lessons from Lockerbie?', 10 *EJIL* (1999) 517; R. Kolb, Ius contra bellum—*Le droit international relatif au mantien de la paix* (Bâle: Helbing & Lichtenhahn, 2003) at 144; E. Cannizzaro, 'A Machiavellian Moment? The Security Council and the Rule of Law', 3 *International Organization Law Review* (2006) 189, at 194; M.I. Papa, *I rapporti tra la Corte internazionale di giustizia e il Consiglio di sicurezza* (Padova: CEDAM, 2006).

[42] C. Gray, 'The Use and Abuse of the International Court of Justice: Cases Concerning the Use of Force after Nicaragua', 14 *EJIL* (2003) 867 *et seq*., at 904–5.

[43] The importance of the UN collective security system in ensuring its effective implementation was emphasized by the International Law Commission; cf. its Commentary to draft Article 49, *supra* note 9, at 246, para. 2. The role of the Security Council was specifically discussed by Special Rapporteur Waldock in the 683rd ILC meeting, *YILC* (1963), vol. I, at 61, para. 14.

[44] Cf. M. Bothe, 'Consequences', *supra* note 3, at 515; Ch. Tomuschat, 'Article 75—Convention de 1969', in O. Corten and P. Klein (eds), *Les Conventions de Vienne*, *supra* note 3, 2657, at 2669 and 2671; M.E. Villiger, *Commentary on the Vienna Convention*, *supra* note 11, at 915.

conflicts,[45] either by setting out peace conditions itself[46] or by endorsing peace agreements concluded by the interested parties, as in the case of the Congo War.[47] The legitimacy of this kind of measure is in principle uncontroversial,[48] as it is an inherent part of the functions entrusted to the Council under Article 24 of the Charter, and is not limited to cases of aggression.[49] Nevertheless, in some instances Security Council action raised very controversial issues as to the limits of its powers in this context. A significant example in this respect concerns resolution 1244(1999), which indirectly endorsed the Military Technical Agreement between the International Security Force (KFOR) and the governments of the Federal Republic of Yugoslavia (FRY) and the Republic of Serbia of 9 June 1999.[50] The validity of the agreement has been questioned in the light of Article 52 of the Vienna Convention;[51] some commentators have held that resolution 1244(1999) too is, at least in part, invalid.[52]

[45] In Dupuy's words, '*il n'est de solution universelle qu'au sein des Nations Unies*; ou, il n'est de restauration de la paix, à tout le moins, sans leur aval ou leur caution, sinon toujours leur participation directe: les Nations Unies, légitimant universel incontournable', P.-M. Dupuy, 'L'unité de l'ordre juridique international—Cours général de droit international public', 297 *Recueil des Cours* (2002) at 235.

[46] See Security Council resolution 687(1991): for a discussion of its treaty-like nature see S. Sur, 'La résolution 687 (3 avril 1991) du Conseil de sécurité dans l'affaire du Golfe: Problèmes de rétablissement et garantie de la paix', 37 *AFDI* (1991) 27 at 39, 42; J.A. Frowein, 'Unilateral Interpretation of Security Council Resolutions—A Threat to Collective Security?', in V. Götz, P. Selmer, and R. Wolfrum (eds), *Liber Amicorum Günther Jaenike: zum 85. Geburtstag* (Berlin: Springer, 1998) at 97; P. Picone, 'La guerra contro l'Irak e le degenerazioni dell'unilateralismo', 86 *Riv. di Diritto Internaz.* (2003) 328 at 356, 364.

[47] Cf. for instance, resolution 1031(1995) as regards the 1995 Paris Framework Agreement for Bosnia-Herzegovina; resolutions 1378 (2001) and 1386 (2001) as regards Afghanistan.

[48] S.S. Malawer, 'Imposed Treaties', *supra* note 19, at 157 and 161.

[49] A. Gattini, *Le riparazioni di guerra*, *supra* note 12, at 410.

[50] 38 *ILM* (1999) 1217. Cf. M. Guillaume, 'Le cadre juridique de l'action du KFOR au Kosovo', Ch. Tomuschat (ed.), *Kosovo and the International Community*, *supra* note 25, at 243; E. Milano, 'Security Council Action in the Balkans: Reviewing the Legality of Kosovo's Territorial Status', 14 *EJIL* (2003) 998, at 1004. It should be recalled that, according to the ICJ, the former Federal Republic of Yugoslavia was not a member of the United Nations at the relevant time: see *Legality of Use of Force* cases, Preliminary Objections, Judgment of 15 December 2004, *ICJ Reports* (2004) 279 *et seq.*, at 900, para. 90 of the judgment against Italy. However, UN practice confirms that the Council may address Chapter VII measures to non-members: cf. L.M. Goodrich, E. Hambro, and A.P. Simons, *Charter of the United Nations* (New York: Columbia University Press, 3rd edn, 1969) at 58–60; B. Conforti, *The Law and Practice of the United Nations* (Leiden–Boston: Nijhoff, 3rd edn, 2005) at 128.

[51] Y. Nouvel, 'La position du Conseil de sécurité', *supra* note 25, and G. Distefano, 'Le Conseil de securité et la validation des traités conclus par la menace ou l'emploi de la force', C.A. Morand (ed.), *La crise des Balkans de 1999. Les dimensions historiques, politiques et juridiques du conflit du Kosovo* (Paris-Bruxelles: LGDJ, Bruylant, 2000) at 167, argue that the transposition of the Agreement in resolution 1244 cancels all doubts as to the binding nature of its content *qua* imposed by the Security Council. Cf., however, O. Corten, 'Article 52', *supra* note 3, at 1897, also for the remark that 'En pratique, le Conseil semble en effet bel et bien s'appuyer sur ce qu'il considère des accords valides, et plus spécialement sur un consentement de l'Etat victime de l'intervention susceptible d'entraîner des effets juridiques'.

[52] E. Milano, 'Security Council Action', *supra* note 50, at 1004 *et seq.*

As a matter of principle, it would seem that the Security Council is not legally precluded from endorsing a treaty concluded by coercion if it deems it to be the most appropriate way to restore peace, as long as the content of that treaty is not inconsistent with *jus cogens*.[53] Still, whatever stance one takes as to the legality of the North Atlantic Treaty Organization (NATO) action and of resolution 1244,[54] it should be noted that Serbia itself does not cast any doubt on the validity of both the resolution and of the Military Technical Agreement. On the contrary, in the case concerning the *Accordance with International Law of the Unilateral Declaration of Independence by the Provisional Institutions of Self-Government of Kosovo*, Serbia qualified resolution 1244 as forming 'the cornerstone of the international legal *regime* of Kosovo',[55] and specifically relied on the Military Technical Agreement which, due to its contractual character, 'could not be subsequently altered unilaterally'.[56] Serbia did recall that the resolution was adopted after the illegal recourse to armed force by some states[57] and that the Security Council would not be in a position to cancel Serbia's sovereignty over Kosovo;[58] however, no specific consequences were drawn from these circumstances, except as regards the interpretation of resolution 1244. The ICJ itself noted that 'none of the participants has questioned the fact that resolution 1244(1999) [...] is part of the law relevant in the present situation' before assessing that it was indeed part

[53] Cf. among others, by J. A. Frowein and N. Krisch, 'Introduction to Chapter VII', in Simma (ed.), *The Charter of the United Nations—A Commentary* (Oxford: Oxford University Press, 2nd edn., 2002) 701, at 711. Article 52 of the Vienna Convention pertains to the way in which the treaty is concluded, not to its content, and is not, *per se*, a peremptory norm (a point to which we will revert later).

[54] It goes without saying that any discussion as to the relevance of Article 52 of the Vienna Convention becomes pointless if the NATO air strikes are assumed to be in conformity with the 'principles of international law embodied in the Charter of the United Nations'. On this very controversial issue see, among others, A. Cassese, '*Ex iniuria ius oritur*: are we moving towards international legitimation of forcible humanitarian countermeasures in the world community?', 10 *EJIL* (1999) 23; C.M. Chinkin, 'Kosovo: a "good" or "bad" war?', 93 *AJIL* (1999) 841; B. Simma, 'NATO, the UN and the Use of Force', 10 *EJIL* (1999) 1; J.-F. Flauss, 'La primarité des droits de la personne: licéité ou illicéité de l'intervention humanitaire?', in Ch. Tomushat (ed.), *Kosovo and the International Community, supra* note 25, at 87.

[55] See the conclusions of the Written Statement of Serbia, 15 April 2009, at 359, para. 1040 (iv), (available at <http://www.icj-cij.org>); cf. also the pleading of Zimmermann, Counsel to Serbia, 1 December 2009, CR 2009/24, 50, para. 4.

[56] Written Statement of Serbia, at 247, para. 268. See further ibid., at 248, para. 674: 'The Military Technical Agreement remains in force, notwithstanding the UDI.' Of course, the statements refer to the provisions of the Agreement confirming that Kosovo is part of Serbia.

[57] Cf. the statement of Batakovic at the hearing of 1 December 2004, CR 2009/24, at 7, para. 7.

[58] Ibid. Cf. G. Gaja, 'Réflections sur le rôle du Conseil de Sécurité dans le nouvel ordre mondial', 97 *RGDIP* (1993) 297, at 300; U. Villani, 'Sul ruolo quasi giudiziario del Consiglio di sicurezza', 51 *La Comunità Internazionale* (1996) 25, at 28; K. Zemanek, 'Is the Security Council the Sole Judge of Its Own Legality?', in E. Yakpo and T. Boumedra (eds), *Liber Amicorum Judge Mohammed Bedjaoui* (The Hague: Kluwer, 1999) 629, at 630; G. Arangio-Ruiz, 'On the Security Council's "Law-Making"', 83 *Riv. di Diritto Internaz.*(2000) 609, at 627; E. de Wet, *The Chapter VII Powers of the Security Council*, (Oxford: Hart, 2004).

of the applicable legal framework.[59] Serbia's attitude is very similar to that taken by the DRC in relation to the Lusaka Agreement. Such clear-cut positions seem to be relevant not only as a way of abiding by Security Council resolutions, but also in the context of the law of treaties.

5. Possibility for the Coerced State to Waive its Claim

The attitude of DRC and Yugoslavia respectively might be read as a sign that the relevant treaties were not concluded on grounds of coercion[60] and that the two countries had kept their freedom of consent. Nevertheless, it seems quite clear that neither the Lusaka Agreement nor the Military and Technical Agreement would ever have been concluded had it not been for the use of force by the other negotiating parties.

These examples, as well as the position taken by the ICJ in the 2005 judgment and in the 2010 Advisory Opinion, rather point at the conclusion that Article 52 is not a *necessary* corollary to the prohibition of the use of force. The victim of coercion seems to be entitled to waive its claim as to the validity of the treaty in the same terms as those set forth by Article 45 of the Vienna Convention, provided that the choice is the result of a free determination of its best interest.[61] The ICJ judgment in *Nicaragua v Colombia* confirms that this conclusion applies to all treaties concluded on grounds of coercion.[62] However, the abovementioned practice conveys the idea that, specifically in the case of peace treaties, the victims of coercion have a strong interest in their implementation even after their freedom of choice is restored.

6. Article 52 and the Protection of Collective Interests

This conclusion has to be appreciated in the light of the fact that Article 52 does not only protect the victim's freedom of consent. The rule is also aimed at ensuring

[59] Advisory Opinion of 22 July 2010, not yet published (available at <http://icj-cij.org>) paras 85, 93.

[60] This option is suggested by O. Corten, 'Article 52', *supra* note 3, at 1888, in whose view Serbia could still decide freely whether to accept the terms of the Military and Technical Agreement notwithstanding the conflict.

[61] It is noteworthy, in this respect, that acceptance of the validity of a treaty under Article 45 should be valid in itself, ie it should be the expression of the free will of the State. See M. Kohen, 'Article 45—Convention de 1969', in O. Corten and P. Klein (eds), *Les Conventions de Vienne*, *supra* note 3, 1667, at 1693.

[62] Cf. the Declaration of Judge Simma in the case concerning the *Territorial and Maritime Dispute (Nicaragua v Colombia)*, *supra* note 17: 'The principle underlying Article 45*(b)* of the Vienna Convention is undoubtedly applicable under the present circumstances.' Judge Abraham takes a different stance in his Separate Opinion, *supra* note 17.

respect for the prohibition on recourse to force in international relations, which is 'at the very heart of international law shaped by community interest'.[63] Doubts may therefore arise as to the legal effects of an acceptance of the validity of a treaty in these circumstances.

Nevertheless, the legal interest of the other members of the international community cannot be equated with the position of the victim of an armed attack, who should have some form of priority in the choice of the most appropriate form of reparation for the wrongful act it has suffered.[64] According to Article 48 of the Draft Articles on State Responsibility for Internationally Wrongful Acts, non-injured states are entitled to claim cessation of breaches of *erga omnes* obligations, as well as assurances and guarantees of non-repetition and reparation in the interest of the injured state.[65] If these objectives are attained by the implementation of the peace treaty[66] or through some other means (such as measures decided by the Security Council or a judicial assessment of responsibility for the breach) the legal interest of the non-injured states is deemed to be satisfied.[67]

On the other hand, the contention that Article 52 is in itself a norm of *jus cogens*[68] cannot be accepted: the cases of the Lusaka Agreement and of the Military Technical Agreement between Serbia and KFOR do not support this view. It is true that acts of aggression such as those that lead to coerced peace treaties contravene the peremptory core of the rule prohibiting the use of force,[69] and entail the consequences envisaged by Article 41 of the Draft on

[63] B. Simma, 'Bilateralism and Community Interest in International Law', 250 *Recueil des Cours* (1994-VI) at 236.

[64] See S. Forlati, 'Azioni di fronte alla Corte internazionale di giustizia rispetto a violazioni di obblighi *erga omnes*', 84 *Riv. di Diritto Internaz.* (2001) 69, at 79, also for further references.

[65] 'Report on the work of its fifty-third session', A/56/10, at 126. See also Article 48 of the Draft Articles on Responsibility of International Organizations adopted on first reading, 'Report on the work of its sixty-first session', A/64/10, at 33.

[66] The relevance of the content of the peace treaty is stressed by O. Corten, 'Article 52', *supra* note 3, at 1899, albeit only as evidence of the coerced nature of the treaty.

[67] Cf. *mutatis mutandis*, *Northern Cameroons (Cameroon v United Kingdom)*, Preliminary Objections, Judgment of 2 December 1963, *ICJ Reports* (1963) 15, in which Cameroon's claims were held to be 'devoid of purpose' (ibid., at 38) also in the light of the assumption that 'the General Assembly was mindful of the general interest when, acting within its competence, it decided the termination of the Trust with respect to the Northern Cameroons and the joinder of the Northern Cameroons to the Federation of Nigeria' (ibid., at 30).

[68] According to E. Milano, 'Security Council's Action', *supra* note 56, at 1018, 'it may well be asserted that Article 52 also represents a norm of *jus cogens*, as it represents both a protection of the legal interests of those who are victims of an unlawful armed attack and of the international community as a whole'. However, the existence of a collective interest in respect of a given obligation points at its *erga omnes* nature rather than at the existence of a peremptory norm (cf. ILC, 'Report on the work of its fifty-third session', *YILC* (2001), vol. II(2) 31, at 110, para. 1 *et seq.*).

[69] Cf. ILC 'Report on the work of its fifty-third session', *supra* note 65, at 112, para. 4. On the distinction between armed attacks and minor breaches of the prohibition of the use of force cf. the ICJ judgment in the *Military and Paramilitary Activities in and against Nicaragua (Nicaragua v United States of America)*, Judgment of 27 June 1986, *ICJ Reports* (1986), 14, at 101–2, para. 190 *et seq.*, and 127, para. 249.

state responsibility[70]—namely, the obligation to cooperate to bring to an end any serious breach of peremptory norms, not to recognize as lawful a situation created by such a breach nor to render aid or assistance in maintaining that situation. Specifically as regards the obligation of non-recognition, the Commentary to Article 41 makes it clear that 'waiver or recognition induced from the injured state by the responsible state cannot preclude the international community interest in ensuring a just and appropriate settlement'.[71] However, this 'just and appropriate settlement' does not necessarily require the declaration of invalidity of a peace treaty that may help to bring it about; endorsement by the Security Council may actually be evidence that this aim can be attained through the treaty's implementation.

[70] Supra, note 65, at 114. Cf. also Article 41 of the Draft Articles on Responsibility of International Organizations, *supra* note 65, at 30.

[71] *Supra* note 65, at 115, para. 9.

20

Absolute Invalidity of Treaties and Their Non-Recognition by Third States

Alessandra Gianelli

1. The 1969 Vienna Convention on the Law of Treaties Provisions Governing Absolute Invalidity and their Shortcomings

Article 53 of the 1969 Vienna Convention on the Law of Treaties (VCLT) provides that a treaty conflicting with a peremptory norm of general international law is void. In such a case of invalidity, no separation of the provisions of the treaty is permitted (Article 44(5)). Parties to a treaty void under Article 53 have a duty, as far as possible, to eliminate the consequences of any act performed in reliance on the treaty (Article 71(1)). These rather severe consequences suggest the use of the expression 'absolute invalidity' in order to distinguish it from other cases, where invalidity may be limited to parts of the treaty, or where acts carried out in performance of the treaty in good faith before the invocation of invalidity are not rendered unlawful by a later declaration of invalidity (Article 69(2)(b)).

On the other hand, the validity of a treaty in conflict with a peremptory norm may be challenged exclusively as provided by the VCLT (Article 42). According to the Convention, only a state party to the treaty may impeach its validity. That state must follow the procedure set out in Articles 65–68. If a dispute arises among the parties as to the existence of this particular ground for invalidity, which cannot be solved through other peaceful settlement means within 12 months, Article 66 entitles each party unilaterally to submit the dispute to the International Court of Justice. The Vienna Convention enables a party to invoke the invalidity of a treaty only at the end of the settlement procedures, and does not provide for any exception in case of conflict of the treaty with a peremptory norm. States not parties to the treaty have no way, under the Vienna Convention, to claim its invalidity, even if the reason is conflict with a norm considered by the international community as a whole not to be derogated from.

In his 1981 Hague Academy lectures, Professor Gaja remarked how these provisions follow two 'hardly reconcilable' approaches.[1] Indeed, it seems contradictory to identify a reason for invalidity of a treaty in its contrast with a fundamental rule of the international community as a whole and then leave to the parties of the treaty the initiative and the choice of invoking the invalidity.[2] Under the VCLT it appears that invalidity cannot be declared before a judgment of the International Court of Justice or an agreement reached among the parties.[3]

The Vienna Convention position has supported the view that peremptory norms do not necessarily give rise to obligations *erga omnes*. According to this opinion, some peremptory norms have a reciprocal nature, that is, they give rise in the specific situation to bilateral relationships.[4] The Vienna Convention would apply to these peremptory rules. Such an opinion is different from the one convincingly maintained, among others, by Professor Gaja and according to which all peremptory norms give rise to obligations *erga omnes*.[5] Whether one follows the opinion that all peremptory norms give rise to *erga omnes* obligations, or that only some of them do, the question remains how third states may raise the issue of invalidity of treaties conflicting with peremptory norms from which *erga omnes* obligations arise.

To add to the complexity of the picture, the Vienna Convention establishes in a specific provision (Article 52) that a treaty concluded under the threat or use of force is void. While a treaty having as its object the illegal threat or use of force is void under Article 53, invalidity under Article 52 affects treaties where the threat or use of force vitiated the consent of one party in the conclusion of the agreement. At least with regard to aggression, both grounds of invalidity are consequences drawn from a contrast with the peremptory norm included in the

[1] G. Gaja, '*Jus Cogens* beyond the Vienna Convention', 172 *Recueil des Cours* (1981-III) 271, at 283.

[2] C.L. Rozakis, *The Concept of* Jus Cogens *in the Law of Treaties* (Amsterdam, New York: North-Holland Pub. Co., 1976) 118 *et seq.*; A. Orakhelashvili, *Peremptory Norms in International Law* (Oxford: Oxford University Press, 2006) 134.

[3] G. Gaja, '*Jus Cogens* beyond the Vienna Convention', *supra* note 1, at 285. As noted by the Federal Republic of Germany during the Vienna Conference (United Nations Conference on the Law of Treaties, *Official Records*, vol. I, 226), an agreement among the parties would not be suitable to establish the presence or absence of a conflict of a treaty with *jus cogens*.

[4] Among Italian scholars, this idea has been supported mostly by P. Picone, 'Obblighi reciproci e obblighi *erga omnes* degli Stati nel campo della protezione internazionale dell'ambiente marino dall'inquinamento', in V. Starace (ed.), *Diritto internazionale e protezione dell'ambiente marino* (Milano: Giuffré, 1983) 15, at 41–2, footnote 56; a more articulated notion of peremptory norms having a bilateral character has lately been put forward in P. Picone, 'La distinzione tra norme internazionali di *jus cogens* e norme che producono obblighi *erga omnes*', 91 *Riv. di Diritto Internaz.* (2008) 5 *et seq.* See also B. Conforti, *Cours général de droit international public*, 212 *Recueil des Cours* (1988-V) 134–5. For further references, see C.J. Tams, *Enforcing Obligations* Erga Omnes *in International Law* (Cambridge: Cambridge University Press, 2005) 146 *et seq.*

[5] G. Gaja, 'Obligations *Erga Omnes*, International Crimes and *Jus Cogens*: A Tentative Analysis of Three Related Concepts', in J.H.H. Weiler, A. Cassese, and M. Spinedi (eds), *International Crimes of States* (Berlin: De Gruyter, 1989) 151; 'First Report, Obligations and Rights *erga omnes* in International Law', 71 *Annu. de l'Inst. de Droit Internat.*, Session de Cracovie (2005) vol. I, at 127–8.

prohibition of use of force. While in the case of Article 52 it is again only the parties who may claim the invalidity, they may not, however, under the VCLT, refer the dispute unilaterally to the International Court; also, the consequences of invalidity in this case are somehow different from those provided in the case of invalidity established under Article 53,[6] even if Article 52 too is considered a case of absolute invalidity.[7]

With regard to the scope of application of the Vienna Convention, the procedure for the settlement of disputes there established applies only to the states parties to the VCLT and to treaties concluded after the entry into force of the Convention. The International Court of Justice has considered that procedure to correspond, in its very general terms, to a customary obligation to act in good faith.[8] The Court referred, however, to grounds for invalidity different from conflict with peremptory norms or coercion, and stressed the duty of the states parties to communicate and to solve the possible resulting dispute by peaceful means. No light is shed on the issue of how third states may claim the invalidity of treaties considered absolutely void.

The unsatisfactory treatment by the VCLT of the invocation of invalidity of a treaty in conflict with peremptory norms has various causes. Facing a range of criticisms, the International Law Commission (ILC) had chosen to merely reaffirm the obligation to resolve disputes through amiable procedures, when a dispute arose about the existence of grounds of invalidity, suspension, and termination of treaties. The Commission had limited itself to recalling Article 33 of the UN Charter in order to preserve the stability of treaties, fully aware that it was not an ideal solution.[9] The specific procedural provisions concerning the International Court of Justice's jurisdiction with regard to nullity and termination because of conflict with *jus cogens* were introduced 'at the eleventh hour' at the Vienna Conference, as part of a more general compromise solution and as a way of limiting the risk of abusive uses of this novel ground for invalidity, as

[6] See Article 69, para. 2, and Article 71, para. 1. See the observations of H. Waldock and other members of the Commission *YILC* (1963), vol. I, 52. W. Czaplinski, '*Jus Cogens* and the Law of Treaties', in Ch. Tomuschat and J.-M. Thouvenin (eds), *The Fundamental Rules of the International Legal Order* (Leiden–Boston: Martinus Nijhoff Publishers, 2006) 83, 90, maintains that the 'only logical explanation' for the separate provision is that 'there was a general consensus among the participants as to the invalidity of a treaty concluded under coercion, but not as to *jus cogens*'. M.E. Villiger, *Commentary to the 1969 Vienna Convention on the Law of Treaties* (Leiden–Boston: Martinus Nijhoff Publishers, 2009) states that the Article 52 ground of invalidity 'does not constitute *jus cogens*', because the use of force is not the object of the treaty.

[7] T.O. Elias, 'Problems Concerning the Validity of Treaties', 134 *Recueil des Cours* (1971-III) 347, 381; G. Gaja, 'Trattati internazionali', *Digesto delle Discipline Pubblicistiche* (Torino: UTET, 1999) vol. XV, 361.

Article 52 has been recognized by the International Court of Justice as a rule corresponding to general international law in the *Fisheries Jurisdiction (United Kingdom v Iceland)*, Judgment of 2 February 1973, *ICJ Reports* (1973) 14.

[8] ICJ, *Gabcikovo-Nagymaros Project (Hungary v Slovakia)*, Judgment of 25 September 1997, *ICJ Reports* (1997) 66.

[9] *YILC* (1966), vol. II, 236, at 262–3.

well as termination.[10] The position of third states was probably not addressed also because the nature and character of *jus cogens*, and its connections with *erga omnes* obligations, were not appreciated by states and doctrine uniformly: a situation that does not appear to have been definitively resolved.[11]

2. Possible Approaches Concerning the Position of Third States with Regard to Treaties Absolutely Invalid

One way to overcome the discrepancies of the 1969 discipline consists in admitting that third states may claim that the treaty in conflict with a peremptory norm or concluded under duress is void, without having to wait for the parties to invoke the invalidity and follow the Vienna Convention procedure.[12] Some practice, like General Assembly resolutions 33/28 A and 34/65 B (1979), questioning the validity of the 1978 Camp David accords with regard to the principle of self-determination of peoples, might be quoted to support the view.[13] To allow such a conclusion would amount to stating that the solution adopted in 1969 has been superseded by subsequent practice, or that it never corresponded to the practice of states, or that at the very least it corresponded only partially, because it does not take into consideration third states. In all of these cases, some more proof about the emergence or the content of a customary rule should be found.

Another possible solution is to leave the issue of the validity of the treaty to the parties, but at the same time to qualify the conclusion of a treaty conflicting with a peremptory norm or vitiated by coercion as a wrongful act toward all states members of the international community.[14] Professor Gaja follows a different reasoning. In his words, '[t]he peremptory norm removes the threat of a violation of the obligations it imposes by invalidating any treaty which, if implemented,

[10] Quotation from G. Gaja, '*Jus Cogens* beyond the Vienna Convention', *supra* note 1, at 279; T.O. Elias, 'Problems Concerning the Validity of Treaties', *supra* note 7, at 397 *et seq.*; F. Capotorti, 'L'extinction et la suspension des traités', 134 *Recueil des Cours* (1971-III) 559 *et seq.*

[11] International Law Commission's Commentary introducing Articles 40 and 41 of the State responsibility text, *YILC* (2001), vol. II(2), 111–12.

[12] S. Rosenne, 'The Settlement of Treaty Disputes under the Vienna Convention of 1969', 31 *ZaöRV* (1971) 35 footnote 97, 54 footnote 168; J.A. Frowein, 'Jus Cogens', 7 *Encyclopaedia of Public International Law* (1984) 329; J.A. Frowein, 'Collective Enforcement of International Obligations', 47 *ZaöRV* (1987) 77–8; B. Simma, 'From Bilateralism to Community Interest in International Law', 250 *Recueil des Cours* (1994-IV) 289; A.L. Paulus, 'Jus Cogens in a Time of Hegemony and Fragmentation', 74 *Nordic JIL* (2005) 305.

[13] G. Gaja, 'Trattati internazionali', *supra* note 7, at 361.

[14] G. Barile, 'La structure de l'ordre juridique international', 161 *Recueil des Cours* (1978-III) 9, at 88, 89, 93–4; W. Czaplinski, '*Jus Cogens* and the Law of Treaties', in Ch. Tomuschat and J.-M. Thouvenin (eds), *The Fundamental Rules of the International Legal Order*, *supra* note 6, at 89–90. See also P. Reuter, *Introduction au droit des traités* (Paris: Presses Universitaires de France, 3rd edn reviewed by P. Cahier, 1995) 159, 162–3.

would entail such a violation'.[15] It would thus appear that, in his opinion, only the implementation of the agreement would constitute a breach of an obligation deriving from a peremptory norm.

The ILC has not given a clear answer to either of these last two approaches. The conduct or omission is not defined by the law of responsibility in case of grave breaches of obligations arising from peremptory norms in any way differently from ordinary breaches of obligations arising from other customary or conventional rules.[16] The ILC chose not to enter into the details of when a breach of an obligation occurs, preferring instead to state a few general rules and to refer the answer to an analysis of the content of the primary rule.[17] The question of whether the conclusion of a treaty which conflicts with a peremptory norm is in itself a (grave) breach of an obligation deriving from a peremptory norm is therefore left by the Commission to the interpretation of the primary, peremptory rule.[18]

Should the answer be positive, the consequences provided for in Article 41 of the 2001 ILC's text on state responsibility would apply immediately at the conclusion of the treaty.[19] This article requires all the states to cooperate to bring the breach to an end and not to aid or assist in maintaining the situation created by the breach; also, and more interestingly for the purposes of this analysis, the provision obliges those states not to recognize as lawful a situation created by the serious breach. If one were to consider that the conclusion of an agreement in conflict with a peremptory norm constitutes a grave breach of an obligation deriving from such norm, the question of the ways open to third parties to claim the nullity of the treaty would lose much of its relevance. If third states were obliged, following Article 41 of the state responsibility codification, not to recognize *as lawful* the situations arising from the treaty, it would indeed come very close to saying that the treaty should be considered void by third parties.[20]

This does not amount to denying that the scope of the two codifications is different. The law of treaties is concerned with the normative level and affirms that conflict with a *jus cogens* rule makes the treaty void, by applying a hierarchic, value-based approach and qualifying as void the lower rule in contrast with the superior rule. The treaty therefore produces no legal effects, does not bind the parties at any time, and does not give rise to situations which third states must

[15] G. Gaja, '*Jus Cogens* beyond the Vienna Convention', *supra* note 1, at 282.

[16] *YILC* (2001), vol. II(2), 56.

[17] *YILC* (2001), vol. II(2), 31, 54.

[18] The International Law Commission did not consider the case of the conclusion of a conflicting treaty, *per se*, among the examples of breach of a primary obligation (*YILC* (2001), vol. II(2), 54 *et seq.*) or of a peremptory rule (*YILC* (2001), vol. II(2), 110 *et seq.*).

[19] W. Czaplinski, '*Jus Cogens* and the Law of Treaties', in Ch. Tomuschat and J.-M. Thouvenin (eds), *The Fundamental Rules of the International Legal Order*, *supra* note 6, 83, at 89–90, refers instead to Article 48.

[20] See H. Blix, 'Contemporary Aspects of Recognition', 130 *Recueil des Cours* (1970-II) 589, for the early use of the expression 'not to recognize as legal' in UN instruments.

confront. How to ascertain this kind of nullity is a question only incidental to such a solution.

The law of responsibility assumes instead that there is a conduct or omission in violation of the peremptory rule, and it qualifies such conduct as wrongful. The law of responsibility is not concerned with rules, but with the behaviour of states.[21] The wrongful conduct may even be required by some other international rule, effective and binding because not necessarily in conflict with the peremptory rule.[22] The wrongful act implies consequences both for the wrongdoer and for the injured state. The content of the law of responsibility is summarized as the new legal relationship giving rise to rights and duties of the states involved.

However, the distinction between the two areas of law is in the specific case less clear. By concluding a treaty in conflict with a peremptory rule, a state adopts at the same time a conduct—which could be considered wrongful *per se* aside from a subsequent implementation of the treaty—and a normative act—which can be legally qualified as void. Also, to oblige all states not to recognize as lawful the situation created by the treaty, because it represents a grave breach of a peremptory rule, would bring the reactions to the wrongful act to the level of legality of the act, a level which is proper to the law of treaties.

Still another possible approach could consist in considering a duty not to recognize treaties concluded in violation of peremptory norms as part of the content of the primary, peremptory rules. The present writer has already maintained this view with regard to the duty imposed on all states by Article 41 of the state responsibility codification.[23]

3. Non-Recognition and Its Meanings

In order not to relegate the discussion on the position of third states to a theoretical analysis, an inquiry into cases where third states have claimed these particular grounds of invalidity seems necessary. The relevant practice consists of cases where states have resorted to the use of the term 'invalidity' but also and more

[21] This is the assumption of Professor Gaja's position, quoted earlier in the text of this paragraph. In the words of the German Constitutional Court's judgment of 26 October 2004, commenting on Articles 53 of the Vienna Convention and 41 of the state responsibility text, 'the legal consequence of voidness is laid down only to the extent that duties under treaties are directed precisely to performance that is prohibited by a peremptory norm', available at <http://www.bundesverfassungsgericht.de/en>.

[22] This may happen if the rule may be implemented in a way which does not give rise to a conflict with the peremptory norm.

[23] A. Gianelli, 'Le conseguenze delle gravi violazioni di obblighi posti da norme imperative tra norme primarie e norme secondarie', in M. Spinedi, A. Gianelli, and M.L. Alaimo (eds), *La codificazione della responsabilità internazionale degli Stati alla prova dei fatti* (Milano: Giuffrè, 2006) 245 *et seq.*

frequently to that of non-recognition of a treaty. In its turn, the last expression is strictly intertwined with the non-recognition of situations arising from a treaty. This relationship deserves a few words.

Generally, the term 'recognition' identifies a unilateral act having as its object the establishment by a state of a factual or legal situation, which cannot later be contested by the same state.[24] As such, it is a basic instrument of legal relationships among states in international law.

The term has long been specifically used with regard to new states or new governments. At the same time, works devoted to the topic of state recognition do not fail to address non-recognition of situations as well.[25] This may be due to the fact that non-recognition very often follows the establishment or enlargement of states, where new states, or significant territorial changes in pre-existing states, emerge. Non-recognition of situations arising from the new establishment may therefore appear simply as a consequence of the non-recognition of a new state or government or of some acts of a pre-existing state.[26] At the very least, non-recognition may assume the guise of a protest to avoid acquiescence towards the newly created situation.[27]

A brief review of the origins of the practice of non-recognition of situations sheds a different light on the notion, however. Non-recognition has in fact long been considered a tool to assert the illegality of situations, at first arising from the establishment of new entities contrary to the rules forbidding resort to war, and later in contrast with the principles of self-determination or forbidding grave forms of discrimination, such as apartheid. This topic has been extensively analysed.[28] The following short investigation will concentrate on whether this practice is relevant with regard to non-recognition of treaties because of their invalidity.

[24] D. Anzilotti, *Corso di diritto internazionale* (Padova: CEDAM, 4th edn, 1955) vol. I, 294–5; V. Rodriguez Cedeno, 'Sixth Report on Unilateral Acts of States', A/CN.4/534, 13.

[25] J. Verhoeven, *La reconnaissance internationale dans la pratique contemporaine* (Paris: Pedone, 1975). For an exhaustive bibliography on non-recognition, which includes works relevant in the present inquiry, see S. Talmon, *Recognition in International Law. A Bibliography* (The Hague: Martinus Nijhoff Publishers, 2000).

[26] J. Dugard, *Recognition and the United Nations* (Cambridge: Grotius Publications, 1987) 31 *et seq.*

[27] J. Verhoeven, *La reconnaissance internationale dans la pratique contemporaine*, *supra* note 25, 309.

[28] Among others, G. Ziccardi Capaldo, *Le situazioni territoriali illegittime nel diritto internazionale* (Napoli: Editoriale Scientifica, 1977); J. Dugard, *Recognition and the United Nations*, *supra* note 26; E. Milano, *Unlawful Territorial Situations in International Law* (Leiden: Martinus Nijhoff Publishers, 2006); S. Talmon, 'The Duty Not to "Recognize as Lawful" a Situation Created by the Illegal Use of Force or Other Serious Breaches of a *Jus Cogens* Obligation: An Obligation without Real Substance?', in Ch. Tomuschat and J.-M. Thouvenin (eds), *The Fundamental Rules of the International Legal Order The Fundamental Rules of the International Legal Order*, *supra* note 6, 99; T. Christakis, 'L'obligation de non-reconnaissance des situations créées par le recours illicite à la force ou d'autres actes enfreignant des règles fondamentales', ibid., 127.

4. The Early Practice Concerning Non-Recognition of Treaties and Situations

The relevant practice dates back to the Americas during the nineteenth century. At that time the American states were trying to prevent territorial changes due to the use of force and to agreements concluded following a conquest, as well as the presence on the American continent of foreign, especially European, powers. In the oldest instruments, a duty not to recognize concerns territorial situations and is coupled with the declaration of nullity of acts of cession of territory, following the use or threat of use of force.[29] In later instruments, like the 1933 Convention on the Rights and Duties of States and the Anti-war Treaty of Non-aggression and Conciliation (the Saavedra Lamas Treaty) of the same year, states parties undertake 'the precise obligation not to recognize territorial acquisitions or special advantages obtained by force'[30] 'nor the validity of the occupation or acquisition of territories that may be brought about by force of arms'.[31] These provisions are the antecedent of Article 21 of the Charter of the Organization of American States, where member states declare that '[n]o territorial acquisitions or special advantages obtained either by force or by other means of coercion shall be recognized'.[32]

In Europe, non-recognition appears at the beginning of the twentieth century, particularly during and after World War I with regard to treaties implying territorial changes.[33] Non-recognition may occur through a unilateral declaration or be stipulated in an agreement.[34] Non-recognition here concerns the treaty con-

[29] Article 13 of the *Continental Treaty*, concluded by seven states in Santiago, Chile, in 1856, stated that '[t]he High Contracting Parties undertake not to cede nor alienate, under any form, to another State or government any part of their territories, nor to permit, within said territories, the establishment of a foreign Power; the other Parties pledge themselves not to recognize such an establishment, on whatever grounds'. The recommendation adopted in 1890 by the International Conference of American States in Washington declared '(2) That all cessions of territory made during the continuance of the treaty of arbitration shall be void if made under threats of war or in the presence of an armed force. (3) Any nation from which such cessions shall be exacted may demand that the validity of the cessions so made shall be void if made under threats of war or in the presence of an armed force.' Texts in R. Langer, *Seizure of Territory. The Stimson Doctrine and Related Principles in Legal Theory and Diplomatic Practice* (Princeton: Princeton University Press, 1947) 35, 36. See also I. Brownlie, *International Law and the Use of Force by States* (Oxford: Clarendon Press, 1963) 410 *et seq*.

[30] Article 11 of the Convention on the Rights and Duties of States, available at <http://avalon.law.yale.edu>.

[31] See also Article II of the Anti-war. Text available at <http://avalon.law.yale.edu>.

[32] Text available at <http://www.oas.org>.

[33] Relevant practice in R. Langer, *Seizure of Territory. The Stimson Doctrine and Related Principles in Legal Theory and Diplomatic Practice*, *supra* note 29, 3 *et seq*.

[34] Examples taken from R. Langer, ibid., 19–20, 27, include the declaration given by the United Kingdom in 1918 about the peace treaty concluded by central European Powers with the so-called People's Republic of Ukraine: 'His Majesty's Government have instructed their agent at Kiev to make a declaration to the effect that they do not recognize the peace recently concluded between the Ukraine and the Central Powers'; and Article 1 of the Treaty between the Soviet Union and

cluded under the use of force; if it affects the territorial situations, it is because this is the object of the treaty itself. That in such cases non-recognition is closest to a declaration of invalidity of the treaty is apparent from the interchangeable use of the two expressions.[35]

The strict interrelationship between non-recognition and invalidity is confirmed by the better-known practice concerning relations between China and Japan in the first half of the twentieth century. The so-called Stimson doctrine was actually formulated in 1915, when State Secretary Bryan sent to those two states a note affirming that 'it cannot recognize any agreement or undertaking, which has been entered into or which may be entered into between the Governments of China and Japan impairing the treaty rights of the United States and its citizens in China, the political or territorial integrity of the Republic of China, or the international policy relative to China commonly known as the Open Door Policy'.[36] The note sent by Stimson to China and Japan on 7 January 1932 deals with the developments of the same dispute. Terms employed are very similar to those referred to above. The note states that the government of the United States 'cannot admit the legality of any situation *de facto* nor does it intend to recognize any treaty or agreement entered into between these governments' having the same object as those quoted in the 1915 note. The note of 1932, however, adds that the US government 'does not intend to recognize any situation, treaty or agreement which may be brought about by means contrary to the covenants and obligations of the Pact of Paris of August 27, 1928 to which treaty both China and Japan, as well as the United States, are parties'.[37] In comparison to the 1915 note, this last sentence broadens significantly the scope of non-recognition.[38] According to part of the doctrine of the time, non-recognition of 'the fruits of aggression' was indeed a duty falling on all states parties to the Covenant and the Briand-Kellogg Pact.[39]

There are further indications that non-recognition was perceived at the time as a tool to affirm international legality.[40] One may recall some positions taken

Turkey of 16 March 1921: 'Each of the Contracting Parties agrees not to recognize any peace treaty or other international agreement imposed against the other against its will.'

[35] The collective declaration of the Allied Powers given one week after the United Kingdom declaration quoted in the previous footnote, qualifies the treaties as invalid. Ibid., 20.

[36] S.N.D. North, 'The Negotiations Between Japan and China in 1915', 10 *AJIL* (1916) 222 *et seq*., quote from 235–6. China agreed to grant Japan some privileges only after an ultimatum from Japan, and clearly stated that it had been forced to accept the demands of the neighbouring state.

[37] Text of the note and further relevant material in Q. Wright, 'The Stimson Note of January 7, 1932', 26 *AJIL* (1932) 342 *et seq*.

[38] Q. Wright, 'The Stimson Note of January 7, 1932', *supra* note 37, 346–7.

[39] Q. Wright, 'The Legal Foundation of the Stimson Doctrine', 8 *Pacific Affairs* (1935) 439 *et seq*.

[40] Stimson wrote to Senator Borah, Chairman of the Foreign Relations Committee of the Senate: 'if a similar decision should be reached and a similar position taken by the other governments of the world, a caveat will be placed upon such action which, we believe, will effectively bar the legality hereafter of any title or right sought to be obtained by pressure or treaty violation'. Q. Wright, 'The Stimson Note of January 7, 1932', *supra* note 37, 343. J. Fischer Williams, 'The

within the League of Nations, and especially the Assembly resolution concerning the Manchuria question, which states that it is 'incumbent upon the Members of the League of Nations not to recognize any situation, treaty, or agreement which may be brought about by means contrary to the Covenant of the League of Nations or to the Pact of Paris'.[41]

This practice was welcomed at the time as a significant step towards the principle that treaties concluded through the use of force are void.[42] While the practice found some application in the *Leticia* affair,[43] later developments concerning the Italian conquest of Ethiopia and treaties concluded by the Nazi government were bound to cool down the enthusiasm for the new doctrine.

In general terms, non-recognition may be said to find its origins in the movement, at first regional and later universal, to ban the use of force. With regard to treaties, the expressions 'invalidity' and 'non-recognition' are at times used interchangeably. This usage is telling about the strict relationship between the nullity of the agreement concluded under threat or use of force and non-recognition not only of territorial changes, but more generally of all the situations—factual and legal—arising from the agreement.[44, 45]

New Doctrine of "Recognition" ', 18 *Transactions of the Grotius Society* (1933) 116 footnote l, notes that Stimson's doctrine 'goes beyond the case of a treaty which violates a previous agreement when it embodies a claim to disregard a treaty resulting from "pressure" '. The United States Senate later debated a resolution affirming to be the policy of this State '2. Not to recognise any treaty or agreement brought about by means contrary to the Covenant of the Pact of Paris which would impair the obligations of that Pact' (ibid., 124). Following the adoption of the resolution by the League of Nations Assembly, quoted in the text and in the following footnote, Stimson stated that '[t]his action will go far toward developing into terms of international law the principles of order and justice which underlie those treaties, and the Government of the United States has been glad to cooperate earnestly in this effort'. Q. Wright, 'The Stimson Note of January 7, 1932', ibid., 344. For various declarations and correspondence, see R.N. Current, 'The Stimson Doctrine and the Hoover Doctrine', 59 *The American Historical Review* (1954) 513 *et seq.*

[41] Resolution of 11 March 1932, as reproduced in A. McNair, 'The Stimson Doctrine of Non-Recognition', 14 *BYIL* (1933), 65 *et seq.*, and Q. Wright, 'The Stimson Note of January 7, 1932', *supra* note 37, 343, where one can find also the note sent by Members of the Council of the League of Nations on 16 January 1932. Members referred to Article X of the Covenant to affirm 'that no infringement of the territorial integrity and no change in the political independence of any member of the League brought about in disregard of this article ought to be recognized as valid and effectual by the members of the League of Nations'.

[42] Q. Wright, 'The Stimson Note of January 7, 1932', *supra* note 37, 344. According to this author, the doctrine also implied that '*[d]e facto* occupation of territory gives no title' and that 'treaties contrary to the right of third states are void'.

[43] The Council of the League of Nations stated in a resolution of 18 March 1933 that member states were obliged not to recognize any situation, any treaty, and any agreement reached by means contrary to the Covenant or to the Briand-Kellog Pact. L.H. Woolsey, 'The Leticia Dispute between Columbia and Peru', 27 *AJIL* (1933) 525–7.

[44] A different opinion is maintained by J. Verhoeven, *La reconnaissance internationale dans la pratique contemporaine*, *supra* note 25, 285. According to this author, in the OAS 'non-reconnaissance y apparait la résultante logique de l'inviolabilité du territoire en droit des gens plutôt que celle de l'interdiction du recours à la force'.

[45] Stimson included in non-recognition the non-application of some rules of the law of war towards the aggressor state, which may probably be rather seen as a countermeasure. R.N. Current, 'The Stimson Doctrine and the Hoover Doctrine', *supra* note 40, 534. A. McNair, 'The Stimson

Non-recognition of a treaty at this time may be described as the determination of the conflict of that treaty with other prior instruments forbidding the use of force. The novelty consists in the fact that the contrast is not treated by way of a wrongful act, but rather considered a reason of invalidity. These statements generally anticipate the implementation of the treaty. The ILC itself, while drafting Article 52 of the VCLT, traced back to this time, and in reference to the Covenant of the League of Nations and the Briand-Kellogg Pact, the opinion that agreements concluded through the use or threat of force 'should no longer be *recognized* as legally valid'.[46]

The change in significance that the notion of non-recognition in this context was undergoing with regard to the more traditional recognition of states or governments did not go unnoticed by the doctrine of the time.[47] The new approach was not free from criticism, both because it was open to political abuse and because of the theoretical difficulty of tracing a cause for nullity to a customary and 'overriding' rule.[48]

Where invalidity of treaties concluded under the threat or use of force starts to be affirmed, the notion of non-recognition by third states appears as well. This seems indeed to be an essential element of the 'new doctrine'. Also, the source of non-recognition is found in the primary rules forbidding, at the time, resort to war—at the universal level, the Covenant and the Briand-Kellogg Pact. A prior collective statement does not appear to be a necessary prerequisite for non-recognition.[49]

5. The Later Practice

Contrary to the Charter of the Organization of American States, the Charter of the United Nations does not mention a duty of non-recognition, either with regard to situations or treaties.[50]

Doctrine of Non-Recognition', *supra* note 41, 72 *et seq.*, considered among the consequences of non-recognition non-application of treaties of commerce, of extradition, of diplomatic protection, however to conclude that '[it] is difficult to see how such a policy can do more harm to the wrongdoing state than to the non-recognizing states', 73. With regard to Manchukuo, Q. Wright, 'Some Legal Aspects of the Far Eastern Situation', 27 *AJIL* (1933) 512 *et seq.*, took into account as consequences of non-recognition the non-admission of the entity to the Universal Postal Union or non-application towards Japan of the obligations of neutral states during a conflict.

[46] *YILC* (1966), vol. II, 246 (emphasis added). See also I. Brownlie, *International Law and the Use of Force by States*, *supra* note 29, 404 *et seq.*

[47] J. Fischer Williams, *supra* note 40, 109 *et seq.*

[48] J. Fischer Williams, *supra* note 40, 121; as a possible example, he mentioned only a treaty reintroducing slavery.

[49] On the positions of states within the League of Nations concerning the Italian occupation of Ethiopia, see J. Dugard, *Recognition and the United Nations*, *supra* note 26, 36 *et seq.*

[50] Some proposals were made by Latin American states during the San Francisco Conference and at the first sessions of the General Assembly towards a provision on non-recognition in a

United Nations practice concerning non-recognition of territorial situations arising from grave breaches of peremptory norms is, however, substantial, and relates to both specific cases addressed by the Security Council and General Assembly Declarations, as well as rulings by the International Court of Justice. This practice is not limited to the consequences of violations of the prohibition on the use of force, but also encompasses violations of the prohibition on apartheid and of the principle of self-determination of peoples. Indeed, the ILC referred to this practice, when drafting in Article 41 of the Articles on State Responsibility a duty not to 'recognize as lawful a situation created by a serious breach'.[51]

Some contemporary practice relating to the present enquiry does also exist, though perhaps less substantial. The preparatory works of the Vienna Convention testify that the issue was not addressed and therefore was left to general international law. The invocation of absolute nullity by third states did not in fact receive much attention, as participating states were more concerned about the establishment of a binding procedure for the parties to the treaty to objectively ascertain the conflict with *jus cogens*. Among the few states who addressed the issue, some declared that the notion of invalidity because of conflict with peremptory norms included its invocability by any state;[52] others merely remarked that the proposed Convention had left open the question as to whether third states could invoke that invalidity.[53]

Some resolutions by the General Assembly—among them, the ones concerning the abovementioned Camp David accords—express in firm, if not precise, terms the 'rejection' of agreements concluded in conflict with the principle of self-determination.[54] Some of these resolutions were adopted with negative votes

Declaration on the rights and duties of states. Non-recognition here was linked to the prohibition of the use of force and to territorial acquisitions. J. Verhoeven, *La reconnaissance internationale dans la pratique contemporaine*, *supra* note 25, 289 *et seq*.; G. Ziccardi Capaldo, *Le situazioni territoriali illegittime nel diritto internazionale*, *supra* note 28, 42 *et seq*.

51 The Commentary to Article 41 recalls, after the Stimson doctrine and its application in the Manchurian question, Security Council resolutions concerning Rhodesia, the apartheid policy by South Africa, the Iraqi invasion of Kuwait, as well as case law by the International Court of Justice and the European Court of Human Rights. *YILC* (2001), vol. II(2), 114–15.

52 See the statements by Chile, Israel, Switzerland in United Nations Conference on the Law of Treaties, *Official Records*, vol. I, respectively at 299, 310, 324.

53 Ethiopia, ibid., 314; Norway, 325; Greece, 438. One cannot agree with L.C. Rozakis, *The Concept of* Jus Cogens *in the Law of Treaties*, *supra* note 2, 119, when he states that 'the Vienna Convention chose only the parties to such a treaty to be the sole executors and trustees of the international community'.

54 GA resolution 34/65 B, 29 November 1979, at para. 2 '[*R*]*ejects* those provisions of the accords which ignore, infringe, violate or deny the inalienable rights of the Palestinian people, including the right of return, the right of self-determination and the right to national independence and sovereignty in Palestine', after having stated in the first preamble that 'the validity of agreements purporting to solve the problem of Palestine required... the full attainment and exercise of the inalienable rights of the Palestinian people' (33 negative votes, 37 abstentions; see also resolutions 36/120 F, 10 December 1981, 37/123 F, 16 December 1982, and 38/180 D, 19 December 1983; resolution 35/118, 11 December 1980, *Plan of Action for the Full Implementation of the Declaration on the Granting of Independence to Colonial Countries and Peoples*, at para. 5 '[*C*]*ategorically Rejects*

or abstentions; the point of disagreement appears, however, to be political, rather than connected with the invalidity proclaimed for the agreements in question.

With regard to other specific cases, in its Advisory Opinion of 1971 on Namibia the International Court of Justice declared that, following the declaration of illegality by the Security Council of the continued presence of South Africa in Namibia, 'member States are under obligation to abstain from entering into treaty relations with South Africa' when this state was acting in relation to Namibia. The Court stated that it gave advice 'on those dealings with the Government of South Africa which, under the Charter of the United Nations and general international law, should be considered inconsistent with the declaration of... invalidity' rendered by the Security Council.[55] In relation to the present inquiry, it is relevant that the Court devoted some attention to states not members of the United Nations. The Court declared that 'no State which enters into relations with South Africa concerning Namibia may expect the United Nations or its Members to recognize the validity or effects of such relationship, or of the consequences thereof'.[56]

The *East Timor* case addressed by the International Court of Justice is also relevant. At issue was the conclusion of a 1989 agreement between Australia and Indonesia concerning the establishment of a zone of cooperation in the Timor Gap and involving the delimitation of the continental shelf between the two countries corresponding to the East Timor coast, as well as negotiations concerning the exploration and exploitation of the continental shelf and of the subsoil of the sea.[57] The Court, while it admitted that according to both Portugal and Australia the people of East Timor had a right to self-determination, found that there was no clearly binding resolution by UN organs stating an obligation not to recognize any authority of Indonesia over the territory. The Court recalled that some states had concluded agreements with Indonesia, without making reservations in relation to East Timor, and that the letter of protest circulated by Portugal at the United Nations after the conclusion of the 1989 agreement had not been followed by actions on the part of the General Assembly or the Security Council.[58] Portugal, in its authority as administering power, had been careful in presenting its claim as a request for the Court to ascertain the breach by Australia of the right of East Timor's people to self-determination and of Portugal's rights,

any agreement... by colonial and racist Powers which ignores, violates, denies or conflicts with the inalienable right of peoples under colonial domination to self-determination and independence'. The resolution was adopted with the abstention of Western Countries and the negative vote of a few.

[55] ICJ, *Legal Consequences for States of the Continued Presence of South Africa in Namibia (South West Africa) notwithstanding Security Council Resolution 276 (1970)*, Advisory Opinion of 21 June 1971, *ICJ Reports* (1971) paras 121–122, at 55.

[56] Para. 126, at 56.

[57] Text of the treaty in J.I. Charney and L.M. Alexander, *International Maritime Boundaries* (1993), vol. II, 1245 *et seq*.

[58] ICJ, *Case Concerning East Timor (Portugal v Australia)*, Judgment of 30 June 1995, *ICJ Reports* (1995) 104.

and to adjudge the reparation of the damage caused to the people of East Timor.[59] Australia had stressed that Portugal's application was really concerned with the validity of the agreement, and that the Court could not decide on this issue without considering whether Indonesia's conduct was lawful.[60] The Court agreed that the dispute necessarily concerned Indonesia, and that it could not render a decision in the absence of this party. The Court considered that a judgment would have had to deal necessarily with the question of the legality of Indonesia's presence in East Timor, and, as a consequence, of its 'treaty-making power' with regard to the delimitation and resources of East Timor's continental shelf.[61]

The conclusion of a treaty has been qualified in this case at the same time as both a breach of a peremptory rule (by a third state) and as a possible invalid act (by a state party).[62] Also, the Court may have implied that a duty not to recognize the treaty could have arisen only from a binding resolution of UN organs, even if the matter concerned self-determination.

Practice includes other cases where individual third states have maintained the invalidity of treaties because of conflict with peremptory norms, such as the position taken by the United States with regard to the Treaty of 1978 between the USSR and Afghanistan,[63] or by Algeria in relation to the Madrid Agreement concluded by Spain, Morocco, and Mauritania in 1975 concerning Western Sahara.[64] It is, however, unclear whether these states, clearly moved by political motivations, believed at the same time that they had a duty not to consider the Treaty valid. The silence of other states might be interpreted against the existence of such a duty, but it might also be due to the uncertainty about the existence of a conflict of the Treaties with peremptory norms.

The fact that the invalidity of a treaty concluded under coercion or in conflict with *jus cogens* has been directly or indirectly affirmed by international jurisprudence, independently from a request by the states parties, is not immediately relevant to the present inquiry,[65] but it strengthens the notion that the declaration of invalidity is not dependent upon the initiative of the parties. When invalidity is ascertained by a court of a third state, this is instead relevant state practice. This is the case of the 1938 Munich Agreement on the transfer to Germany of the Sudetenland, considered void by Dutch courts after World War II, because

[59] Ibid., 94–5. [60] Ibid., 100. [61] Ibid., 105.

[62] E. Milano, *Unlawful Territorial Situations in International Law*, *supra* note 28, 185 sees in the agreement concluded by Australia a breach of the duty of non-recognition of the situation created by Indonesia's denial to East Timor of the right to self-determination.

[63] The United States held that, as far as the Treaty would support Soviet intervention in that country, it was void because of conflict with *jus cogens*. M. Nash, 'US Contemporary Practice Relating to International Law', 74 *AJIL* (1980) 418.

[64] Algeria considered the agreement invalid because it was in contrast with the principle of self-determination. On the dispute see H.P. Gasser, 'The Conflict in Western Sahara', 5 *Yearbook of International Humanitarian Law* (2002) 375–80.

[65] Some cases are reported by A. Orakhelashvili, *Peremptory Norms in International Law*, *supra* note 2, 154–5.

it had been concluded under the threat of force.[66] As national courts refer more frequently nowadays to the concept of *jus cogens*, they seem more willing to acknowledge the invalidity of a treaty in conflict with a peremptory norm, or concluded under coercion.[67]

6. Towards an Obligation for Third States not to Recognize a Treaty as Absolutely Invalid

With regard to non-recognition of territorial situations arising from a grave breach of a peremptory rule, critics have long expressed the view that it is difficult to conceive of their nullity when those situations are effective.[68] Other criticisms affirm that genocide or torture do not give rise to any consequences 'capable of being denied by other States'.[69] These views, whatever their merits, cannot be applied to treaties. Treaties are legal acts; their non-recognition can well express states' appreciation of their validity or invalidity according to the law of treaties.[70]

When the ILC proposed coercion and conflict with *jus cogens* as grounds of invalidity of treaties, it built on some pre-existing practice; and this practice related significantly to the positions assumed by third states. Even a brief review of the origins of the notion of non-recognition shows how this expression was used in relation to both territorial situations and treaties. The term conveys, with regard to treaties, simply the opinion of a state not party that a certain treaty is invalid.

More contemporary practice does nothing to dispel the idea that third states consider a treaty invalid because it is in conflict with peremptory rules

[66] I. Brownlie, *International Law and the Use of Force by States*, *supra* note 29, 405 *et seq.*, 416 *et seq.*; G. Napoletano, *Violenza e trattati nel diritto internazionale* (Milano: Giuffrè, 1977) 402 *et seq.*; J.A. Frowein, 'Nullity in International Law', 7 *Encyclopaedia of Public International Law* (1984) 363. The Munich Pact was declared null in the Federal Republic of Germany–Czechoslovak agreement of 11 December 1973.

[67] For the relevance of peremptory norms, among other examples, see the German Constitutional Court's judgment of 26 October 2004, paras 97–98, available at <http://www.bundesverfassungsgericht.de/en>.

[68] G. Ziccardi Capaldo, *Le situazioni territoriali illegittime nel diritto internazionale*, *supra* note 28, 50 *et seq.* J. Verhoeven, *La reconnaissance internationale dans la pratique contemporaine*, *supra* note 25, 590 *et seq.*, gives to the obligation not to recognize a role only in the promotion of rules.

[69] Separate Opinion by Judge Kooijmans, ICJ, *Legal Consequences of the Construction of a Wall in the Occupied Palestinian Territory*, Advisory Opinion of 9 July 2004, *ICJ Reports* (2004) 232, para. 44; S. Talmon, 'The Duty Not to 'Recognize as Lawful' a Situation Created by the Illegal Use of Force or Other Serious Breaches of a *Jus Cogens* Obligation: An Obligation without Real Substance?', in Ch. Tomuschat and J.-M. Thouvenin (eds), *The Fundamental Rules of the International Legal Order*, *supra* note 6, 120.

[70] As Ch. Tomuschat points out, 'non-recognition is a device through which a juridical situation can be addressed': 'International Crimes by States: An Endangered Species?', in K. Wellens (ed.), *International Law: Theory and Practice—Essays in Honour of Erik Suy* (The Hague–Boston–London: Martinus Nijhoff, 1998) 259.

or concluded under coercion, independently from the initiatives of states parties.[71] As the Vienna Convention preparatory works did not address the position of third states, this may be considered a matter left out of codification.

What seems to result clearly from earlier and later practice is that non-recognition is linked to the primary and peremptory norm. Because the norms evoked (prohibition on aggression, self-determination, prohibition on apartheid) are understood to be addressing all states, states not parties to the treaty consider themselves entitled not to recognize the treaty.

This still does not explain, however, whether the conclusion of a treaty in conflict with a peremptory norm may at the same time be considered a wrongful act, and whether an obligation not to recognize arises as a legal consequence of this wrongful act; or whether third states have a duty not to recognize the invalid treaty simply on the basis of the peremptory norm.

In the absence of different indications from practice, the preferable solution appears to consider non-recognition as part of the content of the primary peremptory rule.[72] A duty of non-recognition has little to do with the consequences of a wrongful act. Non-recognition is an obligation concerning all states, including the wrongdoers, and this by itself is quite exceptional in the regime of responsibility. Also, the obligation is not instrumental in the exercise of some other right, as in the case of obligations which the injured state must fulfil prior to resort to countermeasures. The fact that an obligation in this sense is provided for in Article 41 of the state responsibility codification may be explained by noting that the duty arises in the specific situation only once an invalid treaty has been concluded: a condition similar to the duty of cessation of the continuous wrongful act by the wrongdoer state provided for in Article 30 of the responsibility codification, considered by the ILC to be an effect of the primary rule. The conclusion reached finds some support in the *Wall* Opinion, where the Court links the obligation not to recognize the illegal situation resulting from the construction of the wall in the occupied Palestinian Territory to the 'character and importance of the rights and obligations involved'.[73, 74]

71 A. de Hoogh, *Obligations* Erga Omnes *and International Crimes* (The Hague–London–Boston: Kluwer Law International, 1996) 48, reaches the conclusion that third states may invoke the invalidity of treaties in conflict with peremptory norms according to the customary law of treaties.

72 The view, certainly not a novel one (among others, R.Y. Jennings, 'Nullity and Effectiveness in International Law', in *Cambridge Essays in International Law* (London: Stevens & Sons, 1965) 75; S. Rosenne, 'The Settlement of Treaty Disputes under the Vienna Convention of 1969', *supra* note 12, 35; J.A. Frowein, 'Jus Cogens', *supra* note 12, 329), even if usually limited to brief remarks, has been lately supported by A. Orakhelashvili, *Peremptory Norms in International Law*, *supra* note 2, 143 (see this work's critical review by P. Picone, 89 *Riv. di Diritto Internaz.* (2006) 1240 *et seq.*); E. Milano, *Unlawful Territorial Situations in International Law*, *supra* note 28, 140, 151. See also the Dissenting Opinion of Judge *ad hoc* Skubiszewski in the *Case Concerning East Timor (Portugal v Australia)*, Judgment of 30 June 1995, *supra* note 58, 262.

73 ICJ, *Legal Consequences of the Construction of a Wall in the Occupied Palestinian Territory*, Advisory Opinion of 9 July 2004, *supra* note 69, 200.

74 A similar conclusion has been reached, to some extent, by Professor Gaja with regard to the duty to ensure compliance with obligations *erga omnes*. 'Do States Have A Duty to Ensure

A crucial point which appears to be left open by practice is whether states have a duty, or rather a discretionary power, not to recognize the invalid treaty under general international law and independently from binding resolutions.[75] Because of the absolute character of the invalidity, and of the peremptory primary rule, third states should have an obligation to consider the treaty null. This would furthermore appear consistent with the Opinion on the *Wall* as well as the state responsibility codification, which is admittedly on this point partially a work of progressive development of international law.[76] Practice seems to point out the difficulty of ascertaining the conflict with a peremptory norm—a difficulty resolved by a UN organ resolution—more than the uncertainty about the consequences to be drawn by the contrast, once established.[77]

Compliance with Obligations Erga Omnes by Other States?' in M. Ragazzi (ed.), *International Responsibility Today. Essays in Memory of Oscar Schachter* (Leiden–Boston: Martinus Nijhoff Publishers, 2005) 31.

[75] The existence in general international law of an obligation not to recognize acquisitions of territory by unlawful use of force is already maintained by I. Brownlie in *International Law and the Use of Force by States, supra* note 29, 418 *et seq.*, and reaffirmed by V. Rodriguez Cedeno, 'Sixth Report on Unilateral Acts of States', *supra* notes, 11–12.

[76] J. Crawford, 'Multilateral Rights and Obligations in International Law', 319 *Recueil des Cours* (2006) 473, considers that Chapter III of Part Two is a framework for progressive development, but that the obligation not to recognize 'already reflects general international law'.

[77] In its Commentary to Article 41, the International Law Commission stressed the role of '[c]ollective non-recognition as a prerequisite for any concerted community response', *YILC* (2001), vol. II(2), 115.

21

Desuetude and Obsolescence of Treaties*

*Marcelo G. Kohen***

Since the purpose of the present book is to examine matters related to the Law of Treaties that go beyond the Vienna Conventions of 1969 and 1986 (to paraphrase the title of Giorgio Gaja's course on *jus cogens* at the Hague Academy),[1] I thought it would be of some interest to deal with the topics of desuetude and obsolescence of treaties. As a matter of fact, although the ILC first, and the Vienna Conferences later, did not consider it necessary to include these institutions within the grounds for the termination of treaties, states continue to refer to them, not always in an accurate way. The purpose of this contribution is to briefly analyse whether this apparent gap in the Vienna Conventions is justified, and what are the consequences of this lack of inclusion of desuetude and obsolescence of treaties in the abovementioned codification instruments adopted in Vienna in 1969 and 1986.

1. The Exclusion of Desuetude and Obsolescence from the Vienna Conventions

In his famous *Discours préliminaire* explaining the *Code Napoléon* draft, Portalis explained that no authorization was given to invoke desuetude as a ground for the termination of laws because to do otherwise would have been dangerous. He

* It is a great honour and pleasure to contribute to this collection of essays in honour of one of the most distinguished Italian international legal scholars of today. Many institutions have taken advantage of Giorgio Gaja's rigorous analysis of international legal phenomena, including the International Law Commission (ILC), the International Court of Justice (ICJ), and the *Institut de droit international*, among others. His charming personality, modesty, sense of responsibility, and commitment to collective work has earned him esteem from his colleagues, his students, and all those who have enjoyed the pleasure of working with him.

** The author thanks his assistant, Ms Katherine Del Mar, also teaching assistant at the Law Faculty of the University of Geneva, and Mr Facundo Gómez Pulisich, Ph. D. candidate at the Graduate Institute, for their invaluable help in the preparation of this text.

[1] G. Gaja, 'Jus Cogens beyond the Vienna Convention', 172 *Recueil des Cours* (1981-III) 271–315.

added that this cannot dissimulate the fact that by their unelaborated but nonetheless concerted action, peoples make justice of bad laws.[2] It could be questioned whether the ILC initially, and the Vienna Conferences subsequently, did not act in a similar manner with regard to desuetude and the obsolescence of treaties.

As is known, Part V of the Vienna Conventions dealing with the grounds for invalidity, termination, or suspension of treaties begins with Article 42, the object of which is to limit these grounds to those that are exclusively recognized by the Conventions, and—as far as termination or suspension of treaties are concerned—to the possible grounds foreseen by a treaty itself.[3] As a consequence, in those cases where the Vienna Conventions are applicable to a given treaty, states or international organizations which are parties to these instruments would be precluded from invoking other grounds for the treaty's invalidity, termination, or suspension other than those set out in the Vienna Conventions. The question arises whether outside the scope of application of the Vienna Conventions there exist other grounds for the invalidity, termination, or suspension of treaties at the customary level that have 'survived' the process of codification.

The exclusion of desuetude and obsolescence as grounds for the termination of treaties in the Vienna Conventions was not an act of forgetfulness by the ILC or the Conferences. It was a deliberate decision. In its Commentary to what became Article 42, the ILC considered whether the inclusion of desuetude in the Vienna Conventions was appropriate, and it concluded in the negative, arguing that this situation was covered by what was to become Article 54(b) of the Vienna Convention, according to which all treaties may be terminated by agreement of all the parties. For the Commission, the legal basis of desuetude or obsolescence as a ground for the termination of a treaty is 'the consent of the parties to abandon the treaty, which is to be implied from their conduct in relation to the treaty'.[4] This is a particular understanding of desuetude, i.e. termination by tacit agreement of the parties to the treaty. However, this is not the only possible understanding of desuetude and it is certainly not the traditional understanding of desuetude since post-classical Roman Law.[5] Indeed, the main idea underpinning

[2] Portalis, *Discours préliminaire au premier projet de Code civil* (Bordeaux: Confluences, 1999) 26–7.

[3] For a commentary of Article 42, see, in French: M.G. Kohen, 'Article 42', in O. Corten and P. Klein (eds), *Les Conventions de Vienne sur le droit des traités: Commentaire article par article* (Brussels: Bruylant, 2006) 1593–614; in English: M.E. Villiger, *Commentary on the 1969 Vienna Convention on the Law of Treaties* (Leiden–Boston: Martinus Nijhoff Publishers, 2009) 541–9; and M.G. Kohen and S. Heathcote, 'Article 42' in O. Corten and P. Klein (eds), *Vienna Conventions on the Law of Treaties: A Commentary* (Oxford: Oxford University Press, 2010).

[4] *YILC* (1966), vol. II, 237.

[5] For a brief account of the relationship between *lex* and *consuetudo*, and the possibility of abrogation of the former by *desuetudo*, see A.A. Schiller, 'Custom in Classical Roman Law', 24 *Virginia Law Review* (1937) 268–82; S. Solazzi, *Scritti di Diritto Romano* (Naples: Jovene, 1960) 275–92; J.A.C. Thomas, 'Custom and Roman Law', 31 *Tijdschrift voor Rechtsgeschiedenis* (1963) 39-53; J.A.C. Thomas, 'Desuetudo', XII *Revue internationale de droits de l'antiquité* (1965) 469–83.

desuetude is the termination of treaties by virtue of the passing of a considerable lapse of time during which the treaty is not applied by the treaty parties.[6]

2. The Notion of Desuetude

In his Second Report, Sir Gerald Fitzmaurice asserted that:

While there is no general legal principle of prescription or obsolescence *longi temporis* for treaties, according to which they may lapse by the mere passage of time as such, failure by both or all the parties over a long period to apply or invoke a treaty, or other conduct evidencing a lack of interest in it, may amount to a tacit agreement by the parties to disregard the treaty, or to treat it as terminated.[7]

Faced with two different visions of the phenomenon in question, the ILC adopted the 'contractualist' theory of desuetude, according to which it is a tacit agreement which leads to the termination of a treaty. The other view is nonetheless not only the one which best represents the original meaning of the term, but also represents the core idea of the term, namely the termination of a treaty because of its non-application over a prolonged period of time, which includes a prolonged practice contrary to what is foreseen by the treaty (the so-called *consuetudo abrogatoria*).[8] *Desuetudo* being, in a sense, the flipside of *consuetudo*, this negative practice must be coupled with an *opinio juris*, in other words, the conviction by the parties that the treaty has been extinguished.[9]

Article 54(b) of the Vienna Conventions allows for the termination of a treaty by consent of all the parties. As we have mentioned, in the ILC's view, such consent can also be achieved through tacit agreement. In the same vein, Article 59 of

[6] This paper only deals with desuetude of treaties. As a matter of course, the question also arises with regard to customary rules, resolutions of international organizations, unilateral acts, and other instruments.

[7] *YILC* (1957), vol. II, p. 28. And Sir Gerald commented: 'Indeed it would be possible to point to a number of treaties centuries old, framed in archaic language, and seldom invoked *in terms* or referred to by the parties, which the latter nevertheless regard as being still in force' (ibid., 48).

[8] On the identity of effects of simple inobservance of a rule and the practice contrary thereto, see: F. Geny, *Méthode d'interprétation et sources en droit privé positif, Essai critique* (Paris: LGDJ, 1954) vol. I, 406–7.

[9] For an analysis of desuetude in international law, see A. Vamvoukos, *Termination of Treaties in International Law. The Doctrine of 'rebus sic stantibus' and Desuetude* (Oxford: Clarendon Press, 1985) 325; J.L. Brierly, 'Some Considerations on the Obsolescence of Treaties', II *Transactions of the Grotius Society* (1926) 4–20; A. Goellner, *Pré-caducité, caducité et désuétude en matière de droit international public (essai juridique)* (Paris: Rousseau, 1939), even though the latter two authors mentioned confuse obsolescence or desuetude with fundamental change of circumstances. See also R. Kolb, 'La désuétude en droit international public', 111 *RGDIP* (2007) 577–608 and G. Le Floch, 'La désuétude en droit international public', ibid., 609–42; F. Capotorti, 'L'extinction et la suspension des traités', 134 *Recueil des Cours* (1971-III) 417–587; N. Kontou, *The Termination and Revision of Treaties in the Light of New Customary International Law* (Oxford: Clarendon Press, 1994) 24–31; J. Leca, *Les techniques de révision des conventions internationales* (Paris: LGDJ, 1961) 259–68.

the Vienna Conventions envisages the possibility of terminating a treaty by the subsequent conclusion of another treaty by all the same parties and on the same subject-matter. Both can be forms of tacit abrogation of treaties in which the consent of the parties plays the decisive role. As such, they do not offer theoretical problems. Only in practice can there be difficulties in demonstrating the existence or not of a tacit agreement, and whether the intention of the parties was to abrogate the previous treaty, entirely or only in part. These concerns, however, are far from being related to the matter of the termination of treaties by desuetude. It is true that an earlier treaty can be rendered inapplicable by the entry into force of a subsequent one the content of which prevents the former one from being applied. This situation could be equated with obsolescence. In any case, since this is the outcome of a new treaty reflecting a new coordination of the will of the parties, there is no need to invoke a different ground for termination. Moreover, as will be discussed below, the notion of obsolescence refers to a situation where major changes in the international legal system or in the law governing the parties to the treaty concerned take place.

The question under discussion here does not refer to the termination of treaties by the emergence of a new general customary rule on the same subject-matter but having different content.[10] By virtue of the *lex specialis* rule, there is no automatic termination or modification of the existing treaty: the special rule will take priority over the general rule, whether it is earlier or later in time. Only the emergence of a new peremptory norm will terminate a treaty in force where that treaty is in contradiction with the former treaty's rules, as foreseen by Article 64 of the Vienna Conventions.

3. Is Desuetude a Ground for the Termination of Treaties?

The real question remains whether the traditional understanding of desuetude, based on the passage of a prolonged period of time without the treaty being applied, expresses the existence in international law of a ground for termination not included in the Vienna Conventions.

Some traditional theoretical positions may explain the persistence in invoking desuetude as a ground for termination of treaties. The idea of desuetude is akin to that of prescription. In the case of desuetude, it is the termination of a treaty by the passage of time, whereas in the case of prescription what is at stake is the

[10] The 1964 draft provisionally adopted by the ILC had envisaged the possibility of modification or termination of treaties by means of a new customary rule in contradiction with the treaty concerned, but the idea was abandoned (see Article 68(c), *YILC* 1964, vol. II, 198). In the *France/UK Continental Shelf Delimitation* Arbitral Award, the Court of Arbitration admitted such a possibility but 'under certain circumstances' and as 'evidence [to] the assent of the States concerned to the modification, or even termination, of previously existing treaty rights and obligations' (XVIII *RIAA*, at 37, para. 47).

extinction and creation of subjective rights and obligations. In the former case, the inaction of the parties would allow for termination. In the latter case, it is the inaction of the holder of a right. The discussion about the existence or not of prescription in international law is as old as the science of international law itself, and it is an ongoing debate. As a matter of fact, what is essential for the acquisition of a 'prescriptive' title in international law is not the mere passage of time, but specific conduct by the title holder showing that the holder had abandoned the title.[11]

Another explanation for some theoretical acceptance of desuetude in international law is the Kelsenian notion of the effectiveness of norms as a condition for their existence. If one follows this approach, a rule that is not applied over a certain period of time loses its validity. What is remarkable is that even those authors who adhere to this theoretical position have shown reluctance to categorically affirm the possibility of desuetude of treaties.[12]

Another recent use of the doctrine of desuetude aims to justify illegal conduct on the basis that such conduct, while not challenged and imitated by a sufficient number of other states, leads to the termination of a given rule.[13] However, such a theoretical account is manifestly unsatisfactory if we take the preferred example of Article 2(4) of the UN Charter. It is apparent that this approach overlooks the importance of the legal justifications advanced by the wrongdoers and their potential reaction to similar action that other actors may take. Furthermore, it does not strictly analyse the significance of the attitude of the rest of the international community either, as it equates silence, or the political will not to react to the violation, as being tantamount to accepting the coming to an end of the existence of the rule at issue.[14]

The existence or not of desuetude and obsolescence in international law can be appraised through an examination of international practice, as well as by inference of the logical necessity of their existence, taking into account the nature of the international legal system and the existence of other institutions that could fulfil similar functions in the system. In order to assess the existence or not of

[11] My views on this are essentially presented in 'L'influence du temps sur les règlements territoriaux', in SFDI, *Le droit international et le temps*. Colloque de Paris 2000 (Paris: Pedone, 2001) 129–57. For a recent judicial position, see: ICJ, *Sovereignty over Pedra Branca/Pulau Batu Puteh, Middle Rocks and South Ledge (Malaysia v Singapore)*, Judgment of 23 May 2008, *ICJ Reports* (2008) 12.

[12] R.W. Tucker, 'The Principle of Effectiveness in International Law', in *Law and Politics in the World Community. Essays on Hans Kelsen's Pure Theory and Related Problems in International Law* (Berkeley–Los Angeles: University of California Press, 1953) 31–48, in particular at 34, and at 47–8.

[13] M.J. Glennon, 'How International Rules Die', 93 *Georgetown Law Journal* (2005) 939–91.

[14] For further developments on this point, see my contributions: 'The Use of Force by the United States after the End of the Cold War and Its Impact on International Law', in M. Byers and G. Nolte (eds), *United States Hegemony and the Foundations of International Law* (Cambridge: Cambridge University Press, 2003) 197–231 and 'La pratique et la théorie des sources du droit international', in SFDI, *La pratique et le droit international*, colloque de Genève (Paris: Pedone, 2004) 81–111, especially at 90–2.

desuetude in international law, international practice concerning the continuing legal force of old treaties will first be examined, followed by an analysis of the two leading cases frequently cited in support of desuetude, which will each be discussed in turn.

3.1. Continuing legal force of old treaties

International practice evinces that the mere passage of time, even the passage of considerable time, does not affect the continuing existence of treaties and their applicability to more recent situations and events. Indeed, the International Court of Justice has on occasion applied very old treaties. In the *Right of Passage Case*, for example, the Court examined the Treaty of Poona of 1779 between Portugal and the Marathas.[15] The passage of time from the conclusion of the Treaty in the last quarter of the eighteenth century to its invocation before the Court in this case did not affect the continuing legal force of the Treaty. In a more recent case, the Court in *Case concerning Sovereignty over Pedra Branca/Pulau Batu Puteh, Middle Rocks and South Ledge* referred to a number of treaties from the first quarter of the nineteenth century, including the Anglo-Dutch Treaty of 1814 (the Convention of London), the 1824 Anglo-Dutch treaty signed on 17 March 1824, and a series of treaties concluded with Johor.[16] Certainly, some clauses of these old treaties may have become obsolete,[17] but it was not suggested that these treaties, concluded without any time limit, had been terminated either by the mere passage of time or by its execution.

In the lists of treaties in force elaborated by some states, it is also apparent that the age of the instrument is no bar to its continuing legal force.[18] For example, in the list of treaties concluded by France and still in force published by the French Ministry of Foreign Affairs, the first treaty chronologically notified as being in force between France and Switzerland is that of 30 October 1564, concluded by Duke Emmanuel-Philibert of Savoy and the City of Bern, concerning the restitution by Bern of parts of Savoy conquered in 1536.[19]

3.2. The *Yuille, Shortridge & Co.* Arbitral Award

The case law often cited in support of the existence of desuetude as a ground for the termination of treaties is the arbitral award handed down in the *Yuille,*

[15] ICJ, *Case concerning Right of Passage over Indian Territory (Portugal v India)*, Merits, Judgment of 12 April 1960, *ICJ Reports* (1960) 6, at 37.

[16] ICJ, *Case concerning Sovereignty over Pedra Branca/Pulau Batu Puteh, Middle Rocks and South Ledge (Malaysia/Singapore), supra* note 11, para. 21.

[17] See below.

[18] See for example C. Parry and C. Hopkins, *An Index of British Treaties 1101–1968* (London: Her Majesty's Stationary Office, 1970); M.F. Surbiguet and P. Vagogne, *Liste des traités et accords de la France en vigueur au 1er octobre 1988* (Paris: Ministère des Affaires étrangères, 1988).

[19] M.F. Surbiguet and P. Vagogne, *Liste des traités et accords de la France en vigueur au 1er octobre 1988, supra* note 18, at 309.

Shortridge & Co. case. However, this decision falls well short of clearly recognizing the plain abrogation of a treaty by reason of its non-application over a prolonged period of time. The case dealt with the application to a Portuguese judicial decision of 1834 relative to British subjects, of an Article of an Anglo-Portuguese treaty dating back to 1654 and envisaging procedural privileges for British subjects. The Portuguese government invoked the fact that, over many years, a number of British subjects did not take advantage of the privilege which the Treaty had conferred upon them. After having noted that this did not amount to an application which would bind other British subjects, the arbitrator affirmed that:

> ... [t]he question would be of a different nature if the government of Great Britain had on several occasions refused to intervene, considering that the treaty had fallen into desuetude, or if it had, for the same reason, renounced in its pursuit of an already initiated intervention. For it is without doubt that it is for governments to expressly abrogate a treaty or to suspend its usage, which should be considered by their subjects as a desuetude derogating from the treaty. But this non-application should emanate from the government and manifest itself by the refusal to intervene despite requests from its subjects to that effect, or by the abandonment of an already initiated intervention following calls from Portugal based on the treaty's invalidity. However, at the same time one should only admit the suspending effect of the usage relative to the treaty, with great caution. For in those cases in which there would result from the breach of the treaty but little or no harm to British subjects, the intervention of their government would be futile, it would be a gratuitous lack of politeness towards a friendly government; to abstain thus would be an act of courtesy and not one of renunciation.[20]

The arbitrator did not consider that a contrary application had derogated from Article 7 of the 1654 treaty. In the case at hand, a treaty from the seventeenth century was thus applied to events which occurred in the middle of the nineteenth century, after the passage of a considerable period of time during which the Treaty had not been invoked.

The merit of this award, despite its often equivocal terminology, is to highlight the principal difficulty in admitting the concept of desuetude of treaties, namely, determining the will of the parties to put an end to a treaty. Many reasons may explain the mere non-application of a treaty. Sometimes, it may be that a situation

[20] *Yuille, Shortridge & Co. (Great Britain/Portugal)*, award of 21 October 1861, *Lapradelle et Politis, Recueil des Arbitrages Internationaux* (Paris: Pedone, 1923) vol. II, 105. Our translation of: 'La question changerait de caractère si le gouvernement de la Grande Bretagne avait à plusieurs reprises refusé d'intervenir, estimant que le traité était tombé en désuétude, ou s'il avait, pour le même motif, renoncé à poursuivre une intervention commencée. Car il est certain qu'il appartient aux gouvernements d'abroger expressément un traité ou d'en suspendre l'usage, ce qui devra être regardé par leurs sujets comme une désuétude dérogeant au traité. Mais ce non-usage devrait émaner du gouvernement et se manifester par le refus d'intervenir nonobstant les requêtes de ses sujets à cet effet, ou par l'abandon d'une intervention déjà commencé par suite de réclamations de la part du Portugal fondées sur la nullité du traité. Alors même cependant, on ne devrait admettre la vertu suspensive de l'usage, relativement au traité, qu'avec une réserve extrême. Car dans les cas où il ne résulterait de la violation du traité que peu ou point de préjudice pour les sujets britanniques, l'intervention de leur gouvernement serait oiseuse; elle constituerait une impolitesse gratuite envers un gouvernement ami; s'en abstenir serait donc un acte de courtoisie et non de renonciation.'

permitting its application has simply not presented itself. In other cases, a state may, for political or other reasons, decide not to avail itself of the treaty, without this signifying in any way that it renounces doing so in the future. Also, the mere fact of not applying a treaty may evidence a will to suspend it for a certain time and not necessarily to put an end to it. Finally, as Judge De Castro stated in his Dissenting Opinion in the *Nuclear Tests cases*: '[t]he non-invocation of a treaty may in fact be due to its efficacy in obviating disputes between the parties—and thereby constitute the best evidence of its continuance in force'.[21]

3.3. The Austrian Constitutional Court's judgment in the *Land Sale to Alien Case (Amend v Land Tirol)*

Another case decided at the domestic level often cited as an example of the application of desuetude is the *Land Sale to Alien Case (Amend v Land Tirol)*, rendered by the Austrian Constitutional Court on 13 March 1973. The complainant, a citizen of the Federal Republic of Germany, argued that the application of a law requesting him to pay a guarantee for the purchase of land in Austria was in contradiction with the Austrian–German Commercial Treaty of 12 April 1930. The Constitutional Court decided that, whilst the provisions of the Commercial Treaty had never been formally abrogated, they had fallen into desuetude, which, according to the Court, was a ground for the termination of a treaty under international law.[22] A factual analysis shows that the termination of the 1930 Commercial Treaty can be better explained on other grounds. Indeed, the Treaty ceased to be in force with the Austrian *Anschluss* by Germany in 1938. After the Second World War, the Western Allied Authorities asked the Austrian government to notify them which treaties concluded with the German Reich should be proposed for re-application in the relations between it and the Federal Republic of Germany. The Austrian list did not include the 1930 Commercial Treaty, nor did the German Federal government approach Austria with the view to its possible re-application.[23] Hence, the idea of desuetude is completely alien as a ground for the termination of the 1930 Commercial Treaty.

4. The Distinction between Desuetude and Obsolescence of Treaties

In its abovementioned Commentary, the Commission appears to have assimilated desuetude with obsolescence. France did likewise when it claimed in the *Nuclear Tests cases*, that the General Act of 1928 had fallen into desuetude due

[21] ICJ, *Nuclear Tests (Australia v France)*, Judgment of 20 December 1974, *ICJ Reports* (1974) 253, at 381, footnote 1.

[22] Case No. B 103/71, 77 *ILR* (1988) 433. See B. Simma, 'Termination and Suspension of Treaties. Two Recent Austrian Cases', 21 *GYIL* (1978) 74–96, at 90–6.

[23] Ibid.

to the disappearance of the League of Nations.[24] Belgium also appears to have invoked the concepts indiscriminately in the case concerning the *Legality of the Use of Force (Serbia and Montenegro v Belgium)* when it argued that the 1930 Convention of Conciliation, Judicial Settlement and Arbitration between the Kingdom of Yugoslavia and Belgium, invoked by Serbia and Montenegro to found the Court's jurisdiction, had lapsed due to 'obsolescence or desuetude or on the basis of the implied consent of the parties'.[25]

Yet it is important to distinguish desuetude from obsolescence, which is a distinct concept. Obsolescence (either called *obsolescence* or *caducité* in French) refers to the impossibility of applying a treaty due to the disappearance of a legal situation which constituted one of its essential conditions. In contrast to Article 61 of the Vienna Convention, which deals with the *material impossibility* of performance due to the disappearance of an object indispensable for the performance of a treaty, in the case of obsolescence, what is at issue is a *legal impossibility*. An example of such a scenario is found in the reference to 'Enemy States' contained in Articles 53, 106, and 107 of the United Nations Charter.

The changes which have occurred in Europe since the fall of the Berlin Wall also provide other examples. Thus, on 6 November 1990, Austria notified the state parties to the Austrian State Treaty of 15 May 1955 that it considered the military and aviation clauses of the Treaty to be obsolete. The four contracting parties (France, the United Kingdom, the United States of America, and the USSR) replied by consenting to the Austrian notification.[26] One may query whether in this situation there was in fact a legal impossibility. The fact that Austria and the other state parties expressed their consent to no longer apply the clauses in question shows that they wanted to dispel any possible doubt about the applicability

[24] Letter of the French Ambassador in The Netherlands to the Registrar dated 16 May 1973, ICJ, *Pleadings, Nuclear Tests*, vol. II, 348–54. The Court carefully avoided pronouncing on the question of the maintenance in force of the Act of 1928, both in those cases and in the ICJ, *Trial of Pakistani Prisoners of War (Pakistan v India)*, Provisional Measures, Order of 13 July 1973, *ICJ Reports* (1973) 328 *et seq*. (see the *Statement of the Government of India of 4 June 1973, ICJ Pleadings (Correspondence)*, 143–4); ICJ, *Aegean Sea Continental Shelf (Greece v Turkey)*, Judgment of 19 December 1978, *ICJ Reports* (1978) 17, para. 39; and ICJ, *Aerial Incident of 10 August 1999 (Pakistan v India)*, Jurisdiction, Judgment of 21 June 2000, *ICJ Reports* (2000) 12, at 25, para. 28.

[25] ICJ, *Legality of the Use of Force (Serbia and Montenegro v Belgium)*, Preliminary Objections of Belgium, 5 July 2000, 134–9, paras 412–423. See also CR 2004/6, 32, para. 60 (Bethlehem) and CR 2004/15, p. 14, para.16 (Bethlehem). Serbia and Montenegro replied that the 1969 Vienna Convention 'does not leave room for obsolescence or desuetude' and 'Belgium has failed to produce any proof of implied consent of the parties to terminate the 1930 Convention' CR 2004/14, 59, paras 47–50 (Djeric) and CR 2004/23, 36–7, paras 26–31 (Djeric). As in the *Nuclear Tests* cases of 1974, the Court avoided pronouncing on the issue in its decision of 2004, stating that its jurisdiction could not be founded on the 1930 Convention 'even assuming that that instrument was in force on 29 April 1999 at the date of filing of the Application. The Court therefore does not need to pronounce on the question whether the 1930 Convention was or was not in force on that date': *Legality of the Use of Force (Serbia and Montenegro v Belgium)*, Preliminary Objections, Judgment of 15 December 2004, *ICJ Reports* (2004) 327, para. 126.

[26] See on the question: G. Hafner 'L' "obsolescence" de certaines dispositions du traité autrichien de 1955', 37 *AFDI* (1991) 239–57.

of the said provisions. It was in fact the agreement of the parties (Article 54(b) of the 1969 Convention) which formed the basis of the termination of Articles 12 to 16 of the Austrian State Treaty.

5. Conclusion

The Vienna Conventions rightly did not include desuetude as a ground for the termination of treaties. Indeed, desuetude does not find a place in international law. The mere passage of time without any reference to a treaty or even without its application does not lead to its termination. The fact that states refer in their practice to 'dormant' treaties, which in some cases are many centuries old, is evidence of the basic idea that treaties concluded without time limits are not terminated by the simple fact of their old age.

International law offers other grounds for the termination of treaties that are relevant in the circumstances envisaged by the doctrine of desuetude, such as the agreement (even tacit) of all parties to terminate a treaty, or the conclusion of a subsequent treaty by the same parties on the same subject-matter, both being incompatible. Like other mechanisms relating to the attribution of legal effects by the mere passage of time, such as prescription, there is no need in international law to have recourse to desuetude. As Grotius stated more than three centuries ago: 'time, in fact, in its own nature has no effective force; nothing is done by time, though everything is done in time'.[27]

On the basis of the above, it can be asserted that desuetude does not constitute a ground for termination of treaties that exists in general international law, irrespective of its non-inclusion in the grounds for termination listed in the Vienna Conventions. It is also submitted that obsolescence emerges as a ground for the termination of a treaty (or some of its provisions) outside the regime of the Vienna Convention, when a change in the legal framework of a treaty renders whole or part of the treaty inapplicable.

[27] H. Grotius, *De Jure Ac Pacis Libri Tres*, vol. II, Chapter 4, I, translated by F.W. Kelsey (Oxford: Clarendon Press, 1925) 220.

22

Invalidity and Termination of Treaties and Rules of Procedure

Annalisa Ciampi

1. The Rules of the Vienna Convention

The Vienna Convention on the Law of Treaties[1] provides for a specific procedure to be followed with respect to the invalidity or the termination of the operation of a treaty.

According to the complex international procedure laid down in Articles 65–68 for ascertaining the invalidity or termination of a treaty, a party which, under the provisions of the Convention, 'invokes either a defect in its consent to be bound by a treaty or a ground for impeaching the validity of a treaty, terminating it, withdrawing from it or suspending its operation, must notify the other parties of its claim. The notification shall indicate the measure proposed to be taken with respect to the treaty and the reasons therefore' (Article 65(1)). If, after the expiry of a period which, except in cases of special urgency, shall not be less than three months after the receipt of the notification, no party has raised any objection, the party making the notification may carry out the measure which it has proposed (Article 65(2)). If, however, an objection has been raised by any other party, the parties shall seek a solution through the means indicated in Article 33 of the Charter of the United Nations (UN) but also in compliance with any provisions in force binding the parties with regard to the settlement of disputes. For the general obligation of peaceful settlement restated in the Vienna Convention does not affect the special rights or obligations of the parties under international treaties with respect to dispute settlement (Article 65(3) and (4)).

If no solution has been reached within a period of 12 months following the date on which the objection was raised—either because a stalemate between the parties to the dispute has occurred during negotiations or because one or more parties is reluctant to agree to a particular form of dispute settlement, to participate at all in

[1] 1969 Vienna Convention on the Law of Treaties (VCLT), 1155 *UNTS*, 331.

any such procedure, or to accept the solution proposed thereby, and no provision concerning compulsory jurisdiction between the parties comes into effect—both the notifying and the objecting state (or states) may unilaterally set in motion one of the following procedures, depending on the nature of the dispute. If the dispute concerns the application or the interpretation of Articles 53 or 64, any one of the parties 'may, by a written application, submit it to the International Court of Justice (ICJ) for a decision unless the parties by common consent agree to submit the dispute to arbitration' (Article 66(a)).[2] Where, instead, the dispute concerns the application or the interpretation of any of the other Articles in Part V of the Convention, any one of the parties may set in motion the procedure before the Conciliation Commission set up under the Annex to the Convention, 'by submitting a request to that effect to the Secretary-General of the United Nations' (Article 66(b)).

The latter provisions were only inserted in the Convention during the Vienna Conference, where some delegates criticized the International Law Commission (ILC) for not having dealt with the real problem: the case that parties would not reach agreement on their dispute through any of the means of peaceful settlement provided in Articles 33 of the UN Charter (and no procedure leading to a binding solution would be applicable between—or agreed upon by—the parties). The debate resulted in a compromise.[3] On ratifying the Convention, however, a number of states have sought to exclude the compulsory jurisdiction of the ICJ, while others have rejected these attempts, reflecting the heated debate in Vienna.[4]

Subject to the adaptations necessary to take into account that international organizations have no *locus standi* under the Statute of the ICJ, the Vienna Convention on the Law of Treaties Between States and International Organizations or Between International Organizations of 1986[5] provides for an analogous procedure.[6]

[2] Western states, in particular, perceived the possibility of a judicial settlement by the ICJ as a safeguard against the risk of disruption of the principle *pacta sunt servanda* because of claims based upon the invocation of *jus cogens*, a notion strongly supported and advocated by Third World countries.

[3] While Article 65 was adopted by 106 votes to none, with two abstentions, on the penultimate day of the Conference, a 10-state proposal introduced a package deal including, *inter alia*, a new Article 62*bis* (now Article 66), which was eventually adopted in a spirit of compromise with the lowest number of affirmative votes in Vienna, ie by 61 votes to 20, with 26 abstentions. M.E. Villiger, *Commentary on the 1969 Vienna Convention on the Law of Treaties* (Leiden–Boston: Martinus Nijhoff Publishers, 2009) at 805 and 818 *et seq.*

[4] See the reservations and declarations concerning Article 66(a) and the objections to them, in *UN Multilateral Treaties*, Chapter XXIII.1.

[5] Vienna Convention on the Law of Treaties Between States and International Organizations or Between International Organizations (Vienna, 21 March 1986, A/CONF/129/15, not yet in force). On the reasons why treaties of international organizations were left out of the 1969 Vienna Convention on the Law of Treaties and that Convention came to be the template on which the 1986 Convention was based, see C. Brölmann, *The Institutional Veil in Public International Law: International Organizations and the Rule of Treaties* (Oxford-Portland, OR: Hart Publishing, 2007).

[6] For further details, see P.K. Menon, *The Law of Treaties between States and International Organizations* (Lewiston–Queenstone–Lampeter: The Edwin Mellen Press, 1992) 125 *et seq.*

None of the Vienna Conventions indicates the course of events if—outside the cases concerning Articles 53 or 64, which may be brought before the ICJ—the notifying and the objecting states fail to agree on the solution of the conciliation commission or to submit the dispute to arbitration (or another procedure for a binding settlement thereof). It is generally held that, during the procedure, a state ought to continue to apply the treaty. As to whether the claim to invalidity or termination should remain paralysed indefinitely, it is reasonable to consider that the power to unilaterally take the measures sought is only suspended, and may be exercised at the end of the procedure.[7]

The provisions of the Vienna Convention have never been applied in practice. It is thus difficult to maintain that they correspond to general rules of international law[8] or establish, even in the relations between the parties, the exclusive procedure for the invocation of the invalidity or termination of the operation of treaties falling within their scope of application.[9]

2. National Courts and the Ascertainment of Invalidity or Termination of Treaties

The thesis has been put forward that most causes of invalidity or termination of treaties are subject to a sort of *sui generis* automaticity: national courts, like

[7] G. Gaja, 'Trattati internazionali', *Digesto delle Discipline Pubblicistiche* (Torino: UTET, 1999) vol. XV, 344 *et seq.*, at 367. For the view that, in the context of the Vienna Convention, the principle *pacta sunt servanda* prevails over the principle *in dubio pro libertate*, see, eg, G. Morelli, 'Aspetti processuali dell'invalidità dei trattati', 57 *Riv. di Diritto Internaz.* (1974) 5 *et seq.*, at 12. On the question of the effects of a unilateral denunciation in the absence of agreement, acquiescence, or another solution binding for the other contracting party(ies), see ICJ, *The Gabčíkovo-Nagymaros Project (Hungary/Slovakia)*, Judgment of 25 September 1997, *ICJ Reports* (1997) 7 *et seq.*: in relation to the Hungary's decision, notified to Czechoslovakia, to terminate the 1977 Treaty, the Court excluded that under the circumstances of the case, the decision had produced its intended effect: 'It would be otherwise, of course, if the parties decided to terminate the Treaty by mutual consent. But in this case, while Hungary purported to terminate the Treaty, Czechoslovakia consistently resisted this act and declared it to be without legal effect' (para. 114). On the *Gabčíkovo-Nagymaros* case and the law of treaties, see M. Fitzmaurice and O. Elias, *Contemporary Issues of the Law of Treaties* (Utrecht: Eleven International Pub., 2005) 34 *et seq.*

[8] That the Vienna Convention does not correspond in this part to general international law was stated by the ICJ in the case *Armed Activities on the Territory of the Congo (New application: 2002) (Democratic Republic of the Congo v Rwanda)*, Judgment of 3 February 2006, *ICJ Reports* (2006) 6 *et seq.*: 'in the present case the rules contained in the Vienna Convention are not applicable, save in so far as they are declaratory of customary international law. The Court considers that the rules contained in Article 66 of the Vienna Convention are not of this character. Nor have the two parties otherwise agreed to apply Article 66 between themselves' (para. 125). As to the formal requirements laid down by Article 65 of the Vienna Convention, see Case C-162/96 *A. Racke GmbH & Co. v Hauptzollamt Mainz* [1998] ECR 1-3655, noting that 'the specific procedural requirements there laid down do not form part of customary international law' (para. 59).

[9] On the mandatory character of the procedure and the impact of Articles 65 and 66 on international practice subsequent to the adoption of the Vienna Convention, however, see L. Sbolci, *Obblighi di procedura nell'estinzione dei trattati* (Padova: CEDAM, 2008) 202 *et seq.*, and 239 *et seq.*, respectively.

anyone called upon to apply a treaty, might judge whether the treaty is invalid or has been terminated and hence is not to be applied, even in the absence of a formal act of denunciation or any such similar manifestation of intent at the international level on the part of the state of which the court is an organ (unless, of course, the exercise of a power of denunciation is itself an independent cause of termination, as provided in Article 56 of the Vienna Convention).[10]

In its proponents' view, a domestic judge's finding and a state's denunciation at the international level are not mutually exclusive but alternative, as they fulfil different functions and have different effects: the first one only affects *the particular case at issue*, while, with a formal act of denunciation, a state proclaims its intent to free itself *once and for all* from its contractual commitment. Concurrence is excluded in relation to few grounds of termination only. On the one hand, the expiration of the specific time period provided for in the treaty for its termination and the abrogation by tacit mutual consent (because of incompatibility with a subsequent treaty) are—obviously—not subject to any further international manifestation of intent as they operate automatically for the simple fact of materializing. On the other hand, the exercise of a power, express or implied, of denunciation or withdrawal which is in itself an independent cause of termination, by definition, requires an international act of denunciation or withdrawal. But for these exceptions, when a cause of invalidity or termination arose, it might be found by national courts and 'other domestic legal operators (government officials, public bodies, and in general anyone called upon to apply the law or secure compliance with it within the state)'.[11]

Most of the case law referred to in support of the power of domestic courts to ascertain the invalidity or termination of treaties concerns treaties allegedly concluded under threat of armed force or contrary to peremptory rules of general international law, while a number of decisions cited in favour thereof concern the alleged breach of the internal norms on the treaty-making power (Article 46 of the Vienna Convention). While the first set of cases deserves to be specifically examined (see, *infra*, Section 5), the latter raises the question of whether national decisions actually deal with issues of validity in relation to the internal rules on the competence to conclude treaties from the viewpoint of municipal, rather than international, law.[12] No domestic court supports the view of an autonomous power to terminate the operation of a treaty on the ground of a fundamental change of circumstances or a party's material breach.[13]

At the abstract level, this thesis is 'inspired' by a particular conception of international law according to which the effectiveness of international law is enhanced

[10] B. Conforti and A. Labella, 'Invalidity and Termination of Treaties: The Role of National Courts', 44 *EJIL* (1990) 44 *et seq.*; B. Conforti, 'Cours général de droit international public', 212 *Recueil des cours* (1988-V) 9 *et seq.*; B. Conforti, *Diritto internazionale* (Napoli: Editoriale Scientifica, 7th edn, 2006) 125 *et seq.*

[11] B. Conforti and A. Labella, 'Invalidity and Termination of Treaties', *supra* note 10, at 49.

[12] The authors point out, however, that the international and municipal viewpoints are interwoven to such an extent that they are 'more often than not, inseparable' (ibid., at 55).

[13] Ibid., at 62–3.

by the ability and will of internal operators, national courts in particular, to exploit up to the maximum possible extent the tools provided under national law to ensure the observance of international law. In this perspective, the strengthening of the role of domestic courts would correspond to a higher degree of observance of international law.[14]

The conception that the need to strengthen the role of national courts is justified for the purposes of enhancing the effectiveness of international law, however, when applied to the case at hand, seems flawed. Still *there is no necessary correspondence between the need to strengthen the role of national courts and that of promoting the observance of international law.*

The stability of international relations and certainty of the law, together with the principle *pacta sunt servanda*, risk being threatened by the recognition of an autonomous power to ascertain the validity or termination of treaties in favour of each and every national court (as well as anyone called upon to apply the law), in the absence of a formal act of denunciation or any such similar manifestation of intent at the international level.

The thesis under consideration also has implications at the level of state responsibility.[15] A court's finding that a treaty is not applicable (eg on the ground that the consent to be bound by it is invalid) is an act attributable to the state of which the court is an organ; in so far as it results in a failure to fulfil the treaty commitments, therefore, its lawfulness is challengeable by the other contracting state(s) under the law of state responsibility. These consequences are not diminished by the fact that the effects of a national court's finding are limited to the particular case at issue: even one single instance of disregard for the treaty provisions and commitments, unless it can be justified, is a breach of the treaty and, therefore, entails the international responsibility of its author. Furthermore, if the breach is

[14] '[T]he effectiveness of international law follows from its application by domestic "legal operators" (as defined above), in particular, national judges, and hence must be founded upon a strengthening of the role of the latter', ibid. The idea is not new: see, eg, Justice Powell's remark in *First City Bank v Banco National de Cuba* of 1972 that '[u]ntil international tribunals command a wider constituency, the courts of the various countries afford the best means for a development of a respected body of international law'. That national courts can be instrumental in enforcing and developing international law has been stressed by many (eg R.A. Falk, *The Role of Domestic Courts in the International Legal Order* (New York: Syracuse University Press, 1964), to mention only one).

[15] The need to keep separate the law of the treaties and the law of international responsibility—'as those two branches of international law obviously have a scope that is distinct' (ICJ, *The Gabčíkovo-Nagymaros Project* (*Hungary v Slovakia*), *supra* note 7, para. 47)—tends to obscure the relations and reciprocal interferences between the two. See D.W. Bowett, 'Treaties and State Responsibility', in *Mélanges Michel Virally—Le droit international au service de la paix, de la justice et du développement* (Paris: Pedone, 1991) 137 *et seq.*; A. Yahi, 'La violation d'un traité: L'articulation du droit de traités et du droit de la responsabilité internationale', 26 *RBDI* (1993) 437 *et seq.*; P. Weil, 'Droit des traités et droit de la responsabilité', in *Le droit international dans un monde en mutation—Liber amicorum en hommage au Professeur Eduardo Jimenez de Aréchaga* (Montevideo: Fundación de cultura internacional, 1994) 523 *et seq.*; P.-M. Dupuy, 'Droit des traités, codification et responsabilité internationale', 43 *AFDI* (1997) 7 *et seq.*; P. Weckel, 'Convergence du droit des traités et du droit de la responsabilité internationale', 102 *RGDIP* (1998) 647 *et seq.*

substantial, it may also give rise to a ground for the termination (or suspension) of the treaty by the other party(ies) (Article 60 of the Vienna Convention).[16]

At the concrete level, the thesis of an autonomous role for national courts is grounded on the idea that they may judge whether a treaty is invalid or has been terminated, without an international act of denunciation or some other equivalent international act being necessary on the part of the state concerned, as part of their function to interpret the applicable law (including international rules). National courts as well as anyone called upon to apply a treaty would thus be endowed with a general power to ascertain the validity and termination of treaties.[17] *Not all questions of invalidity or termination, however, can be reduced to a merely interpretative question.*

3. The Nature of the Problem at the International Level

Despite the formulation of a few provisions according to which under certain circumstances a treaty 'is void',[18] the causes for impeaching the validity or terminating the operation of a treaty do not generally operate automatically. On the contrary, but for a few exceptions, they are conceived as giving the party(ies) concerned the *right to claim* the invalidity or termination of the treaty.[19] This right usually accrues to one of the parties to the treaty: the party whose consent to be bound by a treaty has been expressed in violation of a provision of its internal law regarding competence to conclude treaties (Article 46); the victim of error, fraud, corruption, or coercion of a state representative (Articles 48–51); or the party affected by another party's material breach, the impossibility of performance, or a fundamental change of the circumstances at the basis of the consent to be bound by the treaty (Articles 60–62). It is only if the treaty is in conflict with *jus cogens* (Articles 53 and 64) or its conclusion has been procured by the threat or use of force (Article 52), that the Vienna Convention provides that both parties, in the case of bilateral treaties, or all the parties to a multilateral treaty, are entitled to invalidate it or terminate its operation.

16 For a thorough study of the relationship between the law of treaties and state responsibility in this respect see S. Forlati, *Diritto dei trattati e responsabilità internazionale* (Milano: Giuffrè, 2005) 61 *et seq*.

17 'A domestic judge's finding constitutes an integral part of his decision establishing whether a treaty applies to a particular case, a decision which *inter alia* involves the application of all international customary rules relating to the conclusion, modification and termination of treaties.' B. Conforti and A. Labella, 'Invalidity and Termination of Treaties', *supra* note 10, at 50.

18 See Articles 52 and 53, *infra*, Section 5. Under Article 51: 'The expression of a State's consent to be bound by a treaty which has been procured by the coercion of its representative through acts or threats directed against him *shall be without any legal effect*' (emphasis added).

19 In addition to the specific substantive provisions in Part V, see Articles 69(2) ('A treaty the invalidity of which is *established under the present Convention* is void') and 70 (referring to 'the termination of a treaty *under its provisions or in accordance with the present Convention*') (emphasis added).

In this respect, however, a distinction needs to be made with regard to the causes which, by their very nature, operate automatically, ie produce their effects simply by virtue of the fact that they occur. No doubt, the final term provided by the treaty, when the termination date is reached, brings to an end the operation of the treaty, as does a termination condition, when the condition is fulfilled. Similarly, a cause resulting from another conventional undertaking, when the latter enters into force, terminates the operation of the treaty. With the inclusion in the treaty of a termination date or condition or the conclusion of a subsequent treaty incompatible with the former, in fact, the states parties manifest their will that the treaty be terminated when the specified time limit expires, the condition materializes, or the subsequent treaty enters into force, with no further expression of consent being required (a manifestation of intention would instead be necessary to prevent the treaty from being considered terminated, eg a subsequent agreement which extended the time limit of the original treaty).

But for the said exceptions, the causes of invalidity or termination of treaties *entitle* the injured state or all states parties to the treaty (as the case may be) to plead on the basis thereof the invalidity or termination of a treaty. Their operation, therefore, depends on the exercise of a *power* of which the state is the exclusive holder.

Because their invocation implies the ascertainment of situations of fact or law, the grounds of invalidity or termination—whether they arise out of unilateral acts of the parties or events external thereto—are open to abuse. Indeed, the difficulties in their appraisal give rise to such a risk. The question of possible abuses, however, is merely a possible one: it arises only if—and to the extent that—the state (or states) entitled to invoke a certain ground to invalidate or terminate the operation of a treaty to which it is a party, decides to undertake the necessary steps.

Now, the Vienna Convention deals with the procedure to impeach the validity or terminate a treaty as well as with the consequences thereof, ie both with the questions of *how* to invalidate or terminate a treaty and also with *what effects* that may have. It does not touch upon the real and actual issue of *whether* to invoke the invalidity or termination of a treaty, whenever a possible ground to do so arises.

The Vienna Convention, when a ground for invalidating or terminating a treaty arises, gives the party(ies) concerned different options, including that of not taking any form of reaction under the law of treaties.

The lack of invocation of a ground for impeaching the validity of a treaty or terminating its operation can be the consequence of the most varied considerations. For example, in the case of material breach by one of the parties, the affected party may find it preferable—as long as it has a lasting interest in keeping the conventional regime in force—to tolerate the breach in order to induce the other party to comply with the treaty by showing an attitude of cooperation and assistance, or even to invoke the consequences of the commission of an internationally wrongful act in accordance with the rules on state responsibility, rather than to impinge upon the treaty.[20]

Moreover, at least in relation to bilateral treaties, the Vienna Convention gives the affected party the choice between termination and suspension of the operation of the treaty. The effects of these two types of measures are—in theory, at least—substantially different from one another: in principle, the suspension of a treaty affects its legal existence for a certain period only. It is primarily a safeguard against the risk of unfair implementation of the treaty between the parties but is also a measure which shows the party's faith in a future resumption of the treaty. To this end, in fact, Article 72(2) of the Vienna Convention specifically provides that '[d]uring the period of the suspension the parties shall refrain from acts tending to obstruct the resumption of the operation of the treaty', the ground for this obligation being the principle of good faith implicit in the *pacta sunt servanda* principle.[21]

Furthermore, in relation to the causes of invalidity which allow for the separability of treaty provisions,[22] a state has the choice of whether to invoke the nullity with respect of the whole treaty or only with respect to the particular clauses to which the ground for invalidating the treaty relates. The same choice applies in relation to the causes of termination of treaties.

[20] On human rights treaties—but with comments which can be extended to the invalidation or termination of any treaty—see Y. Tyagi, 'The Denunciation of Human Rights Treaties', 79 *BYIL* (2009) 86 *et seq.*, at 107–8: 'generally only extraordinary developments trigger the denunciation of a human rights treaty. Since most states consider the continuity of treaty obligations as a demonstration of good faith, they do not want to give up an inherent advantage by taking an extreme action that may attract public attention. That is the way a number of states manage their treaty obligations without exercising the right of denunciation. Instead of rushing to formal denunciations of treaties, states with developed systems of law resort to amending domestic legislation, restructuring administrative arrangements, or changing policy prescriptions. Others simply ignore troubling treaties or respect them in breach. In sum, the most important reasons for avoiding denunciation of a treaty are the principles of good faith, imperatives of stability, international comity, and diplomatic constraints. Functional necessities, reciprocal benefits, international reputation, and apprehension of retaliatory action also operate as barriers to the denunciation of treaties. Comparatively, there are always more reasons for continuing with treaty relations than for their termination.' On termination or suspension of the operation of a treaty as a consequence of its breach, see C. Laly-Chevalier, *La violation du traité* (Bruxelles: Bruylant, 2005); R. Pisillo Mazzeschi, *Risoluzione e sospensione dei trattati per inadempimento* (Milano: Giuffrè, 1984); B.P. Sinha, *Unilateral Denunciation of Treaty Because of Prior Violations of Obligations by Other Party* (The Hague: Martinus Nijhoff, 1966).

[21] In practice, however, the suspension of a treaty, which is formally a provisional measure, is generally revoked on the basis of an agreement between the interested parties. G. Gaja, 'Trattati internazionali', *supra* note 7, at 363.

[22] See Article 44(4)—which lays down a special rule for cases of fraud and corruption—and Article 45(5), ruling out separability altogether in cases of coercion or where part of a treaty conflicts with *jus cogens*.

Finally, most causes of invalidity or termination are subject to acquiescence, ie to explicit renunciation or renunciation by conduct.[23] And, under Article 68, at any time before it takes effect, there can be a revocation of the notification or the instrument adopted by the party for impeaching the validity of a treaty, terminating it, withdrawing from it, or suspending its operation.

The Vienna Convention is neutral with respect to all these alternatives. It is up to the discretion of the party(ies) concerned, *in principle*, to make the relevant choices.

The issue of who is competent to take the appropriate decisions for the state (or the international organization) concerned is also not a question of international law. The Vienna Convention describes the person(s) with the authority to sign a treaty (Article 7), but does not mention the person(s) who can invalidate or terminate it. It imposes, however, certain formal requirements: the notification triggering the whole procedure has to be made in writing (Article 67(1)), and any act declaring invalid, terminating, withdrawing from, or suspending the operation of a treaty shall be carried out through an instrument communicated to the other parties; moreover, '[i]f the instrument is not signed by the Head of State, Head of Government or Minister for Foreign Affairs, the representative of the State communicating it may be called upon to produce full powers' (Article 67(2)). These forms ensure that the party wishing to invoke any of the grounds for impeaching the validity, or terminate the operation, of a treaty, does so only after the competent organs have been involved in the process.[24] Who exercises the faculties provided for under Part V of the Vienna Convention, however, remains an essentially domestic issue.[25]

As is well known, states are not unitary, one-dimensional legal actors.[26] It is thus for each state to establish the necessary internal procedures and determine which organ or organs shall or may take part in the process leading to impeachment of the validity or termination of the operation of treaties.

[23] Acquiescence does not apply to coercion and conflict with *jus cogens*. On the loss of the right to invoke a ground for invalidating, terminating, withdrawing from, or suspending the operation of a treaty see Article 46.

[24] In relation to renunciation by international organizations, see, however, the more protective solution provided under the Vienna Convention on the Law of Treaties Between States and International Organizations or Between International Organizations (Article 46(2)).

[25] This in turn recalls the more general question of the exercise at the internal level of any faculty, power, or right provided under international law. International freedoms can be dealt with very differently at the domestic level. That the problem is in itself not a problem of international law but one of national law, of course, does not exclude a conventional regulation, which has so far been lacking in relation to the matter under consideration. See, however, Y. Tyagi, 'The Denunciation of Human Rights Treaties', *supra* note 20, at 94, for the view that the Vienna Convention 'takes for granted that the denunciation of a treaty is the prerogative of the executive branch of the denouncing state'.

[26] Nor are international organizations. See D. Badermans, 'The Souls of International Organizations: Legal Personality and the Lighthouse at Cape Spartel', 37 *Va. J Int'l L* (1996) 275 *et seq*.

4. The Solutions at the National Level

While most, if not all, states have internal rules regarding competence to conclude treaties, they do not generally regulate denunciation (whether as an independent cause of termination or on the basis of another ground of invalidity or termination).[27] The problem of attribution and distribution of competences between state organs in matters of international relations, therefore, has been mainly studied in relation to the treaty-making power (including the authority to formulate, or withdraw, reservations), rather than to the unilateral acts through which a state expresses its intent to impeach the validity or terminate the operation of a treaty.

From a comparative study, it emerges that in states which do provide for a specific regulation, provisions on the termination of treaties tend to mirror provisions on the treaty-making power.[28] Where no express regulation under national law of the competence to impeach the validity or terminate treaties exists, the rules on the conclusion of treaties apply by analogy or analogous ones tend to be followed in practice.[29]

[27] See W.E. Butler (ed.), *The Law of Treaties in Russia and the Commonwealth of Independent States: Text and Commentary* (Cambridge–New York: Cambridge University Press, 2002); Council of Europe, British Institute of International and Comparative Law, *Treaty Making: Expression of Consent by States To Be Bound by a Treaty*/ Conseil de l'Europe, Institut britannique de droit international et de droit comparé, *Conclusion des traités: expression par les Etats du consentement à être liés par un traité* (The Hague–Boston: Kluwer Law International, 2001); D.B. Hollis, M.R. Blakeslee, and L.B. Ederington (eds), *National Treaty Law and Practice. Dedicated to the Memory of Monroe Leigh* (Leiden: Martinus Nijhoff, 2005); J.S. Lanftis, *Domestic Constraints and the Breakdown of International Agreements* (Wesport–Connecticut–London: Praeger, 1997); J.S. Lanftis, *The Life and Death of International Treaties. Double-Edged Diplomacy and the Politics of Ratification in Comparative Perspective* (Oxford–New York: Oxford University Press, 2009).

[28] See, eg, Articles 36 and 37 of Federal Law No. 101-FZ of 15 July 1995, in W.E. Butler (ed.), *The Law of Treaties in Russia and the Commonwealth of Independent States*, *supra* note 27, at 182 *et seq.* Depending upon whether the President or the government adopted the decision that the Russian Federation be bound by the treaty, the proposals concerning termination or suspension are sent, respectively, to one or the other. Likewise, the distribution of competence to adopt, if necessary, the decision is resolved by making that dependent upon allocation of competence to adopt the decision to give consent to the treaty in question. See also the constitutional provisions of Cuba, the Netherlands, Spain, and Sweden in D.B. Hollis, M.R. Blakeslee, and L.B. Ederington (eds), *National Treaty Law and Practice* (Leiden–Boston: Martinus Nijhoff, 2005) *passim.*

[29] The Constitution of the United States, for example, specifies the process for making treaties, but it is silent on the question of denunciation. Article II gives the President the power to make treaties, with the 'advice and consent' of the Senate, provided two thirds of the senators present concur. The treaty ratification process, however, has been modified over time. In the Trade Act of 1974 Congress established a system whereby the President may be granted 'fast-track' authority for negotiation of treaties. Moreover, the President may conclude 'executive agreements' for dealing with other countries, which do not require Senate ratification. The first abrogation of a treaty occurred in 1798, when Congress passed a law terminating a 1788 treaty with France. In the nineteenth century, several Presidents terminated treaties after Congress passed resolutions requesting the same. In 1854, however, President Franklin Pierce terminated a treaty with Denmark with the consent of the Senate alone. A Senate committee ruled that it was correct procedure for the President to terminate treaties after being authorized by the Senate alone, and not the entire Congress. President

The question is generally tackled as one of exclusive or concurrent competence between the executive and the legislator. In most states, the impeachment of the validity of treaties and the termination of their operation are the product of a legal process: as a rule, denunciation is a prerogative of the executive, with the legislature being given different roles at different stages.[30]

Moreover, no state explicitly entrusts its national courts with the power to denounce treaties, whether once and for all or with effects limited to the particular case at issue. While the judiciary of democratic states generally has the power to review the validity of its domestic laws, judicial review is a rare vehicle of denunciation. State practice generally demonstrates that courts do not invalidate or terminate treaties, nor do they sit in judgment on the political braches to prevent them from invalidating or terminating a treaty. They may, however, interpret political acts or even political silences to determine whether they implied or intended invalidation or termination.[31]

Pierce's successors, however, returned to the former procedure of obtaining authorization from both Houses. Some Presidents have claimed to themselves the exclusive power of terminating treaties. Abraham Lincoln, for instance, terminated a treaty without prior Congressional authorization, but Congress retroactively approved his decision at a later point. The first unambiguous case of a President terminating a treaty without authorization, granted prior to or after the termination, occurred when Jimmy Carter terminated a treaty with the Republic of China: for the first time, judicial determination was sought but the Supreme Court could not find a majority agreeing on any particular principle, and therefore instructed the trial court to dismiss the case (*Goldwater v Carter*, 444 US 996). See L. Henkin, 'Litigating the President's Power To Terminate Treaties', 73 *AJIL* (1979) 647 *et seq.*; G.S. Krutz and J.S. Peake, *Treaty Politics and the Rise of Executive Agreements: International Commitments in a System of Shared Powers* (Ann Arbor: University of Michigan Press, 2009). On the Belgian legal order, see J. Masquelin, *Le droit des traités dans l'ordre juridique et dans la pratique diplomatique belges* (Bruxelles: Bruylant, 1980) 588 *et seq.*; with regard to Italy, G. Ziccardi Capaldo, *La competenza a denunciare i trattati internazionali. Contributo allo studio del Treaty power* (Napoli: Edizioni scientifiche italiane, 1983); A. Cannone, 'La denuncia dei trattati internazionali nella teoria e nella prassi costituzionale italiana', 67 *Riv. di Diritto Internaz.* (1984) 16 *et seq.*

[30] 'Denunciation is an executive act, although an initiative to this effect may originate from any arm of a state party—the executive, the legislature, or the judiciary—or its political parties. The possibilities for such initiatives may differ in different domestic jurisdictions.' Y. Tyagi, 'The Denunciation of Human Rights Treaties', *supra* note 20, at 192.

[31] The holding of the Supreme Court of the United States in the case of *Charlton v Kelly* (229 US 447, S Ct 232 (1913)) is exemplary of the attitude of the judiciary of a democratic state. It concerned an extradition treaty with Italy of 1868 that Italy had refused to apply in relation to its own nationals, in conflict with the interpretation given by the United States: 'If the attitude of Italy was, as contended, a violation of the obligation of the treaty, which, in international law, would have justified the United States in denouncing the treaty as no longer obligatory, it did not automatically have that effect. If the United States elected not to declare the abrogation, or to come to a rupture, the treaty would remain in force. It was only voidable, not void; and if the United States should prefer, it might waive any breach which in its judgment had occurred and conform to its own obligation as it there had been no breach.' See also *Peroff v Hylton*, 563 F. 2d 1099 (US C of Apps (4th Cir.) 1977, at 1102: 'Even if the claimed lack of reciprocity were construed to be a violation of treaty obligations, it would be for the Executive alone to determine whether to waive such violations or to denounce the extradition agreement.' For an analogous approach, see the judgment of 2 February 1923 of the Swiss Federal Court in *Lepeschkin v Gossweiler* (2 *Annual Digest and Reports of Public*

Whether a role for the judiciary in the exercise of a state's right to invalidate or terminate treaties (even with effects limited to the case at issue) may be construed as implied in the courts' general power to interpret and apply the law, is a question which is independent, at least to a certain extent, of the manner in which national courts operate with respect to questions of international relevance, the general issue of the relationship between the judiciary and the executive in treaty matters, and the degree of deference of the judiciary to other constitutional organs in the application of international law.[32]

No doubt, the courts have the power (and duty) to interpret and apply any treaty in force (and/or its implementing legislation), but not all issues of invalidity or termination can be reduced to a merely interpretative question. As highlighted above,[33] most causes of invalidity or termination of treaties are subject to the initiative by the interested party, whether or not they imply the ascertainment of specific situations of fact or of law (which indeed may fall within the purview of the judiciary) and imply a number of choices among different alternatives.

The question of an autonomous role of the judiciary in relation to the invalidity and termination of treaties, therefore, has to be answered in the negative with respect to all grounds the invocation of which implies the exercise of a discretionary *right* of the state. It shall be given, instead, an affirmative answer in relation to the causes of invalidity or termination which require the ascertainment of circumstances falling within the purview of national courts but do not imply any discretion as to whether and when to be invoked.

This latter category certainly includes termination on the basis of a final term or condition and abrogation (tacit or explicit) by a subsequent agreement, for these causes operate automatically in the sense outlined above.[34] But this category also includes the legal grounds in relation to which—notwithstanding that their operation is *not* automatic—states are endowed under international law with the *duty*, rather than a mere power, to impeach the validity of or terminate treaties. The first ground to be considered is invalidity or termination of treaties in contrast with *jus cogens* (Articles 53 and 64). The other concerns treaties concluded under coercion of the state (Article 52 of the Vienna Convention).

International Law Cases (1923–24) at 323–5), which still reflects the opinion of the Swiss Federal Tribunal today, maintaining that national courts have no power to declare treaties terminated due to a change of circumstances. On the courts' tendency not to apply the principles *rebus sic stantibus* and *inadimplendi non est adimplendum*, see also the cases criticized by B. Conforti and A. Labella, 'Invalidity and Termination of Treaties', *supra* note 10, at 61–3.

32 For a recent study on the role of national courts in the maintenance of the rule of international law, see A. Nollkaemper, *Domestic Courts and the Rule of International Law* (Oxford: Oxford University Press, 2010). See also, D. Sloss, *The Role of Domestic Courts in Treaty Enforcement. A Comparative Study* (Cambridge–New York: Cambridge University Press, 2009).

33 *Supra*, Section 3. 34 Ibid.

5. Treaties Conflicting with *Jus Cogens* or Concluded under Threat of Use of Force

All treaties have to comply with peremptory norms of general international law (*jus cogens*), norms accepted and recognized by the international community of states as a whole, from which no derogation is permitted under the Vienna Convention (and now the corresponding norms of general international law).

The Convention—in Articles 53 (concerning a treaty in conflict with *jus cogens* at the time of its conclusion) and 64 (considering the emergence of a new peremptory norm subsequent thereto)—states that the treaty 'is' or 'becomes void and terminates'. Moreover, Article 52 provides that a treaty 'is void if its conclusion has been procured by the threat or use of force in violation of the principles of international law embodied in the Charter of the United Nations'.

Independently from the value of the reference to the 'principles of international law embodied in the Charter' in Article 52, the nature of coercion envisaged by the Vienna Convention implies that the conclusion of the treaty is the result of a breach of *jus cogens*. This does not mean an overlapping between the provisions of Article 52 and 53 of the Vienna Convention: while the latter concerns the content of the treaty, the first attains to the way it is concluded. The particular nature of the interests protected under the two provisions is, however, at the origin of some common features.

In both cases, the Vienna Convention rules out the separability of treaty provisions and the possibility of acquiescence[35] and dictates special consequences for the invalidity of a treaty conflicting with *jus cogens*.[36] The rationale of such provisions is obviously the importance of the protected values, which belong to the international society as a whole. As the ILC made clear in its Commentary to Article 61 of the Draft Articles on the Law of Treaties (now Article 64 of the Vienna Convention), 'a rule of *jus cogens* is an overriding rule depriving any act or situation which is in conflict with it of its legality'.[37] Nevertheless, in the context of the Convention, the validity of a treaty conflicting with *jus cogens* may be impeached, or its termination may take place, only as a result of the application of the procedural provisions in Part V (Article 42).[38]

It is arguable that in these cases international law today imposes an obligation on all states (and possibly other international actors) to break treaty relations.

No doubt, general international law recognizes the obligation to wipe out the risk, as well as the consequences, of a breach of *jus cogens* for all states *parties* to the treaty whereby such a breach is, or risks being, committed. This implies the possibility of recognizing an autonomous role for national courts, whose specific task

[35] See *supra*, notes 22 and 23 and corresponding text.
[36] See Article 71 of the 1969 Vienna Convention.
[37] *YILC* (1966), vol. II, at 262, para. 1.
[38] See *supra*, notes 18 and 19 and corresponding text.

is to respect and ensure the observance of international law, in the ascertainment of the compatibility with *jus cogens* of treaties that they are called to apply.

Courts usually contribute to the implementation of such an international obligation by way of interpretation of the relevant treaty. The invocation of an alleged conflict with *jus cogens* will lead the court to choose, among different possible meanings, that which allows the treaty not to be inconsistent with *jus cogens*. Indeed, the presumption of conformity of treaties with *jus cogens* is a corollary of the principle *pacta sunt servanda* requiring the stability of international relations and the conservation of international regulations. Should a conflict with *jus cogens* persist notwithstanding interpretative efforts to overcome it, the possibility should be open for the court to raise the issue of the validity or operation of the treaty with the competent organs, so that the appropriate steps can be taken at the international level. By way of provisional measure, it should also be possible for the court to consider the treaty as void or terminated, or suspend its application.[39] Thereby, national courts would contribute to the effectiveness of *jus cogens*, the values of which override those protected under the *pacta sunt servanda* principle.

But the nature of general essential interests of the values protected under the notion of *jus cogens* raises the further question of the position of states and international organizations (and other international actors) *not parties* to the treaty which is null and void in accordance with Article 52 or 53 or which can be terminated under Article 64 (or the corresponding norms of customary law).

As is well known, the regime of international responsibility—under the impact of the work of the ILC—is now firmly established in the sense that, in the presence of serious breaches of an obligation arising under a peremptory norm of general international law, the legal position of any subject other than the injured state is comparable, if not completely correspondent, to that of the party(ies) specially affected.[40] It is reasonable to conceive that a corresponding rule of customary law has emerged allowing any third party to invoke the invalidity or termination of treaties in contrast with *jus cogens* or concluded in breach of the prohibition of

[39] For an example of treaty interpretation in conformity with *jus cogens*, see Italian Court of Cassation, First Criminal Section, *Milde*, Judgment no. 1072 of 21 October 2008, registered on 13 January 2009 (reprinted in 92 *Riv. di Diritto Internaz.* (2009) 618 *et seq.*), affirming jurisdiction over claims for compensation against the Federal Republic of Germany (FRG) for war crimes and crimes against humanity committed during Germany's occupation of Italy in the Second World War. Dealing with the question of the alleged conflict between the Peace Treaty of 1947 and the Bonn Agreements between Germany and Italy of 1961, and a purported *jus cogens* rule entitling private parties to judicially enforce their rights, the Court declared that the 1947 Peace Treaty did not apply because the FRG was a third state in relation to the Peace Treaty. Moreover, the Treaty provision only related to material damages and did not cover moral damages to the families of war crimes victims. As to the Bonn Agreement of 1961, the Court held that the Agreement concerned the final settlement of disputes which were already pending at the time of signature and, therefore, did not apply to disputes, such as the one introduced with the Civitella proceedings, which had not been commenced at that date.

[40] See, in particular, Articles 41, 48, and 54 of the Draft Articles on Responsibility of States for Internationally Wrongful Acts, *YILC* (2001), vol. II (2).

the threat or use of force. *Mutatis mutandis*, therefore, what has been said with respect to the role of the national courts of the states parties can be extended to the courts of *any state* (whether or not party to the treaty allegedly in conflict with *jus cogens* or concluded in violation thereof).

As to the role of *international organizations*, the pertinent practice relates to treaties potentially invalid or susceptible of termination because of a breach of *jus cogens*, to which the relevant organization is not a party, concluded by one or more of its member states.

On occasions, the issue of a treaty's compatibility with *jus cogens* has been raised in proceedings before the ICJ or other international courts or tribunals.[41]

In the *Gabčíkovo-Nagymaros* case,[42] for example, Hungary argued, *inter alia*, that it was entitled to terminate the 1977 Treaty because new requirements of international law for the protection of the environment precluded performance of the Treaty: the previously existing obligation not to cause substantive damage to the territory of another state had, Hungary claimed, evolved into an *erga omnes* obligation of prevention of damage pursuant to the 'precautionary principle'. Slovakia argued, in reply, that none of the intervening developments in environmental law gave rise to norms of *jus cogens* that would override the Treaty. Because neither of the parties contended that new norms of environmental law had emerged since the conclusion of the 1977 Treaty, the Court considered that it was not necessary to examine the scope of Article 64 of the Vienna Convention (*rectius*, the corresponding customary rule). It held, however, that 'the Treaty is not static, and is open to adapt to emerging norms of international law. [...] The responsibility to do this was a joint responsibility' (para. 112).

The arbitration award of 31 July 1989 on the delimitation of the maritime frontier between Guinea Bissau and Senegal tackled the problem of the invalidity of an agreement for conflict with *jus cogens* rules related to the principle of self-determination. The Tribunal found that the Agreement between Portugal and France of 26 April 1960 was valid and could be opposed to Senegal and Guinea-Bissau because, *inter alia*, the principle of permanent sovereignty over natural resources was not applicable and the principle of the restriction of the *jus tractatus* of the colonial power once the process for national liberation was initiated was in a mere logic relation with, not a corollary of the principle of, self-determination: therefore it was an independent legal rule, not a rule of *jus cogens*.[43]

[41] Of course, there is a fundamental distinction between the existence of the jurisdiction of an international court or tribunal and the compatibility with international law of the particular acts which are the subject of the dispute (see ICJ, *Legality of Use of Force (Serbia and Montenegro v United Kingdom)*, Preliminary Objections, Judgment of 15 December 2004, *ICJ Reports* (2004) 1307 *et seq.*, at 1351). This is so even with regard to rights and obligations *erga omnes* or peremptory norms of general international law: the mere fact that a principle has this character is not enough of itself to confer jurisdiction, for this is dependent upon the consent of the parties (*Democratic Republic of the Congo v Rwanda*, *supra* note 8, at 32 and 52).

[42] *Supra* note 7.

[43] See 83 *ILR* (1989) 1 *et seq.*, and 94 *RGDIP* (1990) 204 *et seq.*

The political organs of the UN have also come across the question of invalidity or termination of treaties potentially in conflict with *jus cogens*. Among the historical examples are the Treaty of Guarantee for Cyprus of 1922 between the United Kingdom, Cyprus, Greece, and Turkey, and the Camp David Accords between Egypt and Israel of 1978.

Under Article IV of the Treaty of Guarantee for Cyprus, as a measure to ensure compliance with the Treaty, each of the three foreign powers reserved itself the 'right to take actions'.[44] In the debates on the Cyprus question, in the Security Council, after the Turkish intervention and the creation of the so-called Federated Turkish State of Cyprus in 1974, Cyprus held that the Treaty could not be interpreted so as to allow military intervention, but only political pressures and other measures of the same sort: if intervention by the three guarantor states in Cyprus could take place even against the wish of the territorial state, consent for intervention having being given once and for all, the Treaty would be null and void, because in contrast with *jus cogens*. The UN accepted this view and on that basis held that the Treaty of Guarantee was still in force.[45]

The Camp David Accords of 1978 between Egypt and Israel provided that the territories occupied by Israel during the six-day war of 1977 would be subject to five years of self-government, while their final regime would be discussed by Israel, Egypt, and Jordan (with the participation, in the delegation of Jordan, of Palestinians as representatives of the people in the occupied territories). No independence, at least for a period of time, was envisaged, nor was the involvement of the Palestine Liberation Organization in the negotiations over the future status of the occupied territories. General Assembly resolution 34/65 B[46] noted 'with concern that the Camp David accords have been concluded outside the framework of the United Nations and without the participation of the Palestine Liberation Organization, the representative of the Palestinian people'; rejected 'those provisions of the accords which ignore, infringe, violate or deny the inalienable rights of the Palestinian people'; and declared that 'the Camp David accords and other agreements have no validity in so far as they purport to determine the future of the Palestinian people and of the Palestinian territories occupied by Israel since 1967'. The resolution does not state the grounds of the alleged invalidity, but several delegates pointed to the existence of a conflict with *jus cogens*.[47] Its express invocation, however, would have implied impeaching the validity of the Camp David Accords in their entirety, in accordance with

[44] 'In the event of a breach of the provisions of the present Treaty, Greece, Turkey and the United Kingdom undertake to consult together with respect to the representations or measures necessary to ensure observance of those provisions. In so far as common or concerted action may not prove possible, each of the three guaranteeing Powers reserves the right to take action with the sole aim of re-establishing the state of affairs created by the present Treaty.'

[45] See, eg, UNSC resolution 353(1974) of 20 July 1974.

[46] GA resolution 34/65 (A-D) of 12 December 1979.

[47] According to the delegate of Kuwait, the cause was the non-participation of the Palestine Liberation Organization; South Arabia stressed the contrast with *jus cogens*; Iraq pointed

the principle of non-separability of treaty provisions laid down in the Vienna Convention (Article 44(5)). The declaration of nullity, therefore, would have affected the Accords also in so far as they provided for the withdrawal of Israeli troops from Sinai, an outcome that the General Assembly was willing to avoid. As a matter of fact, due to the opposition of the Arab states and the Palestine Liberation Organization, the transitory regime envisaged by the Camp David Accords was never implemented.[48]

This practice supports the view that not only international organizations are under an obligation, without exception, to respect the peremptory norms of general international law. International law also requires international organizations to ensure that their member states respect *jus cogens* rules, in particular by acting to impeach the validity, or terminate the operation, of treaties conflicting therewith.

6. Concluding Remarks

But for a few exceptions (termination term or condition, and abrogation by subsequent treaty), treaties do not come to an end automatically. This is a consequence of the way most substantive grounds for invalidity or termination are conceived under the Vienna Convention. The *substantive* rules on the invalidity and termination of treaties give rise to a legal position of which the state is the exclusive holder.

The general regime is one that *allows* a party to invoke a cause of invalidity or termination of the treaty. In this respect, no general role of the judiciary can be grounded in specific national provisions or practice, application by analogy of the rules on the treaty-making power, or the courts' general power to interpret and apply international law. In principle, the possibility of a role for national courts to impeach the validity or terminate the operation of treaties is ruled out by the lack of autonomy of the judiciary in the exercise of the *rights* provided for under international law.

to the breach of the prohibition on the use of force as well as of Article 53 of the 1969 Vienna Convention.

[48] See also the Madrid Accords of 1975 between Spain, Morocco, and Mauritania, ending the Spanish presence in the territory of Western Sahara, on the basis of which the territory would be divided between Morocco and Mauritania. The legality of this Agreement was challenged by the UN General Secretary for Legal Affairs and Legal Counsel, Hans Corell, who, in an opinion on the legality of petroleum agreements signed by Morocco, said: 'The Madrid Agreement did not transfer sovereignty over the territory, nor did it confer upon any of the signatories the status of an administering Power—a status which Spain alone could not have unilaterally transferred. The transfer of administrative authority over the territory to Morocco and Mauritania in 1975, did not affect the international status of Western Sahara as Non-Self-Governing Territory' (letter dated 29 January 2002 from the Under-Secretary-General for Legal Affairs, the Legal Counsel, addressed to the President of the Security Council, 12 February 2002, S/2002/161).

National case law and international practice support—or at least show a trend in favour of—the emergence of a customary rule on the basis of which courts are under an *obligation* to impeach the validity, or terminate the operation, of treaties concluded under the threat of use of force or conflicting with *jus cogens* (either at the time of their entry into force or at a subsequent stage). Indeed, international law requires (or aspires) that national courts (like any state organ) as well as international organizations (and other non-state actors) act for the protection of the essential interests of the international community as a whole. The patterns of domestic and international practice mapped here are in line with the implementation of such an international obligation.

Now, where a conflict with *jus cogens*—that cannot be solved by way of interpretation—is ascertained by a *third* party (ie the national court of a non-contracting state or an organ of an international organization not party to the treaty), this does not, *per se*, prevent the application of the treaty as between the parties. Unless at least one of the parties decides to impeach its validity or to terminate its operation, the treaty remains in force and the superior interests protected under the *jus cogens* rule which has been breached could only be defended under the rules of state responsibility. Rather than a reason to underline the complementary and accessory role of the law of treaties with respect to the law on international responsibility,[49] this conclusion stands in favour of strengthening the role of national courts, beyond the Vienna Convention, in relation to issues of validity and termination of treaties conflicting with *jus cogens* or concluded in breach thereof.

[49] S. Forlati, *Diritto dei trattati e responsabilità internazionale, supra* note 16, at 59.

PART V

JUS COGENS BEYOND THE VIENNA CONVENTION

23

The Metamorphosis of *Jus Cogens*: From an Institution of Treaty Law to the Bedrock of the International Legal Order?

*Karl Zemanek**

1. A Doctrine Becomes Law

The idea of curbing the freedom of states to choose the object of their international agreements was put on the political agenda after World War I. Having proclaimed the idealistic proposition that changes of territory between states should be subject to the consent of the affected populations,[1] President Wilson discovered that such changes had already been promised in secret agreements between his allies, though without regard to his lofty ideal. The frustration of his plan generated Article 18 of the Covenant of the League of Nations,[2] which was repeated in modified form in Article 102 of the United Nations (UN) Charter. It requires states to register treaties with the UN Secretariat—which makes them public—if the parties wish to rely on them before UN organs, thus supposedly guaranteeing that states observe their obligations under the Charter when concluding agreements. The result is a mass of valuable material for research and a convenient reference for chancelleries, but it is doubtful whether the provision achieves its original purpose and prevents secret agreements of questionable content. Their secret nature makes it impossible to prove or to disprove its efficiency empirically.

Yet the matter did not rest there. In particular, the natural law school, of which Alfred Verdross was the principal protagonist, argued between the World Wars that certain treaties were actually *forbidden* by international law. In 1932 one of Verdross's disciples, Von der Heydte, published a paper in German entitled 'Die Erscheinungsformen des zwischenstaatlichen Rechts: *jus cogens* und *jus*

* I am indebted to Stephan Wittich for his comments on a draft and to Helmut Prantner for his assistance in assembling the literature.

[1] In his 'Fourteen Points'.

[2] He had proposed 'open conventions openly arrived at'.

dispositivum im Völkerrecht' (The manifestations of the law between states: *jus cogens* and *jus dispositivum* in public international law).[3] Verdross followed three years later with an article in German[4] and in 1937 with an article in the *American Journal of International Law* on 'Forbidden Treaties in International Law'.[5] As a member of the International Law Commission during a decisive phase of the codification of the law of treaties, Verdross was a strong advocate of introducing the concept of *jus cogens* into the draft. He referred to that in an article in which he defended the decision of the Commission[6] against the criticism of Schwarzenberger.[7] Meanwhile, however, the idea had spread beyond this particular natural law school and the thinking of other authors[8] has undoubtedly encouraged the acceptance of the concept by the International Law Commission. Since Suy[9] and Sztucki[10] have analysed these pre-convention currents thoroughly, it is unnecessary to repeat that here.[11]

In the form adopted by the International Law Commission (ILC) and now embodied in the Vienna Convention on the Law of Treaties, the concept copies the late Roman law dichotomy of *jus publicum* and *jus civilis*, the first being absolute law whose operation could not be changed by the private will of individuals. The dichotomy is still found in many European legal orders which are historically rooted in Roman law. Borrowing that concept, natural law schools postulated international *jus cogens*, which they identified with natural law, as the equivalent of *jus publicum*. Depending on the school, this natural law would either exist because of divine ordinance or be the product of human rationality. Characteristically, Verdoss referred to Wolff[12] and Vattel[13] as inspiration and described as *contra bonos mores* the forbidden treaties in his 1966 article.[14]

After the existence of *jus cogens* had been definitely confirmed by the Vienna Convention on the Law of Treaties, a theoretical foundation that would also satisfy positivists was needed. It is generally believed that Hermann Mosler was the first to use the term 'public order of the international community' to describe the ground for the peremptory character of certain norms in his General Course at

[3] F. Von der Heydte, 'Die Erscheinungsformen des zwischenstaatlichen Rechts: *jus cogens* und *jus dispositivum* im Völkerrecht', 16 *Zeitschrift für Völkerrecht* (1932) 461.

[4] A.Verdross, 'Anfechtbare und nichtige Staatsverträge', 15 *Zeitschrift für öffentliches Recht* (1935) 289.

[5] A. Verdross, 'Forbidden Treaties in International Law', 31 *AJIL* (1937) 571.

[6] A. Verdross, '*Jus Dispositivum* and *Jus Cogens* in International Law', 60 *AJIL* (1966) 55.

[7] G. Schwarzenberger, 'International *Jus Cogens*?' 43 *Texas Law Review* (1965) 455.

[8] Particularly the Marxist theory of international law; cf J. Sztucki, Jus Cogens *and the Vienna Convention on the Law of Treaties. A Critical Appraisal* (Vienna–New York: Springer-Verlag, 1974) 65.

[9] E. Suy, 'The Concept of *Jus Cogens* in Public International Law', in *Lagonissi Conference: Papers and Proceedings* (Geneva: Carnegie Endowment for International Peace, 1967) vol. II, 17.

[10] J. Sztucki, Jus Cogens *and the Vienna Convention on the Law of Treaties. A Critical Appraisal, supra* note 8, at 54–93.

[11] For a recent examination of the concept's fate in the various stages of the ILC Draft and in the Vienna Conference see A. Paulus, '*Jus Cogens* in a Time of Hegemony and Fragmentation', 74 *Nordic JIL* (2005) 297, at 300–5.

[12] C. Wolff, *Jus Gentium* (1764).

[13] E. de Vattel, *Le Droit des Gens* (1758).

[14] See *supra* note 6, at 56.

the Hague Academy in 1974,[15] although Sztucki had also used the term in his book[16] which appeared in the same year, but he was, of course, less prominent. Mosler defined the international *ordre public* as the principles and rules of 'such vital importance to the international community as a whole that any unilateral action or any agreement which contravenes these principles can have no legal force'.

This explanation has since attracted the widest following among scholars. With it, and practically unnoticed, a paradigmatic change had taken place. What had been designed as a nullity for transgressing *law* in the form of *jus cogens*, had been turned into a nullity for infringing public *policy*. Yet there is more than a linguistic difference between public *law* and public *policy*. To illustrate the point: it is public *law* which nullifies a contract that stipulates that one person may kill another with impunity. It is a matter of public *policy* that a state, which has a monogamous concept of marriage, refuses to recognize the marriages of a man to more than one wife, even though these marriages were validly contracted under the law of another state which permits polygamy.

The *jus cogens* of the Vienna Convention on the Law of Treaties was simply underogable law of uncertain content. The Vienna Convention described the process by which the norms of *jus cogens* should be discovered in only vague terms. In its Commentary to the respective article the International Law Commission had suggested 'the right course to be... to leave the full content of this rule to be worked out in State practice and in the jurisprudence of international tribunals'.[17] As I have shown elsewhere,[18] reality has not yet come up to these expectations. Positive law only rarely makes treaty provisions non-derogable to underline their *jus cogens* nature.

The public policy concept tries to eliminate the uncertainty by offering the *ordre public international* as a measure of the content of *jus cogens*. It should be noted, though, that this changes the nature of *jus cogens* from a legal technique to a value-based guideline. *Ordre public* is not definitely expressed in the wording of legal norms. It is their understanding in the light of currently shared values which makes up public policy. Instead of reflecting the firm, for some immutable, commands of natural law, *jus cogens* became the expression of fundamental values shared by the international community of states at a certain time and it is, therefore, not absolutely free of contradictions.

[15] H. Mosler, 'The International Society as a Legal Community', 149 *Recueil des Cours* (1974-IV) 2, at 34. In fact, the term had been used by H. Lauterpacht, then Special Rapporteur of the ILC on the Law of Treaties, in his Report of 1953, A/CN.4/63, comment on Article 15, para. 4.

[16] See source, *supra* note 10, eg at 165.

[17] ILC, Report on the Second Part of its 17th Session and on its 18th Session (1966) *GAOR, Twenty-first Session, Supplement No. 9* (A/6309), 76.

[18] See K. Zemanek, 'How to Identify Peremptory Norms of International Law', in P.-M. Dupuy *et al.* (eds), *Völkerrecht als Wertordnung/Common Values in International Law. Essays in Honour of Ch. Tomuschat* (Kehl: Engel, 2006) 1103.

That is, however, also the weak point of the concept. As the Permanent Court of International Justice observed in the *Case Concerning the Payment in Gold of the Brazilian Federal Loans Issued in France*, the definition of national public policy 'in any particular country is largely dependent on the opinion prevailing at any given time in such country itself'.[19] Hence its substance is fluid and adapts to modifications of shared values more readily than law which requires a formal act for this. In a domestic legal order its substance, at a given point in time, has to be determined by a competent organ. Since no such organ exists in the international legal community, *jus cogens* has to be identified through an intellectual operation[20] by those who apply it or discuss it academically. This makes the way free for all sorts of philosophical speculations.

Public policy determines, moreover, legal activities beyond the prevention of contravening contracts by individual actors. It was thus the change from natural law to public policy which encouraged the academic proposals to recognize *jus cogens* as *the* basis of international law and as the ultimate element of its constitutionalization.

Kolb[21] lists five additional schools of thought, classified according to the reason which they give for the existence of *jus cogens* in international law. He himself favours the definition by effect, ie the nullity of contrary treaty provisions, which makes *jus cogens* a simple legal technique.[22] Two of the other opinions classified by Kolb, the idea that *jus cogens* consists of higher ranking norms, or that it is the embodiment of the constitutional principles of the international community, will be examined later.[23]

In the rest of the chapter I propose to examine first the methods to identify the norms of *jus cogens* (Section 2) and then the areas which have been suggested for applying the concept beyond the law of treaties (Sections 3 and 4). Finally, I shall analyse the arguments of authors who object to the concept (Section 5).

2. Identifying the Norms of *Jus Cogens*

As has been argued above, the applicable positive international law of the Vienna Convention on the Law of Treaties does not establish a procedure to identify rules of *jus cogens*. It does not even indicate a manner in which to achieve this

[19] PCIJ, *Case Concerning the Payment in Gold of the Brazilian Federal Loans Issued in France,* Judgment of 12 July 1929, Series A 15 (1929) at 125.

[20] For more details see K. Zemanek, 'How to Identify Peremptory Norms of International Law', *supra* note 18, 1109 *et seq.*

[21] R. Kolb, *Théorie du* ius cogens *international. Essai de relecture du concept* (Paris: Presses Universitaires de France, 2001) 68. S. Kadelbach, *Zwingendes Völkerrecht* (Peremptory International law) (Berlin: Duncker & Humblot, 1992) 130–60, distinguishes ten different schools, to which he adds his own explanation.

[22] Ibid., 172–3. In fact, his book is a plea to return to this original understanding of *jus cogens.*

[23] See Section 3.

identification without the use of subjective evaluations. This is made explicit by the ILC's Commentary to Article 50 of its draft (now Article 53 of the Vienna Convention) which states:[24] '[I]t is not the form of a general rule of international law but the particular nature of the subject matter with which it deals that may, in the opinion of the Commission, give it the character of *jus cogens*.'

Unfortunately, the Commission did not elaborate on 'the particular nature of the subject matter' which would confer the character of *jus cogens*. Academic researchers appear to have utilized three different methods for identification. They are linked to what the respective theory postulates as the source of *jus cogens*.

Historically, the first proposition saw natural law as the source of peremptory rules. The commands of natural law were claimed as the supreme framework of positive law, as an immutable and underogable standard. Although all schools of natural law would agree up to that point, they would not necessarily agree on the norms that are supposed to have that character. Whether the source of natural law is found in some religious belief or is assumed to reside in the rationality of man (rationalism), one must be a follower of the respective school to accept its deductions without question.

The most commonly followed explanation of *jus cogens,* the concept of *ordre public,* relies on an analogy with domestic law. The suitability of that analogy is questionable. A doctrine that was generated in highly developed legal systems does not necessarily fit international law, which lacks the former's development and differentiation. Moreover, *ordre public* may even in a domestic legal system be a vague notion, but when the occasion requires, its content is established by a competent organ of the legal order, in most cases a court, and is thus, at that point in time, definitive. Because the international legal order lacks an appropriate structure, proposing the content of *jus cogens* is largely left to academics, and their reference to *ordre public international* as the manifestation of the guiding principles of the international community is mostly nothing more than the author's opinion on what the essential and indispensible, and therefore non-derogable elements of order in the international community are. Or worse, what they should be.[25] The result is unverifiable assertions.

Tomuschat has suggested a refinement of this method by introducing the requirement of empirical verification. He writes:[26]

> [G]enerally, rules of *jus cogens* will evolve from the common value fund cherished by all nations. To establish them is therefore less a constitutive than a declaratory process.

[24] Source note 15, at 76: Commentary to Article 50, para. 2.

[25] Cf. A. Gómez Robledo, 'Le *Jus cogens* international: Sa genèse, sa nature, ses fonctions', 172 *Recueil des Cours* (1981-III) 17, at 167: '[C]hacun érige telle ou telle norme en norme impérative ou absolument insusceptible de dérogation, car chacun estime que de l'observation de cette norme dépendent la structure même de la société internationale ou les intérêts suprêmes de l'homme.' An example is Chapter 6 (210–330) of Kadelbach's book, *Zwingendes Völkerrecht, supra* note 21.

[26] C. Tomuschat, 'Obligations Arising for States Without or Against Their Will', 241 *Recueil des Cours* (1993-IV) 209, at 307.

Pursuant to what was said above, certain deductions from the constitutional foundations of the international community provide binding rules that need no additional corroboration by practice. However, it will always be necessary to ascertain that indeed the international community sticks to its axiomatic premises. In that regard, the regular criteria of customary law keep an important evidentiary function. The deductive method can never be used to oppose and disregard the actual will of the international community.

Nevertheless, what he proposes remains mainly a deductive method. It is the scholar who formulates the propositions which he deduces 'from the constitutional foundations'[27] (for which one can substitute the ubiquitous international *ordre public*) and then tries to confirm them by exploring the 'will of the international community'.

The third method proceeds in the inverse manner but it is rarely encountered in writings. It requires, following the indications of the Vienna Convention on the Law of Treaties to which it is conceptually linked, to canvas the practice of the vast majority of states, including manifestations of their *opinio juris*. Virally has observed in this respect:[28]

[L]a détermination du contenu du *jus cogens* n'exige pas d'autres méthodes que celles qui s'impose chaque fois que l'on veut établir l'existence d'une règle de droit international général, même simplement dispositive, mais elle n'autorise pas non plus qu'on se dispense d'y recourir.

To that he adds, however, a warning:[29]

[A]pparemment, cette détermination ne peut être fait qu'en prenant en considération des éléments matériels c'est-à-dire le contenu de la norme en question, sa signification éthique et politique. Une telle méthode risque, toutefois, de soulever des difficultés pratiques considérables: les possibilités de contestation sont évidemment extrêmement larges et difficiles à réduire lorsqu'il s'agit de qualifier une norme en raison de sa valeur morale, de son importance pour la société dans son ensemble, ou des besoins de protection auxquels elle répondrait. Une telle appréciation est nécessairement subjective et, par conséquent, ne répond pas à des critères très stricts.

To use an inductive method is thus laborious and only few studies of this kind have been undertaken. Hannikainen[30] purports to examine a broad spectrum of norms which he considers potentially peremptory, eg the prohibition on the use of force, self-determination, certain human rights, or some parts of the international law of armed conflict. More instructive is the recent study of Weisburd on the prohibition on the use of force.[31] He analyses the attitude of states in the

[27] On constitutionalism, see Section 4.

[28] M. Virally, 'Réflexions sur le *jus cogens*', 12 *AFDI* (1966) 5, at 29.

[29] Ibid., 19.

[30] L. Hannikainen, *Peremptory Norms (Jus Cogens) in International Law* (Helsinki: Finnish Lawyers, 1988).

[31] A.M. Weisburd, 'Consistency, Universality, and the Customary Law of International Force', in E. Cannizzaro and P. Palchetti (eds), *Customary International Law and the Use of Force. A Methodological Approach* (The Hague, Martinus Nijhoff, 2005) 31.

United Nations and the ensuing practice of the organization with respect to the use of force with a view to testing the consistency and uniformity of that practice. He has found three firmly established types of conduct, two of which he describes as:

> 1) providing assistance to insurgents fighting against European colonialism, and uses of force against European colonies by third world states are lawful, while European colonial powers cannot lawfully use force against the territory of other states supporting anti-colonial insurgencies, even if the use of force is aimed solely at insurgent bases; 2) using force to seize all or part of another state's territory is unlawful, unless the territory in question is a colony of a European state; however, conquest of a former colony is lawful so long as the colony is arguably not a state itself.[32]

Practice, considered on its own, would thus have pointed at least to an emerging new rule of customary law modifying the existing rule of *jus cogens* on the non-use of force. However, this is one of the instances in which the orthodox maxim, that consistent and uniform conduct permits the assumption of a corresponding *opinio juris*, does not work because there is evidence to the contrary: when force was used to support a liberation movement, the majority in the United Nations favoured justice over the non-use of force, but that argument was strongly opposed by others, which makes a general *opinio juris* doubtful. Weisburd therefore justly cautions that 'it would seem premature to say that a change in customary law has as yet taken place'.[33] Even this careful empirical study leads thus to a result which does not eliminate the uncertainty of whether the supposedly peremptory norm has been changed by custom.

Hannikainen has also examined the 'interpretation of relevant Charter provisions in UN practice',[34] but the result regarding the non-use of force is disappointing. He analyses practically no source material from UN organs but relies heavily on academic writings. Not surprisingly, he comes to the conclusion that 'the *peremptory* obligation to refrain from the use or threat of *aggressive* armed force'[35] is unimpaired. He apparently found what he wished to find.

While the academic world is at least debating, albeit with a bewildering variety of results, the International Court of Justice which, in spite of its lack of mandatory general jurisdiction would, eventually, have to adjudicate conflicts concerning *jus cogens* under the Vienna Convention on the Law of Treaties, has over decades only vaguely hinted at the possible existence of peremptory norms in international law. Nevertheless, even in the limited function established by Article 66(a) of the Vienna Convention the Court is the closest equivalent which the international legal order can manage, to the domestic organs

[32] Ibid., at 69. [33] Ibid., at 76.

[34] L. Hannikainen, *Peremptory Norms (Jus Cogens) in International Law, supra* note 30, 333–9.

[35] Ibid., 356; emphasis in text.

competent to pronounce on public policy. The 1986 *Nicaragua* judgment,[36] although it did not use the term *jus cogens*, is an example. In order to establish the customary nature of the principle of the prohibition of the use of force the Court argued 'that it is frequently referred to in statements of State representatives as being not only a principle of customary international law but also a fundamental or cardinal principle of such law'.[37] In another part of the judgment the Court found that states, which do not act in conformity with a legal rule, but cite it nevertheless to demonstrate that it either does not apply to the case or that an exception allows the conduct under the specific circumstances, were in fact confirming the rule rather than denying it. Neither argument is conclusive, especially in respect of custom. At best, they prove the existence of *opinio juris* while conduct (practice) is either not taken into account (first quote) or is even contrary to what was required (second quote). No additional evidence is offered in support of the (implied) peremptory character of the customary rule. In contrast, Weisburd[38] has recorded three firmly established types of conduct which are at variance with the principle, though he admits that this does not mean that a corresponding *opinio juris* exists. But his research underlines the unreliability of statements in the General Assembly in the third case which he examines, the policy of the United Nations towards interventions by great powers in what they consider their sphere of influence. States may be united in verbal condemnation of foreign domination of peoples but do not always mean the same by it.

Another example is the Advisory Opinion on the *Legality of the Threat or Use of Nuclear Weapons*, where the Court found that 'a great many rules of humanitarian law' had acquired the legal quality of being intransgressible.[39] The Court neither explained how it had arrived at this conclusion nor did it elaborate on the difference between 'intransgressible principles of international customary law' and *jus cogens*. The difference may be that the first term refers to executive action, the second to law-making. But that is only a guess.

Only quite recently, in the *Congo v Rwanda* case,[40] did the Court explicitly mention *jus cogens* by referring to: '... the fact that a dispute relates to compliance with a norm having such a character [being a peremptory norm of general

[36] ICJ, *Military and Paramilitary Activities in and Against Nicaragua (Nicaragua v United States of America)*, Merits, Judgment of 27 June 1986, *ICJ Reports* (1986) 14, at 100, para. 190.

[37] G. Gaja, '*Jus Cogens* Beyond the Vienna Convention', 172 *Recueil des Cours* (1981-III) 279, at 287 comments on the evidence which the Court used for its assumption: 'For ascertaining the existence of an effective norm, mere assertions on the part of governments or State delegates about the existence of a norm can hardly be accepted as conclusive... The declarations which can be attributed to the respective governments do not fully indicate those governments' attitude.'

[38] *Supra* note 31.

[39] ICJ, *Legality of the Threat or Use of Nuclear Weapons*, Advisory Opinion of 8 July 1996, *ICJ Reports* (1996) 226, para. 83.

[40] ICJ, *Case on the Territory of the Congo (New Application: 2002) (Democratic Republic of Congo v Rwanda)*, Jurisdiction of the Court and Admissibility of the Application, Judgment of 3 February 2006, *ICJ Reports* (2006) 6, at 27, para. 64.

international law (*jus cogens*)], which is assuredly the case with regard to the prohibition of genocide...'

It seems that, in arriving at this conclusion, the Court did not follow either of the abovementioned methods. This pronouncement, with respect, rather gives the impression of being the result of a spontaneous concurrence of opinion among the judges, each using his or her undisclosed method to reach it. Careful research is not discernable. The result is a terse statement in the form of a judicial dictum.

The Vienna Convention on the Law of Treaties assigns the eventual decision on the nullity of an agreement which allegedly violates *jus cogens* to the International Court of Justice. Gaja[41] mentions an example which illustrates the danger of undermining that monopoly. He refers to General Assembly resolution 34/05 B of 29 November 1979, which resolved that the Camp David agreements 'have no validity'. He suggests that 'the conflict with *jus cogens* [is] the most likely cause for the agreements to be declared void'. He observes, however, that under the Vienna Convention on the Law of Treaties 'conflict with a peremptory norm would not make a treaty void unless one of the parties took some action to this end'.[42] That is, of course, true and one may add that under the same Convention it is the International Court of Justice, not the General Assembly of the United Nations, which should eventually adjudicate an alleged violation of *jus cogens*. The latter has clearly no legal standing in the matter, whatever the political value of its pronouncement may be. I can, on the other hand, not follow Gaja's conclusion that 'one can use a concept of peremptory norm wide enough to encompass both norms which invalidate a treaty irrespective of the attitude taken by the contracting States and norms which only grant to one of the contracting States the possibility of invalidating the treaty'.[43] The two options entail different consequences. The first instance is one of absolute nullity, the second one of relative nullity, meaning that the respective act has to be rendered invalid. The second case naturally requires the intervention of an organ but, for the sake of legal certainty, so too does the first. If the evaluation is left to the individual members of a legal order chaos may result. Even if they act in common, the situation does not change unless the common action is invested with the authority to declare the voidness with binding effect. I share Gaja's misgivings about the necessity of a complaint by a contracting party for obtaining an authoritative determination of invalidity,[44] but balancing that inconvenience against the danger of a divided community of states argues decidedly in favour of the present solution.

The problems which the foregoing analysis has revealed are essentially two. The first is the non-consensual character of *jus cogens*, to which Tomuschat has

[41] G. Gaja, '*Jus Cogens* Beyond the Vienna Convention', *supra* note 37, at 282.
[42] Ibid., 283. [43] Ibid.
[44] G. Gaja, '*Jus Cogens* Beyond the Vienna Convention', *supra* note 37, at 288.

devoted his Hague lectures,[45] but which is a novel element in international law. Macdonald has remarked in this respect:[46]

[T]he essential non-consensual basis of the doctrine is emphasized by the test for determining whether a given rule has the status alleged. It is not necessary that every state gives its consent to the rule but that the rule is accepted by the vast majority of states and by a majority in each of the world's major political groupings. This point was made by Yassen in his explanation of the insertion of the words 'as a whole' by the Drafting Committee at the Vienna Conference. Further, it is the essence of the concept that a peremptory norm is applicable against states that have not accepted the rule.

He then points to the role of General Assembly resolutions as evidence of *jus cogens* or even as the means of its creation:[47] '[I]n such a controversial area of law, where the true facts of state practice are difficult to distil, it is clearly impossible to build up a rule of customary international law by a universal survey of state practice. A relevant General Assembly resolution offers a ready starting point for such a task.'

Citing the *Nicaragua* judgment,[48] he adds:[49] '[I]f a resolution may be binding in itself, it is difficult to see why, if that is the stated intention and the above features are fulfilled, a resolution cannot form part of the emerging public order.'

This is evidently a very optimistic and idealistic view, but I doubt that it is a realistic reflection of the *opinio* of states. I can only reiterate what has been said above in respect of the *Nicaragua* judgment of the International Court of Justice and refer again to the opinion of Gaja, quoted above,[50] which I share.

The second problem arises because no convincing theory has as yet been proposed to deal with a split between *opinio juris* and frequent practice. An international organ faced with an issue of that sort cannot rely on a scholarly consensus. With regard to the 1986 *Nicaragua* judgment of the International Court of Justice Orakhelashvili remarks approvingly:[51] '...what the Court's judgment affirms is that once a norm is part of *jus cogens*, its customary status can be proved by criteria different from those applicable to other norms and the consent by individual States as opposed to the community acceptance is not crucially relevant'.

I do not think that this is the appropriate way to resolve the dilemma. That the International Court of Justice, and the ICTY whose jurisprudence Orakhelashvili has also examined, forgo research into state practice in favour of statements by state representatives,[52] which may or may not reflect the true *opinio juris* of the

[45] See source in note 26. In contrast, S. Kadelbach, *supra* note 21, at 198–200 argues that the persistent objector rule would also apply to *jus cogens*.

[46] R.St.J. Macdonald, 'Fundamental Norms in Contemporary International Law', 25 *Canadian Yearbook of International Law* (1987) 115, at 130–1. References omitted.

[47] Ibid., 140.

[48] Source *supra* note 33, para. 188.

[49] R.St.J. Macdonald, 'Fundamental Norms in Contemporary International Law', *supra* note 46, at 140–1.

[50] See *supra* note 37.

[51] A. Orakhelashvili, *Peremptory Norms in International Law* (Oxford: Oxford University Press, 2006) 119.

[52] Cf. G. Gaja, '*Jus Cogens* Beyond the Vienna Convention', *supra* note 37.

respective state, is a fact but does not—with respect—canonize the method. Although the existence of a customary rule is not infrequently inferred from manifestations of *opinio juris*[53] that inference is not admissible in the face of contradictory practice. As the 'Panel on United Nations Peace Operations'[54] under Lakhdar Brahimi succinctly put it in commenting on Security Council decisions: *res* not *verba*. If international law were reduced to a mere verbal exercise, unrelated to reality, it would become nothing more than an academic construct—even when declared by the International Court of Justice. Applying the general theory of law one would be inclined to believe that constantly unremedied violations of a rule evidence a contravening state practice[55] and put the continued existence of the binding character of the rule in doubt, notwithstanding the presumed *opinio juris* of 'the international community as a whole', making the rule rather a moral prescription. Academic insistence on its peremptory character is unreasonable. One should remember Tomuschat's opinion[56] on the will of the international community and try seriously to discover it instead of substituting personal convictions.

3. Widening the Scope of Application

3.1. A forgotten point in treaty law?

Until today, no case has been brought before the International Court of Justice in which the applicant invoked Article 66(a) of the Vienna Convention on the Law of Treaties as the basis of the Court's jurisdiction, in order to request a decision on the violation of a norm of *jus cogens* by an agreement. Some would say that this is due to the preventative effect of Article 53 of the Vienna Convention. Be that as it may, no authoritative judicial practice exists in the matter of treaties, although the Court sometimes referred incidentally to *jus cogens* in cases concerning other matters, as discussed above.

Scholars, on the other hand, have devoted a great deal of writing to the subject. In the course of this academic examination some problems have surfaced which are not expressly regulated in the Vienna Convention. One such problem should be mentioned here because it is a good example for demonstrating how the different approaches to *jus cogens* influence the result. Linderfalk[57] has exposed the

[53] See K. Zemanek, 'What is State Practice and Who Makes It?' in U. Beyerlin *et al.* (eds), *Recht zwischen Umbruch und Bewahrung. Festschrift für R. Bernhard* (Berlin: Springer, 1995) 289, at 292–3.

[54] A/55/305—S/2000/809, of 21 October 2000, para. 276.

[55] Even A. Orakhelashvili, *Peremptory Norms in International Law*, *supra* note 51, points out at 113: '[T]he prohibition of aggression ... is indisputably "accepted as law". But it is questionable if these norms are based on "general practice", because too high a non-compliance rate.'

[56] *Supra* text at note 26.

[57] U. Linderfalk, 'The Effect of *Jus Cogens* Norms: Whoever Opened Pandora's Box, Did you Ever Think About the Consequences?' 18 *EJIL* (2007) 835, at 868.

problem in the following argument: '[I]f normally a state has the possibility of excluding or modifying the effects of a treaty by making reservations to it, a reservation to a treaty will not have the purported effect if it is incompatible with a norm of *jus cogens*.'

In a footnote he refers to an earlier paper of his which addresses the question of reservations to human rights treaties in particular and in more detail. Indeed, these reservations put his quoted claim to the test. As many provisions of human rights treaties are heralded as peremptory norms—though often without substantive proof—states parties to the respective treaty could regard another state's reservation concerning such a provision as a violation of *jus cogens*. Although reservations to human rights treaties have occasionally been objected to on the ground that they conflicted with the object and purpose of the treaty, the argument of their possible nullity as a consequence of their violating *jus cogens* has not yet found entry into state practice.

If one wants to speculate about the possible outcome should the problem ever come up in practice, there will be two options.

Although not explicitly regulated by the Vienna Convention, the problem can nevertheless be treated as one of treaty law. Alain Pellet, the Special Rapporteur of the International Law Commission on the law of reservations, assimilated the case to a conflict with the object and purpose of a treaty.[58] That is a stopgap measure which does not get to the heart of the matter, namely maintaining the control of the International Court of Justice over disputes concerning *jus cogens*. A reservation may be a unilateral legal act but, in respect of another party that does not object to it, it amounts to a bilateral agreement not to apply the reserved provision or provisions between them. Since Linderfalk assumes in his example that the reservation—and hence the agreement—is incompatible with a norm of *jus cogens*, it seems a straightforward case under Article 53 of the Vienna Convention. That deduction is, however, deceptive. First, because only a contracting party can assert the nullity and if a state objects to a reservation no agreement and consequently no contracting parties exist. Secondly, because if a state has not objected to the reservation at first but asserts its nullity afterwards, the lack of an agreement in written form prevents the application of the Vienna Convention (Article 3). Thought should therefore be given to the possibility of construing the relevant articles of the Vienna Convention in a manner that would establish the ultimate jurisdiction of the International Court of Justice in the case.

If one approaches the problem from the point of view of the public policy doctrine, however, the result may be different. It could be argued that the reservation, because it infringes the *ordre public*, is absolutely and hence automatically void, without the need of an objection by another contracting state and without a decision of the International Court of Justice. It may be doubted that this solution would promote the certainty of the law.

[58] In his *Tenth Report*, A/CN.4/558/Add. 1, para. 146, rule 3.1.9. The Commission concurred.

3.2. Unilateral legal acts

Predating the adoption of the concept of *jus cogens* in the Vienna Convention on the Law of Treaties, the Carnegie Endowment had organized in 1966 a conference of scholars to discuss the subject. In an introductory report Erik Suy stated briefly:

> [I]f an international *jus cogens* exists it must, indeed, make necessarily null and void any of those legal acts and actions of States whose object is unlawful. If an agreement which does not conform with the rules of *jus cogens* is considered null and void the reason is that its *effects* [italics in text] are contrary to international public policy. In that case it is inconceivable that this effect should not extend to any act or action having in the hierarchy of legal norms a lower rank than treaties.[59]

Although he referred to several authors in support, he did not cite any relevant state practice but rested his argument solely on a logical deduction from the dogmatic conception. In what seems to have been a Geneva in-house controversy, Krystyna Marek[60] retorted that a single state could violate international law through a unilateral legal act, but it could not create law and could therefore not derogate from it. The only question with regard to unilateral legal acts was thus whether they were legal or illegal; *jus cogens* and the possible nullity attaching to its violation were irrelevant.[61] The matter has remained controversial and Orakhelashvili[62] provides a good overview of the differing opinions.

Marek's critique is not conclusive. To mention but one example, an illegal recognition, though unlawful, is still a recognition that needs nullification if it contravenes *jus cogens*. Illegality does not *ipso facto* obliterate the relevant act or else the latter's illegality could never be established. But Suy's generalizing analogy is also too sweeping.[63] The violation of a norm of *jus cogens* in an agreement makes the agreement null and void, which means that the rights and obligations of the parties under the agreement cease to exist. Not all unilateral legal acts produce legal rights for another state and are, as Kolb puts it, a 'source de droits'[64] which can be nullified. Inflicting nullity on a unilateral legal act that violates a norm of *jus cogens* is only appropriate if that act has created an obligation vis-à-vis another state and consequently a right for the latter, like the recognition of a territorial

[59] E. Suy, 'The Concept of *Jus Cogens* in Public International Law', *supra* note 9, at 75. It is interesting to note that in his monograph on *Les actes juridiques unilatéraux en droit international public*, published four years earlier in 1962, Suy had not mentioned *jus cogens* and its possible impact on unilateral legal acts. E. Suy, *Les actes juridiques unilatéraux en droit international public* (Paris: Librairie Générale de Droit et de Jurisprudence, 1962).

[60] K. Marek, 'Contribution à l'étude du *jus cogens* en droit international', in *Recueil d'études de droit international en hommage à Paul Guggenheim* (Geneva: IUHEI, 1968) 426, at 441.

[61] Cf. A. Gómez Robledo, 'Le *Jus cogens* international: sa genèse, sa nature, ses fonctions', *supra* note 25, at 198–201.

[62] A. Orakhelashvili, *Peremptory Norms in International Law, supra* note 51, 207–12.

[63] G. Gaja, '*Jus Cogens* Beyond the Vienna Convention', *supra* note 37, at 295 is of a different opinion.

[64] R. Kolb, *Théorie du* ius cogens *international. Essai de relecture du concept, supra* note 21, at 91.

acquisition achieved through the use of force. Orakhelashvili has singled out that issue for closer examination[65] and suggests that the international community's tolerance of certain forcible acquisitions of territory, for example in the cases of East Timor, North Cyprus, Goa, or Western Sahara, should be attributed to the operation of primary norms, like the principle of self-determination, rather than to 'a deviation from the regime of voidness applicable to breaches of *jus cogens*'.[66]

That explanation is not really persuasive. Weisburd's findings[67] in respect of the prohibition on the use of force suggest that the tolerance of the international community (in the United Nations) of the acquisition of territory by force has developed into a fairly solid pattern in the anti-colonial context. To explain this by the assumed precedence of the principle of self-determination over the prohibition on the use of force is based on Orakhelashvili's subjective conviction of the former's superiority, because the Charter does not establish a hierarchy among the principles enshrined in it. Moreover, even if one were to agree with Orakhelashvili's value judgement, the question would still arise how the preference was expressed in practical terms. Only acquiescence and *silent* recognition by the other states explain the 'tolerance' legally. And yet, until now nobody has suggested that this 'recognition' was null and void because the situation recognized was achieved in violation of a norm of *jus cogens*. Quite to the contrary: on the basis of empirical material Weisburd found that it was rather the content of the norm of *jus cogens* expressing the prohibition on the use of force that had changed with practice. Assuming a change in the understanding of the prohibition seems by far a better explanation of what actually happened than having recourse to a supposed but unverifiable hierarchy among the principles of the Charter.

3.3. Custom

Does *jus cogens* have the same effect on customary international law as the Vienna Convention stipulates that it has on treaty law? In other words: is a rule of customary law void if it conflicts with a norm of *jus cogens*? Whatever theory one subscribes to, the answer to this question should be affirmative. The concept of peremptory norms would not make sense if such norms affected only one source of legal rights and obligations, and not the other. Since, however, the structure of customary law differs considerably from the structure of the law of treaties, applying *jus cogens* to custom requires some adjustments. Crucial points are the non-formalized source of custom and the uncertain date of the entry into force of one of its rules. One cannot identify all states which have generated a customary rule, because even the most painstaking empirical research cannot ensure that all

[65] A. Orakhelashvili, *Peremptory Norms in International Law, supra* note 51, 218–23.

[66] Ibid., 223.

[67] See A.M. Weisburd, 'Consistency, Universality, and the Customary Law of International Force', *supra* note 31, 69.

states which have contributed by their practice are included in the review. And one cannot specify from exactly which point states acting in conformity with the rule do so because they consider it a legal obligation (*opinio juris*).

These differences are particularly relevant when the peremptory norm is also one of custom, as in a case of *jus cogens superveniens* similar to the situation envisaged by Article 64 of the Vienna Convention on the Law of Treaties. In the 1986 *Nicaragua* judgment the International Court of Justice affirmed that the prohibition on the use of force was not only a customary norm of general international law independently of the Charter, but also a 'fundamental' or 'cardinal' principle,[68] which was tantamount to declaring it peremptory.[69] The Court had apparently no doubt that custom could generate peremptory norms (*jus cogens*). Yet the Court's dictum does not specify the process in which the nullity of a previous customary rule, now conflicting with a new peremptory customary rule, could be claimed in practice. Nor is it clear that the provisions of Article 71(2) of the Vienna Convention apply by analogy to the legal situations created under the previously valid customary rule. While there is no doubt about the applicability of the concept to customary law, it would need further elaboration to operate smoothly and effectively in practice.

Glennon has pointed to what he sees as a further problem of customary *jus cogens* by arguing that once a peremptory customary rule is established, it becomes immutable because the process by which a change of customary law intervenes is excluded by the definition of *jus cogens*.[70] Although writing 40 years earlier, Virally has provided the answer to that objection:[71]

> [O]n pourrait être tenté, en effet, de considérer que puisque aucune dérogation n'est permise, un traité ne peut pas modifier une norme de *jus cogens*; d'autre part, le mécanisme de la coutume semble s'opposer à ce que celle-ci soit utilisée pour une telle modification. En effet, la coutume se forme par une succession de précédents et si elle peut évoluer, c'est grâce aux variations apportées par chaque nouveau précédent par rapport à la règle déjà établie. Ces variations sont considérées comme juridiquement valables parce qu'elles ne rencontrent pas d'opposition et que la coutume, telle qu'elle se transforme, continue à être acceptée par l'ensemble de la société internationale. Les variations des précédents par rapport à la règle établie représentent donc toujours une dérogation acceptée.

It is indeed inherent in the modification of custom, whether the disappearing norm is peremptory or ordinary in nature, that the reaction of other states decides whether conduct deviating from the old rule is a violation of it or the beginning of

[68] Source note 33, para. 190.

[69] See the text at note 38.

[70] M.J. Glennon, 'De l'absurdité du droit impératif (*jus cogens*)', 110 *RGDIP* (2006) 529, at 533: '[N]ous savons tous que les nouvelles normes impératives se forment quand les anciennes sont violées. Cette violation, quand elles est suivie par un nombre suffisant d'Etats, devient une non-violation et établit une nouvelle norme. Mais la violation initiale, nécessaire à la survenance d'une nouvelle norme impérative, est interdite: l'article 53 insiste sur le fait qu'aucune dérogation n'est permise... Une norme de *jus cogens* coutumière ne peut changer que par un moyen explicitement prohibé par sa doctrine.'

[71] M. Virally, 'Réflexions sur le *jus cogens*', *supra* note 28, at 15.

a new rule. In the case of customary *jus cogens* it could be argued that the absence of negative reactions by other states was proof that the old rule had lost its peremptory nature in the *opinio* of these states. Being dynamic and adaptable to social change is the advantage of custom over treaty law, and that applies to ordinary customary rules as well as to those of a peremptory nature. Gaja argued long ago[72] that this dynamism was essential for the viability of the concept of *jus cogens*.

The question of whether a norm of *jus cogens* generated by a multilateral treaty could nullify an existing customary rule has been answered by the UN Charter and hence by positive law. Since then, provisions in conventions and human rights treaties have done the same to some customary rules, the most conspicuous among them being perhaps the rule that reserved the relation between a state and its citizens to domestic jurisdiction, a rule which still worried the drafters of the Nuremberg Charter which established the International Military Tribunal in 1945.[73] Having these precedents in mind one may consider that aspect to be settled.[74]

3.4. Responsibility

It is obvious that the possible nullity of treaty provisions, customary rules, or unilateral acts which had created rights and/or obligations for states raises the question of responsibility. Giorgio Gaja was the first[75] who systematically examined the effect of the Vienna Convention on the Law of Treaties on the law of state responsibility in his Hague lectures of 1981.[76] At a time when the International Law Commission was working on the codification of responsibility this inquiry was clearly well-timed since the question of whether non-derogable norms might cause special problems in the law of state responsibility had not yet been explored by scholars. Gaja suggested three such cases:[77] (1) A new peremptory norm may require the breach of the existing obligation under a previously effective norm; (2) the obligation imposed by a peremptory norm may prevent an injured state from reacting in the manner in which it usually could, either with the consent of the injurer, or in a state of necessity, or as countermeasure; (3) the breach of an obligation imposed by a peremptory norm may entail some consequences which are more serious than those attached to an ordinary wrongful act.

The ILC Articles on State Responsibility, which the General Assembly of the United Nations commended to the attention of governments in 2001,[78] do not treat these situations conclusively.

72 G. Gaja, '*Jus Cogens* Beyond the Vienna Convention', *supra* note 37, at 284.

73 See, eg, the references in E. Schwelb, 'Crimes Against Humanity', 23 *BYIL* (1946) 178, at 187 and 198.

74 This is the opposite of what L. Hannikainen, *Peremptory Norms (Jus Cogens) in International Law*, *supra* note 30, 226 defends. He doubts that conventions can generate peremptory norms.

75 Earlier writings concentrated on the relation between *jus cogens* and 'international crimes of States which, at that time, featured in the ILC Draft.

76 G. Gaja, '*Jus Cogens* Beyond the Vienna Convention', *supra* note 37.

77 Ibid., at 290.

78 A/RES/56/83.

The first point is not explicitly addressed, although the answer may be inferred from Article 26.[79] Accordingly, compliance with an obligation arising under a new peremptory norm which necessitates the violation of an already existing international obligation does not give rise to state responsibility. This interpretation coincides with the rule stated in Article 71(2)(a) of the Vienna Convention on the Law of Treaties.[80]

The second point is also covered by Article 26, at least as far as the consent of the injurer or the state of necessity are concerned. In respect of countermeasures, Article 50(1) specifically prohibits measures that would violate obligations for the protection of fundamental human rights or obligations of a humanitarian character prohibiting reprisals, or, in a general clause, other obligations under peremptory norms of general international law. In this connection it is interesting to note that the inviolability of diplomatic or consular agents, premises, archives, and documents merits a separate sub-paragraph (2)(b) for exempting it from countermeasures. One may speculate that the ILC's members could not achieve a consensus on the peremptory nature of the rules protecting the diplomatic or consular inviolability and had thus to exempt them in a neutral separate paragraph. The question which the judgment of the International Court of Justice in the *Teheran Hostage* case had provoked, as to whether the Court, though it had avoided using the term,[81] had really meant that the relevant rules were peremptory, thus remains unanswered.

Gaja's third point is inadequately addressed. The notion of 'crimes of the state', which had appeared in earlier drafts of the International Law Commission,[82] but had met with stiff opposition from the representatives of states on the Sixth Committee of the General Assembly and in written comments by states, was not retained. Article 40 deals with the 'serious breach' of an obligation arising under a peremptory norm of general international law and defines as serious a breach which 'involves a gross or systematic failure by the responsible State to fulfil the obligation'. Article 41 states the consequences of such a breach in a disappointing way. Special consequences are only alluded to in sub-paragraph 3 by the reference to 'such further consequences that a breach to which this chapter applies may entail under international law'. The formulation apparently refers to relevant provisions of multilateral conventions but it is so broad that it may include currently non-existing customary rules.

[79] It reads: '[N]othing in this chapter [on circumstances precluding wrongfulness] precludes the wrongfulness of any act of a State which is not in conformity with an obligation arising under a peremptory norm of general international law.'

[80] It reads: '[I]n the case of a treaty which becomes void and terminates under article 64, the termination of the treaty: (a) releases the parties from any obligation further to perform the treaty.'

[81] See G. Gaja, '*Jus Cogens* Beyond the Vienna Convention', *supra* note 37, at 286.

[82] For an informative and sympathetic discussion of the problems raised by the proposition in the earlier drafts cf P.-M. Dupuy, 'The Constitutional Dimension of the Charter of the United Nations Revisited', 1 *Max Planck UNYB* (1997) 1, at 15–18.

4. 'Constitutionalizing' International Law?

Over the past few decades reflection on the 'constitutionalization', at first of the United Nations but more recently of international law in general, has become a topical subject in international legal writing.[83] It is particularly popular among German scholars, who also teach national constitutional law. The idea is not novel. Already in 1926 Verdross had published a book under the title *Die Verfassung der Staatengemeinschaft* (The Constitution of the International Community of States). And indeed, if one understands by constitution an order which comprises not only a sum of substantive legal norms but also basic principles and functional rules about norm-creation, norm-application, and so on, the international legal community had and has a fragmentary constitution, albeit not a written one.

4.1. *Jus Cogens* as a higher order

That, however, is not what modern 'constitutionalists' have in mind. Their campaign began with the proposition that *jus cogens* was not only non-derogable law but law of a higher order than ordinary norms of international law. Authors like Macdonald[84] or Fassbender[85] relied on Article 103 of the UN Charter, which imposes the priority of obligations under the Charter over those arising from other international agreements, in support of their proposition; and Macdonald, writing at a time when the membership of the United Nations was not yet near-universal, specifically referred to the effect which Article 103 had, in his opinion, on the rights of non-members.[86]

[83] See, eg, P.-M. Dupuy, 'The Constitutional Dimension of the Charter of the United Nations Revisited', *supra* note 82; R.St.J. Maconald, 'The Charter of the United Nations in Constitutional Perspective', 20 *Australian YIL* (1999) 205; D.M. Johnston, 'World Constitutionalism in the Theory of International Law, in R.St.J. Macdonald and D.M. Johnston (eds), *Towards World Constitutionalism. Issues in the Legal Ordering of the World Community* (Leiden: Martinus Nijhoff, 2005) 3; and B.-O. Bryde, 'International Democratic Constitutionalism', ibid. 103.

Entries by German scholars are, eg, C. Tomuschat, 'Obligations Arising for States Without or Against Their Will', *supra* note 26, 209–40; J.A. Frowein, 'Reactions of Not Directly Affected States to Breaches of Public International Law', 248 *Recueil des Cours* (1994-IV) 353, 355–65; ibid., 'Konstitutionalisierung des Völkerrechts', 39 *Berichte der Dt. Gesellschaft für Völkerrecht* (2000) 427; and B. Fassbender, 'The United Nations Charter as Constitution of the International Community', 36 *Columb. J of Transnat' l L* (1998) 529; and ibid., *The United Nations Charter as the Constitution of the International Community* (Leiden-Boston: Martinus Nijhoff Publishers, 2009).

[84] R.St.J. Macdonald, 'Fundamental Norms in Contemporary International Law', *supra* note 46, at 125: '[I]n their deliberations leading up to the Vienna Convention states took the view that Article 103 was a forerunner of the *jus cogens* doctrine.' Ibid., note 84, at 213: '[A]rticle 103, even more forcefully, assigns the Charter a quasi-constitutional relevance ...'

[85] B. Fassbender, 'The United Nations Charter as Constitution of the International Community', *supra* note 83, at 577 citing Article 103, asserts: '... the Charter clearly gives expression to such a hierarchical model ...'.

[86] R.St.J. Macdonald, 'Fundamental Norms in Contemporary International Law', *supra* note 46, at 120–5.

The proposition neglects the essential features of a hierarchy of norms in any legal order. It requires a community mechanism which designates the norms of the higher order so that they can be identified. Furthermore, when norms of a lesser quality or acts supposed to implement the higher norm directly conflict with the higher norm, the system must either declare them void *ipso facto* or make them subject to an annulment process. The higher norms thus form the framework which determines the legality of activities carried out under it. If one of the two elements—identification and nullity—is missing, one cannot properly speak of a hierarchy of norms.

Article 103 does not establish such a system.[87] It deals with a problem which is not infrequently encountered in inter-state relations: at a certain moment and in a given situation a state may have conflicting obligations under international agreements with different partners. Normally, the state would choose the obligation which it would perform and accept responsibility for non-performance towards the party or parties of the other agreement. The choice would be his. Article 103 pre-empts the choice by ordering that obligations under the Charter must be given priority. Sanctions ordered by the Security Council which require violating obligations under a trade agreement of a UN Member with another state would be one example. If that other state is not a UN member, Article 103 does not exclude the responsibility which may arise because of the non-performance of the obligation under the trade agreement. And, in contrast to a violation of *jus cogens*, the validity of the conflicting agreement is not affected; it is only its performance which is in abeyance for the duration of the sanction. Hence proving a hierarchy of norms by Article 103 of the Charter leads to a dead-end.

A different, now more common, approach justifies the hierarchical superiority of *jus cogens* simply by its nature, as an expression of *ordre public*. And indeed, the provisions of the Vienna Convention which provide for the nullity of agreements that violate *jus cogens*, a sanction which possibly extends to customary rules and even some unilateral legal acts, satisfy one of the two criteria named above. In contrast, the designation of the norms forming the 'higher order' is left to processes which are partly obscure and their results therefore open to challenge.[88] Macdonald[89] argued that 'during the last twenty years or so there has been a trend in the literature of international law, in judicial practice, and in state utterances to regard certain norms of international law as fundamental or of a constitutional nature', but that can hardly be taken for an orderly process. The second condition for a hierarchy of norms is thus not met. It was apparently not felt

[87] P. Paulus, '*Jus Cogens* in a Time of Hegemony and Fragmentation', *supra* note 11, at 317, calls it 'a mere conflict rule for the relationship between different treaty regimes'.

[88] See Section 2.

[89] R.St.J. Macdonald, 'Fundamental Norms in Contemporary International Law', *supra* note 46, 135.

necessary for the purposes of the Vienna Convention to create a 'higher order' of norms. I share the opinion of Virally:[90]

> [O]n peut se demander, cependant, s'il s'agit, ici, d'une véritable hiérarchie. Les normes impératives, en réalité, prennent place non pas au-dessus des règles dispositives mais bien à côté d'elles, dans le cadre du droit international général. En effet, le *jus cogens*, comme l'on a vu, exprime une hiérarchie rigoureuse entre les normes qui lui appartiennent et les normes issues de traités particuliers. En revanche, aucune hiérarchie de cette sorte n'apparait entre les normes du *jus cogens* et les autres normes du droit international général, qu'elles aient un caractère dispositif ou supplétive.
>
> La distinction du *jus cogens* et du *jus dispositivum* ne constitue pas, par conséquent, la base d'une véritable hiérarchie juridique.

4.2. *Jus cogens* as source of constitutional principles

The next step in the doctrinal development consisted in postulating the Charter of the United Nations as 'constitution' of the organization,[91] different from a multilateral treaty, even a very special one. That opinion is now fairly popular, although the protagonists have somewhat different ideas of the consequences which that entails; one has even cautioned that it may be a constitution *in fieri*.[92] When the membership of the UN increased to nearly all states of the world more and more writers suggested that the Charter was not only the constitution of the United Nations Organization but of the international legal community as such.[93] The latest entry is *The Constitutionalization of International Law*,[94] a monumental blueprint for remodelling international law, reminiscent of Louis Sohn's grandiose design for an improved United Nations,[95] with the same dim chance of becoming reality soon. Significantly, its many suggestions do not include one on how to persuade states to adopt the project. However, no comment on the general

[90] M. Virally, 'Réflexions sur le *jus cogens*', *supra* note 28, at 18.

[91] See J. Crawford, 'The Charter of the United Nations as a Constitution', in G. Abi-Saab (ed.), *The Changing Constitution of the United Nations* (London: The British Institute of International and Comparative Law, 1997).

[92] The expression was coined by Macdonald, 'The Charter of the United Nations in Constitutional Perspective', *supra* note 83, at 228 but the underlying idea is shared by others, eg J. Crawford, 'The Charter of the United Nations as a Constitution', *supra* note 91, at 15.

[93] See P.–M. Dupuy, 'The Constitutional Dimension of the Charter of the United Nations Revisited', *supra* note 82, 11: '... from a substantial point of view, it seems possible to pretend that the Charter constitutes the constitutional "Law of Nations"...'. Cf. also B. Fassbender, 'The United Nations Charter as Constitution of the International Community', *supra* note 83, at 532 and ibid., 'Rediscovering a Forgotten Constitution: Notes on the Place of the UN Charter in the International Legal Order', in J.L. Dunoff and J.P. Trachtman (eds), *Ruling the World? Constitutionalism, International Law and Global Governance* (Cambridge: Cambridge University Press, 2009) 133; M.W. Doyle, 'The UN Charter—A Global Constitution?', ibid., 113; and Johnston *supra* note 83.

[94] J. Klabbers, A. Peters, and G. Ulfstein, *The Constitutionalization of International Law* (Oxford: Oxford University Press, 2009).

[95] G. Clark and L. Sohn, *World Peace Through World Law* (Cambridge MA: Harvard University Press, 2nd edn, 1964).

proposition is required in this chapter. For the purposes of the following discussion it is assumed that the proposition is sustainable.

What connects constitutionalism with *jus cogens* is the quality of constitutional principles. Logic dictates that constitutional principles must be peremptory if they are to function as guidelines that cannot be manipulated at will. Fassbender argues that peremptory norms and constitutional law are not identical,[96] and that 'at present the number of rules that undisputedly have the quality of a peremptory norm is much smaller that that of constitutional rules'.[97] This is surprising because the title of his paper suggests that it is the UN Charter which 'constitutionalizes' the international community. The institutional rules[98] of the constitution of an international organization, including that of the United Nations, must necessarily be peremptory or else the organization could not function. To explain the non-derogable nature of principles solely by Article 108 of the Charter, as Fassbender suggests,[99] overlooks that this would not protect their content from modification by simple custom unless they were for another reason. Moreover, an agreement between a few states to accept a decision of the Security Council as binding only if it was adopted by a majority of 11, would evidently be null and void and not only inoperative because of Article 103 of the Charter. Fassbender's argument only makes sense when *jus cogens* is understood as manifestation of *ordre public* and the term 'peremptory' reserved for the norms of this category. If used in this sense, it may indeed be confusing to call the institutional law of international organizations 'peremptory', but what other adjective should then describe their character? Wittich calls them 'mandatory rules'.[100] A possible difference between the two types of peremptory rules lies, perhaps, in the fact that in respect of mandatory rules there is no 'counterparty' and hence no one needed to assert the nullity of an act violating the mandatory rule.

It is obvious that the terminology confuses the issue. As part of the institutional law of the United Nations the principles and purposes enshrined in the Charter are peremptory. But are they all *jus cogens* in the sense of the Vienna Convention on the Law of Treaties? The question would have only theoretical significance if one believed Macdonald's assertion that '[a]lmost all principles listed in Article 2 have achieved the status of *jus cogens*',[101] an assertion which widens

[96] B. Fassbender, 'The United Nations Charter as Constitution of the International Community', *supra* note 83, at 589.

[97] Ibid., at 590.

[98] Cf. R. Kolb, *Théorie du* ius cogens *international. Essai de relecture du concept*, *supra* note 21, at 211–12.

[99] B. Fassbender, 'The United Nations Charter as Constitution of the International Community', *supra* note 83, at 590.

[100] St. Wittich, 'Permissible Derogation from Mandatory Rules? The Problem of Party Status in the Genocide Case', 18 *EJIL* (2007) 591, at 610.

[101] R.St.J. Macdonald, 'The Charter of the United Nations in Constitutional Perspective' *supra* note 83, at 208.

the—equally unsubstantiated—comment in the American Restatement,[102] where it was confined to the principles prohibiting the use of force. But can such wholesale assertions be defended without empirical proof? One could probably argue[103] that principles which are imperatively formulated, ie stated in the form of a legal rule prescribing the conduct which they require, like non-intervention or non-use of force, are likely candidates.

Less convincing are principles expressed in a maxim, like justice or sovereign equality. They are normative catchword expressions of values. For establishing the content of the respective norm, reference must be made to the underlying philosophy. If that philosophy is not generally shared, no authoritative statement is possible. It seems bizarre under these circumstances to entertain the idea that agreements could be void *ab initio* because they violated the vague and undefined principle of 'justice'. International relations would be in a shambles.

Principles which are formulated as a programme that UN organs are to implement with the cooperation of states, like the protection of human rights or solidarity in socio-economic matters have, as such, no detailed predefined content. The substance is supplied during the process of their implementation and by it. They function as true 'constitutional principles', directing law-making in the form of multilateral conventions and their interpretation and administration, but it is hard to credit that a norm (principle) of uncertain content could be part of *jus cogens* and nullify contravening agreements.

The foregoing leads to the conclusion that, as far as the law of the United Nations is concerned, the terms 'peremptory norm' and *jus cogens* are not identical. Charter principles are peremptory within the system but do not necessarily belong to *jus cogens* in the sense of the Vienna Convention on the Law of Treaties.

Some authors maintain that constitutional principles of a peremptory nature exist outside the Charter in customary international law.[104] They follow the International Court of Justice's *Nicaragua* judgment[105] in citing the principle of non-intervention as an example. Yet to maintain the parallel existence of the same principles and norms in the Charter and in customary international law after the United Nations have achieved near-universality seems now even more artificial than it appeared in 1986, unless one shares the Court's opinion that 'the rules do not have the same content'.[106] It seems an unnecessary confusion of an already bewildering issue. Moreover, since in general international law only *jus*

[102] Restatement (Third) of the Foreign Relations Law of the United States para.102, comment k (1987).

[103] For a more ample discussion of this problem see K. Zemanek, 'The Basic Principles of UN Charter Law', in R.St.J. Macdonald and D.M. Johnston (eds), *Towards World Constitutionalism: Issues in the Legal Ordering of the World Community* (Leiden-Boston: Martinus Nijhoff Publishers, 2005) 401.

[104] eg P.–M. Dupuy, 'The Constitutional Dimension of the Charter of the United Nations Revisited', *supra* note 82, at 8–9.

[105] Source note 34, para. 202.

[106] Ibid., para. 176.

cogens norms are peremptory, extensive evidence would be required to sustain such an assertion; a mere analogy to Charter principles and their (peremptory or mandatory) nature in institutional law is not sufficient.

What happens to a norm of *jus cogens* when it doubles as 'constitutional principle'? It does not change its quality but acquires a new function: it is not longer simply a legal obstacle to the free choice of the object of a treaty but becomes the supreme guide as well as the ultimate limit of the legislative and executive power in the community that is governed by the constitution.[107] One purpose of 'constitutionalizing' international law is the consequent possibility of interpreting international legal rules 'constitutionally' instead of 'contractually', which means that they can be checked as to their compatibility with the basic (constitutional) principles.[108] Most national constitutions know some sort of mechanism to ensure that the legislative and executive activity is exercised in conformity with the principles enunciated in them. The absence of such a mechanism in the UN system is 'almost universally seen as serious problem[s] for the constitutional perspective'.[109]

Owing to the particular structure of the international community, its constitutional principles would, in the first instance, be addressed to states which exercise, by custom or treaty, its legislative power. But the advocates of the idea sometimes neglect the side-effect that would bind specialized organs, which the international legal community has established to exercise at least part of the executive power, in particular the Security Council of the United Nations, to these constitutional principles. And it has indeed been suggested—though at variance with the available evidence—that even when it was acting under Chapter VII of the Charter, the Council was bound by *jus cogens* (which would include some of the constitutional principles).[110] The usual supportive argument for this opinion is the wording of Article 25 of the Charter by which the member states accept to carry out decisions of the Security Council 'in accordance with the present Charter'. Some argue that these words refer to the obligation of the member states but a majority holds them to apply also to the decisions of the Council.[111] Weisburd has shown the flaw in that argument by pointing out:

> [A]fter all, the fact that the Council takes an action necessarily signifies that the states making up the Council do not believe that action violates a rule 'from which no

[107] B.-O. Bryde, 'International Democratic Constitutionalism', *supra* note 83, at 106.

[108] B. Fassbender, 'The United Nations Charter as Constitution of the International Community', *supra* note 83, at 577.

[109] R.St.J. Macdonald, 'The Charter of the United Nations in Constitutional Perspective', *supra* note 83, 229. The weakness is discussed in detail by J. Crawford, 'The Charter of the United Nations as a Constitution', *supra* note 91, 11–13 and P.-M. Dupuy, 'The Constitutional Dimension of the Charter of the United Nations Revisited', *supra* note 82, 27–8.

[110] B. Fassbender, 'The United Nations Charter as Constitution of the International Community', *supra* note 83, 591.

[111] For the latter argument see R.St.J. Macdonald, 'The Charter of the United Nations in Constitutional Perspective', *supra* note 83, 209–10. Judge *ad hoc* Lauterpacht reasoned in a similar

derogation is permitted'. And if the members of the Security Council do not so characterize the action, it can hardly be said that 'the international community as a whole' sees the matter differently—to argue otherwise is to suggest that one can exclude the Security Council's membership from the international community as a whole.[112]

Weiburd has a point. The peremptory nature of a norm of *jus cogens* is not established once and for all. A norm is peremptory as long—but only as long—as the *opinio juris* of the international community as a whole affirms that it is such a norm. A deviant decision of the Security Council suggests that its members do not—or no longer—share this *opinio*. In view of the important part of the international community which the members of the Security Council represent it can, therefore, be argued that the respective norm no longer meets the condition of being recognized as peremptory by the international community as a whole. Hence, what Weisburd's argument really means is that the Security Council can in fact manipulate *jus cogens* in its decisions under Chapter VII of the Charter, which signifies that its norms do not effectively limit the executive power of the Council. That prompts Dupuy to complain:[113]

[I]f the Security Council is no longer the representative of the world community but rather that of a very small minority of powerful countries acting to some extent under pressure exercised by the only super-power, then the international community lacks its main tool for the promotion and defence of its main rules.

It is a matter of speculation whether judicial supervision of UN organs by the International Court of Justice, if it were politically possible, would remedy the situation. The Court sent ambivalent signals in the *Lockerbie* case,[114] the only one that seems relevant. It affirmed, on the one hand, its jurisdiction despite Security Council resolutions 748 (1992) and 883 (1993), which the defendants claimed had rendered the Libyan action without object. On the other hand, however, it declined to rule immediately on the objection of the defendants because that would 'inevitably be ruling on the merits'.[115] This may simply have been a strategy to give the parties time to settle the matter out of court.[116] But it also shows a certain reluctance to examine the validity of Security Council resolutions, given the precarious balance between the two organs under the Charter. The crucial

manner in the *Application of the Convention on the Prevention and Punishment of the Crime of Genocide case (Bosnia and Herzegovina v Serbia and Montenegro)* Order of 13 September 1993, Provisional Measures, *ICJ Reports* (1993), Separate Opinion of Judge Lauterpacht, at 440–1, paras 101–102.

[112] A.M. Weisburd, 'The Emptiness of the Concept of *Jus Cogens*, as illustrated by the War in Bosnia-Herzegovina', 17 *Michigan JIL* (1995) at 36.

[113] P.–M. Dupuy, 'The Constitutional Dimension of the Charter of the United Nations Revisited', *supra* note 82, at 30.

[114] ICJ, *Questions of Interpretation and Application of the 1971 Montreal Convention Arising from the Aerial Incident at Lockerbie* (*Libyan Arab Jamahiriya v United Kingdom*), Preliminary Objections, Judgment of 27 February 1998, *ICJ Reports* (1998) 9. The judgment in the parallel case against the USA is identical in substance.

[115] Ibid., para. 50.

[116] In fact, both cases were removed from the list on 30 September 2003.

weakness of the scheme lies, however, in Article 94(2) of the Charter, which entrusts the eventual execution of the Court's judgment to the Security Council. It is not likely that the Council would sanction itself.

This all tends to show the limited usefulness of introducing the notion of 'constitutional principle' into international law and linking it to *jus cogens*. The analogy with national constitutional models does not hold.

5. Dissidents

Where appropriate, the views of critics or objectors have been cited throughout this chapter. Since it is, however, difficult to evaluate arguments taken out of context, fairness demands that the gist of the principal protagonists' reasoning is presented in concise form.

When, in 1963, the International Law Commission had definitely incorporated the concept of *jus cogens* in its Draft Articles on the Law of Treaties, Schwarzenberger wrote an extremely critical article against it.[117] The principal elements of his criticism, the indeterminable substance of *jus cogens* and the ineffective (if not impossible) enforcement of the norms having supposedly a peremptory character, have remained the main arguments of those who are critical of the concept or reject it altogether. Schwarzenberger stated:

> [I]nternational law on the level of unorganized international society does not know of any *jus cogens*. The explanation lies in the absence of any center of government with overwhelming physical force and courts with compulsory jurisdiction to formulate rules akin to those of public policy on the national level... In organized world society... these efforts are too precarious... to constitute more than international quasi-orders.[118]

Thereupon he concluded:

> [I]n a system of power politics in disguise, apparent 'progressiveness' can readily be made to serve hidden sectional interests, not apparent at first sight. In this particular case, the beauty of a general, as distinct from more specific, formula of international *jus cogens* is that it leaves everybody absolutely free to argue for or against the *jus cogens* character of any particular rule of international law.[119]

He particularly warned that *jus cogens* would be used 'as a justification of non-compliance with a burdensome treaty'.[120] These fears have not materialized. States have, in their practice, not undermined 'the sanctity of the pledged word'[121] through invoking violations of *jus cogens*.

While Schwarzenberger objected to the concept of *jus cogens* primarily for reasons of legal policy, Glennon[122] denies its existence on principle. He attacks the

[117] G. Schwarzenberger, 'International *Jus Cogens*?', *supra* note 7. [118] Ibid., 476.
[119] Ibid., 477. References omitted. [120] Ibid. [121] Ibid., 478.
[122] M.J. Glennon, 'De l'absurdité du droit impératif (*jus cogens*)', *supra* note 70.

concept with rigorous and stringent positivist logic. His arguments crystallize in two essential points: first, that international law is based on consent. States are only bound by the norms to which they have consented.[123] This is the exact opposite of what Tomuschat had argued in his Hague lectures.[124]

Secondly, the international community as a whole has never consented to establish *jus cogens*:[125]

> [L]'article 53 [de la Convention de Vienne] demande qu'une norme impérative soit 'acceptée et reconnu par la communauté internationale des Etats dans son ensemble', et l'article 53 n'a pas obtenu cette reconnaissance. 'Dans son ensemble' indique un tout. Or toute la communauté internationale n'est pas partie à la Convention de Vienne sur le droit des traités.

This argument makes an assumption which Glennon does not substantiate, namely that the normative category of *jus cogens* was *created* by the Vienna Convention. Critics might retort that *jus cogens* had existed in customary international law before the Vienna Convention recognized it as a category and incorporated appropriate provisions.[126] Without convincing proof that *jus cogens* was unquestionably invented by the Vienna Convention, Glennon's resultant argument that neither the UN Charter nor the Genocide Convention can contain peremptory norms because they predate the Vienna Convention,[127] is not persuasive.

Using the principle of the non-use of force in Article 2(4) of the Charter as example, Linderfalk[128] deconstructs the concept of *jus cogens* with a strictly normative method. He argues that:

> ...in order fully to reconstruct the contents of a legal norm having a regulative character, we need to be able to state, first, the specific kind of conduct or state of affairs prescribed, prohibited, or permitted, and, secondly, each and every single condition on which the prescription, prohibition, or permission is to be dependent, including to whom it applies.[129]

According to this opinion, the *jus cogens* norm which states the prohibition on the use of force is only partly expressed in Article 2(4) of the Charter. To satisfy Linderfalk's normative requirements a full rendering of its content would also have to include the exceptions, namely the right of self-defence[130] and the use

[123] Ibid., 529: '...le principe, à présent bien établi, selon lequel les règles de l'ordre juridique international ne contraignent que les Etats qui y consentent'.

[124] C. Tomuschat, 'Obligations Arising for States Without or Against Their Will', *supra* note 26.

[125] M.J. Glennon, 'De l'absurdité du droit impératif (*jus cogens*)', *supra* note 70, at 532.

[126] L. Hannikainen, *Peremptory Norms (Jus Cogens) in International Law, supra* note 30, devotes the first two chapters of his book and 156 pages to the examination of the history of the idea and its realization.

[127] M.J. Glennon, 'De l'absurdité du droit impératif (*jus cogens*)', *supra* note 70, at 533: '...ni la Charte ni la Convention sur le Génocide ne peuvent ainsi créer de norme impérative'.

[128] U. Linderfalk, 'The Effect of *Jus Cogens* Norms: Whoever Opened Pandora's Box, Did you Ever Think About the Consequences?' *supra* note 57.

[129] Ibid., 857.

[130] Ibid., 860.

of force pursuant to a decision of the Security Council.[131] It would further have to include the limitations conditioning the right of self-defence, ie observance of the rules and principles of international humanitarian law in its exercise and the necessity and proportionality of its measures.[132] Would these incorporated norms or norm-complexes then also have *jus cogens* character? If not, must the exceptions be considered unlawful derogations from *jus cogens*?[133] To avoid this unattractive choice, Linderfalk explores three ways to 'establish some new definition of the *jus cogens* concept that corresponds better to the effects that we can agree to afford on *jus cogens* norms',[134] none of which he finds satisfactory, however. This leads him to the gloomy conclusion: '[*J*]*us cogens* is a term used for rhetorical purposes, but on closer analysis we should admit that in positive international law *jus cogens* norms simply do not exist.'[135]

Linderfalk makes the same mistake as Hans Kelsen.[136] A rigorous normative legal method may be suitable for some, though not all, domestic legal orders. But it does not fit the loose and fractured structure of the international legal order, characterized by the coexistence of custom and treaty as sources of law and of states and UN bodies as its organs. Its use in international law leads to results which may be logical in the framework of the postulated theory, but are unrealistic and only assemble deviations from what the normativist considers the *right* dogmatic deductions. This is best shown by the possible answer to Linderfalk's query whether the norm-complex he has arranged has *jus cogens* character. The answer may simply be yes. Or should an agreement between two states, in which one relinquishes its right of self-defence, be valid?

Weisburd[137] agrees with the *jus cogens* concept of the Vienna Convention on the Law of Treaties, but argues against its transformation by the public policy doctrine into what he calls for the sake of convenience, but inaccurately so, 'Verdrossian *jus cogens*'.[138] He rejects, in particular, the position of the American Restatement of Foreign Relations Law and of some scholars 'that *jus cogens* can control the content of customary international law'.[139] Having compared the war in Bosnia-Herzegovina with the demands of the public policy doctrine, he concludes:

> [O]f course, any legal system needs some standard against which the justice of its enactments is evaluated. The difficulty with the concept of *jus cogens* is that it purports to be, not a standard for evaluating law, but law itself.

131 Ibid., 863.
132 Ibid., 865.
133 Ibid., 869.
134 Ibid., 867.
135 Ibid., 871.
136 Especially in his *Law of the United Nations* (London: Stevens & Sons Ltd, 1951).
137 A. M. Weisburd, 'The Emptiness of the Concept of *Jus Cogens*, as Illustrated by the War in Bosnia-Herzegovina', *supra* note 112.
138 Ibid., 32. At 34 he deplores that: '... there are two concepts, each called *jus cogens*'. On the difference between the *jus cogens* concept of Verdross and of the public policy doctrine see Section 1.
139 Ibid., 35. For the reference to the Restatement see *supra* note 102.

As law, *jus cogens* fails. Its content is inevitably uncertain, reflecting intellectual confusion as to the core of the doctrine. Correspondingly, its claim to legitimacy in international law is murky. It is applied as a characterization to rules which, if treated as though they really were non-derogable, would do more harm than good in many contexts. And the means most often suggested for determining its content lack both the authority and the capacity to carry out the task.[140]

The main thrust of Weisburd's criticism is thus not directed against *jus cogens* but against assigning it other tasks than those provided for by the Vienna Convention on the Law of Treaties. Yet he adopts a peculiar concept of law when he implies that a 'standard for evaluating law' cannot itself be 'law'. Principles enunciated in constitutions for measuring ordinary laws against them are in most legal systems considered to form part of constitutional 'law'; they just have a special function. In many respects, however, Weisburd's diagnosis coincides with mine, despite the different approach.

Christenson[141] is an odd case. His *recherché* terminology makes the paper a difficult read. As far as I managed to understand, his central thesis is that he wishes to 'distinguish the power of participants invoking the peremptory norm from the concept itself'.[142] He doubts that, in a society of sovereign states, invoking a norm of *jus cogens* can be separated from the power-potential of the invoking state. '*Jus cogens*,' he writes, 'is a normative myth masking power arrangements that avoid substantive meaning until later decisions, thereby both postponing and inviting political and ideological conflict'.[143] And a little later:

[T]he conflict between States and the world community is between different kinds of political systems of control. In this situation then, the most powerful elites speaking for the international community may simply impose their version of a suitable ideology in the guise of peremptory norms. However, the interests of international society intervening between a government and its citizens will not easily transform the nation-state system of order.[144]

However, all in all Christenson's attitude is more sceptical than negative and slightly optimistic. As the title of the paper implies, he sees at least the prospect of a future development. 'While the concept *jus cogens* in international law surely conceals substantive emptiness, it also symbolizes a hope for a humane public order.'[145] And further: '[I]t is enough to assert that *jus cogens* analysis reveals and challenges odious conduct from the nation-state system by introducing a possible secondary system of norms of validation and change.'[146] Except for the use of 'might' he comes to the rather conventional conclusion that '[*j*]*us cogens*

[140] Ibid., 50–1.

[141] G.A. Christenson, '*Jus Cogens*: Guarding Interests Fundamental to International Society', 28 *Va. J Int'l L* (1988) 585.

[142] Ibid., 608.

[143] Ibid., 590; cf. also 599. The paper was published in 1988, before the implosion of the Soviet Union, hence the reference to 'ideological conflict'.

[144] Ibid., 602.

[145] Ibid., 590.

[146] Ibid., 645.

norms... might form a normative public order to guide change in ordinary rules of international law'.[147]

6. Conclusions

Summing up the foregoing considerations permits the conclusion that the concept of *jus cogens* as expressed in the provisions of the Vienna Convention on the Law of Treaties is, by and large, accepted by the majority of scholars and is slowly reflected in the jurisprudence of international courts and tribunals and in the practice of states,[148] though no case has yet been brought before the International Court of Justice in which it was claimed that an agreement was void because it violated a norm of *jus cogens*.

Applying the concept to customary law and to certain unilateral legal acts which create a right for another state is theoretically warranted, but the process in which the consequence of a violation of *jus cogens* could be asserted needs further elaboration. A review of state practice, jurisprudence, and literature reveals furthermore that the apparent consensus often stops at the notion, its meaning being subject to a variety of explanations.

This becomes apparent in the attempt to present *jus cogens* as a hierarchically higher form of international law, the higher level containing, among other norms, the constitutional principles of the international legal community. The academic history of the concept before the Vienna Convention shows that *jus cogens* is apparently a necessary and essential element of certain legal theories. The variations, caused by the characteristics of the different schools, generate a lively academic discourse but that discourse finds only a marginal reception in the real world, the world of states and international organs. This may one day change, but presently the idea that a set of commonly accepted principles effectively guides the legislative and executive activities of the world community is an academic construct.

When scholars claim *ad libidum* norms as *jus cogens* or raise unwarranted expectations about the latter's function, they confuse those who are not specialists in international law but must nevertheless make decisions involving it. In the *Kadi* case[149] the Court of First Instance of the EU implied its power to pronounce on the lawfulness of Security Council decisions in case they violated *jus cogens*, which was defined 'as a body of higher rules of public international law binding all subjects of international law, including the bodies of the United Nations [sic],[150]

[147] Ibid., 647.

[148] Cf. some examples in G. Gaja, '*Jus Cogens* Beyond the Vienna Convention', *supra* note 37, at 288–9.

[149] Case T-315/01 *Yassin Abdullah Kadi v Council and Commission* [2005] ECR II-3649. See introductory note by A. Reinisch, 45 *ILM* (2006) 77.

[150] The UN is a subject of international law, but its 'bodies' are not.

and from which no derogation is possible'.[151] Without any deeper study the right to property, the right to be heard, and the right of access to court were qualified as *jus cogens,* though the Court did not find them violated. On appeal, the Grand Chamber of the European Court of Justice rejected the whole construction and examined only the implementation of the Security Council decisions in EU law, with the human rights standards of that law as parameter.[152]

As an omen of the future, the judgment of the Court of First Instance does not bode well. If the idea catches on with domestic courts we may soon find a fragmentation of *jus cogens* in a multitude of different systems, each filled by the imagination of the respective judges. That is exactly the fate which the UN Conference on the Law of Treaties wanted to avoid by establishing the International Court of Justice as sole arbiter of disputes over *jus cogens.*

It would be better to keep a sense of proportion and *jus cogens* at its original task.

[151] Judgment, ibid., para. 226.

[152] ECJ, Jointed Cases C-402/05 P & C-415/05 *P Yassin Abdullah Kadi and Al Barakaat International Foundation v Council and Commission* [2008] ECR I- 6352. See note by A. Reinisch, 47 *ILM* (2008) 923. I do not wish to imply that I agree with the Court's approach, which creates a different problem for UN members since it makes it impossible for them to perform their duty under Article 25 of the Charter.

24

The Distinction between *Jus Cogens* and Obligations *Erga Omnes*

Paolo Picone

1. The prevailing view in international legal scholarship tends to regard the notions of peremptory norms of international law, or *jus cogens*, and norms which impose obligations *erga omnes* as interchangeable. In the final draft on the responsibility of states approved in 2001 by the International Law Commission, this view eventually led Special Rapporteur Crawford to replace the second type of rules with the first (literally, in the title of Chapter III of Part II), as rules that, if seriously breached, would give rise to the aggravated regime of responsibility provided for violations *erga omnes* (previously defined as international 'crimes').[1] This equation is often justified on the basis of a number of rather vague elements. Among these, a prominent role is played by empirical evidence, according to which—as it is usually said—the two categories of norms, covering essentially the same cases (from the prohibition on the use of force to aggression, the prohibition on torture to genocide, and so on) would, in their practical operation, end up overlapping and/or conflating with one another, thus representing, as is often said, 'two facets of the same coin'.

For our part, we have tried to counter this approach, in a quite recent contribution devoted to the necessary distinction between the two specified categories of rules, a view which is receiving growing support in legal scholarship.[2]

Indeed, by way of introduction, we might point out that the equivalence between the two concepts is based on a theoretical misunderstanding, consisting of the confusion between the *material characteristics* of the relevant rules and a possible, and merely hypothetical, *quality* of these rules. Single international

[1] See extensively, on the latest developments of the codification, P. Picone, 'Obblighi *erga omnes* e codificazione della responsabilità degli Stati', 88 *Riv. di Diritto Internaz.* (2005) 893.

[2] See again P. Picone, 'La distinzione tra norme internazionali di *jus cogens* e norme che producono obblighi *erga omnes*', 91 *Riv. di Diritto Internaz.* (2008) 5; and, for some concurring opinions, F. Salerno, *Diritto internazionale. Principi e norme* (Padova: CEDAM, 2008) 414; C. Focarelli, *Lezioni di diritto internazionale* (Padova: CEDAM, 2008) vol. I, 216; R. Monaco and C. Curti Gialdino, *Diritto internazionale pubblico. Parte generale* (Torino: UTET, 3rd edn, 2009) 122.

rules can exist between different subjects and can obviously be at the origin of very different legal positions. They may, in fact, on the one hand, regulate (as traditionally happens) only bilateral and reciprocal relationships between one or more pairs of states, or the conduct of one state vis-à-vis a group of other states taken collectively, or the conduct which every state is required to comply with in respect of the entire international community, or else the conduct of a state towards other subjects of international law, such as international organizations, and so on. On the other hand, it is clear that the behaviours which are normatively relevant can from time to time give rise to different deontic modalities. That is to say that, as appropriate, they can attribute rights, give rise to obligations, confer powers or authorizations, and so on. These features and these effects relate to the specific material content (in the strict sense) of each single 'primary' norm which comes to be relevant, and, where this norm is breached, they are the basis of the consequences attached to the unlawful conduct by the rules that are usually defined as 'secondary'. However, a separate issue is whether a particular rule which falls within one or another of the categories mentioned is also (because of its hierarchical and/or formal relevance, its prescriptive content, or for other reasons) a peremptory rule which cannot be derogated from by the contrary will of the subjects of the legal order (namely, the autonomy of the potential contracting parties). Indeed, this question relates to each possibly relevant norm, and in principle is reflected in an ancillary effect, independently of the consequences which might follow from a breach of that norm *stricto sensu*, an effect which consists of the invalidity (and not the illegality) of the contrasting 'contractual' behaviour.[3]

Claiming, then, that the rules of *jus cogens* generally correspond to those which impose obligations *erga omnes*, apart from the uncertainties of the terminology used, would either mean that, in the international legal order, only the latter rules may be classified as peremptory, or that all norms of *jus cogens* produce, if breached, obligations *erga omnes*. Both of these conclusions, as we shall see, are unacceptable.[4]

[3] See also briefly D. Alland, 'Countermeasures of General Interest', 13 *EJIL* (2002) 1221, where, at 1237, after having distinguished between 'bindingness' and 'responsibility', the author underlines that 'bindingness is a technique determining the effect of certain norms (non-derogability); it is not, strictly speaking, substantive law, *nor a category of norms*, but *an attribute pertaining to certain norms* (from which one may not derogate)' (emphasis added). Highlighting the distinction between the two concepts in an earlier work, see P. Picone, 'Obblighi reciproci e obblighi *erga omnes* degli Stati nel campo della protezione internazionale dell'ambiente marino dall'inquinamento', in V. Starace (ed.), *Diritto internazionale e protezione dell'ambiente marino* (Milano: Giuffré, 1983) 15, at 39 *et seq.* (reproduced in P. Picone, *Comunità internazionale e obblighi* erga omnes (Napoli: Jovene, 2006) 1 *et seq.*).

[4] See previously P. Picone, 'Obblighi reciproci e obblighi *erga omnes* degli Stati nel campo della protezione internazionale dell'ambiente marino dall'inquinamento', *supra* note 3, at 29 *et seq.*, also for the demonstration of the existence of peremptory norms that govern mere reciprocal relationships between states (a point that I recently reaffirmed in 'La distinzione tra norme internazionali di *jus cogens* e norme che producono obblighi *erga omnes*', *supra* note 2, at 33 *et seq.*).

2. The distinction between the concepts under consideration, ie the peremptory nature and the production of obligations *erga omnes*, is already clear from the literal wording of the provisions and normative passages in which the same notions were originally formulated.

Peremptory or non-derogable international norms are provided for by Article 53 of the Vienna Convention of the Law of Treaties of 1969 as norms accepted and recognized 'by the international community of States as a whole' from which no derogation is permitted. These norms are of such a nature that, if parties sought to contract out of them by agreement, the attempt would produce the radical and irremediable invalidity of a treaty.

For our purposes, the wording of the provision raises three considerations.

First, it can be said that 'inderogability' is the only essential and invariable effect of the rules of *jus cogens*, belonging as they do to the field of the validity of legal acts.[5] Their significance 'beyond the Vienna Convention', which seems now the most emphasized in legal scholarship, is currently accepted in cases where those rules don't limit themselves to ensure the operation of the principles '*d'ordre structurel*' of the international legal order (such as those related to the '*création, validité, modification et fin des traités*') but aim at respecting the essential and higher values of the international community; values of which the peremptory nature of a norm as an ancillary effect is certainly an expression, but which—as we have said—are materially and directly protected by the norm itself, not because of its peremptory character, but because of its prescriptive content and its effects concerning the unlawful conduct and the responsibility of the states.[6]

Secondly, as regards the formation of the rules of *jus cogens*, it is significant that Article 53 refers to 'the international community of States as a whole' simply to assert the existence of a rule of the type under consideration. As we have pointed out elsewhere, in this case the international community is the material source of these norms (as is ultimately the case with all the customary or general rules of the international legal order), but not the exponential entity to which certain behaviours are collectively due. It is the 'static' moment of the non-derogability of a norm that is pertinent here, not the 'functional' moment (which is emphasized, as we shall see shortly, by rules producing *erga omnes* obligations).

Finally, the exclusive relevance of Article 53 in the area of the invalidity of treaties, as a norm aimed at limiting (as happens in domestic law) the autonomy of the contracting states, is proven by the fact that—in the Convention itself—the *entitlement* to invoke the cause of invalidity in question is reserved to the *contracting*

[5] See, in a very radical fashion, R. Kolb, *Théorie du* jus cogens *international. Essai de relecture d'un concept* (Paris: PUF, 2001) who, however, excessively extends the scope of 'non-derogability', isolating it from the content of the various material norms.

[6] It is in the light of this consideration that the classification of the various rules I made in 'La distinzione tra norme internazionali di *jus cogens* e norme che producono obblighi *erga omnes*', *supra* note 2, at 9, and 14 *et seq.*, should be reinterpreted.

states only. As shown by the preparatory works, this solution was adopted in full awareness, in contrast with the positions advanced by some states in favour of an extension of the entitlement at least to any other state party to the Convention.[7] Accordingly, no relevance can be attributed to the solutions currently advanced by some authors (sometimes even assuming that, from the standpoint of obligations *erga omnes*, all states of the international community should be considered as entitled to invoke this ground of invalidity), because, finding no support in the original provisions, they should at least be able to rely on subsequent evolutionary practice, which is nevertheless entirely lacking.[8]

3. Independently of the rules of *jus cogens*, the norms which impose obligations *erga omnes* were first envisaged in a well-known passage (a brief *obiter dictum*) contained in the judgment given by the International Court of Justice in 1970 in the *Barcelona Traction* case.[9] In this passage, the Court, in opposition to the purely reciprocal obligations of states, spoke of the existence of obligations of states 'towards the international community as a whole', which, by their nature, are 'the concern of all States'. These should be defined as obligations *erga omnes*, as 'all States can be held to have a legal interest in their protection' (ie they may require their implementation). Later, in 1976, these obligations were again recalled, albeit by implication, in Article 19 of the Draft Articles on the Responsibility of States approved on first reading by the International Law Commission, in order to launch the well-known distinction between international 'delicts' and 'crimes', basing the latter on the serious breach of an international obligation 'so essential for the protection of fundamental interests of the international community' as to be recognized 'as a crime by that community as a whole'.[10]

The category of rules which impose obligations *erga omnes* has been kept distinct from the category of rules of *jus cogens* from the very beginning.

First, on a literal level, it is significant that, in defining the concept, the International Court of Justice makes no reference to Article 53 of the Vienna

[7] See, for instance, G. Gaja, '*Jus Cogens* Beyond the Vienna Convention', 172 *Recueil des Cours* (1981-III) 271, at 304; L. Hannikainen, *Peremptory Norms (Jus Cogens) in International Law. Historical. Developments, Criteria, Present Status* (Helsinki: Finnish Lawyers, 1988) 179 *et seq*.; C. Tams, *Enforcing Obligations* Erga Omnes *in International Law* (Cambridge: Cambridge University Press, 2005) 146 *et seq*.

[8] See, for instance, in the sense here criticized, F. Voeffray, *L'*actio popularis *ou la défense de l'intérêt collectif devant les juridictions internationales* (Paris: PUF, 2004) 263 *et seq*., and 272 *et seq*.; A. Orakhelashvili, *Peremptory Norms in International Law* (Oxford: Oxford University Press, 2006) 142.

[9] See ICJ, *Barcelona Traction, Light and Power Company, Limited (Belgium v Spain)*, Judgment of 5 February 1970, *ICJ Reports* (1970) 3 *et seq*., at 32 (and the reference at 47); and in the legal scholarship M. Ragazzi, *The Concept of International Obligations* Erga Omnes (Oxford: Oxford University Press, 1997) 1 *et seq*.

[10] See extensively P. Picone, 'Obblighi *erga omnes* e codificazione della responsabilità degli Stati', *supra* note 1, 31 *et seq*., and 44 *et seq*.

Convention, adopted just a year before.[11] Speaking rather of the obligations of states 'towards' the international community as a whole, the Court distinguishes them clearly from all other general international rules, including the peremptory ones, which are only 'produced' by the international community as a whole.

Secondly, the Court does not take pains to clarify whether the rules which impose obligations *erga omnes* are peremptory or not, but tends to briefly outline their content, stressing that all states would have an 'interest' in their implementation. The Court therefore does not intend to impose limits on the will of states: rather, it recognizes that they have functional powers (or, if one prefers, collective rights) to be managed on behalf of the international community as a whole.[12] The international community, with its inorganic nature, cannot in fact use its own bodies to further the values or goods that are directly related to it (or that it intends to directly protect); rather, for this purpose, it must necessarily avail itself of the activity carried out by states acting *uti universi* (in a perspective, so to speak, of the classic '*dédoublement fonctionnel*'), as keepers of the international legal order.

Thirdly, one must consider that the rules which impose obligations *erga omnes* perform not only the function of protecting absolute and 'supreme' values of the international community (as would be the case, according to some authors, with regard to the rules of *jus cogens*) but also the wider role of making it possible, through the collective action of states, to protect goods and values that might otherwise be ineligible for protection. The rules in question can in fact operate in three different kinds of hypotheses: a) protection of the *internal* values of the state taken into consideration (eg the protection of citizens' human rights or the environment within that state); b) protection of values existing *outside* the jurisdictions of individual states (such as the case of major pollution on the high seas); and c) protection of goods and values of such an importance (as in the case of an aggression, with the ensuing collective self-defence under Article 51 of the UN Charter) that they entail that the injured state should and/or could be 'supported' by the reaction of third-party states. As is evident, in the first two cases, the limitation of the relationship of responsibility to the traditional reciprocal perspective of the breach of an international rule by one state against another would impede the guarantee of protection of the goods mentioned before. As there is no injured state, only the potential entitlement of all states to make a claim concerning the good or value in question, in the name and on behalf of the international community, makes it possible to achieve the desired

[11] For a clear assertion that Article 19 should be 'better read as an attempt to express the notion of obligations *erga omnes*', see J. Crawford, 'First Report on State Responsibility', A/CN.4/490/Add.1, para. 51, note 33, restated literally by N. Jørgensen, *The Responsibility of States for International Crimes* (Oxford: Oxford University Press, 2000) 53.

[12] On this aspect, see extensively P. Picone, 'La distinzione tra norme internazionali di *jus cogens* e norme che producono obblighi *erga omnes*', *supra* note 2, 11 *et seq.*

outcome.[13] In the final Draft Articles on the Responsibility of States this reality is obscured by the fact that there is always a distinction between the 'injured state' and states 'other than an injured state', almost as if there could be no cases (which are potentially the most numerous) in which the *erga omnes* unlawful conduct does not involve the very existence of an injured state (thus causing the violation of the values and interests of the international community itself, regarded as a whole).[14]

Finally, and this is the fourth point, the distinctions just outlined show that, in the case of norms which impose obligations *erga omnes*, it is not justified in principle to postulate their general non-derogability (although, certainly, this is often a recurring feature of these norms). The norms in question may actually take very different directions, as they often tend, as we have seen, to ensure community values that might otherwise remain completely ineligible for protection. It is therefore quite possible that they constitute, at least in some cases, potentially derogable norms for the will to the contrary of the states (under the conditions provided by the international community itself).[15] The fact that the scholarship does not address the point (showing, instead, the tendency to mistakenly equate the rules of *jus cogens* with those which impose obligations *erga omnes*) is simply the result of the insufficient level of elaboration of these latter norms, both in the legal literature and in the work of the International Law Commission on the codification of the responsibility of states.

4. According to international legal scholarship, the substantial equivalence between the two categories of rules was established precisely in the abovementioned 2001 final draft of the International Law Commission. Following a number of factors and considerations that cannot be analysed here, the International Law Commission decided, under the influence of Special Rapporteur Crawford, to expunge the old Article 19 (still present in the preliminary draft of 1996) from the final text in order to eliminate the 'international crimes', and to reconnect violations *erga omnes* (broadly downsized in their specific effects) to serious breaches no longer of obligations *erga omnes* but of 'obligations under peremptory norms of general international law'. Thus, hastily and without careful examination,

[13] See also B. Simma, 'From Bilateralism to Community Interest in International Law', 250 *Recueil des Cours* (1994-VI) 219 *et seq.*, at 296 *et seq.*; and further E. Uhlmann, 'State Community Interests, *Jus Cogens* and Protection of the Global Environment: Developing Criteria for Peremptory Norms', 11 *Georgetown International Environmental Law Review* (1998–1999) 101 *et seq.*, at 102; D. Shelton, 'Normative Hierarchy in International Law', 100 *AJIL* (2006) 291 *et seq.*, at 318.

[14] It should be noted that a subdivision of the various hypotheses, with an autonomous emphasis on those characterized by the absence of an injured state, was still drawn by the Special Rapporteur Crawford in the preliminary draft of 2000; see 'Third Report on State Responsibility', A/CN.4/507/Add.4, 20 *et seq.* (paras 403–405), but the proposal was not accepted in the final text of 2001. In this regard, see the important considerations of M. Koskenniemi, 'Solidarity Measures: State Responsibility as a New International Order?', 71 *BYIL* (2001) 337 *et se*q., at 345 *et seq.*

[15] See P. Picone, 'Obblighi reciproci e obblighi *erga omnes* degli Stati nel campo della protezione internazionale dell'ambiente marino dall'inquinamento', *supra* note 3, at 43, note 57.

the theoretical perspective that had driven codification for over 20 years was removed.[16]

In the legal scholarship, the change in question was commonly attributed to the fact that the two categories of norms (those which are peremptory and those which produce *erga omnes* obligations) would end up regulating, in practice, the same cases. But this justification does not make sense in general, and it is not even supported by the final text of the Draft Articles.

Indeed, from a general point of view the peremptory nature of certain rules is, as we noted earlier, a particular characteristic or quality of such rules beyond the typical effects they produce at a material level and with regard to the possible consequences of unlawful conduct. In national law, to give just one example, criminal laws are certainly 'peremptory' with respect to the contrary intent of the parties, but they produce, if violated, their material and specific effects as criminal norms, and not as... peremptory rules! Furthermore, it should be borne in mind that norms may be peremptory in so far as they protect the basic structural principles of the international legal order, and not the absolute or supreme values likely, if violated, to result in the unlawful conduct of states. One must therefore reject the proposition that the consequences of unlawful conduct can be unitarily looped back to the peremptory character of the norm infringed, since even in international law, peremptory norms may have the most varied content, and therefore they certainly do not coincide only with norms which can produce obligations *erga omnes*.[17]

Moreover, the solution adopted in the final draft on the responsibility of states is not even developed in a consistent manner, whatever the conceptual construction that lies at its base.

A first approach indicates, in line with the literal wording of Article 40(1) of the draft, that the provision in question actually and directly takes as its point of reference all of the peremptory norms of general international law (and not just those involving *erga omnes* obligations), by stating that a 'serious' breach of these norms entails the commission of *erga omnes* unlawful conduct, and the possible reaction to that violation on the part of all states. Such a position was adopted by Rapporteur Giorgio Gaja, in the *Projet de résolution* of the *Institut de droit*

[16] See extensively P. Picone, 'Obblighi *erga omnes* e codificazione della responsabilità degli Stati', *supra* note 1.

[17] See again P. Picone, 'La distinzione tra norme internazionali di *jus cogens* e norme che producono obblighi *erga omnes*', *supra* note 2, at 25 *et seq.* As has been rightly observed by A. Paulus, '*Jus Cogens* in a Time of Hegemony and Fragmentation', 74 *Nordic JIL* (2005) 297 *et seq.*, at 316, before the International Law Commission accepted in the text the solution here indicated, 'there was no indication that the effect of *jus cogens* was to create obligations for third States. On the contrary, the impact of *jus cogens* was to void any contrary agreement, not to produce additional obligations for other parties. This was however the impact of obligations *erga omnes*, the *omnes* being the States composing the international community.' Many examples of international peremptory norms regarding only the mutual reciprocal relationships between states can be derived from L. Hannikainen, *Peremptory Norms (Jus Cogens) in International Law. Historical. Developments, Criteria, Present Status*, *supra* note 7, *passim*.

international in 2005 on 'Les droits et les obligations erga omnes en droit international', in a provision, not fortuitously later eliminated, which stated that '*les règles de jus cogens imposent toujours des obligations erga omnes*'.[18] This opinion is unacceptable because it is not supported by practice. It contrasts—as we have said—with Article 53 of the Vienna Convention of the Law of Treaties (according to which the possibility of asserting the invalidity of a treaty on the ground that it breaches peremptory norms of general international law is limited to the contracting parties). Moreover, in the framework of the final draft of codification of the responsibility of states the solution contradicts, on the one hand, the still predominant importance attributed by the project, as we shall see, to the rules which impose obligations *erga omnes*; and, on the other hand, the fact that some of the rules considered likely, in the event of violation, to lead to *erga omnes* wrongful conduct are (in contrast with the premises) incapable by their very nature of establishing non-derogable or peremptory norms of general international law![19]

A different interpretative approach, more autonomous with respect to the literal wording of Article 40(1) of the draft, is that advanced by some authors, within or outside the negotiations, according to which all international norms, and not only those of a peremptory character, would be likely to produce, in the event of serious breach, a possible reaction on the part of all states (and more severe 'sanctions').[20] This approach can theoretically be related to the idea expressed by Crawford according to which the elimination of obligations *erga omnes* as a basis of international crimes is justified by the impossibility of believing that 'only *specified* norms can give rise to the most serious breaches';[21] and it seems to be supported in the draft by the fact, already pointed out, that the final text multiplies, under Articles 42 and 48, the instances of multilateral and conventional norms to be taken into consideration in order to determine the 'state injured'

[18] See Article C of the project, 71 *Annu. de l'Inst. de Droit Internat.*, Session de Cracovie (2005) vol. II, at 86, and for other similar assertions in doctrine, the bibliographic references in P. Picone, 'Obblighi *erga omnes* e codificazione della responsabilità degli Stati', *supra* note 1, at 932, note 106.

[19] These are the rules laid down in the final draft for identifying the injured state (Article 42) or the subjects entitled to react 'other than an injured state' (Article 48(1)). These rules envisage the scenarios where the obligation breached exists toward a *group* of states, and thus conventional regimes governed by the Vienna Convention on the Law of Treaties, and are therefore beyond the scope of a project aimed at codifying the rules governing the responsibility of states under general international law: see more extensively P. Picone, 'La distinzione tra norme internazionali di *jus cogens* e norme che producono obblighi *erga omnes*', *supra* note 2, 22; I. Papa, 'Protezione diplomatica, diritti umani e obblighi *erga omnes*', 91 *Riv. di Diritto Internaz.* (2008) 669, at 700 *et seq.*

[20] This solution, already expressed by Riphagen as Rapporteur of the codification (see, for bibliographic references, P. Picone, 'Obblighi *erga omnes* e codificazione della responsabilità degli Stati', *supra* note 1, 909 *et seq.*, and 913), was then taken up by other authors: see, for example, with nevertheless significant nuances of thought, M. Byers, 'Conceptualising the Relationship between *Jus Cogens* and *Erga Omnes* Rules', 66 *Nordic JIL* (1997) 211, at 229 *et seq.*, and 232 *et seq.*; C. Dominicé, 'The International Responsibility of States for Breach of Multilateral Obligations', 10 *EJIL* (1999) 33, at 36 *et seq.*

[21] See J. Crawford, 'Multilateral Rights and Obligations in International Law', 319 *Recueil des Cours* (2006) 325, at 470.

or states 'other than an injured state', whilst these same norms may not—even potentially—be qualified as peremptory norms of general international law. Elsewhere we have already critically discussed this second interpretative variant: it is clear, however, that it is not only unsupported by past practice, but that in its hypothetical implementation it would create theoretical and practical difficulties of an almost insuperable nature.[22]

In conclusion, there does not seem to be sufficient interpretative room to justify, in the light of either of the last two variants analysed here, the solution adopted in the final text of the draft. In any event, it needs to be added that both constructions, connecting, in the case of an *erga omnes* unlawful conduct, the possible reaction of all the states either to the peremptory character of the norm infringed, or only to the 'degree of gravity' of the violation in question, in practice attribute this reaction (mostly without expressing it so explicitly) to the *modus operandi* of *secondary* rules, those that determine and regulate the consequences of the commission of an international crime. Whereas, as we have already shown elsewhere,[23] there is clear evidence to suggest that, even in the final text of the draft, the possibility for everyone to 'invoke' the responsibility of the state offender is not set out as an independent and additional sanction opposable only to 'international crimes'; but that it will continue to represent, in line with the viewpoint adopted during the whole of the negotiations, a direct and connatural consequence of the nature of the very primary rules violated, which impose obligations *erga omnes*.

5. The criticism of the strategy adopted by the final draft of codification of the responsibility of states is increased by an additional argument, this time decisive, if one considers that, despite the literal wording of Article 48(1), and despite the 'fashionable' statements recurrent in the scholarship, it is not true that the peremptory norms of international law have in all respects replaced, as the basis of the 'serious' violations that may give rise to *erga omnes* wrongful conduct, the rules which impose obligations *erga omnes*. These are in fact still very present, and, as will be maintained here, they are the central point of reference of the codification with respect to the aim indicated.

Consider Article 42(b) and Article 48(1)(b), both of which make explicit reference to 'obligations' of the states 'owed to... the international community as a whole', that is, to quite traditional obligations *erga omnes*, 'claimable' by states acting *uti universi* on behalf of the entire international community. While the reference in the first provision is partly spurious, since it literally deforms in letter (b)(ii) the content and the mode of operation of the rules which impose obligations *erga omnes* (and contradictorily in the comment refers only to provisions of a

[22] See extensively P. Picone, 'La distinzione tra norme internazionali di *jus cogens* e norme che producono obblighi *erga omnes*', *supra* note 2, 23 *et seq*.

[23] See again P. Picone, 'La distinzione tra norme internazionali di *jus cogens* e norme che producono obblighi *erga omnes*', *supra* note 2, 26 *et seq*.

conventional nature!), the second provision, instead, regulates in detail (in Article 48(2)) the reactions that 'third-party' states (ie states other than the 'injured state') may put in place against a state which has committed an *'erga omnes'* wrongful act, and therefore specifies the way in which Article 41 generally operates.

The rules which impose obligations *erga omnes* are therefore still taken into consideration in the final draft on the responsibility of states, as a separate category of primary rules, and as a likely base of legitimacy for all states to react to an international crime.[24] On closer examination, it is indeed the only category of rules which is relevant and which can be used to reach the goal indicated, considering that Article 48 makes further reference to the obligations 'owed to a group of states' without realizing that such a case is beyond the scope of the codification, since it does not concern general norms of international law but conventional norms likely to give rise to simple obligations of solidarity or '*inter omnes partes*'.

At this point, we can only briefly examine the manner in which 'peremptory' rules are intended to tie in with those which impose obligations *erga omnes*. In our view, given that the former cannot, even in the final text of the draft, replace the rules which impose obligations *erga omnes*, or be deemed interchangeable with them, it is clear that the reference in Article 40(1) of the draft to 'peremptory norms of general international law' should not be considered as decisive, but the mere result of the error frequently mentioned here (concerning the alleged coincidence between the rules of *jus cogens* and those which create obligations *erga omnes*). One may then ask whether, in the light of a more adequate systematic interpretation of the whole draft (with the central role attributed by Article 48(2) to international norms to be respected by states towards the international community as a whole), it can be concluded that the two categories of norms mentioned should be read together so as to justify the solution for which, behind the commission of violations *erga omnes*, there are still (in continuity with the perspective opened by Article 19 of the draft approved by the Commission as early as 1976, and unchanged until 2000) serious breaches of rules producing obligations *erga omnes* of a *non-derogable nature*.[25]

[24] According to F. Voeffray, *L'*actio popularis *ou la défense de l'intérêt collectif devant les juridictions internationales, supra* note 8, 294, the current text of the Draft Articles would even grant '*de manière justifiée une importance capitale au concept d'obligations* erga omnes'! See also M. Toufayan, 'A Return to Communitarianism? Reacting to "Serious Breaches of Obligations Arising under Peremptory Norms of General International Law" under the Law of State Responsibility and United Nations Law', 42 *Annuaire canadien de droit international* (2004) 197, at 208 *et seq.*, 213, and 232.

[25] An indirect confirmation of our solution is derived from the Advisory Opinion delivered on 9 July 2004 by the International Court of Justice in the well-known and much discussed case of the *Legal Consequences of the Construction of a Wall in the Occupied Palestinian Territory* (*ICJ Reports* (2004) 136 *et seq.*), which relates directly to the violation of obligations *erga omnes* the consequences arising for third-party states under Article 41, paras 1 and 2, of the final draft on the responsibility of states, without being distracted by the literal wording of the draft (see also, for

The solution proposed here does not only take into account the central importance attributed by Article 48(1)(b) of the draft to the norms 'due' by states to the international community as a whole, and thus to 'primary' international rules which produce obligations *erga omnes*. It also takes account of the fact that, as the history of codification is to demonstrate, there has always been a correlation between those provisions and the possibility of all states to ensure their implementation, and to 'invoke', in the event of *erga omnes* unlawful conduct, the responsibility of the offender. The latter possibility is indeed inherent in the nature of the same primary rules violated: 'third-party' states (or states 'other' than the injured state, to use the misleading headline of Article 48) are therefore entitled to react not as bearers of an autonomous sanction against the offending state, but as 'direct' material addressees of the norms in question.

6. The need to keep the peremptory nature of general international law rules separate from the ability of such rules to produce obligations *erga omnes* is proven by the fact that the two aspects raise separate problems which are the subject of different regulations and solutions.

With regard, firstly, to their peremptory nature, it is known that the non-derogable character of international norms is currently reconstructed by many scholars in a radical and absolute fashion, ie as likely to give rise to a series of consequences that automatically characterize the norms in question, regardless of their relevance in practice. Thus, just to give a few examples, *jus cogens* has been used in the field of international crimes, as a basis, in the event of infringement, for the principle of the non-prescriptibility of the crime, or to justify the disappearance of the obligation to grant immunity from civil jurisdiction to foreign organs or states, and so on.[26]

This approach may be criticized from various angles. In the light of the considerations discussed earlier, the peremptory nature of certain international norms is a characteristic that goes beyond the specific effects stemming from these rules, because of their material content, in the field of wrongful conduct and the responsibility of states. Non-derogability therefore covers a very wide range of rules which are not at all, because of the mere fact that they are peremptory, a single category of material norms. In my view, this explains, by way of premise, the reason why some authors assert, rightly, that each special effect stemming from non-derogability, far from being automatically derived from a superior hierarchical rank with respect to any other rule in question, must in any case be verified on the basis of the elements (practice plus *opinio iuris*) suitable for establishing the

instance, A. Bianchi, 'Dismantling the Wall: The ICJ's Advisory Opinion and its Likely Impact on International Law', 47 *GYIL* (2004) 343, at 378 *et seq.*, and 389).

[26] A radical perspective of the type shown is followed, for example, by A. Orakhelashvili, *Peremptory Norms in International Law*, *supra* note 8 (which I reviewed critically in 89 *Riv. di Diritto Internaz.* (2006) 1240 *et seq.*).

existence of an international custom.[27] And the solution is easily understood if one considers that the admission of an additional effect generally operates in the sense of extending or modifying, at least indirectly, the material content of the international norm in question.

But the solution we have adopted leads to a different analysis of the various hypotheses, and to determining whether and to what extent a certain further effect is really attributable to a norm's peremptory character (eg producing effects in respect of a legal 'fact' and not an 'act'); whether some effects can really be inferred from a wider interpretation of Article 53 of the Vienna Convention; whether they present themselves differently, as seems logical, if the peremptory norm in question is an international norm which only produces pure reciprocal effects, or, instead, obligations *erga omnes*, and so on. Recently, an author has undertaken a survey of this kind, to demonstrate, with a radical critique, that in most cases the effects in question do not *stricto sensu* (or formally) arise from the non-derogability but are justifiable on different grounds.[28] Thus, for example, autonomous theoretical solutions could in each case justify the rule (laid down in Article 26 of the final Draft Articles on the Codification of the Responsibility of the States) whereby the various circumstances precluding the wrongfulness of a particular type of conduct, as enshrined in Articles 20–25, may not function if an obligation under a peremptory norm of general international law has been breached.[29] While in other cases the issue is not really the peremptory nature of a rule of *jus cogens* but its ability to positively depart from other norms of general international law, so as to transform (or help to transform), with the support of the practice, the rules themselves.[30]

These issues cannot be clearly set out here. For our purposes it is only important to stress that they too are an expression of the fact, pointed out above, that it is necessary to keep the effects of the peremptory nature of an international norm (covered by Article 53 of the Vienna Convention or deducible from the same provision in the strict sense) distinct from the consequences, in terms of wrongful conduct and responsibility of states, resulting directly or indirectly

[27] In this sense, see C. Focarelli, *Lezioni di diritto internazionale*, *supra* note 2, 215 *et seq.*

[28] See K. Kawasaki, 'A Brief Note on the Legal Effects of Jus Cogens in International Law', 34 *Hitotsubashi Journal of Law and Politics* (2006) 27 *et seq.*

[29] In summary, whereas in the case of the circumstance precluding wrongfulness represented by the consent of the injured state, since it actually consists of an agreement between this state and the state responsible for the wrongful conduct, the invalidity of that agreement for its incompatibility with a norm of *jus cogens* falls wholly within the scope of Article 53 of the Vienna Convention; in the case of necessity, the impossibility of invoking the circumstance in question would result, in the opinion of the author, through the same provision of Article 25, para. 1, letter b); and in other cases (self-defence, countermeasures), the impossibility of violating a peremptory rule would be due to the fact that the reaction may affect the position of third states, at least when the same provision creates obligations *erga omnes*, and so on: see K. Kawasaki, 'A Brief Note on the Legal Effects of Jus Cogens in International Law', *supra* note 28, at 36 *et seq.*

[30] See again K. Kawasaki, 'A Brief Note on the Legal Effects of Jus Cogens in International Law', *supra* note 28, at 39 *et seq.*, with regard to the possible existence of a 'derogatory rule in the case of torture from, for example, the general rule of State immunity' (at 40).

from a breach of the international norm in question (in the cases considered here, the norm able to produce obligations *erga omnes*). Indeed, while current opinion tends to confuse the peremptory or non-derogable nature of a norm with the material content typical of the norm itself, the critical solutions listed above correctly reconstruct this nature as the (possible) source of further additional effects, which must be identified and assessed independently of those—so to speak—typical of the international norm in question.

7. The rules that produce obligations *erga omnes* can also be further distinguished and qualified, on the basis of their typical material content, and are still waiting to be adequately examined in the legal scholarship.

In the draft on the codification of the responsibility of states, the norms in question, if breached, give rise to international crimes, but only on condition that their breach may be regarded as 'serious': so that, first, apart from the difficulty of ascertaining in some cases the condition of seriousness, it is not yet clear what consequences should and/or may be derived from a less serious violation of these norms. Secondly, the need to look more deeply into how the rules of the type under consideration of a derogable nature operate has been completed ignored. Finally, focusing on aspects regarding wrongful conduct and responsibility, it has not been taken into account that the same rules may also serve to prevent the commission of wrongful conduct, and/or to establish appropriate monitoring mechanisms: aspects which are increasingly destined to gain importance in the framework of the 'responsibility to protect', if it is true, as we believe, that the principle at issue is the succinct expression of a number of *erga omnes* obligations owed in various directions by states to the international community.[31]

One of the most sensitive points to be examined concerning the way the rules which impose obligations *erga omnes* operate, however, arises from how the circle of states entitled to require compliance therewith is determined, and how to react in the event of violation. As is known, the possible entitlement of all states was hypothesized from the outset in the famous *obiter dictum* of the International Court of Justice in the *Barcelona Traction* case, mentioned above. It was historically asserted until the provisional draft of the International Law Commission in 1996, being also justified on the basis of the erroneous contention that all states would in such cases have similar individual rights.[32] Article 48(1)(b) of the final draft of 2001 equally states that, in the case of an obligation owed to the 'international community as a whole', every state 'other than an injured State' would have the power to invoke the international responsibility of the offending state, albeit

[31] See my review of C. Verlage, *Responsibility to Protect* (Tübingen: Mohr Siebeck, 2009) in 93 *Riv. di Diritto Internaz.* (2010) 289 *et seq.*

[32] See extensively P. Picone, 'Obblighi *erga omnes* e codificazione della responsabilità degli Stati', *supra* note 1, 907 *et seq.*; I. Papa, *I rapporti tra la Corte internazionale di giustizia e il Consiglio di sicurezza* (Padova: CEDAM, 2006) 515 *et seq.*; I. Papa, 'Protezione diplomatica, diritti umani e obblighi *erga omnes*', *supra* note 19, 685 *et seq.*

limiting itself, under para. 2, letter b), to require reparation only 'in the interest of the injured state or of the beneficiaries of the obligation breached':[33] the possibility, alluded to above, that *erga omnes* unlawful conduct may not involve the existence of an injured state (and thus gives rise to the violation of interests and values of the international community alone, considered as a whole) is then completely overlooked.

From the outset, I have maintained on the contrary—even though legal scholarship has only rarely taken a position on this point—that the rules which impose obligations *erga omnes* could theoretically allocate entitlement to react by individual states in a different way, so that possible reaction by all would constitute 'nothing more than a trend'.[34] This solution was consistent with the fact that, as submitted here, the 'omnes' would not have enjoyed traditional individual rights, all of the same scope, but collective rights, or rather, powers and duties or functional powers allocated by the international community itself. Despite the fact that the state of elaboration of international law on this point is still very rudimentary, one might wonder whether the perspective here indicated is not destined to prevail in the future, also considering that the 'obligation' at least literally imposed on the states by Article 41(1), of the final draft on the responsibility of states, to 'cooperate' in order to bring a case of *erga omnes* unlawful conduct to an end, cannot leave aside in practice a more precise definition of the content of international norms which produce obligations *erga omnes*, and with it a definition of the states entitled to react as material addressees of these norms.

[33] On the significance of this latter solution, see extensively I. Papa, 'Protezione diplomatica, diritti umani e obblighi *erga omnes*', *supra* note 19, 700 *et seq*.

[34] See, from the very outset, P. Picone, 'Obblighi reciproci e obblighi *erga omnes* degli Stati nel campo della protezione internazionale dell'ambiente marino dall'inquinamento', *supra* note 3, 59 *et seq*.; and, for some concurring opinions, S. Villalpando, *L'émergence de la communauté internationale dans la responsabilité des Etats* (Paris: PUF, 2005) 305; I. Papa, 'Protezione diplomatica, diritti umani e obblighi *erga omnes*', *supra* note 19, 688 *et seq*.

25

A Higher Law for Treaties?

Enzo Cannizzaro

1. Introductory Remarks: *Jus Cogens* across the Boundaries between the Law of Treaties and the Law of State Responsibility

Articles 53 and 64 of the Vienna Convention establish special rules of conflict applicable in the relationship between treaties and *jus cogens* rules. Treaties conflicting with a prior *jus cogens* rule are invalid; treaties conflicting with a rule of *jus cogens* that emerges after their conclusion terminates. It is well established that the mere existence of a conflict triggers the normative consequences envisaged by these provisions, regardless of whether the treaty has been implemented, and regardless of whether an actual breach of a *jus cogens* rule has occurred.

Jus cogens can also be offended, and this is a more frequent occurrence, by unilateral conduct. The idea that the notion of *jus cogens* is not confined to the law of treaties but also produces consequences under the law of state responsibility was pioneered by legal scholars[1] and eventually inspired the drafting of the Articles on State Responsibility, adopted by the International Law Commission (ILC) in 2001.[2]

In this context, the notion of *jus cogens* is employed in order to establish a special form of state responsibility which arises for serious violations of fundamental interests of the international community as a whole.[3] As is well known, conduct in breach of *jus cogens* entails, beyond the ordinary form of responsibility, additional obligations incumbent on third states. According to Articles 41(1) and 41(2), states must cooperate in order to bring the *jus cogens* breach to an end; they

[1] This idea was expressed in particular by Giorgio Gaja in his famous cycle of lectures, 'Jus Cogens *Beyond the Vienna Convention*', at the Hague Academy. See 172 *Recueil des Cours* (1981-III) 271 *et seq*.

[2] The text is reproduced in *YILC* (2001), vol. II (2), A/CN.4/SER.A/2001/Add.1 (Part 2).

[3] See J. Crawford, 'First Report on State Responsibility', A/CN.4/490/Add.2, paras 68 *et seq*. For various views on the use of the *jus cogens* notion in the field of state responsibility, see J.H.H. Weiler, A. Cassese, and M. Spinedi (eds), *International Crimes of State* (Berlin–New York: de Guyter, 1988); N. Jorgensen, *The Responsibility of States for International Crimes* (Oxford: Oxford University Press, 2000).

must not recognize as lawful a situation created by the breach, and they must not render aid or assistance in maintaining such a situation.

The two legal regimes—ie the rules of conflict established by the Vienna Convention and the additional secondary rules established under the law of state responsibility—are formally distinct. Indeed, they were developed to govern distinct situations. The law of treaties concerns normative conflicts and tends to provide, *ex ante,* for a preventative defence in cases where states intend to violate *jus cogens*. The secondary rules on state responsibility apply once actual measures in breach of *jus cogens* have already been performed.

In practice, however, the strict separation between these two legal regimes is less clear than it might appear, and this can create uncertainty and difficulties. It is not uncommon for states to conclude treaties in the aftermath of a *jus cogens* breach with a view to regulating the factual situation created by the breach.

According to the classical view, the conclusion of a treaty of this type must be treated as a measure whose legality must be assessed in the light of the law on state responsibility and, in particular, in light of the secondary obligations entailed by the breach for the responsible state and for third states.

Yet this view is not entirely convincing. First, the law of state responsibility does not provide an exhaustive list of the consequences of a breach of *jus cogens*. After stating, in paragraphs 1 and 2, the consequences of a *jus cogens* breach for third states, Article 41 refers in its third paragraph to further consequences provoked by a *jus cogens* breach under international law, among which one can also reasonably group normative consequences.

Secondly, and perhaps more importantly, the law on state responsibility establishes secondary obligations flowing from a *jus cogens* breach, but it does not determine the fate of a treaty inconsistent with these obligations.[4] States parties to a treaty regulating the consequences of a *jus cogens* breach would thus be under conflicting obligations, deriving respectively from the treaty and from the secondary rules on state responsibility. For example, states are under an obligation not to recognize the illegal situation arising from a breach under the law of state responsibility. However, a treaty containing such a recognition would nonetheless be valid and binding upon the parties.

This difficult situation could be avoided if one addressed the issue from the different methodological angle of the law of treaties. However, this perspective encounters a preliminary difficulty. As mentioned above, Articles 53 and 64 of the Vienna Convention provide for the invalidity or the termination of a treaty conflicting with *jus cogens*. Undoubtedly, treaties governing situations created by breaches of *jus cogens* interfere to a certain extent with *jus cogens*. Yet the Vienna Convention does not pronounce on the invalidity or termination of treaties interfering with *jus cogens*. Rather, it refers to the technically more precise

[4] For an analogous notation, see A. Gattini, 'A Return Ticket to Communitarisme, please', 13 *EJIL* (2002) 1181, at 1190.

notion of conflict. It follows that the scope and content of the notion of conflict assumes a decisive role for evaluating whether the normative sanctions envisaged by Articles 53 and 64 of the Vienna Convention also apply to treaties concluded in the aftermath of a *jus cogens* breach.

Undoubtedly, the notion of conflict is among the most obscure of the Vienna Convention. Not only does the Convention shed no light on the subject; one also finds that subsequent practice is scant, and, all in all, it is hardly sufficient to sustain a legal doctrine. Furthermore, an analogy with other possible notions of conflict of laws in international law could be misleading.[5] It cannot be taken for granted that a notion of conflict between rules having the same rank is immediately transposable to situations of conflict between rules whose relation is determined by a hierarchical order.

Nonetheless, an attempt to illuminate this notion is well worth the effort.[6] Not only can a clearer understanding provide useful guidance in a number of possible different contexts, as evidenced by the increasing tendency to invoke *jus cogens* in a variety of situations. Determining the notion of conflict between treaties and *jus cogens* can also have a more systematic significance. Indeed, it might contribute to the shaping of a general doctrine on hierarchical methods of conflict resolution in international law, and to that extent it may promote a better grasp of the relationship between the legal regime of *jus cogens* under the law of treaties and its counterpart regime under the law of state responsibility.

2. Conceptualizing the Notion of Conflict under Articles 53 and 64: The Classical Forms of Conflict

First of all, Articles 53 and 64 refer to classical conflicts of laws: those which arise from the coexistence of obligations requiring materially inconsistent lines of conduct. It is unanimously recognized that treaties, whereby the parties purport to contract out of the application of *jus cogens* rules, are in conflict with *jus cogens* and are therefore invalid or terminated.

This quite obvious point can be drawn literally from the phraseology of Article 53 of the Vienna Convention. The provision defines *jus cogens* as a body

[5] It is worth noting that the issue of conflict between treaties and *jus cogens* is not addressed in recent legal writings concerning the notion of conflict in international law. These writings are mainly focused on treaty conflicts, and specifically on conflicts between the WTO Agreements and other treaties. See J. Pauwelyn, *Conflict of Norms in Public International Law: How WTO Law Relates to Other Rules of International Law* (Cambridge: Cambridge University Press, 2003); E. Vranes, 'The Definition of "Norm Conflict" in International Law and Legal Theory', 17 *EJIL* (2006) 395.

[6] See A. Orakhelashvili, *Peremptory Norms in International Law* (Oxford, Oxford University Press, 2006) 136 *et seq.*

of rules to which 'no derogation is permitted, which can be modified only by a subsequent norm of general international law having the same character'. The term 'derogation' typically indicates a legal effect whose purpose is to address the impossibility of applying two mutually exclusive rules simultaneously.[7] The paradigm of conflict referred to in Articles 53 and 64 is thus given by a treaty by which the parties contract out of the binding effect of a peremptory obligation. This conceptual scheme can be indicated as a conflict by derogation. Classical examples of treaties conflicting with *jus cogens* refer mostly to that scheme: treaties by which the parties undertake to commit genocide, to use unlawful force, and so on.[8]

This is the scheme presupposed by the International Court of Justice (ICJ) in deciding the dispute between Iran and United States in the *Oil Platform* case. The Court decided that Article XX(1)(d) of the 1955 Treaty, which gives to either party the power to adopt measures 'necessary to protect [their] essential security interests', must be interpreted in accordance with international customary law, and therefore according to the Court it could not be invoked 'in relation to an unlawful use of force'.[9] By curtailing the scope of the provision through a *jus cogens*-consistent interpretation,[10] the Court thus excluded the possibility that the treaty was meant to contract out of the rules of international customary law on the use of force, and it thereby prevented a conflict from arising.

If this were the only type of conflict falling within the scope of Articles 53 and 64, the effect of these provisions would be very limited. Indeed, the conclusion of a treaty containing provisions aimed at contracting out of a *jus cogens* rule among the parties should be considered a rare occurrence. More frequently, an issue of consistency arises when the parties exchange obligations in regard to situations arising out of a *jus cogens* breach that has occurred in the past. These might be conflicts of a particular nature, where there is no direct clash but a different form of interaction among legal rules.

[7] This is the classical definition adopted by, *inter alia,* W. Jenks, 'The Conflict of Law-Making Treaties', 30 *BYIL* (1953) 401. Jenks expressly addresses his analysis to treaty conflicts. Yet even in that narrow field of inquiry he finds a difference between conflict in the strict sense and various forms of divergence (see especially 425 *et seq.*). See also J. Klabbers, *Treaty Conflicts and the European Union* (Cambridge: Cambridge University Press, 2009).

[8] This is the case of the Treaty of Friendship between the USSR and Iran of 1921, whose Article 6 expressly provided that the USSR had the right 'to advance her troops into the Persian interior' in case of an armed attack against Iran by a third state or in case of a threat to Russia coming from the Iranian territory, without any need for Iran's consent.

[9] ICJ, *Oil Platforms (Islamic Republic of Iran v United States of America),* Judgment of 6 November 2003, *ICJ Reports* (2003) 161, paras 40–41. A few lines earlier, in para. 38, the Court provided an admonition regarding the function of the rule which prohibits the unilateral use of force 'to all members of the international community'. The Court pointed out that 'both Parties are agreed as to the importance of the implications of the case in the field of the use of force, even though they draw opposite conclusions from this observation'.

[10] See the Separate Opinion of Judge Simma, ibid., at 324 *et seq.*

3. Conflict by Divergence

A classical conflict by divergence arises when states conclude a treaty on the exploitation of the resources of, or on the commercial intercourse in respect of the products of, a non self-determined territory. If the legality of the treaty were to be assessed in the light of the derogation test, the assessment would inevitably favour the full consistency between these treaties and the principle of self-determination. By no means do the parties to the treaty undertake an obligation to violate that principle.[11] However, one can hardly say that the conduct of the parties is inspired by the wish to re-establish a situation of full conformity with *jus cogens*. They not only fail to abide by their obligation to bring the breach to an end, as they are required to do by Article 41(1) of the Articles on State Responsibility; they also tend to aggravate the misconduct by cooperating with the responsible state in relation to a situation created by the *jus cogens* breach.[12]

Certain trends in practice, though the cases have been few, might provide further guidance on the issue. The problems raised by a treaty concerning the exploitation of resources of a non self-governing territory and its compatibility with the principle of self-determination was considered, albeit indirectly, in the *East Timor* case, decided by the ICJ in 1995.[13] The facts of the case are well known, and there is no point in dwelling on them here at any length. Portugal asked the Court to decide, *inter alia*, that by concluding a treaty on the delimitation of the continental shelf off the coast of East Timor with Indonesia, the occupying power of the territory of East Timor, Australia, violated the right of Portugal as administering power of that territory and the principle of self-determination and permanent sovereignty over the natural resources of the people of East Timor.

It is worth noting that the Portuguese claim was based on the principle of self-determination, and not only on the secondary obligations deriving from its

[11] The existence of rules governing this conduct is controversial. Some authors are inclined to assume that the conclusion of treaties relating to exploitation of unlawfully occupied territory falls within the prohibition against recognizing a situation created by a breach of *jus cogens* or rendering aid or assistance in maintaining that situation, a prohibition laid down by Article 41(2) of the Articles on State Responsibility adopted by the ILC in 2001 (see, for instance, S. Talmon, 'The Duty Not to "Recognize as Lawful" a Situation Created by the Illegal Use of Force or Other Serious Breaches of a *Jus Cogens* Obligation: An Obligation without Real Substance?', and T. Christakis, 'L'obligation de non-reconnaissance des situations créées par le recours illicite à la force ou d'autres actes enfreignant des règles fondamentales', both in C. Tomuschat and J.-M. Thouvenin (eds), *The Fundamental Rules of the International Legal Order* (Leiden–Boston: Martinus Nijhoff Publishers, 2006) at, respectively, 99 and 127, with further reference to diplomatic practice and to judicial case law). Even if this were the case, however, one can hardly contend that a breach of Article 41(2) entails, by itself, the invalidity of treaties concluded by the state responsible for a *jus cogens* breach with a third state.

[12] In its Commentary on Article 41, the ILC specified that the obligation not to recognize the serious wrongful act 'not only refers to the formal recognition of these situations, but also prohibits acts which would imply such recognition' (*YILC* (2001), vol. II(2), at 114, para. 5).

[13] ICJ, *East Timor (Portugal v Australia)*, Judgment of 30 June 1995, *ICJ Reports* (1995) 90.

breach. Thus, the request of Portugal was based on the conceptual paradigm that *jus cogens* is breached not only by way of derogation, but also by a treaty which regulates a factual situation in a way that diverges from that which would have existed if *jus cogens* were duly complied with. However, Portugal refrained from asking the Court to declare the Treaty invalid; rather, it insisted on the unlawfulness of its conclusion.[14]

The Court, basing its conclusion on the precedent of the *Monetary Gold* case,[15] declined to decide the case for want of jurisdiction. Yet the Court seemed to sympathize with the idea that an actual conflict might have been deemed to exist between the principle of self-determination and a treaty regulating the exploitation of resources of a non self-governing territory. In the famous passage contained in paragraph 29 of the judgment, the Court qualified as 'irreproachable' the assertion 'that the right of peoples to self-determination, as it evolved from the Charter and from United Nations practice, has an *erga omnes* character'. Furthermore, said the Court, the right of self-determination 'is one of the essential principles of contemporary international law'. It concluded, however, that, in spite of the *erga omnes* structure of the principle of self-determination, and arguably also of its *jus cogens* character, 'the Court could not rule on the lawfulness of the conduct of a State when its judgment would imply an evaluation of the lawfulness of the conduct of another State which is not a party to the case'. Nothing in this passage conveys the idea that there was no conflict between the Treaty and the rule of self-determination.

A different course was taken by the European Union (EC/EU) in 2006 when it concluded a fishery partnership agreement with Morocco, whose territorial scope does not exclude the waters off the coast of the Western Sahara.[16] Morocco occupies this territory in violation of the right to self-determination of the Saharawi people.[17] In spite of the sharp objection raised by private and institutional actors, who pointed out the dubious compatibility of the agreement with international

[14] In one of the final submissions, Portugal asked the Court to 'adjudge and declare that Australia, inasmuch as in the first place it has negotiated, concluded and initiated performance of the Agreement of 11 December 1989, [...] (a) has infringed and is infringing the right of the people of East Timor to self-determination, to territorial integrity and unity and its permanent sovereignty over its natural wealth and resources, and is in breach of the obligation not to disregard but to respect that right, that integrity and that sovereignty; On the right to invoke *ius cogens* as a ground of invalidity of a treaty by an entity which is not party to that treaty, see *infra*, next page.

[15] ICJ, *Case of the Monetary Gold Removed from Rome in 1943 (Italy v France, United Kingdom of Great Britain and Northern Ireland and United States of America)*, Preliminary Question, Judgment of 15 June 1954, *ICJ Reports* (1954) 19.

[16] Council Regulation (EC) No 764/2006 of 22 May 2006 on the conclusion of the Fisheries Partnership Agreement between the European Community and the Kingdom of Morocco [2006] OJ L141/1.

[17] For a recent analysis of the different legal implications of Morocco's illegal presence in Western Sahara, see K. Arts and P.P. Leite (eds), *International Law and the Question of Western Sahara* (Leiden: International Platform of Jurists for East Timor, 2006).

law, the validity of the agreement was not questioned by the parties at the international level.[18] According to the bilateralist approach adopted by the Vienna Convention in Articles 65 and 66(a), only the parties to a treaty might invoke *jus cogens* as a ground for impeaching the validity of a treaty or for terminating it. One can only speculate that the EU's position was influenced by political and economic considerations related, in particular, to the interest of having new fishing fields for the EU's troubled fishing industry. The vicissitudes of the agreement are thus clear evidence of the insufficiency of a bilateralist approach where there is a need to safeguard collective or universal interests such as those enshrined in *jus cogens*.

The idea that circulated in institutional and academic circles was that the provisions of the agreement in question must be interpreted in a manner consistent with the principle of self-determination. On this view, the Treaty would apply to the zones where Morocco exercises its jurisdiction lawfully.[19] A conflict could thus be prevented through the use of a classical technique of conflict-avoidance, namely, the doctrine of consistent interpretation. Logically, however, this approach tends to confirm, and not to obviate, the existence of a potential conflict between these provisions of the agreement and *jus cogens*.

Consistent interpretation as a technique of conflict avoidance seems to have been used by the ECJ in order to settle another potential conflict between the principle of self-determination and an agreement whose scope potentially covers a non self-determined territory. In *Brita*,[20] the ECJ held that the association agreement between the EC and Israel must be interpreted as excluding from its scope goods coming from the Palestinian territories. The Court grounded this finding on international principles of interpretation according to which the association

[18] In an opinion released upon request of the Security Council, the Legal Counsel to the Security Council expressed a position cautiously in favour of the legality of contracts concluded by Morocco with foreign companies for the exploration of mineral resources in Western Sahara, if undertaken for the benefit of the people (see letter dated 29 January 2002 from the Under-Secretary-General for Legal Affairs, the Legal Counsel, addressed to the President of the Security Council, UN Doc.S/2002/161 of 12 February 2002, available at <http://www.arso.org/Olaeng.pdf>. However, in a speech to an academic conference held in Pretoria on 5 December 2005, the Legal Counsel, speaking in his private capacity, held that 'an agreement which does not make a distinction between the waters adjacent the Western Sahara and the waters adjacent to the territory of Morocco would violate international law'. See V.H. Corell, 'The Legality of Exploring and Exploiting Natural Resources in Western Sahara', contribution to the conference on *Multilateralism and International Law with Western Sahara as a Case-Study*, Pretoria, 5 December 2008, 7 *et seq.*, available at <http://www.havc.se/res/SelectedMaterial/20081205pretoriawesternsahara1.pdf>.

[19] This view was, for instance, endorsed by EU institutions in the debates leading to the approval of the Fisheries Partnership Agreement with Morocco, where it was stressed that the Agreement was to be interpreted in conformity with the principle of self-determination. See the legal opinion rendered by the Legal Office of the European Parliament on the 20 February 2006, Doc. N. SJ-0085-06, available at <http://www.europarl.europa.eu>. See also the position expressed by the Commission during the debate in the Parliament on 15 May 2006, Doc N. CRE 15/05/2006—18, available at <http://www.europarl.europa.eu>.

[20] Case C-386/08 *Brita GmbH v Hauptzollamt Hamburg Hafen*, Judgment of 25 February 2010, not yet reported.

agreement with Israel was to be interpreted in accordance with the cooperation and trade agreement between the EC and the Palestinian Authority, which concerns precisely those goods. In spite of its persuasive force, this approach can hardly have a legal basis in the international principles on treaty interpretation, which limit the relevance of other international rules to those applicable between the parties. One fails to see how the agreement between the EC and the Palestinian authority can be taken into account in the interpretation of another unrelated agreement between the EC and Israel. The conclusion could be different if one assumed that the obligation to interpret the two treaties in accordance with each other follows from a superior principle of *jus cogens–freundliche Auslegung*.

The cases briefly referred to above illustrate one of the dilemmas left open by Articles 53 and 64. Do they apply only to normative conflicts, arising prior to an actual breach of *jus cogens*, or do they also apply to treaties which do not derogate from *jus cogens* but establish forms of cooperation with the responsible state in relation to a situation already created by a previous *jus cogens* breach?

4. The Ambiguity of the Notion: Divergence and Convergence

There are still greater difficulties if one thinks of how easily divergence can turn into convergence. The latter might be viewed as a conceptually reversed situation in which a treaty creates a situation which tends to converge toward the situation required by *jus cogens,* without, however, attaining full conformity.

With this situation in mind, it has been argued that, if there are clauses in a treaty on exploitation of the resources of non self-governing territories which are aimed at ensuring that a part of the profits from exploitation go to the benefit of the non self-determined people, this would offset the balance in favour of the legality of the treaty.[21] This argument rests ultimately on the consideration that a treaty reserving substantial advantages to the holder of the right to self-determination is to be preferred over the absence of any treaty, which would leave the occupying power practically free to dispose of the territorial resources for its own benefit.

Logically, the thread separating convergence from divergence is very thin. In the course of the debate within the General Assembly of the UN on the legality of the Camp David Accords, concluded in 1978 between Egypt, Israel, and the United States, the positions of states tended to boil down to two main options. According to the majority of states, the Accords, by recognizing a limited right to

[21] This was the position held by a number of member states and certain EU institutions in regard to the Fisheries Partnership Agreement with Morocco. For a full account, see E. Milano, 'The New Fisheries Partnership Agreement between the European Communities and the Kingdom of Morocco: Fishing Too Far South ?', 22 *Anuario Español de Derecho Internacional* (2006) 413.

self-government on the part of the Palestinian people, had the effect of rendering impossible, or more difficult, the full attainment of self-determination: a typical divergence argument. The antithetical position was taken by a minority, but not insignificant group of states, who maintained that the Accords, although not realizing in full the right to self-determination, nonetheless constituted a first step in this direction: a typical convergence argument. In the end the first position prevailed and resolution 34/65 B of 29 November 1979 was adopted. This resolution rejected 'those provisions of the accords which ignore, infringe, violate or deny the inalienable rights of the Palestinian people' and concluded, in paragraph 4, that these agreements 'have no legal validity in so far as they purport to determine the future of the Palestinian people and of the Palestinian territories'.[22]

Thus, the question arises whether respect for *jus cogens* can be graduated; whether, in other words, a treaty which aims at alleviating the violation of fundamental values of the international community, without bringing about a situation of full compatibility, is nonetheless in conflict with *jus cogens* and therefore invalid.

The question raises momentous legal and political issues.[23] Politically, it is difficult to determine what is the best approach to re-establish a situation of full compliance with *jus cogens* after a breach: whether it is an approach based on intransigence, or one based on flexibility. Legally, the issue is even more complicated, as the absence of consistent practice makes it necessary to rely on mere logical deduction from premises which are far from clear. It is difficult, in particular, to determine whether individual states, acting on their own behalf, can lawfully conclude treaties, among themselves or with the responsible states, which are objectively inconsistent with *jus cogens* even though they gradually promote compliance with *jus cogens* norms, on the ground that in doing so they act in the interests of the international community as a whole, which is the ultimate holder of the rights and duties deriving from a rule of *jus cogens*.

On the basis of the current state of the law, drawing precisely the line between convergence and divergence remains highly controversial, as is the question of what are precisely the constitutive elements of each of these situations. These

[22] See the discussion held at the Plenary Meeting of the General Assembly of 29 November 1979, *GAOR, Thirty-fourth Session,* Plenary Meetings, 83rd Meeting, vol. III, at 1534. In particular, a proposal by Egypt to delete para. 4 of the resolution was rejected by a narrow majority, with many states voting against or abstaining. The majority was 56 to 51, with 30 abstentions. Interestingly enough, although not immediately relevant for the aim of the present chapter, some states also cast doubt on the competence of the General Assembly to declare the invalidity of treaties. See, in particular, various interventions to explain the vote, ibid., at 1535 *et seq.*

[23] The same reasoning should also apply to the secondary obligation not to recognize the unlawful situation created by a breach of *jus cogens*. See S. Talmon, in 'The Duty Not to "Recognize as Lawful" a Situation Created by the Illegal Use of Force or Other Serious Breaches of a *Jus cogens* Obligation: An Obligation without Real Substance?', *supra* note 7, at 106. In the author's view, however, this reasoning would not apply in the relations between the responsible state and third states. The responsible state is under the obligation to ensure the full respect of the violated rule, a duty owed to the international community as a whole (at 124–5).

questions would be better left to future development. What seems important, for the purposes of the present study, is only to point out that the divergence/convergence dyad can intuitively serve as a possible logical framework aimed at determining the existence of a conflict on a case-by-case analysis.

5. The Farthest End of the Spectrum: Occasional Collision

Situations of collision arise when the application of ordinary rules, which logically and, in most cases practically as well, are consistent with *jus cogens* rules, creates occasional interference. In these instances, the way the ordinary rules are applied can make the full achievement of the aim of *jus cogens* norms more difficult, or even deprives such norms of their effectiveness.

This situation is also theoretically interesting, as it provides an opportunity to observe in practice a conflict between customary international law and peremptory law which in theory is quite difficult to conceive of. Indeed, the classical conception of conflict of laws is patently incapable of explaining the clash with *jus cogens* arising from the application of a *superveniens* rule of general international law. Conduct leading to the formation of custom would be, from the very beginning, inconsistent with *jus cogens,* and would therefore be inappropriate for establishing new law. A conflict is practically conceivable only as a form of indirect and occasional collision between the effects created, in a particular context, by a customary law rule and by a *jus cogens* rule.

The most obvious example of collision is the relation between peremptory substantive rules and ordinary procedural rules. The two sets of rules have different contents and therefore do not impose incompatible obligations. In practice, however, procedural rules can collide with substantive rules, in particular when they prevent the system of remedies from properly functioning, or when they affect, in a variety of ways, the effectiveness of that system.

Some indication in this direction can be drawn from the interesting decision of the ICJ in the *Armed Activities in the Congo* case.[24] The Congo contended that the reservation made by Rwanda to Article IX of the Genocide Convention, which establishes the jurisdiction of the ICJ over disputes related to the interpretation and application of the Convention, was inconsistent with substantive provisions of the Convention that have a peremptory nature.[25] The Court

[24] ICJ, *Armed Activities on the Territory of the Congo (New Application: 2002) (Democratic Republic of the Congo v Rwanda)*, Jurisdiction and Admissibility, Judgment of 3 February 2006, *ICJ Reports* (2006) 6.

[25] The tacit underlying premise was that the effects of the reservation were analogous to that of a treaty contracting out of the effects of Article IX of the Convention in the relations between Rwanda and the other parties to the Convention, at least those who did not object to the reservation. This premise, however, does not appear to be altogether correct, as it tends to equate the effect of a reservation, which indicates the lack of consent to assume an obligation, with the effect of a treaty which derogates from obligations established in a previous treaty.

rejected the Congo's claim using the classical scheme of conflicts by derogation. According to that scheme, in order to proclaim the invalidity of a reservation to Article IX of the Genocide Convention, it must be demonstrated that a peremptory rule requires the states to recognize the jurisdiction of the ICJ for disputes regarding the interpretation or application of the Convention. In the absence of such a rule—and, quite to the contrary, in the presence of a conspicuous practice of reservations to Article IX—the Court declined to review the validity of the reservation.[26]

However, in an earlier passage of the decision, concerning the compatibility of the reservation with the object and purpose of the Convention, the Court alluded to a subtler and more nuanced form of conflict. It found that the reservation of Rwanda did not affect the substantive obligations of the Genocide Convention, as it was simply aimed at excluding a particular method of settling a dispute under the Convention.[27] One could thus infer, on the basis of an *a contrario* reasoning, that a reservation to procedural provisions would be inconsistent with the object and purpose of the Convention if these reservations proved capable of affecting the Convention's substantive obligations.

This approach would appear to be entirely reasonable. A treaty can be composed of an inextricable pattern of substantive and procedural provisions, so that a reservation to the latter inevitably affects the normative balance on which the entire system of the treaty rests. This is probably the rationale behind the position of human rights treaties bodies, according to which reservations to the special mechanisms of compliance with a human rights treaty that authorize individuals to raise a claim are inconsistent with the treaty's object and purpose.[28]

More controversial is the determination of the fate of the reservation. Even assuming that a reservation to a treaty provision embodying a *jus cogens* rule is invalid,[29] it does not automatically follow that a reservation to a treaty provision

[26] In para. 68 the Court recalled previous occasions in which it gave full effect to reservations to Article IX, namely, *Legality of Use of Force (Yugoslavia v United States of America)*, Provisional Measures, Discontinuance, Order of 2 June 1999, *ICJ Reports* (1999), at 924; and *Legality of Use of Force (Yugoslavia v Spain)*, Provisional Measures, Discontinuance, Order of 2 June 1999, *ICJ Reports* (1999), at 772.

[27] *ICJ Reports* (2006), at 32, para. 67.

[28] See the General Comment No. 24 of the Human Rights Committee: *Issues relating to reservations made upon ratification or accession to the Covenant or the Optional Protocols thereto, or in relation to declarations under article 41 of the Covenant*, especially para. 11. In their Joint Separate Opinion to the ICJ decision mentioned in the *Armed Activities in the Congo* case, Judges Higgins, Kooijmans, Elaraby, Owada, and Simma emphasized the importance of the role of the ICJ for the object and purpose of the Genocide Convention. They also recalled the case law of human rights bodies, which tends to consider that reservations to provisions which establish mechanisms aimed at securing compliance with the substantive provisions of human rights treaties are incompatible with the object and the purpose of the treaty.

[29] This is the prevailing view among legal scholars. See A. Pellet, 'Tenth Report on Reservations to Treaties', A/CN.4/558/Add.1, para. 35. It seems natural to assume that reservations aimed at contracting out of a peremptory rule enshrined in a treaty conflict with *jus cogens* and are therefore invalid. This conclusion is not altered by the consideration that the effect of reservations is limited to the plane of the law of treaties, and cannot contract out of the effect of peremptory rules

which sets up a special mechanism aimed at securing compliance with *jus cogens* is equally invalid.

This idea is acceptable only in as much as a treaty establishing special remedies for *jus cogens* expresses the belief of the international community that these remedies are necessary in order to preserve the effectiveness of *jus cogens,* and that they are necessarily connected with it. The functioning of the system of remedies thus becomes a corollary of the existence of substantive *jus cogens* obligations, whose effectiveness can be affected by a radical malfunctioning of that system. The conclusions of the ICJ in *Congo v Rwanda* might imply that Article IX of the Genocide Convention, which contains a classical compromissory clause conferring jurisdiction to the ICJ for disputes regarding the interpretation or application of the Convention, is not an indispensable tool for preserving the effectiveness of the prohibition on genocide.

Issues connected with special remedies provided for by treaties in order to secure the effectiveness of *jus cogens* have been discussed in regard to Article 66(a) of the Vienna Convention, which confers jurisdiction on the ICJ for disputes concerning the validity or the efficacy of treaties conflicting with *jus cogens.* Different views have been expressed in this regard. On the one hand, there are no indications in the Vienna Convention that the existence of an objective dispute settlement mechanism was conceived of as an indispensable part of the *jus cogens* regime.[30] It is well known that reservations to Article 66(a) have been made by a large number of states which, by so doing, evidenced their belief that the regime of *jus cogens* enshrined in Articles 53 and 64 is not legally linked to the question of whether the ICJ has jurisdiction.[31]

This conclusion might change only if one demonstrated that the development of a category of higher law designed to protect fundamental collective values of the international community includes, as a corollary, the need to have the validity of inferior law assessed through an objective system of dispute settlement. Considerations of this kind might have inspired the objections of certain states to the reservations to Article 66(a), which indicate a certain tendency of the

of general international law. As stated above, hierarchy as a conflict-settling technique expresses the collective interest not to tolerate the presence of conflicting acts within the international legal order.

[30] The inclusion of Article 66(a) was rather inspired by the attempt to discourage unilateral invocation of *jus cogens,* which would have endangered the stability of international legal relations. This consideration might have prompted the conclusion that this rule can be hardly 'considered as an element of the concept of peremptory norm'. See G. Gaja, 'Jus Cogens *Beyond the Vienna Convention*', *supra* note 1, at 285.

[31] See Multilateral treaties deposited with the Secretary-General, the Vienna Convention on the Law of Treaties, Status as at 25 June 2010, available at <http://treaties.un.org/Home.aspx?lang=en>. See J. Verhoeven, 'Jus Cogens and Reservations or "Counter-Reservations" to the Jurisdiction of the International Court of Justice', in K. Wellens (ed.), *International Law: Theory and Practice. Essays in Honour of Eric Suy* (The Hague: Martinus Nijhoff, 1998) 195; H. Ruiz Fabri, 'Article 66', in O. Corten and P. Klein (eds), *Les conventions de Vienne sur les droit des traits. Commentaire article par article* (Bruxelles: Bruylant, 2006) vol. III, 2391.

objecting states to regard the jurisdiction of the ICJ as a necessary part of the legal regime of *jus cogens*.[32]

6. *Jus Cogens* and Rules on Sovereign Immunity

The controversial existence of a conflict between substantive peremptory rules and procedural rules has assumed a central role in the *jus cogens* versus sovereign immunity saga. Given the limited scope of the present chapter, there is no point in dwelling unnecessarily on all the aspects of this well-known issue, which concerns a typical case of occasional and indirect interference between customary law and *jus cogens*. The analysis will therefore focus on one particular issue, the most controversial one, concerning the possibility to lift state immunity in a civil claim for damages allegedly arising from a violation of *jus cogens*. Even this limited aspect will be explored concisely. In the following paragraphs, only some views will be considered, which epitomize diverse, maybe antithetical, views about the existence of a conflict between the two legal regimes.

The first view, maintained by a small but not insignificant number of cases and scholarly works, seems to consider that a conflict arises when rules on state immunity are invoked with a view to avoiding the judicial assessment of conduct allegedly in breach of *jus cogens*. The need to apply *jus cogens* would therefore justify disregarding the rules on state immunity.[33]

This position has been expressed with exemplary clarity by Judges Rozakis Caflisch, Wildhaber, Costa, Cabral Barreto, and Vajić in their Dissenting

[32] This conclusion is not easily drawn if one considers that Article 66(a) is fashioned as a classical compromissory clause concerning disputes on the validity or the efficacy of treaties allegedly conflicting with *jus cogens*. There is undoubtedly an incoherence in shaping *jus cogens* as a body of rules protecting fundamental values of the international community, on the one hand and, on the other, in assigning only to the states parties to a treaty the power to invoke *jus cogens* as a ground for impeaching the validity of that treaty or for terminating it. Maybe in an attempt to escape this incoherence, the idea was put forward that invalidity or termination of treaties conflicting with *jus cogens* follows automatically from the existence of higher law and need not be determined through the procedure set out in Articles 65 and 66 of the Vienna Convention (see, for example, B. Simma, 'From Bilateralism to Community Interest in International Law', 250 *Recueil des Cours* (1994-VI) 217, at 289). This incoherence seems to reflect the difficulty of reconciling the new communitarian approach inherent in the notion of *jus cogens* with the traditional bilateralistic dynamics of the international community. A system of objective remedies designed to protect collective values vis-à-vis treaties should have been fashioned differently. However, one can certainly doubt that, at the present historical stage, states are ready to accept a mechanism aimed at assessing objectively the priority of collective interests over individual interests. For consideration of this issue, see B. Simma, 'Bilateralism and Community interests in the Law of State Responsibility', in Y. Dinstein (ed.), *International Law at a Time of Perplexity. Essays in Honour of Shabtain Rosenne* (Dordrecht– Boston, London: Martinus Nijhoff, 1989) 821, at 837 *et seq*.

[33] See in particular A. Bianchi, 'Denying State Immunity to Violators of Human Rights', 46 *Austrian Journal of Public and International Law* (1994) 195–229; M. Reimann, 'A Human Rights Exception to Sovereign Immunity: Some Thoughts on *Princz v. Federal Republic of Germany*', 16 *Mich. J Int'l L* (1995) 403 *et seq*.

Opinion to the *Al Adsani* decision of the European Court of Human Rights. The judges took the view that, 'due to the interplay of the *jus cogens* rule on prohibition of torture and the rules on state immunity, the procedural bar of state immunity is automatically lifted, because those rules, as they conflict with a hierarchically higher rule, do not produce any legal effect'.[34]

The opposite view relies on the classical conception of conflict by derogation. The House of Lords, in *Mitchell and Jones*, expressed this view in the following terms: 'The *jus cogens* is the prohibition on torture. But the United Kingdom, in according state immunity to the Kingdom, is not proposing to torture anyone. Nor is the Kingdom, in claiming immunity, justifying the use of torture. It is objecting in limine to the jurisdiction of the English court to decide whether it used torture or not.' A few lines later, the Court added: 'to produce a conflict with state immunity, it is therefore necessary to show that the prohibition on torture has generated an ancillary procedural rule which, by way of exception to state immunity, entitles or perhaps requires states to assume civil jurisdiction over other states in cases in which torture is alleged'.[35]

These two excerpts highlight the existence of philosophically different notions of conflict. Whereas the House of Lords relies on the classical notion of conflict by derogation, the dissenting judges in *Al Adsani* advanced a different notion, rooted in a broader conception of *jus cogens*, conceived of as overriding all inferior rules that interfere with their application. In the classical view, *jus cogens* is regarded merely as a limit to the consensual capacity of the parties to a treaty, whereas under the broader approach it is seen, rather, as the overarching system of values of the international community.[36]

[34] *Al Adsani v the United Kingdom*, Judgment of 21 November 2001, Application no. 35763/97, Joint Dissenting Opinion of Judges Rozakis and Caflisch joined by Judges Wildhaber, Costa, Cabral Barreto, and Vajić, para. 3. A somewhat similar approach, which further highlights the effect of hierarchical methods of normative conflicts, has been adopted by Italian courts. In the well-known *Ferrini* case, the Court of Cassation denied immunity to Germany in a civil suit brought by the victims of war crimes committed during World War II (*Ferrini v Germany*, decision of 11 March 2004, No. 5044, reprinted in 87 *Riv. di Diritto Internaz.* (2004) 539 *et seq.*). A consistent pattern of cases has confirmed this approach (see, for example, Court of Cassation, first criminal section, case no. 1072, 21 October 2008, not yet reported) giving rise to a dispute between Germany and Italy, referred by Germany to the ICJ (the application is available at <http://www.icj-cij.org/docket/files/143/14923.pdf>). See P. De Sena and F. De Vittor, 'State Immunity and Human Rights: The Italian Supreme Court Decision on the *Ferrini* Case', 16 *EJIL* (2005) 89.

[35] House of Lords, *Jones v Ministry of Interior Al-Mamlaka Al-Arabiya AS Saudiya (the Kingdom of Saudi Arabia) and others*, Judgment of 14 June 2006, paras 44 and 45. An analogous position is maintained by, among others, H. Fox, *The Law of State Immunity* (Oxford: Oxford University Press, 2002) 525; A. Zimmermann, 'Sovereign Immunity and Violations of International *Jus Cogens*—Some Critical Remarks', 16 *Mich. J Int'l L* (1995) 438; C. Tomuschat, 'L'immunité des Etats en cas de violations graves des droits de l'homme', 109 *RGDIP* (2005) 51.

[36] For a critique of a purely normative approach and attempts to solve the conflict through a functional analysis of the relevant international norms, see J. Bröhmer, *State Immunity and the Violation of Human Rights* (The Hague–Boston–London: Martinus Nijhoff, 1997); L.M. Caplan, 'State Immunity, Human Rights, and Jus Cogens: A Critique of the Normative Hierarchy Theory', 97 *AJIL* (2003) 741. Considerable emphasis on the hierarchical effect of superior law as a conflict-settling technique is put by A. Orakhelashvili, *Peremptory Norms in International Law*, *supra* note 6,

It is not easy to say which of these perspectives corresponds to the current state of the law. In terms of intuitive logic, the existence of a conflict should be denied. Rules on immunity do not require conduct inconsistent with *jus cogens*. Nor, conversely, does *jus cogens* require states to exercise their jurisdiction over the conduct of foreign states, either in general or in particular circumstances. Uncontroversially, no logical conflict between the two sets of rules can be deemed to exist.[37]

In most cases, *jus cogens* and immunity rules do not collide. Substantive *jus cogens*, not unlike other substantive international rules, must be carried out and enforced in the context of the system of remedies of international law, including mechanisms and procedures which determine the conditions under which primary rules must be applied. In principle, this should inevitably lead to the conclusion that the two sets of rules are simultaneously applicable: *jus cogens* as a standard for assessing the legality of conduct of states, and immunity as a standard for determining the conditions under which a state can be sued in the courts of another state.

However, a collision in the application of these two normative systems can indeed occur when the mechanisms and procedures for the implementation of primary rules create conditions so restrictive that they deprive *jus cogens* norms of their effectiveness.

A possible way out of the dilemma might begin from the notion that a conflict between *jus cogens* and immunity can arise only if it is proven that the grant of immunity entails the nullification of legal protection for the values and interests underlying a *jus cogens* rule. The existence of a conflict would thus be dependent upon a careful balancing of interests to be conducted on a case-by-case basis, with a view to determining whether the full satisfaction of the interests protected by one of the two competing sets of rules completely subdues the interests protected by the other. Needless to say, the balancing test in this case is not a conflict-settling technique but rather a logical operation designed to determine whether there is actually a conflict. If there is such a conflict, it must be resolved by applying the usual *jus cogens*-based hierarchical method of conflict-settling. Determining exactly the standard which should be applied in order to reach such a conclusion falls well beyond the scope of this chapter.

at 341; ibid., 'State Immunity and Hierarchy of Norms: Why the House of Lords Got It Wrong', 18 *EJIL* (2008) 955–70.

[37] This conclusion is endorsed by prevailing scholarly views. See, in particular, P. d'Argent, *Les réparations de guerre en droit international public* (Bruxelles: Bruylant, 2002) 801; T. Giegerich, 'Do Damages Claims Arising from *Jus Cogens* Violations Override State Immunity from Jurisdiction of Foreign Courts?', in C. Tomuschat and J.-M. Thouvenin (eds), *The Fundamental Rules of the International Legal Order* (Leiden–Boston: Martinus Nijhoff, 2006) 203; B. Stern, 'Vers une limitation de l'"irresponsabilité souveraine" des Etats et chefs d'Etat en cas de crime de droit international?', in M. Kohen (ed.), *Promoting Justice, Human Rights and Conflict Resolution through International Law/La promotion de la justice, des droits de l'homme et du règlement des conflits par le droit international. Liber Amicorum Lucius Caflisch* (Leiden: Martinus Nijhoff, 2006) 511.

7. Concluding Remarks

The analysis undertaken in previous paragraphs prompts two observations.

First, the notion of higher law seems to be more useful in the phase subsequent to a *jus cogens* breach than in the phase prior to its violation. Practice reveals a thick net of cases in which *jus cogens* has been invoked with a view to opposing the application of treaties, or other international law rules, which govern the situation emerging as a consequence of a *jus cogens* breach.

Secondly, in order to deal with these cases, the adoption of a broad notion of conflict under Articles 53 and 64 seems, in principle, appropriate. This notion encompasses not only the classical conflicts by derogation but also other sophisticated types of conflicts characterized by various forms of interferences between higher law and inferior law. Yet, at the present stage of development of international law, the precise scope of this notion and, in particular, the conditions under which potential interference turns into an actual conflict, are doomed to remain controversial.

These two remarks seem, however, to demonstrate the shortcomings of the traditional conceptual framework based on the strict separation between the legal regimes of *jus cogens* under, respectively, the law of treaties and the law on state responsibility. This artificial state of things, which is probably due to historical contingencies surrounding the codification of these two branches of international law, can be remedied, to an extent, by a broader notion of conflict under Articles 53 and 64. This notion would apply not only to treaties by which the parties contract out of the application of *jus cogens* but also to treaties, or other ordinary rules, which make it more difficult, once a breach has occurred, to re-establish full compliance with *jus cogens* or to meet the secondary obligations entailed by the breach.

This solution also accords better with the need to preserve the *effet utile* of Articles 53 and 64. As stated above, the conclusion of treaties by which the parties undertake the commitment to violate *jus cogens* is a very rare occurrence. If this were the only normative effect of *jus cogens*, its proclamation in the Vienna Convention would be little more than symbolic. It is in the context of situations created by *jus cogens* breaches that the normative sanctions provided for by the Vienna Convention can fully attain their objective. It would be logically absurd if *jus cogens* had the effect of invalidating treaties which impose merely the obligation to derogate from *jus cogens*, even if this obligation is not put into effect, but did not invalidate treaties or other law rules which give full effect to, and bestow legal stability on, an actual violation of *jus cogens* norms.

This idea is also sensible from a theoretical perspective. In the course of its history, international law has developed an ample and variegated set of conflict-settling methods and techniques. However, until the entry into force of the Vienna Convention, recourse to hierarchical methods of conflict-settling was quite extraneous to the international legal dynamics, mainly inspired by the logic of bilateralism. The theoretical novelty introduced by Articles 53 and 64 is the conceptualization of the typical effect of a hierarchical mechanism of conflict-settling, invalidating inferior law in the presence of a collective interest in expunging from the legal order any obligation inconsistent with its fundamental principles.[38]

From a more general perspective, the notion of conflict under Articles 53 and 64 can contribute to grasping the implication of this theoretical novelty. Rudimentary notions of conflict, conceived of as the impossibility of complying simultaneously with two obligations, are fully appropriate in a bilateralist conception. However, they do not appear adequate in the collective interest perspective which inspires the legal regime of *jus cogens*, and its very *raison d'être*. A different notion of conflict is taking shape in the somewhat 'primordial brew' of the practice subsequent to the Vienna Convention. Arguably, this notion, whose precise contours are still uncertain, is more appropriate to the hierarchical model of the relationship between ordinary law and higher law presupposed by Articles 53 and 64. If *jus cogens* is to be conceived as a category of rules expressing collective fundamental values, a broader notion of conflict ought to be adopted, more consistent with the role and function normally discharged by higher law in a constitutional community.

[38] Hierarchical techniques of conflict-settling are based on the recognition that certain values or interests enjoy overall 'supremacy' over others; supremacy is formalized in a superior rank of the norms which protect superior values and interests. Consequently, higher rules take priority over inferior rules in all situations. Here lies the difference with other techniques, which tend to recognize limited priority to certain values over other competing values and interests, conditional, however, on the search for an appropriate balance among them. The basic distinction is that in these techniques, typically referred to as interest-balancing or value-balancing, priority to prevailing values is not formalized in a higher normative rank but depends, rather, on the particular context in which the balancing must be carried out and on the case-by-case search for the appropriate balance among the diverse competing interests. Hierarchy as a conflict-settling technique thus emphasizes the existence of an emerging sphere of fundamental collective interests in the international legal order, which take priority over interests of individual states. However, the conditions under which the diverse legal interests are prioritized, and the instrument granting full effect to this scale of priority, are still to be determined. This explains the enduring uncertainties in practice and in legal scholarship, which still linger about *jus cogens* and related notions.

Index

VCLT = Vienna Convention on the Law of Treaties
VCLT II = Vienna Convention on the Law of Treaties between States and International Organisations 1986

Printed and bound by CPI Group (UK) Ltd, Croydon, CR0 4YY